# Surveying Social Life

Herbert H. Hyman

# Surveying Social Life

## Papers in Honor of
## Herbert H. Hyman

Christian Bay, Lawrence Bobo, Leo Bogart, Jonathan R.
Cole, Stephen Cole, James S. Coleman, Sigmund
Diamond, Robert Fiorentine, Charles Y. Glock, Robert B.
Hill, Elliott Jaques, Daniel Katz, Stanley Lebergott,
Charles C. Lemert, Robert K. Merton, Daniel R. Miller,
Elisabeth Noelle-Neumann, Hubert J. O'Gorman,
Leonard I. Pearlin, Morris Rosenberg, Howard Schuman,
Eleanor Singer, Robin M. Williams, Jr., Charles R. Wright,
Harriet Zuckerman

## Hubert J. O'Gorman, editor

 Wesleyan University Press
Middletown, Connecticut

Copyright © 1988 by Wesleyan University

All rights reserved.

All inquiries and permissions requests should be
addressed to the Publisher, Wesleyan University Press,
110 Mt. Vernon Street, Middletown, Connecticut 06457.

Library of Congress Cataloging-in-Publication Data

Surveying social life: papers in honor of Herbert H. Hyman / edited
by Hubert J. O'Gorman: Christian Bay . . . [et al.].—1st ed.
p.    cm.
Bibliography: p.
Includes index.
ISBN 0-8195-5138-4
1. Social surveys—United States.   2. Hyman, Herbert Hiram,
1918-1984.   3. United States—Social conditions.   I. Hyman,
Herbert Hiram, 1918-1984.   II. O'Gorman, Hubert J.   III. Bay,
Christian, 1921-
HN29.S736  1987
301'.0723—dc19                                    87-26371
                                                      CIP

Manufactured in the United States of America

FIRST EDITION

# Contents

## Part III. Social Psychology

## Part IV. Public Opinion

## Part V. Inequality

## Part VI. Mass Media

# Tables

# Figures

# Contributors

| | |
|---|---|
| *Christian Bay* | Professor Emeritus<br>Department of Political Science<br>University of Toronto |
| *Lawrence Bobo* | Assistant Professor<br>Department of Sociology<br>University of Wisconsin, Madison |
| *Leo Bogart* | Executive Vice-President<br>Newspaper Advertising Bureau,<br>Inc. |
| *Jonathan R. Cole* | Professor<br>Department of Sociology<br>Director, Center for the Social<br>Sciences<br>Columbia University |
| *Stephen Cole* | Professor<br>Department of Sociology<br>State University of New York<br>Stony Brook |
| *James S. Coleman* | University Professor<br>Department of Sociology<br>The University of Chicago |
| *Sigmund Diamond* | Giddings Professor of Sociology<br>and<br>Professor of History Emeritus<br>Columbia University |
| *Robert Fiorentine* | Assistant Professor<br>Department of Sociology<br>Pennsylvania State University |
| *Charles Y. Glock* | Professor Emeritus<br>Department of Sociology<br>University of California, Berkeley |

Robert B. Hill                    W. E. B. Du Bois Distinguished
                                  Professor of Behavioral and
                                  Social Sciences
                                  Atlanta University

Elliott Jaques                    Director of the Institute of
                                  Organization and Social Studies
                                  Brunel University
                                  Uxbridge, Middlesex, U.K.

Daniel Katz                       Professor Emeritus
                                  Department of Psychology
                                  Survey Research Center
                                  University of Michigan

Stanley Lebergott                 Chester D. Hubbard Professor
                                  of Economics and Social Science
                                  Wesleyan University

Charles C. Lemert                 Dean of the Social Sciences
                                  Wesleyan University

Robert K. Merton                  University Professor Emeritus
                                  Columbia University

Daniel R. Miller                  Professor
                                  Department of Psychology
                                  Wesleyan University

Elisabeth Noelle-Neumann          Professor of Communication
                                  Research
                                  University of Mainz
                                  Director, Institut für Demoskopie
                                  Allensbach
                                  West Germany

Hubert J. O'Gorman                Professor
                                  Department of Sociology
                                  Wesleyan University

Leonard I. Pearlin                Professor and Director
                                  Human Development and Aging
                                  Program
                                  University of California, San
                                  Francisco

Morris Rosenberg                  Professor
                                  Department of Sociology
                                  University of Maryland

Howard Schuman                    Professor
                                  Department of Sociology
                                  Director, Survey Research Center
                                  University of Michigan

# Contributors

*Eleanor Singer*

Senior Research Scholar
Center for the Social Sciences
Columbia University

*Robin M. Williams, Jr.*

Henry Scarborough Professor
of Social Science Emeritus
Department of Sociology
Cornell University

*Charles R. Wright*

Professor of Communications and
Sociology
Annenberg School of
Communications
University of Pennsylvania

*Harriet Zuckerman*

Professor
Department of Sociology
Columbia University

# Acknowledgments

The preparation of this *Festschrift* would have been impossible without the help of many individuals. I want to thank the twenty-four authors for their papers written for this occasion. I owe a particular debt to Sigmund Diamond, Eleanor Singer, and Charles Wright, whose personal support was indispensable. I also want to thank Nathan Brody, Morris Rosenberg, and Helen Strauss for the special help they offered, and to express my gratitude to Anne Dunham for her repeated help. To Leanore Bona, associate registrar of Columbia University, and to Stanley Presser of the National Science Foundation, I am in debt for helping me to locate needed information. The general counsel and concrete recommendations of Jeannette Hopkins, Eliza Childs, and Molly McQuade of Wesleyan University Press were always valuable, and I am grateful to them. My deepest debt is to Irene Spinnler who worked closely with Herbert Hyman for many years. She assembled Hyman's bibliography and provided the administrative and secretarial labor without which this volume would not have been completed. Lastly, I want to thank Colin G. Campbell, president of Wesleyan University, for his warm personal and generous financial support.

H. J. O'G.

# Surveying Social Life

# Hubert J. O'Gorman

## Introduction: Herbert H. Hyman
## His Life and Work

Modern survey research has increased our knowledge of social life more than any other tool in the social sciences. In survey research, studies of large numbers of people, who have been selected by rigorous sampling techniques, are conducted in normal life situations using standardized procedures. Such studies yield quantitative measurements that allow researchers to survey the social landscape with an effectiveness unmatched in the history of human societies. Its familiar limitations notwithstanding, survey research has rapidly become such a prominent and indispensable source of knowledge during the last four decades that it is difficult to imagine how a modern society could function without it.[1]

This technological revolution created the status and role of the survey researcher. The responsibilities of this new status included a working knowledge of psychology, sociology, and applied statistics, plus a practical understanding of research design, sampling, questionnaire construction, interviewing, and data analysis. These role requirements weakened the conventional distinction between applied and basic research, narrowed the gap between theory and research, and blurred traditional disciplinary boundaries. They also put a premium on imagination and innovation. Above all, they called for sensitivity to the tactics of data collection and analysis that only a comprehensive

For their comments on an earlier version of this chapter, I would like to thank Sigmund Diamond, Anne C. Dunham, Jeannette E. Hopkins, Helen Kandel Hyman, Molly McQuade, Robert K. Merton, Paul B. Sheatsley, Eleanor Singer, and Charles R. Wright.
[1] For informed, critical, and thorough assessments of modern sample survey research, see Schuman and Kalton 1985; Turner and Martin 1984.

1

grasp of the strategy of large-scale research could insure. No less important, the new status of survey researcher called for an informed, critical attitude toward survey research that, considering its novelty and complexity, was necessary to its vitality and sometimes difficult to find.

It should come as no surprise, therefore, that the status of survey researcher quickly attracted creative and enterprising individuals. In some instances, the talents of these pioneering investigators were so closely associated with the field's rapid growth, remarkable accomplishments, and ongoing controversies that their professional careers and reputations became virtually indistinguishable from the field of survey research itself. Few came as close to embodying this fused pattern of outstanding accomplishment as Herbert H. Hyman, whose distinguished work has long been an integral part of survey research and in whose honor this *Festschrift* is written.

## The Early Years

Herbert H. Hyman was born in New York City on March 3, 1918. His parents, Dr. David Elihu Hyman and Gisella Maunter Hyman, were immigrants, his father from Russia and his mother from Yugoslavia. The second of two sons, Hyman grew up on the upper east side of Manhattan (where his father practiced medicine), and, aside from a chronic heart murmur acquired during a severe case of diphtheria, his childhood was normal and healthy. He attended the neighborhood public elementary school, went to De Witt Clinton High School in the Bronx, and enrolled in Columbia College in 1935.

Like his older brother Richard, who became a surgeon, Hyman began college with the intention of preparing for a career in medicine. Throughout his undergraduate years, however, he found other fields, especially psychology and anthropology, more appealing. Among twenty-eight elective courses, he took eight in psychology—his field of concentration—five in anthropology, and three in sociology with the legendary William C. Casey. Hyman was stimulated by his psychology courses, particularly those taught by B. F. Skinner's protégé, Fred S. Keller; by Otto Klineberg, the social psychologist who was deeply involved in studies of black intelligence; and, most of all, by the eclectic and charismatic Gardner Murphy, then conducting surveys of college students. Inspired by Keller, Klineberg, and Murphy, and profoundly moved by the writings of the great psychologist William James, Hyman decided to become a social psychologist.

After graduation in 1939 from Columbia College with honors in psychology, he enrolled in the university's graduate psychology program. During the next year, working under the supervision of Fred Keller, Hyman designed a learning experiment with six albino rats to test the validity of Gordon Allport's concept of functional autonomy. As reported in his 1940 master's essay, he found no evidence that the behavior of the rats had become independent of their original hunger motives, at least as measured by the time spent training them to push food-releasing levers.[2] In the following two years he managed, remarkably, to complete all of the doctoral course requirements, including a memorable year-long anthropology seminar with Ruth Benedict; and he prepared, wrote, and defended an extraordinary thesis. In 1942, at the age of twenty-four, he received the Ph.D. in social psychology.

Hyman's doctoral dissertation, "The Psychology of Status," was an enormously rich and far-reaching contribution to social psychology and sociology. Written under the supervision of Otto Klineberg and John Volkmann, it investigated the subjective aspects of social status. Introducing the terms "reference groups" and "reference individuals," Hyman explored the dynamics of personal and social comparisons and their effects on self-appraisal through a series of intensive interviews and several experiments. As in most significant innovations, Hyman's reasoning appears deceptively simple and straightforward. He proceeded on two assumptions. First, he assumed that we cannot know, based on objective status characteristics, what a status generally means to those who do and do not occupy it. This information, he insisted, can be obtained only by reference to individuals' personal conceptions of statuses, their own and others'. His second assumption, a corollary of the first, was that an individual's actual identification with a specific status cannot be inferred from the individual's objective position. He based this assumption on the finding—as reported, for example, by Hartman and Newcomb (1940) in their study of industrial conflict—that individuals' levels of aspiration, a variable influencing their social-class identification, were imperfectly correlated with their objective income and wealth.

The technical problem Hyman faced was how to tie these two assumptions into a formulation that gave order to varying subjective judgments. After all, if individuals' identification and evaluation of their own social positions were inaccurate and arbitrary, with no patterned relationship to their objective positions, there would seem to be no reason to examine them except as instances of distortion. Part of the problem was solved by extending, as Hyman did, the notion of

[2] Herbert Hyman, "An Experimental Approach to the Problem of Functional Autonomy," May 1940. This and all other references to Hyman's work in this *Festschrift* will be found in the bibliography of his writings at the end of the book. All other references appear at the end of chapters.

psychophysical perception to include judgments of social stimuli. This implied that individuals' assessments of social status, as with subjective assessments of size, weight, color, and smell, would form a scale anchored by end stimuli. Hyman resolved the other part of the problem by recognizing the implication of John Volkmann's finding that an individual's values and aspirations often anchor perceptions of the social world (Chapman and Volkmann 1939; Hunt and Volkmann 1937; Volkmann 1936). The critical step occurred when Hyman came to realize that social units and aggregates like groups, organizations, social strata, and even total populations, could provide, in a parallel fashion, the necessary anchor for judging any status. "With reference to the status scale, the reference group is," he wrote, "analogous to anchoring by the end stimuli" (Hyman 1942; p. 25). His trailblazing exploration of reference-group phenomena, *The Psychology of Status*, was published in 1942; it earned seven dollars in royalties, quickly went out of print, and remained in unjustified obscurity until rescued eight years later by Merton and Rossi (1950).

## The War Years

Ineligible for military service because of his heart murmur, Hyman went to Washington, D.C., in the spring of 1942 to hunt for a war-related job. At Gardner Murphy's suggestion, he went to see Murphy's former student, Rensis Likert, director of the division of program surveys at the U.S. Department of Agriculture. At the time the department had what was probably the largest social research organization in the world.[3] In addition to its own research, it regularly carried out,

[3] The complete story of the part played by the U.S. Department of Agriculture in the growth of sample survey research has yet to be told. New Deal legislation to help the farm population during the early years of the Depression legally required that the department actively cooperate with farmers in planning and administering programs. This requirement was sympathetically accepted by many department officials who had close personal and political ties to their constituents and clients. In particular, some of the top administrators, notably Henry A. Wallace, then Secretary of Agriculture, were especially sensitive to the needs of farmers and, later, of unemployed urban residents, who were not represented by organized interest groups. Department officials, quickly discovering that the usual methods of obtaining information through institutional channels were too cumbersome and unreliable, organized small groups of interviewers (often farmers or individuals familiar with farm issues) who roved the countryside collecting opinions as best they could. The results seemed intuitively relevant but they were difficult to assess or apply, and the process of assessment and application was time-consuming. Finally, in 1939, impressed with the efficiency of the new techniques of political and commercial polling and the promising results of efforts to measure basic attitudes, the department established the Division of Program Surveys and appointed Rensis Likert its director. The first sample surveys were carried out in 1942, about the time of Hyman's arrival. By the end of 1942 there were more than 100 social scientists on Likert's staff. (See Dreis 1951; Skott 1943; Wallace and McCamy 1940.)

under contract, studies for other government agencies. Likert hired Hyman as a social science analyst and assigned him to the division's methodology section, which was directed by Richard Crutchfield.

In his new assignment, Hyman dealt with a wide assortment of surveys about reactions of the civilian population to the experiences of war, wrestled with the relative merits of open and closed questions, worried about the standards of interviewing, and pondered the merits of the division's move from quota to full-scale probability sampling. He also made close and lasting friendships with Angus Campbell, John Riley, Jules Henry, and, in particular, with Dan Katz. When, in November 1942, a budget crisis forced Likert to cut his staff drastically, Hyman, along with Katz, Riley, and Crutchfield, moved to a similar job in New York City with the Survey Division of the Office of War Information (OWI).

The official goals of the OWI (Davis 1943; Hawkins and Pette 1943) and the rationale for the existence of its surveys division sharpened Hyman's interest in the methodological components of survey research. Many specific war measures like salvage campaigns, purchase of war bonds, recruitment for jobs in war plants, and the control of information depended on voluntary compliance and not on sanctions. Thus, people had to be informed and urged to participate. Conveying the information and motivating popular participation were among the OWI's major tasks, and the principal function of its surveys division was to collect data that would help make the information campaigns more effective. Since the OWI knew what information it wanted to communicate, and since the informational content (of pamphlets, posters, radio broadcasts, and so forth) was known to the OWI, the attention of the division's analysts focused increasingly on the subjective understanding of the population as reflected in its sample surveys. Thus, the validity and reliability of the collected data had a substantive and political significance that matched its methodological significance.

This growing concern with the quality of subjective data led the National Opinion Research Center (NORC), which was conducting the field work for OWI surveys, to look closely at the ways in which characteristics of the interviewers and of the respondents, and also of the context of the interviewing situation itself, influenced the quality of data collected. In the spring of 1942, for example, NORC had studied the effects of black and white interviewers on the responses of large samples of blacks in Memphis, Tennessee, and in New York City (Hyman et al. 1954, p. 159). During his work at OWI Hyman began, in collaboration with Paul Sheatsley, NORC's project director of the OWI surveys, to pursue these problems of interviewing, problems that he had previously encountered and discussed with Katz during their work at the Department of Agriculture.

The diversity of Hyman's work during his twenty months at OWI suggests the breadth of survey experience that social scientists encountered during their wartime service with the government. The problems studied by Hyman ranged in interest and urgency from the minor details of the distribution of OWI posters by Boy Scouts in twelve cities, through the redemption of war bonds in various parts of the country, to the Harlem riot of August 1943 when he, Kenneth B. Clark, and Hylan G. Lewis served simultaneously as observers, interviewers, and analysts in an early example of "firehouse" research. He carried out, in addition, a number of longer, larger, and more complex field surveys, often with Dan Katz. These included, for example, studies of absenteeism in eighteen war plants, worker morale in five shipyards, and, in three urban communities, the resistance of qualified men and women to war industry employment.

Hyman continued to work for the OWI surveys division until July 23, 1944, when the division was unexpectedly abolished. A few months later he was hired, again by Rensis Likert (who had recently left the Department of Agriculture), to work on a historic but by now largely forgotten research mission: the United States Strategic Bombing Survey of Germany (December 1946; May 1947). Hyman was assigned to the survey's morale division, which Likert directed, and which was responsible for designing and administering the complex and unprecedented field surveys in Germany. The goal of the survey was to determine the effects of bombing on the civilian population, especially its willingness to support the German war effort. After recruiting Hyman, Likert added others to his survey staff, among them David Krech, Richard Crutchfield, Dan Katz, Helen Peak, Howard Longstaff, and W. G. Cochran. From its headquarters, first in London and later in Bad Nauheim, near Frankfurt, Likert's research team carried out its extraordinary and grim task from January to July 1945. It was, for Hyman, an unforgettable experience.

Even in retrospect, the multiple requirements of the project seem staggering: to draw up a feasible research design; to devise a means of selecting a probability sample of German civilians; to construct a meaningful questionnaire in German; to find and train appropriate German-speaking interviewers; to locate and interview 3,711 civilian respondents in thirty-four cities for two separate surveys; to analyze the resulting mountain of data; and to prepare a report summarizing the effects of massive bombing on an enemy civilian population. That this gigantic task was carried out within a seven-month period while the war in Europe was still going on must rank as an episode unparalleled in the short history of modern survey research. It is also profoundly paradoxical that this gifted team of survey researchers, while systematically depicting the horrors of massive bombing, consistently and explicitly documented the diminishing effects of increased levels of bombing on civilian morale, a finding subsequently confirmed in a similar study of Japanese morale (United States Strategic Bombing Survey, June 1947).

After the completion of the German bombing survey, Hyman participated in a small study of public opinion in the U.S.-occupied zone of Austria, served for a short time as a planning consultant to the Japanese bombing survey, and then, with the European war over, returned home to New York.

## The NORC Years

In the fall of 1945 Hyman secured a full-time position as assistant professor of psychology at Brooklyn College, where Dan Katz had returned as department chairman. He also went to work on a part-time basis at NORC's New York office, then run by Paul Sheatsley. At Brooklyn College Hyman was primarily responsible for teaching statistics and research methods; his work at NORC consisted largely of helping Sheatsley to conduct national sample surveys for the U.S. Department of State. With his financial and professional future reasonably secure, in October he married Helen Kandel, the daughter of Isaac L. Kandel, a noted professor of comparative education at Columbia's Teachers College. A graduate of Barnard College, and, at the time, a writer for the Columbia Broadcasting System, Helen Kandel was Hyman's lifelong companion and the mother of their three children: Lisa, David, and Alex.

Hyman had pursued his dual life—teaching with Katz and doing surveys with Sheatsley—for a year when Clyde Hart began to urge him to join NORC on a full-time basis. Hart had become director of NORC in 1946 when Harry Field, its founder and first director, died in a plane crash. Hart was determined to improve NORC's already excellent record as a major research center. With this in mind, he worked out an affiliation with the University of Chicago, moved NORC's headquarters from the University of Denver, and began to recruit talented researchers for his staff. He was particularly anxious to keep Hyman, whose skills and experiences were not only well known, but who seemed especially qualified for a new and demanding NORC project on interviewing. Hart's offer to Hyman included directing the project, and, as an added inducement, a trip to Japan as Hart's representative to an Expert Mission on Public Opinion and Sociological Research.[4]

In 1947 Hyman resigned from Brooklyn College, spent three months in Japan, and returned to become a full-time research associate at NORC. While the move was prompted by several considerations, including Katz's decision to accept a similar offer from the University of Michigan and its newly acquired Survey Research Center, it was Hart's project that was decisive. As part of his new duties, Hyman was put in charge of a massive and novel inquiry into the process of interviewing as a method of data collection. The study was sponsored by the Committee on the Measurement of Opinion, Attitudes, and Consumer Wants, established two years earlier by the Social Science Research Council and the National Research Council. The committee, chaired by Samuel Stouffer, sponsored the investigation as part of its effort to promote inquiries into fundamental methodological problems of survey research.

This project occupied much of Hyman's attention during his years at NORC. Before it was completed he had written or coauthored eight technical papers on one or another aspect of interviewing. During this long project he still found time for other work. For example, he published some of the results of his wartime research with Dan Katz (Katz and Hyman 1947*a*; 1947*b*); with Paul Sheatsley (Hyman and Sheatsley 1948) he wrote a probing but sympathetic analysis of Alfred Kinsey's research on sexual behavior; and, late in 1948, he spent a hectic five weeks preparing and writing a long chapter as part of the critique of the preelection polls of 1948 initiated by the Social Science Research Council (Mosteller et al. 1949). However, the publication that probably drew the most attention during Hyman's early NORC years was "Some Reasons Why Information Campaigns Fail," written with Sheatsley (Hyman and Sheatsley 1947). This respected article was designed to show "those charged with the task of informing the public" that, regardless of the nature and amount of information presented, psychological barriers always interfere with the absorption of that knowledge. In addition to research and writing, and with Hart's strong encouragement, Hyman accepted invitations to teach at the University of California, Berkeley, in the spring of 1950 and in Norway as a Fulbright Lecturer at the Oslo Institute for Social Research during the 1950–51 academic year.

---

[4] Hart, as director of NORC, had been asked to nominate one of three members to this mission, which had been requested by the Army of Occupation. Clyde Kluckhohn, the anthropologist, and Raymond Bowers, the sociologist, were the other members. For some of Hyman's reflections on his three-month visit to Japan, see Hyman 1947.

## The Columbia Years

In the spring of his Fulbright year in Oslo, Hyman received an offer from Paul Lazarsfeld to join Columbia's graduate department of sociology as an assistant professor. He was pleased and excited at the prospect of joining what was then one of the most prestigious and influential sociology departments in the world, but was ambivalent about leaving NORC. Not only did he take pride in its accomplishments and standing as a national research center; he had strong bonds of friendship and loyalty to both Sheatsley and Hart and felt obliged to finish ongoing projects. His dilemma was resolved when the university and the department agreed to allow him to continue his affiliation with NORC after his appointment to the Columbia faculty. Hyman accepted this generous offer and assumed his new duties as a full-time member of the department in the fall of 1951.[5]

That Hyman's name and work have come to be closely associated with Columbia is understandable in view of the eighteen years he spent there. Still, his relationship with NORC remained strong during his first five years at Columbia. For instance, three years after his new appointment he worked diligently, as NORC's representative, with Stouffer on the planning and analysis of the *Communism, Conformity and Civil Liberties* study (Stouffer 1955). Another sign of his persisting ties to NORC was the frequency with which his publications continued to rely on its survey findings. These included a series of important articles written with Paul Sheatsley about monitoring public attitudes toward civil liberties (1953) and white attitudes toward desegregation (1956), and the first of two frequently cited studies of membership in voluntary associations, written with Charles Wright (1958). Hyman also drew extensively on NORC data in two of his most celebrated essays, both published two years after his move to Columbia. One, coauthored with Sheatsley (1953), a long methodological assessment of *The Authoritarian Personality* (Adorno et al. 1950), remains one of the most incisive, technically sophisticated, and instructive critiques to be found in the literature. The other, "The Value Systems of Different Classes" (1953), is Hyman's best-known paper. It brought together a rich array of data to describe the extent to which individuals in different classes hold the values and beliefs needed for economic success, a

---

[5] His new colleagues, listed in the official department roster, included Professors Edmund de S. Brunner, Paul F. Lazarsfeld, Robert S. Lynd, and Robert K. Merton; Associate Professors Theodore Abel, Conrad M. Arensberg, William C. Casey, Kingsley Davis, Mirra Komarovsky, and C. Wright Mills; Assistant Professor Seymour M. Lipset; Instructor John W. Alexander; Lecturers Jeremiah P. Shalloo and Bernhard J. Stern; Visiting Lecturer Benjamin B. Wolman; and Tutorial Assistants Allen H. Barton, Joan Gordon, Hanan Selvin, and Charles R. Wright.

key issue in Robert Merton's theory of social structure and anomie, and a fundamental problem in social stratification.

But by far the most visible evidence of Hyman's persistent identification with NORC was the publication in 1954 of the long-awaited *Interviewing in Social Research.* It was a technical report summarizing the results of the NORC research project Hyman had been directing for seven years. Written by Hyman, with chapters by William J. Cobb, Jacob J. Feldman, Clyde W. Hart, and Charles H. Stember, the NORC monograph was quickly acknowledged as a major contribution to social science methodology. Long recognized as a classic in the field, it was republished in 1975 and is still widely used.

Hyman's principal pedagogical responsibility at Columbia was to take over the courses in sociology on methods of survey research, courses previously taught by Paul Lazarsfeld and Patricia Kendall. To these he added the first graduate course devoted explicitly to the secondary analysis of survey data, a course that attracted students from quite different parts of the university. In addition to his teaching, Hyman began to prepare, at Lazarsfeld's request, a combination text and casebook on the collection and analysis of survey data. The request was part of a project proposed by Lazarsfeld and Merton to establish a professional school for social research at Columbia. The university eventually turned down the project, but Hyman, with the help of Lazarsfeld and Patricia Kendall, completed his assignment, and the book, *Survey Design and Analysis: Principles, Cases and Procedures,* published in 1955, became enormously successful and influential. It went through nine printings, was translated into Italian, Spanish, and Portuguese, and, for at least a decade, was the most frequently used methods text in graduate departments of sociology. Like *Interviewing in Social Research,* it became a classic in the social sciences.

Several years after his arrival at Columbia, Hyman, by then an associate professor, became involved in the Bureau of Applied Social Research, the famed research arm of the university's sociology department. His first project, financed by a Ford Foundation grant, called for an inventory of what was known about political behavior. It was conducted by an interdisciplinary committee chaired by Seymour M. Lipset and made up of Hyman, Richard Hofstadter, William Kornhauser, and David Truman. Hyman's role was to pull together findings and hypotheses about what he called political socialization, that is, how people learned about politics. The results of his inquiry, which drew heavily on the secondary analysis of survey data, were published in 1959 in *Political Socialization: A Study of the Psychology of Political Behavior.* It opened up a neglected line of research that subsequently became a thriving specialty. In Niemi's words, Hyman's book "indelibly impressed upon political scientists and psychologists that political learning is indeed a challenging and worthy subject in its own right" (Niemi 1973, p. 120). Republished in 1969, it remains in print more than twenty-five years after its initial publication.

Hyman's second bureau project was quite different. An organization called the Encampment for Citizenship had asked the bureau to evaluate the effects of a summer training program it ran for youth leaders from diverse ethnic backgrounds. At the suggestion of Charles Glock, the bureau's director, Hyman assumed responsibility for the study, brought in Charles R. Wright as the project's codirector, and later recruited Terence K. Hopkins to help them. The study was long and complex, involving a number of replications and panel surveys over several years. In addition to showing that the Encampment achieved many of its goals, the final report opened up systematic methods of thinking about principles for evaluating programs of social action (Hyman, Wright, and Hopkins 1962).

Hyman's contributions to Columbia's department of sociology and the bureau were soon rewarded with his promotion to full professor in 1956 and appointment as associate director of the bureau in 1957. The growing influence of his work was, of course, recognized far beyond his home institution. He received the Julian L. Woodward Memorial Award from the American Association of Public Opinion Research (AAPOR) in 1956, accepted a visiting professorship in Turkey at the University of Ankara in 1957, and was elected president of AAPOR in 1959. He continued to participate actively in major professional associations and on editorial staffs of leading professional journals.[6]

During the same period, he began to reap a delayed harvest for his pioneering but neglected dissertation on reference groups. Throughout the 1950s and well into the next decade, reference group theory and research became such an active area of inquiry that Hyman's study emerged as one of the most frequently cited in the literature. Hyman, as he himself noted (1960, p. 386), had little to do with this development. The explosion of interest in reference groups was directly attributable rather to Merton and Rossi, who, in 1950, brilliantly reconceptualized diverse findings from Stouffer's *The American*

---

[6] Hyman served on the Executive Council of the Society for the Psychological Study of Social Issues, 1955–57; he chaired the Social Psychology Section, 1970–71, and the Methodology Section, 1962–63, of the American Sociological Association; he was president of the Sociological Research Association in 1974; and from 1952 to 1978 he was a member of the Social Science Research Council, serving on four major committees: Comparative Sociological Research, Cross-Cultural Education, Comparative Politics, and Mass Communication and Political Behavior. In the late 1960s, he also served on the National Science Foundation's advisory panel for their programs in sociology and social psychology.

*Soldier* (1949) in terms of reference groups and drew explicit attention to Hyman's 1942 monograph. Merton's later elaboration of reference group theory (1957) added considerably to the monograph's stature. Thus, *The Psychology of Status* was rediscovered, reread, eventually republished (1980), and, belatedly, recognized as a landmark.

Throughout the rest of Hyman's tenure at Columbia, even while serving as department chairman (1965–68), the quantity and quality of his research and writing remained impressive. Although he had tours of duty in England in 1961 as a Guggenheim fellow, and in Geneva in 1964 as a program director for the United Nations Research Institute for Social Development, the pace and diversity of his interests never slackened. There were further monographs and books: *Evaluation of Statistical Methods Used in Obtaining Broadcast Ratings* (1961), with William Madow and Raymond Jessen; *Inducing Social Change in Developing Communities* (1967), with Gene Levine and Charles Wright; and *Readings in Reference Group Theory and Research* (1968), with Eleanor Singer. There were, in addition, papers with Sheatsley (1964) and Wright (1964) on desegregation and evaluation; a pair of new articles on the mass media (1961, 1963); a subtle analysis of climates of tolerance and intolerance in England and the United States (1968); and a remarkable essay on social psychology and race relations (1969).

The most original and imaginative piece of research by Hyman during the 1960s was a complicated sample survey of totally blind adults and children carried out with the assistance of Helen M. Strauss. The idea for the project grew out of conversations he had with his father-in-law, Professor Isaac Kandel. Hyman intended to use an empirical investigation of the phenomenology of the blind to understand the phenomenology of the sighted. As he explained in his proposal to the National Science Foundation,[7] he chose to study the blind "as a powerful vehicle to explore fundamental problems of social psychology, a tool to magnify and sharpen our understanding of the ways in which behavior is guided by perception and communication. . . . The mere contemplation of the blind forces us to think in new ways about old problems." He had problems of race relations primarily in mind. However, he was quite explicit in spelling out the ways in which thinking about the blind had implications for theories of occupational choice, reference groups, stratification, social comparison, and label-

[7]"Communication, Perception and Social Behavior: Explorations in These Fundamental Processes through the Study of the Inter-group Relations and Attitudes of the Blind," Supplementary Report on Phase 1, by Herbert H. Hyman and Helen M. Strauss, March 1, 1963. For this document and other related material, I am indebted to Dr. Stanley Presser of the National Science Foundation and to Dr. Helen M. Strauss.

ing. The NSF financed a small pilot study in 1961, and, in 1963, funded the much larger project.

The many and formidable sampling and interviewing problems associated with this unusual study cannot be briefly summarized, but it should be noted that no comprehensive national list of the blind population existed and that many of the incomplete state and local lists were guarded by officials and agencies not always eager to assist Hyman. The final adult sample, drawn primarily from Detroit, New York City, and Atlanta, consisted of 227 white and 151 black, non-institutionalized, totally blind respondents between the ages of eighteen and seventy. In addition, 116 sighted parents, spouses, or siblings of the blind respondents were interviewed in order to report on the socialization of their blind relatives and to serve as a control group. Finally, a sample of 102 blind children, ten to fifteen years of age, plus nearly all of their sighted mothers and many of their sighted siblings, were interviewed.

Hyman never wrote a final report on this provocative project. Since many of the rich and intriguing findings are still not readily accessible, it is worth citing just a few of them.[8] Among the totally blind respondents, the Hyman study found:

— A large minority, about forty percent, of those defined as blind by public and private agencies did not regard themselves as blind.
— With a few exceptions, the blind were more likely to use the sighted as a reference group rather than other blind.
— The more isolated the blind were from the sighted, the less likely they were to make comparisons with anyone blind or sighted.
— Among poor white and black blind children, those who had high occupational aspirations did so because of, not in spite of, the handicap of being blind.
— The white blind reflected and endorsed the racial values and norms of the regions in which they lived. Thus, southern blind whites were more racially intolerant than northern white blind.
— Nevertheless, regardless of regional norms and values, blind whites were consistently more racially tolerant and less prejudiced than sighted whites.

As an undergraduate, graduate student, and faculty member, Hyman had always been proud of his long affiliation with Columbia University. It was therefore all the more painful when, in the late 1960s, he and an increasing number of the Columbia community became aware of the serious problems facing the university. In the spring

[8]See Hyman, Stokes, and Strauss 1973; Lorenz 1968; and Strauss 1966, 1968.

of 1968, Columbia University was virtually paralyzed while students, faculty, administrators, and New York City police literally battled for control of offices, classrooms, and buildings. This tragic and violent turn of events erupted during the course of student demonstrations provoked, as they were at California, Michigan, Harvard, and other universities, by racial injustice at home and the Vietnam war abroad. But according to the Cox Commission (1968), the intensity of the demonstrations at Columbia was fueled by an interlocking and persistent set of seemingly intractable problems that had plagued the university for years.[9] Thus, even in the absence of disruptive student demonstrations, Columbia University had apparently become, for a substantial proportion of its faculty, a less rewarding place to work. By 1966 the number of senior faculty leaving the university had become a matter of serious concern. Most faculty, of course, did not leave, but the proportion who had become receptive to unsolicited offers from other institutions almost certainly increased.

The extent to which the student demonstrations made some of the Columbia faculty more receptive to outside offers is difficult to say. In Hyman's case, they probably played an important, and perhaps decisive, role. As much as he deplored the American military policy in Vietnam and the persistent patterns of American racial discrimination, he was shocked by the violence of the 1968 disturbances. Like most, though certainly not all, of the senior faculty, Hyman opposed the demonstrations (Cole and Adamsons 1970). He had little sympathy for the student demonstrators and their faculty supporters, though as department chair he had to deal with both.

## The Wesleyan Years

Hyman left Columbia University in 1969 to accept a position as full professor in Wesleyan University's new sociology department.[10] Although there were, then and subsequently, periods of serious unrest and tension at Wesleyan, Hyman quickly adjusted to the smaller, more cohesive, largely undergraduate university. He offered well-received

[9] The problems identified, which surely had their counterparts at other major universities, included: hostile relationships between Columbia and the surrounding neighborhoods; inadequate campus facilities; an ineffectual administration; an indifferent Board of Trustees; a decline in prestige of many graduate programs; a downward slide in faculty salaries; and chronic low morale among many students, younger faculty, and nonacademic employees (Cox Commission Report, 1968).

[10] The Wesleyan department was established in 1967 with my appointment as professor and chair and the successive appointments of Philip H. Ennis from NORC and Vernon K. Dibble from Columbia to senior positions. All three of us had Columbia Ph.D.'s. Albert Hunter and John Brewer, both Chicago Ph.D.'s, joined the department in 1968 and 1969 as assistant and associate professors, respectively.

courses on public opinion, mass communication, social sentiments, and secondary analysis; did his share of committee work; took his turn chairing the department; and served as advisor and consultant to students, faculty, and administrators on a variety of research problems.

Hyman's professional interests continued to be remarkably diverse. He wrote articles and chapters on mass communications, voluntary associations, black matriarchy, unemployment, the social psychology of race, reference individuals, and job aspirations of the blind.[11] Underneath the diversity was, characteristically, the ever-present reliance on sample surveys, his methodological lifeline. As he so often said, he remained addicted to survey research. But at Wesleyan his addiction took a specialized turn as he devoted more of his time to applying survey techniques to the study of social change. Given the extraordinary difficulties of carrying out very long-range studies, he urged the use of secondary analysis as a technically feasible procedure for examining patterns of change. That the reanalysis of cross-sectional data originally collected for one purpose could be fruitfully analyzed for quite a different purpose (e.g., for the study of change) was, of course, not new. The problem was, how to do it effectively? Hyman tackled this difficult question in *Secondary Analysis of Sample Surveys,* published in 1972.[12]

But he went further. In the subsequent decade he conducted, with the financial support of the Spencer Foundation, a series of ingenious secondary analyses to document the long-lasting effects of particular but widely shared experiences. In each of these remarkable studies, an array of national sample surveys, done over relatively long periods of time and involving large numbers of respondents, was combined into a research design allowing for the simultaneous control of aging and cohort effects. As an example, the first, carried out with Charles R. Wright and John S. Reed, drew on fifty-four national surveys done between 1947 and 1971 and used data from 80,000 respondents to relate 250 discrete items of information to respondents' educational background. Published in 1975, *The Enduring Effects of Education* was a tour de force showing that, regardless of when respondents received their education, the retention of knowledge and the continued search for new knowledge are directly and positively related to the number of years spent in school.

The second inquiry, *Education's Lasting Influence on Values,* also done with Charles Wright, was essentially an extension of the first to the realm of values, and the results, published in 1979, were similar. They

[11] See Hyman 1972, 1973, 1974, 1975, 1979; Hyman and Reed 1969; Hyman, Stokes, and Strauss 1973; Hyman and Wright 1971.
[12] Republished by the Wesleyan University Press in 1987.

found that support for selected values like civil liberties, due process of law, and equal opportunity become more prevalent with increasing levels of formal education. The last in the series, *Of Time and Widowhood*, Hyman's final publication, appeared in 1983. It focused ironically on the enduring effects of being widowed. Using cross-sectional and longitudinal data and carefully chosen control groups, his analysis confirmed on a nationwide basis what previous and more circumscribed studies had suggested: the damaging effects of widowhood are less severe among women than men, regardless of their age and the time they are widowed. More surprisingly, Hyman also found that bereavement is generally less traumatic than divorce or separation.

Although his years at Wesleyan were productive and satisfying, they did include a brief period in early 1973 when Hyman's attempt to publicize the futility of the American bombing strategy in Vietnam was rebuffed; the rebuff left him frustrated and bitterly angry. Like millions of others, he had anguished over the horrors and senselessness of the Vietnam war. When, however, he read, heard, and saw the news stories on the intensified massive bombings of Hanoi in December of 1972, he wrote a carefully prepared article for the general reader. This paper, which wholly ignored the principal point of his celebrated 1947 essay, written with Sheatsley, on why information campaigns fail, was intended to enlighten the American public. The paper summarized the results of the World War II bombing surveys of the German and Japanese civilian populations; emphasized the statistically supported finding that, both in Germany and Japan, increased levels of bombing were self-defeating; and raised questions about the current American policy of relying on large-scale bombing in Vietnam.[13] He sent the article to some of the best-known magazines in the country, but not one was willing to publish it. He was led to believe that since the bombings seemed to be decreasing (which was true), his story of the earlier surveys was no longer newsworthy. Hyman's protest that the bombings could be resumed (as they were) brought no response. The article was never published.

Hyman spent the rest of his career at Wesleyan. Elected to the American Academy of Arts and Sciences in 1970 and to the presidency of the Sociological Research Association in 1974, he was a visiting professor at the Italian universities of Catania and Turin in 1972 and at Massachusetts Institute of Technology in 1976. From 1977 to 1982 he served as Wesleyan's Crowell University Professor of the Social Sciences, and in 1983 he received the Helen Dinerman Memorial Award from the World Association for Public Opinion Research. In 1984 he

---

[13] Wilensky (1967, pp. 24–34) had made essentially the same point several years earlier.

retired, planning to devote more time to a project that, with the support of the Russell Sage Foundation, he had been pursuing for years: a history of modern sample survey research based largely on his own experiences.[14] A year later, he gave an invited paper at the "All-China Conference on the Uses of Sociology," held at Zhongshan University in the People's Republic of China. He died unexpectedly of cardiac arrest on December 18, 1985, in China, a few days after delivering his paper, "The Use of Surveys in Developing Societies."

## Hyman's Role Orientations

Any overview of Hyman's career in objective terms would be seriously deficient without some complementary reference to its subjective dimensions, particularly his conception of what he thought he, as a social scientist, was doing. In his case it was certainly this professional sensibility, this configuration of personal perspectives and technical issues, that gave such distinctive coherence to his research. As we have seen, his professional life as a social psychologist was tied to the rise of modern sample survey research,[15] and he plainly had much in common with that small band of pioneers who shaped the new research technology. But he was, in his own right, a leader and an influential role model, a singular "significant other" for the survey research community. A wise intellectual, a special voice, with gifts that transcended trained experience, he was a man, as the *Public Opinion Quarterly* (Fall 1960, p. 383) pointed out, with "few equals in the range and profundity of his intellectual explorations." What Hyman studied, wrote, and said usually went beyond the occasion at hand because his work characteristically brought together several major themes that gave his role as a researcher unmistakable personal meaning: an abiding concern with ethnography, a wide range of substantive interests, a clear stance as a social psychologist, and a comparative and relational style of thought.

Hyman thought of social psychology, sociology, and sample survey research as sciences.[16] He considered himself a social and behavioral

---

[14] To be published by the Russell Sage Foundation.

[15] The specific contributions made to contemporary social psychology by Hyman through his work in survey research are described by Katz in Chapter 9 of this volume.

[16] To be more specific, he thought of survey research as a device for making sociology and social psychology more scientific. A statement written with Katz early in his career summarizes a position he never seriously questioned: "Laboratory experiments on motivation have yielded valuable information about the biology of basic drives but they have given us few generalizations for controlling and predicting human behavior in the complex social situations of practical life. . . . Fortunately, the scientific logic of laboratory procedures can be applied to such problems through the field, or survey method. This method, through observation and interviewing by a field staff of investigators,

scientist. Such images of work were, of course, part of the professional environment, of the thought collective, as Fleck (1979, p. 38) has so aptly named it, within which he worked. Although widely shared throughout the social sciences, the imagery never went unchallenged, even in principle. More significantly, in the context of the different, often inconsistent, and sometimes contradictory conceptions of the concrete meaning of science among those who counted themselves as social scientists, the imagery when applied to survey research rarely failed to provoke criticism. Indeed, as Hyman knew, there were respected advocates of the scientific method, notably in psychology and economics, who openly rejected the subjective data and correlational techniques of survey research as intrinsically unscientific.[17] Hyman disagreed strongly with this proscience but antisurvey research perspective, as did Floyd Allport, Stouffer, Lazarsfeld, Murphy, Likert, Katz, and Campbell, to cite only a few of many like-minded social researchers who saw surveys as an important scientific tool. But Hyman's disagreement grew, in part, out of an ethnographic orientation that was not shared by many other advocates of survey research.

To Hyman's mind, survey research, as a scientific tool, was ethnographic in two related senses. First, in the more primitive or uncritical sense, its roots, like those of science, were in the ethnography of everyday life. Though acutely aware of the difficulties imposed by a commonsense view of the world, he was impressed by the similarities between that view and scientific knowledge. He saw survey research as an elaboration of those information-seeking efforts that are part and parcel of ordinary social life, a familiar view in the philosophy of science (Rouse 1987). In Quine's (1976, p. 229) words: "Science is not a substitute for common sense, but an extension of it. The quest for knowledge is properly an effort simply to broaden and deepen the

---

identifies and measures the factors operative in the social situation outside the laboratory and so builds up the principles necessary for a science of social psychology" (Katz and Hyman 1947, p. 437).

[17] These "scientific" critics of survey research shared with Hyman, and other advocates of survey research as "science," a faith in experimental design as the paradigm for verifying causal relationships. They differed in the extent to which they thought survey research could realistically match the criteria of a well controlled experiment. The formal objections to utilizing experimental methods, in the laboratory or in surveys, for the purpose of establishing causal relations had been spelled out in accessible terms by the 1930s (Cohen and Nagel 1934, pp. 265–67). But neither the "scientific" critics nor the "scientific" defenders of survey research paid much heed, preferring to define and debate the issues within the technical vocabulary of validity and reliability. The controversy, which never took into account the often agonistic criticisms directed at any social research modeled on the natural sciences, has largely died down. However, it is still capable of arousing moral indignation, as, for example, the recent dispute over the use of survey data to establish a causal link between marijuana and heroin use (Baumrind 1983; O'Donnell and Clayton 1982) testifies.

knowledge which the man in the street already enjoys, in moderation, in relation to the commonplace things around him." What could be more natural, Hyman often remarked, than to ask people for needed information? Or, to seek out those who seem to represent the best sources of information? Or, to try to avoid asking foolish or misleading questions and to attend seriously to questions that would provide needed knowledge? The procedure of asking questions of a sample of people is such a part of our usual routine as to constitute an integral part of everyday existence.

In the second place, survey research is approximately the same, if a more standardized, procedure as that followed by anthropologists when they conduct field studies. Thus, as an effort to acquire information from individuals in a particular culture, survey research is ethnographic in this more technical sense. To be sure, survey research was characteristically more quantitatively and substantively restricted than conventional anthropology; but it was, as Hyman saw the matter, no less ethnographic in intent and in effect.

This ethnographic orientation undoubtedly grew out of Hyman's long-standing fascination with anthropology. But it was also strongly reinforced by two psychologists. One was his teacher Otto Klineberg, whose ability to combine social psychology and cultural anthropology set a standard that Hyman never ceased to admire (Hyman 1979). The other was Kurt Lewin, whose field theory, with its emphasis on individual and social space and its insistence on the need for subjective and objective data (Lewin 1951), seemed to Hyman consistent with the principles of effective survey research and good anthropological practice.[18]

The view of survey research as ethnography was, it should be noted, not only or simply a part of Hyman's private orientation. When he began his career, nonexperimental studies of social life, whether based on observation, participant observation, or sample surveys, were frequently referred to collectively as "field studies," connoting a strong family resemblance to anthropological fieldwork. Similarly, in those days, respondents in surveys were often called "informants," and surveys were often preceded by fieldwork in the communities to be studied. One of Hyman's (1945) earliest papers described the importance of these preliminary field studies for sample surveys, and especially the critical role of "key informants." Although this ethnographic frame of reference eventually dropped from sight among survey researchers, it persisted as an active and characteristic ingredient in Hyman's own thinking.

[18] For the same reasons, he greatly respected the work of Solomon E. Asch, whose 1952 text on *Social Psychology* was, Hyman thought, unsurpassed.

This tendency is quite evident, for example, in Hyman's innovative analyses of interviewers' assessments of their respondents' behavior (Hyman et al. 1954; 1975). Viewing the interviewer as an active informant about a cultural experience shared with interviewed members of the same culture is a procedure that many social anthropologists would presumably find familiar and enlightening. It is one of Hyman's innovations that has never been seriously pursued. Sometimes, especially in his early survey work with Katz on morale in war industries, Hyman came close to playing the roles of anthropologist and survey analyst simultaneously. But, as a rule, his ethnographic orientation was simply woven, more or less explicitly, into his formulation of a research design. It is understandably made explicit in his 1964 United Nations study, done with Gene Levine and Charles Wright, of the "opinions, beliefs, and experiences of 445 experts working in various spheres of social development activity, distributed among thirteen countries in four regions of the developing world" (Hyman et al. 1967). But the same orientation was just as salient twenty years earlier in his famous dissertation on reference groups. There he had occasion to remark, modestly, that in interviewing his subjects about the meaning they assigned to social status, he was simply following the reasonable lead of ethnologists.[19]

Hyman's ethnographic perspective largely accounts for his persistent interest in an unusually wide range of dissimilar substantive topics. From his anthropological point of view, almost any technical issue in any of the social sciences could, in principle and often in practice, be examined to illuminate the cultural world within which it was located. Interviewer effects, for instance, were for Hyman not just a technical problem in survey research but a manifestation of the much broader phenomenon of group membership.[20] He was consequently prepared to see in any particular problem an opportunity to learn about the cultural, structural, and psychological variables that, in vari-

[19] "When the ethnologist reconstructs the social organization of a society, he does so mainly from the reports of informants and the observation of the behavior of individuals. Hence, the only way to find out the criteria for status is by an actual field study of the way people view the matter of status" (Hyman 1942, p. 7).

[20] He never tired of insisting that most technical problems in survey research were also substantive problems. In a paper read before a University of Chicago Seminar on Communications and Public Opinion in September 1949, he emphasized this point, using a situational theory of attitudes as his illustration: "We can fill in some of the concrete details for such a theory by interpreting the interview situation as a miniature of the larger social setting and seeing some of the interviewer effects as analogies to the influence of social factors on the expression of attitudes. . . . Such reactions by the interviewer to the group membership of the respondent and the corresponding reactions of the respondents to the group membership of the interviewer . . . provide incidental evidence of the pervasive influence of group membership on human behavior" (Hyman 1949–50, pp. 366–67).

ous combinations, constituted the broader social environment. Interest in a problem is usually a necessary but hardly a sufficient condition for making, as Hyman so often did, a recognized contribution to its resolution. Still, he probably would not have had the perceived opportunity to apply his fertile mind to so many areas of substantive inquiry in the absence of his ethnographically induced outlook, a view that allowed him to move confidently and creatively into the study of industrial morale, public opinion, race relations, voluntary associations, education, unemployment, political socialization, stratification, civil liberties, mass communication, the blind, the widowed, and, of course, his own specialty, reference groups.

As wide-ranging as Hyman's substantive interests were, they were almost always expressed openly or tacitly in the language of survey research. This had notable consequences. It meant, for one thing, that the terms he used to depict or explain, for example, changing attitudes toward civil liberties, the effects of gender on being widowed, or the occupational aspirations of the blind were drawn from the grammar and vocabulary, and hence the logic, of survey research. This had the further effect of spreading both the word about survey research, and, in almost Whorfian fashion, the inclination to view the researchable world primarily through the eyes of its technical idiom. This not only meant that specialists in, say, civil liberties or aging were learning to think in the categories derived from this one mode of research; it also meant that the esoteric language of survey research was increasingly employed, more or less explicitly, to formulate empirical and theoretical questions among an ever-widening circle of social scientists who were predominantly consumers rather than practitioners of survey research. Hyman played a leading role in this historic diffusion of ideas. Modern sample survey research was a response to a widely felt need among those with otherwise divergent interests for an efficient method for collecting and analyzing data about large numbers of people. But it received its intellectual legitimacy as a powerful and prestigious research technique in large measure because it was accepted, and therefore validated, by academic consumers of research, the overwhelming majority of whom did not conduct surveys. Hyman was, of course, not the only survey analyst with multiple interests. But Hyman's portfolio of diversified interests, combined with his command of survey methodology, enabled him, more than any other survey researcher of his generation, to reach repeatedly this critical and exoteric audience of social scientists. He helped to persuade social scientists of the value of survey research by allowing them to see how it could illuminate their own areas of specialized concern.

If Hyman's ethnographic turn of mind nourished his appetite for a variety of substantive problems, and if his command of the intricacies of survey research gave logical unity to his diverse interests, it was his abiding commitment to a Durkheimian social psychology that made the problems and the research so salient for him. He was, in his own eyes, primarily a social psychologist. Though he recognized the merits of quite different conceptions, the core of social psychology was, in his mind, the description and explanation of the subjective dimensions of the objective social world. Unlike many American social psychologists, he did not believe that social phenomena could be reduced to any form of psychology, social or otherwise. Sociology was, in his judgment, correctly concerned with the external cultural and structural world. That some people were rich and powerful while others were poor and powerless; that blacks and whites did not have the same life chances; that not everyone held the same values and norms; that many could see but some were blind; these and other similar regularities were, he thought, undeniable sociological facts of life. Furthermore, he had no doubt that these and other constraints often operated independently of how they were psychologically defined and experienced. In fact, some of his most thoughtful and persuasive criticisms were directed at what he considered to be misguided attempts to psychologize about the social world, to locate, for example, the irrational elements of collective human existence in individual personality configurations (Hyman and Sheatsley 1953), or to see in public opinion nothing but aggregated psychological attributes (Hyman 1957).

Nonetheless, as a social psychologist Hyman was convinced beyond doubt that understanding the social world would never be complete without a systematic analysis of its subjective dimension, a dimension that varied with the differing psychological worlds of the participants in it. For him the pattern of differential phenomenology was the organizing principle of social psychology: people do not subjectively respond in uniform ways to the social world they share. Thus, Hyman's rule, as extracted from his work, augments Thomas' theorem: individuals with the same objective social characteristics do not define their situation in the same way. From his 1942 doctoral dissertation on the psychology of social status to his 1983 monograph on the experiences of being widowed, the subjective social psychology of the objective sociological world was a controlling theme found in all of Hyman's research.

Finally, beneath his ethnographic outlook, his diversified interests, and his commitment to social psychology, Hyman developed a habitual way of thinking governed by an almost intuitive reliance on a comparative syntax. As is so often the case with gifted scholars and scientists, his natural turn of mind was to arrange words, ideas, facts, theories, hypotheses, predictions, and conclusions comparatively. This personal capacity was strongly reinforced by his training and experience in cultural ethnology, statistical reasoning, and research design. This trained capacity is most openly spelled out, naturally enough, in his methodological writings, where he emphatically insisted on the irreplaceable role of control variables and subgroup comparisons, warning time and again of the dangers of fictitious comparisons. His advice was not restricted to the logical and empirical imperatives of sound research practice. It applied across the board to every stage of problem solving in the social sciences, with Hyman arguing, in effect, that the logic and substance of research, like the logic and content of theories, always involved a relational analysis. Although his counsel plainly touches the known rudiments of intellectual work and seems self-evident for any form of empirical inquiry, the principle on which it is based seems to have slipped into oblivion among many social scientists. Hyman's advice needs to be heeded, if only to retrieve what we know. For example, consider two instances in which he chided researchers for their insensitivity to the relational dimensions of the phenomena they were investigating. If, Hyman noted emphatically, we want to understand an authoritarian personality or the alleged pattern of black matriarchy, the characteristics of personalities *free* of authoritarian traits and the characteristics of *white* mothers are essential to all phases of the inquiry (Hyman and Sheatsley 1953; Hyman and Reed 1969).

A more telling example is his discussion of the obstacles to a theory of public opinion (Hyman 1957). Before such an explanation can be formulated, he said, we need to think carefully about *nonpublic* opinion, its meaning, measurement, and possible explanations. The same point applies implicitly to other areas: the study of small groups requires a comparison with large groups; bureaucracies can be understood only in contrast to nonbureaucratic organizations; the imputation of ideological thought requires a clear conception of nonideological ideas; and so forth. Even more broadly, the distinctive meaning of psychological, social, cultural, and structural concepts ultimately depends upon a process of contrasting each with the others.

Hyman's principle of comparative thought goes well beyond the self-evident, but often neglected, routine of controlling relevant variables in experimental and survey research. Generalizing about his recommendation regarding public opinion, this principle asserts that the identification of significant phenomena, the distinction between their correlates and components, and the transformation of both into problems worth investigating require at each step of the way a comparative frame of reference. That this principle applies, and is known to apply, to daily life is hardly news to anyone familiar with the large literature

(Suls and Miller, 1977) on social comparison processes. Hyman's exemplary work suggests that it might profitably be made a more explicit and organized part of theory and research in all corners of social psychology and sociology. Although the suggestion will not, of course, provide the sagacity for knowing what comparisons will work in particular cases, it should help us understand more clearly what we are doing as social scientists. In that sense, it constitutes a valuable and altogether fitting bequest from a pioneer in the exploration of reference groups.

## A Gift in Common

The full extent of Hyman's legacy to the fields in which he labored is difficult to measure, but its enduring value is beyond question. The contributions to this *Festschrift* represent a special public acknowledgment of that value. They were written to honor Herbert Hyman, as only scholars, scientists, and artists honor the best among themselves, with a gift made of their individual work. The contributed papers that make up this gift have been grouped under six headings: survey research, reference groups, social psychology, public opinion, inequality, and mass media.

Part I, "Survey Research," follows this introduction. It includes essays by Charles Glock, a personal account of persistent problems encountered in survey research; by Howard Schuman and Lawrence Bobo, on experimentation within sample surveys; by Sigmund Diamond, on the involvement of the Federal Bureau of Investigation in survey research; and by Charles Lemert, on some theoretical reactions to perceived deficiencies in survey research. In Part II, "Reference Groups," there are papers by Harriet Zuckerman, on the effects of being chosen as a role model; by Hubert O'Gorman, relating reference group theory to pluralistic ignorance; by Robert Merton, discussing invisible colleges and deviance among scientists within a reference group framework; and by Christian Bay, urging a reformulation of the normative basis of political obligation. In Part III, "Social Psychology," there are contributions by Dan Katz, on the impact of survey research on social psychology; by Morris Rosenberg, on the link between sensitivity to self-threatening situations and participation in political discussions; by Leonard Pearlin, on the ways in which cultural values control experience in social structures; and by Dan Miller and Elliott Jaques, on an interaction conception of psychosis.

Part IV, on "Public Opinion," consists of two papers; one, by Elisabeth Noelle-Neumann, describes the events and ideas that led to the development of her well-known theory about "the spiral of silence";

the other, by Stephen Cole and Robert Fiorentine, analyzes public attitudes toward nuclear power. In Part V, "Inequality," there are papers by Robin Williams, assessing the conflicting evidence regarding white racial attitudes and actions; by Robert Hill, discussing racism in terms of unintended institutional effects; by James Coleman, exploring the conflict between equality and excellence in education; and by Stanley Lebergott, explaining why some signs of economic inequality are misleading. The last section, Part VI, "Mass Media," includes contributions by Eleanor Singer, describing the images of survey research as presented by the mass media; by Jonathan Cole, examining the different views of cholesterol found in the mass media and the scientific community; by Charles Wright, on the use of the mass media by the elderly; and by Leo Bogart, on the impact of cable television and videocassette recorders on the Hollywood film industry.

"No work of social research is perfect," Hyman once reminded us. "Human beings, scientists no less than critics, are fallible. Practical limitations impose themselves on every empirical investigation and force departures from the ideal. Unexpected contingencies destroy the most perfect of research plans. . . . But while perfection cannot be expected, sound canons of criticism require . . . the adoption of high standards. . . . If it is unfair to expect perfection, it is no less than fair to expect a great deal."[21] During his more than forty years of research, we learned to expect a great deal from Hyman. He gave us far more than we expected.

## Coda

William James was Herb Hyman's hero. He cited the eminent psychologist and philosopher frequently in his writings and countless times in conversation. Of all of James's observations, Herb's favorite was the conclusion that while there is very little difference between one human being and another, that difference makes all the difference. As sociologists and social psychologists we understand James's point. The recent histories of our fields cannot be written without close attention to Herb's work; his footprints are everywhere. As family, friends, colleagues, and students we painfully recognize the truth, power, and beauty of James's remark. Herb made a personal difference in the lives of all of us. Our individual and collective biographies cannot be properly recorded, our autobiographies cannot be faithfully narrated, without taking into detailed account the part that he played. His presence so obviously enlivened and enlightened us that it

[21] Hyman and Sheatsley 1953, p. 51.

is hard to imagine what life would have been without him. Each of us knew him, of course, in different ways. So it would be presumptuous and futile to try to compute the sum of what he gave to us, or of what we lost so suddenly and irretrievably. Still, our personal recollections will not go unnoted, nor will they go away: Herb's love for his family; his affection and loyalty to friends; his concern for students; his deeply felt commitment to scholarship and science; his outrage at the needless blunders of life; his affinity for animals; his irrepressible sense of humor; his unfeigned modesty; his shining and restless intelligence; his diffusive wisdom and pervasive gentleness.

An unpretentious man of enormous stature, Herbert Hiram Hyman made a difference.

## Bibliography

Adorno, Theodor W., Else Frenkel-Brunswik, Daniel J. Levinson, and R. Nevitt Sanford. 1950. *The authoritarian personality.* New York: Harpers.

Asch, Solomon E. 1952. *Social psychology.* New York: Prentice-Hall, Inc.

Baumrind, Diana. 1983. Specious causal attributions in the social sciences. *Journal of Personality and Social Psychology* 45, pp. 1289–98.

Chapman, Dwight W., and John Volkmann. 1939. A social determinant of the level of aspiration. *Journal of Abnormal and Social Psychology* 34, pp. 225–38.

Cohen, Morris R., and Ernest Nagel. 1934. *An introduction to logic and the scientific method.* New York: Harcourt, Brace and Company.

Cole, Stephen, and Hannelore Adamsons. 1970. Faculty status and faculty support of student demonstrations. *Public Opinion Quarterly* 34, pp. 389–94.

Cox Commission Report. 1968. *Crisis at Columbia.* New York: Vintage Books.

Davis, Elmer. 1943. OWI has a job. *Public Opinion Quarterly* 7, pp. 5–14.

Dreis, Thelma. 1951. The Department of Agriculture's sample interview survey as a tool of administration. Unpublished doctoral dissertation. Washington, D.C.: American University.

Fleck, Ludwik. 1979. *Genesis and development of a scientific fact.* Chicago: The University of Chicago Press.

Hartmann, George W., and Theodore M. Newcomb. 1940. *Industrial conflict.* New York: Dryden Press.

Hawkins, Lester G., Jr., and George S. Pette. 1943. OWI—organization and problems. *Public Opinion Quarterly* 7, pp. 15–33.

Hunt, William A., and John Volkmann. 1937. The anchoring of an affective scale. *American Journal of Psychology* 49, pp. 88–92.

Lewin, Kurt. 1951. *Field theory in social science.* New York: Harper and Brothers.

Lorenz, Gerda K. 1968. Attitudes toward racial desegregation among the blind, and patterns of consensus between blind and sighted relatives. Unpublished doctoral dissertation. New York: Columbia University.

Merton, Robert K., and Alice Kitt Rossi. 1950. Contributions to the theory of reference group behavior. Pp. 40–105 in Robert K. Merton and Paul F. Lazarsfeld (eds.), *Continuities in social research.* New York: The Free Press.

Merton, Robert K. 1957. *Social theory and social structure.* New York: Free Press.

Mosteller, Frederick *et al.* 1949. *The pre-election polls of 1948.* New York: Social Science Research Council, Bulletin No. 60.

Niemi, Richard G. 1973. Political socialization. Pp. 117–38 in Jeanne N. Knutson (ed.), *Handbook of political psychology.* San Francisco: Jossey-Bass.

O'Donnell, John A., and Richard R. Clayton. 1982. The stepping-stone hypothesis—marijuana, heroin, and causality. *Chemical Dependencies: Behavioral and Biomedical Issues* 4, pp. 229–41.

Quine, Willard V. 1976. *The ways of paradox and other essays.* Revised and enlarged edition. Cambridge, Mass.: Harvard University Press.

Rouse, Joseph T. 1987. *Knowledge and power: toward a political philosophy of science.* Ithaca, New York: Cornell University Press.

Schuman, Howard, and Graham Kalton. 1985. Survey methods. Pp. 635–97 in Gardner Lindzey and Elliot Aronson (eds.), *Handbook of social psychology.* Vol. 1. New York: Random House.

Skott, Hans E. 1943. Attitude research in the Department of Agriculture. *Public Opinion Quarterly* 7, pp. 280–92.

Stouffer, Samuel A. 1955. *Communism, conformity, and civil liberties.* New York: Doubleday and Company.

Stouffer, Samuel A., et al. 1949. *The American soldier,* 2 vols. Princeton, New Jersey: Princeton University Press.

Strauss, Helen M. 1966. A study of reference group and social comparison processes among the blind. Unpublished doctoral dissertation. New York: Columbia University.

———1968. Reference group and social comparison processes among the totally blind. Pp. 222–37 in Herbert H. Hyman and Eleanor Singer (eds.), *Readings in reference group theory and research.* New York: The Free Press.

Suls, Jerry M., and Richard L. Miller. 1977. *Social comparison processes.* New York: John Wiley and Sons.

Turner, Charles F., and Elizabeth Martin. 1984. *Surveying subjective phenomena,* 2 volumes. New York: Russell Sage Foundation.

United States Strategic Bombing Survey. 1946–47. *The effects of strategic bombing on German morale,* 2 volumes. Washington, D.C.: U.S. Government Printing Office.

———1947. *The effects of strategic bombing on Japanese morale.* Washington, D.C.: U.S. Government Printing Office.

Volkmann, John. 1936. The anchoring of absolute scales. *Psychological Bulletin* 33, pp. 742–43.

Wallace, Henry A., and James L. McCamy. 1940. Straw polls and public administration. *Public Opinion Quarterly* 4, pp. 221–23.

Wilensky, Harold L. 1967. *Organizational intelligence.* New York: Basic Books, Inc.

*Part I*  Survey Research

# Charles Y. Glock

## 1 Reflections on Doing Survey Research

Herbert Hyman's *Survey Design and Analysis* (1955) was the first comprehensive effort to codify then existing knowledge about the conduct of survey research. Since then there have been numerous additional codifications, some seeking to be comprehensive and others focusing on one or another element in the survey process (e.g., Hyman 1972; Rosenberg 1968; Sudman 1976).

The codification is never completed. This is because new innovations make the process an ongoing one. It is also a result of many practitioners not reporting their own experience and of prospective codifiers not being privy enough to the thought processes of particular investigators to do the job for them.

All of this led to the thought, as I was contemplating a subject for this essay, that older practitioners might be of assistance to codifiers by offering observations about things learned and problems faced in designing and executing surveys deemed to be of more than incidental interest. There is danger in such an enterprise of no more being accomplished than documenting what is already obvious to everyone. Documenting the obvious is an element in codification, however, and insofar as anyone's experience may raise new issues or be at odds with others' perceptions about correct procedure, it can contribute to clarifying what needs to be done and what differences need to be reconciled before codification can be achieved. Moreover, if this kind of endeavor works, others might be stimulated to similar effort.

For those unfamiliar with it, a brief introductory word about my experience in survey research might be in order. I was first exposed to survey research in market research courses taken while an undergraduate at New York University in the late 1930s. While at NYU, I worked part time as an interviewer for the Psychological Corporation and, later, as a research assistant to Darrell B. Lucas on the surveys supervised by the then Magazine Audience Group for *Life, Collier's, Look,* and *Liberty* magazines. I received some further training in survey research while pursuing an M.B.A. at Boston University. Upon graduation in 1941, my goal was to pursue a career in advertising and market research. With a 1A draft status, however, it was hard to find a permanent job, and I spent most of the summer of 1941 on temporary assignments as an interviewer for various advertising agencies.

A chance encounter on Madison Avenue in New York with Matthew Murphy, an NYU faculty member with whom I had taken a course or two, dramatically changed the course of my barely launched career. When informed of my unemployment, Murphy suggested that I consider making an application to the Office of Radio Research (ORR) at Columbia University which, he understood, had open a number of coding jobs. Murphy was right about the availability of jobs. I applied and was hired. The job lasted only several weeks, but before my expected departure the supervisor, Hazel Gaudet, later Erskine, introduced me to Paul Lazarsfeld, director of the ORR, and recommended that I be considered for one of the Rockefeller Fellowships which the ORR commanded. The fellowship was forthcoming, and I remained at ORR until the end of January 1942, at which time I entered the army. The few months at Columbia were spent mostly in running cross-tabulations for Lazarsfeld on a Hollerith counter-sorter. The data sets, coincidentally, were the surveys conducted on behalf of the Magazine Audience Group, of which, it turned out, Lazarsfeld was a member.

My army career afforded no further exposure to survey research per se, although a good part of my time was spent in doing field research in England for the finance arm of the Army Air Corps. During the war, Lazarsfeld dropped me a note once a year or so, extending greetings and inviting me to consider returning to Columbia when the war was over and I was released from service. When this happened in November 1945, I took Lazarsfeld up on his invitation and joined the staff of the Bureau of Applied Social Research, the successor organization to the ORR. My initial assignments were to serve as office manager and apprentice researcher.

The choice to return to Columbia also represented a decision to pursue a Ph.D. in sociology at Columbia. In so doing, I received considerable additional formal training in survey research. And, at the bureau, I became actively engaged in doing survey research, first under Lazarsfeld's supervision and later on my own. While at Columbia, I became director of the bureau and eventually a member of the faculty.

It was at Columbia that I first became acquainted with Herb Hyman. His appointment to the Columbia faculty was not accompanied immediately by an association with the bureau because he retained research commitments to the National Opinion Research Center. Subsequently, however, the opportunity to work on the project that resulted in the monograph *Applications of Methods of Evaluation: Four Studies of the Encampment for Citizenship* (Hyman, Wright, and Hopkins 1962) produced a bureau connection and shortly thereafter an appointment as one of the bureau's associate directors. Herb and I became friends, and we maintained close professional and personal contact throughout his life.

I remained at Columbia until 1958 when I accepted an offer to found the Survey Research Center and to join the sociology faculty at the University of California, Berkeley. I headed the center until 1968 but remained associated with it until my retirement from the university in 1979. I cannot conceive of trying to count the number of surveys with which I have been associated. Suffice it to say, there have been a goodly number of them and on such diverse topics as girl scouting, the appeal of Betty Crocker, radio listening in the Middle East, attitudes toward the oil industry, higher education, public responses to the Eichmann trial, the uses of the wilderness, the new religions and the old ones, anti-Semitism, racial attitudes, the structuring of reality, and so on.

Except in one instance (Glock 1967), I have not previously subjected my work in survey research to inner reflection about it. What follows will include some reference to points made in the earlier essay. For the most part, however, this is the first time these reflections have been written down. They are organized around the following rubrics: survey design, the nature of survey research, concept formation, theory, instrument construction, variable building, and causal analysis.

## Survey Design

Most of the surveys with which I have been associated have employed a standard cross-sectional design and do not warrant any further comment in the present context. There have been a few departures from convention, however, among them several designs that justify inclusion if and when someone should attempt a codification of survey designs akin to what Campbell and Stanley (1963) have done for experimental designs.

I was not party to the invention of my favorite design, although I feel a strong association with it because it produced the data on which my doctoral dissertation was based (Glock 1952). I include it on the assumption that it may not be familiar to many in the present generation of survey researchers.

The design I have in mind is the one employed in the 1941 study of voting behavior whose results were published in *The People's Choice* (Lazarsfeld, Berelson, and Gaudet 1944). Substantively, that study attempted to assess the impact of the mass media on the public's voting decisions. Methodologically, Lazarsfeld and his associates wanted to examine the effects of "mortality" and response conditioning in panel studies.

The design invented to serve these purposes called for interviewing 3,000 persons representing a cross-sectional sample of the eligible voting population of Erie County, Ohio, where the study took place. (A community study was chosen to insure common respondent access to newspapers and radio stations.) From the first interview wave, four groups of 600 persons were selected by stratified sampling, thus constituting four matched groups. One of these groups was designated the main panel and reinterviewed five times before the November election and once after. Each of the remaining three groups was reinterviewed only once: Control Group 1 was reinterviewed when the main panel was being interviewed a third time, Control Group 2 was reinterviewed at the time of the fourth main panel interview, and Control Group 3 was reinterviewed at the time of the sixth main panel interview.

The design allowed the substantive purposes of the study to be pursued using the seven interviews conducted with the main panel. At each interview, data were collected both on media exposure and on voting expectations or behavior, thus allowing study of the interplay between the two. The main panel also enabled an examination of panel mortality. It was possible not only to determine the size of mortality from one wave to another but also to find out who the dropouts were and how they compared with the active participants. By comparing change and stability of the responses of the main panel and the control groups between the first and subsequent interviews, it was also possible to assess how much response conditioning took place, to determine its direction, and to learn if it increased, decreased, or remained the same with additional interview waves (see Glock 1952 for the results).

The beauty of the design lies in its incorporating into a panel survey a field experiment of considerable complexity. The design has wide applicability to the study of attitude formation and change. To my knowledge, however, the design has not been repeated in as complex a form.

Of the survey designs with which I have been personally involved, the one I admire most is one whose invention I think I share with Hanan Selvin. One never knows for sure about such things, however, and it could be that without being conscious of it we were borrowing from someone else. In any case, I cite it because it impresses me as a design that has applicability to situations far beyond the one in which it was employed initially.

The design grew out of a request in 1952 from the then Protestant Episcopal Church (the Protestant has since been dropped) to the Bureau of Applied Social Research for a study of Episcopalians' knowledge of and agreement or disagreement with a wide range of social policies adopted by the Church over a number of years at its national conventions. It was standard bureau practice to accept such commissions only where the project under consideration could serve a scholarly purpose as well as the applied needs of the prospective client. The client, of course, had to agree to the two purposes being served. The study thus became the attitude survey the Church wanted and an inquiry into the nature, sources, and consequences of Church involvement, which the bureau representative, namely myself, saw as the project's potential scholarly contribution (Glock, Ringer, and Babbie 1967). In both connections, it seemed useful to inquire into how context might influence parishioners' attitudes and behavior; hence the contextual design I now describe.

The design involved the following elements: first, the administration of a questionnaire to a national sample of parishioners using a two-stage sampling design with a sample of parishes chosen first and the sample of parishioners chosen from members of the sampled parishes. The design called for enough parishioners to be included in each sampled parish to allow individual questionnaire responses to be aggregated so as to produce variables characterizing the parish context. Parishes could be classified, for example, according to the proportion of their members who had attended worship services the previous Sunday. In addition to the questionnaire administered to parishioners, two questionnaires were sent to the rector of each of the sampled parishes: one for him to fill out about himself (no herselfs then, although there are now) and the other for him to describe the characteristics of his parish—size, budget, geographical location, and so on. The Episcopal Church is organized into dioceses presided over by a bishop. The design also called for administering a questionnaire to all of the bishops of the Church.

The analytic features of the design are perhaps self-evident. The design allows analysis at the levels of the parishioners, the rectors, the parishes, and the bishops. At each level, data about the other three levels can be introduced in analyzing the level at issue. For example, in analyzing the data collected from parishioners, data about their bishops, their rectors, and their parishes can be introduced to understand parishioner behavior and attitudes. Especially to be noted is that two kinds of data about parishes can be utilized in this way: the data about the parishes supplied by the rectors and the aggregated data from the parishioners surveyed in each sampled parish.

This design lends itself to application to a wide variety of situations where the subjects to be studied share contexts of one kind or another. It has been used, in a less elaborate form than just described, in a study of academic social scientists. In that study (Lazarsfeld and Thielens 1958), a two-stage sampling design was used. A sample of the nation's colleges and universities was drawn first after which a sample of social science faculty was chosen from within the sampled schools. Independent data were also collected about each of the sampled schools. The design would also be applicable in studies, for example, of patients and staff of an area's or of the nation's hospitals, of members of a union which is divided into locals and of members of organizations such as the Boy Scouts and Kiwanis which have local chapters.

A third design, which I believe to be a classic, is one whose invention was the result of a group effort. I was part of the group as were, if I recall correctly, James S. Coleman, Elihu Katz, Herbert Menzel, David Sills and Joseph Precker. All, except Precker who represented the client, were bureau research assistants or associates at the time. In 1953, the bureau had been approached by a drug company to help it decide whether or not the company's advertising of a new drug in a medical journal represented a good investment. After considerable discussion, the client was persuaded that the question they should be addressing is how doctors come to innovate new drugs into their practices. The company agreed with this reformulation and commissioned a study to get the answers. The agreement, as usual, gave the bureau the right of publication. The major subsequent publication was *Medical Innovation: A Diffusion Study* (Coleman, Katz, and Menzel 1966).

As background to a description of the study design, it is to be noted that a new species of drugs—the tetracyclines—had been introduced recently on the market; the sponsoring drug company was among a number of firms marketing a brand of the species. Also to be noted is that a preliminary examination of the innovation literature suggested that physicians' adoption of new drugs might be influenced in significant ways by their status in the medical community.

Resources would have permitted a study of a national sample of physicians using a traditional cross-sectional design. Such a design would have had the advantage of allowing results to be projected to the national physician population. The design was not judged ideal, however, for learning about physicians' status in the medical community or for obtaining accurate information on their use of the new drug. Relying on physicians' self-reports in these regards would not be reliable, it was felt. And we were not able to conceive of an affordable procedure for obtaining independent checks on physicians' self-reports using a national cross-sectional survey design.

To overcome these obstacles, a design was chosen that called for doing the study in only four communities and for interviewing therein all practicing physicians who had the opportunity to prescribe the new drug. The limit of four communities was dictated by available resources. The four were chosen to provide variation in the availability of hospital facilities and proximity to a medical school so as to assess possible differences in patterns of innovation in different settings.

Interviewing all of these doctors allowed us to ask each of them sociometric questions about which other doctors in the community they respected and went to for advice. This provided a powerful means for assessing each physician's influence on other physicians.

In the interviews conducted with them, physicians were asked about their use of the new drug. Primary reliance for such information, however, was placed on records of drug prescriptions obtained from the communities' pharmacists. With the approval of the local medical associations, pharmacists made their prescription records available to the investigators. These provided accurate data on when and how frequently each physician had prescribed the new drug since its innovation.

Sociometric designs were not foreign to studies of innovation when the study just described was undertaken, nor was the use of independent sources to obtain information on the adoption of innovations. The study described, however, combined the two in a unique way and represents a design useful not only for the study of innovation but for investigating power relationships in closed systems as well.

These examples, it will have been noted, were all drawn from studies done at the Bureau of Applied Social Research. Virtually all of the surveys I was associated with at the Survey Research Center at Berkeley employed conventional cross-sectional designs. There were some variations, which warrant brief mention here because they represent innovations that could be more widely used.

One of the problems with cross-sectional designs is that they do not ordinarily provide enough cases to allow analysis of units with attributes in which the investigator may have a special interest. There are various well-known ways to oversample such units, of course. A procedure that may not be so well known is one adopted by S. M. Lipset and Earl Raab in a study of political extremism which they conducted at the Survey Research Center. They were interested in comparing, on a number of characteristics, persons with extreme right-wing tendencies with the average member of the population. During the design phase of their project, they learned of a politician who had been the recipient of a considerable amount of hate mail from the Right. Gaining access to this mail, Lipset and Raab screened it to sort out those correspondents showing the greatest extremism. These persons were then interviewed along with a cross-sectional sample of the population to produce sufficient extremist respondents for comparative analysis (Lipset and Raab 1970).

Another variation on a cross-sectional design, which impresses me as being more widely serviceable, was invented by M. Brewster Smith and Jane Allyn Piliavin for a study of adolescent prejudice (reported on in Glock et al. 1975). They were especially interested in examining how the number of Jewish students in a school might be related to the amount of anti-Semitism exhibited by non-Jewish students. For this purpose, they chose to do their study in three communities, reasonably matched on other criteria but differing in the proportion of students who were Jewish: 43 percent of the students were Jewish in one of the communities chosen, 23 percent in another, and less than 1 percent in the third. In each school district, they arranged to administer their research instrument to all students in the eighth, tenth, and twelfth grades. This enabled them to ask sociometric questions on friendship choices within classes and in analysis to assess for non-Jewish students how many, if any, of their friends were Jewish. Collecting data on students at three grade levels also proved useful by allowing comparisons of anti-Semitism and other forms of prejudice by grade.

## The Nature of Survey Research

Survey research, as I have experienced it, is usefully conceived as being concerned with the study of variation. In cross-sectional studies, variation has to do with how the units being surveyed differ from one another. In trend studies, that is, studies repeated over time with equivalent but not the same samples, the variation principally at issue is how aggregates differ from each other from one time period to another. In so-called panel studies, studies in which data are collected repeatedly from the same samples, variation between units and within units over time becomes the focus of attention.

Survey research calls for or allows three questions to be asked about variation: What is its nature, what are its causes, and what are its consequences? By the nature of variation, I refer essentially to how it is ordered or classified. This is never a given in the sense of its being inherent in the phenomenon being studied. When we classify the colors of a rainbow, for example, we are ordering the perceived variation in light. The colors do not come built-in, so to speak. Conceptualizing the nature of variation is a task that arises repeatedly in survey research: when we ask open-ended questions, when we formulate the answer categories to close ended questions, and when we anticipate the scales and indices to be constructed from question answers. Open-ended questions are a means we adopt to discover what variation exists in our sample population. When we formulate close ended questions, presumably we already have a good idea of the variation to be expected. Similarly, when we phrase the questions, the answers to which will form the basis for building scales and indices, the variation expected is already explicit or implicit in our minds.

Surveys inherently call for consideration of the nature of variation. They allow for but do not require consideration of its causes or consequences. Questions of cause or consequence do not arise, for example, in purely descriptive surveys concerned only to learn how variation of one or more kinds is distributed in a sample population. When the causal question is addressed, the matter at issue is how the variation is to be accounted for, how it is produced. What leads some people to be prejudiced, for example, and others not, assuming for the moment that it is sufficient to order the variation within a dichotomy? In turn, when the consequences of variation are the focus of inquiry, attention shifts to what follows or can be expected to follow from a given variation. What consequences, if any, follow from the varied beliefs people harbor about God, for example?

Whichever question about variation is being addressed, at least tentative answers must be formulated before a design can be decided upon or data collected. It takes a while in a career to learn that the outcome of a survey is determined much more by the strength of its formulation than by the power of its analysis. Sometimes, in survey analysis, it is possible to arrive at an answer to a question that had not been anticipated beforehand (I will give an example later, in the section on analysis). Mostly, however, analysis is a means for assessing answers arrived at initially in the formulation stage. On this score, I judge the widespread belief that analysis is paramount in survey research to be misguided.

Addressing the causes and consequences of variation calls for the construction of theory; addressing questions about the nature of variation requires conceptualization. This distinction is not always made. I find it useful to make it in order to avoid confusing the two. It has also helped in my comprehension of what survey research is about. I turn first to some observations about conceptualization in survey research and then to some about theory.

## Concept Formation

Concept formation in survey research sometimes involves no more than adopting what someone else has already done. The doing may be embedded in the language and may represent long-term everyday ways to order variation. Age is one such concept. It has been both specified and operationalized for us; it is not necessary to start anew. The same might be said for gender, although with the growing acceptance of alternative sexual orientations, we may come to adopt a more elaborate specification than simply male and female.

Borrowing of concepts also takes place when a scale or index is utilized that is already in the literature. Here, once again, the specification and operationalization have already been done for us. As is evidenced by the spate of compendiums of scales and indices in the literature, there is a growing storehouse of concepts from which survey researchers may borrow (e.g., Chun, Cobb, and French 1975; Miller 1977; Robinson, Rusk, and Head 1968; Robinson and Shaver 1973 [1969]).

Commonly, however, some invention of concepts is called for in survey research. This often happens because there is nothing to be borrowed or because an existing concept requires modification in either the way it is conceived or the way it is operationalized to serve our needs. The invention called for, in such instances, may be relatively simple, as, for example, when responses to a single question will adequately order the variation to be studied. Sometimes, of course, what appears simple at first glance becomes, on reflection, complex. For example, the question "Do you own an automobile?" suggests that the variation with respect to car ownership may be specified as yes or no. This might be an adequate specification for some purposes. It is self-evident, however, that considerable residual variation exists in a yes and in a no answer that one might wish to specify if car ownership is a major focus of study. What about leasing a car, for example, or having exclusive use of one owned by a spouse?

Concept formation becomes a major task in survey research when the variation to be ordered is complex and has not been studied before or has been studied in ways that seem inadequate. In such instances, concept formation may, and often does, require a series of studies before an acceptable classification and means of measurement are produced. Indeed, in some instances, the matter may remain in controversy for extended periods of time; IQ is an example, which perhaps may never be resolved.

In my own work in concept formation, I have found Lazarsfeld's delineation of imagery, specification, and operationalization useful as a guide (Lazarsfeld and Rosenberg 1955). Imagery is constituted by a vague sense or feeling of how variation is ordered. To achieve it requires deep immersion in whatever information and data exist about the variation. Sometimes new data have to be collected. Concept formation is not accomplished, at least not effectively, without adequate data. As the immersion in data continues, one begins to discern an order, which slowly allows a tentative specification of the variation. Thereafter, exposing the tentative specification to others can lead to its further refinement and can bring one, finally, to the step of operationalization.

I think I have used all of the various extant approaches to concept formation in my career. Only twice, however, has concept formation become for me a task of major proportion. I cite one of the instances to illustrate some of the complexities.

The social psychology of religion has been an abiding interest of mine. For as long as I can remember, I have been curious about what leads people to be religious and, in turn, what the consequences are of being religious. Given these interests, it behooved me rather early to consider how religious persons are to be distinguished from non-religious ones. Once I addressed this question, it became apparent immediately that it would take more than a dichotomy to represent the variation.

An examination of the literature revealed that William James had attempted to specify how people vary religiously in his *Varieties of Religious Experience* (1902), as had the sociologist Joseph Fichter (1951). Their formulations, though helpful, I judged incomplete either because they dealt with only one element in religiosity (James) or because the conceptualization was culture-bound. On the latter score, James was concerned with Western religious experience, Fichter with the religiosity of Roman Catholics. Other investigators, interested in religiosity and using survey research to investigate it, had been satisfied to accept everyday conceptualizations as adequate. For them, whether or not people went to church, how often they went, and/or whether or not they expressed a belief in God were sufficient grounds for judging religiosity. It is common practice, of course, to adapt everyday conceptualizations of variation to survey use, and I have often done it myself. It must be recognized, however, that such conceptualization is almost always culture-bound and likely to harbor a considerable amount of residual variation in some or all categories. There is more than one way, for example, to believe in God.

Dissatisfied with what others had done, I set out to discover a conceptualization of religiosity that would more wholly comprehend the phenomenon and still lend itself to operational use in surveys. As a source of data, there was the extant social science literature on the topic. There was also the extensive historical and comparative literature on religion. This material suggested that there are common grounds in different religions to distinguish religious from nonreligious or less religious persons and that the grounds are not classifiable on a single dimension.

An initial effort to specify these dimensions produced a list of four: belief, practice, experience, and consequences. A friend, Yoshio Fukuyama, suggested that faithful adherents are also expected to be informed about their religion, so I added knowledge to the original list of four. Common to all of the world's religions, I proposed, are expectations that their adherents will subscribe to certain religious beliefs, that they will engage in religious practices, that they will experience their religion emotionally, that they will be knowledgeable about their religion's scriptures, and that by virtue of being religious in these ways certain consequences will follow in the way adherents live their lives. I recognized that the content of the expectations on these several dimensions varies in different religions as does the relative emphasis given to each of them. The dimensions themselves, however, I believed to be universally applicable.

I reported this specification, without at the time attempting to operationalize it, in a paper entitled "On the Study of Religious Commitment" (Glock 1962). The next step, taken somewhat later in collaboration with Rodney Stark, was an attempt to subject the dimensions to measurement for use in surveys of a national sample of the U.S. population and of a sample of Northern California church members. (I do not report the details here since no unusual procedures were involved; see Stark and Glock 1968).

The operationalization was not undertaken at a level of abstraction to make it applicable to the study of religiosity in all cultures at all times. The specification, however, was so intended. On this score, I believe that we are well advised to seek to specify concepts at as high a level of abstraction as our knowledge allows, with the hope eventually of achieving universal applicability. I advocate this even when the research being planned may be limited to one culture or to a society within a culture. In such instances, practical considerations may oblige investigators to operationalize concepts in a parochial way. The opportunities for eventual cross-cultural comparison will be enhanced if specifications are as close to being culture-free as possible.

My experience in trying to conceptualize religious commitment also revealed that it is useful in forming concepts to entertain the possibility of variations in kind as well as variations in degree. Variation is seldom so simple in the real world that it can be comprehended by distinctions in degree alone. (This point is elaborated on later in the section on variable building.)

The response to the conceptual paper on religiosity and to the book reporting on its operationalization was at once both receptive and critical. Since their publication, acceptance of a multi-dimensional specification of religious commitment has become virtually the norm. Considerable disagreement remains, however, about whether the five dimensions I proposed are the correct ones and about whether there are more or less than five dimensions. The literature on the topic has by now become enormous but among those who make the study of religion a specialty, there is still no agreed-upon way to conceptualize, much less measure religious commitment (see Roof 1979 for a critical review).

The situation with respect to religiosity is not an isolated one. I suspect that most of the concepts invented by survey researchers couldn't stand muster if there were a concentrated effort to evaluate them. This is a result, in part, of the conceptual task not being addressed collectively and with sufficient frequency, rigor, and concentration. It is also a consequence of our not having produced a codification of concept formation that includes agreed-upon criteria to decide if and when closure has been achieved.

This is not a problem peculiar to survey research. It is endemic to all of social science and is at the root of Thomas Kuhn's conjecture that we are devoid still of a common paradigm (1962). Survey research is about as effective a tool as exists to help move forward in this realm. It is to be regretted that the codification of concept formation does not enjoy high priority among us and that, so often, we settle for less than we are presently capable of in the formulations we undertake.

## Theory

The formulation of theory in survey research is called for, as has already been noted, when the causes and/or the consequences of variation are addressed. In such instances, theory is necessary to enable decisions to be made about the variables on which data are to be collected. If prejudice, for example, is to be accounted for, theory to the effect that prejudice is grounded in motivational dynamics would lead to a quite different selection of independent variables than would theory conceiving prejudice to be a result of social conflict. In turn, if the consequences of religious commitment are to be investigated, theory would suggest what consequences to look for and what dependent variables to measure.

Survey research need not, of course, always be oriented to testing theory. The goal may be purely descriptive as, for example, when polling organizations seek to assess the amount of support for opposing candidates in an election or when the U.S. Bureau of the Census conducts a sample survey between decennial censuses to assess what shifts, if any, have occurred in population characteristics since the previous census. Rarely, if ever, will a survey be conducted solely for such narrowly descriptive purposes. Almost inevitably, there is interest as well in discovering how the distribution on dependent variables may vary under conditions introduced by independent variables. Thus, pollsters are usually not content to learn how the population as a whole intends to vote. They also want to see whether support for candidates comes more from one sector of the population than from another. Similarly, the Census Bureau will want to compare population characteristics for different subgroups.

There is an element of theory in such differentiated description. In deciding what comparisons to make, pollsters and the Census Bureau will choose on the assumption that important differences will be uncovered. The assumptions may not be grounded in anything more than speculation or past experience. Still, the choices are not made at random. Otherwise, eye color, for example, would be an independent variable as often as age.

Theoretically oriented research begins, to my mind, when the reasons for making comparisons are made explicit and when this is done before rather than after data are collected. This is not to say that research cannot make a contribution to theory after data are collected. Theory, after all, can no more be formulated in a vacuum than concepts. The two must be grounded in some kind of data even if the data are only imagined. It seems useful, in this connection, to keep in mind the sometimes neglected rule that theory derived from data does not constitute a test of the theory. For a test to occur, the theory has to precede the collection of data. This means, however, that there is a constant interaction between theory and data; data are necessary to formulate theory, theory then guides data collection, the newly collected data may suggest a refinement of theory or even new theory; and so on.

This process became quite real to me in a sequence of projects that began with a study whose findings suggested a new theory rather than affording a test of a known theory. The project is the one on Episcopalians to which I have already referred in the section on study design. One of the scholarly purposes of that project, it will be recalled, was to explore the sources of religious commitment.

This was one of the first projects for which I had prime responsibility, and I was more interested to insure that the client's applied purposes be served than to use the survey for my own ends. At the time, I had not thought very much about the topic of religious commitment; the conceptualization of it mentioned earlier was produced somewhat later. Theory was something I had learned about in the classroom, not something I had thought about with respect to conducting a study. Thus, the main questionnaire of the study, the one to be administered to parishioners, was designed without the benefit of any formal theory of religious commitment. Rather, in the differentiated description tradition just described, we included a number of items in the questionnaire that would allow some comparison of the relative commitment of different subgroups in the population. There must have been reasons why we chose the particular items we did. We never sought to make these reasons explicit, however, and the analysis proceeded in an essentially rank-empirical way to find out which of the items worked, meaning, which items were associated with how deeply these Episcopalians were involved in the Church. (Church involvement rather than religious commitment became the dependent variable after the data were examined. It refers basically to the extent to which the lives of the sampled parishioners are caught up in the agenda and affairs of the Church; see Glock et al. 1967.)

In brief, the major findings were that women are more deeply involved on the average than men; older parishioners more than younger ones; people without or with limited family ties more than those with full ties; and the less well-to-do more than the well-to-do. Not only did each of these factors relate independently to involvement, but the effect was accumulative: the greater the number of predisposing factors, the greater the involvement.

In contemplating these results, it occurred to me and my collaborators that one or both of two things might be happening. The results might simply be a reflection of the fact that women, older persons, the familyless, and the less well-to-do have more time on their hands to become involved in the Church. Alternatively or in addition, it could be that these people became involved as a compensation for being deprived, relative to their counterparts, of access to the rewards of the larger society. The data, having suggested these explanations, did not afford a means to test them, although further analysis gave more credence to the second than to the first of the hypotheses.

The Episcopal study affords, then, an example of survey data suggesting theory. The next step was not another study that would allow a formal test of the theory. Rather, I did what I should have done before; namely, I examined the literature to see what it might have to say on the matter. As might be expected, this exposed me to additional data and to what others were thinking theoretically or speculatively about religious commitment. As a result, the simple theoretical idea that relative deprivation may be a factor influencing church involvement was elaborated into a more general theory; namely, that relative deprivation is an element in the origin and evolution of religious groups as well as in the religious behavior of individuals. There followed then a wholly theoretical paper to this effect which, incidentally, included an attempt to conceptualize relative deprivation (Glock 1964).

Subsequently, I had the opportunity to test the theory with new data, not in its entirety but with respect to its relevance to the question of how to account for variations in individual religiosity. The test was made using survey research as the major methodological tool. My collaborator, Rodney Stark, has reported the results in a series of papers (1968, 1971, 1972). By and large, the tests were in accord with the theory: Persons experiencing relative deprivation of the rewards afforded by the larger society were more disposed than others to be religious in the variety of ways specified in the conceptualization of religious commitment reported upon earlier. The tests also showed, however, that relative deprivation falls considerably short of affording a total explanation of why people turn to religion.

Once this research was completed, it would have been eminently reasonable to engage in further exploration of the sources of religiosity. Indeed, the data collected in this last study suggested the direction that further exploration might take. Moreover, there was the prospect of engaging in research to test deprivation theory with regard to religious groups rather than individuals. At that point, however, Stark left Berkeley to accept an appointment to the faculty of the University of Washington where he turned to other problems. As for myself, the resources to do anything further were not readily at hand; and by then I had had enough of the topic of religiosity to discourage me from making a special effort to raise funds. Besides, as director of the Survey Research Center, I was responsible for other projects. Several years later, when I was ready to take on new assignments, other opportunities presented themselves that proved more attractive than trying to find support to advance my earlier work on religiosity.

As I reflect now on the decision to change directions then, my feelings are mixed. On the one hand, I would hate to have missed participating in the new projects on new religions (Glock and Bellah 1975) and on racial attitudes (Apostle et al. 1983). On the other hand, I feel some remorse, even guilt, at having left a topic while still believing I had a contribution to make to it.

## Instrument Construction

Instrument construction, in my experience with survey research, is done most effectively if it is preceded by the formulation of theory, if theory is called for, and by conceptualization carried to the point where all variations to be operationalized have been specified. A main contribution that theory can make to instrument construction is to delineate the topics on which questions have to be asked. Having such information ahead of time facilitates instrument construction by affording, in effect, a blueprint of what has to be done. Conceptualization affords instruction in the framing of questions and answer categories. Done ahead of time, it makes instrument construction more efficient by keeping the specification of concepts distinct from their operationalization. The latter, of course, is what instrument construction is essentially about.

The meaning and significance of these observations can be conveyed best by an illustration. The illustration I shall use is the study that first made these observations clear to me. It was an attempt to examine possible religious sources of contemporary anti-Semitism and was undertaken as part of a larger program of research on "Patterns of American Prejudice" by the Survey Research Center under a grant from the Anti-Defamation League of B'nai B'rith (Glock and Stark 1966).

The dependent variable of the study—secular anti-Semitism—was determined by the terms of the grant. The decision to explore possible religious sources of anti-Semitism was my own idea, a natural consequence of my interest in studying the consequences of religious commitment. In this instance, theory construction preceded data collection and, indeed, deciding on a study design. The theory was derived from Stark's and my reading of the literature, from qualitative interviews conducted with church members of various denominations, and from our own personal church experiences during our youth.

Simply stated, the theory postulated that Christians who believe deeply and firmly that salvation is possible only through Jesus Christ, what Stark and I later labeled particularism, will experience feelings of religious hostility toward Jews because of their rejection of Christ. This religious hostility, in turn, will dispose those who harbor it to secular anti-Semitism. This initial formulation identified three topics—namely, particularism, religious hostility, and secular anti-Semitism—to be addressed in the study.

In elaborating on these theoretical ideas, we added that a precondition to being particularist in one's faith is to be orthodox, that is, to accept the central tenets of Christianity. We also postulated that the causal chain—orthodoxy to particularism to religious hostility to anti-Semitism—might be muted or derailed among persons who have internalized American values of religious liberty. Thus, orthodoxy and religious libertarianism were added to the topics for study.

Our theorizing also led us to consider possible alternative explanations that might demonstrate our central thesis to be spurious. This led to the identification of still additional topics for study. By the time we turned to developing a research instrument, virtually all of the topics to be included therein had been identified.

In the formulation of the theoretical ideas, we were inexorably drawn into conceptual considerations. How do people vary with respect to their response to the particularist claims of some versions of Christianity? What is the range of possible responses to the Jews' rejection of Christ? Can people be classified simply as being or not being anti-Semitic, or is the variation more complicated than this? Similar questions arose with respect to each of the other variations identified by the theoretical model.

In retrospect, I cannot claim that prior to instrument construction we pursued answers to each of these questions to the point of having clearly in mind how each variation was to be classified. We were simply not sufficiently aware at the time that it would constitute good practice. Intuitively, however, this was the direction in which we were heading. By the time instrument construction was begun, concept formation, though not complete, had been advanced well beyond any previous study on which I had been engaged. For example, based on an examination of the literature, not only had we specified anti-Semitism as having cognitive, affective, and behaviorial components, but we had also decided to distinguish religious hostility toward the historic Jew from religious hostility to contemporary Jews.

The net effect of all this activity was to make the task of instrument construction significantly more efficient and, I believe, effective. As we began that task, we had a very clear idea of the variations for which questions had to be constructed. We were also well served in framing questions and answer categories by specifying how these variations might be ordered. Mostly, instrument construction involved decisions about how to operationalize what had gone before. Proceeding in this way also facilitated the analysis and the writing of the subsequent book. The lessons learned in this project have been applied and with more rigor in the later surveys to which I have been a party, all, I believe, to positive effect (see especially Apostle et al. 1983; Wuthnow 1976, 1977).

## Variable Building

Variable building is, at once, both the most and the least codified step in the survey process. On the one hand, there is the range of scales and indices—Gutman and Likert scales, for example—where construction and validation procedures have been spelled out in great detail. On the other hand, there is a wide range of ad hoc procedures which investigators invent because the data do not meet scale or index requirements. Most measurement in survey research is probably of the ad hoc variety, which suggests that there is an enormous amount of codification still to be done.

Whether undertaken on an ad hoc basis or in accord with a formal scaling or index construction procedure, variable building involves essentially following the instructions implicit in how the concepts were specified and operationalized in the research instrument. These instructions are not always infallible, of course, since all they constitute are expectations as to what will happen. Sometimes, specifications are simply not reflected in reality. At other times, the means adopted to operationalize them may be flawed. There are occasions where both of these things happen.

A relatively recent study of racial attitudes affords an example of what may happen in these connections (Apostle et al. 1983). In that study, several collaborators and I attempted to specify the various ways white Americans explain the relative deprivation suffered by black Americans in levels of employment, education, and quality of housing. Among the explanations specified was a cultural one, namely, that blacks' relative deprivation is a result of differences in the cultural backgrounds of blacks and whites. To operationalize this specification, a number of questions were formulated so that responses to them would distinguish respondents who accepted a cultural explanation of racial differences from those who did not. In the variable-building stage, however, it was discovered that the cultural explanation was being accepted both by respondents who, in other respects, showed open hostility to blacks and by respondents who, in answering other questions, were highly sympathetic to blacks. Upon further examination, it became apparent that the cultural questions failed to discriminate between those who harbor a distinct preference for white over black culture and those who are neutral in this respect or prefer black culture. In this instance, the operationalization, not the specification, was at fault.

The more that concept specification and operationalization are grounded in data, the greater the likelihood that they will hold up in the variable-building stage. A major source of such data in survey research is the qualitative interview conducted during the planning phases of a project. Such interviews, with a small but roughly representative sample of the population to be surveyed subsequently, afford an indispensable way to learn about the nature of variation and how to go about operationalizing it. In many instances, such interviews provide data helpful to the development of theory as well. Using experts as an adjunct to such interviews in the planning stages of a project is also to be recommended, though they are rarely a satisfactory substitute for the interviews.

Survey researchers learn early in their careers that variables may be nominal, ordinal, or interval. When it comes to variable building, however, they are likely to find themselves thinking, virtually always, in ordinal terms. In part, this is because the conditions necessary for interval measurement are so rarely met in the social sciences. It is also because prevailing multivariate statistics can be employed, albeit sometimes making unwarranted assumptions, with ordinal data but are ordinarily quite inappropriate for use with nominal variables, except dichotomies.

The ordinal bias thereby created is widespread and rarely challenged. When nominal measurement is called for, most of us accommodate to it by some transformation of the nominal categories into ordinal form. The loss from making the accommodation has not been evaluated seriously, and it is difficult to know how such evaluation might be accomplished, given survey researchers' relative lack of experience in analyzing nominal variables. Once the matter is attended to, however, it is difficult to avoid the nagging feeling that something is wrong; to aver that all human variation can be ordered by degree simply defies common sense. Yet, most multivariate statistical procedures virtually oblige us to make the assumption.

The case for nominal or typological over ordinal measurement can best be made by example, that is, through a demonstration that more can be learned through retaining nominal categories than by transforming them into ordinal form. It will take more than one example to make the case, of course. The following study is intended only to illustrate the possibilities.

The purpose of the research project was to explore the political and social attitudes of devotees of the new religions that sprouted, especially in the western United States, in the late 1960s and early 1970s. An opportunity arose to explore this topic in conjunction with a study of the population of the San Francisco Bay area being undertaken by the Berkeley Survey Research Center (Glock and Wuthnow 1979).

One option in conceptualization was to conceive of openness to new religions in ordinal terms and to try to distinguish respondents on a continuum ranging from very receptive to very hostile. This would have been easy to do, and since the study was to be done in the Bay area, the chances were good that sufficient cases would fall on the receptive side of the scale. Moreover, on that end of the scale, such a conceptualization would probably have done an adequate job of identifying devotees of the new religions. It was the probable residual variation in the rest of such a scale that gave us pause. Included there would be atheists and agnostics as well as those committed to traditional religion. It seemed self-evident that these latter types would differ markedly in political and social outlook.

These considerations led to the following specification of categories: devotees of the new religions, adherents to a traditional religion, the nonreligious, and a residual group comprising those unsure of what they are religiously. Doing it this way led us to the discovery that those involved in new religions were much more similar in their political and social attitudes to the nonreligious than to either the traditionally religious or the religiously unsure. For example, 13 percent of the conventionally religious and 22 percent of the nominally religious identified themselves as liberal or left of liberal in politics. In contrast, 40 percent of the nonreligious and 56 percent of the devotees of new religions did so. On issues relating to the religious realm (but not in traditional terms)—thinking about the meaning of life, for example—those into new religions were most at odds with the nonreligious. These results would not have been revealed if an ordinal measure, as described above, had been used. Moreover, differences by scale score would have been muted because of the residual variation in the lower part of the scale.

Finally, it is helpful in variable building to examine how the items in typologies, scales, and indexes relate individually to the other variables to be included in whatever causal analysis is planned. This step sometimes reveals that scale items relate differently to dependent or independent variables. Consider, for example, a situation in which three items are being considered on which to build a measure of political orientation. On the first two of the three items, it is found that younger respondents answer in a liberal direction more often than older ones do. The third item, however, produces the opposite result; older respondents are now the more liberal. Given these findings, the third item would appear to have a different meaning than the first two items and consequently ought not to be included in the same scale. Following this procedure in building summary measures may seem tantamount to "cooking the data." It is not, of course, if what is done and found is duly reported. Thomas Piazza has elaborated on these observations (1980).

## Causal Analysis

My views on causal analysis are old-fashioned and may no longer have currency. Still, they have served me well, and I report on some of them more to reassure those who share my biases than out of any expectation of converting those who do not. The most helpful analytic tool I have encountered is the "elaboration" formula developed originally by Kendall and Lazarsfeld (1950) and enlarged upon subsequently by Hirschi and Selvin (1967) and Rosenberg (1968), among others. It affords extraordinary insight into the logic of not only survey analysis but all effort in the social sciences to explore and test theory. It is to be regretted that it is possible these days to earn a Ph.D. in the social sciences without being exposed to it.

Also to be regretted is the absence of anything equivalent to the elaboration formula for situations where the dependent variable is nominal and more than a dichotomy. Log linear analysis may appear to fill the gap, but Goodman (1972, 1978, 1984) and other developers of this technique (e.g., Davis 1974) have not worked out the logic for the analysis of nominal variables to anywhere near the extent that the elaboration formula provides for ordinal, including dichotomous, variables.

This is not to say that the elaboration formula solves all of the problems of ordinal analysis. It is, after all, restricted to the analysis of only three variables, and there remain ramifications of three variable analyses that the formula does not address. Path analysis affords a logic for analyzing many variables, of course. Its assumptions, however, are rarely met by the data, and although there have long been techniques for identifying interactions, or specifications, as they are labeled in the elaboration formula, it remains awkward, sometimes misleading, and often uninformative to use path analysis to deal with them.

My own devotion to cross-tabular analysis is partly a result, I am sure, of having been brought up with it. All those tables I ran for

Lazarsfeld in the early days have had a long-lasting effect. Socialization, however, does not fully explain my devotion despite the advent of newer analytic procedures and their ready application with computers. In this regard, it is simply a matter of my continuing to believe that it is possible to learn more and to gain more insight into the problems being investigated with cross-tabular than with other procedures. Other procedures are all right and, indeed, to be desired if their use is informed by what cross-tabulations have revealed. To use them exclusively poses, for me, the dangers of being underinformed or misled about what the data are capable of reporting.

It is not possible in short compass to offer a full-scale demonstration of these assertions. My testimony lies in the entire corpus of my work. Having made the assertions, however, it behooves me to offer, at least illustratively, some evidence that cross-tabulations can still be significant in survey analysis.

One of the important, although not unique, advantages of cross-tabulations is their capacity to reveal specifications or interactions. Having this capacity is essential to an analytic procedure because of the profound impact specifications may have on the entire course of analysis. The experience I recall most vividly in this regard occurred during analysis of a survey undertaken to assess American public responses to the Eichmann trial (Glock, Selznick, and Spaeth 1966).

The legality of that trial, it may be recalled, came into question because Eichmann was taken secretly by Israeli agents from a suburb of Buenos Aires, Argentina, and brought to Israel on an El Al airliner. One of the questions in our survey asked respondents their views on the legality of the trial. A majority—59 percent—thought it was legal, although included in this figure were 18 percent who qualified their answers. Analysis revealed that more educated respondents and those knowledgeable about the details of Eichmann's capture were less likely to judge the trial legal than the poorly educated and the uninformed. This result seemed perfectly understandable to us. After all, the more educated and knowledgeable should be more likely to see the ambiguities in any situation.

The specification, in this instance, came about as a result of repeating the cross-tabulation separately for white and black respondents. Among the former, the relation between level of education and knowledge and views of the trial's legality was stronger than in the total sample. Among black respondents, the relation was reversed; well-educated and knowledgeable blacks were more likely to judge the trial legal than poorly educated and uninformed blacks.

Given this result, we were obliged to redo much of the analysis, this time separately for white and black respondents. Moreover, we had a new analytical question to ponder: how to account for the different results in the two subcommunities. Specifications are seldom so dramatic. When they occur, as they often do in survey analysis, their implications for analysis are rarely trivial.

A more distinctive advantage of tables is that they provide more details about what is taking place than do summarized statistics. One example is hardly sufficient to demonstrate the variety of ways this advantage manifests itself. Still, one example may be sufficient to illustrate the general point. I take it from the aforementioned study of the religious sources of anti-Semitism.

In one part of the analysis for that study, we were engaged in testing our hypotheses about the possible religious sources of religious hostility toward Jews. Our expectations were that Christians who are orthodox (e.g., believe absolutely in Christ's divinity), particularist (e.g., believe salvation is possible only through Christ), and who conceive of the historic Jews as responsible for the Crucifixion would be much more likely than their opposite numbers to agree with the assertion that "Jews can never be forgiven for what they did to Jesus until they accept him as the True Saviour." The results of the cross-tabulation undertaken to test these expectations are reproduced as Table 1.1. (The table reports the results for Protestants. The table for Catholics is similar in direction, but the relationships are not as strong and there are many more empty cells because of the small number of cases; see Glock and Stark 1966, p. 70.)

Table 1.1 tells us, as for example a path analysis would also, that each of the three independent variables is related independently of each other to seeing the modern Jew in religiously negative terms. Unlike other procedures, the table also reveals the astounding additive effect of the three independent variables. Note especially in this connection that 86 percent of the Protestants who are highly orthodox, highly particularist, and who judge the Jews responsible for the Crucifixion show religious hostility toward modern Jews. Among their opposite numbers—those low on orthodoxy and particularism and who do not see the Jews as responsible for the crucifixion—1 percent show such hostility. This is a finding of considerable importance substantively and, indeed, practically. In the latter regard, it is also of significance to those struggling to combat anti-Semitism that of the 1,634 respondents reported on in the table, a substantial 15 percent of them (242) fall in the cell expressing the most hostility, another finding, incidentally, not readily revealed by other procedures.

The final advantage of cross-tabulations that I shall mention is their suitability for deviant-case analysis. If we look back to Table 1.1, for example, some 14 percent of the respondents with the attributes

**TABLE 1.1.** *Influence of Orthodoxy and Particularism on Linking of Modern Jews with the Crucifixion*

(Percent who agreed "The Jews can never be forgiven for what they did to Jesus until they accept Him as the True Saviour.")

| | ORTHODOXY INDEX | | | | | |
| | High | | Medium | | Low | |
| | Group most responsible for Crucifixion | | Group most responsible for Crucifixion | | Group most responsible for Crucifixion | |
| RANK ON PARTICULARISM INDEX | Jews | Not Jews[a] | Jews | Not Jews[a] | Jews | Not Jews[a] |
|---|---|---|---|---|---|---|
| **Protestants:** | | | | | | |
| High | 86% (242) | 70% (78) | 52% (103) | 28% (54) | 40% (21) | 0% (22) |
| Medium | 69 (152) | 59 (49) | 25 (221) | 13 (123) | 10 (114) | 7 (85) |
| Low | 19 (16) | [b] (5) | 9 (67) | 2 (46) | 1 (135) | 1 (101) |
| **Catholics** | | | | | | |
| High | 33 (80) | 33 (15) | 12 (17) | [b] (9) | [c] (4) | [c] (2) |
| Medium | 15 (92) | 3 (34) | 6 (35) | 4 (27) | [c] (9) | [c] (11) |
| Low | [b] (12) | [b] (5) | [c] (10) | 0 (15) | [c] (13) | [c] (9) |

*Note:* Figures in parentheses show total number of respondents.

[a] Includes persons who answered "the Romans," "the Christians," "none of these."

[b] Too few cases to compute meaningful percentage.

[c] Although too few cases to compute meaningful percentage, none of the respondents agreed with the statement.

judged to be most predisposing to religious hostility against Jews do not exhibit that hostility. On the other extreme, 1 percent of the respondents with all of the attributes considered least predisposing to religious hostility are religiously hostile. Now that the thought occurs to me, I regret that we never attempted to learn who these "deviants" were. If we had, however, cross-tabulation and, indeed, examining the cases one by one would have been suitable ways to proceed. We did engage in deviant-case analysis in the aforementioned study of public responses to the Eichmann trial. The number of cases was too small to produce anything statistically significant. The cross-tabulations did, however, afford what we judged to be a plausible account of what might be taking place.

Analysis is the most exciting part of survey research, for one finally finds out how all the theory, speculation, hunches, guesses that went into a project come out. Unfortunately, the excitement is greater when things work out than when they do not. I say it is unfortunate, because there is something to be learned, whatever the results. Too often, investigators do not feel this way, which can have the effect, I am afraid, of not reporting results when they do not conform to one's expectations.

If I limit myself to three, I judge the following to be the analytic highlights of my career. The confirmation in three sets of data of the theoretical model we had postulated on how Christian beliefs may lead to anti-Semitism constitutes one of these highlights (Glock and Stark 1966; Stark et al. 1971). The intellectual rewards were enhanced by the personal satisfaction gained from learning that West German Cardinal Bea had referred to our findings in introducing the Statement on the Jews to Vatican Council II.

A second analytic highlight also involved a study of anti-Semitism, but in this instance the theoretically based expectations were not confirmed. In a study of adolescent prejudice, we anticipated, based on theoretical considerations and what turned out to be a mistaken projection from past research, that adolescent anti-Semitism would be less, the larger the Jewish presence in a school's population. The results were just the opposite (Glock et al. 1975).

Faced with this kind of result, it would not be possible ordinarily to use the same data to find out why. This is not what data are designed to do. We decided in this case to try, nevertheless, hoping that serendipitously we had collected data that would afford a clue to an answer. The answer we arrived at cannot be judged definitive. We were enough convinced by it, however, to experience the excitement that discovery seems always to bring.

We learned, in accord with the findings of previous research, that anti-Semitism is less among non-Jews who have Jewish friends than among those who do not. This does not, however, warrant the additional assumption that a Jewish presence, without friendship, has the same effect. On this issue, we learned that the potential in prejudice to distort reality and to function in ways akin to self-fulfilling prophecies is greater in the presence of "outgroup" members than in their absence.

Of all of the projects on which I have been engaged, the sense of discovery was greatest in the study of racial attitudes to which brief mention was made earlier (Apostle et al. 1983). Here, there were not one but a number of discoveries that produced emotional as well as intellectual satisfaction. Of these, the most exciting findings, at least for me, were (1) that the same perception of racial differences can be accompanied by very different explanations of these differences and (2) that how blacks are responded to by whites is much less a function of how racial differences are perceived than of how they are explained. As far as we knew, these were not things that anyone else had discovered. This makes discovery even more exciting and especially if it is not trivial.

## Bibliography

Apostle, Richard A., Charles Y. Glock. Thomas Piazza, and Marijean Suelzle. 1983. *The anatomy of racial attitudes*. Berkeley: University of California Press.

Campbell, Donald T., and Julian C. Stanley. 1963. *Experimental and quasi-experimental designs for research*. Chicago: Rand McNally.

Chun, Ki-Taek, Sydney Cobb, and John R. P. French, Jr. 1975. *Measures for psychological measurement: A guide to 3,000 original sources and their application*. Ann Arbor: Institute of Social Research, University of Michigan.

Coleman, James S., Elihu Katz, and Herbert Menzel. 1963. *Medical innovation: A diffusion study*. New York: Bobbs-Merrill.

Davis, James A. 1974. Hierarchical models for significance tests in multivariate contingency tables: An exegesis of Goodman's recent papers. In Herbert L. Costner, ed., *Sociological methodology, 1973–1974*, pp. 189–231. San Francisco: Jossey-Bass.

Fichter, Joseph. 1951. *Southern parish: The dynamics of a city church*. Chicago: University of Chicago Press.

Glock, Charles Y. 1952. Participation bias and re-interview effect in panel studies. Doctoral thesis, Columbia University.

———. 1962. On the study of religious commitment. Research supplement to *Religious Education*, July/August.

———. 1964. The role of deprivation in the origin and evolution of religious groups. In Robert Lee and Martin E. Marty, eds., *Religion and social conflict*, pp. 24–36. New York: Oxford University Press.

———. 1967. Survey design and analysis in sociology. In Charles Y. Glock, ed., *Survey research in the social sciences*, pp. 1–62. New York: Russell Sage Foundation.

Glock, Charles Y., and Robert M. Bellah. 1975. *The new religious consciousness.* Berkeley and Los Angeles: University of California Press.

Glock, Charles Y., and Thomas Piazza. 1981. Exploring reality structures. In Thomas Robbins and Dick Anthony, eds., *In gods we trust*, pp. 67–86. New Brunswick and London: Transaction Books.

Glock, Charles Y., Benjamin Ringer, and Earl R. Babbie, 1967. *To comfort and to challenge: A dilemma of the contemporary church.* Berkeley: University of California Press.

Glock, Charles Y., Gertrude J. Selznick, and Joe L. Spaeth. 1966. *The apathetic majority: A study based on public responses to the Eichmann trial.* New York: Harper and Row.

Glock, Charles Y., and Rodney Stark. 1966. *Christian beliefs and anti-Semitism.* New York: Harper and Row.

Glock, Charles Y., and Robert Wuthnow. 1979. Departures from conventional religion. In Robert Wuthnow, ed., *The religious dimension: New directions in quantitative research*, pp. 47–68. New York: Academic Press.

Glock, Charles Y., Robert Wuthnow, Jane Allyn Piliavin, and Metta Spencer. 1975. *Adolescent prejudice.* New York: Harper and Row.

Goodman, Leo A. 1972. A general model for the analysis of surveys. *American Journal of Sociology* 77:1035–86.

———. 1978. *Analyzing qualitative/categorical data.* Cambridge: Abt Books.

———. 1984. *The analysis of cross-classified data having ordered categories.* Cambridge, Mass.: Harvard University Press.

Hirschi, Travis, and Hanan C. Selvin. 1967. *Delinquency research: An appraisal of analytic methods.* New York: Free Press. Revised as *Principles of survey analysis.* New York: Free Press, 1973.

James, William. 1902. *The varieties of religious experience.* London: Longmans, Green.

Kendall, Patricia L., and Paul F. Lazarsfeld. 1950. Problems of survey analysis. In Robert K. Merton and Paul F. Lazarsfeld, eds., *Continuities in social research: Studies in the scope and method of "The American Soldier,"* pp. 133–96. New York: Free Press.

Kuhn, Thomas S. 1962. *The structure of scientific revolutions.* Chicago: University of Chicago Press.

Lazarsfeld, Paul F., Bernard Berelson, and Hazel Gaudet. 1944. *The people's choice: How the voter makes up his mind in a presidential campaign.* New York: Duell, Sloan, and Pearce. 2nd ed. (with a new preface), New York: Columbia University Press, 1948. 3rd ed. (with a new preface), New York: Columbia University Press, 1968.

Lazarsfeld, Paul F., and Morris Rosenberg, eds. 1955. *The language of social research: A reader in the methodology of social research.* New York: Free Press.

Lazarsfeld, Paul F., and Wagner Thielens, Jr., 1958. *The academic mind: Social scientists in a time of crisis.* New York: Free Press.

Lipset, Seymour M., and Earl Raab. 1970. *The politics of unreason.* New York: Harper and Row.

Miller, Delbert C. 1977. *Handbook of research design and social measurement.* 3rd ed. New York: McKay.

Piazza, Thomas. 1980. The analysis of attitude items. *American Journal of Sociology* 86:584–603.

Robinson, John P., Jerrold G. Rusk, and Kendra B. Head. 1968. *Measures of political attitudes.* Ann Arbor: Institute of Social Research, University of Michigan.

Robinson, John P., and Phillip R. Shaver. 1973 [1969]. *Measures of social psychological attitudes.* Ann Arbor: Institute of Social Research, University of Michigan.

Roof, Wade Clark. 1979. Concepts and indicators of religious commitment: A critical review. In Robert Wuthnow, ed., *The religious dimension: New directions in quantitative research.* New York: Academic Press.

Rosenberg, Morris. 1968. *The logic of survey analysis.* New York: Basic Books.

Stark, Rodney. 1968. Age and faith: A changing outlook or an old process? *Sociological Analysis* 29:1.

———. 1971. Psychopathology and religious commitment. *Review of Religious Research*, spring.

———. 1972. The economics of piety. In *Issues in Social Inequality.* Boston: Little, Brown.

Stark, Rodney, Bruce D. Foster, Charles Y. Glock, and Harold Quinley. 1971. *Wayward shepherds: Prejudice and the Protestant clergy.* New York: Harper and Row.

Stark, Rodney, and Charles Y. Glock. 1968. *American piety.* Berkeley: University of California Press.

Sudman, Seymour. 1976. *Applied sampling.* New York: Academic Press.

Wuthnow, Robert. 1976. *The consciousness reformation.* Berkeley: University of California Press.

———. 1977. Is there an academic melting pot? *Sociology of Education* 50:pp. 7–15.

*Howard Schuman and Lawrence Bobo*

## 2 An Experimental Approach to Surveys of Racial Attitudes

This chapter illustrates how the introduction of simple experimentation into surveys can fruitfully address substantive problems difficult
to resolve through standard survey analysis. Our substantive concern
is with a number of interpretive uncertainties that arose in the course
of a secondary analysis of archival data on racial attitudes collected by
three major survey organizations (National Opinion Research Center
[NORC], Institute for Survey Research [ISR], and Gallup). All of the
primary themes of the chapter—the use of formal experimentation to
improve surveys, secondary analysis of archival data, an interest in racial attitudes as a central issue in American life, and a focus on social
change—echo methods and concerns pioneered by Herbert Hyman
at one point or another in his career. If there is a contribution in the
pages that follow, it comes from putting these themes together in a
new way that indicates the value of regularly combining experimental
and survey approaches to the study of social issues.

Both NORC's General Social Survey (GSS) and ISR's National Election Study (NES) are widely regarded as major national resources for
social research. Each data set is the increasing focus for analysis by
scholars across the country, and as a consequence these periodic surveys contribute greatly to what we know about the attitudes, beliefs,
and values of the American public. For example, a small number of
questions in the GSS and its NORC predecessors have formed the

Experiments drawn on in this chapter were carried out with the support of a grant
from the National Science Foundation (SES–8411371). We are also grateful to Charlotte
Steeh, who was an author with us of the book for which some of these data were first
developed.

basis for the most widely cited writings that trace and interpret racial attitude change among white Americans over the past forty years (Greeley and Sheatsley 1971; Hyman and Sheatsley 1956, 1964; Schwartz 1967; Taylor, Sheatsley, and Greeley 1978). Add a dozen more questions from the NES and even fewer from Gallup and we have almost the entire stock of survey information about trends in this important area since World War II. Thus, the questions bear a heavy weight, and the more we can learn about their meaning and resolve their ambiguities, the more informed their use and users will be. Similar comments could be made about data on many other social issues.

A second and more modest development in survey research has been renewed emphasis on using randomized experiments within surveys in order to explore methodological problems of question form, wording, and context. The first author of this paper was one of the reinventors of this particular wheel (Schuman and Presser 1977, 1981; see also Bishop, Oldendick, and Tuchfarber 1978), although the real invention goes back to the beginnings of survey research with the creation of the "split ballot," probably by Gallup. Much of the recent work has been driven, however, by formal methodological concerns, such as the general effect of question order on answers, the extent to which acquiescence occurs with agree/disagree items, the study of "don't know" responses, and so on. The work has been valuable in providing a deeper understanding of the nature and complexity of the question–answer process in surveys, but it must be admitted that it has seldom led to simple principles that can be applied directly to the design of survey questions. More often the conclusion of such research has been that either of two ways of constructing questions can be perfectly legitimate, even though mixing the two ways in the measurement of trends is exceptionally hazardous to the health of one's conclusions.

How then can we draw on this methodological work in order to improve *substantive* survey research? We illustrate here one direction: Instead of concentrating on the search for timeless methodological generalizations that can then be applied mechanically to future substantive studies, we should use both the techniques and the ideas developed thus far in methodological work in order to illuminate important substantive data sets such as the GSS and the NES. The illustrations draw partly on experiments from our recent report on existing trend data on racial attitudes (Schuman, Steeh, and Bobo 1985) and partly on new but related experiments.

The experiments share a common concern with white attitudes toward racial integration, especially school integration. In the first case, we investigated question context effects in order to understand a

highly unusual trend over time for general attitudes toward segregation. The second experiment also involved possible context effects,
this time as sources of unexpectedly high levels of willingness to participate in substantial school integration. A third experiment varied
question wording in order to explore the effect on attitudes of different meanings of the term "busing." The final experiment used a
formal variation in questioning—inclusion or omission of a middle alternative—to study ceiling effects on the item having the longest history of any of those available to assess changes in racial attitudes. All
four experiments started from standard attitude items included in either the General Social Survey or the National Election Study, then
introduced a second order or wording variation to test points at issue
for those studying racial attitudes.

## The General Segregation Item

There are approximately thirty survey items from NORC, ISR, and
Gallup surveys that allow us to chart changes in white racial attitudes
over a substantial set of time points between World War II and the
present. Eleven of these items deal with broad principles of integration and equal treatment; for example, "Do you think white students
and black students should go to the same schools or to separate
schools?" Ten of the eleven "principle items" show a clear positive monotonic trend over the period in which they were asked, as portrayed
in Figure 2.1. In each case, regardless of the starting or ending time
point, it is obvious that white Americans have moved strongly in the
direction of at least verbal support for principles of racial integration
and equal treatment, although the levels of support (intercepts, in a
linear sense) vary by particular context (mixed-race marriages always
receive much less support than does school integration). We should
add that when these graphs are broken by education and region, we
find higher education and northern residence to be unvaryingly associated with more liberal sentiments on these general principle issues,
though the same positive monotonic pattern prevails for each educational and regional category.[1]

However, the one remaining principle item, shown in Figure 2.2
rather than in Figure 2.1, departs strikingly from this monotonic pattern. This NES question, which is the most general of all the available
items and is therefore called the General Segregation item, indicates
that support for the principle of desegregation rose steadily until

---

[1] For question wordings and more detailed results for all the items in Figure 2.1, see
Schuman, Steeh, and Bobo (1985).

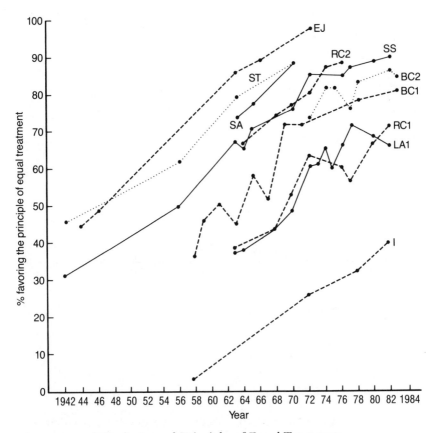

FIGURE 2.1. *Attitudes toward Principles of Equal Treatment:
National Trend Lines.*

EJ = Equal Jobs
ST = Segregated Transportation
SA = Same Accommodations
RC2 = Residential Choice,
     2 alternatives (ISR)
SS = Same Schools

BC2 = Black Candidate (NORC)
BC1 = Black Candidate (Gallup)
RC1 = Residential Choice,
     1 alternative (NORC)
LAI = Laws against Intermarriage
I = Intermarriage

1970, just as it did for the ten questions in Figure 2.1, but thereafter
dropped just as steadily through the last point at which it was asked
(1978). Moreover, this curvilinear trend is clearest for northern college-educated whites (the subsample shown in Figure 2.2)—exactly
those white Americans who have otherwise shown the most support
for the principle of integration over the past forty years.

    Thus, when we first saw these results in our study of racial trends, it

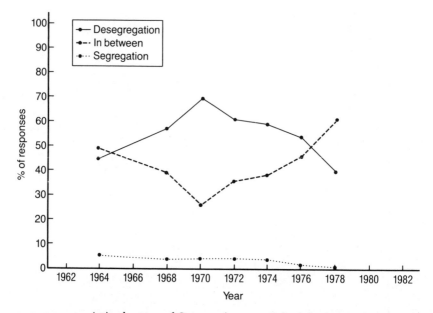

FIGURE 2.2. *Attitudes toward Segregation as a Principle, among Northern, College-Educated Whites.*

> *General Segregation (ISR):* "Are you in favor of *desegregation,* strict *segregation,* or something in-between?
>     1. Desegregation     2. Something in-between     3. Strict segregation

was crucial to determine whether there was something peculiar and perhaps artifactual about the trend for this question *or* whether it told us something of broad and profound importance that was being missed by the other ten principle questions.

The General Segregation question has one obvious feature that distinguishes it from the ten questions presented in Figure 2.1: inclusion of a middle alternative ("something in-between") as a legitimate choice between pro and con responses. We know from previous research that such explicit inclusion of a middle alternative increases the percentage choosing it (Schuman and Presser 1981; Stember and Hyman 1949–50). However, this research finding can account only for a lower level of responses favoring desegregation; it does not in itself explain the curvilinearity—unless somehow the middle alternative was able to pick up a suddenly rising white "backlash" that was being missed by the other essentially dichotomous items. This was indeed an alarming possibility—alarming both in what it said about racial attitude trends and in what it said about the limitations of dichotomous survey items for tracking such trends.

However, a more restricted possibility is suggested by recent research on context effects in surveys. Highly general attitude questions have been shown to be especially susceptible to context effects due to placement within the questionnaire, apparently because respondents need some way to specify the frame of reference and locate their response within it (Schuman and Presser 1981; Smith 1979). For example, asked how much interest they have in politics or religion, respondents are influenced by previous questions that help them think they see how "interest" is being defined and measured (McFarland 1981). Because the General Segregation item is also highly general, respondents may seek help in deciding exactly what the words "desegregation" and "segregation" are intended to refer to.

We therefore looked for one or more other questions that always preceded the General Segregation item and that could have influenced its meaning in a way that would account for the curvilinear trend in Figure 2.2. Our search quickly led to the question shown in Figure 2.3, which deals not with broad principles but rather with the *implementation* of principles by direct government action. "Implementation questions" are in fact the one type of racial question that has not generally shown a positive monotonic trend over time. (Some nine of the available trend questions can be classified as dealing with government implementation of integration or equal treatment.) Responses to the question in Figure 2.3 on Federal School Intervention were stable until 1970, but at that point support for such intervention began to drop—the decline being largely limited to northern respondents and especially pronounced among the college-educated. The reason for the decline was almost certainly the beginnings of court-ordered busing in the North around 1970, which we know from other data was opposed by most whites.

The Federal School Intervention question always preceded the General Segregation item. The two were not always contiguous, but other research has shown that contiguity is not essential for a context effect to occur (Schuman, Kalton, and Ludwig 1983).

Our final step was to test this chain of reasoning using experimentation. Although we could not subject the time trend itself to direct test, we could determine if the Federal School Intervention question would produce a clear context effect on the General Segregation item. The test, carried out as part of a national telephone survey in 1983, is shown in Table 2.1, where the General Segregation item is preceded on one form by the Federal School Intervention question and on the

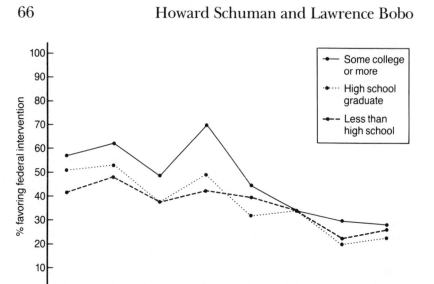

FIGURE 2.3. *Federal School Intervention by Education (North only).*

TABLE 2.1. *Context Effect on General Segregation Question*

| General segregation responses | Preceded by equal jobs | Preceded by school intervention |
|---|---|---|
| 1. Desegregation | 61.4% | 38.9% |
| 2. Something in between | 36.1 | 57.1 |
| 3. Segregation | 2.5 | 4.0 |
| Total | 100 | 100 |
| (Base N) | (158) | (149) |

*Note:* $\chi^2 = 15.6$; d.f. = 2; $p < .001$.

other by a noncontroversial question dealing with the principle of equal treatment in employment ("EJ" in Figure 2.1, where by 1970 there was near-perfect support for the principle). The hypothesized context effect appears not only in terms of statistical significance but with a difference large enough to account for all of the decline in the General Segregation item reported earlier.

Thus, we feel fairly confident that the curvilinear trend in Figure 2.2 was due to the contextual sensitivity of the General Segregation item and that it represented not a basic backlash having to do with principles of integration and equal treatment as such, but rather resistance to court-ordered desegregation of schools, in fact probably to court-ordered busing specifically. Such a curvilinear finding is not unimportant, but its importance has much more limited scope and meaning than would be inferred from the highly general wording of the question.

## Half and Half

We have mentioned thus far two conceptual types of racial questions, those dealing with broad principles and those dealing with government implementation of principles. We classified most of the remaining NORC, ISR, and Gallup questions into a third type dealing with the preferred social distance between the (white) respondent and one or more blacks. Figure 2.4 presents recent data for three social distance questions that have always been asked in the same order in both Gallup and NORC surveys. It is perhaps not surprising that by the 1970s only a tiny percentage of whites objected to having their child in a school where a few other children would be black. However, it is more surprising that more than two-thirds of the white population claimed to have no objection to their child being in a school where half the children are black and that some 40 percent claimed not to object to a school where the majority of children are black. If these claims reflect actual or intended behavior, then maintaining stable school integration should be a good deal easier than in fact it has been, especially in cities where the black proportion of the school population is rising rapidly.

Since the first of the three questions seemed so innocuous once the principle of school integration was accepted *and* since it always preceded the other two more problematic questions, one possibility again is that a context effect is occurring. Having said yes to the first question about a few black children, respondents may find it difficult to change their answers as the proportion of black children increases in later questions.

We tested this possibility by asking the few/half sequence to a random half of a national sample in 1983, with the remainder of the sample receiving only the half item in that section of the questionnaire. Contrary to our hypothesis, the trend that occurred was opposite to prediction: Respondents were more likely to endorse the half item when it came first than when it came second, though the difference did not quite reach statistical significance. Thus, in this case we did *not* demonstrate a context effect but instead felt somewhat re-

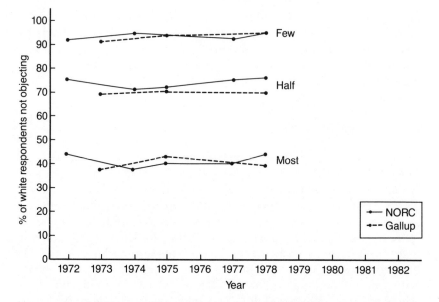

FIGURE 2.4. *Gallup and NORC Results for Three Questions about Schools with Different Proportions of Blacks.*

> *Few:* "Would you, yourself, have any objection to sending your children to a school where a few of the children are black?"
>     1. Yes    2. No
> *Half:* (If No to Few) "Where half of the children are black?"
>     1. Yes    2. No
> *Most:* (If No to Half) "Where more than half of the children are black?"
>     1. Yes    2. No

assured that the survey results were not due to an artifact resulting from question order. Sometimes negative experimental findings can be almost as useful as positive ones.

## A Wording Experiment on Busing

A different kind of problem on which an experimental approach can throw light has to do with the manifold ways in which a question can be worded. Consider, for example, the issue of the use of busing to integrate public schools. NORC's General Social Survey has yielded only about 15 percent of the white population in favor of "the busing of black and white school children from one school district to another." An even smaller proportion, around 10 percent, has chosen the pro-busing side of a scale presented in the National Election Study, where the question contrasts "busing children to schools out of their own neighborhoods" and "letting children go to their neighborhood schools," with an explicit "don't know" alternative offered as well. Yet "busing" can and sometimes is implemented in ways other than these widely used questions imply. In particular, it can involve only "one-way busing."

In order to learn whether one-way busing is reacted to differently from two-way busing, we employed a split-ballot experiment that posed the standard NORC question on one form and a question about busing "black children from inner city schools to predominantly white areas" on the other form. The results show that whereas only 23 percent of a white national subsample support two-way busing, 41 percent of a comparable subsample support one-way busing as described in the question ($\chi^2$=41.5, 1 df, p<.001). Thus one form of busing registers appreciably more support than is suggested when survey reports are cited as unofficial referenda—as they usually are—without qualification in terms of the exact wording of the question. The split-ballot approach to examining this difference allows one to avoid the order effects that might well occur if both questions were asked to the same sample, as well as the various confounding factors that could account for differences discovered between the questions had they been asked in two entirely separate surveys.

Although the difference in thinking about and measuring attitudes toward busing is fairly large, the background correlates of the two attitude questions are similar: older whites, southern whites, and more educated whites tend to be disproportionately opposed to busing regardless of whether it is one-way or two-way. (It may be noted that the direction of the education relationship is opposite for busing to that usually found for racial attitudes, but since the association does not differ between the two versions of the busing question we do not consider that finding further here.) However, another experiment illustrates not only a change in question marginals, but also an important change in the relation of the attitude responses to education.

## Education and Support for the Principle of School Integration

This last experiment deals with the trend question that has the longest history of any of those available in surveys of racial attitudes: "Do you think white students and black students should go to the same schools or to separate schools?" First posed by NORC in 1942 when only 32 percent of a white national sample favored "same schools," it continues to be asked in the General Social Survey, with the percentage for whites most recently having reached 93 percent. Even in 1976, with the figure at 84 percent, the authors of one trend report noted that the "item is coming to elicit such broad agreement that it will soon not be useful in discriminating racial opinion" (Taylor, Sheatsley, and Greeley 1978).[2]

We administered this standard item on school integration to half a white national sample over a four-month period in 1985–86, and for the other half we simply added at the end of the question the phrase "or do you favor something in between?" The original item split 94 percent to 6 percent between "same" and "separate"; the split for the amended item is 85 percent to 4 percent, with the balance (11 percent) choosing the rather odd middle alternative. The shift in response is not massive, but nevertheless the "ceiling" for "same schools" has been raised by 9 percentage points ($\chi^2$=24.9, 1 df, p<.001), and a non-trivial part of the white population has been shown to seek a way of avoiding the integration vs. segregation choice.

More important, perhaps, the addition of the middle alternative throws a somewhat different light on the regularly reported positive relation of education to the choice of the "same schools" response (e.g., Hyman and Sheatsley 1964). When "separate schools" and "in between" are combined and opposed to "same schools," as they should be if we are interested in distinguishing those who support school integration from all others, the association (gamma) of the item with education drops from .55 on the form omitting the middle alternative to .18 on the form where the collapsing occurs; the former coefficient is highly significant (p<.001), the latter misses even conventional significance (p>.06), and the decrease itself is highly reliable (p<.01). Thus when respondents are offered an alternative between "same schools" and "separate schools," the relatively higher support for school integration by more educated white Americans almost disappears.

## Conclusions

We draw three conclusions from the preceding examples.

1. Every survey question or set of questions must be regarded as a single treatment in an incomplete experiment. There are always other substantively important ways to ask and order the questions, and some of these variations can have potential effects on univariate distributions and in some cases on associations with time or other important variables as well. The most effective way to deal with such possibilities is to carry out between-subject experiments in which question form, wording, and context are varied. Although there are always many such

---

[2] From the 1985 General Social Survey Code Book. A small number of "don't know" responses are omitted from this percentaging.

variations possible, in most practical cases only a few are serious candidates for experiment, so one should not be intimidated by visions of an infinite number of experiments.

2. Sample surveys and randomized experiments can usefully be wedded much more closely than is generally assumed. The between-subject experiment incorporated into a general population survey combines the power of random sampling with the power of random assignment, to the advantage of both.

3. Finally, at least when dealing with language, the separation of methodological and substantive sides to research is generally a harmful one. In the examples we have given here, it is hard to know where one stops and the other starts.

## Bibliography

Bishop, George F., Robert W. Oldendick, and Alfred J. Tuchfarber. 1978. Change in the structure of American political attitudes: The nagging question of question wording. *American Journal of Political Science* 22:250—69.

Greeley, Andrew M., and Paul B. Sheatsley. 1971. Attitudes toward racial integration. *Scientific American* 225:13—19.

McFarland, Sam G. 1981. Effects of question order on survey responses. *Public Opinion Quarterly* 45:208—15.

Schuman, Howard, Graham Kalton, and Jacob Ludwig. 1983. Context and contiguity in survey questionnaires. *Public Opinion Quarterly* 47:112—15.

Schuman, Howard, and Stanley Presser. 1977. Question wording as an independent variable in survey analysis. *Sociological Methods and Research* 6:151—70.

———. 1981. *Questions and answers in attitude surveys: Experiments on question form, wording, and context.* New York: Academic Press.

Schuman, Howard, Charlotte Steeh, and Lawrence Bobo. 1985. *Racial attitudes in America: Trends and interpretations.* Cambridge, Mass.: Harvard University Press.

Schwartz, Mildred A. 1967. *Trends in white attitudes toward Negroes.* Chicago: National Opinion Research Center.

Smith, Tom W. 1979. Happiness: Time trends, seasonal variations, intersurvey differences, and other mysteries. *Social Psychology Quarterly* 42:18—30.

Taylor, D. Garth, Paul B. Sheatsley, and Andrew M. Greeley. 1978. Attitudes toward integration. *Scientific American* 238:42—51.

## Sigmund Diamond

## 3 Informed Consent and Survey Research: The FBI and the University of Michigan Survey Research Center

Recent years have seen a prolonged, sometimes acerbic, debate on the issue of the use of human subjects in research. Medicine was perhaps the first area of concern, but the ever-widening perimeter of research brought awareness that the issue did not lie exclusively in the realm of medicine or in the realms of the physical sciences and the biological sciences more generally. Nor was it self-evident that even in medicine awareness of the issue produced agreement as to its solution. It existed—or at least it had close counterparts—in the social sciences as well. Nor has the debate been limited to the academy. As government support for and participation in research of all kinds—medicine, natural sciences, and social sciences—has increased enormously, the use of human subjects has become a political as well as professional problem; that is, it has come to be seen as raising issues of public policy, not only—perhaps not even primarily—of academic policy.

For many, the propriety of this concern seemed easier to accept when what was at issue was the body of the human being. But in re-

EDITOR'S NOTE. Although the events described in this chapter occurred some years ago, Diamond's account prompted me to inquire about the current practices of the Survey Research Center with respect to their contact with law enforcement officials. In April 1986, Dr. Robert L. Kahn, then acting director of the Center, was kind enough to provide the following information to me. The Survey Research Center does not notify the Federal Bureau of Investigation of its surveys. It does routinely send a letter to communities where interviewers will be working. More specifically, the letter is sent to agencies, such as the local police department, the local Chamber of Commerce, and the local Better Business Bureau, that people might contact to determine the bona fides of the Center's interviewers. The names and addresses of interviewers are not included in the letter, nor are the identities of individuals, household addresses, or neighborhoods where interviews are to be conducted. General information about the study, usually limited to a few sentences, is included, and sources of financial support may or may not be mentioned.—Hubert J. O'Gorman

cent years scientific research has involved the borrowing and use not only of the bodies of human subjects, but also of their minds and characters—their opinions, beliefs, hopes, expectations, fears—and their social behaviors and attributes as well: sex, age, race, ethnicity, consumption habits, occupation, income, recreational preferences. Did the use of human subjects as sources of evidence relating to these matters involve consideration of the same range of questions as was admittedly involved in medical and biological research? The explosive increase in the use of the questionnaire and the application of computer technology to the processing of the information collected by means of the questionnaire lent urgency to these questions and put them on the political as well as the professional agenda.

Concern with the use of human subjects has focused on the doctrine of "informed consent." That doctrine has been repeatedly set forth in a form that reveals that medical research was its point of departure and remains its primary interest. Informed consent, the Pure Food and Drug Administration has stated, means that the person experimented upon has the legal capacity to consent to being used, can exercise free power of choice, and "is provided with a fair explanation of all material information concerning the administration of the investigational drug or his possible use as a control, as to enable him to make an understanding decision as to his willingness to receive said 'investigational drug.'"[1] The Code of Regulations promulgated by the Department of Health and Human Services for the protection of human subjects stipulates that in seeking informed consent the following information must be provided to each subject: (1) a statement that the study involves research, an explanation of its purposes, a description of the procedures to be followed, and identification of any experimental procedures; (2) a description of reasonably foreseeable risks or discomforts; (3) a description of reasonably expected benefits; (4) a "disclosure of appropriate procedures or courses of treatment"; (5) a guarantee of the maintenance of the confidentiality of records; (6) a statement concerning compensation for injury; (7) sources from which the subject may obtain further information; (8) a statement that participation by the subject is voluntary.[2]

Is there—should there be—an equivalent doctrine of "informed consent" when nonphysical attributes of the subject are being studied? If so, what information must be provided to the subject to guarantee that the consent is "informed"?

Testifying at the Special Inquiry on Invasion of Privacy of the House

[1] Quoted in Barber 1980, p. 43.
[2] Code of Federal Regulations, 45 CFR 46; revised as of March 8, 1983, par. 46.116.

of Representatives, even before the Camelot, Sanchez, and other exposés stimulated discussion, Francis Ianni, then acting commissioner for research of the Office of Education, listed the minimal guarantees for subjects who lent their minds to the government for purposes of research:

The Office of Education recognizes the essential need to protect the public against questionnaire items which needlessly infringe on individual privacy. . . . the Office of Education will carefully review all questionnaires submitted to it, to prevent injuring public sensitivities in such matters as the challenging of established morals, the invasion of privacy, the extraction of self-demeaning or self-incriminating disclosures, and the unnecessary or offensive intrusion of inquiries regarding religion, sex, politics, et cetera. . . . The responses are used solely for statistical purposes and are not identified with any particular individuals.

Replying to the question from Congressman Benjamin S. Rosenthal, "How extensive is the information you give to [parents and children] prior to executing their consent?" Ianni said, "They should know the types of tests used, the purpose of the research, the fact that they will be kept confidential, and try to relate all of these factors to the specific purpose of the test" (*Special Inquiry* 1966, pp. 303–4, 319).

Many of the problems involved in the use of respondents and informants could have been, and were, easily anticipated: protection of privacy rights, guarantees against self-incrimination or self-degradation, safeguarding the anonymity of the human subjects and guaranteeing security for their responses, and informing them of the scope and purposes of the studies for which their cooperation was being sought. But continued experience with the use of respondents revealed facets of these problems that had previously been unnoticed or neglected. Respondents may be informed of the purposes for which their opinions and other information about them are sought. Later investigators may, however, piggy-back on the original survey and use it for purposes about which the respondents were told nothing and of which, indeed, some of them might disapprove. Some organizations, piggy-backing on a government survey, may use the threat of government retaliation to coerce responses to questionnaires and to secure personal interviews. Arthur A. Miller has reported that a number of people complained that "workers on a government-sponsored Harvard–MIT urban planning project harassed and threatened them in connection with a questionnaire they felt invaded their privacy." One investigator on the project apparently implied that it was a federal crime not to respond to the questionnaire and that the uncooperative subject's name would be turned over to governmental authorities if the documents were not fully answered (Miller 1971, pp. 64ff.). The Federal Bureau of Investigation has acknowledged that its agents have misrepresented themselves as census enumerators while collecting information on New Left political activities in the 1970s. The FBI maintained that the use of this pretext was a proper use of a legitimate investigative technique; U.S. Census Bureau officials, though concerned that the disclosure might erode public confidence in the confidentiality of its records, found that no law had been broken (*New York Times,* April 10, 1980).

Providing security for the information obtained from respondents means more than keeping the files locked. How will the tongues of the interviewers be kept locked? Miller finds it difficult to believe that "all census takers are immune from gossip or impervious to the entreaties by one neighbor for information concerning the replies of another"— even though it is a violation of federal law for census takers to disclose such information. What about nongovernmental employees? And what protects respondents when employees—whether governmental or private—are subjected to either threats or blandishments by government investigative agencies or feel that their principles, moral or political, require that they make known what they have learned about a respondent (Miller 1971, p. 136)?

Notwithstanding the great stimulus given to consideration of the doctrine of informed consent in social research, especially as a result of the inquiries into the Camelot and Sanchez affairs and, even more generally, into the relations between government agencies and private research organizations, specific protections for the subjects of social research are strikingly sparse. Indeed, research "involving survey or interview procedures" is explicitly exempted from the law establishing informed consent, except where *all* of the following conditions exist: (1) responses may be linked to particular respondents; (2) responses may subject respondents to criminal or civil liability or "be damaging to the subject's financial standing or employability"; and (3) the research deals with "sensitive aspects of the subject's own behavior, such as illegal conduct, drug use, sexual behavior, or use of alcohol."[3]

This limitation in the degree to which federal law protects the subjects of social research—especially those studied by the techniques of survey research—is in contrast to the concern shown by the Swedish Council for Research in the Humanities and Social Sciences. Proceeding from the premise that the "demand for research" and the "demand for [personal] integrity" must be balanced, the council laid down the following rules, among others:

[3] 45 CFR 46, par. 46.101.

Rule 1. The research should inform the suppliers of information and those participating in the investigation concerning all features of the investigation that could effect their willingness to take part. . . . It should emerge clearly that participation is voluntary and that the information collected will not be used for any other purpose than research. It is further desirable that information be furnished concerning how and when the results of research will be made public, and who has financed the project. . . .

Rule 2. . . . the research should obtain the consent of the suppliers of information and participants in the investigation. . . . no pressure involving the threat of sanctions of any kind must be applied.

Rule 4. The research should inform all intended participants and suppliers of information for a project that they have a right to discontinue their participation without this involving any negative consequences so far as they are concerned.

Rule 5. All personnel in research projects involving the use of ethically sensitive information on private, identifiable persons should sign an undertaking to keep such information confidential.

Rule 6. All information on private, identifiable persons shall be registered, stored and reported with due maintenance of confidentiality. . . . Personal data on private individuals must not be disclosed to outside persons.[4]

In the contrast between the American and Swedish statements the issue is sharply drawn, but fairness demands recognition of the fact that in the United States some social scientists have expressed a concern more acute than the concern reflected in public law. Writing in the aftermath of Camelot and the revelation of Central Intelligence Agency involvement in some social research at MIT, Michigan State, and elsewhere, Gideon Sjoberg emphasized the danger of overidentification by social scientists with the objectives of administrative agencies; he showed how that overidentification was revealed in manipulation of respondents (1969 pp. 152ff.).

For Ralph Beals, former president of the American Anthropological Association, national, even international, political issues provided the context for the discussion of ethical issues in social research. Coop-

---

[4]Swedish Council for Research in the Humanities and Social Sciences, n.d., pp. 4, 5, 7, 8. The existence of a formal set of rules does not, of course, eliminate *all* controversy. The Swedish Data Inspection Board, created twelve years ago "to license private individuals, organizations and businesses that want to keep computerized files on individuals," recently ordered a group of sociologists to "de-identify" its files so that individuals cannot be identified in their study. According to *Dagens Nyheter*, Stockholm's leading morning newspaper, the Board had for some years pressed the sociologists "to curtail data collection until [they] had obtained the 'informed consent' of the people" being studied. Information concerning "criminal deviance," "leftism," and "social radicalism" was involved. The director of the study justified it on professional grounds: "It is sometimes unethical not to do research if we can get answers we should know about" (*New York Times*, March 11, 1986).

eration with government in the pursuit of legitimate research interests was proper, but in order to gain the public confidence and support needed for the success of the enterprise, social researchers had to maintain autonomy. Autonomy required that respondents be protected from all forms of manipulation, that they be informed of all aspects of the research for which their information is vital, and that their participation be voluntary. Given the political context of Beals's concerns, it is not surprising that he emphasized investigators' ulterior purposes, concealment of the true sources of project funding, and invasion of the privacy of respondents as among the worst of the poisons vitiating the integrity of social research. Far from exempting, or virtually exempting, survey research as a technique of research in need of scrutiny, he took special pains to call attention to the ubiquity of social research and therefore to the need that it be carefully observed:

The problem of individual privacy recently has become acute in the United States, particularly with respect to certain types of survey research and psychological and biomedical research. . . . Recent scientific developments have made possible the invasion of privacy to a point that society must now create workable rules for the protection of private personality. If that is not done . . . public revulsion may produce arbitrary laws too inflexible to reconcile the needs of society and of individual privacy. [Beals 1969, pp. 16, 29, 30–31, 33]

Beals advanced a number of general and specific proposals to reconcile the needs for research and privacy and to guarantee the integrity of the research process itself. As to the utility of professional codes of ethical practice, some of his specific recommendations are of particular interest, especially for their relevance to the case study presented in this essay. Concerning informed consent, he said: "The express or implied consent of the informant usually is considered necessary in most social science research." What should be revealed to the subject?

Every researcher must be prepared to disclose his source of finances, sponsorship, and, in terms appropriate to the understanding of those wanting to know, the purpose of this research. If revealing the source of funds or sponsorship will endanger the research, the solution is not concealment but the seeking of a new source of funds or a new sponsor. False statements of purposes to conceal intelligence-gathering activities . . . is [*sic*] indefensible and fatal to the future of research.

As to the protection of privacy, he said: "The research data obtained for one purpose should not thereafter be used for another without the consent of the individual involved or a clear and responsible assessment that the use of the data transcends any inherent privacy transgressions" (Beals 1969, pp. 34, 173, 180).[5]

Private organizations as well as government, perhaps even more than government, have been alive to such questions and have made them a matter of professional concern. Section II, paragraph D, of the Code of Professional Ethics and Practices of the American Association for Public Opinion Research (1979–80, pp. iv–v) pledges these guarantees of informed consent and privacy:

1. We shall not lie to survey respondents or use practices and methods which abuse, coerce, or humiliate them.
2. We shall protect the anonymity of every respondent, unless the respondent waives such anonymity for specified uses. In addition, we shall hold as privileged and confidential all information which tends to identify the respondent.

The first of the eight "Principles of Disclosure" of the National Council on Public Polls states that "all reports of survey findings of member organizations, prepared specifically for public release, will include reference to the . . . sponsorship of the survey."[6]

Acknowledgment of the need for such guarantees as a matter of professional responsibility is reassuring, but, as Justice Oliver Wendell Holmes suggested of the law, experience sometimes shows the limitations of logic. The American Association for Public Opinion Research promises not to lie to respondents. But what of concealment of the truth rather than outright deceit? The National Council on Public Polls promises that reports of survey findings will include reference to the "sponsorship of the survey." Does this include reference to the "real" sponsorship as well as to "dummy" sponsorship when the survey organization is aware—or becomes aware—that both forms exist? A decade ago Miller (1971, p. 151) was concerned that the current political climate jeopardized the security of information in university files:

[5] Beals's skepticism concerning the efficacy of professional codes of ethics in limiting dubious methods of opinion probing is well taken. Notwithstanding the fact that many organizations have such codes and notwithstanding assurances like Ianni's, government agencies and private research organizations still seem on occasion to collaborate in the use of such methods. An assistant superintendent in the Corvallis, Oregon, public school system recently told teachers not to participate in a federally financed survey that asked, among other things, whether they prayed, how often they had sexual relations, their views on abortion and mercy killing, and whether they had voted for Ronald Reagan or Walter F. Mondale. The study was conducted by the National Center for Education Information under a $72,461 grant. The director of the center justified the use of the questions on the grounds that they are "standard on public opinion polls" and were necessary to "get a profile of the nation's teachers" (*New York Times,* November 10, 1985).

[6] *AAPOR Newsletter* 7 (2) (1980): 2.

Investigative efforts certainly would be expedited if data collected by the FBI, the Justice Department, local law-enforcement agencies, and the academic institutions could be coordinated. If anyone thinks that this notion is farfetched let him consider the implications of President Nixon's request of September 22, 1970, for funding and increased statutory authority to use one thousand new FBI agents on university campuses.

What happens when private survey organizations, including academic survey organizations, in an understandable effort to provide unimpeachable credentials and greater security for their interviewers, place the names of interviewers on record with the FBI and thereby jeopardize the anonymity of the respondents to interviewers who are subject to FBI pressure or cajolery?

Are these questions, which test the limits of the meaning of such terms as "informed consent" and "privacy rights," paranoid fancies? Do they merely point to logical possibilities that have small chance of occurring? Or do they suggest practices that have already occurred and show, therefore, the existence of serious problems and the need to devise solutions for them?

A few years ago, Richard Stephenson of Rutgers University learned that a study he had conducted after the Hungarian uprising of 1956 had been sponsored by the CIA. He felt that he, his university, and his profession had been used by the CIA, and he was concerned that information he had obtained from informants might be used to embarrass or harm them. What, if anything, could justify the "deliberate deception and misrepresentation" that had compromised him and possibly victimized others? In 1980 eight members of the faculty of the John Jay College of Criminal Justice protested that a detailed questionnaire about the "professional and private lives" of faculty members, administered by the Center for Social Research of the CUNY Graduate Center, solicited full cooperation from respondents but failed to inform them that the "survey was being conducted for the specific purpose, as revealed in the trial proceedings, of providing material for the defense" of the Board of Education in the largest class action suit brought by women against a university. Suppression of information, as well as falsification, they argued, violated one of the canons for ethical research of the American Psychological Association: "Ethical practice requires the investigator to inform the participant of all features of the research that reasonably might be expected to influence willingness to participate" (Glazer 1979, p. 62; *New York Times*, June 19, 1980).[7]

---

[7] That secret relations between professors and the CIA still exist, with attendant ethical problems, may be seen in the current controversy concerning Nadav Safran, professor of government at Harvard University and director of its Center for Middle

What might historical knowledge reveal to us about the contours of the problem—the many shapes in which it has presented itself to us in the past, the debate over how, even whether, it should be addressed, the conditions that affected the nature of the responses to it? Martin S. Pernick's brilliant essay on the social history of informed consent in medicine has the great merit of reminding us that informed consent is more than a legal doctrine or practice, that it is affected by "changes in medical technology, medical theory, professional power, and social structure," that neither consciousness of the problem nor solutions are mere matters of technical or professional expertise (Pernick, 1982, p. 3).

Documents that have become available through the Freedom of Information Act have made it possible to reconstruct one situation in which life rather than logic generated the subtleties that both policy makers and professionals must deal with but often fail to recognize. The specific circumstances of this case study allow us to probe more deeply into the politics and psychology of the Cold War and into the relation of government agencies to professional research organizations, and, at the same time, permit us to observe the variety of forms in which general problems like the ethics of research, professional autonomy, and personal privacy—the problems we have been concerned with, which involve the balancing of the need for research and the protection of the respondent—are presented squarely in the area of survey research. Legal statutes and professional codes should last for more than a day; to do so, they must be based on the experience of more than a day.[8]

---

Eastern Studies. Safran did not tell university authorities or participants in a proposed conference on politics and Islam that the conference was being financed by the CIA. It was first reported, moreover, that he had failed to reveal to the Harvard authorities that his recently published book on Saudi Arabia (Harvard University Press) had been produced under a "private . . . confidential" contract between him and the CIA, under which he received $107,430 and promised not to "specify Agency sponsorship" of his research. The contract affirmed "the Government's right to review and approve any and all intended publications" and stressed "the Government's right to deny permission to publish." In his official report on the matter, A. Michael Spence, dean of the Harvard Faculty of Arts and Sciences, found that Safran did notify former dean Henry Rosovsky of the CIA contract. Rosovsky did nothing about the matter, a fact both he and Spence now admit to be an "administrative error" (*New York Times*, November 5, 1985; *Harvard University Gazette*, January 10, 1986).

[8] The FBI documents on which this case study is based were obtained as a result of requests filed under the Freedom of Information Act and a suit in the Southern District of New York of the U.S. Federal District Court to compel the FBI to provide uncensored copies of the documents I had requested. To conserve space, the documents will not be referred to by their FBI serial numbers, but all will be identified in the text by author, recipient, date, or some other distinguishing characteristic. Personal names appearing in the FBI documents that I have quoted or paraphrased have been permitted to stand when they were the names of FBI officials or other officials of government. Names of

On June 24, 1952, FBI Director J. Edgar Hoover read a clipping from the *Washington News* datelined Ann Arbor, Michigan, June 23, 1952, and headlined, "What Are Russians Like?" The article concluded that

The Russian communists are able to keep putting the Soviet system over on the Russian people chiefly because every once in a while the minor official forgets he is a communist and, in spite of himself and the spies who watch him, "backslides" into brotherly, affectionate and easy-going human relations.

This study of Russian national character, the article went on, was based on "confidential interviews" with twenty-nine recent Russian arrivals, ranging from peasants to professionals, conducted by "Dr. Henry V. Dicks for the Rand Corp. and is reported to the Research Center for Group Dynamics, here, and to the Tavistock Institute of Human Relations, London." When Hoover had finished reading the clipping, he attached it to a buck slip on which he wrote, "Just what project is this?" and routed it to a number of FBI officials.

That very day, an "urgent" teletype, signed "Hoover," was sent from Washington FBI headquarters to the special agent in charge (SAC) of the Detroit field office, summarizing the article, mentioning the Research Center for Group Dynamics and the Tavistock Institute, and requesting additional information:

A syllabus of the Russian Research Center, Harvard University, date January, fifty one [*sic*] reflects Dicks submitted for publication to quote Human Relations unquote an article captioned quote Some Observations on Russian Behavior unquote. The Bureau desires to be immediately advised regarding the identity of Dicks, the nature of the project in which he is engaged including its purpose, organization, scope, sponsors, etc.

The next day SAC Detroit replied by teletype: "Top officials and confidential sources at University of Michigan, Ann Arbor, have no knowledge regarding source of instant release. No record of Dicks ever being connected with U.M." SAC Detroit continued that *Human Relations,* jointly published by the Tavistock Institute and the Research Center for Group Dynamics, listed both Dicks and Rensis Likert of Ann Arbor as members of its advisory board and that volume 5, number 2, published in June 1952, contained an article by Dicks, "Observations on Contemporary Russian Behavior," which "work reportedly was quote commissioned and carried out with the aid of generous grants from Rand Corporation, Santa Monica, and the Russian Re-

---

persons associated with the Survey Research Center and appearing in the documents have been deleted. In a few cases, I have also deleted the names of persons whose association with the FBI was only tangential.

search Center, Harvard University, USA, which in turn received support for this work from the Human Relations Research Institute, USAF, under contract AF three three paren zero three eight paren— one two nine zero nine unquote." Dicks had acknowledged receiving an invitation to participate in the study from "Dr. Hans Spier [*sic*], chief of social sciences division, Rand Corp., Washington, D.C. and Professor Clyde Kluckhohn, Director of Harvard University Russian Research Center."

On the same day, June 25, 1952, SAC Detroit sent a second teletype to Washington headquarters with additional information: "No local publicity on instant matter recalled by Bureau agents assigned Ann Arbor," but he informed FBI headquarters about the existence of the Institute for Social Research, headed by Rensis Likert and composed of the Survey Research Center, under Angus Campbell, and the Research Center for Group Dynamics, under Dorwin Cartwright of the University of Michigan faculty. Nearly ten lines of the final paragraph of this teletype have been blacked out by the FBI, ostensibly to protect the personal privacy of another person, but what remains suggests that a series of Survey Research Center studies of "attitudes toward international affairs and civil defense" since 1946 had been the subject of lengthy correspondence among FBI offices in Detroit, Ann Arbor, and Washington. The teletype concludes: "confidential sources at the Univ. of Mich. will be contacted tomorrow regarding Dicks and instant matter. Will advise."

All of this information was summarized in a memorandum dated June 26, 1952, prepared for Hoover by D. M. Ladd, assistant director of the FBI.

Because I have been engaged in research on the relations between the FBI and universities during the McCarthy period, my curiosity was aroused by SAC Detroit's reference to "confidential sources at the University of Michigan" and to earlier correspondence concerning the Survey Research Center (SRC). The documents I had received earlier about the Dicks study had been filed with material dealing with the Russian Research Center at Harvard; until I read those documents, I had no idea that the FBI might be interested in the Survey Research Center. Their interest turned out to be persistent.

On August 13, 1948, SAC Edward Scheidt of the New York field office notified Hoover that a member of the SRC staff had called on him earlier that day with two letters addressed to him: one from John F. Stearns, chief of the Air Research Unit of the Reference Department of the Library of Congress; the other from the staff member himself. Scheidt told Hoover the letters dealt with an SRC project "undertaken for the Library of Congress," which involved "interviewing people who have lived under the Soviet government at least six months since 1939, including American citizens, displaced persons, repatriated Americans, and Russian immigrants, asking them about the reaction of the people to the Soviet government and living conditions under the Soviet regime." The New York phase of the national study would last for three or four months, Scheidt added. He reported that the SRC staff member "stated the project is a restricted one for the Library of Congress and the findings will probably not be published." He sent copies of the two letters to Hoover. The first, from Stearns, identified the staff member and discussed the survey:

The Survey Research Center has undertaken a research project for the Library of Congress—the exact nature of which [the staff member] can explain. Since the project entails the interviewing of many displaced persons and other aliens in your area, it was thought best to notify you of the activity.

[The staff member] will provide a list of the New York area interviewers for your records if you so desire and I shall be glad to supply you any further information you require.

The second of the two letters, written before Scheidt had even seen Stearns's promise to provide the FBI with a list of the names of the interviewers "if you so desire," was from the staff member to Scheidt. It contained the names and addresses of the seven interviewers in New York and promised that additional "names will be forwarded to you whenever additions to the staff are made."

On August 25, 1948, SAC New York notified Hoover of a telephone call he had received five days before from a Mr. A. [name deleted by me—S. D.] of Fifth Ave., Brooklyn, concerning someone who "had a letter in his possession indicating that he was representing the Library of Congress. He claimed to be a student of Michigan University and was making a survey for the Library of Congress. . . . He also stated that his supervisor in N.Y." was an SRC staff member. A. told the FBI that the student had a list of people who had visited Russia within the last ten years and that A.'s mother's name was on the list; she had refused to be interviewed, and he had "answered the questions for her, which interview took two days." Most of the questions "seemed to be the ordinary routine questions as to conditions in Russia," A. said, but "one of the last questions asked him, which made him very suspicious, was somewhat as follows: What city in his opinion would be a good city to bomb without getting in wrong too much with Russia or the Russian people, one of less sentimental value?"

SAC New York concluded his report to Hoover by noting that his letter of August 13 had included the name of the student as one of the

SRC interviewers for the survey. Someone in the Washington head-quarters of the FBI wrote at the bottom of the report: "No action necessary this time."

On October 8, 1948, Mr. B. [name deleted by me—S. D.] of New York wrote FBI headquarters in Washington that he had been asked by an SRC employee "for information regarding 'social conditions in Eastern Europe.'" He enclosed a copy of the letter to him and of his reply and called attention to the writer's statement that he was employed by the Survey Research Center of the University of Michigan and that "his organization and project are registered with the F.B.I." As to himself, Mr. B. told the FBI that he had been a clerk in U.S. military attaché offices in Moscow, Warsaw, Bucharest, and Budapest from September 1938 to September 1940 and was now, having completed the examination for a position in the Foreign Service, waiting for an appointment. "If you need further information about me," he added, "you will undoubtedly find it in your own files." He appealed for verification of the SRC employee's story.

Hoover himself wrote in the margin of the letter: "No record of [the employee] in Bureau files." The employee's letter to Mr. B., dated October 3, 1948, solicits his cooperation as someone whose "name has been submitted to us as among those who are in a position to give us some of the information we seek. . . . Because of the special nature of this project I am unable to supply further details or present my credentials until I see you. You may verify the above by calling Dr. Atkinson of the Library of Congress. Also, we are registered at the F.B.I." B.'s reply, dated October 7, 1948, requested that he see the writer's credentials and that he be given the full name and title of Dr. Atkinson of the Library of Congress and the "department or section of the F.B.I. with whom you are registered."

Hoover replied promptly to B.'s inquiry about the survey:

I desire to advise that this Bureau is in possession of no information relating to the official nature of the Survey Research Center nor is it registered with the FBI. Your thoughtfulness and interest in bringing this matter to my attention is indeed appreciated.

Although Hoover disclaimed knowledge of the SRC, he had been informed about it and about this very survey.

An internal office memorandum of the FBI, dated October 7, 1948, reported that the New York field office had already submitted three letters on the survey and had suggested that upon completion of the survey the bureau should "obtain the results of these interviews of these various individuals since the interviews may contain information of an intelligence nature which could be of interest to the Bureau. . . .

Some of the persons interviewed might be subjects of current Bureau investigation and . . . information of possible value would be derived from such interviews."

The memorandum concluded:

It is suggested that the Liaison Section contact the appropriate representatives of the Library of Congress for whom this survey is being made and determine if the results of this survey can be made available to the Bureau for possible intelligence purposes.

At the bottom of this final paragraph, J. Edgar Hoover himself wrote: "Determined Air Force is backing the Survey & arrangements made to get CC."

Moreover, SAC Detroit had sent to Hoover on October 12, 1948, a lengthy report on the organization and operations of the SRC:

The center is self-supporting and conducts . . . surveys for business, labor and any group who contract for surveys. However, the biggest contractor with the SRC is the United States Government

. . . The nucleus on which the center was formed were former employees of the Department of Agriculture who conducted surveys of a similar nature with the Department of Agriculture. However, all connection with the Government is now severed and the work done by the center is done on a contract basis by Governmental Agencies who contract for most of the surveys.

SAC Detroit went on to report that an SRC administrator had been interviewed by the FBI in connection with "several security matter complaints from various field divisions."

The administrator had pointed out that most of the complaints he had received concerned "surveys wherein Russia was involved" and that sometimes in the past FBI offices in areas where interviews were being conducted were notified. According to the FBI files he told SAC Detroit that the SRC was about to begin a national survey on attitudes toward American-Russian relations. "He pointed out that this is the fourth such survey which the SRC has undertaken," and, so the FBI reported, he gave SAC Detroit

the names and addresses of interviewers along with the places where the interviews will be conducted. Forty-nine interviewers will question people in 32 localities in the United States. . . . [This same person] has advised that he will be glad to furnish the nature of the survey, the names and addresses of interviewers, and the localities where they are making interviews in all cases where the Survey Research Center believes the investigations may cause complaints to be received by the FBI.

There is at least a bit of evidence that the FBI interviewed some of the respondents of the SRC survey. On November 30, 1949, SAC Chi-

cago sent a memorandum to Hoover, the first three lines of which
have been deleted by the FBI. Immediately after the deletion the
memo begins:

were recently interviewed by agents of the Chicago Office. In connection with
the interviews they advised that during the early part of 1949 a woman had
interviewed them at length pertaining to Russia. The [word deleted] first got
the impression that the woman was making a survey for the Library of Congress which was being conducted by the University of Michigan but later decided that the survey was being made by the University of Michigan and that a
copy of the results of the survey would be furnished the Library of Congress.
This woman was talking with American soldiers who had been in Russia during World War II and with Russian war brides.

The memo contains a description of the woman interviewer and concludes—as did the earlier memo from SAC New York—that it "would
appear that the results of the survey might be of some assistance to the
Bureau."

That the auspices of the SRC study were somewhat obscure (Was it
done for the Library of Congress? Was it done for the Air Force?);
that the names of the interviewers were made known to the FBI; that
the FBI was interested in obtaining the results of the study; that the
respondents were not told who the ultimate client was, all seemed
clear enough from these documents. But some questions still remained obscure. How many such surveys had the SRC conducted?
Did even it know who the sponsor was? What was the reason for giving
the names and addresses of the interviewers to the FBI? I wrote to the
SRC for clarification of the situation. Angus Campbell responded to
the first of my letters by advising me that the

SRC did indeed conduct a survey of Russian expatriates in 1948. The contract
was with the Library of Congress but I think the Air Force provided the
money. There was only one study (not four). All the records of this study,
including the interviews, were turned over to the Russian Institute at Harvard
in about 1950. Professor Kluckhohn was very interested in these materials at
one time. We did not publish anything from this study. It is my understanding
that the materials are public.[9]

[9] Angus Campbell to Sigmund Diamond, April 22, 1980. In connection with Professor Campbell's statement that "all the records of the study were turned over to the
Russian Research Center at Harvard," note Beals's warning that "the research data obtained for one purpose should not thereafter be used for another without the consent
of the individual involved" (Beals 1960, p. 180). There is no evidence that the respondents in the SRC study were asked for permission to send the records to the Russian
Research Center. There may be doubt about the auspices and financing of the SRC
study. There is none about the Russian Research Center study; it was done under Contract no. AF33(038)12909 with the Human Relations Research Institute, U.S. Air Force,
Maxwell Field, Montgomery, Alabama.

I followed with a number of additional questions: Were the respondents only Russian "expatriates" or, as the FBI documents state, "people who have lived under the Soviet Government at least six months since 1939, including American citizens, displaced persons and repatriated American and Russian immigrants"? Was this study conducted for the "Air Research Unit" of the Library of Congress? Were respondents told that it was the Library of Congress or the Air Force that desired the information? If they were not told, was it because the SRC did not at that time inform respondents of the organization or agency sponsoring its surveys? What were the respondents told about the confidentiality of their responses? Why did the SRC give the names and addresses of its interviewers to the FBI? Is there any indication that the FBI ever contacted any of these interviewers? Was it at Kluckhohn's request that all the records of the survey were turned over to the Harvard Russian Research Center?[10]

I wrote to Campbell about other studies as well. His full response to my questions concerning this study is as follows:

I was not involved in the original negotiations concerning the Library of Congress Study. It was one of the first studies we undertook after the SRC was established and was the only "restricted" study we have ever accepted. I am surprised at your description of the subjects; I would have thought they were all previous Soviet citizens. [The SRC staff member] was correct in describing the study as having a "restricted" classification although I believe all the material became public after it was transferred to Harvard. The title, "Air Research Unit," is not one I remember although it was clear that the Air Force was interested in the study. The names of our interviewers were given to the F.B.I. and the local police because the intended respondents often wanted to check their credentials. We have notified the police of ongoing studies for over 30 years. So far as I know the F.B.I. never contacted any of the interviewers. I do not have a letter in hand but it is my memory that Professor Kluckhohn asked that the material be sent to Harvard, otherwise they [*sic*] would not have been sent.[11]

[10] Diamond to Campbell, June 24, 1980.
[11] Campbell to Diamond, July 9, 1980. Does the SRC still give the FBI and local police agencies the names of its interviewers? I have been reliably informed that it does not notify the FBI now and has no record that that was its policy in the past. But Angus Campbell said flatly that the "names of our interviewers were given to the FBI and the local police because the intended respondents often wanted to check their credentials," and his statement is abundantly confirmed by the FBI documents cited here. That the SRC has no record now that that was its policy does not prove that that was not its practice; it may prove that there is a gap in its records or that its policy was never made a matter of written record. The SRC continues to notify local police forces of its surveys and provides them with a facsimile of the identification badges and cards used by the interviewers. The same information is given to local chambers of commerce and better business bureaus. Some light is shed on the practice of registering the names and addresses of interviewers with the FBI in the recent report on survey research by the

Some questions remain. Was there only one such study, as Campbell remembered, or four, as reported to the FBI? What were respondents told about sponsorship of the study, government interest in it, and the confidentiality of their answers? Did the SRC authorities realize that in giving the names and addresses of their interviewers to the FBI, to protect them from possible harassment, they might at the same time increase their vulnerability to pressure from the FBI? Was the identity of the respondents kept confidential when the questionnaires were turned over to the Harvard Russian Research Center? What use was made of the information obtained in the survey?

We are not likely to learn what use the government made of the information, but there is a tantalizing reference in one of the reports of the Harvard Russian Research Center Project on the Soviet Social System that whets the appetite for more information and, coincidentally, demonstrates how the simplest question can be raised to a high level of theoretical abstraction. Mr A. had told the FBI that one of the last questions asked him made him very suspicious: "What city in his opinion would be a good city to bomb without getting in wrong too much with Russia or the Russian people, one of less sentimental value?" One Harvard report on its Soviet study states that a major research interest is to develop a set of propositions indicating the probable consequences for any part of the system and for the system as a whole of particular types of social action or change under specified conditions, including the impact of external forces: "This is probably the most difficult area in which to state reliable propositions. Examples, however, would be to specify the probable reaction to a proposal from the United States for complete bilateral disarmament, or the consequences for the system of simultaneous atom-bombing of twenty specified major cities." [12]

The question that bothered Mr. A. might, then, have been used as evidence for the Russian Research Center's conclusions concerning

---

Panel on Survey Measurement of Subjective Phenomena (Turner and Martin 1984, 1 : 73). Discussing "pseudo surveys" as one of the misuses of polls, the authors point out that sometimes the solicitation of funds and the selling of products are disguised as polls. Some major polling organizations try to avoid this by providing interviewers with "notification of clearance by the Better Business Bureau." Even if one were to agree that the Better Business Bureau is the organization to provide such "clearance," it would not necessarily follow that the FBI should be used to provide its form of "clearance." The Better Business Bureau is not, after all, the FBI, and the consequences of the one form of "clearance" are not as far-reaching and uncontrollable as those of the other.

[12] Office memorandum, SAC New York to the Director, FBI, August 25, 1948; "The Harvard Project on the Soviet Social System, Survey of Research Objectives," Harvard Russian Research Center, October 1, 1951, Officer Education Research Laboratory, Maxwell Air Force Base, Montgomery, Alabama.

the "consequences" for parts of the system and for the system as a whole of the impact of "external forces."

Another subject of SRC surveys in which the FBI showed particular interest was atomic energy. Since the issues presented by this second case are—with one exception—the same as those presented by the first (What information about the sponsorship of the study was provided to the respondents? What guarantees were given as to the confidentiality of their responses? What information about the surveys, respondents, and interviewers was given to the FBI?), our analysis of the FBI documents concerning this case need not be so lengthy. But one difference between the two situations is worth pointing out at the start. In the first case, the SRC did not disclose who the sponsor of the study was. In the second case, there are indications that it was under instructions *not* to disclose such information and apparently acceded to the command.

The first reference to the "Public Opinion Poll—Atomic Energy Matters"—as the FBI called the SRC study—is contained in an FBI interoffice memorandum of September 1, 1949, which reports that an official in the Washington area office of the Atomic Energy Commission (AEC) had "confidentially advised Agent [name deleted by FBI] that the Commission" had recently contracted with the University of Michigan for a public opinion poll on atomic energy; the first sample poll would soon be held in Detroit. The AEC official said that "he was anticipating that some of the individuals interviewed would contact the local Bureau offices with information that an individual had been asking numerous questions concerning atomic energy." Attached to the memorandum was a copy of the preliminary questionnaire, which the AEC official was furnishing "confidentially since the person handling this project did not know that [he] had obtained any information concerning it."

The preliminary questionnaire, designated Project 53 and dated July 15, 1949, consists of twenty-three questions. They deal with sources of information about atomic energy, whether more information is needed by the public, whether plants in the neighborhood of the respondent are making use of atomic energy, whether the respondent feels that it is dangerous to live near or work in a plant using "atomic materials," and the dangers of atomic war. In the light of recent events, some of the 1949 questions seem almost prophetic:

> 10. Suppose it were decided that they were going to build a plant using Atomic Materials close to where you live. How would you feel about it?
>     a. Why?

     b. (if says "dangerous") How do you mean?

     c. Any other reasons?

     d. (if says "dangerous") What would you try to do about? [*sic*]

11. Suppose they offer you, or someone in your family, a good job in this plant. Would you say it is all right to take it?

     a. Why?

     b. (if says "too dangerous") In what ways do you think it would be dangerous?

     c. (if says "too dangerous") What could happen to you?

If said "Dangerous" in Q. 10:

12. How far from here would you want the plant to be so you'd feel really safe? . . .

14. Do you think there are any dangers that can come from plants using or making Atomic Energy? . . .

21. Is there anything special that makes Atom Bombs worse than regular Bombs?

In a letter to all FBI field offices, dated September 1, 1949, but sent September 7, J. Edgar Hoover notified all SACs of the impending SRC survey and alerted them to the possibility that they might be receiving "complaints from individuals that persons have been asking questions of them concerning atomic energy." Hoover was quite right in suggesting that the public might be nervous in answering questions about atomic energy. Replying to his letter, SAC New Orleans informed Hoover on October 5, 1949, that the business manager of the Southern Forest Experiment Station, U.S. Forestry Service, had called the New Orleans office of the FBI with information that he had received a mail questionnaire concerning atomic energy from the Bureau of Editorial Research of New York. He sent the FBI a copy of the questionnaire and "stated he had no intention of replying to" it. SAC New Orleans could not find any connection between this questionnaire and the SRC study about which the FBI had been alerted.

Due to the incompleteness of the documents provided by the FBI, it is not altogether clear—but highly probable—that the next reference to an SRC survey on atomic energy refers to the one Hoover mentioned on September 1, 1949, rather than to yet another. In any case, on July 19, 1950, SAC Detroit notified FBI headquarters that another SRC administrator had advised that the SRC was about to undertake a survey in thirty-nine localities throughout the United States on "Public Thinking Regarding Atomic Energy . . . authorized by Mr. John Derry, Executive Office, Division of Biological Medicine, Atomic Energy Commission." On August 4, all SACs were notified of the impending survey: "This is being brought to your attention in the event inquiries are received by your office regarding this matter. The work is being performed on a contractional [*sic*] basis for the Atomic Energy Commission."

SAC Newark had already been notified of the survey. On August 2 he teletyped Hoover that the New York office of the AEC had advised that "employees of the University of Michigan" would soon begin a survey in Totowa and Little Falls Township, New Jersey. "Interviewers will possess credentials and have interview sheet and personal data sheet to be filled out." At least a few more details concerning these surveys and what respondents were and were not told about their sponsorship may be obtained from FBI field office reports. On August 11, 1950, for example, SAC Albuquerque wrote FBI headquarters that the director of the Office of Security, AEC, Los Alamos, had notified him of the SRC survey:

The persons conducting the interviews in this study have been instructed to refer anyone having any doubt as to the authenticity of this survey to the FBI or the local police.

According to [name deleted] this survey is being made with the full knowledge and approval of AEC and possibly for AEC. It is not desired, however, that anyone be informed that this study is being conducted for the Atomic Energy Commission.

On August 15, SAC San Francisco notified Hoover that the security officer of the Radiation Laboratory at Berkeley had told him that the Survey Research Center would be making a survey in the San Francisco and Los Angeles areas "relative to the knowledge of certain individuals regarding atomic energy." According to SAC San Francisco, the security officer "stated that this survey was not under the auspices of the Atomic Energy Commission, but that [it] was aware that the survey was being made." SAC San Francisco also reported that two members of the SRC staff had already contacted his office, identified themselves as they "had been instructed," and discussed the purposes of the survey.

Although it is clear that the SRC was using the FBI, in effect, to provide credentials for its interviewers and reasonably clear that it was not informing its respondents as to the auspices of the survey, it is not altogether clear even now, given the discontinuities in the FBI documents, who the sponsor really was. Among the documents released by the FBI is a letter dated September 15, 1950, on the stationery of the chairman, National Security Resources Board, Executive Office of the President. Except for the names of the recipient (J. Edgar Hoover) and the author (W. Stuart Symington), the entire letter has been blacked out by the FBI. At the bottom, however, there is a handwritten comment by Hoover: "Alert our field offices in these cities so they will know—but they must treat it confidential [*sic*]."

But another document released by the FBI—a letter from Hoover
to SAC New York, September 18, 1950—quotes Symington's blacked-
out letter in full:

By letter dated September 15, 1950, Honorable W. Stuart Symington,
Chairman, National Resources Security Board, furnished the following
information:
    "The Survey Research Center, Institute of Social Research University of
Michigan, has been engaged by this Board to perform a survey on the psychological aspects of civil defense. This survey will be a field interview program
which will be conducted by trained personnel of the Institute in the eleven
cities as follows: Baltimore, Boston, Chicago, Cleveland, Detroit, Los Angeles,
New York, Philadelphia, Pittsburgh, San Francisco and St. Louis.
    "The Institute has been notified that under no circumstances can the
people to be interviewed be told that this study is being conducted for the
Civil Defense Office of this Board. If it were known that this study was sponsored by the Resources Board, it might be misinterpreted with resulting damage to the study and to the Civil Defense Program. . . ."

The National Security Resources Board notified FBI headquarters
in Washington about this study; SRC notified the Detroit field office.
On September 27, SAC Detroit reported that an SRC administrator
had called about this eleven-city survey:

The survey will concern civilian defense and atomic attack to determine the
public attitude, awareness and concern. The survey is being conducted by the
Survey Research Center under contract with the National Security Resources
Board, Civil Defense Division. However, in the survey this information will
not be disclosed and under no circumstances should a Bureau representative
divulge the fact the NSRB is interested in the study.

This may or may not have been the first of such surveys undertaken
by the SRC for the National Security Resources Board. It was not the
last. On April 3, 1952, SAC Detroit reported to Washington FBI headquarters that the same SRC administrator had called with information
that still another survey would be conducted in the same cities from
March 19 to April 1, 1952.
    Some light on the climate of the period is shed by the correspon-
dence concerning this study among Hoover, Congressman J. Harry
McGregor of Ohio, and Mrs. D. [name deleted by me—S. D.], a part-
time SRC interviewer. Humorous or serious, the episode is enlightening, for it suggests, among other things, that the Survey Research
Center, responding to public fears by seeking legitimacy from the FBI,
was, in fact, increasing those fears.
    On April 9, 1952, Congressman McGregor sent Hoover a copy of a
letter he had received from Mrs. D., one of his constituents. It was a
complaint about the FBI. She had been approached about a month

earlier by a representative of SRC, who had obtained her name from the local Chamber of Commerce, about "doing some surveying in this locality for them." Since the offer was attractive and she had had experience as a census enumerator, she accepted. But "the news was just breaking about the communistic element found in this particular university," and, not wishing "to unknowingly or innocently filter information into Un-American hands," she wrote to the Ann Arbor Chamber of Commerce and to the University of Michigan to inquire into the SRC and its representative who had approached her about the job. She "established the fact that there was such a Center, but still did not know whether it was Un-American or not." She decided to accept the job to learn what she could about the SRC; "in the mean time [*sic*] I could contact the F.B.I." Mrs. D. never received from the FBI the reassurance she wanted. Because of illness she was not able to work as efficiently as she would have liked, but a friend did the interviewing for her. The pay was good and the work enjoyable, "but we still do not know whether this job was for the government or not. We were told that the Civil Defense Commission in Washington hired the University of Michigan to make this survey on civil defense. We do not know. . . . We got no help from the FBI; they made us spend money for useless telephone calls to the extent of $2.75."

McGregor felt that Mrs. D.'s complaint deserved an answer "because her efforts were for the good of our government and she did not wish to partake in any communistic activities." At the bottom of McGregor's letter, Hoover wrote: "Get facts at once. H." When he wrote McGregor on April 15, he provided him with some of the facts:

For your information, another Government agency has in the past advised that it contracted with the Survey Research Center to conduct certain research. We do not know if the project on which Mrs. [D.] was employed was for the Government.

The relationship between the SRC, the government agency or agencies that sponsored these studies, and the FBI, cagily described in Hoover's letter, persisted. On January 22, 1954, SAC Detroit informed FBI headquarters that the SRC had notified the Detroit field office of still another survey being done under "contract with the National Office for Civil Defense" on public awareness of "danger of war . . . and related matters." He also, the FBI said, provided the names of the SRC interviewers in the Detroit area. On February 9, all FBI field offices were notified of the survey.

In response to questions I submitted to him, Angus Campbell told me: (1) that the SRC had conducted a single study in 1950 "in the environs of certain nuclear installations. We have a report of this study.

It was not published but it was not classified and it is available for your inspection"; (2) that in the period 1942–62 SRC did "some six studies" for the National Office of Civil Defense; they "were not published but they are public documents and are available in our library." In answer to my questions as to what the respondents were told about the sponsoring agency of these surveys ("Were they told that it was the Atomic Energy Commission, the Civil Defense Office of the National Security Resources Board, or the University of Michigan?") and why the names of the interviewers were given to the FBI, he replied:

> The names of our interviewers were given to the F.B.I. and the local police because the intended respondents often wanted to check their credentials. We have notified the police of ongoing studies for over 30 years. . . .
>    The report of the Atomic Energy Study, published in December 1951, states, "The research reported here was conducted under contract with the U.S. Atomic Energy Commission." I cannot tell you what the interviewers were told about the sponsorship but I doubt if it was the Civil Defense Office of the National Resources Board. That name is not familiar to me. The interviewers identified themselves with police officials so that they could reassure suspicious citizens who might ask if they knew about the study.[13]

So ends our story—but not our problem. The story deals with an episode in the history of the Cold War and with a chapter in the history of public opinion research. The problem concerns the ethics of research involving human subjects: Does the doctrine of "informed consent" require that they be told under whose auspices the study soliciting their opinions, feelings, and beliefs is really being carried out? May the documents relating to their responses be used without their permission for a second and different study? What guarantees must an opinion-polling organization provide for the confidentiality of responses when it knows that those responses are of particular interest to government agencies, including those in the intelligence-gathering field? Cannot means be found to provide credentials for interviewers without seeking legitimacy from police agencies, whose bona fides in these matters may be open to question?

Clearly these questions, though they are suggested by the case we have examined, are not limited to that case. What is the present policy of the survey research community in general, and of the Survey Research Center in particular, regarding such practices? Recent statements suggest that, on both levels, practice may not have changed much, though technique has vastly improved.

[13] Diamond to Campbell, March 31, June 24, 1980; Campbell to Diamond, April 22, July 9, 1980.

The most recent authoritative examination of the problems and methods of survey research—*Surveying Subjective Phenomena* (Turner and Martin 1984), a report of the Panel on Survey Measurement of Subjective Phenomena—notes that, in general, existing "standards for the conduct and reporting of surveys appear to have had a limited impact on survey practices. When systematic evaluations have been possible, we find that current practice leaves much to be desired" (1 : 90). Why has the effect of codes of professional ethics been so limited? "First, codes of professional practice bind only the members of professional organizations." *Others* (my emphasis) "will not be subject to review or sanction." But the historical record demonstrates, in this case at least, that it was not "others" who were at fault but the members, and some of the leading members at that, of the professional organizations themselves. The assumption that members of professional organizations will feel obligated to abide by the ethical standards of those organizations seems naive, and the impression of naiveté is strengthened by the conclusion of the same report as to federal surveys:

A different set of standards has been applied to surveys conducted by the federal statistical agencies, in part because many of the issues are simpler. Information collected by the government is (supposed) to be made available to the public and so there is no motive for secrecy. In addition, as both a sponsor and performer of its own survey research, federal agencies have greater power to enforce standards and control the quality of their surveys. [Turner and Martin 1984, 1 : 67–68]

Who, at least since Watergate, can believe that because information "is (supposed) to be made available to the public . . . there is no motive for secrecy"? And who can believe that, because the federal government has "greater power to enforce standards and control the quality" of its surveys, it will use its power to that end and not to some other?

But naiveté is not the only, or the principal, reason for the panel's position as to informed consent. It agrees that "some of the practices might be questioned on the grounds that a respondent is not fully informed before he consents to be interviewed," but its general view seems based on an assumption as to the relation between ethical and professional considerations that does not necessarily obtain. "In this regard," the panel concludes, "it is worth noting that Singer (1978) finds that fully informing respondents about the purpose of the interview results neither in lower response rates nor in less complete responses to sensitive questions" (Turner and Martin 1984, 1 : 269). Is the panel suggesting that "fully informing the respondent about the purposes of the interview" is appropriate because it does not reduce participation in the study?[14] Ethical and professional considerations seem happily wedded. Singer (1978, p. 159) states:

Finally, since a more detailed, informative, and truthful introduction adversely affects neither overall response rate nor responses to individual questions, there appears to be no reason to withhold such information from respondents.

What are the larger implications of this finding? These are "far from clear," Singer says (p. 160), but one might

conclude optimistically that none of the elements of informed consent, except the request for a signature, has sizable effects on the response rate to surveys or the quality of response, and that therefore ethical imperatives do not conflict with practical considerations.[15]

That ethical considerations may be taken into account because they "do not conflict with practical considerations" is not entirely reassuring. Professor Singer's conclusion of "no conflict" may be an artifact of her study. Suppose another study—such as this one—should disclose a conflict between ethical and practical considerations? Which would prevail? A recent statement by Professor Howard Schuman of the Survey Research Center, and a member of the panel, suggests that the "professional" interest would dominate over the ethical: "substantial deception should be avoided *except when necessitated by important scientific goals and not likely to be especially vexing to respondents if revealed*" (Schuman 1983, p. 603; emphasis added).[16]

It is not likely that, on this score, the practice of the Survey Re-

---

[14] The phrase, "fully informing the respondents about the purposes of the interview," is ambiguous, because the purpose of the interview and the purpose of the study are not necessarily the same. Respondents may be told that the purpose of the interview is to obtain their opinions as to foreign policy; the purpose of the study may be to locate sources of support for or disaffection from some aspect of foreign policy in order to provide information needed by the Department of State or an intelligence agency. Which "purpose" will be revealed to the respondents? Years ago, Paul F. Lazarsfeld pointed to similar problems concerning the question, "Why?" The naked question "Why?" can be answered in a variety of ways, making it difficult to compare responses. Lazarsfeld was writing in the infancy of scientific polling, and it is understandable that the weakness he was pointing to resulted from lack of experience. But it is now half a century later, and lack of experience can no longer account for the failure to see the dangers of ambiguity. Lazarsfeld's point was that ambiguity endangered the scientific validity of the survey and therefore was to be avoided. Perhaps the danger of ambiguity is selectively perceived. Where ambiguity is felt to be necessary for the completion of the survey, then clarity is to be avoided (Lazarsfeld 1935, pp. 32–43).

[15] Moreover, if we look at the matter from only a methodological point of view, it would seem difficult to draw any conclusions whatever concerning the importance of informed consent as a variable until that variable is itself controlled explicitly in the research design.

[16] This is in strong contrast to Beals: "If revealing . . . the sponsorship will endanger the research, the solution is not concealment but the seeking of a new . . . sponsor" (Beals 1960, p. 173).

search Center is on a higher level than that of the profession generally. The panel has found that organizations differ in the instructions they give to interviewers on how to approach respondents. SRC tells its interviewers to "provide the respondent with a minimal amount of information. . . . 'the doorstep introduction should be just enough to get you inside the house.'" And the panel concludes that neither the Census Bureau nor NORC places "quite as much emphasis as does SRC on not telling respondents the purpose or nature of the interview" (Turner and Martin 1984, 1:259–60).

That current practice and policy in survey research are virtually silent on the serious discussion of ethical issues is perhaps not surprising given the view that the profession apparently has of itself. The last words to appear at the end of the second volume of *Surveying Subjective Phenomena* (Turner and Martin 1984), on the last page, where nothing else is printed, are a quotation from Bernard Gui's treatise of ca. 1321, *Manual of the Inquisition*. The prominence given to the quotation suggests that the panel sees in it something more than the final word of its report:

If a person spoke openly and clearly against the faith, offering the arguments and authorities upon which heretics usually rely, it would be very easy for the faithful learned of the Church to convict him of heresy. . . . But since present day heretics attempt and seek to conceal their errors rather than to avow them openly, men trained in the learning of the Scriptures cannot convict them, because they escape in verbal trickery and wily thinking. Learned men are even apt to be confounded by them, and the heretics congratulate themselves and are all the stronger therefore, seeing that they can thus delude the learned to the point of escaping artfully by the twists and turns of their crafty, cheating and underhanded replies.

The analogy is powerful, and the more telling because it must have been chosen unreflectively. No one would suggest seriously that survey analysts see themselves as hounds of heaven whose duty is to expose heretics; but surely the analogy implies that they do see themselves as having a mission—albeit a professional rather than a religious one—and that that mission is the completion of the research project, even in the face of recalcitrant respondents and contrary ethical norms. The issue is a real one and it is a living one, not a "mere" matter of history. Carl-Gunnar Janson of the Stockholm University sociology department feels that it "is sometimes unethical not to do research if we can get answers we should know about." Who wants to know? Howard Schuman of the University of Michigan sociology department feels that "substantial deception should be avoided except when necessitated by important scientific goals." What goals? Janson and Schuman are not Torquemadas; they epitomize a phenomenon well recognized in the sociology of knowledge: How does a particular point of view come to be taken as having more general sanction, as resting on the authority of the "profession"? But, of course, not all members of the profession see the practice of deceit as justified by the project mission. Herbert C. Kelman, professor of social ethics at Harvard University and chairman of its Middle East Seminar, writes that "central to the ethical conduct of scholarly work is the obligation to reveal its sponsorship and source of funding, whenever this information may be relevant to the decisions and evaluations of others. . . . The principle of informed consent, which lies at the core of research ethics, requires investigators to reveal any information which might be material to a person's decision to cooperate." Nor is this requirement for openness a safeguard only for the subjects of research. It is indispensable for the scholarly community itself:

> Our academic affiliations and scholarly credentials are crucial to public trust in us and, hence, readiness to cooperate in our projects and accept our conclusions. Unless informed otherwise, people expect us to act as independent scholars. Failure to make known any conditions that might limit our independence—or public perception of it—is a violation of the trust placed in us when we present ourselves as independent scholars. Such violations of trust are ethically problematical and damaging to the scholarly community.[17]

Writing about the situation in South Africa nearly twenty years ago, Pierre van den Berghe said, "The one salient conclusion which the South African scene confirms is that the distinction between ethics and politics in an actual research situation is analytical rather than empirical" (1969, p. 195). It is a conclusion that is borne out by every study in the ethics of research, no matter the time and no matter the place. The methodology of research may be a matter of professional competence, but that methodology is applied in a context in which professional competence is only one—and not invariably the most important—of the issues to be considered. When professionals remember that there are things on heaven and earth that are more important than the "project mission," they will be wise as well as competent.

## Bibliography

American Association for Public Opinion Research. 1979–80. *Directory of members.*

Barber, Bernard. 1980. *Informed consent in medical therapy and research.* New Brunswick, N.J.: Rutgers University Press.

Beals, Ralph L. 1960. *Politics of social research.* Chicago: Aldine Publishing Co.

---

[17] *New York Times*, March 5, 1986. See also nn. 4 and 16.

Glazer, Myron. 1979. Controlling ourselves: Deviant behavior in social science research. *Research in Social Problems and Social Policy* 1:43–64.

Kaiser, Fred M. 1980. Secrecy, intelligence, and community: The U.S. intelligence community. In Stanton K. Tefft, ed. *Secrecy: A cross-cultural perspective*, pp. 273–96. New York and London: Human Sciences Press.

Lazarsfeld, Paul F. 1935. The art of asking why. *National Marketing Review* 1:32–43.

Miller, Arthur R. 1971. *The assault on privacy: Computers, data banks, and dossiers*. Ann Arbor: University of Michigan Press.

Pernick, Martin S. 1982. The patient's role in medical decision-making: A social history of informed consent in medical therapy. In President's Commission for the Study of Ethical Problems in Medicine and Biomedical and Behavioral Research, Studies on the Foundations of Informed Consent, *Making health care decisions: The ethical and legal implications of informed consent in the patient-practitioner relationship*, vol. 3, Appendixes. Washington, D.C.: U.S. Government Printing Office.

Schuman, Howard. 1983. Review of Serge Lang, *The file*. *Public Opinion Quarterly* 42:pp. 601–607.

Singer, Eleanor. 1978. Informed consent: Consequences for response rate and response quality in social surveys. *American Sociological Review* 43: pp. 144–62.

Sjoberg, Gideon. 1969. Project Camelot: Selected reactions and personal reflections. In Gideon Sjoberg, ed. *Ethics, politics, and social research*, pp. 141–61. Cambridge, Mass.: Schenkman Publishing Co.

*Special inquiry on invasion of privacy*. 1966. U.S. Congress, House, Committee on Government Operations. 89th Cong., 1st sess., June 2, 3, 4, 7, 23, and September 23, 1965. Washington, D.C.: Government Printing Office.

Swedish Council for Research in the Humanities and Social Sciences. N.d. *Ethical principles of research in the humanities and social sciences*. Stockholm.

Turner, Charles F., and Elizabeth Martin, eds. 1984. *Surveying subjective phenomena*. 2 vols. New York: Russell Sage Foundation.

van den Bergh, Pierre. 1969. Research in South Africa: The story of my experiences with tyranny. In Gideon Sjoberg, ed. *Ethics, politics, and social research*, pp. 183–97. Cambridge, Mass.: Schenkman Publishing Co.

# Charles C. Lemert

## 4 What's Become of Talk? From Hyman to Foucault

In sociology, as in other liberal disciplines, the 1960s were disruptive. Through most of the decade sociology enjoyed unprecedented popularity with students and prestige among the powerful. At least through the end of the Johnson administration, in 1968, Washington welcomed sociologists and other social scientists to presidential task offices, White House conferences, and high-level executive positions.[1] But, as the Great Society gave way to Nixon's New Federalism, social science's easy compact with the high-rolling political liberalism of the early sixties was broken, a divorce founded upon a broad disenchantment with liberal values. Within academia, changes in student priorities were the surest sign that the marriage was failing. By the midseventies enrollments in sociology began to collapse.[2] At the very time students were transferring to business courses, sociologists were experimenting with new models that, far from being appropriate preparation for future masters of business administration, were not even consistent with liberalism. By the midseventies ethnomethodology, neo-Marxism, critical theory, world systems theory, and various structuralisms excited graduate students and younger professors, a good number of whom had been student radicals in the sixties. The end-of-ideology debate was at an end. Many were attempting to reconstruct sociology on grounds

[1] Robert C. Wood, himself a liberal political scientist who served as secretary to the Department of Housing and Urban Development in the last days of the Johnson administration, is the source of this observation. Wood is currently engaged in a study of the role of intellectuals and academics in presidential administrations from Eisenhower to the present.

[2] The nationwide level of majors in sociology peaked in 1974. By 1980 the number had declined by 50 percent, according to the executive offices of the American Sociological Association.

that explicitly attacked its earlier liberal faith that sociology by becoming the true science of social life could contribute to social progress.

With the twentieth anniversary of the May 1968 disruptions close at hand, it is time to assess what we have done since and, perhaps, because of the turmoil. This is a not altogether inappropriate theme in a volume honoring Herbert Hyman. Herb was perceived by many of my sociological generation to have been on the other side of the political barricades in those spring days when Columbia came apart. And for many who became sociologists in and after the sixties Hyman is an exemplar of the accomplishments of the perspective many have since opposed.

Throughout his career Herb believed social science could be an inherently scientific endeavor. In 1955 Hyman began *Survey Design and Analysis* with a remark that reveals the completeness of his faith in science: "The formal features of survey analysis are no different at an abstract level from the procedures of more traditional scientific work" (Hyman 1955, p. 8). Thirty years later he responded to the suggestion that the scientist might have been the model for his life's work with brisk, visceral enthusiasm:

Oh, that I like. I don't want to flaunt it, but that I like. I think that's perfectly true. I'd be happy to be called a scientist, or a social scientist. And there's a sense in which I'd even be happy to be called a positivist, an empiricist, which I fundamentally am.[3]

Much of the debate generated by younger sociologists in the late sixties and seventies challenged this central principle of Hyman's sociology.

Though Hyman himself never joined the post-1960s debate, his work was the subject of one of its earliest important critiques of scientific sociology. Aaron Cicourel's *Method and Measurement* (1964) devoted the larger part of two chapters to Hyman's important methodological textbooks, *Interviewing in Social Research* (1954) and *Survey Design and Analysis* (1955). Cicourel's book, a comprehensive attack on then dominant quantitative methods in American sociology, was to become ethnomethodology's most substantial early program statement. Hyman's texts had already become leading sources for those who used interviewing and other survey techniques in scientific sociology. Hyman had codified important aspects of sociology's grandest technical achievements. His ideas were, therefore, natural data for Cicourel's theoretical question: Can methods generate numbers that fairly represent social reality?

[3] Personal interview with Herbert Hyman, August 28, 1984. Much of the background for observations about Hyman's view of science and the changes in sociology is from recorded and transcribed interviews on February 13, 1984; August 28, 1984; and July 31, 1985.

Arguments about whether sociology is a "science" or its theories and findings are amenable to quantification are premature if we cannot agree on what is theory or whether our theories can be stated so that they generate numeric properties that will have correlates in an observable world. [Cicourel 1964, p. 5]

Cicourel—like other ethnomethodologists, critical theorists, and neo-Marxists—became a leader of new postsixties schools of thought precisely because he questioned the scientific status of sociology. From the hindsight of more than twenty years, a comparison of the two positions is a bit shocking. So accustomed have we become to thinking of those on the other side as ignorant of our concerns that one is jolted by the extent to which each understood the other very well. Cicourel, a founder of ethnomethodology, knew his numbers. Hyman, the self-declared positivist, knew the problems of the natural world. This was, after all, an issue not of ignorance but of choice. One side chose science. The other chose something else. Each will was competently informed. Indeed, this is, I suspect, one of the good reasons Cicourel selected Hyman as a case study. Hyman's sophistication as an interviewer, survey researcher, and secondary analyst of survey data lies, in part, in his keen appreciation of the effects of the "natural frame of reference" on his subjects (Hyman 1955, p. 28). Successful formal interviews or surveys are anything but imperious when it comes to the problems created by subjects' abilities to lie, conceal, or seduce themselves and their interviewers. This is why Cicourel must have selected, as the lead quotations in the two chapters on Hyman, passages that demonstrate Hyman's ample sensitivity to the vagaries of everyday life: first, in the problem of reliability loss for validity gain (that is, living with the fact that differences among interviewers reflect unstandardizable but valid access to social reality) (Cicourel 1964, p. 77; Hyman et al. 1954, p. 30); second, in the obligation to build into survey designs technical strategies for capturing qualitative influences on response, coding, and analysis (Cicourel 1964, pp. 106–7; Hyman, 1955, pp. 27–28). Hyman's science, therefore, reflects the scientist's attitude: The world is a solvable mystery. Or, in sociology: The natural social world is a mess we can, nonetheless, order by our technical skills. "Consequently," says Hyman in reference to survey research, "the analyst engages in a *series of prior planning procedures to insure that the standardized procedure will nevertheless be adapted to the natural frame of reference of most of the subjects under study*" (Hyman 1955, p. 28; emphasis in original). The standardized procedures must be refined and adapted. But they can be made to work.

This Cicourel doubts. The now famous claim of early ethnomethodology was that scientific sociology errs fundamentally in assuming a qualitative difference between the scientist and his world. Though later ethnomethodologists often took this idea to outrageously relativistic extremes, Cicourel did not. His position was not that the social world lacked discoverable order but that its order could not be discovered without a sufficient theory of discovery.

Overcoming uniqueness of interviews in field research requires that we examine our cases for invariant properties which are not affected adversely by the noncomparable character of present decisions for assigning meanings to observations and extracting the data. The model for deciding what is observed and what the observation means to us within the framework of our theory must view some part of the world of everyday life as a system of invariant relevance structures. *Studies of interviewing procedures and common sense "rules" of everyday life are essentially studies on the same phenomena: the same model will explain the data of both kinds of study.* [Cicourel 1964, p 81; emphasis added]

This is an early formulation of ethnomethodology's identifying principle: Social science and the social world are governed by the same rules because everyday-life activity is sociological. Though, to many, this insistence was bizarre and frivolous, Cicourel was first among those who meant it constructively. He was seriously intent upon reformulating sociology as a kind of sciencelike endeavor. His plan irritated many. But the fact is that sociologists are social actors even, and especially, when they (or their agents) are interviewing. If so, then it is perfectly reasonable to consider the idea that the prior invariant rules are those of the everyday-life world. From this it is a short step to the notion that rules for sociological practice are, at some crucial level, subsumable under those of daily life. The sociologist is not special. He is, even as sociologist, a social person. Sociology, the intellectual activity, is but a variant of sociology, the universal human practice. Both are attempts to live by understanding what is going on. Both are reflexive activities, differing only in their degree of self-consciousness and formality.

For Cicourel this led, ultimately, to an attempt to identify invariant interpretive procedures of social behavior (structural attributes of consciousness comparable to Chomsky's deep structures of language). Thus, Cicourel's *Cognitive Sociology* (1974) broke decisively, in name and substance, with those ethnomethodologists who believed that social life is little more than context-bound negotiations. Because Cicourel sought invariant properties in social life, he was one of the first and most compelling antiscientific sociologists to propose a cryptoscientific reconstruction of sociology. Not incidentally, this involved a reaffirmation of measurement procedures, but now, of course, by arguing that measurement is simply sociology's way of reflexively interpreting the social world.

Admittedly, this could not satisfy scientific sociology, but it does illustrate the extent to which one important source of post-1968 anti-science sociology retained an important loyalty to the concerns of opponents. As such, it is precisely analogous to Hyman's highly naturalistic examination of interview effects and definition of the interview situation in *Interviewing in Social Research.* In other words, Hyman and Cicourel, representatives of very different camps, shared at a crucial point views that were mirror images of each other. The scientist attempted to understand (and control) natural context effects. The contextualist looked for a theory of measurement based on invariant properties. These were irreconcilable projects, to be sure, but their common ground says a lot about the true intellectual origins of the great divide in sociology after the sixties.

Beyond sociology the same was true. As radical sociology took shape in the seventies, it took the shape of these revolutionary appeals which were, with notable exceptions, mostly for participation and dialogue. In the barricaded streets and occupied buildings, students, blacks, and eventually women demanded little more than the right of participation free of oppression, the fire in their rhetoric notwithstanding. Participatory democracy, the ideal of Students for a Democratic Society (SDS), was, after all, mild stuff as revolutions go, and it was very close kin to the ideals of postsixties sociology. Critical theory's search for communicative competence and ethnomethodology's insistence that common, everyday-life talk contained the standards of all social knowledge were appeals similar to those voiced by students from California to Frankfurt.

Talk—free, common, and universal—was the preoccupation of sixties politics in America, and of the sociology that grew there from them. The Free Speech Movement in 1964 in Berkeley was the opening public moment of the student rebellion. But in its then quiet background was the Port Huron Statement of SDS policy, which in 1962 called for participatory democracy as a way toward "the creation of bridges," a task "made more difficult by the problems left over from the generation of 'silence'" (Port Huron Statement, in Albert and Albert 1984, p. 191). Students rebelled against the expectation that they remain passive listeners to their parents' moral silence. Likewise, the Student Non-Violent Coordinating Committee (SNCC), moving away from civil rights toward black power in 1965, demanded a climate in which "blacks can express themselves" (SNCC Radical Education Project, in Albert and Albert 1984, p. 120). Black men separated themselves from whites in order to speak, a move thousands of white women would soon make away from their men, for the same purpose. The sixties were many things. But, if there was a common denominator among demands made and goals sought, it was talk—the right to free voice in public affairs.

Likewise, the divide between the generations in sociology was largely (though not entirely) over talk. Language appealed to many younger sociologists as it bored their elders. To be sure, not all of the post-sixties critique of science in sociology was devoted to language. But a good deal was, enough so that language prevailed, in the seventies, as the topic of informed conversation. In addition to ethnomethodology, Habermas resuscitated German critical theory with his ambitious project of discovering in the speech act a universal pragmatics on the basis of which he could found a postpositivist science. Just as ethnomethodology put traditional American sociology—including symbolic interactionism—on the defensive, so Habermas did to the nascent but rapidly growing American Marxism. From another quarter, some turned to the new French social theorists as an alternative to ethnomethodology's excess of reflexivity and critical theory's overwrought communicative competence. Soon Lévi-Strauss's structuralism, Foucault's studies of early modern discursive formations, and Barthes's formal semiotics were read. And, in a kind of counterrevolutionary action, a new generation of scientific sociologists had its own interest in language. The then new theory constructionism was fundamentally a mild positivist language analysis of variables (Lemert 1979, chaps. 2, 3).

The decade or so after 1968 was breathtaking. Talk, discourse, signs, speech acts—language by whatever name—became the means for reformulating the science in sociology. The infatuation with conversation no doubt bore an important connection to all the exaggerated enthusiasm for defining sociology as an essentially pluralistic discipline (e.g., Friedrichs 1972). Sociology was seen by many as a highly stimulating critical conversation over the truth of the social world in which the world's plurality was the gentle standard of its reality.

The euphoria was short-lived. Students disappeared with a vengeance beginning with the economic crisis of 1972–74. Today the sociological domain is more sober, its future uncertain. But for a time the thrill of good talk reigned supreme. Talk had entered the public sphere in Sproul Hall at Berkeley in 1964, at the Sundial at Columbia, and in the Latin Quarter in 1968. Later, many of the participants in these public dramas made free speech the revolutionary flag of seventies sociology. And now they are all quiet, except for several echoes important enough to cause us to ask, What's become of talk?

If the sixties destroyed America's liberal ethic in politics, so the seventies threatened sociology's dream of becoming a unified science. To be sure, there is good science in sociology and there will be more, in large part because of the accomplishments of Hyman and his generation. What has been lost is not just the courtesy visits to the White House and the other signs of prestige and influence but something basic to the discipline's self-confidence. Sociology, like others of the social sciences, was so interdependent with, in Godfrey Hodgson's terms, the postwar liberal consensus that "sociology, history, economics, political science . . . followed parallel paths rejecting those who argued for radical change and emphasizing the virtues of the American way" (1978, p. 95). This pre-1968 experience is past because, like America in the sixties, liberal sociology ate itself up from within. Whatever happened to it because of its environment, sociology did much to undercut its own scientific bravado. For good or ill, this was largely the work of the seventies linguistic turn.

Three very different adventures led to this result: ethnomethodology, critical theory, and European (mostly French) postmodernism. What Cicourel, Habermas, and Foucault—and their respective confederates—have in common is more than an interest in discourse. Each has held that a diagnosis of practical language use in the modern world is the key to a proper social theory of that world—that is, its analysis and critique.

Ethnomethodology is, of course, only an implicit social theory. Though it is frequently accused of being amoral and politically reactionary, ethnomethodology did serve to shake the world and our understanding of it. In its heyday it was a kind of political force. The proposition that all talk is the same is, after all, a highly revolutionary idea. Hugh Mehan and Houston Wood, students of Cicourel, made the only partly tendentious claim that ethnomethodology is fundamentally a destratifying practice. "All speech is alienating when it ignores its origins and treats world and speaker as things, rather than as essentially practical activities" (Mehan and Wood 1975, p. 220). If so, then any activity like ethnomethodology that systematically reveals the practicality of speech also, by identifying the universality of practical talk, puts at risk all explicitly alienating forms of talk. Few ethnomethodologists followed Mehan and Wood to the conclusion that Marx was an ethnomethodologist. But we should not forget that the movement's critical work was often addressed to the alienating function of modern society's official talkers. Cicourel, for example, lumped judges, linguists, the police, and prosecutors with sociologists in the category of those whose job it is to manage social meanings. "Anyone engaged in field research will find that the short hand vocabulary of social science is very similar to the general norms stated in some penal codes" (Cicourel 1974, p. 13). Subsequent ethnomethodologists extended this theme to include teachers, medical practitioners, congressional hearings (Cicourel 1981; Fisher 1986; Molotch and Boden 1985). Hence ethnomethodology's contributions to the great divide in recent sociology. Its strength was in explaining the risks of any social practice that ignores the everyday-life context of language. Sensitivity to the natural frame of reference is insufficient. Nothing less than a full acknowledgment of the centrality of discourse to social life was called for. Underlying this radicalization of the naturalistic perspective was the assumption that all talk—ordinary and scientific—is created equal. This, in turn, was the basis for a radical political sentiment, resonant with sixties politics but largely undeveloped by ethnomethodology.

Why then did ethnomethodology fail to develop its implicit political line? For the same reason that it has failed so far to become a coherent alternative in sociology. Ethnomethodology in taking talk seriously took it too seriously. Talk may well be the one and only social universal, but it cannot be the social exclusive. If sociology is reflexive talk on talk, then one enters an infinite regress in which the very social context in which talk is founded becomes talk itself. In another guise this is no better than the famous riddle of the hermeneutic circle. How can there be explanatory understanding if understanding relies on preunderstanding? In ethnomethodology's case this is the dilemma of extracting specific statements about the world when all statements are endlessly subjected to metastatements. Likewise, in politics, how can there be compelling critique and effective action when all truth claims are subject to gloss?

Habermas's *Knowledge and Human Interests* appeared in German in 1968, just as ethnomethodology was surfacing and radicals were going underground. Presumably this is no accident. Yet, *Knowledge and Human Interests* (Habermas 1971, English edition) is a confusing book, and for reasons that go beyond its intellectual and literary density. Imagine those unfamiliar with German critical theory who came to the book for some other than intellectual reason, like the fact that their graduate students were suddenly talking about Habermas. They must have expected something radical, probably Marxian. What they found behind a thinly Marxian philosophical anthropology was Kant. True, the book sought to ground knowledge—especially social scientific knowledge—in human interests. But, amazingly, Habermas also proposed that the human interests in question were both universal and transcendental. Many must have shared Hyman's view of critical theory: "There's something obtuse when they elevate those criticisms to a level so all-encompassing. I don't find them at all persuasive."[4] What Habermas proposed was indeed disarmingly encompassing. Though critical of the interest in technical control behind scientific sociology, Habermas did not dismiss science. He was in fact just as critical of hermeneutical adventures like Cicourel's. Here he addressed the problem of the hermeneutical circle and argued persuasively that any knowledge based primarily on preunderstanding relies so heavily on a tradition of knowledge that it cannot detect and criticize systematic evil in that tradition. One can well appreciate why the intellectual leader of post-Nazi German social theory would be sensitive on this point, and why Habermas would in some crucial ways be worlds apart from an interpretive sociology like Cicourel's. Nonetheless, what Habermas shared with Cicourel was an interest in the centrality of language. "What raises us out of nature is the only thing in nature we can know: language" (Habermas 1971, p. 314). Here was an early clear statement of the language-based social theory that was to develop from a widely read essay appearing several years later, "Toward a Theory of Communicative Competence" (1970a). As Alford (1985), among others, has shown, the design of a reconstructive theory of science was Habermas's major preoccupation after 1964, and language was central to that project.

In criticizing both technical scientific and hermeneutic social science, he sought to include the universal interests of both—control and understanding—in a more comprehensive science that incorporated a third transcendent human interest, emancipation. Habermas insisted on having it both ways—science and liberty. Even more, consider the mind-boggling audacity of a project that wants science founded in human interests which, though they transcend human history, lead somehow to both truth and practical historical action. This was, after all, the 1970s, long after Hegel had been inverted and dismissed.

Beginning with "Toward a Theory of Communicative Competence" (1970a), all this was to be discovered in the universal pragmatic features of spoken language. The ideal speech situation was both model and resource from which we were to deduce truth that could free us. "Truth is the peculiar compulsion toward universal recognition; this is, however, bound to an ideal speaking situation and that means a way of life in which unforced universal agreement is possible" (Habermas 1970b, p. 126). Though he then drew heavily on language theory— Chomsky, Wuenderlich, Austin, Searle—there can be no mistaking

[4] Personal interview, August 23, 1984.

Habermas's goal of summarizing and responding to the virtual whole of modern knowledge to present a social theory that could be, among other things, responsive to the same demands to which ethnomethodology conformed: the student movement's insistence on a free and public voice.[5] Again, like Cicourel, an appeal was made to the invariant properties of speech.

But the difference in Habermas's approach to language clarifies two of the reasons why talk about talk eventually was silenced by the 1980s. If ethnomethodology's talk led to an infinite regress without specifics, Habermas's ideal speech situation established a standard so elevated that all actual claims for truth could only suffer for their insufficiency. The one made sociology a talmudic reflection on the meaning of meaning; the other made it a puritan search for the word of an inscrutable god. Both so overplayed the linguistic ante that only the most irreverent would stake their academic lives on a sociology unable to talk convincingly about anything but talk. Neither talk of talk nor talk judged by ideal talk could issue in concrete statements about a larger social reality. Few, then or now, can say that we will explain social life or correct social evil with such an exclusive reference to language. Both ethnomethodology and critical theory succeeded brilliantly in demonstrating the limits of scientific sociology, but neither has come close to matching its results. In sociology at least, salvation is still by good works, however insensitive to or controlling of natural life one may think them to be.

If ethnomethodology and critical theory illustrate two of the reasons why talk eventually lost out in sociology, recent French social theory suggests a third: a tendency to destroy talk by formalizing it. Actually all three reasons owe to the very nature of oral discourse. It is very hard to be concrete about speech because voice is so ephemeral. Hence the dilemma of a science of things spoken: How can science, necessarily writing, be rigorously applied to speech without turning it into something it is not? "In speech," said Roland Barthes, "everything is held forth, meant for immediate consumption, and words, silences and their common mobility, are launched toward a suspended meaning superseded: it is a transfer leaving no trace and brooking no

---

[5] One of the most direct links between sixties politics and the linguistic turn in seventies social theory was John Searle. A source of Habermas's ideas, Searle was also counselor to participants in the Free Speech Movement at Berkeley in 1964 and author of *The Campus War: A Sympathetic Look at the University in Action* (New York: World Publishing, 1971). The last sentence of Searle's *Speech Acts* is: "But the retreat from the committed use of words ultimately must involve a retreat from language itself, for speaking a language . . . consists of performing speech acts according to rules, and there is no separating those speech acts from the commitments which form essential parts of them" (Searle 1969, p. 198).

delay" (Barthes 1970a, p. 121). That which leaves no trace cannot be encoded and counted without submitting to some form-destroying alteration. The voice is made available to science only in transcription—literally, by conversion into writing. In this act the unique quality of speech, the secret intention of the speaker, is lost because "writing is always rooted in something beyond language" (Barthes 1970a, p 20). That which is written cannot be taken back or otherwise glossed. The original voice, when denying, for example, a newspaper account of his meaning, can say, "I didn't mean that," but, once printed, the words are the speaker's burden of proof. They stand intractable against him. Transcribed speech is always out of context. In sociology this problem arises equally across all attempts to encode talk—from close transcripts of naturalistic methods (like field notes or transcribed conversations) to the precoded survey questions of interviewers. Here, of course, is Hyman's opening for a retort he never made to Cicourel: You say the data of interviews lack context. Now show me how ethnomethodology even in using full transcripts of conversations does appreciably better. Hyman, thus, could have had Cicourel at his own game. All written transcripts are the same. They commonly collapse the infinity of intended meanings of speech and, in Barthes's sense, introduce something beyond language—the limits of the medium, the social interests of the transcriber, the political economy of archives. If, then, science must subject itself to writing, then scientific sociology's compelling defense might be: Given the unavailability of pure speech, why not enjoy the benefits of technical controls for the regularly occurring uncertainties of our data, nearly all of which begin with what we cannot capture, voiced intentions? This is sociology's equivalent to the indeterminacy problem.

The impossibility of keeping talk natural under analysis leaves structuralism only two alternatives. One makes talk itself—as opposed to the concrete references of talk—the object of analysis. This is the path of both ethnomethodology and critical theory. The other is to restrict analysis to the formal properties of language. This was the temptation to which many of the French structuralists succumbed.

The formalizing temptation is rooted in Lévi-Strauss's earliest, and most famous, program statement, "The Structural Study of Myth" (1955, in English), in which he revived Saussure's classic distinction between *la langue* (language as a formal system) and *la parole* (speaking). Language (*la langue*), said Lévi-Strauss (1955, pp. 172–73), "belongs to revertible time, whereas *parole* is non-revertible." Speech, once uttered, is overtaken by time; language holds its form through time. Structuralism is, therefore, the study of specific "properties found *above* the ordinary linguistic level," properties that are more complex than "those found in any kind of linguistic expression" (Lévi-Strauss 1955, p. 174). In Lévi-Strauss's hands structuralism remained a concrete empirical method. But with those who wished only to appropriate and adopt his theory of formal properties the results were frequently quite different. Most notably, in sociology, Harrison White's *Anatomy of Kinship* (1963) used Lévi-Strauss's ideas to launch a series of studies of the formal properties of social relations, from which came one of today's most mathematical sociological specialties, network analysis (see Mullins 1973, chap. 10). As it evolved, network analysis soon lost all meaningful contact with Lévi-Strauss's complicated theory of language. This is precisely the kind of fate that led Boudon, and others, to ask what is the usefulness of structuralism (Boudon 1971). Why bother with the linguistic rigmarole if this is only a way of doing what other, less complicated structural methods do just as well?

The path from language to the formal structures of language leads one into a dilemma of no lesser difficulty than that faced by ethnomethodology. Talk loses its concreteness now by receding into the form of language. Claim that the form of language is central to social studies, and language becomes a metaphor for social relations. Either this, or one must insist there is nothing important outside language. In the former case, the original metaphor is soon surpassed and language is irrelevant. In the latter case, social analysis becomes a subspecialty of linguistics or semiotics. Neither alternative provides a very strong foundation for reconstructing social science around language. The one is not linguistic at all; the other is so massively linguistic that, as in ethnomethodology, concrete social life is nil. Structuralism was either a closet scientism or a megalomaniacal linguistics. Thus, to talk of talk, and talk judged by talk, we must add talk frozen in its own form. Ethnomethodology's talmudic mediations and critical theory's puritan quest are joined by structuralism's scholasticism. Language becomes its own form; talk is a location in an abstract system of relations just as, in scholastic theology, salvation was an assigned status in a cosmic hierarchy. No surprise, therefore, that Umberto Eco, the unchallenged master of the most formal of structuralist enterprises (Eco 1976), was originally a medievalist and is currently a novelist of medieval intrigues.

Structuralism's formalism led to the poststructuralist revolt in France against its overly abstract scientism. The revolt took many forms, especially in the seventies. But for a moment in the sixties there was a seeming consensus on the shape of the new social theory. In 1968, *Tel Quel,* then the leading review of New Wave social theory, published a special issue, *Théorie d'ensemble.* Texts included those by all the poststructuralist masters: Foucault, Barthes, Derrida, Julia Kristeva, and

Philippe Sollers. The issue began with a declaration of collective purpose, which included the vision of "articulating a politics bound logically to a non-representative dynamic of writing" (*Tel Quel* 1968, p. 10). The major theme was to derive a politics from language theory, but the revolt lay in the minor theme: an intentional shift to nonrepresentative writing. This actually meant two things at once. First, the choice of writing over speech entailed a critique of subjectivism (the voice was seen as the articulation of pure consciousness). Intentions, thus, were dismissed as a topic of inquiry. Here, the new movement shared structuralism's rejection of the subjectivist excesses of postwar existentialism. But, second, the choice of nonrepresentational writing was intended to open discourse to politics, which could be done only if the field of language was open and dynamic. Hence the critique of structuralism. If structuralism was right in turning from speech (*la parole*), an inherently subjective practice, it was wrong in taking the form of language (*la langue*) as a representation of the form of social structures. This led to objectivism, which was seen as doubly flawed. As the mirror image of subjectivism, objectivism was no less apolitical; as the couplet of subjectivism, it maintained a closure on thought and action, freezing both in a worn-out metaphysical category (Derrida 1970).

The New Wave idealized writing as only a group of Parisians can (Lemert 1981, chap. 1). The goal of making writing political involved a simple formula: Writing (*écriture*) is a historically open social field. The practice of writing extends that field. Writing is the politics of telling the truth of social reality by reconstructing reality in writing. "To write" is an intransitive verb (Barthes 1970*b*). In Derrida's terms, to write is to defer the meaning of language by deconstructing an original text (whether an archive or a novel). Deconstruction relativizes history. The truth of the social world is not in the enduring form of literature or historical fact but in the political space opened by demonstrating that what we know about the world is linked to past events available to us in transcripts (letters, ledgers, statistical archives, novels, etc.). If we try to see through these transcripts either to the original intentions of actors or to the pure form of an epoch we are trapped in a regression that idealizes a past but unknowable world. The alternative is to rewrite that world and in so doing to open up its only available truth: the way in which it, in being different, clarifies the present.

Such is hardly the stuff to inspire brick throwing on the boulevard St. Michel, though it did lead to considerable intellectual passion in France in the late sixties and elsewhere thereafter. To the same degree, it inspired skepticism, even rage, on the part of those who held more traditional empiricist standards of truth.

The case most interesting to sociology is Michel Foucault. His opponents raged against the presumed empirical inaccuracies of his social historical studies of nineteenth-century modernity, *The Birth of the Clinic* (1963), for example. Foucault's declaration that modern medicine arose from the discovery of the body in postrevolutionary France is truly arguable if one's scientific goal is to establish the pure truth of late eighteenth-, early nineteenth-century medicine. There were bodies, to be sure, and physicians attended them. But, if one's project is an archaeology of the many disjunctive historical layers upon which the present is founded, then the book reads differently. *Birth of the Clinic* is but one of several studies designed to answer the central question of modernity: How did industrializing capitalism succeed in converting generations of peasant farmers into an army of disciplined urban factory workers? Only by the superficially gentle means of shaping and controlling bodies—in hospitals, schools, and prisons. The laboring body was the unit of surplus value and the key to capitalist development. Thus, Foucault reconstructs in *Birth of the Clinic* the sociologically relevant truth of the birth of modern medicine. The teaching hospital was one of the mechanisms for calling attention to and fashioning labor power, working bodies. This truth was not part of early nineteenth-century knowledge. The early teaching doctors could not have uttered it, in so many words. It cannot be found in or behind any archive. The truth of Foucault's political economy of bodies in early capitalism can be conveyed only in the nonrepresentative texts of those in our time who live with the consequences of an original but silent fact. Only a political judgment conveyed in writing can assert an unprovable reality that answers the riddle: How is it that doctors and teachers now do the work once done by the threats of despots and overlords?

Foucault, more than anyone, represents the limits of the utility of talk in social science. But it is important to see that his discovery of the limits of talk depended upon a similar, transforming limit on the second great theme of the sixties, politics. For Foucault, as for others in the poststructuralist revolt, the limits of talk were but an instance of the limitations of the deep epistemological faith at the heart of science, the false belief that knowledge is a contract between subjects and objects. But to challenge this epistemological doublet is necessarily to confront its political equivalent: the idea that radical politics is the informed voice of subjects confronting oppressive objective structures. This, indubitably, was the model of student activists at Berkeley, Columbia, and Nanterre, of which Foucault was explicitly critical. "The intellectual of the Left has claimed speech for his own and has viewed himself as having the right to speak insofar as he is master of truth

and justice" (Foucault 1981, p. 301). Foucault's alternative was remarkably simple. He collapsed power and knowledge into each other—no
subject/object dichotomy, hence no politics/science dichotomy. (See
Lemert and Gillan 1982, chap. 3.)

So what's become of talk? Simply, it so spent itself in excess that, like
the politics of the sixties, it came to its own limits. If we can, for simplicity's sake, consider ethnomethodology, critical theory, and French
postmodernism as the collective progression of the linguistic turn in
social science, then they also eventually formed the horizon beyond
which that turn cannot move. Though they are anything but direct
linear descendants, there was an important sense in which they necessarily entailed each other. Viewed from within a regional field of endeavor, like postsixties radical sociology, they provided intellectual
terrain that must be explored by a sociology rooted in the American
sixties. That the long journey did not yield the discovery of a north-
west passage to open pacific seas does not mean the explorations were
in vain. A considerable domain was mapped and settled which, had it
remained uncharted, would have left sociology hunkered down in the
coastal colony of a grand but confined scientific sociology. Once the
equality of all talk is broached, the original colony is at risk. The faith
of fifties sociology has been shaken, at least for the new generation.
One can no longer believe, with impunity, that sociology can be a unified science or that, in its unity, it can be at one with the progressive
realism of liberal politics. Both liberal politics and liberal sociology are
now set, defensively, within their own limits, limits that thirty years
ago were inconceivable. This does not mean there can be no liberalism
or no science. Only that these cannot be our exclusive governing
principles.

In American sociology, ethnomethodology first breached this boundary of expectations. This observation has little to do with whether or
not everyone, even every radical sociologist, reads ethnomethodology.
It has only to do with the way in which the radicalization of language,
especially talk, surreptitiously intruded upon a collective sense of what
is permissible in sociology's self-understanding. Compared to the
spirit prevailing in 1955 when Hyman published *Survey Design and
Analysis*, it is now far more difficult to treat the natural frame of reference as a mere obstacle to be overcome. The natural frame of everyday life is, for many, a resource as much as an obstacle, as one learns
from many and various social theorists who are not even remotely
ethnomethodologists—Geertz, Giddens, Gouldner, Bourdieu, Shal-
ins, Collins, to say nothing of the new wave of postannalist social historians. None of these makes claim to reduce social inquiry to everyday

life. They simply assume it must be accounted for. And the thematizing of talk was the major source of this compulsion.

But ethnomethodology's own limits were evident from the beginning. Hence the plunge in the seventies for critical theory. If talk about talk is not the way, what about the universal ideal properties of talk? And, then, full circle, if this is not the answer, can we not return to empirical specifics by means of the form of language? In the progression of collective thinking, if not in the direct historical descent of ideas, structuralism arose out of the limits of critical theory, as critical theory did out of ethnomethodology. All three came to the same horizon. Talk, in limiting science, limited itself.

In our time Foucault and the French social theorists, like Habermas and modern critical theory, seem utterly remote from the concerns of Cicourel's attack on Herb Hyman. But, when that small exchange is viewed through the lens of the sixties turmoil, its frame is large. If, a century from now, an archaeology of these past twenty years is performed, surely ethnomethodology, critical theory, and postmodernism will appear as the field of thought that arose on the other side of the barricades from science like Herbert Hyman's and the liberal politics that for good or ill sponsored that moment of scientific sociology.

## Bibliography

Albert, Judith C., and Stewart E. Albert. 1984. *The sixties papers: Documents of a rebellious decade.* New York: Praeger.

Alford, Fred C. 1985. Is Jürgen Habermas's reconstructive science really science? *Theory and Society* 14 : 321–40.

Barthes, Roland. 1970a. *Writing degree zero and elements of semiology.* Boston: Beacon Press.

———. 1970b. To write: An intransitive verb. In Richard Macksey and Eugenio Donato, *The structuralist controversy,* pp. 134–45. Baltimore: Johns Hopkins University Press.

Boudon, Raymond. 1971. *The uses of structuralism.* London: Heinemann.

Cicourel, Aaron. 1964. *Method and measurement in sociology.* New York: Free Press.

———. 1974. *Cognitive sociology.* New York: Macmillan.

———. 1981. Notes on the integration of micro- and macro-levels of analysis. In K. Knorr-Cetina and A. V. Cicourel, eds., *Advances in social theory and methodology,* pp. 51–80. Boston: Routledge and Kegan Paul.

Derrida, Jacques. 1970. Structure, sign, and play in the discourse of the human sciences. In Richard Macksey and Eugenio Donato, eds., *The structuralist controversy,* pp. 247–64. Baltimore: Johns Hopkins University Press.

Eco, Umberto. 1976. *A theory of semiotics.* Bloomington: Indiana University Press.

Fisher, Sue. 1986. *In the patient's best interest.* New Brunswick, N.J.: Rutgers University Press.

Foucault, Michel. 1963. *The birth of the clinic: An archaeology of medical perception.* New York: Random House.

———. 1981. "Trust and power." In Charles Lemert, ed., *French sociology,* pp. 293–307. New York: Columbia University Press.

Friedrichs, Robert. 1972. *A sociology of sociology.* New York: Free Press.

Habermas, Jürgen. 1970a. "Toward a theory of communicative competence." In H. P. Dreitzel, *Recent sociology, no. 2,* pp. 115–48. New York: Macmillan.

———. 1970b. "Summation and response." *Continuum* 8:123–33.

———. 1971. *Knowledge and human interests.* Translated by Jeremy J. Shapiro. Boston: Beacon Press.

Hodgson, Godfrey. 1978. *America in our time.* New York: Vintage Books.

Lemert, Charles. 1979. *Sociology and the twilight of man.* Carbondale: Southern Illinois University Press.

———. 1981. "Reading French sociology." In Charles Lemert, ed., *French sociology,* pp. 3–32. New York: Columbia University Press.

Lemert, Charles, and Garth Gillan. 1982. *Michel Foucault: Social theory and transgression.* New York: Columbia University Press.

Lévi-Strauss, Claude. 1955. "The structural study of myth." *Journal of American Folklore* 78:428–44.

Mehan, Hugh, and Houston Wood. 1975. *The reality of ethnomethodology.* New York: Wiley.

Molotch, Harvey, and Deidre Boden. 1985. "Talking social structure." *American Sociological Review* 50:273–87.

Mullins, Nicholas. 1973. *Theories and theory groups in contemporary American sociology.* New York: Harper and Row.

Searle, John. 1969. *Speech acts.* Cambridge: Cambridge University Press.

*Tel Quel.* 1968. *Théorie d'ensemble.* Paris: Editions du Seuil.

White, Harrison. 1963. *An anatomy of kinship.* Englewood Cliffs, N.J.: Prentice-Hall.

## Part II  Reference Groups

# Harriet Zuckerman

## 5 The Role of the Role Model: The Other Side of a Sociological Coinage

More than forty years have passed since Herbert Hyman published his doctoral dissertation, *The Psychology of Status* (1942). In that landmark study, he sought to understand how individuals assess their "subjective status," how they conceive of their "own position relative to other individuals" ([1942] 1968, p. 147). Using an ingenious combination of interviews and experiments, he found that subjective assessments of social class, prestige, and even physical appearance, and the extent to which people are satisfied with them, shift, depending on the groups with which they compare themselves. These Hyman called their "reference groups" ([1942] 1968, p. 149).

That twenty-four-year-old Ph.D. could not have anticipated that his central thesis would be taken up by fellow social scientists with such enthusiasm that, by 1950, the usually restrained Ralph Turner would describe its rise as "meteoric" (Hyman and Singer 1968, p. 7). Making a major and enduring contribution in one's doctoral dissertation is not standard practice, even among those who ultimately go on to shape their fields. Indeed, only 10 of the 370 scientists named Nobel laureates up to 1985—a reasonably elevated reference group—reported the research that eventually won them their prizes in their doctoral dissertations. Among these rare few, five were in their thirties at the time, indicating delayed dissertations as much as precocious discovery.

In the intervening years, reference group behavior, positive and negative (Newcomb [1952] 1968), comparative and normative (Kelley [1952] 1968), and the array of associated phenomena, such as anticipatory socialization (Merton and Rossi [1950] 1968, pp. 319–22 et

This inquiry was supported by grants from the National Science Foundation (SES-84-11152), the Josiah Macy Jr. Foundation, and the Russell Sage Foundation.

passim) and relative deprivation and gratification (Merton and Rossi [1950] 1968, pp. 282–90; Stouffer et al. 1949, 1 : 52), have been subject to intensive theoretical analysis and empirical investigation not just in social psychology and sociology but in economics, political science, history, education, public health, and anthropology; not only in the United States but in places such as Australia, Israel, Sweden, and South Africa. The underlying concept has proved so amenable to empirical research and so powerful in explaining seemingly paradoxical social patterns of attitudes and behavior that it has provided the basis for decades of research activity.

Not surprisingly, Hyman's own research provided the basic model for much of what came later. He was interested in accounting for the formation, organization, and distribution of attitudes among individuals and social groups, their connections to objective social position, and ultimately the ways in which attitudes affect conduct. As the research program associated with reference groups has evolved, it has focused mainly on how individuals select their reference groups, that is, what criteria are typically used, which groups were chosen by which individuals, and what effects such choices had on the acquisition of attitudes, norms, and values, and on behavior. The first quarter-century of developments in reference group research were incisively reviewed by Hyman (1968) and by Hyman and Eleanor Singer (1968) in the volume they coedited, which also reprints some of the signal contributions during that period. (For a later examination, see Schuman and Johnson 1976, pp. 185–89.)

A hasty review of the journal literature on reference groups published in the last five years or so shows that the determinants of selection of reference groups by individuals with specified characteristics and the attitudinal and behavioral consequences of choosing particular reference groups continue to be at the center of research attention. The cast of characters figuring in recent research is as varied as that reviewed by Hyman (1968, p. 355); recent studies, for example, treat teenagers, parents, middle managers, architects, prisoners, teachers, and policemen among others. The attitudinal and behavioral outcomes being studied are as diverse as sex morality, norms of family size, occupational aspirations, substance abuse, and bias in rating tasks. The findings of these recent studies continue to be substantively interesting and at times even surprising in one or another detail, but the underlying concepts and the logic of the research have not changed much.

With all this research and analysis, it is odd that sociologists have examined reference group behavior primarily as a one-way rather than as a two-way social relationship with effects on both those who choose reference groups or individuals and those who are chosen as reference groups or individuals. After all, sociologists are professionally committed to the notion that all social relations involve *interaction*, potential and actual. Yet reference group behavior has been treated as unidirectional or asymmetrical which, by the hypotheses adopted here, it need not be. In this, research on reference groups is not unique. Like other departures from the general pattern which take the form of looking at social process from only one vantage point, reference group research, like studies of socialization, typically focuses on changes in the *recipient* of socialization rather than on changes in the *agents* of socialization. Similarly, studies of criminal justice have long neglected defendants' views of the process while emphasizing those of agents of social control. (See Ericson and Baranek 1982, pp. 5–29; and Smith 1985, p. 340, who emphasizes this gap in the criminological literature.) And, to take one more case in point, studies of leadership and the exercise of authority often focus on the characteristics of leaders in spite of the substantial theoretical tradition reaching back to the work of Max Weber ([1922–24] 1957, pt. 3, p. 360) and Chester Barnard ([1938] 1962), among others, which emphasizes that authority and leadership involve social relations rather than being only characteristics of individuals.

There may of course be other cases in the sociological literature, but I have encountered only one instance referring to the possible merit of examining the reciprocal nature of the relationships between those choosing reference groups and those chosen, and this instance is rather oblique. In discussing the need for consolidating "the findings and hypotheses concerning influentials and opinion leaders, and those concerning group behavior," Merton ([1957] 1968, p. 382) observed that "since such 'behavior' involves social relationships which are, of course, two-sided, . . . the next steps in investigation of this field of behavior will require simultaneous analysis both of the individuals adopting various reference groups and of the groups which provide these frames of reference." For reasons that are far from clear, those next steps were not taken. Nor has any work I have encountered gone on to specify the problem of the effects on reference groups or reference individuals of their having been chosen as such.

It is no easy task to account for the neglect of certain problems in science and scholarship while others, which are closely related, are actively pursued. So it is here. If one were to inquire into the neglect of the reciprocal relations of reference groups and those who choose them, analysis in the tradition of the sociology of knowledge would be one direction to follow and another would be cognitive psychology and an investigation of the tendency to consider causal connections as unidirectional. In any event, such an inquiry would take us far afield from the principal subject here. It is enough to reiterate that, in the forty-five years that have intervened since Hyman's first investigations of reference individuals and groups, the focus of research attention has been on those who choose them rather than on those who are chosen.

This paper aims, then, to reverse the reference group coin and to identify the principal sociological problematics of *being chosen* rather than of choosing and to focus primarily on role models, a special class of reference individuals. It is too early to say, of course, whether knowing more about the effects of being chosen will further enhance the explanatory power of reference group ideas. It may be that reference groups and reference individuals who become aware that they have been chosen as frames of reference, in as yet unidentified ways, alter their attitudes and conduct and thus reinforce or undermine their influence as standards for comparison and as sources of norms and values.

Because there is conceptual and terminological overlap between reference groups and individuals on the one hand and the cognate idea of role models, this will be briefly examined. I then take up the three central questions that focus on the processes and consequences of serving as reference individuals and role models. I leave to others the related and, in some respects, more complicated questions involving the effects on groups, as distinct from individuals, of being chosen as a frame of reference.

First, what affects the probability of individuals being chosen as frames of reference generally and as role models specifically, either for comparative or for normative purposes? The idea here is to identify the characteristics of those most likely to be chosen as frames of reference rather than focusing, as much prior research has done, on the reasons for specific kinds of choices by specific kinds of individuals.

Second, how do individuals learn that they have been chosen, that is to say, discover that they "are" reference individuals and role models? What can be said about social perception and the structure of communication that leads the chosen to believe that they serve in those capacities?

Third, and a virtually untouched question, even by way of preliminary speculation, what are some of the attitudinal and behavioral consequences of being selected as a reference individual or role model?

## A Family of Concepts: Reference Groups, Reference Individuals, and Role Models

At the risk of repeating what everyone knows, I review some of the history associated with the notion of role models and its kinship to reference groups and reference individuals. I do so in part to underscore their differences and also, in part, to identify their affinities, particularly those related to the central issue at hand, the problematics of being chosen as a reference individual or as a role model.

Role models are, in one standard formulation, "individual[s] whose behavior in a particular role provides a pattern or model upon which another . . . bases . . . behavior in performing the same role" (Theodorson and Theodorson 1969, p. 355). Like reference individuals more generally, role models can be a source of norms and values and serve as standards for comparison. The *Supplement to the Oxford English Dictionary* (1982, 3 : 1325C) locates the first published appearance of the term in Wagner Thielens's 1957 analysis of entrants to medical and law schools. In that report, which appeared in *The Student-Physician*, Thielens (1957, p. 137) observed that medical students are inclined to "choose a figure in the profession, a practitioner, known personally or one known only by repute, as a model to imitate and an ideal with which to compare their own performance. In short, they adopt a role model." That text does not make it clear whether he coined the term or encountered it elsewhere. In any event, Merton ([1957] 1968, p. 356), in the second long paper on reference groups published that same year, notes that "the *reference individual* has *often* [*sic*] been described as a *role model*" and gives no reference for the term. This suggests that the idea and its associated term had some currency at the time, surely, in the Columbia context and probably elsewhere, although priority is scarcely the point here.[1]

What is interesting is that as late as 1968, when Hyman (1968, p. 355) reviewed the status of reference group research, he agreed with the observation made a decade earlier that "research and theory have tended to focus on reference *groups* to the relative neglect of reference *individuals*" (Merton [1957] 1968, p. 356). Hyman then went on to observe that this was so "despite the emphasis on reference individuals as points of social comparison in the early work and . . . [their] connection to such prestigious concepts as 'role model.'" That emphasis on reference groups rather than individuals has continued with few connections having been yet made between the reference group research tradition and research on role models.

[1] The memories of Thielens and Merton being defective on this matter, interviews brought forth some interesting speculation but no hard information.

The distinction between the concepts, reference individual and role model, resides in their differing specificity, with reference individuals being the more general and role models functioning as a delimited type. Thus, role models are a special class of reference individuals, "more restricted in scope, denoting a more limited identification with an individual in only one or a selected few of his roles," whereas a reference individual is one with whom an individual identifies as he "seeks to approximate the behavior and values of that individual in his several roles" (Merton [1957] 1968, pp. 356–57). The conceptual difference between role model and reference individual has, however, tended to be obscured as the term "role model" has been applied in a blanket fashion, regardless of the number of roles involved, to anyone who becomes a subject of emulation, as a reference point for norms and for comparison. Thus, role models are treated in the literature as having a variety of functions; they serve as aspiration levels,[2] as living evidence that certain achievements are possible, and as models for emulation in achieving and maintaining certain social positions. Little effort, however, has gone into systematic analysis of the scope of modeling: the extent to which it involves emulation of role models' behavior within specific roles, the internalization of role models' attitudes but not the emulation of their behavior, or the extent to which role models' behavior *and* attitudes in a given role are acquired, all of a piece. Rather, the term is taken to be synonymous, in most cases, with reference individual. This presents no great problem except that the disappearance of the terminological distinction reduces the chance that research on role models will be linked to the accumulating research tradition on reference groups and individuals.

Role models and role modeling have recently become part of the popular vernacular and now constitute a flourishing area of research. In the last five years, for example, at least eighty-five articles, books, and dissertations with the term "role model" in the title have turned up in psychological and social scientific literature (*Dialog Social Scisearch Database; Psychinfo Database*). But these of course constitute only the works focused on role models, excluding a far greater number of analyses and discussions of role models where the idea is not central and the term does not appear in the title. A swift review of these usages finds that the work on role models focuses on who is chosen and on the emulation of their assumed attitudes and behavior by the individuals who aspire to be like or to acquire the positions of those

[2] Hyman ([1942] 1968, p. 157) noted this function of reference individuals and indeed used the term in his dissertation in referring to the reference individuals of a psychologist/subject who compared himself to Pavlov and Helmholtz and wished he could have brought one of Pavlov's dogs back from Russia.

after whom they model themselves. Although rarely stated explicitly, it is usually assumed that role models occupy more lofty statuses, have greater expertise, and have achieved more than those who choose them. The relationship is not one of actual or imputed equality. It is also largely assumed rather than stated explicitly that role models are seldom affectively neutral figures for those who choose them; they are thought to matter a great deal.

In the research literature as well as the popular press, the term "role model" is applied far more often to women than to men. This presumably results from the rapid and noticeable structural change in the special roles becoming accessible to women and in the structural result that women pioneering in new roles come to be adopted by later-comers as role models. However, it is evident that the term, concept, and processes of role modeling are no more sex-specific than they are occupation-specific or specific to ethnic groups or any social category. Thus, in interviews done some years ago with Nobel laureates, almost all of whom were men, senior scientists were described time and again as having been role models in effect (although the term was never used) (Zuckerman 1977, chap. 4). There is no reason to think that men scientists differ from other men in this regard.

Both concepts, reference individual and role model, have been treated by researchers as if influence flows only from those chosen to those who choose them. As a result, phenomena of interest are taken to reside in or with the chooser rather than in or with the chosen. This is the outcome, of course, of focusing on such fundamental questions as processes of socialization (how people acquire values and norms), relative deprivation (how satisfied or dissatisfied they come to be), and structural determinants (how conduct is shaped by social position). Once the problems are defined in such terms, it is no surprise that the effects of being chosen have received little or no attention. It is symptomatic that we have a set of standard terms for the individuals chosen as frames of reference (role model, reference individual, opinion leader, influential, significant other, reference idol, and sociometric star) but no standard terms for the chooser or for the relationship between the chooser and the chosen.[3]

## Conditions Affecting the Probability of Being Chosen as Reference Individual or Role Model

The research literature has not yet produced an inventory of differential probabilities of people variously located on the social structure

[3] Members of what may be thought of as the extended family of concepts associated with reference individuals and role models share their unidirectional character and em-

being selected as role models or reference individuals. Being chosen is not a random event. To the extent that prior research has raised this question, it has focused on the characteristics of role models chosen by particular groups. Thus, recent work treats such questions as whether college students and graduate students choose role models of the same or different sex (see the review of such studies in Speizer 1981) or how role models affect behavior (see Lunneborg 1982, who examines influences of role models on women in professions largely populated by men). Much of the current work focuses on congruence of statuses—the extent to which those chosen are like those who choose them—and it follows in the now long tradition of studies of the criteria governing the selection of normative and comparative reference groups by individuals with specified social characteristics.

The problem, however, is not to identify the social or personality attributes of choosers and chosen but to identify the types of role or status occupants apt to be selected as role models or reference individuals, regardless of who chooses them. There are several reasons, I think, for attempting to investigate the status attributes that predispose their occupants to being chosen as role models. First, some status occupants are expected to be subjects of emulation. They know this, and so do others. Since the central purpose of inquiring into this matter is to understand the effects of being chosen as a role model, it is useful to have some clues to the kinds of individuals who have reason to believe they are likely to be taken as role models of designated types. The belief that they may be chosen may have consequences for

---

phasize effects on those who choose rather than effects on those who are chosen. These include the "generalized other," Mead's (1934) basic concept of individuals' abstraction of the expectations, attitudes, and meanings held by the community; "significant others," Harry Stack Sullivan's ([1940–45] 1953) term for those who matter greatly to an individual; "influentials," Merton's tag for "People to whom [others] turned for help or advice regarding various types of personal decisions" ([1949] 1968, pp. 443–44); "opinion leaders," those from whom information and advice are sought on specific issues (Katz and Lazarsfeld 1951, pp. 3–5); "reference idol" (Sherif 1948, p. 336); and "sociometric star" (Moreno and Jennings 1938). New research programs are needed to understand the ways in which the attitudes, values, and conduct of significant others, influentials, opinion leaders, reference idols, and sociometric stars are affected by their having been chosen to serve in these capacities.

Three cognate terms, "mentor," "master," and "sponsor," also appear, on occasion, in the literature on role models. They refer to the role played by older, experienced, and established individuals in inducting newcomers into the tacit lore of organizations and institutions, in protecting them and in acting on their behalf. Research on mentors, masters, and sponsors (Epstein 1970b; Kanter 1977; Reskin 1979; Zuckerman 1977), like research on role models generally, has focused on their effects on the junior members of the role partnership, although Epstein (1970b) comments on the significance for sponsors of having appropriate protégés and Zuckerman (1977) on the facilitating effects of having able scientific apprentices. See Speizer 1981 for a review of research on role models, mentors, and sponsors.

their own attitudes, values, and conduct, all apart from the fact of their actually being chosen. A second reason for trying to identify the sorts of individuals apt to become role models is that this may provide some clues to the communication network and the processes of perception through which status occupants learn that they have been chosen. Third, such preliminary inquiry can direct us to significant consequences of being chosen. A conjectural list of likely prospects for the role of role model should move us toward a formulation of the processes and consequences of serving in that capacity.

One set of clues as to those most apt to be chosen comes from Hyman's own study of the men and women designated as "most admired" by Americans in the "Admiration Derby," the annual polls taken by the Gallup organization (Hyman 1975, pp. 274–75). His purpose there was to identify the features of "reference idols," that evocative term coined by Sherif (1948, p. 336) but hardly put to analytical use since then. The reference idols of the American population are not, Hyman (1975, p. 268) observes, borrowing from Leo Lowenthal, "idols of production" or "idols of consumption," not business leaders or film stars, but, for men, are largely confined to political and military leaders. Among women, the scope of choice is somewhat enlarged to include the wives of political leaders, women who are hereditary rulers, and a few who "do good." This secondary analysis of the Gallup data takes us a certain distance toward identifying those whom Americans admire most, but the connections between admiration and the choice of role models and reference individuals have yet to be worked out.

A second set of clues may be found in the principles thought to guide the selection of reference *groups* although, so far as I know, no efforts have been made to investigate the extent to which these apply to the selection of reference *individuals* and role models. These principles, neatly summarized by Hyman (1968, pp. 356–57), are the "pleasure principle" (reference groups are chosen so as to "enhance [individuals'] self regard or . . . protect [their] egos"); the principle of similarity (the social status of reference groups does not differ greatly from that of those who choose them) (see Festinger [1954] 1968; Runciman [1966] 1968); and the "reality principle" (social circumstances may compel the choice of certain reference groups, regardless of pleasure and social similarity).

At this telling, however, the principles guiding the selection of reference groups do not seem entirely applicable to the choice of individuals as role models. The so-called principle of similarity, which has people acquiring norms and values from and comparing their lot to groups not much better off than themselves, seems not to hold in the selection of role models. These are often selected precisely because they occupy positions of significantly higher rank than those who choose them. At least, the extent of disparity in status of role models and their selectors remains an open question for research. Moreover, role models have been found to be selected because they exemplify what their choosers hope to become rather than being similar to what their choosers currently are, and it is far from clear whether and how such choices square with the pleasure principle. The criteria for choosing role models are therefore not well understood.

What, then, can be said about the characteristics of those most likely to be selected as role models or reference individuals? If we take role models rather than reference individuals as a case in point—that is, those who serve as frames of reference in one role rather than in multiple roles—analysis might proceed by examining the selection of different kinds of role models rather than the selection of role models generally. It would appear that some role models are chosen because they play a particular role in a manner deemed exemplary. Such role models serve as *performance prototypes* in that they not only "possess skills and display techniques" (Kemper 1968, p. 33) but also set a standard of achievement to which others aspire and hope, by emulation, to achieve. Those chosen as performance prototypes should then be drawn from the ranks of those who play their roles in exemplary fashion, however that is defined, in particular groups at particular times. Beyond this, there should be as great a variety of exemplary role performers as there are roles. The point is that such prototypes are selected because they play their roles particularly well and because others believe they can learn through emulation to play the same roles equally well or better. The clearest case of a performance prototype is one who plays the *same* role as the individual who chooses him or her. In this instance, the performance prototype is chosen because individuals wish to improve their role performance and elect to emulate those whom they believe perform especially well *in the same* role. By way of example, consider the choice of Vladimir Horowitz by amateur pianists who emulate his piano technique so as to improve their own playing but have no expectations of becoming a professional, much less meeting the Horowitz standard. Or consider the athletes who emulate the techniques and skills and internalize the standards of excellence of those officially designated as exemplary, the Most Valuable Players, Olympic gold medalists, and world record holders, in hopes of achieving maximum performance. Such designations in sports and their equivalents in other domains serve not only to reward those who receive them but also to earmark the quintessential performance prototypes in each category.

Other role models seem to be chosen for a different reason: because they occupy a particular position that others think of as desirable, not because they play a given role particularly well. Those who choose this kind of role model do so because they would like to occupy a similar position and believe that emulation will make that more likely. These role models therefore serve as *mobility prototypes*.[4] Again, concrete examples of this kind of role model are highly varied; they are apt to include those who, by virtue of occupying a given position, are accorded more than average esteem, wealth, and power and have a greater range of opportunities. In general those chosen as mobility prototypes will occupy comparatively lofty positions in the social structure. Again, by way of example, consider the choice of local physicians as prototypes by aspiring youngsters who wish to become doctors of medicine. These physicians need not be especially competent, nor need they be especially successful. All they need be are models; that is, pertinent aspects of their role behavior as physicians need to be visible and capable of emulation. Quite clearly, the processes of role modeling involved in selecting and then following a mobility prototype are much the same as those involved in anticipatory socialization (Merton and Rossi [1950] 1968, pp. 319–22), the only difference being that analysis of anticipatory socialization has been somewhat more comprehensive, focusing both on its part in individuals seeking admission to groups they wish to join and their acquiring statuses they deem desirable.

If these role model prototypes are separable analytically, they nonetheless sometimes overlap in practice. To take two extreme contemporary examples, it is not self-evident that one can easily separate the cases in which young basketball players choose Larry Bird as a performance prototype from those instances in which he is chosen as a mobility prototype. He is, of course, a superlative basketball player and, as a key member of a major winning professional team, the Celtics, he has won fame and fortune. Thus, he holds a position young basketball players are apt to think is highly desirable. Similarly, it is not self-evident whether business managers who emulate Lee Iacocca do so because, by conventional measures, he has done very well managing Chrysler or because he heads a now thriving industrial empire and is copiously rewarded for doing so. How often performance proto-

---

[4] As we shall see, mobility prototypes must evidently be perceived as exemplary or at least adequate role performers to be selected as role models.

types are one and the same as mobility prototypes is obviously an open question. In short, some care is needed to differentiate empirically between performance and mobility prototypes and to determine whether being chosen as one type rather than the other is differentially consequential.

An important class of mobility prototypes calls for special attention. It differs from the rest by combining one comparatively disadvantaged status or social category with new access to a comparatively advantaged status. The first to scale or breach the walls of social discrimination become *social pioneers* and are apt to be chosen as role models by members of the disadvantaged group and to be subjected to special demands by the larger community. In our time, such composite mobility prototypes include women, blacks, certain ethnic groups, and physically handicapped individuals who enter prized occupations and other statuses still largely closed to their peers.

The historical variety of previously disadvantaged social groups and categories that are beginning to have enlarged social access indicates that such structural change is hardly unique to recent times. However, this type of structural change has become sufficiently marked for recent sociological research on role models to respond by focusing almost exclusively on the emergence of such composite mobility prototypes, particularly but not exclusively among women.

The processes involved in the selection of social pioneers as composite role models are summed up in the emblematic case of Jackie Robinson, the first black man to play major league baseball.[5] Robinson's move into the major leagues, engineered with finesse by Branch Rickey, manager of the Brooklyn Dodgers, was recognized at the time as a "sociological experiment" (Rowan with Robinson 1960, pp. 193–94). It brings together all the principal elements of the composite mobility prototype: an acute awareness of being a role model, the derivative requirement that one must excel as a role performer, and the further derivative obligation to help others like oneself succeed both in their own specific roles and more generally. Robinson wraps all this up:

[5] It is only appropriate that G. H. Mead should often have used the example of a baseball team to bring out the ways in which child socialization occurs: The actions of each player are influenced or controlled by all "the others who are playing the game" (1934, p. 154). Rather than centering on the particular pattern of the role model, Mead's innovating interest lay in how "the team [became] the generalized other in so far as it enters—as an organized process or social activity—into the experience of any one of the individual members of it" (1934, p. 154). The concepts of reference individual and role models, however, go on to focus on the social process through which *particular* members of the immediate social group or a general social category are selected for emulation and self-appraisal, thus moving to a further set of theoretical problems.

I understood that my being on that field was a symbol of the Negro's emerging self-respect, of a deep belief that somehow we had begun a magnificent era of Negro progress, a period in which Negroes could walk onto a baseball field, or into another area of life, asking no quarter, no special concession and compete creditably with white men. [Rowan with Robinson 1960, p. 142]

As we shall see, the Robinson case is also instructive in specifying how role models learn they have been chosen and particularly so in specifying the effects of being a role model.

The Robinson case points to a research program based initially on diaries, memoirs, autobiographies and biographies of historical role models, and, for recent cases, based also on interviews with the first members of disadvantaged social categories to enter other prized social categories. As we have seen, these *firsts* or *social pioneers* are apt to be chosen as role models and apt to see themselves as such. Such case histories should generate the clinical materials for research focusing on the extent to which the social pioneers saw themselves as role models, on how they learned that this was so, and on the consequences of their having been chosen. Thus, one might want to examine the case histories of Israel Jacobs who, in 1791, was the first Jew elected to Congress; of Joseph Hayne Rainey, in 1870, the first black elected to Congress; and of Jeannette Rankin, the first woman member of Congress, elected first in 1917 and again in 1941. Or, for another batch of cases, inquiry might focus on Roger Brooke Taney, the first Catholic to serve as a Supreme Court justice (1836); Louis Dembitz Brandeis, the first Jew (1916), Thurgood Marshall, the first black (1967), and Sandra Day O'Connor, the first woman named to the Court (1981). And, finally, one should focus especially on *double firsts* or social pioneers twice over such as Jane Matilda Bolin, the first black woman judge (1939), to identify the dynamics of such role models compared with single firsts. (See Kane [1950] 1980, the standard reference book on "firsts," and Epstein 1973 on "multiple negatives.")

Systematic study of these and other types of role models has barely begun, perhaps as a result of the focus in research on the influence of the models upon others (as in studies of child and adult socialization). The distinctions between performance and mobility prototypes, simple and composite, and between single and double firsts, are useful for tracing the processes through which individuals become aware that they are being adopted as role models.

## Awareness of Being a Role Model

Not all who actually serve as role models know that they do. It is not inevitably the case that they are aware of being emulated. This is often so for role-models-at-a-distance, those not in any form of interaction with those who choose them; however, it is sometimes also the case for role-models-close-at-hand, those who do interact with their selectors. Yet, as we shall see, such awareness is of course necessary to their playing *the role of being a role model*—or, put in other words, to the influence on their *own* behavior of having been singled out for the emulation.

In one type of situation, individuals may have a general sense of serving as a role model for some others without knowing who those others are. This pattern emerges in Jonathan Cole's and my detailed interviews with three age cohorts of American men and women scientists. It turns out that the 120 interviewees, selected through a stratified random sampling procedure and not for a study focused on role modeling, include five pairs of role models and their selectors.[6] In these instances, just one role model identified the younger scientist who had in fact designated the senior as such. The other seniors who had been selected were aware that they were probably serving as role models but did not name any particular selector, much less the ones in our study who had named them, although they know these younger selectors well. More assiduous interviewing may have uncovered a larger number of identified selector-model pairs, but this evidence suggests that the processes of social interaction do not automatically alert individuals to their having been *assigned the role of being a role model*. Eminent senior scientists are the ones most likely to think they serve as models in the absence of specific knowledge to that effect. This is especially the case with eminent women scientists, presumably as the result of marked structural change in the place of women in the sciences.

Quite another pattern appears, in almost institutionalized form, for those celebrities who serve as role models for large numbers of devoted followers. They are publicly, and often noisily, defined as such. These role-models-at-a-distance learn of their role through ample modes of communication: fan mail and mass media devoted to celebrities. These mass responses can, in turn, be exploited by image building and associated commercial products (those T-shirts replete with celebrity pictures). Just as studies of fan mail addressed to presidents of the United States, senators, and other public figures have indicated how such mail influences the making of public decisions (Sussman

---

[6]"Interview Protocols: Research Careers of American Men and Women Scientists." The study focuses on the careers of both eminent and rank-and-file scientists in three age cohorts. Since the bulk of young scientists are trained by a comparatively small subset of older scientists owing to the concentration of graduate education in a small number of universities, it is not entirely surprising that our 120 interviewees include as many as five pairs of senior role models and their junior selectors.

1963), so studies of fan mail should provide materials for a better understanding of the role of the role model.

The mass media define certain individuals as appropriate role-models-at-a-distance, both performance and mobility prototypes. The national press, radio, television, and magazines are full of stories about individual role performance in almost every domain of activity, legitimate and illegitimate; in sports, politics, business, the arts and sciences. These accounts report and evaluate the achievements of those whose role performance is of world (or national) class, and the local media focus on the role performance of local heroes and heroines. When it comes to mobility prototypes, news stories about Miss America may serve as the quintessential case of sudden propulsion into the ranks of organized celebrity. As Charlene Wells, the Miss America of 1984, observed in the *New York Times,* "We now know and we've always known what Miss America is—she's always been a role model." In the familiar script of unblemished virtue, the account of this announced prototype went on to say that "Miss Wells, a Mormon who teaches Sunday school, said she did not smoke, drink, or gamble. She also said she did not believe in pre-marital sex, and [quite tellingly] opposed abortion and the proposed equal rights amendment." "Miss Wells," it is reported, "pledged to be a role model for young women" (*New York Times,* September 17, 1984). Even the dimmest Miss America cannot fail to learn from the mass media that she is publicly defined as a role model for some indeterminate but goodly number of girls and women. The same learning, one suspects, occurs in the case of mobility prototypes generally, leaders of institutions, organizations, and groups covered in the press who are held up as models[7] for those who aspire to like positions.

When it comes to composite mobility prototypes, those combining disadvantaged and advantaged statuses, the media, both general and specialized, publicly identify appropriate candidates. Thus, Jackie Robinson emerged, after his first year on the Dodgers and the "most exciting of all World Series, as the most talked about and written about Negro in the world" (Rowan with Robinson 1960, p. 196). Robinson plainly knew he had become a role model, with results we shall consider in detail.

Especially in the case of women, pioneers symbolize the extent to which they depart from the stereotype of what those occupying the advantaged status are usually like. Thus, an article in the *New Scientist,*

[7] For just one example, see Bianco 1985, p. 98, on John Gutfreund of Salomon Brothers, the Wall Street firm he runs, which is both respected and "feared by its competitors."

entitled "A Role Model for Female Physicists," describes the subject of the story as

light years away from the Einsteinian image of a theoretical physicist. With a cascade of curly fair hair that catches the light, she seems more likely to have stepped straight out of a pre-Raphaelite painting. But a theoretical physicist she is, and a good one at that. [September 13, 1984, p. 53]

This woman physicist, along with others who read about her, cannot fail to get the message that she is being socially defined as a role model, acceptable both as a physicist and as a woman, stereotyped in terms of her womanly appearance. Mass media accounts of men physicists being proposed as role models probably do not as often include such vivid portrayals of their appearance although descriptions of Albert Einstein, emphasizing his distinctive dishevelment, provide one stereotypic image of the scientist.

In any event, the mass media have plainly discovered the notion of role models. They are central channels for designating role-models-at-a-distance and for diffusing the term "role models." The public identification of role models may encourage people to choose them.

Third-party reports, standing between direct communication through fan mail and the mass media, operate to inform role-models-at-a-distance of their emerging role. In the words of a senior woman biochemist, "A Japanese . . . quite eminent in his field . . . told me that all the young Japanese women look up to me and want to be just like me. . . . I've been to Japan once but, I mean, I couldn't have met all these young women!" So too, a letter from a former student who had spent the year in India informs another senior scientist, "The younger generation looks to you with awe and feels a sense of reverence for you. I thought I should let you know." It may be that the context of vicarious pride leads third parties to "let" the role models know in a gesture of their own respect. That they are role models becomes semipublic knowledge rather than remaining private knowledge.

At times, role-models-close-at-hand are informed that others regard them as such. One senior scientist reported how he learned of his having helped to shape the role performance of one of his most distinguished and autonomous students. Couched almost in the language of George Herbert Mead, a letter to him reads:

I sent the paper to you [not] because I need[ed] your comments. All I needed was to send the paper to you, *and then begin to see it through your eyes.* The end result, which was achieved even before I talked to you and received your comments, is a synthesis in which it is still me . . . but with a corrective applied.

Role-models-close-at-hand also learn of being chosen by inference from direct observation. They notice emulative behavior on the part of others, and the more distinctive it is, the more readily it is identified as emulative. Such behaviors, major and minor, can involve details, more symbolic than instrumental, such as styles of dress, speech, stance, even the style of signing one's name or acquiring the same appurtenances such as writing paper. As one senior scientist wrote to another, even more senior, "P.S. Notice the [new] stationery—it's a direct copy [of yours] (I am a strong believer in good role models)." Beyond these symbols of identification are efforts to adopt work styles and styles of thought.

Both role-models-at-a-distance and those close at hand are less likely to know that they have been chosen as negative role models rather than positive ones. Negative role models are not as apt to be informed of their unenviable role, and it is difficult to identify countermodeling behavior. The same seems to hold for individuals who are at once positive and negative models. The brilliant physician revered by medical students as a model diagnostician but rejected as a clinician because of his ruthless treatment of patients is more apt to learn of the former than of the latter.

Finally, some publicly declare themselves to be appropriate models. The familiar words of *Poor Richard's Almanack* tell us how Ben Franklin's life might serve as a mobility prototype.

Having emerged from the poverty and obscurity in which I was born and bred, to a state of affluence and some degree of reputation in the world . . . the conducing means I made use of . . . my posterity may like to know, as they may find some of them suitable to their own situations, and therefore fit to be imitated. [N.d., pp. 7–8; the Franklin example is used effectively in Kemper 1968]

If years and light years separate Ben Franklin and Miss America, his self-designation bears a formal resemblance to her promise to be a worthy "role model." The *Times* has her say that she has "lived her life 'above reproach—I live my values seven days a week'" (*New York Times*, September 17, 1984).

Role-models-at-a-distance and role-models-close-at-hand evidently learn with varying degrees of accuracy and specificity of their having been assigned that role through somewhat different modes of communication. These differences are not incidental. They involve variations in the extent and kind of obligations the models are expected to fulfill (or believe they are expected to fulfill) and variations in the aspects of their role behavior that are being emulated, rejected, or ignored. In short, these variations affect the consequences of being chosen as a role model.

## The Role of the Role Model

Like other elements in the reward systems of society, being adopted as a role model can be gratifying and reinforcing. As we shall see, it also has its complement of pain, with the distribution of pleasure and pain yet to be determined. In certain contexts, it represents vindication of one's self, way of life, and ways of thought. In effect, it is an emphatic vote of confidence. This is especially the case when that vote comes from one for whom the model has great respect. A sense of this kind of deep gratification is conveyed in the response from the model to the now distinguished scientist who wrote the letter quoted earlier, emphasizing the importance of seeing his own work through the model's eyes. That response reads:

I am moved beyond ready measure by your letter. . . . To have you say what you did about the perspective you gained by seeing things as I presumably would while not necessarily agreeing with what you then see, is for me a culminating tribute to those years of sustained intellectual excitement you and I were privileged to share.

By definition, role models influence others' values, norms, and standards of role performance. Performance prototypes, in particular, believing in the worth of their own perspectives, engage in modes of interaction that directly transmit these perspectives. Thus, Max Delbrück, a founding father of molecular biology, did so in the role of incessant and fearsome critic:

After my seminar [Delbrück] took me by the arm to his office to tell me in confidence that it was the worst seminar he had ever heard. It was not till years later, after I had met dozens of people, each of whom had been told that *his* had been the worst seminar Delbrück had ever heard, that it dawned on me that Delbrück told this to (almost) everyone. [G. Streisinger quoted in Zuckerman 1977, p. 126]

Norms, standards, and behavior are internalized. Thus, Delbrück's influence was felt not just then and there but in his absence and through the years. Gunther Stent, a onetime junior colleague and now eminent senior, describes it this way:

Delbrück managed to become a kind of Gandhi of biology who, without possessing any temporal power at all, was an ever present and sometime irksome spiritual force. "What will Max think of it?" became the central question of the molecular biological psyche. [Quoted in Zuckerman 1977, p. 126]

However, as we have noted, influence flows not only from role model to selectors but in the reverse direction as well. Serving as a performance prototype, being chosen as an exemplar of role performance, gives the role models extra incentives to do well. Learning that one is cast in the role of role model serves to reinforce the behavior that led to the choice in the first place while, at the same time, emulation seems to improve the selectors' role performance.

Not all role models find that role gratifying. It has social and psychological costs as well. Sherry Lansing, who at thirty-five years of age became the first woman to head a major film studio, 20th Century-Fox, states: "I want to slit my throat . . . when girls tell me that I've been their role model" (*New York Times*, October 10, 1985, p. 63). Her response is not unlike that of a distinguished woman biologist who, when asked about her response to young women scientists wanting to emulate her, said, "I can't deal with that. I don't even try. I won't try."

Judging from reports of role models, the main reasons for such discontent are unwanted obligations and limited leeway in conformity to norms. Sometimes, discontent is produced also by feeling one has been chosen as a role model for the wrong reasons or by the wrong people. Sources of discontent vary no doubt among different types of role models as do role models' structured capacities to keep them under control.

## Social Obligations

When role models are publicly defined rather than remaining privately defined by this or that follower, a complex process of social interaction is set in motion. It is as though public acknowledgment of their accomplishments imposes obligations on role models to those celebrating their accomplishments. The expressed loyalty of the followers induces a reciprocal obligation of the role model while the follower acquires rights by following.

## Role Models as Social Pioneers

This process is greatly reinforced in the case of social pioneers, where the shared experience of exclusion reinforces the reciprocal sense of loyalties. Demands upon pioneer role models come to be mutually defined as legitimate. They experience a social obligation to the collectivity of their still disadvantaged peers who expect the model to remain loyal to them. As in all forms of social interaction, here too there is a degree of socially expected reciprocity, but such beneficently imputed obligations can readily get out of hand. The sense of burden is presumably reduced when role models have actively sought that role or accepted it when it is thrust upon them.

So it is that a successful black athlete and successful women scientists alike express this sense of responsibility to their still disadvantaged peers. Jackie Robinson expresses the special obligation of the social pioneer.

People can lose their prejudices when they get to know another group—. . . . So I decided that . . . I had a responsibility to do something to make the . . . fellows [on the team] feel that they had nothing to fear from Negroes—that they were just as valuable to the team as [Bartlett and I] were. [Rowan with Robinson 1960, p. 43]

The eminent women scientists similarly testify to a sense of obligation to help other women to get on with their research and their careers, an obligation that has no counterpart among comparable male role models. A senior woman physicist reports that she took on difficult jobs more often than she liked, owing to a sense of representative obligation to her still excluded peers.

I took this job because no woman had ever been asked to be a lab director. This is one of the large laboratories . . . and I thought it would be bad for women [at this university] if I didn't take it. . . . That was a major consideration. . . . I don't need to be a lab director. . . . I [also] do a great deal of service to the country and a lot of that is in the context [of increasing the] visibility of women in the sciences and also to demonstrate that we can do it too. [Zuckerman and Cole, "Interview Protocols"]

As we have seen, strategically located third parties have expectations about how the role models ought to behave. In the case of Jackie Robinson, the prime mover, Branch Rickey, served as a special kind of third party reinforcing Robinson's own sense of his symbolic role as a social pioneer and the associated obligation to other blacks. Rickey speaks to Robinson when he was first signed to play for the Dodgers: "Jackie, I just want to beg two things of you: that as a baseball player you give it your utmost; and as a man you give continuing fidelity to your race and to this crucial cause that you symbolize" (Rowan with Robinson 1960, p. 119).

At times, efforts to meet these obligations can, ironically, get in the way of maintaining the high level of role performance that led to preeminence. Again, the experiences of the black ballplayer and the women scientists exhibit formally similar patterns. For the women scientists, the problem becomes one of finding the time and focused attention to advance the cause of women in science while keeping their research going. Mixing civil politics with serious science, they report, proves to be difficult and costly for their scientific work.

For Robinson, the obligations that came with being a social pioneer were closely intertwined with the temptations that came with sheer celebrity of the kind familiar to many white ballplayers. Robinson's wife, Rachel, reports that Rickey understood this well: "[He] cautioned us not to accept the many invitations we received . . . and to concentrate on our job. He felt that for us to get snowed under with social obligations would adversely affect Jack's playing" (Rowan with Robinson 1960, p. 191). But after the World Series, caution was thrown to the winds. Robinson made a great many personal appearances, and his admirers "fed him until he was fat and futile." He showed up for training the following spring "twenty-five pounds over playing weight" and felt, he said, like "an ingrate to have . . . shown up so fat" (Rowan with Robinson 1960, p. 196).

Some social pioneers, aware of the ironic consequences of meeting their obligations to the group, nonetheless continue to do so. Their activities on behalf of the groups they are taken to represent are designed to set the stage for accelerated social change set in motion by their being emblematic firsts.

Social pioneers, in particular, find that their behavior is symbolically magnified. Their failures are taken to reflect not merely on themselves but on the groups they are socially defined to represent.[8] Branch Rickey's injunctions to this effect are reinforced by Rachel Robinson:

I want you to play baseball as hard as you know how, but I want you also to remember that every eye in America will be on you. I want you to remember that many sports writers will be looking for incidents, will be out to prove that, in effect, integration won't work in baseball. [Rowan with Robinson 1960, p. 171]

## The Caesar's Wife Phenomenon

As usual with members of the upper strata in systems of social stratification, role models in general and pioneering composite models in particular are subjected to special constraints on their public behavior as counterparts to the special privileges they have acquired. The high visibility of public role models and the demanding expectations of them combine to produce the "Caesar's wife phenomenon." Caesar is said to have observed, in the course of divorcing Pompeia, his second wife, on the grounds of her having allegedly violated the secret rites of Bona Dea, that though she was probably innocent of the charge, "Caesar's wife must be above suspicion" (*Roman Apothegms*). Like other constraints on public figures, the Caesar's wife phenomenon is espe-

[8] Heightened visibility has similar outcomes for "token" women in organizations, as Kanter (1977) notes.

cially acute for the composite role models who constitute social pioneers. Geraldine Ferraro, the first woman and, incidentally, the first person of Italian descent nominated for the vice-presidency of the United States, had ample opportunity to discover that "Ferraro's husband must also be above suspicion." And again, the paradigmatic case of Jackie Robinson exemplifies this pattern. Branch Rickey, intent on opening the gates to black talent, chose Robinson because he "wanted to be sure that the Negro selected to end Jim Crow in baseball would be the right man *off* the field—a clean living family man whose character was above reproach" (Rowan with Robinson 1960, p. 107).

Owing to the Caesar's wife phenomenon, role models are required, at least in public, to be punctilious; in the process, they feel far more constrained than others. Even the Olympic champion Mary Lou Retton, free of the special burdens of being a social pioneer, is said to "acknowledge that the business of being a role model has its dictatorial side. She is told what to wear, when to smile (even if her mouth happens to be jammed with Wheaties) and whom to court" (*New York Times,* November 25, 1985, p. C6). There appears to be a process of enlarged expectation of role models: It is not enough that they excel in one specialized role; they must excel in a larger range of roles. In other sociological words, the tendency is to convert specialized role models into generalized reference individuals.

Those role models who are also social pioneers are socially expected to do better than others in precisely those respects that stereotypes hold their disadvantaged group to be weakest. For Robinson, this meant that apart from being an outstanding ballplayer he must not appear "lazy" or undisciplined. Branch Rickey warned Robinson:

You've *got* to get in there, sore arm or not. For anybody else, it would be all right, but remember that you're here under extraordinary circumstances. You can't afford to miss a single day of practice or other players will start rumors that you're goldbricking that you're dogging off with the pretense that you have a sore arm. [Rowan with Robinson 1960, p. 143]

For women pioneers, the same rule of countering the stereotype would presumably require them to be "unemotional," physically sturdy, tough-minded, and possessed of other positively valued but "unwomanly" attributes. In both types of instances, many social pioneers, aware of the process, have come to reject these discriminatory demands.

The social pioneers are also subjected to the social expectation that they continue as role models. If they did otherwise, they would confirm their detractors' convictions and some of their followers' fears that "failure" would occur. Robinson early recognized that "There could be no quitting, because so much more than my own sensitivity was at stake" (Rowan with Robinson 1960, p. 142). As if echoing his thoughts, a distinguished woman biologist who, from time to time, considered leaving science told of her response to receiving a major award for her work:

the tears rolled down my face. . . . I didn't want this. This now means that as a woman I have to stay with the game . . . at least until women catch up. . . . I was not elated. . . . I didn't have the sense of freedom that I had. I just knew [then] that I couldn't let women down. . . . [It would be] a black mark for women. [Men] would say "Just look at that. That's what they do." [Zuckerman and Cole 1987]

Yet, again, failure and triumph alike hold an enlarged significance for pioneering role models. These are taken not simply as their own potentials in action but to symbolize the potentials of their disadvantaged group. The Robinson experience is again in point:

Almost every Negro who had ever heard of baseball followed that [1947] series, knowing almost instinctively that because Robinson was still thought of as a Negro first and a ball player second, his triumph would be the Negro's triumph, his failure that of black men everywhere. [Rowan with Robinson 1960, p. 195]

Those role models who serve as social pioneers bear living sociological witness to the persistence of discriminatory systems of restricted or closed opportunity. This provides context for such pioneers to want to disengage from the structurally induced role of being a pioneering role model. Thus, Jackie Robinson looked forward to "the day . . . when I can be just a player," as did his wife, Rachel: "I live for the day when you won't be 'Jackie Robinson, the first Negro player in organized ball' any longer" (Rowan with Robinson 1960, p. 193). Much the same symbolic wish for more structural change is expressed in the tart observation by the meteorologist Joanne Simpson: "I would like to retire from being a role model" (quoted in Zuckerman 1985, p. 87).

There are indications that some structural change has been taking place in these domains and that there is popular recognition of the role played by role models in that change. As the fortieth anniversary of Jackie Robinson's rookie year in Brooklyn approaches, his widow observes:

Progress is always slow, and always less than you want it to be. I applaud the number of minority players now not only in baseball but in all sports. But there have been a token number of black managers, and a token number of opportunities for black front-office people. And what I want now is to see Jack remembered as a role model in school history books. [*New York Times*, December 31, 1983]

Frank White, one of the sixteen black and Hispanic players among the fifty in the 1985 World Series, alludes to the dynamics of his experience: "[Robinson] was my role model. . . . In high school there weren't any black-history courses but when I went to a Kansas City community college, I read everything I could about him. And my father talked about him a lot. I know everything about him" (*New York Times*, December 31, 1983). And White's teammate, Darryl Motley of the Royals, says of Robinson that "He's the reason why I'm playing in this World Series."

Role models are not, it would appear, consigned to be passive objects of emulation but, in ways yet to be established, are actively engaged with those who select them. Yet research of role models, as we have seen, has been confined to their effects on selectors and has neglected their reciprocal effects on the models themselves. As a result, the social role assigned to role models of various sorts, performance and mobility prototypes, have yet to be examined systematically. Similarly, the extent and kinds of influence exercised by role models, depending on their awareness of having been selected and their active acceptance of the role, are still open questions. Like other roles, the role of the role model entails rights and obligations, obligations that may be particularly constraining for that socially consequential mobility prototype, the social pioneers, who are taken to represent not just themselves but the disadvantaged groups of which they are a part. Role-modeling behavior long predated the emergence of the concept. But, when social scientists identified the concept and provided an evocative term for it and when that term passed into the language, social reality was reconstructed much as other social science concepts and terms have also helped to reconstruct social reality.

## Bibliography

Barnard, Chester. 1938. *The functions of the executive.* Cambridge, Mass.: Harvard University Press, 1962.

Bianco, Anthony. 1985. The king of Wall Street. *Business Week,* December 9, pp. 98–102.

Epstein, Cynthia Fuchs. 1970a. *Women's place.* Berkeley: University of California Press.

———. 1970b. Encountering the male establishment: Sex-status limits on women's careers in professions. *American Journal of Sociology* 75:965–82.

———. 1973. Positive effects of the multiple negative: Explaining the success of black professional women. *American Journal of Sociology* 78:912–35.

Ericson, R., and P. Baranek. 1982. *The ordering of justice: A study of accused persons as dependents in the criminal process.* Toronto: University of Toronto Press.

Festinger, Leon. 1954. A theory of social comparison processes. *Human Relations* 7:117–40.

Kane, Joseph Nathan. 1950. *Famous first facts.* 4th ed. New York: Wilson, 1980.

Kanter, Rosabeth Moss. 1977. *Men and women of the corporation.* New York: Basic Books.

Katz, Elihu, and Paul F. Lazarsfeld. 1955. *Personal influence.* Glencoe, Ill.: Free Press.

Kelley, Harold H. 1952. Two functions of reference groups. In G. E. Swanson, T. M. Newcomb, and E. L. Hartley, *Readings in social psychology,* pp. 410–14. New York: Holt, 1968.

Kemper, Theodore D. 1968. Reference groups, socialization, and achievement. *American Sociological Review* 33:31–45.

Lunneborg, Patricia. 1982. Role model influences of non-traditional professional women. *Journal of Vocational Behavior* 20:276–81.

Mead, George H. 1934. *Mind, self and society.* Chicago: University of Chicago Press.

Merton, Robert K. 1949. Patterns of influence: Local and cosmopolitan influentials. In *Social theory and social structure,* pp. 441–74. Rev. ed. New York: Free Press, 1968.

———. 1957. Continuities in the theory of reference groups and social structure. In *Social theory and social structure,* pp. 335–440. Rev. ed. New York: Free Press, 1968.

Merton, Robert K., and Alice S. Rossi. 1950. Contributions to the theory of reference group behavior. In *Social theory and social structure,* pp. 279–334. Rev. ed. New York: Free Press, 1968.

Moreno, Jacob L., and Helen H. Jennings. 1938. Statistics of social configurations. *Sociometry* 1:342–74.

Newcomb, Theodore M. 1952. Attitude development as a function of reference groups: The Bennington Study. In H. Hyman and E. Singer, eds., *Readings in reference group theory and research,* pp. 374–86. New York: Free Press, 1968.

Reskin, Barbara. 1979. Academic sponsorship and scientists' careers. *Sociology of Education* 52:129–46.

Robinson, Jackie. 1964. *Baseball has done it.* Edited by Charles Dexter. Philadelphia: Lippincott.

Rowan, Carl T., with Jackie Robinson. 1960. *Wait til next year.* New York: Random House.

Runciman, W. G. 1966. Reference groups and inequalities of class. In H. Hyman and E. Singer, eds., *Readings in reference group theory and research,* pp. 207–21. New York: Free Press, 1968.

Schuman, Howard, and Michael P. Johnson. 1976. Attitudes and behavior. In Alex Inkeles, James Coleman, and Neil Smelser, eds., *Annual Review of Sociology* 2:161–207. Palo Alto, Calif.: Annual Reviews.

Sherif, Muzafer. 1948. *An outline of social psychology.* New York: Harper.

Smith, Trudee F. 1985. Law talk: Juveniles' understanding of legal language. *Journal of Criminal Justice* 13:339–53.

Speizer, Jeanne J. 1981. Role models, mentors, and sponsors: The elusive concepts. *Signs* 6:693–712.

Stouffer, S. A., E. A. Suchman, L. C. De Vinney, S. A. Star, and R. M. Williams. 1949. *Adjustment during army life*. Vol. 1 of *The American soldier*. Princeton, N.J.: Princeton University Press.

Sullivan, Harry Stack. 1940–45. *Conceptions of model psychiatry*. New York: Norton, 1953.

Sussman, Leila A. 1963. *Dear FDR: A study of political letter-writing*. Totowa, N.J.: Bedminster Press.

Sutton, Christine. 1984. A role model for female physicists. *New Scientist*, September 13, p. 53.

Theodorson, George A., and Achilles G. Theodorson. 1969. *A modern dictionary of sociology*. New York: Crowell.

Thielens, Wagner. 1957. Some comparisons of entrants to medical & law school. In R. K. Merton, G. Reader, and P. Kendall, eds., *The student-physician*, pp. 131–52. Cambridge, Mass.: Harvard University Press.

Weber, Max. 1922–24. *The theory of social and economic organization*. Translated and edited by A. M. Henderson and T. Parsons. Glencoe, Ill: Free Press, 1957.

Zuckerman, Harriet. 1977. *Scientific elite: Nobel laureates in the United States*. New York: Free Press.

———. 1985. My daughter, the scientist. Review. *Science* 85(6):86–88.

Zuckerman, Harriet, and Jonathan R. Cole. 1987. Unpublished interview protocols.

## Hubert J. O'Gorman

# 6 Pluralistic Ignorance and Reference Groups: The Case of Ingroup Ignorance

Empirical and theoretical access to reference group phenomena has become indispensable for comprehending the group basis of social action. For this reason, Herbert H. Hyman's pioneering work on reference groups (1942, 1960, 1968; Hyman and Singer 1968) ranks as an enduring contribution to sociology, social psychology, and our collective understanding of our common social life. It is therefore appropriate to honor Professor Hyman with an essay on pluralistic ignorance, an important but neglected social phenomenon that has particular significance for the study of reference groups, as he himself occasionally intimated (Hyman 1969, 1973).

Reference group theory is basically concerned with explaining the various ways in which individuals and groups take other individuals and groups as a frame of reference for defining and evaluating their ideas, feelings, and conduct (Merton 1968). Pluralistic ignorance refers to false social knowledge of other people (Katz and Allport 1931; O'Gorman 1986). It bears directly on reference group theory because the knowledge that individuals have of other people, a self-evident requirement of reference group phenomena, is frequently false. Consequently, explanations of reference group processes are faced with the complex task of spelling out the conditions that facilitate the accurate perception and cognition of other individuals and groups. But because an adequate understanding of the accuracy of empirical beliefs entails an explanation of their distorted counterparts, the identification of these conditions requires explicit attention to the specific circumstances under which individuals acquire and act upon false beliefs

I want to thank Anne C. Dunham, Howard Schuman, and Eleanor Singer for their comments on an earlier version of this paper.

about others. From this perspective, pluralistic ignorance is, I will argue, a major reference group phenomenon.

Although the acquisition, cultivation, and use of false social ideas are of particular concern to reference group theory, they are also of general interest, providing a common perspective on a large array of otherwise diverse problems in sociology and social psychology. For when nontrivial discrepancies emerge between shared beliefs about what others are doing and thinking and what others are, in fact, doing and thinking, patterns of false beliefs are likely to play an influential and often decisive role in defining social actions. These discrepancies are an integral part of the human condition, constant companions of social actors who, to act socially, always need, as Max Weber (1968, pp. 22–24) emphasized, to take each other into account. The generic nature of pluralistic ignorance is further recorded in the intriguing fact that everywhere it usually occurs unnoticed, unintended, and unwanted, an abiding reminder that consequences we might choose not to contemplate can happen.

Despite its profound importance, pluralistic ignorance has aroused little theoretical interest. The lack of attention can be traced to the persistent and ironic supposition that shared misconceptions of other people do not require special explanation. This unwarranted assumption is routinely made when evidence of pluralistic ignorance is taken to be nothing more than another manifestation of some already recognized form of irrational thought or cognitive deficiency. This assimilation occurs for several reasons: because the distinctive characteristics of pluralistic ignorance are not recognized, because well-known explanations for known forms of error appear to be adequate, and because data that are inconsistent with conventional accounts go unattended. To perceive the new within the established vocabulary of the known may be necessary, but it runs the risk of misconstruing the unfamiliar. The assimilation process is a potential and potent source of false beliefs. The obscuring of pluralistic ignorance itself as a distinct phenomenon is particularly disturbing because it shifts attention away from a fundamental sociological question: What are the processes through which a social environment misinforms its inhabitants and observers about the characteristics of themselves and their environment? Since there are relatively few lines of empirical inquiry other than the study of pluralistic ignorance that lead directly to this serious question, issues that help to clarify its meaning and to identify its sources and effects need and deserve extensive discussion.[1]

---

[1] In sociology, lines of inquiry associated with Marxian thought and the sociology of knowledge have not developed a sustained interest in the accuracy of shared cognitive beliefs about others apart from their association with other cultural characteristics, usu-

The following discussion will be informed generally by two controlling ideas. Using the general case of an ingroup, I want to explore the extent to which the values of a reference group contribute to a state of pluralistic ignorance among its members, some of whom do and some of whom do not hold those values. At the same time, I want to demonstrate that these patterns of reference group ignorance cannot be accurately described or adequately explained by assimilating them into more familiar phenomena. I will restrict myself to a pair of well-known and frequently cited hypotheses. One, involving a cultural pattern of cognitive rationalization, claims the values that people share distort their factual beliefs in such a way that the latter normally support or justify the former. The second refers to a psychological process and claims that the same distorting influence of values on facts is the result of the tendency of individuals to view the world egocentrically.[2]

I will begin by discussing the meaning of pluralistic ignorance, its cognitive and social characteristics, and its relationship to reference groups. I will next consider the process through which false beliefs are socially validated, underscoring the significance of this validation process by members of a cognitive reference group, a group that defines the object and assesses the accuracy of social beliefs for its members. Then I turn to the classic problem of how values tend to distort cognitive beliefs about the social world. However, I formulate the problem in a special way in order to highlight a basic question that is usually begged rather than posed. *How do the values of ingroup members distort their cognitive beliefs regarding other ingroup members' values?* To address the question I draw on national sample survey data pertaining to whites' perceptions of other whites' racial values and estimates by the elderly of the severity of problems among most other elderly. Although the data consistently confirm the cognitive rationalization and egocentric views, they repeatedly point to the conclusion that neither view provides a satisfactory account of the reported misconceptions.

---

ally within a context of imputed group interests. Similarly, whatever else the term may mean, "false consciousness" almost always seems to imply, to judge by the same literature, something more than a shared cognitive error. In social psychology, studies of social perception in general and social attribution in particular have not produced a research tradition that centers on shared cognitive accuracy regarding the social world except within a framework of applied problems like prejudice or pathology.

[2] Throughout this paper I use the term "egocentric" to refer loosely to the tendency of individuals to "assume that others are more similar to them in beliefs, feelings, and behavior than they in fact are" (Ross and Fletcher 1985, p. 85). This well-documented and variously labeled psychological disposition does not necessarily lead to a state of pluralistic ignorance (Ross, Greene, and House 1977), but it is a familiar enough process to which the condition of ignorance can readily be assimilated. Equally important, this egocentric process, as we shall see, seems to play a central role in the emergence of ingroup ignorance, providing a common if mistaken basis for ethnocentrism.

To defend this conclusion, I rely on the persistent and important finding that many respondents in the cited studies imputed to others values they themselves did *not* endorse. I then attempt to challenge the validity of this central finding by examining as a source of possible spuriousness the *value* that some respondents may put on expressing themselves in socially desirable ways.

## Pluralistic Ignorance

Pluralistic ignorance refers to the erroneous cognitive beliefs shared by two or more individuals regarding other individuals. In contrast to the value accorded to accurate beliefs, patterns of pluralistic ignorance, when they become known, are usually deplored as representing an unfortunate state of affairs. But such patterns are not easy to identify. A condition of pluralistic ignorance is in many important respects a remarkably elusive feature of social life, almost always escaping the notice of involved participants and frequently eluding the understanding of more detached observers. It will be helpful, therefore, to discuss certain points that must be kept in mind if pluralistic ignorance is to be recognized and properly understood.

To begin with, pluralistic ignorance is a misnomer. It is not ignorance in the ordinary sense of not knowing. On the contrary, it is knowledge of others that individuals mistakenly and with matter-of-fact certainty believe to be correct. In addition, it is knowledge that the knowing individuals believe they share with other individuals. The social validation of false knowledge through the awareness that it is shared not only increases the sense of cognitive confidence but introduces an additional unrecognized error. Individuals do not normally endorse ideas they think are false. When they do, the fact of that endorsement, precisely because it is unknown to them, becomes an imperceptible part of their lives. Strictly speaking, then, pluralistic ignorance invariably involves at least two related errors: the mistake that individuals make in their judgments about other people and the mistake they make in judging themselves to be correctly informed about others. Unaware of either mistake, individuals in a state of pluralistic ignorance live in error but not in doubt.

The absence of doubt is particularly important in maintaining the error. The sense of social competence that individuals have about themselves is tied to their own perceived ability to perceive others accurately. From this point of view, to call into question the accuracy of facts that they rely on to characterize others is to call into question their social standing as competent observers. In other words, individuals may be expected to value their cognitive ideas of others for the simple but powerful reason that such beliefs are part and parcel of their own social identity, in their eyes presumptive evidence that the beliefs are accurate. By definition, the study of pluralistic ignorance means, of course, the examination of shared false ideas. As obvious as this may seem, it should not be allowed to blur the important, but perhaps less evident, point that individuals who share false beliefs routinely believe those beliefs to be true. Though this is a necessary condition for a self-fulfilling prophecy (Merton 1968), false beliefs do not have to become true to affect the actions of those who think they are true.

A second important point is that the type of collective error under review is an empirical or factual mistake. Pluralistic ignorance is a concept that denotes shared *cognitive* illusions, that is, socially validated but empirically false propositions about others in the social world. They are closely implicated with, and for that reason need to be carefully distinguished from, other cultural patterns like norms, values, and attitudes. Once made, the distinction allows us to explore the multiple and reciprocal processes through which cognitive beliefs and the other components of culture are related to each other. As studies in the sociology knowledge demonstrate (Mannheim 1936), attempts to analyze distortions in social thought without making the vital distinction between cognitive and noncognitive elements have limited utility.

Not only are these false beliefs cognitive; they are *shared*. It is important not to lose sight of this third point, a critical social fact, by confusing pluralistic ignorance with the psychological distortions that individuals happen to employ in perceiving others. Although individual cognitive bias undoubtedly reflects general psychological processes of perception and judgmental heuristics (Kahneman, Slovic, and Tversky 1982), in any given situation these mechanisms may or may not contribute to a condition of pluralistic ignorance. There is, after all, a difference between the distortion of accurate information and the veridical perception of false information; and, equally important, there is a difference between the ways in which information is acquired, stored, and transmitted by an individual and the ways in which it is processed by groups and organizations. Consequently, it is difficult to identify, describe, and analyze pluralistic ignorance unless it is sharply distinguished from the psychological mechanisms of perceptual and cognitive bias (O'Gorman 1986).

What sets pluralistic ignorance apart from psychological processes of social misperception is that it always involves a plurality of individuals who share the same substantive error about specific other individuals or categories of individuals. Thus my fourth point: Like language, patterns of comunications, the division of labor, rates of behavior, and other social phenomena, pluralistic ignorance is a property of a social environment within which a number of individuals are differentially located. Although it refers to misinformed individuals, pluralistic ignorance is, technically speaking, a cultural property of a plurality of individuals in a social system.

Social systems vary enormously, of course, in size and complexity. Nonetheless, it is useful to think of them in terms of two analytically distinct but empirically overlapping patterns of pluralistic ignorance. One involves situations in which the same false ideas regarding other people are shared by an *aggregate* of individuals who are *not* directly related to each other except for their common membership in some large social system. That university and college students are often markedly wrong in characterizing most other students at their institutions (Davis 1963; Katz and Allport 1931; Korte 1972) is a good example. Erroneous ideas expressed by respondents in national or regional sample surveys (Fields and Schuman 1976–77; O'Gorman 1975) about others not personally known to them are another. In contrast to the aggregate level, the second pattern of pluralistic ignorance refers to mistaken ideas about others shared by individuals who are *associated* in smaller social systems, networks of mutually recognized relationships (Breed and Ktsanes 1961; Fields 1971). Individuals who belong, for instance, to the same family, or reside in the same community, or live in the same neighborhood, or work at the same place, or worship at the same church frequently misperceive each other. Schanck's (1932) classic study of pluralistic ignorance in a small, rural, and isolated community drew attention to these kinds of associational patterns.

## Ingroup Ignorance

The distinction between aggregate and associational patterns of ignorance helps to raise important questions about the reciprocal relationship between misconceptions that grow out of everyday experience with specific individuals and particular groups and false beliefs about more general categories of individuals and groups. However, this relation is difficult to explore without drawing the additional and equally important distinction between groups and categories to which individuals belong and those to which they do not. The sense of perceived similarity, of consciousness of kind, in Giddings's famous phrase, is indispensable for understanding the formation of shared cognitive beliefs. We can refer to these patterns of belonging and not belonging as indicative of ingroup and outgroup membership. This simple dichotomy separates analytically ingroup ignorance, where members of the same group or category hold false ideas about other members of the same group or category, from outgroup ignorance, where individuals share erroneous beliefs about groups and categories in which they do not hold membership.[3]

As we shall see, this classification is necessary to understand that outgroup ignorance in general and ethonocentrism in particular frequently rest upon ingroup ignorance. But we need to remember that ingroup and outgroup members, no matter how they are defined, always hold in common some social characteristics, like age, gender, and group membership, a central fact that they and observers sometimes forget. Here as elsewhere, perceived differences can only occur against a background of some recognized similarities. The utility of the classification depends largely on the purpose of the investigation. Given that individuals normally identify and affiliate with multiple groups, and given that they can be categorized by themselves and others in a number of ways, the imputation of ingroup or outgroup membership is necessarily relative to some context. Instances subsumed under the terms "ingroup" and "outgroup" may vary, depending on the context, to denote individuals who interact with each other on a sustained basis, who share the same status, who hold the same beliefs, who belong to the same organization, or who can otherwise be identified as members of some relevant social category, a crowd, for example.[4]

In any event, once we recognize that the analysis of false beliefs requires attention to multiple groups and categories, it becomes easier to see that studies of pluralistic ignorance and reference group research are dealing with overlapping problems. Reference group phenomena cannot be described without implying the preexistence of empirical beliefs concerning the identity and characteristics of the individuals and groups used as frames of reference. And there are good empirical and theoretical reasons for expecting that under many conditions this indispensable prior knowledge is likely to be in error. Studies of pluralistic ignorance, on the other hand, have repeatedly reported that the contents of shared false beliefs usually refer to individuals and groups toward whom the believers are affectively oriented for normative, comparative, and other instrumental purposes. In short, the study of reference groups always implies knowledge of

---

[3] This dichotomy necessarily bypasses, at least for the purposes of this paper, otherwise important patterns of pluralistic ignorance that occur *within* groups and categories, patterns that grow out of their internal structural differentiation. These cluster primarily around obstacles to effective communication in hierarchies, status sets, and role sets (Merton 1968) within whatever reference groups or categories are under review.

[4] A crowd is, I believe, most usefully thought of as a transitory and sometimes powerful ingroup that frequently misleads its members and its observers about its own characteristics (Simmel 1950; Turner and Killian 1972).

others, and the study of pluralistic ignorance always implies the perceived existence of reference groups. From this joint point of view, pluralistic ignorance is a cultural manifestation of reference group processes in which members of groups and categories acquire, maintain, and transmit false cognitive beliefs about those who do and do not share their common membership.

To grasp more firmly the connection between pluralistic ignorance and reference groups, we need to remember that the cognitive accounts we must take of others, even as they make possible the countless achievements of everyday life, are, as Simmel (1950) taught us, necessarily incomplete, usually misleading, and frequently false. Most of us most of the time have neither the incentive nor the resources to explore the social world systematically. Suppose, for example and to anticipate my later discussion, whites want to take into account other whites as a normative reference group in matters pertaining to race. This requires some minimal information about the racial norms and values of other whites. Similarly, suppose aged individuals want to consider other elderly as a comparative reference group for purposes of self-appraisal. To make the appraisal they need have some impression of the number and severity of personal problems encountered by most other elderly people. Finally, suppose there are blacks and non-elderly who have no normative or comparative interest in whites' racial values or problems of the aged but who do have to take both into account as part of their immediate environment. In these and similar cases the operation of reference group processes entails a set of prior factual beliefs, a cognitive scheme, that takes the form of estimates of frequency distributions among other people (see Chapter 13). Here, as elsewhere, social life is so complex, reliable information so limited, and the range of personal, interpersonal, and collective experience so narrow that we can safely assume that social perceptions of frequency distributions, the basic mechanism in virtually all reference group phenomena, will always be, in some important respect, pluralistically ignorant.

The close relationship between reference groups and pluralistic ignorance can be made more systematic by subdividing both ingroup ignorance and outgroup ignorance into their associational and aggregate forms. The resulting fourfold classification yields a typology of social error within which the sources and consequences of each type, and of the relations among them, can be analyzed.[5] The need for such a systematic analysis is clear enough, but even a programmatic state-

[5] Within each of these types we would in due course have to distinguish patterns of ignorance involving individuals' relationships to equals, superordinates, and subordinates.

ment to fill the need would go far beyond the scope of this chapter. However, I would like to move toward this goal by examining the badly neglected fact that ingroups often carry out what can be called their cognitive function by contributing inadvertently to the misinformation of their members.

Whatever their historical origins, nearly all patterns of pluralistic ignorance become consequential only within a framework in which the false cognitive beliefs are believed by some members of some ingroup to have credibility among some other members of that same ingroup. For instance, neither "ideological" nor "utopian" ideas, in Mannheim's (1936) sense of the terms, can establish themselves among ingroup members unless this condition obtains. The same condition is necessary for the emergence of cultural phenomena that are *not* necessarily distorted, for example, Marx's class consciousness, Durkheim's collective conscience, and Mead's generalized other. The perceived consensus, however limited, presupposes a process of social validation that presumably vouches for the veracity of the cognitive beliefs. But this validating process is itself open to misperception and may mislead ingroup members about the nature and the extent of their own cognitive consensus.

## Validation of False Beliefs

False ideas become culturally misconstrued as true as a result of the same process of social validation that legitimates other kinds of knowledge. Pluralistic ignorance emerges out of and is maintained through direct and indirect communication in which verisimilitude is displayed, conveyed, and confirmed in the avowed and assumed assent of others presumed competent to judge. Depending on the situation and the specific knowledge deemed relevant, different individuals and groups may do the judging.[6] But in every case their recognized competence derives from membership in different and often conflicting groups, organizations, strata, collectivities, and categories inevitably present within a larger culture. Consequently, although the validating process takes place against a common cultural background, it will reflect the prevailing forms of social differentiation, prestige, and power. These forms provide different perspectives to which the judging individuals can refer themselves in weighing the merits of beliefs to be commonly accepted. Individuals and groups selectively use other individuals and groups as a frame of reference in evaluating the truth of cognitive propositions.

[6]One significant subset of cognitive judges includes "status judges," identified by Merton (1973, p. 460) as those "who are charged with evaluating the quality of role performance in a social system."

This cognitive function is undoubtedly supplied by most human groups in the everyday exercise of social control; and in some cases—courts of law, commissions of inquiry, peer reviews in science, and military intelligence come immediately to mind—it may be the group's primary function. Indeed, the function is so pervasively important that groups, whatever normative and comparative purpose they serve, should be characterized in terms of it.[7] Certainly, for the task of describing and explaining how factual beliefs come to be socially validated, whatever particular groups or categories are immediately involved are accurately designated as *cognitive reference groups*. To be more specific, a cognitive reference group is a referent relied on by individuals to form their cognitive beliefs (Katz 1967, p. 152), in the same way that a normative reference group refers to a group whose norms and values individuals assimilate, and a comparative reference group refers to a group used to make individual and social appraisals.[8]

Cognitive reference groups come into play in two interdependent ways. First, they perform a referential function when they identify the groups (including themselves) and other social and nonsocial phenomena to which particular beliefs are to be imputed. Second, they perform a verificational function by providing types of criteria, evidence, and reasoning to be employed in confirming such imputations. This verificational function can, of course, be carried out only by a group that is believed to possess enough cognitive authority so that its confirming judgment stamps the referential belief as empirically correct. For this reason, membership groups—groups and categories to which individuals objectively belong—are ordinarily important cognitive reference groups. Their authority in cognitive matters is presumed to derive from a common group label, shared experiences, and similar interests. Such cognitive groups generally exert a powerful influence over their members, often leading them to accept as factually true false propositions about their own membership. Just how powerful this influence can be will become more evident when we look at instances in which the majority of ingroup members accept as true a false belief about their group even though the group's majority does not accept the belief as an accurate characterization of themselves as individual members. This exemption principle—what is true of others is not true of me—has the self-validating effect of decreasing the probability that contrary evidence will be recognized.

[7] Including those individuals who may serve the same cognitive function. On reference individuals, role models, and status judges, see Hyman 1975; Merton 1968, 1973; and Chapter 5, herein.

[8] Like normative and comparative reference groups, cognitive reference groups can of course influence nonmembers who adopt its cognitive patterns.

Although it represents an analytically distinct frame of reference, a cognitive reference group may serve other functions, and it will ordinarily be selected on normative grounds within a comparative context involving still other groups. Usually, a given reference group is a single membership group, like a family or work group, simultaneously performing normative and comparative functions for its members and nonmembers, functions that always presuppose, in turn, patterns of common cognitive knowledge. But the point I want to emphasize here is that beliefs—false, accurate, uncertain, or indeterminate—can be socially validated, and therefore certified as culturally true, only through the use of reference groups. For most individuals most of the time, these cognitive reference groups are the ingroups with which they most strongly identify. When this is not the case, the appropriate cognitive reference groups are normatively designated in accordance with ingroup values and practices.

If patterns of pluralistic ignorance achieve their standing as accurate beliefs only through a process of social validation, it is equally true, as I have said, that the validating process itself is often misperceived. For as individuals and groups participate in the process, they may misunderstand what each of them actually believes. When this happens, a set of false beliefs about others may, paradoxically, emerge out of the false estimates of widespread support for those very beliefs. Ingroup members may hold, for example, distorted images of outgroup members largely because they falsely believe most other ingroup members endorse the same stereotypes.[9] What is no less important is that these mistaken estimates of ingroup support may be made both by members who privately subscribe to the outgroup stereotype and by those who do not. In either case, perceived support among ingroup members everywhere plays such a dominant role in the process of validating false cognitive beliefs that its shared misperception is, I believe, the core problem in the study of pluralistic ignorance.

Broadly conceived, this core problem appears whenever social support for a cognitive belief is either overestimated or underestimated. Nearly all distorted images of cognitive consensus are either derived from or are variations on these two related misjudgments, for example, when the perceived consensus is the absolute opposite of the actual or when it is a relative distortion of the magnitude of support for majority or minority views (Korte 1972). These and related misconceptions largely result from misperceptions of similarities and dif-

---

[9] What ingroup members believe about themselves is the ultimate cognitive authority for what they believe about nonmembers. The latter is a special case of the former in the sense that conceptions of others outside of the group are formulated and validated within the overall belief system of the ingroup.

ferences. The beliefs of those to whom individuals look for guidance and support, their cognitive reference groups, are thought to be more similar or more dissimilar to the individuals' own beliefs than they in fact are. As significant as these patterns of misperceived similarity and dissimilarity are, both can reflect, as we shall see, the same and a more far-reaching ingroup error, a collective miscalculation shared by these otherwise divergent perceptions.

Ingroup errors are, as already noted, often associated with judgmental heuristics and individual defense mechanisms. But such psychologically distorting processes are, by and large, apt to have limited social consequences unless activated and reinforced by properties of the surrounding social system.[10] Furthermore, and quite apart from the interlocking of psychological and social mechanisms, specific cultural and structural characteristics of the social context usually play an independent and critical role in shaping the accuracy with which the prevailing cognitive consensus is perceived. Among these characteristics, two of the most significant are the cultural *values* of the participants and the *visibility* of the social structure in which the participants are differentially located. Both are significant determinants of shared beliefs because they direct attention toward some features of the social environment and away from others and thereby control access to important information regarding what those in the environment are doing, thinking, and feeling. Values and visibility, like their parental concepts of culture and social structure, are often difficult to disentangle empirically. Analytically, however, they are distinct, and they need to be examined separately in order to understand how, as components of the validation process, they contribute together to a systematic distortion of the social environment. For the purpose of this present analysis, my primary concern is with the ways in which cultural values facilitate the formation of false cognitive beliefs among ingroup members.[11]

## Values and False Beliefs

The relationship between values and cognitive beliefs has been of long-standing interest in the social sciences. Although there is consid-

[10] As Ross, Greene, and House (1977) pointed out some years ago, the tendency to overestimate similarity between ourselves and others does not itself lead to error. Much depends on the context and whether, for example, we happen to be part of a minority or the majority in that context, a point clearly documented in Sanders and Mullen 1983.

[11] My discussion may be viewed as complementing the structural analysis of visibility and pluralistic ignorance found in the work of Wheeler (1961) and Cloward (1959) and derived from Merton's (1968) theory of visibility.

erable variation in how the concepts have been defined and used, Weber's (1949) comments on the differences between value judgments and empirical statements of fact are particularly pertinent to my concerns in this paper. Values may be said to denote states of affairs or goals that are considered to be socially *desirable,* preferential frameworks within which interests are forged. Cognitive beliefs, on the other hand, refer to social conceptions of what actually *exists,* that is, socially perceived facts. Each constitutes a component of a culture and is shared by a number of individuals. The reciprocal relationship between the two is generally acknowledged as a matter of course. Values are irrelevant unless there are facts to which they apply, and facts cannot be identified apart from values. Each presupposes the other. Most of the interest in the relationship, however, has centered on the ways in which cultural values influence social definitions of facts. This preoccupation with the shaping of facts by cultural preferences has characterized investigations of the place of empirical knowledge in everyday life and the validity of scholarly and scientific research. In both cases, the dominant orientation has been the distortion of cognition by one or another value, frequently with specific attention to the hypothesis that the distortions benefit those individuals, groups, and strata who support the values. Briefly put, cognitive beliefs—so-called facts—defend, support, justify, or, more generally, rationalize the values of those who accept the beliefs as accurate. This cognitive rationalization hypothesis, regardless of its particular expression in the writings of any one thinker like Marx, Mannheim, Pareto, Sumner, Myrdal, or Tajfel, to cite only a few who come to mind, plainly suggests that cultural values are a major source of pluralistic ignorance.

I say "suggests" because, except for Myrdal (1944) and Tajfel (1981), these and other scholars who have addressed the issue of false ideas rarely draw and maintain the distinction between value and belief. They also have little to say about situations where individuals or groups with *different* or *conflicting* values share the same cognitive beliefs. In addition, and more important, most of them, perhaps because of their concern with distortions, virtually ignore the otherwise undeniable relationship between values and truth. That is, undistorted cognitive beliefs also clearly reflect the influence of values. People put a high value on knowing accurately what is existentially going on in their natural and social worlds, even if such beliefs turn out to be inconsistent with some of their other cherished values. And nowhere in the seemingly countless descriptions of false beliefs has anyone seriously proposed that shared cognitive distortions known to be false are consciously and intentionally formulated and validated by their believers to deceive themselves.[12] It is precisely for these reasons that pluralistic ignorance presents such intriguing problems; it occurs among those who put a premium on correct knowledge. If cultural values do distort cognitive beliefs in such a way as to benefit those who endorse those values, they can do so only in a context where accurate cognitive beliefs are valued and where the distorted beliefs are misconstrued as true. But how can this happen?

I want to approach the question by looking at one specific but fundamental version of the cognitive rationalization hypothesis, namely, the degree to which it applies to the perception of ingroup support for important cultural values. To be more explicit, to what extent does a value (or set of values) influence the degree to which that value is attributed by ingroup members to other ingroup members? This is the core of the rationalization hypothesis because it is unlikely that cognitive beliefs that seemed to support a set of values could be seriously considered unless, as I pointed out, some ingroup support was anticipated by those initially espousing them. But, if the hypothesis is true, this would apply to the perception of social support itself; and the perception of that support would probably be overestimated by those holding the values in the first place. There is considerable evidence that this is in fact the case. Thus, one major reason why people's values influence their cognitive knowledge is that they overestimate the number of others who hold their values. This may seem plain, but what is equally true, but certainly far from obvious, is that overestimates of social support for certain values are also made by those who do *not* endorse those values. What is especially ironic is that this distortion of support for a set of values by individuals who do not hold them helps indirectly to validate those very values by providing perceived support for those who do endorse them.

It is important to recognize that the pattern just described is a special case of the cognitive rationalization hypothesis. The general claim is, to repeat, that the values individuals hold influence their cognitive beliefs in such a way as to justify support for those values. But now we are considering the particular case where those same values are being strengthened, as it were, through the misperception of those who do *not* share them. What they do share with those who support the values is the mistaken idea that the values have widespread support. In this sense, their perception—their cognitive beliefs—conforms with the views of the misperceived majority. That individuals may be unduly swayed by what others think and do, especially the majority, has been

[12]Though, to judge by Allport's summary (1985, pp. 9–10) of his work, Felix Le Dantec's *L'Egoisme* (1918) represents a close approximation.

of profound concern to many students of social life. But it was the insight that this influence may result more from faulty perception than from group pressure that led to the discovery of pluralistic ignorance by Floyd H. Allport. And it was his conjecture that the mistaken beliefs of many individuals will lead them to conform to a set of norms or values neither they nor the presumed majority support that initiated the study of pluralistic ignorance as a distinctive line of inquiry (O'Gorman 1986).

Allport's conjecture has, of course, been developed over the years as a plausible explanation for discrimination against blacks by whites, many of whom, it is argued, are simply conforming to what they consider to be white majority values rather than their personal preferences (Pettigrew 1976, p. 487). This line of reasoning rests on the presumed value of reference group conformity and assumes falsely, as we shall see, that whites are reasonably accurate in knowing the racial values of other whites. For my purposes, however, Allport's insight about misperceiving others is more relevant than his conjecture because it raises serious difficulties about the relevance of cognitive rationalization for an understanding of pluralistic ignorance. Although it may be true that individuals who endorse certain values are often likely to hold distorted beliefs consistent with their preferences, that in no way explains why those same distorted beliefs are accepted by others who reject or do not adopt those values. The same difficulty emerges if we turn from the cultural level and consider values and beliefs from a social psychological point of view.

The social psychological literature on social perception contains ample evidence substantiating the expectation implied by the cognitive rationalization hypothesis, namely, that individuals will tend to overestimate support for their values among others like themselves. A number of findings consistently show that individuals tend to perceive others as being very much like themselves (Fields and Schuman 1976–77; Granberg 1984; Holmes 1968; Kassin 1979; Ross and Fletcher 1985; Ross, Greene, and House 1977). This egocentric bias often results in what is sometimes referred to as a self-generated consensus. The perceived similarity is understood, however, in terms that seem to play down personal preferences reflecting cultural values. The perceived homophily between self and others is explained on the grounds, first, that individuals assume that their behavior and views are primarily a reaction to, and in that sense induced by, the external environment rather than by their personal dispositions; and second, that because the environment rather than individual traits is perceived as the cause, they believe that others will react as they do

(Kassin 1979). Thus, individuals who endorse a particular value are apt to see it as a realistic preference imposed by environmental restraints and, therefore, impute the value to others as a reasonable reaction to some specific external situation. Or, to put this last point more accurately, individuals who hold a given value in a given situation are more apt than those who do not to impute that value to others whom they generally perceive as reacting like themselves. This is, of course, just what the cognitive rationalization hypothesis would, on somewhat different grounds, predict. The cognitive belief that others share my value certainly supports the importance I impute to the value and makes them seem more like me; and those who share the value with me are more likely than those who do not to believe that others also share the value. From this point of view, the cognitive belief defends the value, as Tajfel (1981) so often noted, by marshaling perceived support for it.

There is little doubt that under some conditions the egocentric bias operates to influence the impact of values on cognitions. But, as I have said, it does not explain situations in which individuals impute values they do *not* hold to others, a serious omission related to other problems with an egocentric interpretation. The most important other difficulty is the failure to take into account the interpersonal and intergroup context involving others. Though the egocentric bias sometimes produces distorted cognitive beliefs, it also generates accurate conceptions in any context where individuals happen to be part of the majority (Sanders and Mullen 1983). Which pattern will in fact appear depends primarily not on the bias but on the extent to which others objectively share the experiences of the egocentric individuals. In addition, it does not provide conceptual room for individuals' perception of the social and historical context that they share with others. Without this contextual information, there is no way to account for the fact that individuals attribute values to others that they themselves do not hold. In short, as relevant as the egocentric bias is, it is, like the pattern of cognitive rationalization, neither a necessary nor a sufficient condition for a state of pluralistic ignorance. Since this is basically an empirical claim, we need to examine it in the light of empirical evidence directly relating values to cognitive beliefs. To make this assessment I will review data from a cluster of studies of white perceptions of white racial values and estimates made by the aged of the serious personal problems among the elderly. I will proceed on the assumption that whites and the elderly are important ingroups and cognitive reference groups for whites and the elderly in matters pertaining to race and old age, respectively.

## Perceived White Segregationist Support

Let me begin the assessment by looking at patterns involving individuals who hold *different* values and explore how differentials in cultural preferences influence cognitive beliefs. The case of whites' perception of the degree to which the value of strict racial segregation is supported by most other whites is an unusually important example. Without in any way implying the absurd idea that widespread patterns of racial prejudice and discrimination no longer prevail as compelling elements in American life, it is nonetheless true that white support for the *principle* of racial segregation has markedly declined in the past several decades (Schuman, Steeh, and Bobo 1985; see also Chapters 15 and 16, herein). Forty years ago most whites, northerners and southerners, openly advocated a racial policy of rigorous segregation. In the subsequent decades, that racial preference lost nearly all of its public and most of its private support. Whatever reservations whites may harbor about implementing interracial practices in specific settings, and whatever the magnitude of residual segregationist sentiment may be, relatively few whites in the society at large, or in major segments of the population, now assign a high value to the principle of strict racial segregation.

Despite this significant cultural change, the cumulative evidence indicates that whites are in fact more racially liberal than they think other whites are, that whites in general grossly overestimate the degree to which strict segregation as a principle is still supported by other whites. This "conservative bias," as it is sometimes called, was first detected by Katz and Allport in 1931 in their pioneering study of pluralistic ignorance among Syracuse University students. Many fraternity members, they discovered, overestimated the opposition of other members to admitting blacks and certain other types of students to their fraternities. Subsequently, the overestimation of white segregationist support was reported in 1947 among white department store managers in New York City with reference to their white customers (Saenger and Gilbert 1950); in 1957 among white members of a segregated Protestant congregation in the South with reference to other members of the congregation (Breed and Ktsanes 1961); among white residents of New Orleans in 1958 (Breed and Ktsanes 1961); among white residents of Detroit in 1969 with reference to most other whites in their cities (Fields and Schuman 1976–77); and in 1969 among white residents of Detroit with reference to other whites in their neighborhoods (Fields 1971).

This pattern of exaggerating white segregationist strength was not restricted to these circumscribed samples. The same conservative bias appeared in national sample surveys conducted in 1968, 1970, and 1972 among white respondents with reference to "most other whites in their areas" (O'Gorman 1975, 1979; O'Gorman with Garry 1976–77). In each of these studies the research design employed enabled investigators to gauge objectively the prevailing magnitude of white segregationist support and to compare it with white respondents' subjective estimates of that support. One of the most impressive things about the conservative bias is that it appears to be largely unaffected by important demographic variables. For example, in the three national surveys, white support for strict racial segregation was greatly exaggerated in every major region of the country, in large and small communities, by men and by women, by young and old and rich and poor, regardless of religion or political party affiliation and irrespective of marital status and occupation. Most surprising of all, this distorted belief was unaffected by formal education. To be sure, the better-educated whites were less likely to favor segregation than other whites, but they, too, overestimated by far white segregationist strength (O'Gorman 1975, 1979).

Although Katz and Allport explicitly addressed the implications of their data on pluralistic ignorance for American race relations in general, neither they nor most later investigators considered the possible effects of white values on their distorted beliefs. This effect became plainly evident in the analyses of the 1968, 1970, and 1972 national survey data showing the distortion of the degree of white segregationist support to be systematically influenced by the racial values held by whites themselves. The finding in each of the surveys was simple, straightforward, and monotonic. The more closely whites endorsed the value of strict racial segregation, the more likely they were to claim that most other whites around them favored segregation; and, conversely, the more whites leaned toward favoring racial desegregation, the less likely they were to believe that most whites in their communities were segregationists. Further, the finding remained unimpaired when relevant control variables, including education, were introduced into the analysis. If these data show that individuals' values affect their cognitive beliefs about other individuals' values, they clearly did *not* eliminate the original finding. In each of the three surveys, regardless of their racial values, whites greatly overestimated the prevailing strength of white segregationist support. The grossest relative errors were made by white segregationists themselves, who, though they everywhere constituted a small minority, overwhelmingly and incorrectly thought of themselves as part of the white majority. On the other hand, although whites in favor of desegregation gave the lowest estimates of segregationists' support, their estimates were still unrealistically high, though nowhere near as high as those of the small segregationist minority. Estimates of white segregationist support provided by whites who favored some sort of racial compromise between integration and segregation were appropriately higher than those of the desegregationists and lower than those of the segregationists; but they were still, compared to the actual distribution of white values, seriously exaggerated. In brief, whites with different racial preferences subscribe more or less to the same collective error. If the distorting power of values is unmistakable in these findings, so is the distinctive power of a shared false belief sustained by markedly different values.

## Perceiving the Problems of the Elderly

The distinctive character of pluralistic ignorance can also be demonstrated by exploring the effect of values on cognitive beliefs among those who, although they share the *same* values, encounter varying degrees of difficulty in realizing them. Whatever other functions they perform, values give meaning to life because they define problems worth attending to. Consequently, when individuals express concern over a serious problem, an important value is invariably implicated. Normally, it is the perceived discrepancy between a cognitive belief regarding an existing state of affairs and the desired state that constitutes the problem; and, other things being equal, the greater the perceived discrepancy, the more severe the problem is judged to be.[13] In this sense, the identification of a serious problem activates and makes salient a given value, and the more serious it is judged to be, the greater its priority compared to other values. In this sense, the subjective assessment of individuals' own personal problems should provide a key to how salient a particular value happens to be. For example, among adult members of the population we would assume that, though all would place a value on some minimal level of good health, the salience of that value would be greater among those with severe medical problems than among others. If this reasoning is correct, the hypotheses of cognitive rationalization and egocentric imputations should apply to individuals for whom the same value has differential salience. That is to say, among those evaluating their personal problems, the more serious individuals judge their own problems to be, the more likely they should be to impute that degree of

---

[13] This is, of course, essentially the same process through which social problems are diagnosed (Merton 1976).

severity to others like themselves. But, and more to the point, we should still find widespread patterns of pluralistic ignorance that remain beyond the explanatory reach of either hypothesis.

These expectations are systematically confirmed in the analysis of data from two national sample surveys of elderly and nonelderly respondents conducted in 1974 and 1981 (O'Gorman 1980, 1985). In both studies respondents were asked, among other things, to assess the seriousness of problems in their own lives. Most of the problems— for example, lack of money, poor health, and fear of crime—reflect values that most adults of all ages share: financial security, good health, and personal safety. The respondents were also asked to judge the severity of these same problems in the lives of "most people over 65 in this country today." Both studies showed that the proportion of elderly respondents reporting very serious problems in their own lives ranged from 3 to 23 percent in 1974 and from 5 to 25 percent in 1981 and that in both years the distribution of self-reported difficulties among the aged was similar to the distribution of those under sixty-five years of age. The findings make it clear that the overwhelming majority of the aged did *not* see themselves as facing such serious problems; and there is good reason to believe that the self-evaluations were reasonably accurate (O'Gorman 1980).

In sharp contrast to these patterns of self-reports, the perception of very serious problems among most other aged by these aged respondents revealed quite a different picture. They grossly overestimated the difficulties faced by most other elderly people. More specifically, the proportions of the aged who characterized each of the problems as very serious for most people over sixty-five exceeded by far the proportions of the same respondents who described each problem as very serious in their lives. What is more relevant for this discussion is that in both studies the self-reports of the elderly were related monotonically to their perceptions of others: The more serious they thought a problem to be for them personally, the more likely they were to characterize that problem as very serious for the majority of the aged. Thus, the personal salience of a value, as indicated by their self-assessment, shaped their cognitive beliefs concerning others in the same age stratum. And the tendency to make egocentric imputations to the majority also varied with self-assessment: The more serious respondents considered their own problems to be, the more they egocentrically assumed that they were like most other aged. However, and for us this is again the significant finding, most of the elderly respondents, regardless of their perception of their personal problems, greatly overestimated the presence of very serious problems among the majority of the aged. In other words, the patterns of pluralistic ignorance persisted irrespective of the salience of respondents' values and regardless of their tendency to make egocentric attributions. And this remained true when a number of important control variables like age, sex, education, race, and income were introduced.

My contention that pluralistic ignorance cannot be assimilated into phenomena addressed by the cognitive rationalization and egocentric hypotheses rests mainly on the pivotal finding that values were falsely imputed to ingroup members by other members of the group who did *not* themselves endorse those values. Given the widely held, largely intuitive, and traditionally unexamined assumption that ingroup members are accurately informed about their own kind (Allport 1937, p. 514), this empirical regularity seems strikingly at odds with common knowledge and professional wisdom. The disparity seems great enough to make us somewhat suspicious about the validity of the generalization. Are the specific findings incorporated into the empirical generalization valid? The question deserves more than a passing comment, and not only because it raises the always serious issue of spuriousness. In this instance, the source of the potential spuriousness is a cultural *value* that is often the cause of actions that misinform observers about actors' predispositions. This link betwen spuriousness and pluralistic ignorance is worth our attention as a substantive problem in its own right.

The principal reason for suspecting spuriousness is that the questions used in the interviews about racial values and personal problems could have prompted respondents to give socially desirable and self-serving answers. For example, it can be argued that the reported distribution of white values is not accurate because many whites with genuine racist sentiments were reluctant to express openly their preferences which, they think, are no longer socially approved. As a result, they give what they believe to be the proper, nonsegregationist reply and then impute their true segregationist values to most other whites. Basically, the same argument can be offered to question the relevant data about the elderly. Assuming that the acknowledgment to an interviewer of a severe personal problem could threaten their self-esteem, many of the aged respondents may have been reluctant to convey how serious their personal problems actually were. Instead, they may have given a less threatening answer by reporting the absence of serious personal problems and then imputed their true condition to most other aged people. In both lines of research, then, the survey results may not have reflected accurately the racial values or the problems of the respondents. If this line of reasoning is correct, then the conclusion that the data constitute evidence that individuals attribute values they personally do not endorse to other group members must be false.

This criticism raises an important possibility. The missing test factor alluded to, the potential source of the spuriousness, refers to an important value: the desire of respondents to answer questions in a normatively proper way. The interview situation may have posed for some of them a common dilemma: how to tell the truth without losing face, their own or others? At one time or another most of us have probably tried to resolve the dilemma by honoring in our visible behavior one salient value while masking, through temporary inattention, other equally significant values. The value of acting appropriately often calls forth instrumental and expressive actions that are inconsistent with other values. Such value-induced, or situationally provoked, actions commonly mislead others about actors' actual values and other dispositions. False cognitive beliefs easily emerge when individuals engage in verbal and nonverbal behavior that is intended by them to appear desirable to themselves and others but, when done effectively, has the effect of misinforming others. The problem of spuriousness is as pervasive in everyday meanings, conventions, and practices as it is in survey or experimental research.

There are several significant reasons for doubting that the research findings under discussion are spurious. In the first place, some respondents obviously reported openly their support for strict racial segregation or the fact that they were experiencing very serious personal problems. Second, the expressed racial values and the assessment of personal problems were consistent with other characteristics of the respondents and could have been predicted on the basis of many other studies. For example, those respondents who favored strict segregation were more likely to come from the South, to be older, and to have less education than others in the sample; among the elderly, those reporting very serious personal problems in their lives were more likely than other aged respondents to have low incomes, little education, and to be black or Hispanic. Third, if a substantial proportion of the respondents were masking their own preferences and problems by imputing them to most others, it is highly unlikely that the relationship between values and beliefs would take the form it did. Recall that the closer white respondents came to personally endorsing segregation, the more they were apt to believe that most other whites were also segregationists; and the more the elderly respondents reported severe personal problems, the more they imputed such problems to the majority of the aged. In both cases the relationship was monotonic. And in both cases it was those who gave the presumably socially desirable response in characterizing themselves—the whites in favor of desegregation and the aged with no self-reported serious problems—who were the *least* likely to project their values or condition onto the majority. Since this pattern was found repeatedly in all of the surveys referred to, it is consistently inconsistent with the possibility that the data were primarily the result of dissembling and projecting.

Finally, it is worth noting that the data I have cited to document the widespread pluralistic ignorance among white and elderly ingroups are similar to and consistent with complementary data on outgroup ignorance among blacks and the nonelderly. Blacks, like whites, overestimate white segregationist strength; but because of their value commitment to desegregation, their estimates are ironically lower than those of most whites (O'Gorman 1979). And similarly, the nonelderly, like the aged, overestimate the problems of the aged, and the extent of these overestimates by the nonelderly also varies with the severity of their own self-assessed personal problems (O'Gorman 1985). It seems highly improbable and implausible that blacks were projecting their "true" segregationist values to most whites or that the young and the middle-aged were disguising the "real" nature of their own personal difficulties in the form of their attributions to the aged.

It is, however, the findings pertaining to ingroup ignorance that are our prime concern. The analysis just presented allows us to draw three reasonable inferences. First, regarding the degree of perceived white support for strict racial segregation and the estimated severity of problems facing the elderly, a pervasive state of pluralistic ignorance was found among members of the ingroups involved. Whites overestimated white segregationist strength, and the elderly overestimated the seriousness of older people's problems. Second, these distorted cognitive beliefs were systematically related to the racial values explicitly endorsed by whites and to the values reflected in the self-reported problems of the aged. Individuals were more apt to attribute their values or problems to most others if they themselves favored the value of strict segregation or confronted very serious personal problems than if they did not. These empirical patterns clearly confirmed the hypotheses based on cognitive rationalization and egocentric imputations; and the patterns held for values that were not shared by everyone and those that were.

Third, and most important of all, the two cognitive distortions were found throughout the samples *regardless* of the racial values or personal problems of the white and the aged respondents. The fact that pluralistic ignorance was found as a persistent and pervasive set of false beliefs among ingroup members who held *different* values and experienced *different* degrees of personal difficulties means that it cannot be assimilated to processes of cognitive rationalization or egocentric bias. As important as they are, these processes are, to repeat, neither necessary nor sufficient for the emergence of pluralistic ignorance.

These inferences about pluralistic ignorance, and the findings on which they are based, would not have emerged without the idea of a cognitive reference group. It was this specific concept that led us to investigate the accuracy of ingroup members' cognitive assessment of other members. As we reported, not only are there conditions under which ingroup members are seriously inaccurate in their judgments of their own ingroup. These inaccurate beliefs provide, in addition, a cognitive frame of reference such that the majority incorrectly impute to the majority characteristics they correctly do not apply to themselves. The finding may seem unusual, but it is not uncommon, even among smaller and more cohesive groups (Fields 1971; Toch and Klofas 1984); and its significance is not lessened by knowing that there are undoubtedly cognitive frameworks conducive to more veridical judgments. The point is that the finding brings to mind how little we know regarding the accuracy of the kind of cognitive knowledge that we all assume to be one of the prerequisites of social life. It also strongly suggests that further work in reference group theory and research would benefit if more explicit systematic attention were paid to cognitive reference groups.

## Conclusion

To study the conditions inhibiting and facilitating the emergence and maintenance of pluralistic ignorance is an urgent sociological problem. To acknowledge this problem sociologists need to recognize that these patterns of shared false beliefs are not simply another form of human error. They are, I contend, worth investigating on their own distinctive merits and within the context of cognitive reference groups. Assuming that this is true, I will conclude this discussion with several observations that, I think, future investigators of pluralistic ignorance ought to bear in mind.

To begin with, the specific empirical work used in this paper to illustrate my major points needs to be replicated. I obviously do not know, for example, what new studies would reveal about current perceptions of white racial values or problems of the aged. Equally important, I have not attempted to explain the reported patterns of collective ignorance. As matters now stand, there is no adequate explanation of why whites should so persistently overestimate white segregationist support in the face of the well-documented and important shift in the racial climate, or why so many elderly should exaggerate the severity of problems faced by most other aged. Undoubtedly, there is some tendency for misconceptions to emerge when older and once accurate beliefs fail to take into account new patterns of social change (Breed and Ktsanes 1961); and undoubtedly these misconceptions are reported in the mass media and crystallized in public opinion (Katz 1982; Noelle-Neumann 1984). However, social changes are often reflected accurately in both public knowledge and the mass media so that this cognitive lag interpretation needs to be supplemented with other explanations. Let me suggest one hypothesis. Both white segregationists and elderly people with severe personal problems constitute very small minorities *relatively* speaking but include very large numbers in *absolute* terms in a historical setting where treatment of blacks and the aged are culturally salient issues. In such a context, the absolute size of minorities, their views and problems, become *highly visible* to themselves and others and, so magnified, are more likely to become part of the public agenda. In short, I suspect that in any social situation where specific central values activate certain issues the characteristics of a relevant minority are apt to be mistaken for the majority whenever their absolute numbers make them a more visible presence than their relative position would otherwise warrant.

In any event, whatever theoretical framework turns out to be satisfactory, there is no doubt that an important phenomenon exists and needs to be explained. The findings regarding perceptions of racial values and severity of personal difficulties are, of course, substantively important as applied problems, but I have used them primarily to draw attention to pluralistic ignorance as a reference group phenomenon that requires serious sociological attention. Furthermore, in a volume honoring Professor Hyman, whose name is justly associated with survey research, it is especially worth noting that the logic and techniques of sample survey research were directly responsible both for the discovery of pluralistic ignorance and for much of the relevant data subsequently accumulated (O'Gorman 1986). The phenomenon, of course, was known before it was discovered, as Tocqueville's (1955, p. 155) analysis of the public's perception of the Catholic Church in eighteenth-century France shows. Tocqueville's diagnosis also serves to remind us that descriptions and measurements of pluralistic ignorance do not require the use of survey research. In fact, one of the more promising research developments for examining false beliefs is a procedure for studying in an experimental design the minimal conditions needed for the manifestation of behavior associated with ingroup membership (Tajfel 1970). For my purposes, the most compelling finding to emerge out of this line of work is the fact that, within a quasi-experimental setting, members of small ingroups discriminate against members of small outgroups not because of their own preferences but in deference to their mistaken views of what other ingroup members are doing (Allen and Wilder 1975).

As this pertinent finding illustrates, in small, artificial, and transitory ingroups, just as in their larger, more realistic, and more lasting counterparts, pluralistic ignorance is frequently implicated in reference group processes. How then do we explain the failure over the years to perceive and explore the link between these processes and ingroup ignorance? Part of the failure is, I am convinced, due to the general neglect of pluralistic ignorance. But our orientation to reference group problems is also to blame. The most distinctive notion associated with reference group theory and research is the simple idea that individuals are influenced positively and negatively by groups to which they do not belong (Singer 1981). Once made explicit, this idea, which then manages to be both "obvious" and "counterintuitive," leads us to inquire about the mechanisms through which individuals acquire information regarding groups to which they do not belong. This is of course an important question, but it inadvertently leaves unexamined the assumption that such individuals already are competently informed about the groups to which they do belong. Perhaps we have been unwittingly applying an empirical principle of cognitive charity, analogous to the philosophers' methodological principle of charity (Davidson 1980). That is, we may have simply taken for granted that ingroup members in order to employ their common membership class must assume that they accurately know what their classmates think, do, and feel. The assumption, we now know, is untenable, and it is surely time to return to inquiries concerning precisely how accurate group members are in perceiving the characteristics of the reference groups to which they objectively belong or with which they subjectively identify. Certainly, we should not be surprised to discover that, among group members, the extent of pluralistic ignorance about their own ingroups is closely related to their pluralistic ignorance of other, more distant, positive and negative reference groups. We may in due course learn that pluralistic ignorance, like charity, begins at home.

## Bibliography

Allen, Vernon L., and David A. Wilder. 1975. Categorization, belief similarity, and intergroup discrimination. *Journal of Personality and Social Psychology* 32:971–77.
Allport, Gordon. 1937. *Personality*. New York: Holt.
———. 1985. The historical background of social psychology. In Gardner

Lindzey and Elliot Aronson, eds., *Handbook of social psychology*, 1 : 1–46. New York: Random House.

Breed, Warren, and Thomas Ktsanes. 1961. Pluralistic ignorance in the process of public opinion formation. *Public Opinion Quarterly* 25:382–92.

Cloward, Richard A. 1959. Social control and anomie. Doctoral dissertation, Columbia University.

Davidson, Donald. 1980. *Essays on actions and events.* New York: Oxford University Press.

Davis, James A. 1963. Intellectual climates in 135 American colleges and universities. *Sociology of Education* 37:110–28.

Fields, James M. 1971. Perceptions of others' opinions in a city and its neighborhoods. Doctoral dissertation, University of Michigan.

Fields, James M., and Howard Schuman. 1976–1977. Public beliefs about the beliefs of the public. *Public Opinion Quarterly* 40:427–48.

Granberg, Donald. 1984. Attributing attitudes to members of groups. In J. Richard Eiser, ed., *Attitudinal judgment*, pp. 85–108. New York: Springer-Verlag.

Holmes, David S. 1968. Dimensions of projection. *Psychological Bulletin* 69: 248–68.

Kahneman, Daniel, Paul Slovic, and Amos Tversky. 1982. *Judgment under uncertainty: Heuristics and biases.* Cambridge: Cambridge University Press.

Kassin, Saul M. 1979. Consensus information, prediction, and causal attribution: A review of the literature and issues. *Journal of Personality and Social Psychology* 37:1966–81.

Katz, Daniel. 1967. The practice and potential of survey methods in psychological research. In Charles Y. Glock, ed., *Survey research in the social sciences*, pp. 145–215. New York: Russell Sage Foundation.

Katz, Daniel, and Floyd H. Allport. 1931. *Student attitudes.* Syracuse, N.Y.: Craftsman Press.

Katz, Elihu. 1982. Publicity and pluralistic ignorance. In Horst Baier, Hans Mathias Kepplinger, and Kurt Reumann, eds., *Offenliche Meinung und sozialer Wandel: Für Elisabeth Noelle-Neumann*, pp. 28–38. Wiesbaden: Westdeutscher Verlag.

Korte, Charles. 1972. Pluralistic ignorance about student radicalism. *Sociometry* 35:576–87.

Le Dantec, Felix. 1918. *L'Egoisme: Seul base de toute societé.* Paris: Flammarion.

Mannheim, Karl. 1936. *Ideology and utopia: An introduction to the sociology of knowledge.* New York: Harcourt Brace.

Merton, Robert K. 1968. *Social theory and social structure.* Enlarged ed. New York: Free Press.

———. 1973. *The sociology of science: Theoretical and empirical investigations.* Chicago: University of Chicago Press.

———. 1976. The sociology of social problems. In Robert K. Merton and Robert Nisbet, eds., *Contemporary social problems*, pp. 3–43. New York: Harcourt Brace Jovanovich.

Myrdal, Gunnar. 1944. *An American dilemma: The Negro problem and modern democracy.* Vols. 1 and 2. New York: Harper.

Noelle-Neumann, Elisabeth. 1984. *The spiral of silence: Public opinion—our social skin.* Chicago: University of Chicago Press.

O'Gorman, Hubert J. 1975. Pluralistic ignorance and white estimates of white support for racial segregation. *Public Opinion Quarterly* 39:313–30.

———. 1979. White and black perceptions of racial values. *Public Opinion Quarterly* 43:48–59.

———. 1980. False consciousness of kind: Pluralistic ignorance among the aged. *Research on Aging* 2:105–28.

———. 1985. Pluralistic ignorance and false consciousness of kind: The impact of perceived personal problems on the perception of others' problems. Paper presented to the 55th Annual Meeting of the Eastern Sociological Society, March 17, Philadelphia.

———. 1986. The discovery of pluralistic ignorance. *Journal of the History of the Behavioral Sciences* 22:333–47.

O'Gorman, Hubert J., with Stephen L. Garry. 1976–1977. Pluralistic ignorance: A replication and extension. *Public Opinion Quarterly* 40:1–19.

Pettigrew, Thomas F. 1976. Race and intergroup relations. In Robert K. Merton and Robert Nisbet, eds., *Contemporary social problems*, pp. 459–508. 4th ed. New York: Harcourt Brace Jovanovich.

Ross, Lee, David Greene, and Pamela House. 1977. The "false consensus" effect: An egocentric bias in social perception and attribution processes. *Journal of Experimental Social Psychology* 13:279–301.

Ross, Michael, and Garth J. O. Fletcher. 1985. Attribution and social perception. In Gardner Lindzey and Elliot Aronson, eds., *Handbook of social psychology*, 2:73–122. New York: Random House.

Saenger, Gerhart, and Emily Gilbert. 1950. Customer reactions to the integration of Negro sales personnel. *International Journal of Opinion and Attitude Research* 4:57–76.

Sanders, Glenn S., and Brian Mullen. 1983. Accuracy of perceptions of consensus: Differential tendencies of people with majority and minority positions. *European Journal of Social Psychology* 13:57–70.

Schanck, Richard L. 1932. A study of a community and its groups and institutions conceived of as behaviors of individuals. *Psychological Monographs* 43, no. 195.

Schuman, Howard, Charlotte Steeh, and Lawrence Bobo. 1985. *Racial attitudes in America: Trends and interpretations.* Cambridge, Mass.: Harvard University Press.

Simmel, Georg. 1950. *The sociology of Georg Simmel.* Glencoe, Ill.: Free Press.

Singer, Eleanor. 1981. Reference groups and social evaluations. In Morris Rosenberg and Ralph H. Turner, eds., *Social psychology: Sociological perspectives*, pp. 66–93. New York: Basic Books.

Tajfel, Henri. 1970. Experiments in intergroup discrimination. *Scientific American* 223:96–102.

———. 1981. *Human groups and social categories.* Cambridge: Cambridge University Press.

Taylor, D. Garth. 1982. Pluralistic ignorance and the spiral of silence: A formal analysis. *Public Opinion Quarterly* 46:311–35.

Toch, Hans, and John Klofas. 1984. Pluralistic ignorance, revisited. In G. M. Stephenson and J. H. Davis, eds., *Progress in applied social psychology*, 2: 129–59. New York: Wiley.

Tocqueville, Alexis de. 1955. The old regime and the French Revolution. Garden City, N.Y.: Doubleday (Anchor Books).

Turner, Ralph, and Lewis M. Killian. 1972. *Collective behavior.* 2nd ed. Englewood Cliffs, N.J.: Prentice-Hall.

Weber, Max. 1949. *The methodology of the social sciences.* Glencoe, Ill.: Free Press.

———. 1968. *Economy and society.* 3 vols. Totowa, N.J.: Bedminster Press.

Wheeler, Stanton. 1961. Role conflict in correctional communities. In Donald R. Cressey, ed., *The prison,* pp. 229–59. New York: Holt, Rinehart and Winston.

## Robert K. Merton

## 7 Reference Groups, Invisible Colleges, and Deviant Behavior in Science[*]

I begin this occasion of his retirement from the established routines of university life by welcoming my esteemed friend, Herbert Hyman, into the venerable ranks of, shall we say, mature middle age. I bear witness, Herb, that most of what we were told about these years turns out to be thoroughly misleading. All those rumors one heard about the inevitable terrors and miseries of advanced age evidently derive from the provincial belief system of an exceedingly youth-centered society. In any case, don't believe half of what you've been told about these oncoming years of your full maturity. This can be said, without a trace of hubris: Just stay well, give accessible possibilities a decent chance, and you will find that, truly, what's past is still prologue. I can report to you from the vantage point located well into an eighth decade that, given that indispensable condition of being in reasonably good health, these are not merely endurable days. Often enough, they are interesting, even captivating days as freedom from the time schedules imposed by organizational life makes for sustained periods of relaxed concentration in which one can do precisely what one most wants to do. Work can be continuous for long stretches of time, rather

 *This paper was presented in honor of Professor Herbert H. Hyman, May 15, 1984, on the grand and amiable occasion signaling his retirement from the faculty of Wesleyan University. (At the request of Helen Hyman, these cheerful opening paragraphs remain intact, just as they were read far too soon before his death.)

 Aid from the MacArthur Foundation and the Macy Foundation in the preparation of parts of this paper is thankfully acknowledged. The section on "Fraud and Other Deviant Behaviors in Science," a sociological reprise of the papers composing part 4 of Merton 1973, is largely reprinted from "Scientific Fraud and the Fight to Be First," *The Times Literary Supplement*, November 2, 1984, with the kind permission of *The Times Literary Supplement*, London.

than subject to the interruptions of organizational life. Then comes the joy of relaxed concentration—so different from the lesser joy of concentrated relaxation. There's nothing else quite like it.

As Herbert Hyman looks forward to the next phase of his diversely fruitful life as a scholar, the rest of us can glance backward at his many and many-sided contributions to social psychology and sociology. The roll call is as familiar as it is impressive: the fundamental work on the art of interviewing in social research; the magisterial and creative codifying of survey design and analysis; the pioneering work on political socialization; with Charles Wright and Terence Hopkins, the innovative work on systematic modes of auditing and evaluating programs and structures of social activity; the typically perceptive sociological studies, with Charles Wright, of the enduring (rather than only short-term) effects of education; the important directive for the secondary analysis of sample surveys; and, for immediate purposes here, the earliest and perhaps the most consequential of all these consequential contributions, the pathmaking concept of reference groups. To herald his career of continuing accomplishment, it is symbolically apt that Herbert Hyman should have introduced that fundamental concept in his dissertation (Hyman 1942).

## Reference Groups and Invisible Colleges

So intellectually consequential has the concept of reference group proved to be that it has found its way into the language, and authoritatively so. The passage into the vernacular has been registered in that grand depository of the language, the unabridged dictionary. So it is that in *Webster's Third New International Dictionary* (1963), a running head atop page 1908 boldly announces "**reference group**," following this by the rather wooden and incomplete entry:

**reference group** *n, sociol* : a group toward whose interests, attitudes, and values the individual is oriented

The involuted syntax of the Webster definition is scarcely designed to commend this important term-cum-concept to the reader seeking clarification of it—nor, I suspect, is the author of the concept apt to be keen about its truncated location in "*sociol*" alone. But all is not lost. As dictionary buffs have reason to expect, the *Oxford English Dictionary* does better on both counts. The defining entry, in volume 3 of *A Supplement* (1982), reads:

**reference group** *Sociol.* and *Psychol.* a group to which a person may or may not belong but which he, perhaps subconsciously, refers to as a standard in forming his attitudes and behaviour

Here, we note, the concept is properly located in both sociology and psychology as it goes on to differentiate membership and nonmembership reference groups, thus incorporating conceptual developments of the central idea. And, in this instance, the *OED* surely succeeds in its announced effort to identify "the first use of each word and sense" through its "first example in the set of illustrative quotations"; thus:

**1942** H. H. Hyman *Psychol. of Status* ii 37 Satisfaction with status is consequently also a function of the reference group, since the reference group is a variable of the judgment.

Those of us interested in the fate of social science ideas and words as they diffuse, typically with distortion, into the vernacular, can take heart from the detailed and informed entry in the dictionary-compendium, *The Harper Dictionary of Modern Thought* (Bullock and Stallybrass 1977). This, in its entirety, reads thus:

**reference group.**   Term introduced by Herbert H. Hyman (in *Archives of Psychology*, 1942) for a social collectivity, real or imagined, in relation to which an individual regularly evaluates his own situation or conduct. A *comparative* reference group is one which serves as a standard against which the individual appraises his achievements, social circumstances, life-chances, rewards, etc., and which thus influences the level of his expectations and, in turn, his degree of relative satisfaction or deprivation; thus the structure of comparative reference groups among members of different occupations has been shown to be important in determining the extent to which wage differentials are regarded as legitimate and the level at which wage claims are made. A NORMATIVE reference group is one which the individual perceives as a source of values and GROUP NORMS of which he approves, and with whose members he would wish to identify himself; thus a socially aspiring individual may take the ELITE of his local community as a normative reference group, and seek to emulate their LIFE STYLE, manners, tastes, opinions, etc. in the hope of being himself accepted into the elite.                                                                    J.H.G.
   Bibl: R. K. Merton, *Social Theory and Social Structure* (N.Y., 2nd ed., 1957), chs. 8, 9.

Two decades after the first appearance of the term-cum-concept "reference group" in social psychology and general sociology, a kindred term-cum-concept, "invisible college," was being introduced into another, rather more specialized, sector of learning: the sociology and history of science. In a felicitous stroke of terminological recoinage, the polymath Derek J. de Solla Price (1961, p. 99, [1963] 1986, pp. 83 ff.) had adopted and conceptually extended the seventeenth-century term that the twenty-year-old Robert Boyle had used to describe the small group of natural philosophers (scientists) who antedated the formation of what was to become the highly visible college of the Royal Society. All of us who have vicariously lived in seventeenth-century

England of course knew of Boyle's intriguing term, but it was Price who, in a double transfer of metaphor, recognized that it could designate the informal collectives of dispersed but closely interacting scientists conspicuously emerging at the research fronts of science in our own century.

One can almost reconstruct the reflective moment in which Price converted the metaphoric *term,* invisible college, into the *concept,* invisible college. In his *Science since Babylon* (1961), he finds himself alluding to "the new Invisible Colleges [which have] begun to trespass upon the traditional functions of the printed paper in a published journal" by circulating "prepublication duplicated sheets" to a limited number of fellow scientists. Evidently discovering his latent thoughts on that emerging pattern of behavior *as he hears what he says*[1]—the text is being delivered as a public lecture at Yale in 1959—he proceeds to elucidate the notion and records his further thoughts about it in a segregated footnote:

The new Invisible Colleges, rapidly growing up in all the most hard-pressed sections of the scholarly research front, might well be the subject of an interesting sociological study. Starting originally as a reaction to the communication difficulty brought about by the flood of literature, and flourishing mightily under the teamwork conditions induced by World War II, their whole *raison d'être* was to substitute personal contact for formal communication among those who were really getting on with the job, making serious advances in their fields. In many of these fields, it is now hardly worth while embarking upon serious work unless you happen to be within the group, accepted and invited to the annual and informal conferences, commuting between the two Cambridges, and vacationing in one of the residential conference and work centers that are part of the international chain. The processes of access to and egress from the groups have become difficult to understand, and the apportioning of credit for the work to any one member or his sub-team has already made it more meaningless than before to award such honors as the Nobel Prize. Are these "power groups" dangerously exclusive? Probably not, but in many ways they may turn out to be not wholly pleasant necessities of the scientific life in its new state of saturation. [Price 1961, p. 99n]

Two years later, Price begins to sketch out the composition, structure, dynamics, and cognitive consequences of invisible colleges in terms such as these: The scientist

arriving at the research front finds others with the same basic training in the same subject looking at the same problems and trying to pick apples off the same tree. [S]he will want to monitor the work of these similar individuals who are . . . rivals . . . and peers [in an effort] to leapfrog over their advances

[1] Recall E. M. Forster's telling anecdotalized aphorism: "How can I tell what I think till I see what I say?"

rather than duplicate them. How many such individuals can be handled? I suggest that the answer is on the order of a hundred. [Price (1963) 1986, p. 64]

Writing well before the time of electronic networks and bulletin boards, Price continues to note that the invisible colleges "devise mechanisms for day-to-day communication. There is an elaborate apparatus for sending out not merely reprints of publications but preprints and pre-preprints of work in progress and results about to be achieved" (p. 75).

And then, in the *locus classicus* that crystallizes the concept of invisible colleges, Derek Price, as a physicist and historian of science, and all unknowing of the concept of reference group as set forth twenty years before in a monograph entitled *The Psychology of Status*—since, after all, he was not remotely a member of the invisible college initiated by Herbert Hyman—proceeds, in effect, to link the two concepts in this observation:

[Invisible colleges give each scientist] status in the form of approbation from his peers, they confer prestige, and, above all, they effectively solve a communication crisis [in part, deriving from the vast yet slow publication of new work] by reducing a large group to a small select one of the maximum size that can be handled by interpersonal relationships. [Price (1963) 1986, p. 76]

Much of Price's early observations and interpretations has been confirmed and extended by the studies of Crane (1972) and Mullins (1973, 1985) and further explored in several hundred articles and monographs identified in the annotated bibliography by Chubin (1983).

To be sure, the two ideas of reference group and invisible college have, in their origins, substance, and usual applications, only a cousinly conceptual relation. Still, it is indicative of the frequent segregation of differentiated contemporary thought that, for quite some time, these ideas went their separate ways. Their conceptual kinship remained unnoticed even by the hybrid scholars known as sociologists of science who had reason, after all, to be privy to pertinent ongoing work in sociology, the history of science, and, to a degree, social psychology. By taking myself as a clinical specimen, as a case in point, I have instant access to documentary evidence of this prolonged segregation of thought developed in different spheres. It will soon appear that this provides another instance of selective attention (and inattention) in the sociology and psychology of scientific knowledge—or an instance of "the Burke theorem": "A way of seeing is also a way of not seeing—a focus upon object *A* involves a neglect of object *B*" (Burke 1935, p. 70; Merton 1984, p. 264).

The prolonged segregation of reference group and invisible college is registered in this partial series:

In 1950, as Herbert Hyman likes to remind us (Hyman 1960; 1968, 13:353–61; 1975; Hyman and Singer 1968), there appeared an intensive paper entitled "Contributions to the Theory of Reference Group Behavior" (Merton and Rossi 1950, 1957), which aimed to extend the Hyman concept in a sociological rather than primarily sociopsychological direction. Drawing upon the great body of substantive materials consolidated by Samuel Stouffer and his colleagues in *The American Soldier* (Stouffer et al. 1949), this theoretical paper had no occasion to consider reference group behavior among scientists. A focus on *A* preempted attention to *B*.

There follows a lapse of a decade, in printed if not oral publication. There is discernible but slight movement toward applying the notion of nonmembership reference groups to the behavior of sociologists, thus:

The case for the significance of problems of reference-group behavior . . . stems from the cumulative recognition, intimated but not followed up by sociologists from at least the time of Marx, that the behavior, attitudes, and loyalties of men are not uniformly determined by their current social positions and affiliations. Puzzling inconsistencies in behavior are becoming less puzzling by systematically following up the simple idea that people's patterned selections of groups other than their own provide frames of normative reference which intervene between the influence of their current social position and their behavior. [Merton (1961) 1973, p. 61]

Then, moving to

*Reference groups of sociologists.* Conflict is found also in the sometimes implicit selection of reference groups and audiences by sociologists. Some direct themselves primarily to the literati or to the "educated general public"; others, to the so-called men of affairs who manage economic or political organizations; while most are oriented primarily to their fellow academicians and professionals. The recurrent noise about jargon, cults of unintelligibility, the overly abundant use of statistics or of mathematical models is largely generated by the sociologists who have the general public as their major reference group. The work of these outer-oriented sociologists, in turn, is described by their academic critics as sociological journalism, useful more for arousing public interest in sociology than for advancing sociological knowledge. They are said to persuade by rhetoric rather than to instruct by responsible analysis—and so on. It would be instructive to study the actual social roles and functions of these diversely oriented sociologists, rather than to remain content with offhand descriptions such as these, even though again we cannot expect that the results of such study would modify current alignments. [Merton (1961) 1973, pp. 67–68]

This is being set forth in the year of Derek Price's footnoted introduction of the notion of invisible college. Two years later, there is an inching forward in the use of reference group data for psychologists and an observation on locals and cosmopolitans in the scientific community but still no explicit connection between the concepts of reference groups and invisible colleges:

K. E. Clark's study of American psychologists found that especially productive psychologists were more apt than a control group to report that their significant reference groups and reference individuals—the people "whose opinions of their work they care about"—were composed of other outstanding psychologists in the United States and in other countries, rather than by their local colleagues. [Merton (1963) 1973, p. 374]

And then this, still without awareness of the soon-to-be-reiterated Price concept of invisible college:

Historians of science and other scholars have long used the phrase, "the community of scientists." For the most part, this has remained an apt metaphor rather than becoming a productive concept. Yet it need not remain a literary figure of speech, apt and chaste, untarnished by actual use. For we find that *the* community of scientists is a dispersed rather than a geographically compact collectivity. The structure of this community cannot, therefore, be adequately understood by focusing only on the small local groups of which scientists are a part. The sheer fact that multiple discoveries are made by scientists working independently of one another testifies to the further crucial fact that, though remote in space, they are responding to much the same social and intellectual forces that impinge on them all. In a word, the Robinson Crusoe of science is as much a figment as the Robinson Crusoe of old-fashioned economics. [Merton (1963) 1973, p. 375]

Not long after, the concepts of reference groups and of "status judges" are linked with regard to the behavior of scientists concerned to reassure themselves of their capacity for original and significant discovery (Merton [1968] 1973, p. 340). Finally, a decade later, the concepts of reference group and invisible college are explicitly joined in fairly general terms:

Invisible colleges can be construed sociologically as clusters of geographically dispersed scientists who engage in more frequent cognitive interaction with one another than they do with others in the larger community of scientists. At the outset, members of an emerging invisible college regard themselves as major reference figures and regard themselves collectively as a reference group, whose opinions of their work matter deeply and whose standards of cognitive performance are taken as binding. As the field of inquiry grows in numbers of investigators and differentiates cognitively, another structural adaptation of progressively pinpointed informal communication between specialized scientists seems to develop. This takes the form, as Jonathan Cole has suggested to me, of invisible colleges developing *within* the onetime invisible college, now grown amply visible through networks of publication. Subsets of people at work in the developing field of inquiry come to adopt differing sets of reference individuals and reference groups. Cognitive disagreements are reinforced by social conflict. All this makes for a social structure that corresponds more or less closely to the differentiating cognitive structure of the field. [Merton (1977) 1979, p. 6]

When the concepts of reference groups and invisible colleges are put to work to help us understand the institutionally induced or reinforced competitive behavior of scientists, we come upon certain pathogenic components in the culture of science.

## Fraud and Other Deviant Behaviors in Science

As I have been reiteratively maintaining for the past thirty years, no doubt in redundant fashion, we confront the seeming paradox that certain values in the institution of modern science, such as the premium placed upon significant originality, which provide or reinforce incentives for doing often arduous and important science, can lead some scientists to violate other fundamental values and norms of science. The reward system of science depends upon the evaluation of scientific contributions by competent peers; in the last analysis, upon the judgments by members of invisible colleges who serve collectively as reference groups and individually as reference figures. A few scientists, at the margin of their still unrealized aspirations for such peer recognition, undergo a displacement of goals. They are ready to substitute the appearance of scientific achievement for its reality. They engage in such deviant behaviors as plagiarizing the work of others or preempting the ideas of others or, at the extreme, concocting fraudulent data.

The culturally reinforced if not culturally induced lust for great recognition is manifested by those occasional scientists ready to run the risk of having their deviant behaviors eventually detected, when others attempting to use the false data come upon their falsity or when peers come upon the original of a plagiarizing text. Uncertain of prime achievement, they displace goals, centering on the achieving of however temporary applause of peers, with its possible material accompaniments, rather than on doing the work that might warrantably win that applause and possible legitimate fame. For those who have displaced the goal of rewarded scientific accomplishment for the goal of immediate reward itself, deviant behavior becomes the unanticipated and unintended consequence of certain values obtaining in the community of science.

Chief among those values, as I have suggested, is the premium placed on originality, on being the first to make a scientific discovery. Being second, let alone a subsequent *n*th, hardly counts at all. Moreover, scientists know that much the same discovery is often made independently by two or more investigators at about the same time. They not only know it, but many of them act on that knowledge. This often brings about a rush for priority. So it is that the culture of science and its reward system combine with the cognitive fact of multiple independent discoveries to make for intense competition among scientists. The annals of science are punctuated by hundreds of disputes over priority during the past four centuries. What interests us here is, to give it its due emphasis by reiteration, that the value placed upon such originality, which has reinforced intrinsic motives for advancing scientific knowledge, has pathogenic components. Self-assertive claims to have got there first, the hoarding of data to avoid being forestalled in discovery, reporting only the data that support a favorite hypothesis, trimming and fudging the data to have them come in closer accord with theoretical expectations, falsely imputing plagiary to others who have independently come upon the same results, the occasional theft of ideas, and, in relatively rare known cases, the fabrication of data— all these have appeared in the history of science.

These types of deviant behaviors, which variously violate the folkways and mores of science, can be thought of as responses to the gap between the enormous emphasis placed upon original discovery and the great difficulty a good many scientists experience in making one, with the more inventive scientists confronting the ever-present risk of being forestalled. Under such stressful conditions, a variety of would-be adaptive behaviors and misbehaviors is sometimes called into play. The recent spate of news stories about actual and alleged fraud in science invites the belief that such deviant practices have greatly increased in our time.

When the institution of science works effectively and equitably— and, like other social institutions, it does not always do so—peer recognition accrues to scientists who have made authentic contributions to the common stock of knowledge. Such recognition is communally validating testimony that one's ideas or findings are truly new and variously significant. And from these incessant appraisals of work by competent peers comes much of the self-image of individual scientists. As Darwin once reported, "My love of natural science . . . has been much aided by the ambition to be esteemed by my fellow naturalists." Since such peer recognition is the coin of the scientific realm, we can understand how it is that, through the centuries, scientists, including the greatest among them, have been deeply concerned with safeguarding their priority.

Why, then, the frequent reluctance to acknowledge this concern with priority? Why the ambivalence expressed by a Darwin, before he learned of Wallace's parallel ideas, in this way: "I rather hate the idea of writing for priority, yet I should certainly be vexed if anyone were to publish my doctrines before me" (Darwin 1925, 1:426–27)? Why the curious notion that a thirst for significant originality and for having that originality accredited by competent peers is rather depraved—somewhat like a thirst for, say, whiskey and Coca-Cola—or, in Freud's self-deprecatory words, that this is an "unworthy and puerile" motive for doing scientific work?

In one aspect, the ambivalent attitude of a Darwin or a Freud toward his own reluctantly acknowledged interest in priority is based upon the tacit assumption that behavior is actuated by a single motive, which can then be appraised as good or bad, as noble or ignoble. It is assumed that the truly dedicated scientist must be moved *only* by wanting to advance knowledge, whether the source of the contribution is recognized or not. Interest in having one's priority acknowledged is seen as marring one's nobility of purpose (although it might be remembered that "noble" once meant being known, or famous).

There is, however, a grain of psychological and sociological truth in the suspicion enveloping the drive for recognition. Any extrinsic reward—fame, money, position—is potentially subversive of other socially esteemed, *intrinsic* values. For the extrinsic reward can displace the morally respected intrinsic motive: Concern with recognition and its derivative rewards can displace the primary concern with advancing knowledge, as we observe at the extreme in cases of fraudulent practices in science.

Those mixed feelings about concern with priority often stem from the superficial belief that it simply expresses naked self-interest. On the surface, the hunger for peer recognition appears as mere personal vanity, generated from within and craving satisfaction from without. But when we reach into the institutional complex that gives added edge to that hunger, it often turns out to have quite other functions. Vanity, so-called, is then seen as the outer face of the inner need for reassurance that one's work has measured up to the demanding standards exacted by the scientists whose opinions one respects. As we sociologists like to put it more generally—ever since we happily assigned priority to Herbert Hyman for having fixed the composite thought-and-term systematically in our minds—each of us has reference figures, those people whose opinion of us matters greatly.

Again, Darwin serves us well by way of example. He writes to Huxley about *The Origin of Species* "with awful misgivings" that "perhaps I had deluded myself like so many have done, and I then fixed in mind three judges, on whose decision I determined mentally to abide. The judges were Lyell, Hooker, and yourself." In choosing reference figures, Darwin was replicating the behavior of many another scientist, both before and after him. Thus, before his feud with Newton, the astronomer John Flamsteed wrote: "I study not for present applause. Mr. Newton's approbation is more to me than the cry of all the ignorant in the world." In almost identical language, Schrödinger writes Einstein that "your approval and Planck's mean more to me than that of half the world." And a Leo Szilard and a Max Delbrück, widely known as tough-minded judges who, all uncompromising, would not relax their standards of critical judgment to provide even momentary comfort to their associates, were reference figures whose approval of work accomplished had a multiplier effect, influencing in turn the judgments of many another scientist.

The now understandable concern with priority often evolves—some would say, devolves—into a race for priority. Scientists know, at times from hard-won experience, that multiple independent discoveries constitute an occupational hazard. That the consequent rush to achieve priority is common in our time hardly needs documentation. The evidence is there on every side. Some years before James Watson reached his much wider audience with *The Double Helix,* the Nobel physicist Arthur Schawlow reported that another laureate, Charles Townes, and he had been "in a hurry, of course. We feared that it might be only a matter of time before others would come up with the same idea. So we decided to publish before building a working model. . . . Subsequently, Theodore Maiman won the frantic race between many experimenters to build the first laser. Our theory was verified." (Merton 1973, p. 329) Townes in particular had ample biographical reason to be in a hurry. In the early 1950s, he had been involved in that fivefold independent discovery of the maser, along with Willis Lamb, Joseph Weber, Nikolai Basov, and Aleksandr Prokhorov.

The scientific woods are full of investigators spurred on to more intense effort by the knowledge that others are on much the same track. In her interviews with Nobel laureates, Harriet Zuckerman (1977a) found many of them testifying, in words crisply summed up by one of them, that the prizewinning discovery "was bound to happen soon. Had I not done it . . . it was there, waiting for somebody . . . [probably] at the Rockefeller Institute." Or, to turn from the moving frontier to its somewhat interior regions, Warren Hagstrom (1974) found that two-thirds of a sample of some 1,700 scientists reported having been anticipated by others, a good number of them on more than one occasion. For further signs that an awareness of impending multiple discovery intensifies the race for priority, we need only turn to the periodic editorials by Samuel Goudsmit in *Physical Review Letters,* where he notes the drive for quick publication to insure priority, sometimes at the expense of physicists "working along the same lines who want to do a more complete job before publishing their findings." Some of his editorials are touched with anguish as he reviews expedients adopted by physicists, often of the first class, who seek publication in the weekly *Letters* in order to "'scoop' a competitor who has already submitted a full article" or who use the newspapers to announce their results (Goudsmit 1968).

There are those who believe that the rough-and-tumble of competition in science is peculiar to our own deteriorating times, who see such competition as merely self-aggrandizing, and who suppose that the drive to be first necessarily displaces the "relish of knowledge" (of which John Locke spoke) by doing away with intrinsic joy in discovery and pleasure in the beauty of a powerful simplifying idea. As one observer has put it, "isolated scientists daily run the risk that they may be repeating experiments already made by others. . . . Let me add that their security is not complete. They are haunted by the work of a competitor. Possibly someone else is gleaning the same field and may, as the saying goes, 'get there first.' The scientist has to hide himself and conduct in haste and isolation work requiring deliberation." Is this observation about trying to get there first drawn from our own harried time, with its exponentially enlarged population of scientists, its monumental budgets assigned to scientific work—though these, as we know, are never quite large enough—and its numerous variety of prizes and other professional rewards? Not quite. It is an observation by the tumultuous French social philosopher, Henri de Saint-Simon, made 150 years ago (Saint-Simon [1828–29] 1958, p. 9).

As with Newton in his controversy with Leibniz over the invention of the calculus, concern with establishing one's priority can lead to the use of dubious means to buttress even valid claims. When the Royal Society finally provided a committee to adjudicate the rival claims, Newton, who was then president, packed the committee, helped direct its activities, anonymously wrote the preface for the second published report—the draft is in his handwriting—and included in that preface a disarming reference to the old legal maxim that "no one is a proper witness for himself [and that] he would be a uniquitous Judge, and would crush underfoot the laws of all the people, who would admit anyone as a lawful witness in his own cause" (De Morgan 1914, app. 2; More 1934, chap. 15). We can gauge the immense pressures that must have operated for Newton to have adopted these tactics to vindicate his claim to priority. It was not alone that Newton was in this instance weak but also that the institutionalized value set on demonstrable originality of conception was central in the developing culture of science that drove him to these lengths.

In earlier times as in our own, intense competition in science has led to similar patterns of misbehavior. It helped bring about what the English mathematician and adumbrator of computer technology, Charles Babbage, picturesquely described in his *Decline of Science in England* (1830, pp. 174–83) as "trimming" and "cooking." The trimmer clips off "little bits here and there from observations which differ most in excess from the mean, and [sticks] . . . them on to those which are too small . . . [for the unallowable purpose of] 'equitable adjustment.'" The scientific cook makes "multitudes of observations" and selects only those that agree with a hypothesis, and, as Babbage says, "the cook must be very unlucky if he cannot pick out fifteen or twenty which will do for serving up."

*Plus ça change* . . . Here, more than a century later, is Alan Gregg, that wise observer of the world of medical research, practice, and education, reporting the case of

the medical scientist of the greatest distinction who told me that during his graduate fellowship at one of the great English universities he encountered for the first time the idea that in scientific work one should be really honest in reporting the results of his experiments. Before that time he had always been told and had quite naturally assumed that the point was to get his observations and theories accepted by others, and published. [Gregg 1956, p. 115]

This eagerness to demonstrate a hypothesis that has been converted into a thesis can lead even provisional truth to be fed with faked data, as it did for the neurotic scientist, described by the psychiatrist Lawrence Kubie (1953, p. 110), "who had proved his case, but was so driven by his anxieties that he had to bolster an already proven theorem by falsifying some quite unnecessary additional statistical data."

Diagnoses of seeming deviant behavior are aided by Harriet Zuckerman's distinctions among *reputable error* (which occurs at times even though methodological precautions called for by the current state of the art have been taken), *disreputable error* (work judged unacceptably sloppy by the methodological standards of the time), and *deviant behavior* (as in the calculated chicane of plagiary, preemptive theft of ideas, or fabrication of data). In the nature of the case, one cannot truly know the extent to which all actual instances of such deviant behavior in science have been detected—then and there, or at varying times later on. As Zuckerman observes:

there is no statute of limitations on scientific fraud, forgery, and plagiarism—and [scientists know] that such deviant behavior not immediately detected will probably be revealed later when scientific interest in the subject is renewed or when new techniques are developed which make it possible to detect certain kinds of forged evidence. Thus, . . . the Piltdown Man specimens were not decisively revealed as forgeries for some 40 years until a new form of X-ray analysis showed them to be much more recent than they were purported to be. [Zuckerman 1977*b*, p. 92]

To bring matters to the more immediate present, we take note of the recent rash of news reports on the fabrication of data, chiefly in the biomedical sciences and grown painfully familiar through public reiteration: William Summerlin's inked-in mouse at Memorial Sloan-Kettering reminiscent of Paul Kammerer's inked-in midwife toad of half a century before; the forgeries by Marc Straus in his cancer research and by John Long in his research on Hodgkin's disease; the irreproducible findings reported by Melvin Simpson; and the tampering with experimental equipment by the psychologist Jay Levy in his studies of extrasensory perception.

Such widely publicized cases have led some to conclude that the rate of these deviant practices has greatly increased in what is described as our competitive age. Thus, the science journalists William Broad and Nicholas Wade write in their *Betrayers of the Truth* (1982) of "the cases of fraud that occur quite regularly in the elite institutions of science"—this observation being based on a grand total of thirty-four "known or suspected cases of scientific fraud," to quote the title of a summarizing appendix that begins with the case of the astronomer Hipparchus two centuries before Christ and ends with the case of the immunologist Arthur Hale of Wake Forest in 1981. But of course there are no statistical series on the extent of these practices and hence no epidemiology of fraud in science. So we cannot truly say. My own studies of cases of multiple discovery in science during the past three centuries suggest, rather to my surprise, an actual decrease in the proportion of cases involving open conflict over priority. But this, of course, is far removed from data sets on frequency of fraud, bearing rather on experienced intensity of competitiveness in science.

The impression that fraud has vastly increased may be the result of a heightened self-consciousness about such matters and their widespread publicity in a more broadly if not more deeply reading public today than, say, in seventeenth-century Europe; the vast proliferation of the mass and elite media of public communication with their reverberating effects; and the strong moral expectation, evolving over the years, that scientists in pursuit of reliable knowledge will live up to the highest standards of probity. When those expectations are seen to have been violated in even a relatively few widely publicized cases, these statistically rare reports attract great public notice and become cumulatively newsworthy. One still remembers the observation made half a century ago by John Bogart, then the city editor of the *New York Sun:* "When a dog bites a man, that's not news. But if a man bites a dog, *that's* news!"

And Bogart might have added: Even more startling and therefore more apt to make headlines would be the episode in which not only does man bite dog but dog does not bite back—as would be the case were the invisible college, the reference groups, and the scientific community at large to take the fabrication of data as a mere quirk or misdemeanor rather than virtually a capital crime. As the iconic sociologist Emile Durkheim might have said, the very rarity of these extreme violations of the mores of science only deepens the sense of moral outrage and intensifies the glare of publicity when they do occur.

The sociological moral of deviant behavior in science can be put more generally. We have heard much in recent years about the precarious condition of a society in which people do not believe deeply enough or strongly enough. If there is a generic lesson to be learned from some of the unintended consequences of an institutionalized belief in the absolute importance of significant originality in science, it is that absolute beliefs have their dangers too. They can give rise to the zeal in which *anything goes.* The absolutizing of aspirations can, in its way, be as damaging as the decay of aspirations to life in civil society.

## Bibliography

Babbage, Charles. 1830. *Reflections on the decline of science in England.* London.

Broad, Nicholas, and Nicholas Wade. 1982. *Betrayers of the truth: Fraud and deceit in the halls of science.* New York: Simon and Schuster.

Bullock, Alan, and Oliver Stallybrass. 1977. *The Harper dictionary of modern thought.* New York: Harper and Row.

Burke, Kenneth. 1935. *Permanence and change.* New York: New Republic.

Chubin, Daryl E. 1983. *Sociology of sciences: An annotated bibliography on invisible colleges.* New York: Garland.

Crane, Diana. 1972. *Invisible colleges.* Chicago: University of Chicago Press.

Darwin, Francis. 1925. *The life and letters of Charles Darwin.* Vol. 1. New York: Appleton.

De Morgan, Augustus. 1914. *Essays on the life and works of Newton.* Chicago: Open Court.

Goudsmit, S. A. 1968. Editorial. *Physical Review Letters* 21:1425–26.

Gregg, Alan. 1956. *Challenges to contemporary medicine.* New York: Columbia University Press.

Hagstrom, Warren O. 1974. Competition in science. *American Sociological Review* 39:1–18.

Kubie, Lawrence. 1953. Some unresolved problems of the scientific career. *American Scientist* 41: 596–613.

———. 1954. Some unresolved problems of the scientific career. *American Scientist* 42: 104–12.

Merton, Robert K. 1973. *The sociology of science: Theoretical and empirical investigations.* Chicago: University of Chicago Press.

———. 1979. *The sociology of science: An episodic memoir.* Carbondale: Southern Illinois University Press.

———. 1984. Socially expected durations, I: A case study of concept formation in sociology. In W. W. Powell and Richard Robbins, eds., *Conflict and consensus: A Festschrift for Lewis A. Coser,* pp. 262–83. New York: Free Press.

Merton, Robert K., and Alice S. Rossi. 1950. Contributions to the theory of reference group behavior. In Robert K. Merton and Paul F. Lazarsfeld, eds., *Continuities in social research: Studies in the scope and method of "The American Soldier,"* 40–105. Glencoe, Illinois: The Free Press. Reprinted in Robert K. Merton, *Social theory and social structure,* pp. 279–334. New York: The Free Press, enlarged edition, 1968.

More, Louis T. 1934. *Isaac Newton: A biography.* New York: Scribner.

Mullins, Nicholas C. 1973. *Theories and theory groups in contemporary American sociology.* New York: Harper and Row.

———. 1985. Invisible colleges as science elites. *Scientometrics* 7:357–68.

Price, Derek J. de Solla. 1961. *Science since Babylon.* New Haven: Yale University Press.

———. 1963. *Little science, big science – – and beyond.* New York: Columbia University Press, 1986.

Saint-Simon, Henri de. 1958. *The doctrine of Saint-Simon: An exposition. First year, 1828–29.* Translated by Georg G. Iggers. Boston: Beacon Press.

Stouffer, Samuel A., et al. 1949. *The American soldier.* 2 vols. Princeton, N.J.: Princeton University Press.

Zuckerman, Harriet. 1977a. *Scientific elite: Nobel laureates in the United States.* New York: Free Press.

———. 1977b. Deviant behavior and social control in science. In Edward Sagarin, ed., *Deviance and social change,* pp. 87–138. Beverly Hills: Sage.

# Christian Bay

## 8  After Liberalism and Nationalism: Toward a Humanist Theory of Political Obligation

This paper explores some consequences for the construction of political obligation, if one adopts a humanist commitment to human rights as the first and possibly the only a priori normative premise and if one attempts to achieve an optimally authentic human rights language in the articulation, defense, and practical application of this perspective. I shall argue that this kind of commitment must lead us beyond the nationalist as well as the liberal assumptions that characterized, until recently, all the constructions of political obligation of influence in our time, from Plato's to Rawls's and Flathman's. Moreover, I hope to show that a reasonably authentic human rights language has interesting consequences for the problematic of peace, security, and defense issues.

First, let me articulate my conception of a humanist as distinct from a liberal conception of human rights, and of the continuum between authentic and inauthentic languages of human rights. Next comes a brief overview of familiar classical and liberal, all state-centered, theories of political obligation and its limits, to be followed by a discussion of some indications that these theories are about to run out of their persuasive power. I conclude with a discussion of elements of an alternate paradigm: an approach that makes a humanist order of human rights, with priorities according to basic need categories, the legitimating normative foundation for governments, and the basis for contingent principles of political obligation. I also suggest some consequences of such a commitment, to the extent that it is adopted, for the possible resolution of contemporary problems of peace, security, and rational defense policies.

## A Humanist Conception of Human Rights and Their Priorities

It is possible to be a monist or a dualist about moral rights and obligations: The monist holds that the two are inseparable, because (*a*) our rights are derived from our obligations, or (*b*) vice versa, whereas the dualist view is that rights and obligations can be validated independently of each other. Thus, the dualist holds that there can be moral rights without corresponding obligations, and vice versa, even though he or she might be ready to concede that most rights have little practical value unless they obligate people to honor them and that most obligations are of scant practical value unless they entitle at least one or a few beneficiaries to the desired expectations that are generally associated with moral or legal rights.

I take the second of the two monist positions: In principle, each moral obligation is validated only to the extent that it reflects, or originates in or is required by, accepted premises of one or more moral rights, or by premises that should or must be accepted, in order to protect the right(s) in question.

This view is adopted here not on ontological grounds (and I shall leave aside ontological issues in this paper) but on pragmatic or practical-political grounds. It is the principal aim of this paper to establish that a humanist construction of human rights as the exclusive basis for all the most basic political obligations will strengthen the prospects for security, dignity, and freedom for all human beings, in each country and in the world.

The project of advancing human civilization must aim at optimum enduring human freedom (that is, freedom with security) for all human beings, with priority for those who at each time are least free and secure. In other words, the degree of civilization achieved at a given time is to be assessed by the degree of secure freedom achieved by those in a given social order who are least privileged. This basic norm I shall refer to as the *humanist norm* (HN).

But the humanist norm is not limited in application to one social order or another. It extends in space and time. It spans all of humanity. It spans the past, the present, and the future generations.[1] I shall not try to articulate any humanist aspirations for past generations, however, for a sufficient pragmatic reason: Nothing can be done to compensate them for past oppression and suffering. It is the present and future generations that humanists must be concerned with.

---

[1] "Society is indeed a contract . . . a partnership not only between those who are living, but between those who are living, those who are dead, and those who are to be born" (Burke 1969, pp. 194–95).

Given the rapidly increasing interdependence of nations and conti-
nents, and given the increasingly acute one-way dependence of the
well-being of future generations, if any, on the health of the habitats
and ecosystems that our generation leaves behind, it is time for humanists and others to reflect on and to champion one particular category of moral rights that is known as *human rights* (HRs), by virtue of
the assumption that these are entitlements that are, or should be, protected for all human beings qua human beings. I shall take the position that the extent of protection for the most basic human rights in a
given social order indicates the degree to which this society is to be
deemed civilized, and thus worthy of loyalty and defense and support
as a political/legal system. Although the human rights of individuals
in any system must be supported, wherever possible, systems merit
support only to the extent that *they* support human rights, internally
and externally.

"Human rights" refers to a category of moral rights defined by four
attributes. Three of them are specified in Maurice Cranston's *What
Are Human Rights?* (1973, pp. 4–7, 21–24): They are *universal*, as has
been discussed above. They are also *paramount:* The task of protecting
these entitlements should take precedence over all other public policy
objectives; Ronald Dworkin suggests the analogy with trumps in a
game of bridge (1978, 11:85, 364). Third, they are *practical*, for Cranston appears to consider impossible entitlements an absurd notion.
However, as I have argued elsewhere (1982a, pp. 61–62), one should
insist on "*in principle* practical," or we arrive at a human rights concept
that is liberal rather than humanist: Only rights that can be achieved
without socioeconomic changes would qualify as human rights. A humanist commitment requires a kind of human rights concept that calls
for advances in freedom and security beyond what appears practi-
cable within the present scheme of things.

Not every kind of advance in freedom will do, however. I have argued that we should be concerned first of all with the freedom of
those who are least privileged. For this reason we adopt a primary
commitment to human rights rather than, like Rawls (to single out
one of the most egalitarian among influential liberal philosophers), a
primary commitment to optimal freedom in the abstract (Daniels
1975; Rawls 1971). "Human rights" weds freedom claims to equality
criteria; the reference is to kinds and levels of freedom that in principle can, and should, be protected for all human beings qua human
beings. It is a device for a just rationing scheme for access to basic
liberties.

It still remains for me to specify the fourth attribute of moral rights that completes my conception of human rights. This attribute is crucial, moreover, for telling humanist human rights apart from liberal human rights, for example, Cranston's liberal human rights: Human rights are entitlements that must be protected in order to insure the meeting of *basic human needs*.

What is gained by this conceptual coupling of human rights with basic human needs?

First, a sharper line is drawn between essential rights of human persons and insistent demands of merely juridical persons, like corporations. The latter's entitlements ought to be subject to constrictions whenever this appears to be advisable in the public interest; and in a humane society the legal rights of business firms should automatically yield in cases of clear conflicts with human rights.

Second, this conception of human rights makes it easier to grasp and explain how (and why) the dire needs of underprivileged individuals and groups are to be safeguarded, ahead of less physically or psychologically crucial wants and demands advanced by members of more advantaged groups, whose dire needs (for example, adequate nutrition) are not in jeopardy.

Third, since some broad human need categories are more basic than others, it is to the same extent possible to propose a rational basis for a widely acceptable *hierarchy* of correspondingly broad human rights categories. This kind of hierarchy opens up a humanist alternative to pluralist competition among rights claims, an alternative to the liberal marketplace of claims, in the political arena or in the courts, where the human rights claims of the well-connected tend to outweigh the pleas of those who are isolated, poor, or badly organized.

What basic need priorities are proposed? Writers as diverse as Marx and Maslow have argued that physical survival and health needs are the most basic, followed by social solidarity (acceptance, dignity) needs and then by the freedom (individuality, spirituality, growth) needs (Bay 1980*a*). I shall not here argue the merits of this conception of the need hierarchy, but it should be noted that many liberals, perhaps almost all liberals, have tended to place our freedom needs ahead of our social solidarity needs, in contrast with the wise insistence of Aristotle that, when perfected, man "is the best of animals, but, when separated from law and justice, he is the worst of all" (Aristotle 1943, p. 55). My humanist perspective recognizes some freedom needs as basic and therefore entitled to protection as human rights: those freedom needs and claims that are advanced in the context of social responsibility; that is, those that can be protected without hurt to the basic needs and rights of less privileged or more endangered people.

There can, in other words, be no human right to exploit others or to attain ownership or control over properties that monopolize access to means of making a living.

The United Nations and some of its agencies have been helping to build at least moral support for a growing number of human rights claims, and this is good. Conspicuously missing, however, is any attempt to assign priorities to some of these rights categories relative to others. Within the Universal Declaration, for example, Article 5 proclaims a right not to be subjected to torture, and Article 24 proclaims a right to rest and leisure and to "periodic holidays with pay" (*International Bill of Human Rights* 1978, pp. 5, 8). Clearly, it requires only common sense to insist that the former human right should take precedence over the latter. One may disagree with any particular formulation of a human rights hierarchy, but it would seem difficult to disagree with the principle that humanistically satisfactory, general priorities must be sought.

What is also needed, as I have implied, is the kind of political theory that will address the problem of priorities in a rational way, as I attempt to do in this paper. This is not an easy task, for the basic need categories available to me are conceptually loose and empirically less than firmly grounded. Moreover, the liberal persuasion prevailing in the First World is suspicious of attempts to develop objective criteria of justice with which to question the justice obtainable in the democratic marketplace (Bay 1980*b*).

But attempt to move beyond the marketplace kind of justice we must, if we are humanists first and liberals, if at all, second. Justice in the end depends on meeting the most urgent needs, not on accommodating the most persistent or most influential demands.

To return to Marx and Maslow, I shall here assume the following universal need categories as a basis for the basic human rights categories, in the following order of priority, regardless of time and place: (1) human survival, when lives are endangered; (2) protection of health, from hazards as well as from deprivation; (3) protection of solidarity, or equal dignity as humans; and, within these limits, (4) protection for the exercise of all desired liberties that do not jeopardize the rights or liberties of others.

As humanists we want to promote and extend human rights according to just priorities. Having indicated what general priorities I consider just, I hasten to add that they need to be questioned, discussed, improved, better formulated; only the *principle* must be insisted on, that just priorities must be sought, to move the human rights agendas forward, away from the nonjustice of the political/economic marketplace. But we need something else, too: We need to press for a wider use of *authentic* as distinct from *inauthentic* human rights language.

"A relationship, institution, or society is inauthentic," writes Etzioni, "if it provides the appearance of responsiveness while the underlying condition is alienating . . . To be involved inauthentically is to feel cheated and manipulated" (1968, pp. 619–20). When governments, any government, espouse a human rights policy, their pronouncements tend to be inauthentic in a somewhat related sense: Human rights are categorized and prioritized *not* according to how basic the need categories are that each right is alleged to protect or, in specific situations, is said to have failed to protect; nor are they categorized and prioritized according to degrees of suffering caused by deficiencies in rights protection of various categories. Instead, and especially in the argument of representatives of the superpowers, the most important rights categories are always said to be those that appear to be badly protected within the domain of the opposite superpower, or at any rate are represented as being better protected on one's own side. This is so for a good reason: There is a lack of genuine concern with human rights promotion as intrinsic purpose; rather, discussions of human rights issues are instrumental to extraneous political or ideological purposes in the competition between states or political systems. In short, the human rights language is inauthentic, in these contexts.

Thus, to Washington, few human rights are more pressing than the freedom to emigrate, for example, from the USSR (less pressing is the right to immigrate, for example, to the United States); or the right to organize free labor unions (in Poland), or to dissent in general (e.g., in the USSR). In Moscow's rhetoric, on the other hand, the really important human rights instead include the right to work, the right to free education and health care, and the right not to be mugged on city streets.

Now, it would be utopian to expect or demand fully authentic human rights discourse from representatives of any government. Governments have other pressing issues to worry about, like national security or diplomatic prestige contests, to name only two.

Yet, to acknowledge the omnipresence of degrees of inauthenticity in high places makes it all the more urgent for the rest of us, and especially for people interested in human rights as intrinsic political objectives, (1) to be able to tell the difference between authentic and inauthentic arguments about human rights; (2) to struggle to achieve optimal authenticity in our own thinking, speaking, and writing about human rights; and (3) to try to subject glaringly inauthentic pronouncements, especially those that insult many people's intelligence or sense of fairness, to unsparing, damaging criticism.

For example, much as I do admire the courage and the steadfastness of a Lech Walesa or an Andrei Sakharov, surely their human right to organize and to speak freely is not *quite* in the same category of urgency of the human right of Guatemalan Indian families not to be massacred, or of the human right of Chileans or Salvadorans not to be tortured and then killed. Is the right of Nicaraguans to read an uncensored *La Prensa* in the same category of urgency as the right of Amazon Indian peoples to keep or gain control of their habitats so that they can survive as peoples?[2]

## State-centered and Liberal Theories of Political Obligation and Its Limits

"The philosopher's interest in political obligation has been mainly in the problem of the *grounds* of political obligation—that is, in the question: Why ought we to obey the government?" (McPherson 1967, p. 4). Thomas McPherson is right: The duty of obedience to the state, within limits, of course, has been taken for granted. The perceived task of theorists of political obligation has been to justify rather than to question established authority; only secondarily, in liberal theories following the time of Hobbes, has there been a concern also with determining limits to obligation, or scope of justifiable civil disobedience. The obligation to obey most laws and public policies laid down by a constitutional, formally democratic regime had until recently never been questioned by liberal theorists. Anarchists, on the other hand, have contested the legitimacy of every kind of state, whereas Marxists have rejected every feudal and every bourgeois state, whether constitutional or not.

In the beginning of political societies there was total submission, under the deities and under the chieftains or kings who persuasively claimed authority derived from them. Such claims were as a rule made more persuasive by force of superior arms. Disobedience was out of the question, or a mark of madness. Many centuries of ancient civilizations went by before the dawn of reflections about the nature of political authority, let alone about its possible limits.

In ancient Athens Plato in the *Crito* has Socrates explain to his friend why he will not take the opportunity offered to him and flee from his city in order to escape the death penalty to which he had been subjected, unjustly but legally. That would be ungrateful and unjust to the people of Athens, he tells Crito. The people might with

---

[2] See Davis 1977. On the situation in Nicaragua and in other countries in Central and South America, see Stein et al. 1982; on the atrocities in Guatemala, see Americas Watch Report, supplement, 1983. See also Bay, forthcoming, and Bay 1984.

justice say that "he who disobeys us, acts unjustly on three counts: he disobeys us who are his parents and he disobeys us who fostered him, and he disobeys us after he has agreed to obey us, without persuading us that we are wrong. . . . You had seventy years in which you might have gone away if you had been dissatisfied with us, or if the agreement had seemed to you unjust" (Plato 1948, pp. 60–61). In other words he is obligated to his city because it has given him his life and his upbringing and his citizenship rights and privileges. By having remained in Athens Socrates has *tacitly* agreed to obey the city's laws, in fair weather and foul, even if someday the city should demand his death.

This calamity did indeed happen, for Socrates was truly a "conscientious objector": He was committed to obey the city's laws, but first of all he was committed to obey "the god" and "the truth" (Plato 1948, p. 35). Socrates in the *Crito* bases his loyalty to the city not on an explicit contract but on an implicit understanding between the city and every citizen: Within the limits of "higher" duties one owes everything to the city that has made civilized life, perhaps life itself, possible for everyone, as each citizen tacitly acknowledges every day of continued residence in the city.

A related and yet very different kind of "understanding" appears in the modern social contract theories of Hobbes and Locke. The modern contract is different chiefly in that it is intended to establish, as well as to reflect, certain natural individual rights. There was natural law in ancient times, but no idea of natural rights. Socrates, and also Antigone in Sophocles' famous tragedy, had claimed not a right but an absolute *duty* to obey the gods before man, and before the state, too. Hobbes, therefore, reversed Socrates on the ultimate limits of what the citizen owed to the state: Hobbes argued that the citizen had given up his right to entertain a private conscience, and more so a public moral conscience, in matters political; on the other hand, Hobbes held that the citizen's right to seek to escape death was inalienable, even in times of war or after a just sentence of death (Hobbes 1968, pp. 190, 199–200).

The importance of Hobbes for today's human rights theories is that he was the first to raise the issue of individual *rights* against the state— if only to deny that there could be any, beyond the basic right of self-preservation and the right to refuse to kill close kin, if ordered to do so (Hobbes 1968, pp. 190, 199–200). Beyond this, Hobbes argued for *unconditional* submission under any regime that remained firmly in power. Adolf Eichmann could have cited Hobbes in his defense. (This is not to say that Hobbes would have exonerated Eichmann's crimes.)

The notion of individual rights against the state was an idea whose time had come; and it was soon to be supplemented by a related, bolder idea, central to Locke and shared by many subsequent theorists of political obligation: that it was indeed the primary and legitimating task of the liberal state to protect individual rights—to protect them better than in the state of nature, and better than they would be protected under alternate kinds of regimes. Locke's social compact established an obligation to obey the laws that was contingent on the state's respect for the basic civil rights of all propertied people (Macpherson 1962, pp. 221–38). Locke pictured the holders of rights as parties to a continuing contract and even acknowledged the people's right to stage a revolution if the contract was grievously violated (Locke 1965, secs. 223–26). The Hobbesian contract was very different: It was a contract of desperation, with which the people had bought protection at the exorbitant price of relinquishing all political power to the Leviathan.

The rational difficulties with Locke's and subsequent liberal contract theories are enormous, however. The most vulnerable premise is that of tacit consent, which Locke owed to the Socratic dialogues. Even if we were bold enough to assume a historical contract in the distant past, how could subsequent generations be construed to give their assent, voluntarily, when only very few among them could in fact choose to leave the country? David Hume, in particular, tore this premise to shreds (Hume 1953, chap. 6).

Subsequent utilitarian writers have constructed political obligation on the basis of enlightened self-interest, in the absence of any hypothetical contract. The utilitarian tendency has been to be less interested in moral than in legal obligation, to parallel the emphasis within the same tradition on prudential as distinct from ethical grounds for political obligation.

Yet there are moral limits, of course, to what laws can stipulate without placing even their own legal authority in jeopardy. There could be no legal obligation, as J. C. Smith writes, "to report to concentration camp X to be exterminated." Regardless of how a law was enacted, according to constitutional rules or not, "the law requires a particular kind of content when it is accepted as, or is assumed to be, binding" (1976, p. 85).

Richard Flathman, a contemporary utilitarian political philosopher, wisely construes obligation behavior as requiring principled practice; the usual political conformity behavior based on practical convenience, habit, and lack of critical reflection is for him something less than the practice of political obligation, or of political practice of any kind. He argues that civil disobedience is an alternative to obedience that the responsible practitioner of political obligation must keep in mind whenever laws or public policies appear to violate rights; in such contexts there may be an obligation to disobey (Flathman 1972, pp. 263–64).

But, to Flathman, the purpose of civil disobedience is not so much to struggle for the defense, let alone for the expansion, of human rights as it is to protect the so-called democratic system from blemishes. When he returns to the argument in the *Crito*, in concluding his book on political obligation, Flathman takes Socrates to affirm first of all that not so much the individual's moral or material well-being as the political order itself is "sacred," and secondarily that the stability and preservation of the political order require a general obedience (Flathman 1972, pp. 254–56). The Socratic position, thus interpreted, and assuredly including the idea that disobedience in the struggle for human rights normally should be punishable under the law, is recommended by Flathman as "the arrangement most conducive to intelligent thinking about obedience and disobedience" (p. 256).

Advanced contract theorists today appear to be just as state-centered as Flathman's Socrates was in their theorizing about political obligation. Joseph Tussman stresses the contrast between the authentic, democratic ideal of informed consent as basis for political obligation and the prevalence in the real world of a phony, inauthentic semblance of consent. He speaks of most native-born (not naturalized) citizens of his so-called democratic country (the United States) as "political child-brides" at best. This is not because human beings are by nature apolitical but because the commercialized civilization of the United States has replaced the political "come let us reason together" with the pseudopolitical "come let us bargain together"; what is strived for is not what is most reasonable or just but what is the most acceptable trade-off between contending moneyed interests.

Where, then, is the moral basis for political obligation to this kind of regime? Tussman does not say, and yet throughout his analysis he keeps on assuming that there must be a political obligation to the nation-state. Wistfully, he concludes by exhorting "the people" to take its function as the fourth branch of government seriously—its deliberative function, to be freed from the bargaining orientation (Tussman 1960). And in a subsequent book Tussman argues eloquently for a strengthening of the democratic system of government, not by way of expanding social equality or socioeconomic rights but by improving on the quality, including the good manners, of political discourse (Tussman 1977).

John Rawls's contractarian theory of justice is rather cautious on the theme of political obligation. Rawls assumes that there are "natural duties" that will be recognized in the Original Position[3] and will have their impact on the working out of the principles and institutions of justice. He assumes that "the natural duty of justice would be agreed to rather than a principle of utility, and that from the standpoint of the theory of justice, it is the fundamental requirement for individuals. Principles of obligation while compatible with it are not alternatives but rather have a complementary role" (Rawls 1971, p. 337). There is no *general* political obligation, for "all obligations arise from the principle of fairness" and are based on explicit or implied but freely extended promises. No society in the real world achieves justice for all. Although people in public office and others who benefit from dealing with the state must be assumed to have taken on political obligations to the state, the same does not hold for members of disadvantaged communities, for "unjust social arrangements are themselves a kind of extortion, even violence, and consent to them does not bind. The reason for this condition is that the parties in the original position would insist on it" (Rawls 1971, pp. 342–43). And yet, for all his concern to limit by making contingent the principle of political obligation to the state, Rawls appears to go further than Flathman in assigning a duty to comply, under many kinds of circumstances, with unjust laws and is rather restrictive on the issues of civil disobedience and conscientious refusal, thus giving back with his left hand what he takes from state-centered obligation with his right hand. And, much like Flathman, Rawls asserts that "the conditions defining justified civil disobedience" should aim at maintaining "the stability of a just constitution" (pp. 333–91, 384).

On the issue of *how* unjust is the actual U.S. Constitution, Rawls is throughout his analysis disconcertingly vague, and it is therefore difficult to assess, for example, what proportion of the American population today he would consider politically obligated to the state, either generally speaking or in relation to specific issue contexts. Like most liberal theorists, Rawls appears to assume that any actual state's achievements toward just institutions are limited by the prior necessity of an efficient system of production and that efficiency to some extent

[3] This metaphor, the Original Position, provides for Rawls the model for rational public choice among principles and theories of justice. He imagines a situation prior to the process of constitution making, a forum open to all, in which the most basic *principles* of justice are selected, discussed, and agreed upon, for the guidance of the framers of the constitution (and, in turn, also for the guidance of legislators, administrators, judges, and citizens in general). To be enabled to produce just principles, the participants in the Original Position must all be free and equal and ignorant of their own and their children's future status and circumstances of life: There must be a universal "Veil of Ignorance" to keep the deliberations and the ensuing choice of principles of justice free from the influence of private interests. See Rawls 1971, chap. 3, and chap. 4, pp. 195–201.

requires class differences and perhaps even victims, among the losers in the competition for efficiency. His egalitarianism prompts him to insist that welfare regulations must be extended to all the disadvantaged, as far as is compatible with maintaining enough incentive-producing inequalities to satisfy production requirements in the general public interest (Rawls 1971, chap. 5).

Thus, the Protestant individualist work ethic looms in the background. Do we still need the work ethic, in a world with increasing proportions of redundant people, from the perspective of production? I find it troubling, too, that Rawls, who very commendably analyzes the issues of justice between generations, is far briefer and more cursory in his references to the issues of justice between the nations (Rawls 1971, pp. 378–79). It seems that under the Veil of Ignorance everyone knows that he or she is going to be the citizen of a comparatively well-off country. Rawls does not in this work articulate any strong concern with the risks of becoming beneficiaries of a state's unjust domination of the resources of other nations.

## A Paradigm Shift in Progress

There is a paradigm shift in progress, I shall argue, away from state-centered and away from liberal constructions of political obligation. By "state-centered" constructions I mean, very simply, those based on the assumption that every citizen prima facie owes a primary loyalty to his or her state, either unconditionally or on the condition that the state benefits or has benefited him or her in some significant way. By "liberal" I mean here, a bit less simply, those constructions of political obligation that are based on certain formal entitlements of citizenship, such as the right to vote in elections and to have one's vote counted as equal with other people's votes, the rights to free assembly and free speech, the right to stand or run for public office, and so on.

My expectation is that a humanist human rights paradigm will take the place, gradually, of the now prevailing paradigm, which is both state-centered and liberal, but this will be discussed in the next section. For now, let us look at the still prevailing paradigm in the perspective of some of its critics. It is a two-pronged one: The state-centered version in one sense dates from prehistory, as has been suggested, but as articulated theory its earliest influential statement is found in Plato's *Crito*. The liberal paradigm was made influential by Hobbes and Locke: The former initiated the perspective that urgent human needs require a powerful state, whereas the latter affirmed the thesis that every citizen owes his loyalty to the state, on a contractual basis, in return for having his own liberty and property protected. A similar understanding of a *quid pro quo,* as ongoing process rather than based on antecedent contract, marks utilitarian versions of the liberal constructions of political obligation.

State-centeredness came naturally with the teleological assumptions of the Greeks, who stressed the continuing civilizing function of the state, an outlook that peaked with Hegel and then was turned upside down by Marx. Marx thought of the feudal as well as the bourgeois state, whether liberal or not, as shackles to be cast aside, after the revolution, and left on the scrap heap of history. Liberalism came with capitalism and the progenitors of the new middle class, who saw the liberal state and general obedience to its dictates as useful in their own quest for economic wealth and power. The liberals had little interest in questions of whether radical moral improvements might be possible, someday, as a result of institutional changes. Unlike Marx, most liberals assumed that evidence of human frailties reflected a perennially weakly endowed human nature rather than an alienating system of economic and political institutions.

Most liberal writers have been and remain champions of freedom rather than equality. To some extent this may reflect a traditional class bias, in that basic subsistence rights have normally been taken for granted within the middle class in economically advanced countries; also, there has been the liberal assumption that the free market should be left undisturbed, enduring at least until the time of J. M. Keynes.

John Rawls, too, is above all else a champion of freedom, but with an emphasis on equality, too, which in the last decade or two has stimulated much rethinking of liberal assumptions. Rawls's First Principle of justice reads as follows: "Each person is to have an equal right to the most extensive total system of equal basic liberties compatible with a similar system of liberty for all" (Rawls 1971, p. 302). But this right to optimal liberties is a curiously abstract one. Access to these liberties, and therefore their worth, is for Rawls bound to exhibit considerable inequalities, given the assumed need for a production system based on individually different incentives. Norman Daniels, a critic of Rawls, reaches the conclusion that people in the Original Position might just as well have chosen to optimize equal *worth* of liberty. He concludes with a rhetorical question and his own answer: "Can a maximally extensive and equal system of liberties be successfully achieved without ruling out all significant inequalities of wealth and power? I believe not" (Daniels 1975, pp. 278, 281).

It is a traditional perversity of liberal thought, I have observed, to place human freedom needs ahead of our solidarity needs. Rawls comes close to giving equality equal rank with freedom (only in his imaginary Original Position is there full equality), although he falls short; but Daniels, a friendly critic, suggests a significant egalitarian revision, as we have just seen. However, as Ronald Dworkin's argument suggests, we must go further, if we are *Taking Rights Seriously* (1978), and insist on placing equality ahead of liberty as the more crucial general value—*followed,* of course, by optimal liberty, within the bounds of social solidarity. This, as we shall see, is the viable way toward a coherent postliberal construction of political obligation, if I am right in maintaining that valid obligations require a basis in valid moral or human rights.

Dworkin takes rights *so* seriously, in fact, that he as a jurist wants to do away with all judicial discretion in the courts, in principle, even in "hard cases"; and he believes that political philosophy will be of help to the conscientious judge. *Rights* is the key concept, he argues, in the philosophical systems most helpful to what Dworkin calls his own "liberal theory of law," as alternative to the "ruling theory of law." Since the latter is so often called liberal, I shall in this paper take the liberty of referring to Dworkin's position as *postliberal.* Dworkin's central claim, in his jurisprudence as well as his philosophy, asserts that scrupulous protection of the basic rights is crucial in determining the extent of our obligation to honor and obey the state.

Among all rights there is one that, to Dworkin, is fundamental to all the others: the right to "equal concern and respect." This is not a right to equal treatment, for individual needs and need priorities may vary. It is a right to be treated as equals; that is, to have our rights claims and other important concerns be given equal weight and consideration with those of others, assuming comparable claims and concerns, regardless of each person's assumed status or merit or other irrelevant characteristics (Dworkin 1978, pp. xii, xv, 227, 273, et passim).

Dworkin refrains, however, from trying to specify the substantive *criteria* by which "equal concern and respect" are to yield decisions in legal contests, let alone in administrative or political situations. How to measure or estimate the relative weight of conflicting individual needs and wants, or of categories of needs and wants? The conscientious judge must, of course, make such attempts as best he can, in relation to specific cases. Political theorists should press attempts to develop more general principles for weighing competing needs and wants categories, beyond such general principles as would have demonstrable needs take precedence over what appear to be mere wants or preferences, and would perhaps recognize a Maslow type of basic needs hierarchy. There are many complications; for example, the normal difficulties of assessing comparatively the various degrees of existing satisfaction of a given kind of basic need (more difficult with emotional needs, less difficult with physiological needs, generally speaking).

The basic rights thesis is for my purposes the most crucial part of Dworkin's critique of liberal political obligation: If a citizen violates a law of doubtful constitutionality, then, even if the court were to uphold that law, the citizen ought to be acquitted, Dworkin argues, if he or she had reasonable grounds for this doubt and acted for a moral or rationally defensible purpose. Historically, such citizens have been the benefactors of their nation, for they have worked to expand the sphere of rights that all Americans enjoy today. In every contest between a nonviolent lawbreaker and the state, the court's first hypothesis ought to be that the law might indeed violate a constitutional right; if so, the lawbreaker deserves not only acquittal but commendation for his service to the nation (Dworkin 1978, pp. 206–22).

I find this line of reasoning persuasive. Also, there are at least two more kinds of argument that in my view promise to push for a paradigm shift away from state-centered, liberal assumptions about political obligation. One raises the issues of democratic legitimation, more explicitly than Tussman does, given a state system like the American or Canadian, in which the cloak of formal democracy with only modest success attempts to hide vast differentials in real political power; beginning with Robert Michels's classic *Political Parties*, there is now a massive behavioralist literature to show that every large and powerful organization, including every state, is run by oligarchies, generally speaking, even though in some regimes the public can exert a significant share of influence (Michels 1949). The other line of argument cuts to the core of the moral status of the tacit-consent theory with this question: Why should I be expected to be loyal to any regime that would keep me comfortable at the expense of other people's suffering, either in my own country or in foreign countries dependent on decisions made or conditions dictated by "my" regime?

The problem of the democratic make-believe, that counterfeit of legitimating democracy, is augmented in Carole Pateman's excellent critique of liberal theories of political obligation by her questioning of the moral capabilities of possessive individualists. She stresses the differences between promises, which create self-assumed political obligations, and supposed obligations laid down on us by other people or agencies, for example, the state. Her most basic contention is that the very concept of *political* obligation is incoherent if we assume, as most liberals have been doing, even Rawls in a qualified manner (Rawls 1971, chap. 6), a world of possessive, narrowly and shortsightedly selfish individualists. However, Pateman writes, if people are held to be capable of promising and of keeping promises, they might also be capable of *building* "a democratic political order based on self-assumed political obligation. . . . Political theorists who show such great ingenuity in formulating voluntarist justifications for political obligation might have been expected to be keenly interested in exploring the possibilities of such a development—were it not for their totally uncritical attitude to the liberal democratic state" (Pateman 1979, p. 36. and, on popular democratic capabilities, Pateman 1970).

The last but not least of the harbingers of a paradigm shift that I shall refer to here is Burton Zwiebach's important work, *Civility and Disobedience* (1975). The central thrust of his critique of the liberal theory of tacit consent as a legitimate source of political obligation is in my opinion utterly persuasive:

> The traditional notion of tacit consent holds that my consent may be inferred from my voluntary enjoyment of the benefits offered me by society. A society which offers real benefits to two-thirds of its members is thus entitled to their consent and the consequent presumptions of legitimacy as long as they enjoy these benefits. Now suppose that I am one of those old-fashioned romantics who has a genuine concern for the wellbeing of my fellow men, who is disturbed by the thought of starving children, or who believes that I am not free where a sizeable number of my fellows is chained. It is entirely plausible that I should conclude that a regime under which such things take place is not entitled to be called legitimate. Yet at this point I discover that while I continue to enjoy benefits I cannot withdraw my allegiance from a regime which denies them to others, that I cannot be my brother's keeper. [Zwiebach 1975, p. 58]

## A Humanist Human Rights Foundation for Political Obligation, and Some Legal and Public Policy Implications

Let me first state the essential case, as I see it, for the humanist human rights construction of political obligation (1), and then attempt to derive some consequences for the legal order (2) and for public policies (3).

1. Neither a Rawlsian liberal democratic nor an anarchist or Marxist construction of political obligation will do, I shall argue: We are better off going back to Rousseau and then moving forward in the direction recently reinforced by Pateman, Zwiebach, and Dworkin.

Rawlsian rationality dictates a distinction, we have seen, between natural duties and deliberately assumed obligations; although the former (like the duty to help others who are in danger when it is easy to do so) would be accepted in the Original Position as essential to any just moral order, the latter require freely given promises in the real world. However, people in the Original Position would nonetheless, Rawls thinks, settle for a system of imperfect justice in which the state would institute imperfect laws and policies, most of which the citizen would be in the wrong to disobey or resist, whether or not he or she had consented to a specific law or policy.

I have no quarrel with Rawls's natural duties, except that I think they can be and should be derived from human rights (HRs) and from the humanist norm (HN). More important, I think the same holds for the construction of political obligation and its limits and the corollary rights and duties of civil disobedience or other kinds of resistance. Here, I think Rawls gives too much too freely to the state.

My HN–HRs alternative differs from anarchist and Marxist constructions of political obligation. Anarchist theories, from Godwin to Wolff, have tended to reject all notions of political obligation beyond the bonds of local communities and have not allowed for the fact that the state in many historical situations can be an ally as well as an adversary of liberty; it can protect as well as destroy human rights; some states have defended revolutionary improvements in human rights.[4] Many Marxists have attached almost unlimited political obligations to the perceived proletarian class interest, or even to whatever political party or state is understood to serve the interests of the working class or its political party. Recent Marxist academic writers, including Habermas, O'Connor, and Alan Wolfe, have developed sophisticated appraisals of so-called legitimation crises in "late-capitalist" societies but have offered no clear alternate conceptions of political obligation (Habermas 1975; O'Connor 1973; Wolfe 1977). From a different perspective, Robert E. Lane has contributed insightful sociopsychological critiques of the legitimation crisis theme; but he has not indicated what approach should take the place of the increasingly inauthentic and moribund pillars of empirical and moral theory on which liberal-democratic obligation theory now rests (1979*a*, 1979*b*).

To begin the humanist reconstruction project, I suggest that we take off from Rousseau's conception of a social contract, which differs as profoundly from the Socratic "understanding" among moral men as from Hobbes's and Locke's purposive contracts between pragmatic individualists. Rousseau's contract aspires to realize HN, the basic humanist norm, which in this paper stipulates that "the degree of civilization achieved at a given time is to be assessed by the degree of secure freedom achieved by those in a given social order who are least privileged."

---

[4] Some new regimes have achieved radical improvements in the socioeconomic terms of life for the least privileged classes, at least for a time; for example, Fidel Castro's regime in Cuba, Allende's regime in Chile, and the Sandinista regime in Nicaragua. On anarchist political obligation, see Godwin 1971, and Wolff 1970; on anarchism versus nationalism in Canada, see Nelles and Rotstein 1973. The state's double role as enemy and ally of freedom is discussed in Bay 1981, pp. 160–165.

Rousseau asks, "Does not the undertaking entered into by the whole body of the nation bind it to provide for the security of the least of its members with as much care as for that of all the rest?" He answers, and a liberal democrat he is not: "So little is it the case that any one person ought to perish for all, that all have pledged their lives and properties for the defence of each, in order that the weakness of individuals may always be protected by the strength of the public, and each member by the whole State" (Rousseau 1973, p. 132).

Rousseau's General Will originates, in different phrasing to be sure, the modern idea of universal protection for human rights as the legitimating foundation for sovereignty and as a determinant of its limits. Every citizen, including the prince, is, according to Rousseau, bound by the system of equal rights: "by the social contract, [all are] equal, all can prescribe what all should do, but no one has a right to demand that another shall do what he does not do himself" (Rousseau 1973, pp. 242, 165–278, also 174 et passim). By contrast with the now prevailing liberal-democratic tradition, which routinely assigns legitimating power even to blatantly, inauthentically established majorities (even El Salvador's 1983 elections, in a land of right-wing death squads immune to prosecution, served to legitimate the regime in the eyes of their sponsor, the Reagan administration),[5] for Rousseau the citizen's loyalty to the state must be contingent on the state's scrupulous protection of every last citizen's human rights.

Many contemporary liberal writers expound eloquently on the theme that the state exists for the sake of man, not the other way around, especially when they wish to draw contrasts with so-called communist or totalitarian systems. But for which classes of men (and women?) does the liberal state exist? When conservatives and Manchester liberals discuss this, they tend to have privileged individuals in mind—those who are creative, energetic, productive, and so on. When left-leaning "social" liberals write, the reference is more democratic: The state is supposed to exist, legitimately, to enhance the freedom and well-being of the greatest number. For Rousseau and for modern

[5] "For decades, opposition groups have indeed attempted to take part in El Salvador's political process, only to be thwarted by the military, with U.S. approval. As late as 1980, some F.D.F. (Democratic Revolutionary Front) leaders openly remained in El Salvador despite threats to their personal safety. The results are well known. The F.D.F.'s moderate leader, Enrique Alvarez, together with the top echelon of the organization, was kidnapped from a political meeting and thereafter tortured and killed. Our Government found these murders 'regrettable' and immediately forgot they occurred. Is it then so surprising that Guillermo Ungo, the man who replaced Mr. Alvarez and a veteran of Salvadoran electoral politics, refuses to return the F.D.F. to open politics within El Salvador while the same army retains power?" (see Maggio 1983). Nobody responsible for such murders of Salvadorans, even after many thousands of them, has yet been convicted or even prosecuted. See also Fisher 1982.

humanists, as their priorities are understood here, governments exist to serve all men and women, but especially the least advantaged among them. The task of the legitimate state is to guarantee not just *order* but a *just* order, one that keeps trying to compensate for the natural (in the sense that the jungle is natural) tendency, reinforced in market-oriented systems, for those who are more resourceful to exploit or push aside those who are less resourceful. As a good hospital operates emergency wards for the sickest, so a just state must operate social services and health protection programs for the less well-off classes and persons, unless or until it can assure free and equal access to adequate benefits for all.

When Burton Zwiebach objects to seeing "a sizeable number of my fellows in chains," his point might have been put more precisely: He objects to seeing even a single person's basic rights violated, just as Rousseau said that *he* did. A social order that produces victims, whether by design or by some structural flaw, is to that extent an illegitimate social order, from which a humanist citizen must withdraw his or her allegiance. Zwiebach makes this construction of political obligation abundantly clear: "obligation, if it means anything at all, must be a product of moral argument which eventuates in judgment. . . . obligation is owed directly to one's fellows and only incidentally [I would say "conditionally," or "contingently"] to the state" (1975, p. 143).[6] To all our fellows, or to all of our neighbors, in the Christian idiom, but above all to those who need our solidarity most badly.

*And,* since human rights are universal, so our political obligation must be transnational. Those who need our solidarity most badly might at a given time be Guatemalan peasants or Campuchean refugees or aboriginal peoples in the process of being destroyed by corporate inroads on their lands.

Carole Pateman in the concluding section of her book on political obligation extends Zwiebach's argument and opts for a "horizontal" kind of political obligation "between citizens," in contrast with the "vertical" liberal construction of political obligation. She endorses Rousseau's democratic collectivism, by way of stating that the "aim of democratic political change is, as far as possible, to transform power relationships into relationships of authority in which citizens collectively exercise political authority" (Pateman 1979, pp. 174–75, 172–78). The difference between power and authority in this statement is analogous, I think, to the difference between decisions based on the liberal bargaining model of reasoning, whose prevalence Tuss-

---

[6]Zwiebach writes, further: "Our primary obligation is to our fellows. Our obligation to the state is prudential" (1975, p. 160).

man laments, and decisions based on rational models of deliberation about human rights, justice, or other conceptions of the common good. Pateman's parting words are these: "Self-assumed obligation, and the vision of social life as a voluntary scheme, are invaluable democratic kernels that deserve to be extracted from the shell of liberal hypothetical voluntarism" (1979, p. 178). Only actual participation in humanist politics can develop, in Flathman's phrase, an authentic *practice* of political obligation—one that helps to make a society more worth supporting and that makes the individual more conscious of what it is in his or her society, or world, that is worth supporting, defending, aiming for. Bargaining and negotiated compromise between elected representatives can determine which side or which brokers have more clout, not which side has arguments or claims more worth supporting.

2. The legal order within actual states of dubious legitimacy is, from a humanist perspective, a system of rules that the prudent citizen nevertheless heeds. The humanist citizen, like the liberal, ought to be prudent. Where he or she differs from the liberal or the nationalist citizen is in the disinclination to consider obedience or disobedience as such a moral issue. To the extent that the state seeks to protect the interests of its nationals at the expense of access to human rights for worse-off people abroad, for example, the humanist should not be, or feel, either morally or politically obligated to that state. His or her duty is, in my view, to ponder whether to disobey, or even resist, the most relevant laws. But it is necessary to weigh both the moral and the prudential issues.

As we have seen, Ronald Dworkin is one jurist who believes that the courts ought to empathize with and to some extent support the conscientious citizen who at times chooses to disobey, because he sees the legal system's legitimacy ultimately based in, and depending on, its defense of the most basic rights.

In his title essay in *Taking Rights Seriously,* Dworkin argues that in the United States "certain moral rights [are] made into legal rights by the Constitution" and that these are rights in the strong sense, entitled to protection against interference, even against interference by constitutionally enacted law. Consequently, a person sometimes has "the right, in the strong sense, to disobey a law. He has that right whenever the law wrongly invades his rights against the Government." He is entitled to violate any such law with impunity, for "it is silly to speak of a duty to obey the law as such, or of a duty to accept the punishment that the State has no right to give" (1978, pp. 190–93, 184–205).

Dworkin's jurisprudence, grounded in his rights-centered philosophy, not only takes rights seriously but makes the enforcement of the basic rights the crucial condition of legal as well as political obligation to the state. Though he does not probe beyond the stipulated most basic right to equal concern and respect, his constructivist method of legal reasoning seeks to insure a continuing dialectical process in the evolution of court-made law, toward a steady broadening of the scope of those rights that the U.S. Constitution is understood to protect. In contrast with what he calls the "natural model" of legal reasoning, his "constructivist model" engages in the construction of a more adequate theory of justice. "It treats intuitions of justice not as clues to the existence of independent principles (of justice), but rather as stipulated features of a general theory to be constructed." In the interest of achieving advances in the protection of basic rights, while at the same time avoiding the risk of increased uncertainty about what is the law, this approach assumes "that men and women have a responsibility to fit the particular judgments on which they act into a coherent program of action, or, at least, that officials who exercise powers over other men have that sort of responsibility." Legal precedents are not to be seen as revelations of justice, and yet the judge cannot ignore them in relevant new cases; the constructivist judge "accepts these precedents as specifications for a principle that he must construct, out of a sense of responsibility for consistence with what has gone before" (1978, pp. 160–61, 150–83).

3. The range of potential public policy implications of a humanist human rights outlook, if it gains influence, is extensive. It amounts to a new kind of Declaration of Independence, from a lot of assumptions and traditions. Increasing mistrust of authorities and demands for easy access to critical political knowledge will come to take the place of present dependency for information on what commercial mass media see fit to print (Bay 1977). The Ralph Nader model of active citizenship will become more widely emulated, with a beneficial impact on the process of shaping public policies: They will become more influenced than they are now by the likelihood that they must stand the test of intelligent, critical public scrutiny.

The Nuremberg judgments, the prosecution of Nazi war criminals in various countries, and the trial of Lieutenant Calley mark the beginning stages, we must hope, toward the development of a new international human rights law. It must come to be widely understood that there are crimes of obedience, in principle punishable nationally as well as internationally, whenever a government has overstepped its bounds of legitimacy and its officials or citizens have been induced to commit crimes against humanity. The Universal Declaration, the two UN Covenants and the Optional Protocol to one of them, as well as the establishment of the UN Commission on Human Rights, can be seen as further steps toward making basic human rights law an enforceable system of international norms, eventually (*International Bill of Human Rights* 1978; Tolly 1983).

While international lawyers and political leaders work on the legal and the diplomatic stage, it is for political theorists and educators to work within each national political arena to argue for the kind of principles of political obligation that make our loyalty to the basic human rights prevail over our nationalist loyalties. "Our team" should no longer be the nation but all the *victims* of the world's liberal economic order of states and private corporations; or, at any rate, those victims abroad and at home for whose lives and basic rights we can hope to do something by way of educational and political and economic action.

This includes, of course, the *potential* victims of a likely nuclear war, of the ongoing poisoning of our environment, and of the ongoing decimation of the many Third World peoples and ethnic minorities now being rendered redundant within the liberal world market system, since their productivity is so hopelessly far behind that of the new liberal superpower nation, Japan.

Let me conclude by way of suggesting what I take to be some *general* public policy implications, loosely speaking, of the kind of human rights commitment that is articulated in this paper. These suggestions are intended to provoke questions and discussion, and I shall be assertive and brief at the risk of sounding dogmatic (for a more extended argument, see Bay 1982b):

— The humanist commitment is to human rights, with the protection of life itself, all human lives, as the most pressing objective. Peace, and above all avoidance of a nuclear holocaust, constitutes the first human right, the most basic collective as well as individual human right.

— As peace is a basic human right, so there must be a right to defend the peace, with appropriate means, along with an obligation to refrain from, and if need be resist, means of defense that threaten the security of other nations and thus also menace the nation's own stake in international security.

— World security requires defense of *all* states against at least four kinds of danger: military attack, accidental war, ecological destruction, and destruction of people by structural (neoimperialist) violence. Current superpower defense postures aggravate world insecurity by focusing on the first danger alone and by seeking to reduce this danger for one side at the expense of undermining the other side's security from military attack.

— As humanists we are obligated to resist these defense postures and indeed to resist our governments' constant appeals to inauthentic patriotism. Authentic patriotism requires a higher loyalty: to human rights everywhere and to each nation's stake in helping to build a human rights world order.

— Humanists must be prepared to defend not their nation's self-interest as defined by authorities but our own and our nation's stake, as we understand it, in achieving a world order of optimal human rights according to humanist priorities.

— All disarmament efforts must be gradual and largely reciprocal, to avoid increasing national fears and the hazards of even temporary instability. Armed forces should in the end be strong enough to protect basic human rights but not strong enough to make war possible.

— Today's military forces, minus most of their arms, might under UN auspices be transformed and equipped for international service tasks geared toward building a new world order; tasks like relief missions, rescue missions, peace-keeping missions, ecological repair missions, and so on. As the present preoccupation with war games and the risks of war enhance distrust and insecurity, so engagement in cooperative projects for humane international tasks will build mutual trust and faith in a better future for our species.

— International education programs must seek to reinforce our awareness, in all countries, of being human, with a shared, most pressing need to build a world of peace and other human rights. To this task, we must come to understand, we owe our supreme political obligation. No matter what our nationality, in today's endangered world, this kind of transnational commitment represents the most rational and authentic manifestation of patriotism.

## Bibliography

Americas Watch Report on Guatemala, supplement. 1983. In *New York Review of Books,* June 2, pp. 13–16.

Aristotle. 1943. *Politics.* Jowett translation. New York: Modern Library.

Bay, Christian. 1977. Access to political knowledge as a human right. In Itzhak Galnoor, ed., *Government secrecy in democracies,* chap. 2. New York: Harper and Row.

———. 1980a. Human needs, wants, and politics: Abraham Maslow, meet Karl Marx. *Social Praxis* 7 : 233–52.

———. 1980b. Peace and critical political knowledge as human rights. *Political Theory* 8 : 293–334.

———. 1981. *Strategies of political emancipation.* Notre Dame, Ind.: University of Notre Dame Press.

———. 1982a. Self-respect as a human right. *Human Rights Quarterly* 4 : 53–75.

———. 1982b. Hazards of Goliath in the nuclear age: Need for rational priorities in American peace and defense policies. *Alternatives* 8 : 441–82.

———. 1984. Human rights on the periphery: No room in the ark for the Yanomami? *Development Dialogue,* nos. 1–2, pp. 23–41.

———. 1987. Postliberal citizenship, human rights, and the defense of indigenous peoples. In Peter Blanchard and Peter Landstreet, eds., *Human rights in Latin America and the Caribbean*. Toronto: CALACS.

Burke, Edmund. 1969 [1790]. *Reflections on the revolution in France*. Harmondsworth: Penguin Books.

Cranston, Maurice. 1973. *What are human rights?* London: Bodley Head.

Daniels, Norman. 1975. Equal liberty and equal worth of liberty. In N. Daniels, ed., *Reading Rawls*, chap. 11. Oxford: Blackwell.

Davis, Shelton H. 1977. *Victims of the miracle: Development and the Indians of Brazil*. Cambridge: Cambridge University Press.

Dworkin, Ronald. 1978. *Taking rights seriously*. Cambridge, Mass.: Harvard University Press.

Etzioni, Amitai. 1968. *The active society*. New York: Free Press.

Fisher, Stewart W. 1982. Human rights in El Salvador and U.S. foreign policy. *Human Rights Quarterly* 4:1–38.

Flathman, Richard E. 1972. *Political obligation*. New York: Atheneum.

Godwin, William. 1971 [1793]. *Enquiry concerning political justice*. Oxford: Oxford University Press.

Habermas, Jürgen. 1975 [1973]. *Legitimation crisis*. Boston: Beacon Press.

Hobbes, Thomas. 1968 [1651]. *Leviathan*. Edited by C. B. Macpherson. Harmondsworth: Penguin Books.

Hume, David. 1953. *Political essays*. Edited by Charles W. Hendel. New York: Liberal Arts Press.

*The international bill of human rights*. 1978. New York: Office of Public Information, United Nations.

Lane, Robert E. 1979a. The legitimacy bias: Conservative man in market and state. In Bogdan Denitch, ed., *Legitimation of regimes*, pp. 55–79. London: Sage.

———. 1979b. The dialectics of freedom in a market society. Edmund Janes Lecture, University of Illinois.

Locke, John. 1965. *Two treatises of government*. Edited by Peter Laslett. New York: New American Library (Mentor Books).

Macpherson, C. B. 1962. *The political theory of possessive individualism*. Oxford: Oxford University Press.

Maggio, Michael. 1983. Letter to the editor. *New York Times*, May 25, p. 24.

McPherson, Thomas. 1967. *Political obligation*. London: Routledge and Kegan Paul.

Michels, Robert. 1949 [1915]. *Political parties*. Glencoe, Ill.: Free Press.

Nelles, Viv, and Abraham Rotstein, eds. 1973. *Nationalism or local control: Responses to George Woodcock*. Toronto: New Press.

O'Connor, James. 1973. *The fiscal crisis of the state*. New York: St. Martin's Press.

Pateman, Carole. 1970. *Participation and democratic theory*. Cambridge: Cambridge University Press.

———. 1979. *The problem of political obligation: A critical analysis of liberal theory*. Chichester: Wiley.

Plato. 1948. *Euthyphro, Apology, and Crito*. New York: Liberal Arts Press.

Rawls, John. 1971. *A theory of justice*. Cambridge, Mass.: Harvard University Press.

Rousseau, Jean-Jacques. 1973. *The social contract and discourses*. London: Dent.

Smith, J. C. 1976. *Legal obligation*. Toronto: University of Toronto Press.

Stein, Heather, et al. 1982. Synopsis of the 1980–81 country reports of the inter-American commission on human rights. *Human Rights Quarterly* 4: 406–31.

Tolly, Howard, Jr. 1983. Decision-making at the United Nations commission on human rights. *Human Rights Quarterly* 5:27–57.

Tussman, Joseph. 1960. *Obligation and the body politic*. New York: Oxford University Press.

———. 1977. *Government and the mind*. New York: Oxford University Press.

Wolfe, Alan. 1977. *The limits of legitimacy*. New York: Free Press.

Wolff, Robert Paul. 1970. *In defense of anarchism*. New York: Harper and Row.

Zwiebach, Burton. 1975. *Civility and disobedience*. Cambridge: Cambridge University Press.

*Part III*  Social Psychology

# Daniel Katz

## 9 The Development of Social Psychology as a Research Science

Social psychology as a field of philosophical inquiry goes back to Aristotle and Plato, but as a research science its history does not reach much beyond the twentieth century. In fact, most of its experimental and empirical studies are a matter of recent decades. The careers and achievements of a number of contemporary scholars like Herbert Hyman reflect the story of the transformation of a speculative social discipline into a behavioral science.

In this development five overlapping stages can be discerned.

1. The first breakthrough came when inquiring minds in the search for answers to specific questions turned from the traditional wisdom and moral precepts of the culture to studies of the world of facts. The point of departure started with naturalistic observation of social phenomena as in the work of early anthropologists influenced by the Darwinian descriptive approach in the study of plants and animals. This was followed in limited instances by controls in the observation process in the form of measurement techniques and primitive experimental procedures.

2. The second advance was the realization that the methods of science were not confined to a few limited questions about social phenomena but could be applied generally to man's relation to his fellows. For centuries questions about social matters were seldom raised because the answers were already provided in societal teachings. When a question did arise, there were accepted authorities, political or religious, to give the proper reply. Even today authoritative assertion, the exercise of power, and argument are often preferred to scientific investigation as methods for dealing with social issues. It took a revolu-

tion in men's thinking at the beginning of this century to view social processes as natural phenomena.

3. A third step forward was taken with the growth of techniques of experimentation, field studies and surveys and their accompanying measurement and analytic procedures. The technology that developed helped to institutionalize the scientific approach in social studies, give status to the behavioral scientist, and provide training for apprentices. Highly significant in this technological progress were the improvements in the methods of field studies and surveys. In the past social scientists were either confined to highly limited experimental findings or had to examine data gathered for various practical purposes by agencies not part of a scientific enterprise. Surveys and field methods made it possible for social scientists to gather their own data with consideration for their reliability, validity, and adequacy. A discipline without control of its own data, relying on secondary sources for its facts, is at a great disadvantage compared to the sciences.

4. Middle-level theories emerged to replace global points of view on the one hand and rank empiricism on the other. Theoretical concepts at this level called for the constant interplay of theory and research findings. Such an interaction of fact and conceptualization, leading to modifications of interpretation, is central to the growth of knowledge, the cumulative nature of which characterizes science in contrast to the humanities, as Conant (1947) has pointed out.

5. Even after social psychology had attained some status as an independent field of inquiry it encountered a major difficulty, common to most areas of science, namely, specialization and fragmentation. This has been aggravated by its two methodologies. One is the controlled experimentation of the laboratory, the other the survey and field study of a wider world of social reality. Two social psychologies were the outcome of specialists following these approaches, the first relatively atomistic and so heavily individual as to be almost indistinguishable from elementary psychology. Recently, there have been stirrings on the part of some specialists to try to counter the tendencies toward bifurcation and fragmentation.

In detailing the stages described above, reference will be made at appropriate places to the significant role of Herbert Hyman in his constant formulation of problems as researchable questions, in his major contributions to methodology, and in his integrative theories and research.

## The Beginnings of Social Psychology as a Research Discipline

The systematic treatises of Ross (1908) and McDougall (1908) are sometimes cited as the beginning of social psychology. These volumes, however, were not based on research findings, though they did address social problems realistically. It was but a step from some of their concepts to empirical investigations, albeit a long step for most of the scholars at the time. Moreover, as texts entitled *Social Psychology*, they directed attention to the discipline and helped to create an identity for the field. McDougall's work reflected the biological and evolutionary trends in British thinking and sought an explanation of man's social actions in instincts and their corresponding sentiments. Ross's text was not sociological in the sense of a social structural approach as in Durkheim's writings. Like his French predecessors Ross took over the mechanisms and concepts of abnormal psychology to explain crowd behavior and mass contagion, thus extending the work of Tarde (1890) and Le Bon (1895). The research origins of social psychology actually go back before the writings of McDougall and Ross, for in 1897 two studies employing scientific methods were reported: Durkheim's *Le Suicide* and Triplett's "Dynamogenic Factors in Pacemaking and Competition."

Durkheim examined the statistics on suicide rates for various regions of France in relation to nationality, religion, age, sex, marital status, family size, place of residence, variations in economic status, seasons of the year, and time of the day. His conclusions about the relationships of various types of suicide to the integration of groups, and the integration of the individual into the group, stimulated other investigators to pursue his theory of anomie and social integration. But from a methodological standpoint Durkheim's work on suicide reflected an even greater advance. He demonstrated how already accumulated data could be subjected to successive tests of various hypotheses and alternative explanations of findings. It illustrates the constant interplay of ideas and quantitative facts. It also shows the possibility of the replication of a relationship in secondary data. It took years, however, before Durkheim's resourceful use of careful statistical analysis was appreciated as a powerful tool of empirical social science. Even this belated recognition would not have been so widespread if it had not been for Herbert Hyman's documenting in detail Durkheim's resourceful methodology in Hyman's *Survey Design and Analysis* (1955) and showing the relevance of these procedures to current investigations.

The other research beginning of social psychology was the Triplett experiment on group influence (1897). Triplett was the first investigator to bring a social process into the laboratory for controlled manipulation and measurement. He studied the effects of competition on human performance and measured the average time of subjects on a simple motor task while working alone and while competing against one another. The idea of using the laboratory for social experiments, however, was slow in gaining acceptance. It was in Germany, where the tradition of the psychological laboratory was well established, that the first systematic group experiments took place. In 1903 Mayer found that schoolchildren did better on mental tasks in the group situation than in the alone situation and that there was convergence on a group norm. Working in the group produced a lower average deviation of scores than did solitary work. In 1920 Moede reported on a series of experiments that extended the alone/together paradigm to additional types of tasks such as word association, resisting ideomotor suggestion, and withstanding pain. He also pitted groups against one another and found that individuals in competing groups did better than individuals competing against individuals. The interest in group effects was broadening in Münsterberg's study (1914) of changes in individual judgment about factual matters when exposed to the judgments of colleagues—early evidence for the theory of *group-think*.

The stage was thus set for the breakthrough in American social psychology achieved by Floyd H. Allport in his programmatic experiments on social facilitation, rivalry, and conformity at the Harvard laboratory in 1916–19. Allport's studies (1920) went beyond previous work in (*a*) the range of psychological functions investigated, (*b*) the carefulness and thoroughness of the controls and methods, and (*c*) the conceptualization and generalization of findings. His results indicated that different processes were at work for simple tasks such as vowel cancellation than for mentally demanding tasks such as detecting flaws in logical syllogisms in their susceptibility to social influences. For the simple task, the together situation was clearly superior to the alone situation. For the problem-solving task, working in the presence of coworkers gave inferior performances to working in isolation. In other experiments Allport compared judgments of the magnitude and intensity of stimuli alone and in the group setting. Individuals made fewer extreme judgments in the group, and evaluations were more moderate and uniform.

Allport formulated the concepts of social facilitation, social increment and decrement, and group conformity as generalizations of his various findings. Both social facilitation and group conformity generated research for decades—and for some aspects of conformity throughout the history of social psychology.

## The General Acceptance of Scientific Procedures in Seeking Answers to Social Problems

Zajonc (1966) has raised the interesting question of why social psychology was relatively late in emerging as a research science. In the natural sciences the velocity of light had been measured in 1675 and the speed of nerve impulses in 1850. The lack of technology is no answer, for Triplett's experiment required no technical instruments and could have been performed centuries earlier. Zajonc suggests that the main reason for the slowness to attack social problems scientifically was the deeply entrenched attitude of seeking answers in custom, the mores, the legal code, religious beliefs, and political authority. But with the erosion of feudal institutions, the decline in political and religious absolutism, and new problems arising from industrialization and urbanization the old norms were in flux. The certain and simple answers they provided were no longer adequate. Gordon Allport (1954) has written similarly about the historical background of social psychology and has pointed out Comte's insightful postulation of three stages in the development of the social sciences. In the first two stages the social studies were under the constraints of the theological and the metaphysical and only recently entered the third stage of positivism.

Recognition of the scientific method as a fruitful way of discovering principles of social behavior came slowly and, outside of academia, in limited fashion. Nonetheless, it did gain acceptance, and the idea that social man was a logical subject for natural inquiry no longer seemed bizarre. The leadership of Floyd Allport helped the creation of the new science in three ways:

1. He fought vigorously for a basic and comprehensive science of social psychology. Interventions of some limited practical problem should not deter researchers from seeking fundamental principles. Nor does any difficult social area lie outside scientific scrutiny, Allport contended. He warned against the conventional fictions accepted by laymen and scholars alike which served as explanations of social phenomena—the group fallacies and institutional fictions generated not by science but in the interests of social convenience or social privilege.

2. Allport brought together the scattered findings of relevant experiments and research studies in a systematic behavioristic text entitled *Social Psychology* (1924). This was the first text in social psychology to be

based upon research. It made the field as courses in the subject sprang up in departments of psychology and sociology the country over. A wave of experimentation followed.

3. The scientific approach was carried by Allport beyond the walls of the laboratory to the observation and measurement of people in real-life situations. He sent his students into communities and institutional settings to record behavior and measure attitudes. R. L. Schanck studied a small community over time, describing and accounting for changes in public and private attitudes and their interrelationships (1932). Other students of Allport measured conforming behavior to institutional symbols in a church, a factory, and a traffic situation. Still others inquired into the patterning of attitudes and values and their relationship to personal and environmental factors. One result was the documentation of Allport's theory of pluralistic ignorance (Katz and Allport 1931). The obstacles encountered by the Allport group in their pioneering work on the measurement of attitudes led Allport to turn to the psychometrician Thurstone for help. The Thurstone scales and the Thurstone method of scaling (1928) were the outcome.

As in other fields of human endeavor, the upward curve of social science progress was irregular and jagged. In spite of the gigantic steps forward taken by Allport and his followers, there were many setbacks to the use of research as an alternative to traditional means of obtaining answers to social problems. In the first place, societies have defenses in depth against change or threats of change. The existing power structure does not willingly support knowledge seeking that may alter present arrangements. Some areas of social behavior are off limits and taboo to the researcher. It took many years before there were scientific inquiries into sexual behavior and power relationships in the United States. In the second place, social science had to contend with the rule-of-thumb practical knowledge of people, which for some problems was ahead of fragmentary research. Even in the less complex natural world it took time for science to outstrip some aspects of the wisdom derived from direct experience. In some instances the research of the behavioral scientists was apparently documenting the obvious or furnishing oversimplified and inadequate explanations. The public wanted immediate answers and were not content with the promise of a payoff in the remote future after the building of a body of scientific knowledge. And the pressure for immediate results produced applied studies of limited use and further postponed the growth of basic knowledge.

In the third place, there was a psychological barrier among social scientists to becoming full participants in experimental and quantitative research. As members of a society they brought many of the preconceptions of that society to their professional careers. They were not accustomed to formulating problems in their own field in researchable terms. They did not know what questions to ask or what methods would be likely to furnish answers. Techniques of research had not been part of the training of the older scholars. But an even greater obstacle was the new way of thinking about social phenomena.

Though progress was uneven because of these factors, the times stimulated a few talented students of human behavior to show the way to their colleagues in the conversion of traditional social disciplines into fields of scientific inquiry. Among the leaders in this movement were four men who combined technical expertise with theoretical creativity—Kurt Lewin, Rensis Likert, Paul Lazarsfeld, and Herbert Hyman. Their specific contributions to methodology and theory will be discussed later, but at this point mention can be made of the continuing work of Herbert Hyman throughout his career in his ingenious use of measurement techniques in making problems researchable, in his search for theoretical generalizations, and in his application of social psychological theory and method to the other social sciences. Political science in the early decades of this century had been philosophical rather than scientific in its theory, and journalistic rather than measurement-oriented in its empiricism. The research and writing of Hyman on public opinion (Hyman and Sheatsley 1950, 1953), electoral behavior, and political socialization (1959) were important in the development of political behaviorism. This movement transformed much of traditional political science into a quantitatively oriented discipline with data banks from surveys one of its major resources and with its official journal carrying many articles of a social psychological character. Similarly, Hyman's studies of race relationships (1969; Hyman and Sheatsley 1964), of voluntary associations (Hyman and Wright 1958), of mass communication, and of industrial psychology have stimulated sociologists to join hands with psychologists in their empirical investigations of societal problems. Another field that has benefited greatly from his active participation is that of cross-cultural and cross-national research (Hyman 1965). He has emphasized the importance of comparable research designs in such ventures to determine the generality of findings and the conditions that limit generalization.

## The Development of an Appropriate and Adequate Methodology

The first experiments in social psychology required little more technically than a knowledge of elementary controls and the random assignment of subjects to experimental and control conditions. The achievement of similar controls in field studies and surveys posed a more difficult problem. Yet much of the substance of social psychology had to be studied outside the laboratory. Social psychology deals with individuals in group settings and with the comparison of group functions, only some aspects of which can be created in the laboratory. In the real world people can rarely be assigned randomly to groups and conditions, save in the armed forces and in an occasional industrial organization. To make up for some of the weaknesses in a nonlaboratory approach, survey researchers gave their attention to three procedures: (1) representative sampling, (2) interviewing, and (3) research design. Sampling becomes critical in comparing groups as they respond to various conditions and situations. Without representative sampling we do not know whether we are dealing with the group factor supposedly under investigation. Before representative sampling it was common practice to select subjects readily available and generalize about differences among them. A great deal of cross-national and cross-cultural research is still based upon conveniently selected respondents not necessarily representative of the cultures being compared. We can find relationships in our data where no sampling design has been used, but we do not know the validity of the relationship or its true nature unless we have faithful measures of the factors supposedly related. To correct for selective errors in the choice of respondents, the naive resort was the use of large numbers as in the *Literary Digest* mail polls. But, where a selective bias exists, increasing the numbers can just increase the bias. And yet mail questionnaires continue to be used in applied research, sometimes even by academic investigators, in spite of their self-selective character.

The first requisite in sampling design is a clear definition of the universe or universes under study. The second requirement is a plan to provide that each respondent in that universe has an equal probability of being selected or, more accurately, that the probability of a respondent's selection be known. A final requirement is that the plan be checked in practice to insure its faithful execution. A methodological victory of major proportions was achieved when probability samples of known populations were drawn by social scientists working for the U.S. Census Bureau in the thirties and forties. Rensis Likert grasped the significance of probability sampling and became its champion in the survey movement. And social psychology moved ahead by leaps and bounds as sampling design came into use. A shortcut to attain the benefits of precise probability sampling had been taken by market researchers in the thirties in their use of the method of quota control. George Gallup applied quota control to national polls, and his lead was followed by all research organizations save Likert's Program Surveys and its successor, the Michigan Survey Research Center. The controversy over Likert's use of probability sampling and Gallup's quota control was long prolonged and attested to the importance of methodological issues in the history of behavioral science. Theoretically, the quota control procedure could provide a representative sample because it called for a number of respondents in the control categories of sex, age, and economic status proportional to their number in the population. In practice, however, the control categories were determined by the individual interviewers whereas in probability sampling particular households were specified as well as the person to be interviewed. The pollsters were willing to sacrifice the greater accuracy of probability sampling because of the expense involved until their failure in the 1948 election predictions. Poor sampling played a part in the debacle, and Hyman (1949) was one of the members of the Social Science Research Council committee assessing the methodological reasons for the failure of the polls.

One aspect of probability sampling had implications for social science research. In setting up samples for regions and for the nation with detailed maps, preliminary enumerations, successive sample stages, and in locating respondents with several call-backs, the costs were high and for most lone investigators prohibitive. Large-scale organizations with considerable funding from foundations, government agencies, and industry were the answer. Such cooperative group effort accelerated the pace and scope of research but also changed the nature of the game.

Another important technical advance was the development of methods of interviewing. Though observational studies of nonverbal behavior have been neglected in spite of their importance, it is true that much of social behavior is verbal or intertwined with verbal responses. Hence, the gathering of social information has depended in good part upon asking people about their attitudes, their beliefs, their expectations, their experiences, and their behavior. Much of the statistical records of the Census Bureau and other governmental agencies comes from the questioning of people, but little attention was given to the interviewing or questionnaire methods employed. Early census inquiries dealt largely with factual materials and not with matters of belief and attitude. Even such supposedly objective data as the census reported were based upon the subjective responses of the individuals questioned. For example, on such a simple matter of fact as the number of children in the family there was an underreporting because some parents omitted the baby in arms. Social psychologists realized the importance of examining and improving interviewing procedures both for more accurate reporting of fact and for describing and accounting for the psychological world of the person. They proceeded to develop techniques for questioning and for the measurement of attitudes. One objective was to get more psychological depth, to explore more dimensions, and to seek more theoretically significant information than in census taking. Another purpose was to find ways to produce standard scales of known reliability and validity.

Reliability of responses could readily be determined by repeated measures over time, by split-half comparisons, and by item intercorrelation. Validity as in all psychological measurement is the difficult problem. In most forms of testing some outside criterion is sought against which a test measure can be correlated. With attitudes and values, criteria are difficult to identify and difficult to measure save in the most global fashion. Another way suggested by Paul Lazarsfeld and Rensis Likert was to take full advantage of the interviewer/interviewee relationship by obtaining a full account from the respondent through open questions and through a succession of probes. Lazarsfeld maintained that people themselves could relate their own experiences with considerable accuracy and could give valid reasons for their own beliefs and behavior, if skillfully questioned. For example, in "The Art of Asking Why" (1935) Lazarsfeld urged a series of questions following the first reason given to explore contingencies and conditions, always pushing to a deeper level of response. Moreover, he shared the belief of Lewin that the world, as people perceived and cognized it, was the subject matter of social psychology. The Lazarsfeld creed of "Ask them" opened the doors to enlisting respondents as informants not about their fellows as in some anthropological investigations but about themselves.

During the same period Rensis Likert had applied the open-ended questioning of the clinician Carl Rogers to social surveys. Here, too, the emphasis was upon the interviewee's own account of things in terms of his own frame of reference with a minimum of suggestions from the questions posed by the interviewer. The Likert open-ended or intensive interview was aimed at gathering rich qualitative materials reflecting the experiences, feelings, and evaluation of the respondent. The verbatim accounts of such interviews, then, had to undergo content analysis by coders, or judges, to provide quantitative measures for the statistical treatment of results. Before Likert's advocacy and demonstration of open questioning in his directorship of Program Surveys, the common practice was to assume the categories and dimensions of people's thinking in advance and precode their responses. This was much less laborious and less expensive than the Likert procedure but more subject to errors of omission and commission. The controversy of the open as against the closed question was aggravated when the Office of War Information during World War II set up two separate survey divisions, one for intensive interviewing and the other for extensive interviewing. Lazarsfeld in a classic paper on methodology (1944) pointed out that the open-ended interview could be used systematically in a small pretest to get at people's own conceptions of a problem and the terms in which they thought. On this basis, closed questions could be formulated for a more extensive survey. Difficulties of interpretation might require a small follow-up intensive study of critical cases. Though the Lazarsfeld ideal was not completely followed by researchers, they did give more attention to some combination of open and closed questions.

A colleague of Likert in Program Surveys and of Lazarsfeld in the Bureau of Applied Research, Herbert Hyman worked effectively to use both methods to maximize research returns with limited resources. He countered the drift toward the closed question by his concern with people's motives, standards, and values. He did much to broaden the scope of surveys in moving from descriptive accounts of public opinion to studies of group interest, group conflict, and group interrelations in general (1953, 1963). He was one of the pioneers in the use of surveys for dealing with the psychology of the worker in studies of industrial morale and industrial disputes (1947*a* and 1947*b*).

The Likert, Lazarsfeld, and Hyman concerns with what goes on between stimulus and response, what goes on in the head of the person, and their techniques for dealing with the problem gave new life to nonlaboratory investigations. The mechanistic approach with a checklist of items was a quick and cheap method compared to the intensive interview, but it often yielded cheap data.

The growing research tradition in social psychology turned in upon itself in the sense of examining its own methods. Procedures for obtaining data themselves became the objects of research. They needed to be evaluated for their efficacy, validity, reliability, and adequacy. Hyman early realized the part that research could play in improving methodology and led the way in his study entitled, "Do They Tell the Truth?" (1944). His continuing interest and thinking about the methodology of data collection resulted in the monumental volume, *Interviewing in Social Research* (1954). This volume was the outgrowth of a National Opinion Research Center (NORC) program, sponsored by a joint committee of the Social Science Research Council and the National Research Council. Its object was to study systematically the sources of error in research that depended on interviewing as a method of data collection. *Interviewing in Social Research* reported both the existing research literature and the findings of new experiments and quasi experiments to test hypotheses about interviewer effects. Its major areas of investigation included (*a*) sources of effect deriving from the interviewer, (*b*) respondent reaction, (*c*) situational determinants of interviewer effect, and (*d*) reduction and control of error. The book, though basically a report of research findings, is also a treatise on interviewing as a method of inquiry. Samuel Stouffer in his foreword to the volume wrote, "there is one link in this effort [surveys] . . . which has thus far not received as much critically constructive examination as its importance deserves. This link is the human middleman in the normal process of eliciting opinions—the interviewer. To help fill this gap, the present volume provides a much needed fund of information" (Hyman 1954, p. v). In the preface Clyde Hart, then president of NORC, stated, "Throughout this work the contributions of Mr. Hyman have been pre-eminent. He directed the research and largely planned and wrote this report" (Hyman 1954, p. vii).

Essential as were the techniques of sampling and interviewing to the growth of social investigations, they were only the tools through which research design could produce a mature science. Research design refers to the precise planning of a study that permits the confirmation of a hypothesis in quantitative terms. Purely descriptive explorations require little in the way of design save for the setting of a broad enough net and the identification of the sample and its universe. More sophisticated inquiries involve the establishment of relationships among variables and the measurement of causal or antecedent factors and of outcome or dependent variables. The model for this purpose comes from the experimental laboratory where an uncontaminated variable is introduced, other factors eliminated or held constant, and the effects upon the dependent variable measured. In field studies and surveys where such direct control is difficult and often impossible, research design tries to apply as much of the essential logic of the experiment as it can. The timing of variables to insure that the independent variable comes before the dependent variable is one major obstacle. Another hurdle is created by the contamination of variables not readily identified or controlled.

Hyman's book, *Survey Design and Analysis* (1955), was addressed to these problems of causal interpretation. His later methodological work, *Secondary Analysis of Sample Surveys* (1972), extended the principles set forth in *Survey Design* to maximize the usefulness of data collected for various purposes. These volumes not only marked the methodological progress of the field but also stimulated further advances. In them Hyman formulated the principles and procedures by which surveys could follow the canons of science. For example, the problem of the timing of variables in a cross-sectional study can sometimes be met by the temporal location of an event, condition, or experience and sometimes by comparing the length of exposure of various subgroups to some independent variable. Nor is the survey researcher limited to a single cross-section in time. Repeated studies with the same design are useful both for showing trends along a given baseline and for timing variables. When the repeated studies are on the same panel of respondents, the problem of the sequence of independent, intervening, and dependent variables is solved. The panel method has finally come into its own in the large-scale studies of the Michigan Survey Research Center in its programs of economic dynamics, political attitudes and behavior, and personal and social development.

Other difficulties in causal interpretation can be helped by independent measures of environmental conditions and contexts, by the use of many values of the independent variable in measuring a relationship, by the introduction of additional variables in the elaboration of the analysis, and by the specification of results. Elaboration and specification were techniques of analysis described by Kendall and Lazarsfeld (1950). Hyman illustrated their application and added the general principles according to which specific modes of elaboration should be followed. Such elaboration and specification of analysis imply some minimal theorizing about causal relationships as they spell out differing outcomes and different degrees of such outcomes under varying conditions.

In 1951 Hyman offered a graduate seminar at Columbia University on Methods and Applications of Secondary Analysis, which served to guide him and his students in subsequent years in the reanalysis of data from already completed studies. In those early years they were limited in securing such data because data banks had not been established. Nor had the methodology of secondary analysis been fully formulated. Finally, in 1972 Hyman brought out *Secondary Analysis of Sample Surveys,* a codification of the principles and techniques for dealing with data already gathered for various purposes. This book went beyond Hyman's *Survey Design and Analysis* (1955) in its detailed and systematic account of the many uses of secondary analysis. One advantage of the method is that it permits replication of relationships across multiple surveys, and replication is indispensable in scientific inquiry. Moreover, the data from comparable surveys can be pooled to allow more elaborate analysis and more comparisons among subgroups.

Secondary analysis opens the door to studies of social change and social trends. We often encounter findings in our research that are more meaningful if related to some previous point in time. Our own work, however, does not include a relevant prior investigation. But we can turn to the data collected by other investigators and reanalyze them to test our hypotheses. To realize the rich possibilities of secondary analysis it was necessary to have available large bodies of data from studies both here and abroad. Fifty years ago, however, survey samples of known universes were scarce, with little access to the isolated study. As research organizations became established with some continuity in their endeavors, they accumulated stores of data and recognized the importance of keeping old punch cards and code books for their own purposes. It was but a step to the next stage of allowing their data files to be used to some extent by other investigators. The final step was the creation of data banks and archives with microfilms available to everyone, sometimes located in a library, or a university, or some central repository.

Hadley Cantril, Herbert Hyman, Warren Miller, and Elmo Roper were conspicuous figures in the movement to establish such data libraries. Hyman (1972) listed some seventeen nongovernmental archives functioning in 1970 with policies not unduly restrictive with respect to access to their materials. The social scientist of today and the historian of tomorrow can now go beyond the official documents and printed records to detailed evidence of how people in various groups, of different occupations, of different social positions thought and felt and acted about the issues and problems confronting them.

## The Growing Use of Theoretical Concepts

Theories in social psychology in its beginning stages were global in character, representing more a point of view, such as behaviorism or Freudianism, than a set of concepts and hypotheses to be tested in specific situations. Thus, they were of little help to the researcher as the pressures for immediate answers to applied problems mounted. As a result, rank empiricism became the order of the day as investigators attempted a quick response to some practical question. And similar problems had to be tackled anew because of the lack of generalization from previous studies that had not dug deep enough.

Against this dominant trend a few stalwarts were able to make progress in their use of theory in building social psychology. Kurt Lewin (1935) rejected the shortsighted pragmatism of the period with his notion that there is nothing more practical than a good theory. He differentiated between the genotype and its particularistic manifestations in the phenotype and sought to establish general principles. Hyman followed his lead and in his research and writings was always bent upon formulating concepts that could build a general body of knowledge. There was always an idea in his studies. His best-known theory is that of the reference group. Lewin had conceptualized the individual's own organizations of beliefs, feelings, perceptions, expectations, and attitudes as the psychological field or life space of the person. Hyman saw as a key part or aspect of the psychological field the groups that were a reference point for comparative judgments and normative influence. The notion of frame of reference had been popularized by M. Sherif (1936) through his experimental and theoretical work. Sherif demonstrated that judgments of stimuli were made with respect to subjective scales, and these scales were often derived from group norms. Other researchers had shown the pressures toward conformity to the values and practices of the group to which the individual was attracted. Thus, a reference group is defined not by objective membership but by psychological belonging. The objective grouping in which the individual is placed has little effect upon him unless he internalizes its standards because he has made it his reference group. In his original research Hyman (1942) asked subjects about their status socially, economically, culturally, and intellectually and then asked about the groups with which they compared themselves in making judgments about their own status. In general, small intimate groups rather than large populations were used as reference groups.

The reference group concept had many interesting outcomes in research for decades after its formulation. Social class was viewed in a new perspective in many studies. It had been common to measure social class by the objective criteria of income, occupation, and education—in fact, these variables had been standard background questions in most surveys. In predicting to attitudes and behavior, however, they did not consistently account for a great deal of the variance. Cantril (1943) was quick to seize upon the desirability of supplementing objective questions about class with questions about subjective class identification. His student R. Centers (1949), in an informative national study on the psychology of social classes, found that a combination of subjective and objective measures of social status gave better predictions to radicalism/conservatism than did either set of measures alone. Subsequently, sophisticated research in the United States and Europe has followed a similar pattern in dealing with social stratification.

Reference group theory has also proved useful in studies of voting, of attitude change, of the stability in changes of attitude and behavior, of conflicting group memberships, of the adjustment of immigrant groups, and of the basis for wage and job satisfaction. In 1968 Herbert Hyman and Eleanor Singer brought out *Readings in Reference*

*Group Theory and Research,* which contained some thirty-three papers related to the concept that had already seen publication in professional journals or books.

A similar conceptualization to reference group is the notion of relative deprivation (Merton and Rossi 1968). People feel deprived relative to the standards of their group. Studies of the morale of American soldiers during World War II (Stouffer et al. 1949) contained a number of puzzling findings, which could be accounted for by the idea of reference groups. Educated soldiers with better chances of promotion were less satisfied with their prospects than the less-educated because of the higher aspiration levels of their group. Negro soldiers stationed in the North were not as happy with their lot as Negro soldiers in the South. In the North Negro soldiers did not fare as well as Negro civilians whereas in the South the comparison with Negro civilians was more favorable.

In addition to reference group theory, the Lewinian emphasis upon the properties of the psychological field has led to research and theorizing about various aspects of cognition. The dominant stream of thought has been devoted to consistency doctrines of various sorts. The balance theory of Heider (1958), the dissonance concept of Festinger (1957), the incongruity notions of Osgood (1960), and the *A-B-X* system of Newcomb (1961) have occupied the attention of researchers for the past three decades. The outcome has been the restoration of the rational model of man, save that the new model sometimes follows a psycho logic rather than an objective logic. Unfortunately, the theoreticians have not specified when the one rather than the other takes over. The current interest in cognitive processes has been in the development of attribution theory and its application to many areas of psychological functioning.

Another victory for theory-oriented research has been the work of the McClelland school on motivational problems. McClelland (1961) tied the growth of achievement striving to independence training in childhood. He saw a parallel between individual and societal history and accepted the thesis of Weber that the Protestant ethic of self-reliance was the motivating force in the rise of capitalism. What distinguished the research of McClelland and his students was their ingenious solving of the problem of the validity of their measures. Their projective test for measuring achievement was derived from content analysis of stories written in two laboratory conditions, one a motivating arousal condition, the other a nonarousal condition. Other checks on validity were devised, but the essential criterion employed was the differential conditions manipulated in the laboratory. Tests of affiliation and power motives were developed in the same fashion as the need for achievement (Atkinson 1958; Veroff 1957). The various combinations of these motive patterns provide a typology of personality. What is promising for social psychology is that measures of these motives can and have been used in nationwide surveys to predict to adjustment to work and other roles (Veroff, Douvan, and Kulka 1981).

## Final Obstacles: Specialization and Fragmentation

Social psychology today suffers from the great weakness of all scientific disciplines—specialization with the resulting fragmentation of knowledge. In the interests of rigorous control and precise measurement, large problems are broken down into smaller problems. Many variables are excluded in any given study. The detailed knowledge in a subarea becomes so great that the researcher has difficulty even in keeping up with the literature in his own specialty. Though knowledge accumulates, the accumulation is in pockets isolated from one another. Communication is much greater among specialists in a subarea than across areas. And this restricted communication is aggravated by its institutionalization in separate journals, separate sections of journals, and separate professional organizations and meetings.

In addition to the splintering of a scientific discipline, we have seen a major bifurcation in the social field between a psychological social psychology and a sociological social psychology, as noted earlier. But divisionism does not stop there; House (1977) has described the three faces of social psychology, and other writers talk of four or more separate disciplines. There have been voices, however, calling for the integration of the discrete areas of inquiry—Gordon Allport in his plea for generalists, Dorwin Cartwright (1979) in his proposal for a combination of the psychological and sociological approaches, and Herbert Hyman in his catholic stance embracing history, method, and theory. In an age when specialists do not relate their findings spatially to work in other content areas or in other cultures, or temporally to what has been done before, Hyman's scholarship furnishes a refreshing contrast. In his own studies he has sought the threads to the research of others. As a leader in cross-cultural research both as a participant in many ventures and as an integrator of findings, he has been interested in testing general relationships across ethnic groupings. In his historical orientation, he has dug into the research of Durkheim and made Durkheim's techniques part of modern methodology. And his sense of history has made Hyman aware of a missing variable in the research of the specialist, namely, the dimension of time. Findings are generally based upon a very limited time span whereas a full understanding of a social process requires a continuing sample of observations and measurements. This is one reason for Hyman's championing of data banks and secondary analysis for their potential for the study of social change and stability.

Hyman has also contributed to the development of a unified science through his insistence upon casting research in terms of theory. Whether an investigation was basic or applied, he fought for making it significant in a theoretical sense. He followed the approach of the Gestalt school in looking for relational properties in situations, but he went beyond the psychological field to include the objective social environment. His best-known theoretical concept of reference group goes to the heart of social psychology, namely, the social tie of the individual to his fellows, and has been used by psychologists and sociologists alike.

In summary, the problems created by specialization, fragmentation, and divisionism can be met by a more thoughtful methodological strategy, by seeking general principles underlying common problems, by a scholarly and historical orientation, and by the utilization of more theory in empirical research. The accomplishments and career of Herbert Hyman show the way in which these objectives of the generalist can be achieved.

## Bibliography

Allport, F. H. 1920. The influence of the group upon association and thought. *Journal of Experimental Psychology* 3 : 159–82.

———. 1924. *Social psychology*. Cambridge, Mass.: Houghton Mifflin.

Allport, G. W. 1954. The historical background of modern social psychology. In G. Lindzey, ed., *Handbook of social psychology*, pp. 3–56. Reading, Mass.: Addison-Wesley.

Atkinson, J. W., ed. 1958. *Motives in fantasy, action, and society*. Princeton, N.J.: Van Nostrand.

Cantril, H. 1943. Identification with social and economic class. *Journal of Abnormal and Social Psychology* 38 : 74–80.

Cartwright, D. 1979. Contemporary social psychology in historical perspective. *Social Psychology Quarterly* 42(1) : 82–93.

Centers, R. 1949. *The psychology of social class*. Princeton, N.J.: Princeton University Press.

Conant, J. 1947. *On understanding science*. New Haven: Yale University Press.

Durkheim, E. (1897) *Le suicide*. Paris: Alcan. English translation, Glencoe, Ill.: Free Press, 1951.

Festinger, L. 1957. *A theory of cognitive dissonance*. Stanford, Calif.: Stanford University Press.

Heider, F. 1958. *The psychology of interpersonal relations*. New York: Wiley.

House, J. S. 1977. The three faces of social psychiatry. *Sociometry* 40 : 167–77.

Katz, D., and F. H. Allport. 1931. *Student attitudes*. Syracuse, N.Y.: Craftsman Press.

Katz, D., and H. H. Hyman. 1947. Morale in war industry. In T. Newcomb and E. Hartley eds., *Readings in social psychology*, pp. 437–41. New York: Holt.

Kendall, P. L., and P. F. Lazarsfeld. 1950. Problems of survey analysis. In R. K. Merton and P. F. Lazarsfeld, eds., *Continuities in social research: Studies in the scope and method of "The American Soldier,"* pp. 133–96. New York: Free Press.

Lazarsfeld, P. F. 1935. The art of asking why. *National Marketing Review* 1: 32–43.

———. 1944. The controversy over detailed interviews. *Public Opinion Quarterly* 8:38–60.

Le Bon, G. 1895. *Psychologie des foules*. Paris: Olean. Translated by T. Fisher, London: Unwin, 1896.

Lewin, K. 1935. *A dynamic theory of personality*. New York: McGraw-Hill.

Mayer, A. 1903. On the school child's work alone and in the group. *Archiv für Gesamte Psychologie* 1:276–416.

McClelland, D. 1961. *The achieving society*. New York: Van Nostrand Reinhold.

McDougall, W. 1908. *An introduction to social psychology*. London: Methuen.

Merton, R. K., and A. K. Rossi. 1968. Contributions to the theory of reference group behavior. In H. H. Hyman and E. Singer, eds., *Readings in reference group theory and research*, pp. 28–68. New York: Macmillan, Free Press.

Moede, W. 1920. *Experimental group psychology*. Leipzig: Hirzel.

Münsterberg, H. 1914. *Fundamentals of psychotechnics*, pp. 266–71. Leipzig: Barth.

Newcomb, R. M. 1961. *The acquaintance process*. New York: Holt, Rinehart and Winston.

Osgood, C. E. 1960. Cognitive dynamics in the conduct of human affairs. *Public Opinion Quarterly* 24(2):341–65.

Ross, E. A. 1908. *Social psychology*. New York: Macmillan.

Schanck, R. L. 1932. A study of a community and its groups and institutions conceived of as the behavior of individuals. *Psychological Monographs* 43, no. 195.

Sherif, M. 1936. *The psychology of social norms*. New York: Harper.

Stouffer, S. A., et al. 1949. *The American soldier*. Vols. 1 and 2. Princeton, N.J.: Princeton University Press.

Tarde, G. 1890. *The laws of imitation*. Translation, New York: Holt, 1903.

Thurstone, L. L. 1928. Attitudes can be measured. *American Journal of Sociology* 33:529–54.

Triplett, N. 1897. The dynamogenic factors in pacemaking and competition. *American Journal of Psychology* 9:507–33.

Veroff, J. 1957. Development and validation of a projective measure of power motivation. *Journal of Abnormal and Social Psychology* 54:1–8.

Veroff, J., E. Douvan, and R. A. Kulka. 1981. *The inner American*. New York: Basic Books.

Zajonc, R. B. 1966. *Social psychology: An experiment approach*. Belmont, Calif.: Wadsworth.

## Morris Rosenberg

## 10 Hypersensitivity and Political Participation

Among the many and varied contributions of Herbert Hyman to social psychology is his book *Political Socialization* (1959). One of the first works of its kind, it is a fascinating and insightful description of how young people learn their political culture and of the social forces that influence children's and adolescents' political orientations, participation, and authoritarian ideologies.

When Hyman's book first appeared, systematic work on the topic was sparse and scattered. When, ten years later, he wrote a preface to the new edition (1969), Hyman was able to report that a large volume of work had appeared in the interim. It is probable that Hyman's initial systematization of the literature on political socialization was an important impetus for the work that was to follow. Since the appearance of Hyman's book, political socialization has represented an important branch of political psychology, a field that currently appears to be bursting with health and vigor. This field is spearheaded by the youthful International Society of Political Psychology and boasts its own journal, *Political Psychology*. The debt that the field owes to Hyman's pioneering work cannot be measured, but it is certainly a significant one.

One of the features of political behavior on which Hyman focused was political participation. This topic has commanded the attention of a number of political scientists (e.g., Carmines 1978; Greenstein 1969; Lane 1959, 1962; Milbrath 1965; Milbrath and Klein 1962). Whereas Hyman's work focused primarily on the social roles influencing par-

The preparation of this paper was supported by a grant from the National Institute of Mental Health (MH 39710). An earlier version was presented at the Annual Meetings of the International Society of Political Psychology, Toronto, June 1984.

ticipation, other writers centered attention on personality factors or interpersonal relations. This paper pursues this line of interest by exploring the influence of personality on political participation among adolescents. The personality influence I propose to explore is the adolescent's self-concept. The self-concept is here viewed in a broad sense; it is the totality of the individual's thoughts and feelings with reference to the self as an object (Rosenberg 1979). So conceived, there are few features of human life that are immune to its influence. Political behavior is no exception. It touches the political realm as it touches most other realms of life.

The self-concept dimension that has commanded the lion's share of attention in the literature has been global self-esteem (Carmines 1978; Lane 1959; Rosenberg 1962; Sniderman 1975; Sniderman and Citrin 1971). The political relevance of self-esteem has long been recognized. The early thinking on the subject viewed low self-esteem as a stimulant and a spur to political involvement. In his classic work *Power and Personality,* Harold Lasswell (1948) advanced the view that the striving for power often represented an effort to compensate for underlying feelings of inferiority. Developing Lasswell's views, Robert Lane (1959) noted that "One of the most common sources of the need for power is a deeper need for reassurance about the self—'I am not weak,' 'I am not insignificant,' 'I am not dependent.' This need for reassurance is, of course, related to lack of self-confidence, feelings of unworthiness, or low self-esteem" (p. 127). In a similar vein, Fromm (1941) argued that individuals who felt small, worthless, or insignificant might attach themselves to a strong political group with a powerful leader in order to gain a much needed feeling of strength and self-confidence.

On the other hand, theory and research also suggested that low self-esteem might actually inhibit participation. Lasswell himself pointed out that if the individual felt too inadequate and hopeless, he or she would retreat from the search for power. Rosenberg (1954–55) found that some adults inhibited the expression of their political views because of (1) threat of ego deflation (fear of revealing ignorance, stupidity, etc.) and (2) feeling of inefficacy (nothing they could do would make any difference). Subsequent quantitative research utilizing samples of adolescents (Carmines 1978; Rosenberg 1962) and adults (Sniderman and Citrin 1971) consistently showed that low self-esteem people were more politically apathetic: less interested in political issues, less knowledgeable about current or historical political facts, less apt to expose themselves to political news in the media, and less apt to take an active role in political discussions.

In this paper I propose to examine the influence of a different dimension of the self-concept, namely, hypersensitivity. However, since hypersensitivity and self-esteem are related, and since low self-esteem has been shown to affect political participation, it will be necessary to take account of self-esteem in our analyses.

In *Political Socialization*, Hyman (1959) considered a number of manifestations of political participation or apathy: interest in politics, level of political knowledge, exposure to political information in the media, political involvement, and tendency to discuss political issues. Subsequently, Milbrath (1965) identified fourteen kinds of participatory activities, suggesting that these could be ordered along a "hierarchy of political involvement." These ranged from such "gladiatorial activities" as holding public and party office, being a candidate for office, or soliciting political funds to such "spectator activities" as attempting to talk another into voting a certain way, initiating political discussion, voting, and exposing oneself to political stimuli. Hyman's work, of course, focused chiefly on children and adolescents whereas Milbrath was primarily interested in adults. The kinds of political participation possible to people at these different life stages obviously differ greatly. Most adolescents, for example, are not permitted to vote, and rarely do they make campaign contributions.

The aim of this study is to understand how one dimension of the self-concept (hypersensitivity) bears on one type of participation (political discussion) in a sample of adolescents. Before examining the data it is helpful to note the relevance of political discussion and the meaning of hypersensitivity.

## Relevance of Political Discussion

In exploring the various manifestations of political participation, Milbrath (1965) observed that "Of all the stimuli about politics which a person may encounter, those which come through personal discussions are probably the most influential. Nearly everyone gets caught in a political discussion once in a while; some persons studiously avoid them, while others enjoy them and seek them out" (p. 23).

The importance of political discussion is apparent. The free expression of political ideas, the open interchange of opinions and judgments, must certainly be seen as one of the central features of the democratic process (Berelson 1952). The competition of ideas that inheres in political discussion and argument is the crucible in which public attitudes are forged.

Political discussion is not only a feature of the political process, however; it is also an "interpersonal occasion." It is a highly complex interactive process involving self-presentations (Goffman 1959), negotiations of identities (Heiss 1981; Weinstein and Deutschberger 1963), and other behavior governed by social norms and personal motives (Lauer and Handel 1983). Factors such as hypersensitivity that influence interpersonal interaction inevitably influence political discussion.

The data for this report are based on a random subsample of 1,681 juniors and seniors in ten high schools in New York State. (Sample details appear in Rosenberg 1965.) In this study, the following three items were combined to form an index of political discussion (alpha = .7422).

1. Would you say that you discuss national or international matters a great deal, a fair amount, very little, or not at all?

2. When you and your friends discuss national or international questions, what part do you usually take? (*a*) Even though I may have strong opinions, I usually just listen; (*b*) I listen a lot, but once in a while I express my opinion; (*c*) I take an equal share in the conversation; (*d*) I have definite ideas and try to convince the others.

3. When national or international topics are discussed in a group, how often do you take the lead in such discussions?

## Hypersensitivity

To live in society is to expose oneself to threats to self-esteem. To avoid or ward off such dangers completely is not humanly possible. As Allport noted (1961, pp. 155–61):

Every day we experience grave threats to our self-esteem; we feel inferior, guilty, insecure, unloved. Not only big things but little things put us in the wrong; we trip up in an examination, we make a social boner, we dress inappropriately for an occasion. The ego sweats. We suffer discomfort, perhaps anxiety, and we hasten to repair the narcissistic wound.

Although no one is immune to assaults on the self, people vary widely in their level of sensitivity to such experiences. To some people the self is a tender and delicate object. The individual is touchy and easily hurt; the slightest hint of criticism or ridicule gives rise to profound depression. The sensitive person seems to be afflicted with a "psychological sunburn"; the most delicate touch generates the most acute anguish. In contrast, there are those who undergo the same experiences but who appear able to shrug it off, laugh at it, or dismiss it as unimportant. These contrasting types might be described as "tough" and "tender" self-concepts.

It is easy to overlook the importance of hypersensitivity because it is less likely to affect what people do than what they do not do—what they do not say, the chances they do not take, the independence and initiative they do not show, and so on. Although the consequences of inhibition may attract little notice, they may nevertheless be pervasive, serious, and profound.

The following six items, scattered throughout the questionnaire, were used to measure hypersensitivity:

1. How sensitive are you to criticism?
2. How disturbed do you feel when anyone laughs at you or blames you for something you have done wrong?
3. How do you feel when you do badly at something you have tried to do?
4. How much does it bother you to find that someone has a poor opinion of you?
5. Criticism or scolding hurts me terribly.
6. I am deeply disturbed when I become aware of some fault or inadequacy in myself.

These six items showed reasonable internal reliability, as reflected in an alpha coefficient of .7377.

Hypersensitivity, as we would expect, is inversely associated with self-esteem. In this study, self-esteem is measured by a ten-item scale that reflects general, content-free feelings toward the self (e.g., "On the whole I am satisfied with myself" or "At times I think I am no good at all"). (Reliability and validity data are presented in Rosenberg 1979, app. A. Analyses and critiques of this measure appear in Carmines and Zeller 1979; Dobson et al. 1979; Hensley and Roberts 1976; Silber and Tippett 1965; Wells and Marwell 1976; Wylie 1974.)

Among these New York State adolescents, the association between hypersensitivity and self-esteem was $r = -.2163$ ($p < .001$). Consistent results are found in a study of 1,988 school pupils from grades three to twelve in Baltimore; in this study, the correlation was $-.2754$. In addition, Luck and Heiss (1972) found a relationship of Somers's $D = -.48$ between hypersensitivity and self-esteem among a sample of retired men. It is also relevant to report the findings from a study of a small sample of normal controls living on the ward of a research hospital (Rosenberg 1965). In this study, ward nurses were asked to complete an adjective checklist describing the subjects. Those subjects with low self-esteem were significantly more likely to be described as "touchy and easily hurt."

## Hypersensitivity and Political Discussion

Hypersensitive youngsters, according to Table 10.1, are somewhat less likely to be active participants in political discussions ($r = -.1489$, $p < .001$). The influence of hypersensitivity is not a powerful one, but it is clear and significant. It is this finding that I shall attempt to explain. Table 10.2 indicates that the explanation does *not* lie in the lower self-esteem of hypersensitive youngsters because, when self-esteem is controlled, the association declines by about one-fifth ($r = -.1208$). The question, then, is: What is there about the hypersensitive personality that inhibits the individual from expressing his or her social and political opinions freely and openly? The following four factors will be considered:

1. *Interpersonal threat.* Potential interpersonal dangers inhere in political discussion. People particularly concerned with such dangers may be especially cautious about expressing their political opinions.

2. *Political incompetence.* People convinced of their political ignorance or doubtful about their political judgments may hesitate to express their political ideas.

3. *Self-absorption.* People wrapped up in their inner problems may experience a loss of involvement in such external matters as social and political events.

4. *Self-consciousness.* People keenly aware of themselves as objects of observation by others may be inhibited from expressing their political opinions.

TABLE 10.1. *Correlation Matrix of Hypersensitivity, Self-esteem, and Political Variables*

|  | 1 | 2 | 3 | 4 | 5 | 6 | 7 |
|---|---|---|---|---|---|---|---|
| 1. Hypersensitivity | — | | | | | | |
| 2. Self-esteem | −.2163 | | | | | | |
| 3. Political discussion | −.1489 | .1489 | — | | | | |
| 4. Political threat | .4223 | −.1690 | −.4618 | — | | | |
| 5. Political incompetence | .3345 | −.2848 | −.3893 | .4298 | — | | |
| 6. Self-absorption | .2219 | −.2044 | −.3492 | .2683 | .2410 | — | |
| 7. Self-consciousness | .2454 | −.2132 | −.4539 | .3830 | .4022 | .2449 | — |

*Note:* All correlations significant at .001 level.

TABLE 10.2. *Correlations of Hypersensitivity and Self-esteem with Political Discussion and Inhibiting Factors*

| | Correlations with hypersensitivity | | | Correlations with self-esteem | | |
|---|---|---|---|---|---|---|
| | Zero order | Self-esteem controlled | Percent reduction | Zero order | Hypersensitivity controlled | Percent reduction |
| Political discussion | −.1489 | −.1208 | 19% | .1489 | .1209 | 19% |
| Political threat | .4223 | .4009 | 5 | −.1690 | −.0877[a] | 48 |
| Political incompetence | .3345 | .2916 | 13 | −.2848 | −.2309 | 19 |
| Self-absorption | .2219 | .1859 | 16 | −.2044 | −.1643 | 20 |
| Public self-consciousness | .2454 | .2089 | 15 | −.2132 | −.1692 | 21 |

[a]Significant at .01 level. All other correlations significant at .001 level.

## Interpersonal Threats

As in any type of discussion, a number of interpersonal threats inhere in political discussion. The first is the danger of *ridicule*. Respondents were asked: "If you were to offer your opinion on some subject of national or international importance, and someone were to laugh at you for it, how would this make you feel?"

The second danger is that the presentation of one's opinions may arouse the *hostility* of others. Any person who discusses national or international affairs faces the peril of antagonizing people. This fear was expressed in two questions. The first asked respondents how they felt about getting into heated arguments about public issues with others; the second whether they agreed that, in discussions of public affairs, "I think I would prefer to say nothing at all than to say something that will make people angry at me."

A third threat lies in the possibility of making a *negative impression* on the minds of others. In advancing one's political ideas, one runs the risk of revealing one's ignorance, expressing views abhorrent to others, saying things that may elicit scorn, and so on. Respondents were asked whether they agreed that "When national or international questions are discussed, I often prefer to say nothing than to say something that will make a bad impression."

People with tender self-concepts, we find, are much more likely than those with tough self-concepts to feel threatened by discussions of social or political issues. Hypersensitive adolescents are more likely to say that they would be "deeply hurt and disturbed" if someone were to laugh at their political ideas; to agree that they would prefer to say nothing at all than to say something that would make people angry at them; to reply, when asked how they felt about getting into heated arguments about public issues with others, that they "dislike it very much; try to avoid it at all costs"; and to indicate that they would rather remain silent than to say something that would make a bad impression on others.

When these four items are combined to form an "interpersonal threat" index, the association of this index to hypersensitivity is $r = .4223$ ($p < .001$). Since low self-esteem is also associated with interpersonal threat, however, one confronts the possibility that the relationship may be spurious. In *Survey Design and Analysis*, Hyman (1955) specified the conditions for identifying a relationship as spurious. "Only those factors which *precede x* in time," he said, "can be invalidating factors" (p. 286). Self-esteem does not meet this criterion, since it is not possible to establish the temporal order of hypersensitivity and self-esteem unequivocally. Since the two are related, however, and since there is reason to think that low self-esteem may be responsible for political passivity, it is necessary to control on self-esteem to see if hypersensitivity has an effect independent of it. Conversely, when examining the effect of self-esteem, we shall control on hypersensitivity.

Table 10.2 shows that the relationship between hypersensitivity and political discussion is not due to the lower self-esteem of hypersensitive youngsters. In fact, the converse is the case. The higher feelings of threat of low self-esteem youngsters are largely due to their hypersensitivity. Specifically, the relationship between self-esteem and interpersonal threat is reduced by nearly half (from $r = -.1690$ to $r = -.0877$ when hypersensitivity is controlled). This finding suggests that certain political effects that may in the past have been attributed to low self-esteem may in part be due to hypersensitivity.

To the hypersensitive youngster, then, the world of political discussion is a realm of interpersonal danger. Unlike those people who find social and political discussion zestful, invigorating, and pleasurable, hypersensitive adolescents approach a political discussion as though it were a minefield, a place where a single misstep can produce an interpersonal explosion.

The hypersensitive person, it seems probable, is characterized by what Arkin (1981, p. 312) calls a "protective" self-presentation style "that derives from presenters' concerns over engendering disapproval rather than garnering approval." He distinguishes this orientation from "acquisitive self-presentation," where the objective is to enhance self-esteem. Arkin suggests that people utilizing a protective style tend to be characterized by low self-esteem, avoidance of interpersonal relations, reticence, conformity, modesty, and other characteristics. In the context of political discussion, I would expect that people exhibiting a protective style would tend to think twice about voicing their opinions; would be reluctant to present their ideas forcefully out of fear of contradiction or concern with antagonizing others; would mostly listen and nod and murmur assent while others carry the conversational burden; would express their ideas tentatively so that they could readily backtrack from their position if challenged, and so on. Such a protective orientation, it is apparent, fosters political inhibition. It is particularly likely to characterize hypersensitive youngsters.

## Political Incompetence

Whether or not we express our social and political ideas to others depends in part on our own faith in those ideas. If we lack confidence in our own judgments or feel that our ideas will have little impact on people, then it is understandable that we should say little when such matters are discussed.

Three questions in the study appeared to reflect the feeling of political incompetence:

1. I think most people's ideas on national or international questions are sounder than mine.

2. Do you ever have opinions about public affairs which you would like to express but feel too unsure of yourself to express them?

3. If I were to present my ideas on public affairs to a group of strangers, I believe they would be impressed by my views.

There is reason to think that both low self-esteem and hypersensitivity would foster feelings of political incompetence. Though it is readily apparent why low self-esteem should foster feelings of political incompetence, it is less evident why hypersensitivity should have such an effect. One possibility, I suggest, is that political incompetence may be a protective strategy. This may sound like an outlandish idea. How can the affirmation of our ignorance and ineffectuality protect us from assaults on our self-esteem? The answer is that this may represent the strategy that Jones and Berglas (1978) and Arkin and Baumgardner (1985) call "self-handicapping." According to Arkin and Baumgardner (1985:169), self-handicapping "refers to an individual's attempt to reduce a threat to esteem by actively seeking or creating inhibitory factors that interfere with performance and thus provide a persuasive causal explanation for potential failure."

Hypersensitive people, by insisting on their political incompetence or ineffectuality, are provided with an excuse to say little and to avoid arguments. Were they politically knowledgeable, they would have reason to express their viewpoints, and this would expose them to the dangers of ridicule, hostility, and rejection. If, on the other hand, they decide that they are politically incompetent, then they can comfortably listen to the views of those of superior knowledge. Or, if they do voice an opinion, they can easily withdraw it in the face of opposition because they make no claims to expertise in that area. Their affirmation of political incompetence may thus protect them from pain and disappointment. It should be noted, incidentally, that there is a base of truth in the hypersensitive adolescent's self-assessment; the association of hypersensitivity to a test of political knowledge is $r = -.1603$.

The affirmation of ignorance may thus serve the interests of self-esteem. If we do make mistakes, then, given our limited knowledge, this is readily excusable. And if by chance we say something brilliant, this is doubly impressive, given our initial handicap.

If it sounds far-fetched to think that people may be protecting their self-esteem by pleading ignorance or ineffectuality (to others or to themselves), I should point out that there is now substantial evidence (Swann 1983) to indicate that people may in some instances reject opportunities offered them to enhance their self-esteem. One reason they do so has been suggested by Jones (1973): The acceptance of the self-enhancing information may pose future threats of failure and disappointment that they would prefer to avoid. This may be particularly characteristic of hypersensitive people, since they are inordinately fearful of ridicule, attack, or rejection.

Both low self-esteem and hypersensitivity may thus foster feelings of political incompetence and inefficacy. The data support these expectations. As Table 10.2 shows, both hypersensitivity and low self-esteem are significantly correlated with feelings of political incompetence ($r = .3345$ and $r = -.2848$), and each variable exercises an effect largely independent of the other.

## Self-absorption

In developing her theory of neurosis, one of the concepts introduced by Horney (1950) was that of "neurotic egocentricity." This concept refers to the individual's tendency to focus attention on the self and to see matters from one's own point of view. In her judgment, neurotics may be so wrapped up in their own problems that they may tend to lose interest in events occurring in the outside world. A somewhat similar idea was expressed by Goldhamer (1950) in his discussion of the impact of neurosis on political behavior. Goldhamer suggested that the person may be so exhausted by inner conflicts that he or she has no energy left for public affairs; this position was further developed by Lane (1959). One might characterize this condition as one of "self-absorption"—an excessive concern with the self to the exclusion of interest in other matters. The individual's attention centers on the self, especially one's inner states, relative to other objects of interest in the world.

There is reason to think that both hypersensitivity and low self-esteem would foster feelings of self-absorption. For one thing, both factors are clearly associated with psychological distress. As far as self-esteem is concerned, it has been shown that people with low self-esteem are much more likely to be high on measures of depression, to report an unusually large number of psychophysiological indicators of anxiety, to report higher levels of tension and distress, and to be characterized by higher levels of irritability, resentment, and anomie (Burns 1979; Kaplan and Pokorny 1969; Rosenberg 1985; Wylie 1979). As Angyal (1951, p. 37) once said: "In the neurotic development there are always a number of unfortunate circumstances which instill in the child a self-derogatory feeling. . . . The whole complicated structure of neurosis appears to be founded on this secret feeling of worthlessness."

Much less is known about the psychological correlates of hypersensitivity. Nevertheless, in the present study of adolescents, hypersensitive youngsters also scored high on a measure of depressive affect ($r = .3131$) and a measure of psychophysiological indicators of anxiety ($r = .2943$). The data thus suggest that both hypersensitive youngsters and low self-esteem youngsters tend to have unusually severe psychological problems. If the concept of neurotic egocentricity applies in this case, these psychological problems might detract from these youngsters' interest in external social or political events.

Respondents were asked to agree or disagree with the following statements:

1. I often find that I am distracted from public affairs by my personal problems.

2. I am too concerned with my inner problems to devote much attention to the broader problems of the world.

Combining these two items into a "self-absorption" index, we find that the relationships of this index to hypersensitivity and low self-esteem are about equal ($r = .2219$ and $r = -.2044$, respectively) and that each relationship declines by a sixth and a fifth when the other self-concept dimension is controlled. Both hypersensitivity and self-esteem are thus associated with a tendency to be distracted from involvement in public affairs by a focus on psychological problems, and each influence is largely independent of the other.

## Self-consciousness

Beginning with the pioneering work of Duval and Wicklund (1972), a number of investigators have conducted research on the topics of "self-awareness" or "self-consciousness" (Buss 1980; Carver and Scheier 1985; Fenigstein 1979; Fenigstein, Scheier, and Buss 1975). This work has made it evident that there are different types of self-consciousness. The type I wish to discuss here is called "public self-consciousness." It is a condition in which one is "excessively conscious of oneself as an object of observation of others" (*Random House Dictionary of the English Language* 1966). People high on public self-consciousness are keenly aware of what others think of them, of what impression they are making on other people.

There is reason to expect public self-consciousness to be positively associated with hypersensitivity. A person who is acutely sensitive to ridicule, criticism, or anger is obviously concerned with how other people respond to him or her. Citing the work of Fenigstein (1979), Carver and Scheier (1985) report that "public self-consciousness has been found to be associated with sensitivity to interpersonal rejection." Carver and Scheier (1985) also point out that people high on public self-consciousness are more likely to be conformist, to avoid making waves, to avoid offending people—behavior that is consistent with the picture of the hypersensitive adolescent.

In the New York State study, respondents were asked to agree or disagree with the following: "When a number of people are together talking about public affairs, I am often a little self-conscious about talking up in front of everyone."

As Table 10.2 shows, both hypersensitivity and self-esteem are empirically associated with public self-consciousness ($r = .2454$ and $r = -.2172$, respectively). When self-esteem is controlled, the relationship between hypersensitivity and public self-consciousness is $r = .2089$ (a reduction of 15 percent). When hypersensitivity is controlled, the relationship of self-esteem to public self-consciousness becomes $r = -.1692$ (a reduction of 21 percent). Public self-consciousness thus appears to be another factor inhibiting political discussion, and both hypersensitivity and self-esteem are associated with this disposition largely independently of one another.

## Intervening Variables

The basic question raised in this paper has been the following: Why are hypersensitive youngsters more likely to be inhibited in expressing their political opinions? (I would expect such inhibition to characterize discussion of other topics as well.) Several factors have been explored. First, hypersensitive adolescents were found to be more threatened by such discussions—more afraid of being ridiculed, of antagonizing other people, of becoming involved in arguments, and of making a bad impression. Second, hypersensitive youngsters hesitated to express their opinions because they viewed themselves as more politically ignorant and inefficacious. Third, hypersensitive youngsters were so absorbed in their personal problems that they were less apt to develop intense involvement in the impersonal and distant events of the world. Finally, their keen awareness of themselves as objects of observation by others caused them to exercise inordinate caution in expressing their views.

Do these four inhibiting factors explain the relationship between hypersensitivity and inhibition of political discussion? The answer appears to be: decidedly so. In fact, these variables exercise what I have elsewhere (Rosenberg 1968) described as a "distorter effect." When they are controlled by means of partial correlation, the original negative relationship between hypersensitivity and political discussion of $r = -.1489$ becomes a positive one (partial $r = .1511$). (A path model shows a similar reversal of signs.) In other words, were it not for these inhibiting factors, hypersensitive youngsters would be somewhat *more* likely to be active political discussants.

In this paper I have made special efforts to show that when speaking of hypersensitivity I am not merely referring to self-esteem. We have long been aware that self-esteem affects political participation, and these data offer additional evidence of such an effect. But hypersensitivity has an effect on political discussion that is independent of self-esteem and is as strong or stronger than self-esteem. The joint effect (multiple $R$) of hypersensitivity and self-esteem on political discussion is $.1909$.

## Discussion

It is obvious that we still have a long way to go before we can achieve an adequate understanding of the impact of the self-concept on political behavior. Although the literature includes some first-rate work on the bearing of certain dimensions of the self-concept on certain aspects of political ideology and participation (Carmines 1978; Lane

1959, 1962; Sniderman 1975; Sniderman and Citrin 1971), it is clear that our knowledge of the influence of the self-concept on political orientations and behavior is still extremely limited. The self-concept is a complex structure, incorporating many aspects, elements, and dimensions, and the impact of these on the varied manifestations of political participation and expressions of political ideology remains largely unknown. The present paper—an investigation of the bearing of one specific self-concept dimension (hypersensitivity) on one specific expression of political participation (political discussion)—represents a drop in the large bucket of knowledge that remains to be filled.

## Bibliography

Allport, Gordon W. 1961. *Pattern and growth in personality.* New York: Holt, Rinehart and Winston.

Angyal, Andris. 1951. *Foundations for a science of personality.* New York: Commonwealth Fund.

Arkin, Robert M. 1981. Self presentation styles. In J. Tedeschi, ed., *Impression management theory and social psychological research,* chap. 15. New York: Academic Press.

Arkin, Robert M., and Ann H. Baumgardner. 1985. Self-handicapping. In J. H. Harvey and G. Weary, eds., *Basic issues in attribution theory and research,* pp. 169–202. New York: Academic Press.

Berelson, Bernard R. 1952. Democratic theory and public opinion. *Public Opinion Quarterly* 16:313–30.

Burns, R. B. 1979. *The self-concept in theory, measurement, development, and behavior.* London: Longman.

Buss, Arnold H. 1980. *Self-consciousness and social anxiety.* San Francisco: Freeman.

Carmines, E. G. 1978. Psychological origins of adolescent political attitudes: Self-esteem, political salience, and political involvement. *American Politics Quarterly* 6:167–86.

Carmines, Edward G., and Richard A. Zeller. 1979. *Reliability and validity assessment.* Beverly Hills, Calif.: Sage.

Carver, Charles S., and Michael F. Scheier. 1985. Aspects of self and the control of behavior. In B. R. Schlenker, ed., *The self and social life,* pp. 146–74. New York: McGraw-Hill.

Dobson, C., W. Goudy, P. Keith, and E. Powers. 1979. Further analysis of the Rosenberg self-esteem scale. *Psychological Reports* 44:639–41.

Duval, S., and R. A. Wicklund. 1972. *A theory of objective self-awareness.* New York: Academic Press.

Fenigstein, A. 1979. Self-consciousness, self-attention, and social interaction. *Journal of Personality and Social Psychology* 37:75–86.

Fenigstein, A., M. Scheier, and A. Buss. 1975. Public and private self-consciousness: Assessment and theory. *Journal of Counseling and Clinical Psychology* 43:522–27.

Fromm, Erich. 1941. *Escape from freedom*. New York: Rinehart.

Goffman, Erving. 1959. *The presentation of self in everyday life*. Garden City, N.Y.: Doubleday.

Goldhamer, Herbert. 1950. Public opinion and personality. *American Journal of Sociology* 55:346–54.

Greenstein, Fred I. 1969. *Personality and politics*. Chicago: Markham.

Heiss, Jerold. 1981. *The social psychology of interaction*. Englewood Cliffs, N.J.: Prentice-Hall.

Hensley, W. E., and M. K. Roberts. 1976. Dimensions of Rosenberg's self-esteem scale. *Psychological Reports* 38:583–84.

Horney, Karen. 1950. *Neurosis and human growth*. New York: Norton.

Jones, E. E., and S. Berglas. 1978. Control of attributions about the self through self-handicapping strategies: The appeal of alcohol and the role of underachievement. *Personality and Social Psychology Bulletin* 4:200–6.

Jones, Stephen C. 1973. Self and interpersonal evaluations: Esteem theories versus consistency theories. *Psychological Bulletin* 79:185–99.

Kaplan, Howard B., and A. D. Pokorny. 1969. Self-derogation and psychosocial adjustment. *Journal of Nervous and Mental Disease* 149:421–34.

Lane, Robert E. 1959. *Political life*. New York: Free Press.

———. 1962. *Political ideology*. New York: Free Press.

Lasswell, Harold D. 1948. *Power and personality*. New York: Norton.

Lauer, Robert H., and Warren H. Handel. 1983. *Social psychology*. 2nd ed. Englewood Cliffs, N.J.: Prentice-Hall.

Luck, Patrick W., and Jerold Heiss. 1972. Social determinants of self-esteem in adult males. *Sociology and Social Research* 57:69–84.

Milbrath, Lester W. 1965. *Political participation*. Chicago: Rand McNally.

Milbrath, Lester W., and Walter Klein. 1962. Personality correlates of political participation. *Acta Sociologica* 6:53–66.

Rosenberg, Morris. 1954–55. Some determinants of political apathy. *Public Opinion Quarterly* 18:349–66.

———. 1962. Self-esteem and concern with public affairs. *Public Opinion Quarterly* 26:201–11.

———. 1965. *Society and the adolescent self-image*. Princeton, N.J.: Princeton University Press.

———. 1968. *The logic of survey analysis*. New York: Basic Books.

———. 1979. *Conceiving the self*. New York: Basic Books.

———. 1985. Self-concept and psychological well-being in adolescence. In R. Leahy, ed., *The development of the self*, pp. 205–46. New York: Academic Press.

Silber, E., and J. S. Tippett. 1965. Self-esteem: Clinical assessment and measurement validation. *Psychological Reports* 16:1017–71.

Sniderman, Paul M. 1975. *Personality and democratic politics*. Berkeley: University of California Press.

Sniderman, Paul M., and J. Citrin. 1971. Psychological sources of political belief: Self-esteem and isolationist attitudes. *American Political Science Review* 65:401–17.

Swann, William B., Jr. 1983. Self-verification: Bringing social reality into harmony with the self. In J. Suls and A. G. Greenwald, eds., *Psychological Perspectives on the Self*, 2:33–66. Hillsdale, N.J.: Erlbaum.

Weinstein, Eugene A., and Paul Deutschberger. 1963. Some dimensions of altercasting. *Sociometry* 26:454–66.

Wells, L. E., and G. Marwell. 1976. *Self-esteem: Its conceptualization and measurement*. Beverly Hills, Calif.: Sage.

Wylie, Ruth. 1974. *The self-concept*. Rev. ed. Vol. 1: *A review of methodological considerations and measuring instruments*. Lincoln: University of Nebraska Press.

———. 1979. *The self-concept*. Rev. ed. Vol. 2: *Theory and research on selected topics*. Lincoln: University of Nebraska Press.

# Leonard I. Pearlin

## 11 Social Structure and Social Values: The Regulation of Structural Effects

Outstanding scholars become many things to many people. The scope of their work encompasses multiple interests and, consequently, over the span of their careers they create multiple audiences. Herbert Hyman, of course, is a scholar par excellence. The extensiveness and the diversity of issues that have captured his attention, his unflagging productivity over the decades, and his sociological innovativeness make his work a banquet at which many appetites are whetted. Certainly, researchers in social stratification, in the sociology of education, in socialization, in the methodology of survey research, in political sociology, or in race relations have had the opportunity to savor some of the rich rewards of his wonderful writings.

In this essay I shall focus on a major interest of Hyman's that cuts across the various substantive areas of his research. It concerns social structure and values and the tantalizing connections between the two. Values, of course, are those norms that define what is good or bad, desirable or undesirable, in the important institutions of society. The structure–values relationships is a thematic thread that runs through much of his work. It is perhaps addressed most directly in his classic study, "The Value Systems of Different Classes" (1953). In this compelling work he traced the linkages between the opportunity structures in which people are immersed and the goals and aspirations they come to value, a process that affects school-aged children no less than adults.

Other work of Hyman's also focuses on various aspects of social structure and values (e.g., Hyman and Wright 1979). For the most part, however, his interest in these constructs and their relationships is more fully reflected in studies that examined very different issues.

His superb research into the interviewing process (1954) is an illustration of what I am referring to here. Although he does not directly focus on structure and values, they nevertheless constitute important elements in his analytic framework. Hyman, in these studies, sought to identify factors in survey interviews that biased responses. Some of these factors, he found, result from the social characteristics that interviewers and subjects bring to the interview situation, characteristics that structure their relationship. The structure, in turn, activates or inhibits the emergence and expression of values in answering interview questions. Thus, the racial, gender, and class mix of interviewer and respondent can have a profound influence on answers to questions that are relevant to these characteristics. Although this research did not directly deal with the connections between structure and values, they were indirectly very much a part of Hyman's analytic orientation.

There are numerous additional examples of Herbert Hyman's interest in the structure–values theme, reflected both directly and indirectly in his work. It is not my intention to review this work; even a partial treatment of it would quickly take me outside the scope of this essay. Instead, I would like to specify and illustrate the ways in which the relationships between social structure and values can be conceptualized and to suggest the analytic uses of the different conceptualizations. For various reasons, I believe that such a conceptual specification is important; in part the reasons are personal, and in part they concern the discipline.

With regard to the importance of this effort to me personally, I must confess to considerable pleasure at the opportunity to take up an issue to which a key mentor has contributed so much. Indeed, for me this is a continuation of something that began over three decades ago. In Hyman's seminar on secondary data analysis, Joseph Greenblum and I produced our paper, "Vertical Mobility and Prejudice" (1953). The analysis that went into that paper, about which I have more to say below, closely reflected what we were learning as students about the interplay of people's positions in a stratified system and their values. As I hope will become evident in this essay, the analytic orientation that I began to acquire in that seminar has had a distinct effect on my work ever since. Incidentally, it was no accident that Hyman's students were writing papers on substantive issues in a seminar designed to explore the methodology of secondary analysis. This was a reflection of his own keen ability to couple his methodological commitments to theoretically important problems. Even thirty-five years ago, his research stood as a clear model for placing method in the service of substance.

Of course, Herb Hyman's interest in the connections between social structure and values reflected the theoretical climate that prevailed during this period, a climate to which his colleague, Robert Merton, contributed so importantly, as well as Talcott Parsons, Robin Williams, and others. But, despite this powerful intellectual past, contemporary sociological studies do not usually look at the interconnection between social structure and values. Indeed, they can symbolize the focal points of theoretically antagonistic sociologic camps. For some of its critics, the notion of social structure represents a positivistic construct invoked by those engaged in a futile search for a social order that is imprinted in the actions of people. Values, on the other hand, to the extent that they serve to define situations, are part of the conceptual armory of sociologists who are more oriented to the meaning that people give to a situation than to the structural properties of the situation. These kinds of ideological stances are among the partisan divisions that seem to characterize present-day sociology.

The very intricateness of the relationships between social structure and values allows several alternative ways to organize the task I have set for myself. However, essentially three approaches to the conceptualization of the structure–values relationships can be recognized. One looks at values as a consequence of structural arrangements; a second regards structural arrangements as a consequence of values; and the third looks at values as conditions regulating the effects of social structure. It should be clear, of course, that there is nothing inherent in the nature of either social structure or values that dictates how they are related to each other. Whether one is conceived as the source or as the consequence or as a regulating condition of the other is strictly a reflection of the sociologist's own theoretical orientations and analytic goals. These constructs do not speak for themselves; what they can teach us is largely dependent on what we seek to learn from them as researchers. What is inherent in their nature is their importance in directing our attention to and in formulating interpretations of patterns of human behavior. There is a large body of research that could be called upon to illustrate the three types of relationships that will be examined. However, I shall draw primarily on those lines of my research that I see as being intellectually rooted in Herb Hyman's contributions.

A brief note concerning the constructs of structure and values is in order. By structure, I refer to the relatively enduring forms that can be discerned in relationships between individuals, groups, or collectivities or in the actions in which they engage over time. Values, which, like structures, are relatively stable, represent people's shared subjective dispositions that help them to distinguish what is good or bad, desirable or undesirable, what is to be strived after or eschewed. The very notion of value implies the presence of a hierarchy, the top of which contains those precepts and goals that we most prize and consider imperative, at the bottom those that are less central and more optional (Williams 1960). It is because they are so vital in guiding social action and reaction that values are of vital concern to sociological inquiry.

## Values as Consequences of Social Structure

Probably the most sociologically congenial conception of the structure–values relationship is to view the latter as a product of the former. The theoretical roots of this view can be found in the writings of Marx and in the work of several other of our sociological forefathers. Despite the long history of this theoretical orientation, Hyman's brilliant analysis, noted above, of the class bases of achievement values represents the outstanding model for the empirical analysis of values as a consequence of social structure. In that work, he was able to clarify certain key issues concerning the relationship of structure and values. Thus, he established that even those values that are considered to be universal in society, such as the valuation of success in the United States, are in fact differentially defined and differentially held. But what, then, determines who subscribes to and internalizes particular sets of values? We can assume, of course, that the distribution of values in society is not a happenstance phenomenon but one that follows a patterned course. With regard to success values, Hyman was able to amass convincing evidence that the goals toward which people strive reflect the realities they face in their class positions. There is a direct correlation, for example, between class position and the value placed on a college education, the status of the occupations to which people aspire, and whether people seek inner growth and personal enrichment in their job as distinct from money and security. Thus, achievement values, by and large, measure actual opportunity for achievement; many people prize what they see within their reach and reject that which is beyond opportunity. The patterned conditions of life embedded in social statuses form the basis for our dreams and cherished hopes.

Any data analyst must come away from a reading of that classic article with a sense of admiration for Hyman's theoretical clear-sightedness and his uncanny ability to array evidence around issues. For me, it was a powerful demonstration of a basic tenet: Much of what we learn is not a reflection of what we are taught but is, instead, a consequence of the structuring of our lives. As testimony to the effect that this study has had on my own sociological work, I should like to describe a study of mine, one that also treats values as consequences of social structure.

In the 1960s I conducted a study of Italian families (Pearlin 1971), part of which involved the cross-national comparison of the values that Italian and American parents hold for their children. My colleague, Melvin Kohn, had recently completed a study in which he found that the values that parents hold for their children vary with their social class. He had speculated that these differences were a consequence of the occupational conditions encountered by working- and middle-class fathers (Kohn 1959). I wanted to bring some of these speculations into my work, for I saw in them an opportunity to determine whether class is a source of parental values as it is of success values. It had already been established that class position was related to parental values. This was to be an opportunity to identify the conditions within the classes that generate these relationships, occupational conditions in particular. Therefore, I built into my survey of over 800 Turinese parents questions about parental values asked earlier by Kohn and, in addition, a host of questions about conditions of work life that had an a priori relevance to the values under examination. The findings from this part of my Italian study were reported with Kohn (Pearlin and Kohn 1968). Since then, Kohn and his associates have considerably extended this area of inquiry.

The core finding, consistent with Kohn's earlier study, was that both Italian and American middle-class parents tend to value self-direction in their children and that working-class parents tend to value obedience. Why is this? As I indicated, we posited that the reasons reside in certain pivotal occupational conditions that tend to be different for middle- and working-class people. The conditions we singled out and measured were (1) the closeness of supervision workers received; (2) whether they worked with things, people, or ideas; and (3) the self-reliance required by their jobs. Close supervision, working with things, and limited self-reliance were all associated with the valuation of obedience in one's children, whereas little or no supervision, working with ideas, and a high level of self-reliance on the job were related to valuing self-direction. As can be recognized, furthermore, the conditions leading to the parental value of obedience are predominantly clustered in working-class occupations, and those related to self-control predominate in middle-class occupations.

Thus, just as class structure shapes success values, so too does it influence parental values. Furthermore, the dynamics through which it exerts its influence are, in each instance, similar. In both cases we can see that the structured realities that one repeatedly encounters in areas of daily life shape our conceptions of our world, what it can offer, what it permits, what it demands, what it prohibits. If in our work we must be obedient and responsive to the direction of others, obedience is what we come to value in our children, out of the conviction, presumably, that this is a characteristic that will eventually contribute to their survival and success. Similarly, when our work demands that we rely on ourselves, we value self-direction in our children. Thus, we come to value those attributes and activities that help us to satisfy the range of imperatives and prohibitions imposed by the social structures of which we are a part and our statuses within them. To examine values as consequences of structures, therefore, informs us not only as to the origins of values but also as to the profound and penetrating effects of social structure on people's lives.

## Social Structures as Consequences of Values

It is not as simple to find examples of research that treat structures as the consequence of values as it is to find the reverse. However, this conception of the structure–values relationship does have a well-established place in sociology. Weber's *Protestant Ethic and the Spirit of Capitalism* (1958) may be taken as a prime example of this orientation. Similarly, theories of stratification (e.g., Davis and Moore 1945) that emphasize the pursuit of universal goals and values as the underpinning of status hierarchies essentially conceive of structure as following from—or sustained by—social values.

Stratified classes are not the only collectivities whose formations and structures are influenced by values. The audiences of mass communications can also be seen as collectivities whose structure is shaped in part by shared values. This was the subject of my thesis research (Pearlin 1956), a subject very much in keeping with the intellectual interests that then had a strong presence at Columbia. As my advisor, Herb Hyman provided more conceptual and methodological guidance and example than he probably recognized at the time. Underlying the work was the assumption that values, since they are the criteria by which people distinguish the more desirable from the less desirable, are active elements in the selection of television programs to which people were willing to expose themselves. Thus, it could be predicted that an audience of a program or type of program is made up of self-selected individuals who are distinguished from other audiences by the relevant values they hold. By way of example, it was found that viewers who feel that a good job is one that results in personal enrichment are also more disposed to watch programs broadcast by the public broadcasting channels than those who judge occupation more in instrumental terms; that is, in terms of pay and security. Thus, people who value occupations according to the inner growth they provide are inclined to select television programs on the basis of the same criteria. The choices people make from a large array of television programs are not a random process, therefore, but an orderly one in which values play a key part. As a result, values serve as an ingredient uniting the individuals who compose audiences of the mass media.

As I indicated, the treatment of values as factors underlying the development of structures is not common in sociology. The reason, of course, is that values themselves may be the result of structural arrangements. Eventually, the sociologist must ask where the values that contribute to the structure and organization of groups and collectivities come from. That is, the existence of value systems cannot be taken as a given; instead, we must search for the conditions that give rise to them. This search is likely to lead the sociologist back to social structure. For example, although values help to give structure and unity to the mass audiences of television, the very values that exercise this influence arise out of the status structure of the society. Even where they are the forerunners of social structure, values are also the consequences of structure.

## Values as Conditions Regulating Structural Effects

Regardless of their contributions to social structure, values, in a real sense, are the subjective extensions of the objective structuring of social life. However, it should not be thought that values are mechanistically and invariably dependent on structure. As any researcher who has looked at these issues can attest, people who are immersed in the same structural contexts may vary widely in the values they hold. This variation in values, in turn, can help to explain variations in the effects that the same structural arrangements have on different people. Values, that is, are powerful intervening conditions that regulate the effects of structure. The treatment of values as regulators of structural effects is, I believe, a most analytically useful approach to the structure–values relationship. It is the explication of this relationship that I shall deal with here.

One of the established currents of research by sociological social psychologists is the observation of social structures and their effect on people's actions, sentiments, and psychological functioning. Encompassed in this work are such diverse structures as stratification orders, systems of authority in factories, the division of labor in families, the distribution of status in neighborhood street-corner groups, and so on. Virtually all arrangements among individuals, groups, and collectivities are potential objects of study. The assumption underlying our interest in these durable arrangements is that individuals' locations within them organize experience over time. Organized experience, in turn, is the basis for how we see the world around us, how we think about it and act toward it. Were people's experience unstructured, their subjective dispositions would also be formless. Despite this fundamental assumption, when we empirically examine relationships between social structure and subjective dispositions, it is not unusual to find that such relationships are either nonexistent or quite modest in magnitude. And where the effects of social structure can be discerned, the reasons that the effects appear are frequently not self-evident or clear. This is where values can emerge as very useful constructs: They are often the conditions that importantly govern the magnitude of structural effects, and at the same time they can provide critical cues as to the processes that bring about the effects.

A number of illustrations can be drawn upon to explicate these points. One, which I referred to earlier, is an article that Joe Greenblum and I wrote while students in Hyman's seminar on secondary analysis (Greenblum and Pearlin 1953). Using data that were originally collected for a panel study of political attitudes in Elmira, New York, we took advantage of a number of questions concerning attitudes toward different minority groups to examine the structural sources of such attitudes.

We compared a variety of attitudes of middle- and working-class respondents and of those who had been occupationally downwardly or upwardly mobile or stationary. The findings were quite complex, and here I shall focus only on the social distance expressed toward blacks by the downwardly mobile. We had expected that this group would be more prejudiced than either the stationary working- or middle-class groups. Indeed they were, but by a surprisingly small margin. However, when the downwardly mobile were further distinguished according to the social class to which they referred themselves, interesting differences appeared. Specifically, the downwardly mobile who continued to identify themselves as belonging to the middle class accounted for all of the difference between the mobile and stationary groups, with the downwardly mobile who identify themselves as working-class members being no more prejudiced than the stationary groups. As we interpreted the findings, the downwardly mobile whose identifications and aspirations remain high feel a greater loss of status and, at the same time, experience a greater threat to their own fragile status from social proximity to ethnic groups whose status is low. Social distance becomes a mechanism to protect against this threat. The impact of movement to a new location in the class structure on social atti-

tudes, therefore, was conditioned by whether there was a corresponding shift in status values.

It is to be noted, then, that neither occupational status nor change
in status by itself was impressively related to prejudice. These structural arrangements matter when they are combined with certain kinds
of dispositions, in this case class identifications. These dispositions and
the status values that underlie them are thus instrumental in shaping
the meaning of structural arrangements and the consequences of
such arrangements. By distinguishing people according to their relevant dispositions, what was a modest relationship between status
structure and prejudice for a pooled group became a substantial and
more theoretically meaningful relationship for a subgroup. And, at
the same time, the dynamic link between status and prejudice could
be further elaborated.

Since this early work, I have had the opportunity to apply the same
basic analytic strategy to a number of very different substantive issues.
One such issue concerns alienation from work. Some years ago, while
doing research in a mental hospital, I became interested in the organization of authority and various of its effects (Pearlin 1962). Among
these effects is the extent to which people feel powerless to manage
the conditions that importantly bear on their work. Because hospitals
are typically hierarchical, it was possible to form a clear picture of the
ways in which authority was formally structured in the work life of
hospital staff. Of particular interest was whether alienation from control over work varied with the structural source of authority, specifically the structural proximity of one's primary superordinate. In some
units workers were supervised by those directly above them, and in
others they were supervised by authorities one or more levels removed. It seemed reasonable to suppose that the more structurally remote one's significant superordinate, the less reciprocal influence the
worker would be able to exercise and the more powerless he would be
to control his work destiny.

The findings were consistent with this expectation: Workers who
were separated from their superordinates by four levels were most
alienated, with the proportions progressively decreasing, being smallest among those whose significant superior was at the adjacent hierarchical level. The assumption underlying the interpretation of these
findings is that people want control over their own work, and when
prevented by the organization of their occupational setting from realizing what they feel is rightfully theirs, they become vulnerable to
alienation. Yet, it was obvious that people embedded in the same authority structure differed with regard to their feelings of powerless-

ness; some are deeply alienated by the very conditions that seem to leave others contented. What accounts for these variations?

In an attempt to answer this query, I turned to a value that seemed quite pivotal, namely, obeisance to authority. Obeisance was measured by a scale that essentially tapped the esteem accorded authority for its own sake. An obeisant person is one who is unquestioningly accepting of and deferential to authority, one who would not assume for himself the rights he accords to his superordinates. The obeisant worker thus sees his supervisor not only as superior in responsibility and authority but also as superior as a person. When obeisance is considered in conjunction with the positional disparities that exist between workers and their supervisors, the differences in alienation originally observed became much more specified. What we learn is that the alienative effects resulting from subordinate/superordinate positional disparity are found predominantly among those who reject obeisance. That is, structural separation from authority is most likely to result in alienation among those who feel that rights over the management of their work do not belong exclusively to superordinates. Workers who feel most powerless under these structural circumstances are those who want power, who do not deferentially yield it to superordinates. By contrast, the obeisant are unaffected by the very structural conditions that alienated the other workers.

There are two points to be taken from these results: First, the analytic introduction of values can identify groups most sensitive to the effects of structural arrangements, and second, the very specification of these effects helps to reinforce and refine the interpretation of why these effects come about.

A final example will further emphasize the analytic use of values as intervening conditions regulating structural effects. In the past two decades there has been an upsurge of interest in stress and its health consequences. To a considerable extent my own program of research has aimed at identifying the processes by which social circumstances result in personal distress. The family and the structure of its interpersonal relations can be, of course, active sources of stress for its members. Among the aspects of family structure that I have examined in relation to psychological distress are the status characteristics that wives and husbands bring to the marriage (Pearlin 1975). One can be hypergamous, marrying a spouse coming from a status background higher than one's own; one can be hypogamous, marrying "down"; or the couple can be of equal status, coming from the same stratum. Some early family sociologists argued that marriages between partners of unequal status harbor more disaffection and are more unstable than those whose partners are of equal status. One of the interesting implications of these arguments is that status is not unitary for the individual members of the nuclear family, as sociologists usually assume, but that the hierarchical arrangements of the larger society intrude on marriage by creating status differentiations within it. This study, then, was an opportunity to put earlier observations and speculations to test and to examine the processes of stress that might be set in motion by marital status arrangements.

Status inequality in marriage does have stressful consequences, but not in the way or under the conditions earlier supposed. First, status inequality per se is less important than the direction of inequality. Thus, the hypogamous—those marrying down—are most likely to score high on a measure of stress whereas the hypergamous are most likely to score low, even lower than people whose spouses come from equal status backgrounds. Not surprisingly, it was found that the hypogamous also experienced the least reciprocity in their marriages— that is, equality of give and take; they also had the least expressive or affective exchange with their spouses; and they were least likely to enjoy consensus about the use of money and the raising of children. It appears, therefore, that the status structure of the marriage can contribute to stress by creating problematic circumstances in the marital relationship. This is especially the case among the hypogamous, with the hypergamous being least stressed.

Once again this set of findings is interestingly specified when certain values are combined with the status structure of the marriage. Specifically, people who currently place great store on status advancement are most affected by the status structure of their marriages. Those who had married down but who are presently striving to move up are by far the most susceptible to stress and its attendant conditions. Indeed, the hypogamous who reject advancement values are notably free of marital stress and the limited reciprocity, affective exchange, and consensual decision making associated with the stress. It is not marrying down that is at issue, therefore, but marrying down in companionship with key values. What about status strivers who married up? The valuation of status has precisely opposite effects among people who had married up than it has when found with those who married down. That is, status strivers who were hypergamous had the most reciprocal, affective, consensual, and stress-free marriages. By contrast, the hypergamous not subscribing to status-enhancement values were indistinguishable from the hypogamous who also reject these values.

Simply put, then, we have here an instance where the structural arrangements, when combined with different values, have quite different effects. For respondents who had married down, aspirations for upward mobility accentuate feelings of deprivation and disappointment in the marriage. This combination shapes the flow of everyday interactions in a way that contributes to a markedly high disposition to stress. Among others who were also hypogamous but who did not hold such status values, the same structural inequality had no effect. The marriages of status strivers who had married up, by contrast, benefited from these status values. In these unequal marriages, strivers were realizing their values, resulting in marital relations that are distinctly harmonious and stress-resistant. Whereas marrying down represents a loss to the striving individual, the same striving results in gain and success when it is joined to marrying up. Neither the marital status arrangements nor the mobility values by themselves can reveal as much about stress and the processes leading to it as they do when analyzed in conjunction with one another. From this example it is again evident that values both govern and help to explain the impact of social structures on the lives of individuals.

## Another Look Back

It will be recognized that some of the roots of current research into the social origins of personal stress can be traced to Merton's treatment of anomie. He clearly showed how individuals can be caught at the juncture of the social structures of which they are a part and the value systems to which they subscribe. A discontinuity between the two—that is, having a location in a social order that is inconsistent or in conflict with what one cherishes and strives after—is the kind of circumstance that researchers need to understand if they are to understand the social causes of psychological distress. Hyman, in effect, clarified why even more people are not exposed to such circumstances. It is, first, because the values that are crucial to this process grow out of the very structures in which people are located; and, second, values engendered by structures tend to be congenial with and supportive of those structures. The seeds of my own program of research into social stress can be found planted in these fundamental sociological issues.

Although Herb Hyman's clear-sightedness and his scholarly skills are found in a number of substantive areas of inquiry, it is clear from this essay that one of these areas that has been important to me involves the intricate interplay of social structure and social values in shaping people's lives. Particularly in research into the forces affecting well-being, these constructs are a necessary complement to one another. We can understand the impact of social structures much more clearly by taking pertinent values into consideration; and we can best assess the role of values in guiding action when they are viewed in the context of the pertinent social structures.

## Bibliography

Davis, Kingsly, and Wilbur E. Moore. 1945. Some principles of stratification. *American Sociological Review* 10:242−49.

Greenblum, Joseph, and Leonard I. Pearlin. 1953. Vertical mobility and prejudice: A socio-psychological analysis. In Reinhard Bendix and Seymour Martin Lipset, eds., *Class, Status, and Power*, pp. 480−91. Glencoe, Ill.: Free Press.

Kohn, Melvin L. 1959. Social class and parental values. *American Journal of Sociology* 64:337−51.

Pearlin, Leonard I. 1956. The structural contexts of television audiences. Ph.D. thesis, Columbia University.

———. 1962. Alienation from work: A study of nursing personnel. *American Sociological Review* 27:314−26.

———. 1971. *Class context and family relations.* Boston: Little, Brown.

———. 1975. Status inequality and stress in marriage. *American Sociological Review* 40:344−57.

Pearlin, Leonard I., and Melvin L. Kohn. 1968. Social class, occupation, and parental values. *American Sociological Review* 31:466−79.

Weber, Max. 1958. *The Protestant ethic and the spirit of capitalism.* Translated by Talcott Parsons. New York: Scribner.

Williams, Robin. 1960. *American society,* pp. 397−470. 2nd ed. New York: Knopf.

# Daniel R. Miller and Elliott Jaques

## 12 Identifying Madness: An Interaction Frame of Reference

> The usefulness of the concept of schizophrenia is amply estab-
> lished by the universal occurrence of the behavioral and
> experimental anomalies to which the term refers, irrespective
> of differences in language and culture; by the biological disad-
> vantage associated with these anomalies . . . ; by the evidence
> that these abnormalities are . . . transmitted genetically; and by
> the influence on them of drugs which lack analogous effects on
> other people. [Kendell 1975]

> Never in the history of modern medicine have so many author-
> ities made so many assertions about the cause of a disease
> [schizophrenia] where the disease could not even be objectively
> identified by means of histopathological or pathophysiological
> criteria and observations; where . . . the very identity of the
> disease which the authorities so self-assuredly . . . set out to re-
> search and cure is shrouded, if not in mystery, then surely in
> controversy. [Szasz 1976]

These quotations illustrate how much discord there still is concerning
the nature of schizophrenia despite more than a century of pro-
digious research on the topic, some of it impressively creative. This
chapter is concerned with the reasons why different specialists become strongly committed to theoretically irreconcilable viewpoints,
and with a possible solution of this problem. It is postulated that the
disagreements are derived from doctrinal differences that are ultimately philosophical rather than biological or psychological or sociological.

Clinicians tend to be affiliated with particular doctrinal groups—
behavioral therapists, psychoanalysts, labeling theorists, and the like.
Members of each group typically subscribe to a system of first principles that serves as a model for constructing theory. Commitment to
such principles is a matter of faith; they are not right or wrong. They
are important because they circumscribe the areas of legitimate inquiry, influence the types of conceptions and dimensions used in the

We are very grateful to Hubert O'Gorman for his helpful comments on an earlier
version of the manuscript.

phrasing of questions, and predetermine the forms of the empirical answers. Hence, the clinician who subscribes to one model often cannot integrate concepts or findings with those reported by a clinician who subscribes to another model.

In what follows, some of these principles and their underlying philosophical assumptions are used to compare two of the most influential types of theoretical models that are used in the study of psychosis. One is derived from the medical conception of disease; it is presumed that psychosis is a "mental illness," akin to paresis, which also produces delusions and hallucinations. Investigators of psychosis and its origins have related it to heredity, biochemistry, stress, inner conflict, and epidemiology. The second type, which is concentrated on social reaction, begins with the indisputable point that the concept of madness is created socially and postulates that psychosis is expressed and identified during social interaction. Usually one of the partners violates a particular kind of social norm, and the other applies the label of madness. According to this view, madness originally exists in the eye of the beholder.

After a critical analysis of the two types of models, the chapter concludes with an alternative in which psychosis is defined in terms of incapacities that cause a breakdown in the individual's participation with another in the attainment of common social goals.

## The Empirical Picture

During the past century, armies of investigators have collected an awesome amount of information about psychotic states. Abundant genetic, constitutional, and biochemical information is now available about the etiology of schizophrenia. Biochemists have learned to modify, if not eliminate, the symptoms of schizophrenia. Psychoanalysts have become increasingly effective in unraveling the therapeutic puzzles posed by borderline patients and schizophrenics, and reinforcement therapists have had considerable success in helping long-term patients from back wards to communicate. There are abundant and convincing epidemiological findings linking psychoses to socioeconomic status, and labeling theorists have made a strong case for their claim that certain psychotic symptoms are the products of socialization and stigmatization in the hospital.

The cumulation of these findings, insights, and practices is impressive. Yet, an overview of the literature reveals a number of common weaknesses that preclude the integration of many findings and make it difficult to use them in the resolution of theoretical disagreements. To begin with, clinical investigators tend to do research that is relevant to the practical problems of clinical practice, but, as a whole, their papers tend to deemphasize interpretation and theory. Comparison of different findings is often frustrated by lack of comparability in concepts, premises, and questions.

It should be noted, parenthetically, that the aforementioned problems of emphasis on empiricism, varied frames of reference, and atheoretical and arbitrary systems of classification are not uncommon in most fields of knowledge. They seem especially handicapping in the clinical field where practitioners often complain that theory interferes with their practical diagnostic and therapeutic goals. Moreover, clinicians are often members of theoretical schools and find that their commitment to particular sets of principles is necessary to maintaining their professional identities. Hence, they are loath to question their dogmas.

## Definitions of Schizophrenia

Given the lack of theoretical foundations, it is not surprising that there is currently no agreement on even the most fundamental attributes of schizophrenia, not to mention its subtypes. The term "schizophrenia" covers a broader range of patients in the United States than it does in Europe. This is particularly true in Germany and Austria, where the disorder is attributed to degenerative lesions in the brain and twenty-five different schizophrenias have been proposed, their properties corresponding to the locations of the hypothetical lesions (Fish 1962).

Like other systems of classification, the current one used by the American Psychiatric Association (1980) lacks theoretical foundations. The manual is frankly descriptive and is aimed at precise formulations that maximize reliability.

There being no independent organic criteria for schizophrenia, Bleuler (1950) arrived at the syndrome by looking for fundamental symptoms: those that occur exclusively in some patients and not in patients with other pathologies. The fundamental criteria that he proposed were ambivalence and disorders of association and affect. Bleuler's syndrome was a modification of Kraepelin's dementia praecox, which was identified on the basis of apathy, thought disorders, and hallucinations. In addition to changing these criteria, Bleuler added psychosis with psychopathic personality, and alcoholic hallucinosis, both without theoretical justification. Since Bleuler's time, the definition of schizophrenia has continued to be revised, usually on the basis of clinical findings and compromises between the advocates of different models.

## Underlying Premises

Various theoretical groups differ in the metaphors they favor in their thinking about schizophrenia. Underlying the metaphors are assumptions about basic premises in the philosophy of science. Following are some of the underlying premises about which there is most disagreement:

1. *Universality/particularism.* Some specialists think that the symptoms of schizophrenia are universal. Like the symptoms of any other disease, they have the same meaning regardless of the society or the historical period. Other specialists think that the syndrome varies with particular cultural conditions and the period in history.

2. *Holism/reductionism.* Reductionists feel that the explanation of psychopathological states, like that of all other forms of human behavior, requires a reanalysis, first in the language of biology and then in the language of chemistry and physics. According to the holistic position, cases of schizophrenia are products of a number of complex interacting forces—societal, social interactional, conflictual, and the like. Their reduction to the concepts of the natural sciences, these theorists feel, can only distort their meanings.

3. *Phenotypes and genotypes.* Some groups assume that the disorder consists of its symptoms. There is nothing else. Behaviorists, for example, define cure as the elimination of symptoms. According to other groups, symptoms are phenotypes, overt manifestations of underlying or genotypic problems. Unless they are resolved, the disorder is not cured, even when the original complaints have been eliminated.

4. *Objective/subjective.* Concerned about the unreliability of information obtained by introspective analysis of mental states, behaviorists originally proposed that the study of human behavior, like the study of animal behavior, be restricted to publicly observable information, without reference to subjective or private mental states. Although they usually subscribe to the common goal of objectively controlled inquiry, critics of behaviorism think that there are clinically significant attributes of psychosis that can be studied only on the basis of subjective experience.

5. *Situation and individual.* Some researchers concentrate on attributes of the environment in deriving their explanations of pathological states. Proponents of cultural determinism, for example, are primarily concerned with environmental forces and pay little attention to the structure of the individual. In contrast, the proponents of certain psychological systems provide detailed accounts of individual

characteristics—dispositions, capacities, values—and summarize attributes of the environment as abstract stimuli.

6. *Temporal/atemporal.* Without the dimension of time, there would be no system of mechanics as we know it today. Some social scientists also try to establish principles by analyzing the variations in different processes with the times during which they run their courses. Most investigators, however, tend to think in spatial rather than temporal terms; their models are concerned with structures rather than development and change.

There are obviously natural combinations of these premises. A partiality to universalism, for example, means that the conclusions must apply at all times and in every society, preferably to every species. The position is, consequently, likely to be associated with reductionism and a deemphasis of social environments and subjective data. Holism, on the other hand, because of its emphasis on the total, complex structure, tends to be associated with particularism and detailed analysis of the cultural environment.

Preference for a particular combination is often determined more by the skills, methods, goals, and theoretical climate within a profession than by theoretical persuasion. Biochemists tend to be reductionists; sociologists are usually holists. Such biases can have profound effects on the welfare of a patient. They can determine whether a confused person is labeled as psychotic and, if so, whether the treatment consists of psychotherapy, medication, or behavioral reinforcement. Faiths in particular models tend to harden, and objectivity diminishes when one group of specialists is convinced that medication in a hospital, involuntary if necessary, provides the only hope of a cure, and another group is positive that the medication is not helpful and that involuntary hospitalization both violates the patient's civil rights and creates new symptoms.

The choices of model and philosophical premises are not solely a matter of personal predilection and professional identification. As illustrated by the models in the following sections, some sets of premises promote the types of analysis most fruitful to the types of problems being investigated and their particular theoretical formulations.

## The Medical Model

The reigning current viewpoint, the medical model, is a product of developments in physical medicine during the nineteenth century. Influenced by the metaphor of the Newtonian clock machine, physicians became mechanists and determinists. Trained in physics, chemistry, and biology, they were confident that all medical problems could be reduced to the categories of the natural sciences.

In their thinking about behavior disorders, physicians accepted Descartes's duality of mind-body: They separated behavior, which was external and physical, from consciousness, which was internal and mental. But whereas some conceived of body as the prime mover, others thought of mind as the prime mover, and still others assumed that body and mind interacted.

Physicians saw their goal as the curing of infectious disease, which they attributed to an invasion of the organism by the bacteria that cause cellular change and organic malfunctioning. Since particular diseases could be identified with reference to specific invading organisms, diseases were reified as discrete entities. Many specialists in physical medicine are now partial to models of interacting biological and ecological systems in which disease is defined by critical points on relevant parameters, but the original discontinuous conception is still the basis for psychiatric classification.

## Positions Concerning Basic Premises

With respect to the basis premises, the medical model is universalistic and reductionistic. The quest for principles that apply to all conditions and even to all species precludes the study of issues that apply only to local social conditions. In fact, medical researchers have tended to be relatively disinterested in society as a source of causal variables and have not appreciated the fact that its organization affects population density, pollution, and the expression of genetic tendencies, all of which are crucial to physical welfare.

The medical model, then, devotes little attention to the external situation and is focused on conditions within the individual. Physicians consider psychosis a disease. They define it with respect to the phenotypic manifestations of delusions, hallucinations, and confused thinking. However, their universalism and reductionism prompts them to look for genotypic infectious or biochemical conditions.

In his attempt to understand the sources of psychosis, Kraepelin took an unequivocally reductionistic stand. Disease, he thought, affects the body, not the mind. His confidence in his reductionism was boosted by two previous findings: that tuberculosis and Sydenham's chorea were identified originally by means of clinical observation, and that some delusions and hallucinations had been shown to be caused by the spirochetes that produce paresis. Unfortunately, too little was known about brain pathology, and, since the presumed diseases were manifested in psychic events, it was, paradoxically, psychological manifestations of psychosis to which Kraepelin actually devoted most of his attention. Logically, the examination of mental phenomena seems like a poor method of searching for underlying, genotypic physical causes. As Szasz notes (1976, p. 13), "The fact that paresis is a brain disease could never have been established by studying the paretic's thinking. Then why study the schizophrenic's?"

A physician like Kraepelin, Freud was also plagued by the Cartesian metaphor and initially assumed that all mental events would ultimately be explained in physical terms. His clinical work, however, led him to reverse the direction of causality. But he never explained the mechanism whereby mental events cause physical ones: how the hysteric's frustrated sexual desire, for example, becomes converted into paralysis or anesthesia.

Concerned as they were with developing a science akin to mechanics, it is puzzling that the originators of the medical model did not concentrate on time, a cornerstone of mechanical theory. There are some hints of interest in temporal variation, as in the conception of chronic schizophrenia or the observation that the symptoms of schizophrenia occur in phases.

More consistent with the aim of becoming a natural science is the concentration on objectivity. To maximize reliability, the authors of the current system of psychiatric classification have attempted to delineate narrow syndromes which they have tried to define in operational terms. A perusal of their lists of symptoms, however, reveals that the criteria of many syndromes are vaguely defined and replete with unstated values. Consider the criteria for schizophrenia: "odd or bizarre ideation" (How odd and bizarre? By what standards?); "unusual perceptual experiences" (How unusual? What kind?); "blunted, flat, or inappropriate affect" (How blunted? Inappropriate in what sense?). The prodromal symptoms of schizophrenia include criteria defined by values that are not at all universal: "marked impairment in role functioning as wage earner, student, or homemaker," "marked impairment in personal hygiene and grooming," and "social isolation or withdrawal." All three violations are inapplicable to societies with different values about achievement, cleanliness, and the establishment of strong emotional bonds.

In line with the Newtonian tradition, the medical model was formulated with the goal of creating a full-fledged, applied physical science. But the premises are unsuitable to the study of schizophrenia. The reduction to biology is unworkable; psychiatrists now conceive of the syndrome of schizophrenia in terms of psychological attributes and social behavior that are culture-bound and vaguely defined.

## Labeling Theory

Psychosis may be viewed as a form of deviance from certain social norms. Proponents of labeling theory are primarily concerned with the societal roots of deviance. They assume that stabilized, deviant behavior is primarily a product of others' reactions, not necessarily of the person's inner state. Psychosis, they think, is the end product of a sequence that causes the individual to be channeled into the role of the mentally ill. The postulated sequence consists of the following steps.

An individual violates a social norm. To be viewed as a possible sign of madness, the person's action must represent a form of "residual deviance" (Scheff 1966), for which the culture does not supply explicit rules. One type is the violation of rules governing the showing of interest and involvement in conversations with others. Although unstated, norms about involvement are universally taken for granted. Lemert (1951) uses the term "primary deviation" for residual rule breaking, which, he thinks, has only "marginal implications for the psychic structure of the individual" (Lemert 1967, p. 17). It is usually rationalized away by others, but occasionally it becomes part of the sequence leading to hospitalization.

Next, the person is labeled. This is the crucial step in the development of psychiatric symptoms. "[D]eviance is not a quality of the act the person commits, but rather a consequence of the application by others of rules and sanctions to an offender" (Becker 1963, p. 9). Observers interpret the action in terms of stereotypes of insanity, which are learned in early childhood and are continually reaffirmed in everyday interactions.

Finally, the identified deviant is brought to the attention of officials, who arrive at a diagnosis. In consequence, the deviant is given the social role of patient (Erikson 1964, p. 16).

There are two connotations of the word "insanity" according to *The Oxford English Dictionary* (1977): utterly senseless or irrational behavior, and an incurable condition. Learning to behave in accordance with these conceptions is reinforced by the degradation and stigmatization rituals of the "asylum" (Goffman 1961). When societal agents react to the deviant in terms of the stereotypes of insanity, unstructured rule breaking crystallizes into conformity with their expectations. Gradually, the patient manifests a "secondary deviation," which pertains to the development of a role "as a means of defense, attack, or adjustment to the overt and covert problems created by the consequent societal reaction" (Lemert 1951, p. 76).

Finally, the process is made irreversible, according to the theory. The labeled deviant is rewarded for playing the stereotyped role and punished for attempting to return to conventional roles. Following discharge, the stigma of psychiatric hospitalization causes others to deny access to social contacts, employment, and marriage. As a result, the deviant withdraws, a response that elicits more stigmatization. The vicious cycle continues with the ex-patient withdrawing further and becoming more disturbed and socially isolated. Symptoms are consequently stabilized and even exacerbated, often insuring a return to the hospital.

## Positions on Basic Premises

A comparison of the medical and labeling models illustrates vividly how much difference contrasting positions on basic premises can make for the conception of psychosis. In contrast to the reductionism of the medical model, the labeling one is uncompromisingly holistic. In formulating his version of labeling, Scheff's goal was to create a "purely sociological model" that would counterbalance the atomism and exclusive emphasis on the isolated individual that are characteristic of medical models. Paradoxically, he commits a comparable sin by reversing the emphasis and completely ignoring individual variation.

With respect to the basic premises, labeling theorists also differ from the physicians in emphasizing the social environment rather than individual structure and in assuming that psychosis, unlike physical disorders, varies with cultural conceptions of insanity, patterns of socialization, and relations within groups. Unlike the medical model, labeling theory is exclusively phenotypic. Analysis of psychosis is based on observable social behavior; no provision is made for genotypic explanations. Not surprisingly, behavior therapists, who also dismiss genotypes, feel very comfortable with labeling theory (Ullman 1969).

The models are similar in two respects: their relative indifference to time as a dimension and their concern with objectivity. Possibly because labeling theory is designed to become part of a social rather than a physical science, it differs from the medical model in its strong emphasis on values. Most labeling theorists, for example, view the deviant as an underdog victimized by the social system (Gouldner 1968), and the descriptions of the psychotics' socialization in the hospital imply a strong negative evaluation of current medical practices.

The two models have a serious shortcoming in common. They turn a blind eye to subject matter the investigation of which is precluded by their premises but which is likely to contribute significantly to the understanding of psychosis. Hence, as will be shown, both models are limited in their capacities to generate the theoretical principles needed to devise criteria of psychosis.

Despite these problems, the labeling perspective has some undeniable assets. Deviants are labeled, and there is convincing evidence that the ways in which they are classified are crucial to their welfare. In various historical periods, sufferers of the same disorder have been identified as witches, village idiots, felons, or schizophrenics—with considerably different consequences. The theory also seems fruitful in its use of interaction as the context within which people are labeled, decisions are made about treatment, and socialization occurs.

The labeling perspective has a special strength: It is sufficiently clear to afford empirical testing. But this provides disclosures of its greatest weakness. There is abundant literature, much of it summarized by Gove (1970, p. 198), that indicates that some of the basic assumptions do not hold up under empirical scrutiny. The data reveal that people are not hospitalized primarily because of others' complaints, that hospitals do not usually stigmatize and degrade their patients, and that patients are not necessarily penalized when they attempt to return to their conventional, socially acceptable roles.

The findings suggest that labeling theorists trivialize the complexity and seriousness of the difficulties a person can have long before coming to the attention of legal and psychiatric authorities and that they overemphasize the importance of labeling and socialization relative to primary deviance. These distortions are attributable, in great part, to the restrictions of underlying premises that proscribe alternate ways of thinking about the problem.

## A Proposed Alternative

The study of schizophrenia entails the investigation of a multiplicity of questions, some social, some psychological, and some biological. No one profession can provide all the answers. In what follows, a social interactional conception of psychosis is proposed that is designed to integrate some of the relevant social, psychological, and biological issues, and to answer the question: What is psychosis?

### Disorders and Society

How does one go about developing criteria for identifying schizophrenia? Psychiatrists can modify some symptoms with medication, but they seem uncertain about whether an imbalance of biogenic amines should be viewed as a definition or a cause of the disorder.

Better etiological leads to defining the problem are available in the sociological and anthropological literature.

Linton (1956), an anthropologist and specialist in documenting behavior disorders in different societies, concludes that there are both universal and relative forms of pathology. Every society, he thinks, provides examples of psychotics, neurotics, and hysterics who are recognized as such by others in the society. Although some symptoms associated with these abnormal states are shaped by local cultural influences, he postulates the existence of underlying tendencies, genotypes, which are universal and probably have physiological bases. Individuals having the required constitutional defects are likely to become deviants in any society. It also seems likely that certain universal trauma and conflicts contribute to psychosis in all societies.

In support of Linton's universalistic view, there is the historical evidence that certain disorders have been identified in all societies. The ancient Greeks and Romans identified melancholia, hysteria, and psychotic states (Menninger, Mayman, and Pruyser 1963). In the thirteenth century, Bracton, an Englishman, described an insane person as "one who knows not what he is doing, is lacking in mind and reason" (Guttmacher, 1962, p. 13). The American colonists distinguished among the poor, the ill, the criminal, and the insane (Fingarette 1972, p. 12). In a treatise on "sicknesses of the soul," the philosopher Immanuel Kant identified the syndromes of hypochondria, melancholia, and psychosis. Characteristic of the latter are deficiencies in reality testing and different kinds of delusions (Zilboorg 1941).

Disorders are universally attributed to the individual's incapacities, which contribute to behavioral deviations. But deviations from what? The universality of labeling suggests that the functioning of the society may provide an answer. The welfare of every society depends on activities that its citizens perform as means of achieving certain functional prerequisites (Aberle et al. 1950). The prerequisites, such as socialization, control of disruptive behavior, and the regulation of affective expression, are general conditions for maintaining the society as a system.

Structural arrangements may differ, but all required social activities have one property in common: People have to work together in defined relationships, usually as part of larger groups. These observations help to identify the dimensions on which the various types of deviants are categorized. The universal ones are not height or income or musical talent, none of which implements the functional prerequisites. They include, among others, adherence to moral standards, intellectual capacity, and competence in social interaction. Deviance on the first identifies criminality; on the second, mental retardation. Deviance on the third, productive interaction, could not be more damaging, since the capacity to work productively with others enters into virtually every activity in which an individual is involved throughout life and is a core condition for the operation of the society. It is this deviation that identifies the disorders that are of interest in this chapter. In short, incapacities that interfere with or disrupt social encounters are universal properties of psychosis.

## Channels of Communication

Further consideration of this criterion requires a preliminary examination of the social encounter, which furnishes the context in which the handicaps of the schizophrenic are manifested. Aimed as they are at the attainment of the participants' shared goals, activities in the encounter require continuing reciprocity in communication. Without adequate reciprocity, the encounter falters and may even be terminated.

Communication is conducted by means of two separate channels (Reusch and Bateson 1968). The one most people are aware of is verbal and literal and contains denotative meanings. Everyone is generally aware of thoughts, and can exert considerable control over their translation into verbal messages. The second channel, of which people are much less aware, is nonverbal, contextual, and connotative. It is typically more loaded with affect. Like everyone else, the schizophrenic is much less aware of, and has less control over, nonverbal than verbal messages. We propose that it is problems in nonverbal communication that cause the psychotic to damage or disrupt social encounters. This is because nonverbal difficulties interfere with the partner's complementary communications and damage the required reciprocity.

The encounter provides a spatiotemporal frame of reference for understanding communication. The key concepts are behavior settings, for spatial dimensions; episode, for temporal dimensions; and script, for spatiotemporal organization. Spatially, the participants find themselves in a behavior setting (Barker 1960), which can be a baseball game or dinner at a restaurant. As a means of facilitating the ongoing activities, the space is divided into regions filled with objects like tables or typewriters. But the setting is more than just spaces filled with objects. It also includes the people, their obligations, and their actions: It is the entire baseball game, including the layout of the field, the rules of the game, the players, and their actions. It may be viewed as a dynamic conception of organized space, a homeostatic system that is partly independent of the characteristics of its occupants.

Temporally, an encounter can be viewed as an episode, a structure that is organized into at least three stages with respect to the participants' goals. An encounter between friends, for example, may begin with greetings: mutual expressions of commitment to the relationship, communications of purpose, and agreement on appropriate activities. Next, the participants engage in the primary activity—it may be work, play, or the unstructured expenditure of time. The episode usually concludes with comments on the activity, possibly plans for future encounters, mutual assurances about the value of the relationship, and departure.

Throughout the episode, the participants are only partially in control of their actions. This is because they are participating spontaneously in a common stream of behavior (Barker and Wright 1955), which is altered constantly by changes in the interaction, the participants' needs, and environmental pressures. The complexity of the participants' changing, intersubjective experiences has been described as the collective contextures of conjunctive meaning (Mannheim 1982) and the thousand-faceted mirroring of each other (Schutz 1968).

So subtle and swift are some of the changes that the participants would probably lose their social bearings were it not for their shared scripts (Abelson 1980). These internal blueprints depict the likely sequence, timing, and spacing of the framing events in their appropriate regions. People in any restaurant can anticipate a sequence of events—waiting to be seated, being conducted to a table, getting the menu, and so on. Also implicit in the script are role pressures, such as the obligation to honor others' rights to keep their conversations private. Based on the overall spatiotemporal frame of reference, people usually know how to conduct themselves, even with strangers and in unfamiliar restaurants.

## Time and Space in the Social Encounter

Why assume that time and space are so crucial to communication generally and to psychotic communication in particular? They are generally important because they are formal parameters for the definition of meaning. "[R]elationships in time and space are ways of describing the various substantive definitions that social actors construct for a specific event . . . social activity is an outcome of these relationships" (Jaques 1982; McHugh 1968). Effective communication and reciprocal activity can occur only when people react to each other with reference to a common spatiotemporal frame of reference. Conversely, communication is impeded, if not precluded, if the participants in an interaction have different orientations in time and space.

Each event has its own temporal and spatial structures, which create pressures for action. If friends are meeting for the first time in fifteen years, the greeting is likely to last much longer than if they last met fifteen minutes earlier. A viable encounter is contingent on the pair concurring about the appropriate duration of each stage. If they do not, one individual may still be conveying greetings while the other is engaged in the second stage of the encounter. Communication thus becomes confused. A relationship such as that between friends also imposes many other temporal pressures during the encounter. Possible examples include standards pertaining to rate of speech that is suitable to the occasion and proportions of time devoted to eye contact and waiting for turns as speaker.

If time is held constant, each event can also be analyzed with reference to its spatial structure, which creates its own pressures for impelling, inhibiting, and directing action. Spaces are commonly mapped with reference to regions, barriers, and boundaries. A vivid illustration is provided by the baseball diamond, with its visual indications of pitcher's mound, home plate, base paths, and the like—all laid out to define the rules about acceptable movement in space (runners must touch each base). Visual cues are not available for most social encounters, but common knowledge about basic social rules enables people in encounters to facilitate one another's attempts to engage in reciprocal actions that achieve mutual goals. Some of the rules pertain to maintaining an acceptable distance between heads, avoiding the touching of certain regions of another's body, and restricting physical movement to a range appropriate to the occasion and one's social status.

In addition to organizing relationships with reference to physical time and space, each participant also organizes the meanings of events subjectively with reference to the present, the temporal point of intersection for all events that may affect action, whether they be present, past, or future. What the child experiences as a serious crisis, for example, is likely to be reinterpreted numerous times during later stages of development. Moreover, each reconceptualization of events in the past requires corresponding changes in the meanings of the present and the anticipated future.

## The Nature of Schizophrenia

It is now possible to be specific about the kinds of deviation that cause people to be labeled as psychologically disturbed. They entail the misuse of space and time, predominantly in nonverbal communication, and in a manner that damages the social encounter. The psychotic may abandon the script or alter it, eliminate a temporal stage of the encounter, invade the partner's personal space, respond asynchronously to the latter's comments, or turn attention inward so that "there is not a dialogue but essentially two people speaking to themselves" (Modell 1980).

There are many possible violations of spatiotemporal rules. All forms of nonverbal deviance are crucial to the encounter because they literally destroy the reciprocity on which every social bond depends. The psychotics' nonverbal responses prevent them from doing the work needed to attain common goals. More important, their disabilities make it impossible for partners who participate in requisite activities to carry out their obligations and to have their rights recognized. No matter how hard they try, no matter how motivated they are, they cannot succeed in maintaining a viable interaction.

Even in a transaction as simple as the purchase of a newspaper, the psychotic spoils the interaction and threatens the shopkeeper's occupational identity by creating confusion and interfering with the latter's use of appropriate reciprocal responses. The shopkeeper is likely to become angry because work has been interrupted, and there is no obvious way of eliminating the difficulty. The psychotic's deviance is expressed by the inappropriate direction of gaze or the exceptionally long pause, responses to which most people do not devote much thought but which can engender considerable anxiety and frustration in others.

## Some Exploratory Research

The concentration here on time and space departs from the traditional clinical emphasis on the schizophrenic's thinking and language. To explore empirically some of the issues just raised, one of the authors and associates conducted a number of studies in which hospitalized schizophrenics were compared with hospitalized depressives and with normals.[1] Each subject participated in informal, unstructured conversations with two members of the research team. The conversations were recorded on audiovisual tapes, which were later coded by the researchers.

An initial study was devoted to the adequacy of conventional psychiatric criteria as indexes of the everyday interpersonal behavior of schizophrenics. We find that twenty-one of a sample of twenty-five patients show none of the classic symptoms of schizophrenia mentioned by Bleuler (1950): the stupor, the clang associations, the echolalias, the hallucinations, the total detachment from reality. Most of the patients seem in touch and very reasonable. In fact, after reading tran-

[1] The research was planned by Daniel R. Miller, Henry B. Mann, Anne Haines, Lisa Black, Evan Nelson, and Sharon Kost. Results of the pilot studies are described in dissertations written at Wesleyan University by Black (1985), Nelson (1985), and Kost (1986).

scripts of the conversations, the average person would have no idea that they were taking place in psychiatric wards.

Although few of the patients seemed like refugees from *Psycho*, they still had a strong emotional impact on the researchers. Asked to review the tapes and write their reactions to different stages in the conversations, the interviewers typically report being bored, frustrated by the patients' inadequate reciprocity, occasionally frightened by an unanticipated invasion of personal space, and, mostly, slowed up by a growing sense of fatigue, which they connected with a constant feeling of tension during the interviews.

In their nonverbal behavior during the interviews, schizophrenics differ significantly from normal subjects and hospitalized depressives in a number of ways. One is congruence with the partner's movements, on which the schizophrenics are the lowest of the three groups. Congruence refers to appropriately timed coordination with the partner's actions by mirroring, inverse action, and other meaningful movements. Not surprisingly, schizophrenics are also significantly higher than the other two groups in incongruent movements, such as looking away after the partner has just made a point.

Other variables on which schizophrenics are lowest are fluidity, which is degree of rhythm when shifting from one movement to another; amount of spatial extension; synchrony, which is the overall smoothness in physical adjustment to one's partner; and intensity of gaze. Schizophrenics are also significantly more inclined than normals to step back and turn away from the interviewer, to speak very slowly, and to restrict the range of their pitch. Finally, there are indications that most of the differences are greater when schizophrenics are listening rather than speaking. The role of listener is less structured than that of speaker. When listening, patients seem more inclined to be distracted by their problems and by events unrelated to the conversation.

The finding that schizophrenics usually do not display the bizarre behavior commonly attributed to psychotics is not astonishing. It is commonly agreed among clinicians that, except for certain extremely disturbed, chronic patients, most psychotics display disorders of thought and association only infrequently, in phases, and, in some cases, only under severe stress. In contrast, our repeated observations of the same patients indicate that their deviant forms of nonverbal communication are always evident, although they may fluctuate in intensity, possibly with degree of personal stress. In other words, schizophrenics always have trouble with their personal encounters, even when they are able to make accurate judgments of what is really happening. There are empirical as well as theoretical reasons, then, for using interpersonal effectiveness as a basis for choosing diagnostic criteria.

## Psychological Sources of Nonverbal Deviance

Every society must attend to madness because it spoils the encounters needed to do the society's work. By interfering with requisite activities, it poses a general threat to the welfare of the society and a specific one to the people who live with the psychotic. Thus far, we have defined madness in terms of its nonverbal effects on interaction. Accounting for nonverbal deviance requires, we think, an understanding of certain internal qualities of the person, which make themselves felt in encounters with others. After all, the label of madness is applied to the individual, not the interaction, particularly to the individual who spoils interactions with many different people.

Because of their holistic premise, theorists who study social interaction are often opposed to the seeking of explanations for social behavior in the psychological attributes of individuals. We find that an adequate accounting for deviant forms of nonverbal communication requires the exploration of the individual's subjective experiences, especially cognitive organization.

Our explanation begins with socialization during the early years. While participating in relationships with parents and siblings, the child learns to behave in a manner that is compatible with the family's style. With experience, conceptions develop of interactions as units, each consisting of the child's self, the self of another, and some type of reciprocal behavior. An integral part of the unit is a set of emotions: The impatient, grumpy father teaches his son to catch a ball, and the latter feels demeaned, hopeless, and resentful. The child's interpretations of the same interactional unit of self–activity–other self keep changing with maturation and increasing success in assessing others' motives, causality, and time.

Everyone incorporates patterns of relationships, as they are experienced, into an inner world (Klein 1975). This is an internal society, which is cognitively organized in terms of the networks of all one's relationships with people who have been significant in one's life and the relationships among these significant people. In the fantasy life of this inner world, the individual keeps reexperiencing the relevant past events, particularly the ones that are emotionally most salient.

The internal society is used as a template for interpreting social events in the external world. We make sense of strangers' behaviors by comparing them with the actions in a similar setting of others close to us who resemble the strangers with respect to social class, sex, and status in the family. We may even evaluate ourselves in terms of strangers' judgments. This is because unknown people are assimilated to occupants of the inner world whom we use as reference groups and reference individuals (Hyman 1968). Such groups furnish the standards of comparison for the appraisals of ourselves and others and serve as sources of values, norms, and attitudes. The inner world can be regarded, then, as a set of multiple reference groups internalized during different periods of development.

Pertinent to psychopathology is Hyman's observation that groups are living structures in the mind of the perceiver. Since many of their norms are implicit, ambiguous, or inconsistent, they provide free rein to autistic perception. Hence, conceptions of groups, relationships, and norms are subject to marked variations in individual interpretation.

Conceptual templates can be misleading if they represent misunderstandings of interactions or if they were formed by relationships that prepared the individual for a world that is very different from the one being experienced. The resultant discrepancy between internal and external societies is bound to create serious confusion. It is this discrepancy, we think, that is at the heart of the psychotic's difficulties with others.

What might cause the development of an inaccurate conceptual template, one leading to the anticipation that people will be more discouraging or attacking or envious than they are in the real world? Klein finds that very young children tend to split their pictures of adults into good and bad parts and to split their own selves accordingly into corresponding loving and hostile components. Normally, the reassurances provided by supportive experiences with loving adults enable the offspring to integrate their conceptions of both self and others into whole persons. This need not happen, however. Some familial relationships are so frequently associated with conflict and pain that they interfere with the conceptual integration and may even cause a regression to an earlier stage of development, which is preverbal and tends to be experienced in the language of the dream instead of the adult's world of time, space, and causality (Miller and Sobelman 1985).

Of course, the difficulties need not be caused by actual rejection. Traumatic events beyond the control of well-intentioned parents can have the same deleterious effects. And since the ambiguous characteristics of groups like the family allow free rein to autistic perception, certain weaknesses, possibly a biochemically induced low threshold for pain, can cause the child to experience contact with even a very supportive adult as persecuting, so that the relationship is internalized as an attacking one.

As stated earlier, people generally reconstruct their conceptions of past and future in terms of unanticipated events in the present. But this may not be possible if the individual's inner society is overweighted with painful relationships from the distant past, ones whose use as a frame of reference keeps causing continual misinterpretations of the present. In that event, an encounter with a friendly authority in the external world can be misapprehended in the light of continuing, obsessive struggles with a significant hostile authority from the past. Moreover, since the misapprehension causes the individual to assimilate the meaning of the event to past ones, there is little likelihood that its unanticipated features will be appreciated. Misunderstandings created by earlier relationships are not, then, readily corrected; the past cannot be rewritten, as it is by most people.

The more the template refers to an unpleasant past, the greater is the likelihood that the individual will be confused about others' intentions, misinterpret events in the behavioral stream, and engage in socially inappropriate behavior. That is the plight of psychotics. Given the persecutory conception of the internal society plus the practical difficulties in the external world that are likely to result from such an inaccurate template, psychotics tend to become increasingly aversive to their fellow beings. Consistent with this deduction are the findings that schizophrenics differ from depressives and normals in their tendencies to step back physically, to look away, and to restrict the extensity of their physical movements.

## Premises Revisited

In the last section, a model was presented that is interactional, like the labeling model. Rather than concentrating on the theme that psychosis is predominantly a product of socialization, we view it as an inclination to behave in ways that disrupt the social encounter; an inclination attributable to certain features of the inner world, and the past experiences and biological predispositions that contribute to the development of those features.

Before the model is considered in light of the six premises, it is first necessary to note that the investigation of schizophrenia is an exercise in applied research. There are many complex topics, which require the expertise of specialists in different professions. The commonly studied topics—social distribution of different pathologies, methods of labeling, hereditary dispositions, and coping mechanisms—indicate how varied are the orientations and methods needed to do research in the field. As suggested earlier, a commitment to premises suitable to the closed system assumed to exist in mechanics or astronomy is handicapping to workers in complex, applied research. Yet, such limited positions, which are adopted by the advocates of the medical and labeling models, are all too common in models of pathology.

The medical model is universalistic in its presumption of underlying disease, which has the same manifestations in every society; the labeling model is particularistic in its premise that the structure of disorders varies with the type of socialization. This, in turn, varies with the society. Both premises are included in the interactional model presented here. Hallucinations, delusions, and depression are clearly universal; they are found in every society. Their different forms and their contents, however, vary with the culture.

The present model resembles the alternatives in two other respects. Like the labeling model, it features situations and social relationships; like the medical model, it also emphasizes the organization of the individual. The second similarity concerns the position on reductionism. The medical model aims at the reduction of psychotic phenomena to the language of physical science; the labeling model is holistic. The present interactional model is antireductionistic in its assumption that social phenomena cannot be reduced to psychology or biology; the three disciplines represent different ways of analyzing the same topics. Unlike other holistic models, however, the present one does not rule out the interrelationship of data from different realms of discourse. It is presumed, for example, that an understanding of the origins of schizophrenia requires an exploration of the social encounter. An exploration of the individual's internal society is also required. The latter is not undertaken, however, to explain away the former. Both types of information are needed to answer complex, etiological questions about schizophrenia.

As for the other premises, the interactional model is like the medical model and unlike the labeling one in its provision for the analysis of genotypes; the schizophrenic's difficulties with time and space are explained in terms of underlying, genotypic phenomena such as splits in the self and hereditary predispositions. Unlike the others, the present model utilizes time and space for reasons already described. This emphasis is based on the presumption that the manifestations of schizophrenia are extreme positions on dimensions, on each of which all humans can be located. It is assumed, in fact, that the similarities among the various syndromes are far greater than the differences and that, ultimately, the names of diseases will be abolished in favor of a classificatory system focused on interacting dimensions and homeostasis (Menninger, Mayman, and Pruyser 1963).

Much work is needed on integrational models like the one proposed here. Before that work can begin, the different theoretical camps will have to begin questioning seriously their dogmatic defenses of their favored philosophical premises and establish the lines of communication needed for coordinated efforts.

## Bibliography

Abelson, R. P. 1980. *Status of the script concept.* New Haven: Yale University Cognitive Science Program, Cognitive Science Technical Report no. 2.

Aberle, D. F., A. K. Cohen, A. K. Davis, M. J. Levy, and F. X. Sutton. 1950. The functional prerequisites of a society. *Ethics* 60:100–11.

American Psychiatric Association. 1980. *Diagnostic and statistical manual of mental disorders.* 3rd ed. Washington, D.C.: APA.

Barker, R. G. 1960. Ecology and motivation. In M. R. Jones, ed., *Nebraska Symposium on Motivation,* pp. 1–49. Lincoln: University of Nebraska Press.

Barker, R. G., and H. F. Wright. 1955. *Midwest and its children.* Evanston, Ill.: Row, Peterson.

Becker, Howard. 1963. *Studies in the sociology of deviance: Outsiders.* New York: Free Press.

Black, Lisa M. 1985. The nonverbal communication of schizophrenics. Master's thesis, Wesleyan University.

Bleuler, E. 1950. *Dementia praecox; or, the group of schizophrenias.* New York: International Universities Press.

Erikson, Kai. 1964. Notes on the sociology of deviance. In Howard Becker, ed., *The other side,* pp. 9–21. New York: Free Press.

Fingarette, H. 1972. *The meaning of criminal insanity.* Berkeley: University of California Press.

Fish, F. J. 1962. *Schizophrenia.* Bristol: Wright.

Goffman, E. 1961. *Asylums.* New York: Doubleday (Anchor Books).

Gottesman, I. I., and J. Shields. 1972. *Schizophrenia and genetics.* New York: Academic Press.

Gouldner, Alvin. 1968. The sociologist as partisan: Sociology and the welfare state. *American sociologist* 3:103–16.

Gove, Walter R. 1970. Societal reaction as an explanation of mental illness: An evaluation. *American Sociological Review* 38:873–84.

———. 1976. The labeling theory of mental illness: Reply to Scheff. *American Sociological Review* 40:242–57.

Guttmacher, M. 1962. *The role of psychiatry in law.* Springfield, Ill.: Thomas.

Jaques, Elliott. 1982. *The form of time.* New York: Crane, Russak.

Kendell, Robert E. 1975. The role of diagnosis in psychiatry. London: Blackwell Scientific Publications.

Klein, Melanie. 1975. *Envy and gratitude and other works, 1946–1963.* New York: Dell (Delacorte Press).

Kost, Sharon A. 1986. Nonverbal communication and schizophrenia. Honors thesis, Wesleyan University.

Lemert, E. M. 1951. *Social pathology.* New York: McGraw-Hill.

———. 1967. *Human deviance, social problems, social control.* Englewood Cliffs, N.J.: Prentice-Hall.

Linton, R. 1956. *Culture and mental disorders*. Springfield, Ill.: Thomas.
Mannheim, K. 1982. *Structures of thinking*. Boston: Routledge and Kegan Paul.
McHugh, Peter. 1968. *Defining the situation*. New York: Bobbs-Merrill.
Menninger, K., M. Mayman, and P. Pruyser. 1963. *The vital balance*. New York: Viking Press.
Miller, Daniel R., and George Sobelman. 1985. Models of the family. In L. L'Abate, ed., *The handbook of family psychology and therapy*, 1:113–371. Homewood, Ill.: Dorsey.
Modell, Arnold H. 1980. Affects and their non-communication. *International Journal of Psycho-Analysis* 61:259–67.
Nelson, Evan S. 1985. Patterns of nonverbal communication in schizophrenics. Honors thesis, Wesleyan University.
Reusch, J., and G. Bateson. 1968. *Communication: The social matrix of psychiatry*. New York: Norton.
Scheff, Thomas J. 1966. *Being mentally ill: A sociological theory*. Chicago: Aldine.
———. 1976. Reply to Chauncey and Gove. *American Sociological Review* 40: 252–57.
Schutz, A. 1968. *The phenomenology of the social world*. Evanston, Ill.: Northwestern University Press.
Siegler, M., and H. Osmond. 1974. *Models of madness, models of medicine*. New York: Macmillan.
Szasz, Thomas. 1976. *Schizophrenia: The sacred symbol of psychiatry*. New York: Basic Books.
Ullman, Leonard P. 1969. Behavior therapy as social movement. In Cyril M. Franks, ed., *Behavior therapy*, pp. 495–523. New York: McGraw-Hill.
Zilboorg, Gregory A. 1941. *History of medical psychology*. New York: Norton.

# *Part IV*  Public Opinion

# Elisabeth Noelle-Neumann

## 13 Toward a Theory of Public Opinion

How is a theory created? In 1957 Herbert Hyman, a young scholar who had already been honored with the Julian L. Woodward Memorial Award, presented his ideas on this subject in an essay in *Public Opinion Quarterly* entitled "Toward a Theory of Public Opinion." Twenty years earlier in the inaugural issue of the *Quarterly* Floyd H. Allport had struck a hopeful note in his article "Toward a Science of Public Opinion." Hyman wrote in a similar spirit of confidence. He agreed with Allport that the development of the method of public opinion research had improved the prospects of establishing a sound theory of public opinion. This was not something to be taken for granted. For, as Hyman observes in the introduction to his article, theory and practice are often viewed as being at cross-purposes: Empiricism is seen as destroying theories, as burying theoretical thinking beneath an avalanche of data. The impression of a conflict between theory and practice may be due to personal differences between scholars who specialize in one or the other. But Hyman stresses that they are related. "Indeed," he writes, "they must progress together" (Hyman 1957, p. 55).

Hyman rejects the proposition that empiricism is destructive of theory. He argues that the development of survey research methods has worked to the advantage of a theory of public opinion in that "today when relevant evidence is so much easier to come by" (Hyman 1957, p. 55) there is not as much dependence on speculation when constructing a theory as there was in previous centuries. It is now possible to test theoretical concepts with the aid of empirical methods, rejecting that which does not stand the test and further developing that which does.

Hyman does not, however, see it as a foregone conclusion that the use of methods to test public opinion research will insure a sound theory of public opinion. He cites a number of deficiencies of public opinion research that impede the development of such a theory. The greatest of these, in his view, is precisely that public opinion research is not directed toward the goal of developing a theory of public opinion.

Public opinion research, he argues, has limited itself to an unduly narrow definition of its scope. Public opinion has been defined as "the views of the electorate on the controversial issues of the day" (Hyman 1957, p. 56). It has thus neglected that which Hyman considers necessary: "We need concepts and corresponding research on what is both fundamental or deep and also *common* to a group or society. The study of values . . . would enrich current theories of opinion formation and broaden what is at present an unduly narrow psychological emphasis" (p. 58).

As Hyman sees it, the concentration on issues works against the development of a theory of public opinion because the interests of those who require public opinion research result in discontinuities—current issues are taken up and then are dropped as soon as they are no longer topical.

As a consequence, the most striking discontinuity in our accumulated body of data is the shift from problem area to problem area with the passage of time. . . . This very movement of problem areas into and out of the sphere of public opinion research, while understandable, is perhaps the crucial deficiency for the growth of a theory. The absence of data which provide a sound description of even the *lack of* public opinion on a problem, at a time when it is not under discussion, means that there is no basis for developing adequate theory as to the formation of public opinion. Similarly, the waning of an issue has generally meant the neglect of it by survey research. Thus, no theory can really be built as to either the formation or decline of public opinion. [Hyman 1957, p. 56]

This criticism still applies today. Hyman's acknowledgment that the pattern is "understandable" reflects his awareness that it is not due to the stupidity of public opinion researchers but rather is the result of a practical problem. The issue is one of demand. Clients are interested in the controversial issues of the day because *their* constituents have no interest in what people think about issues that are not being debated and hence are not topical.

What Hyman has in mind is basic research to be done at universities. But here too problems arise. There are grave doubts in those quarters as to whether public opinion research will really lead to theories of public opinion that have scholarly validity. Hence, funding tends to be allocated to more pressing matters.

Hyman also recognizes that even if the financing of systematic, continuous public opinion research were assured, certain problems would persist: "not all continuities are valuable. We may concentrate on the trivial rather than the important. We may even institutionalize the neglect of some important part of our ultimate larger theory" (Hyman 1957, p. 56).

Yet, despite these problems, Hyman remains optimistic: "if these same areas were dealt with over long spans of time, providing trend data, a theory of public opinion formation and change would be well on its way to formulation" (Hyman 1957, p. 57).

Is this really the way theories are created? The following description of how one theory of public opinion came into being is not intended to imply that this theory has been developed to the point where the problems described by Hyman have been solved. Rather, my account is intended to illustrate certain of Hyman's theses. It also describes some factors important in the formation of a theory of public opinion which he does not mention. Finally, I touch upon the irrational element, which can, and perhaps must, play a role in the formation of a theory.

Before I began writing this contribution, I wondered whether I should follow the accepted structure and style of the American social sciences or whether I might not write as a European and exercise the freedom one enjoys writing a personal essay. I decided on the latter approach because it was precisely in the course of the work I will be discussing that I realized how much personal experiences influence a social scientist's work. Such influences can certainly be disguised, and may even be denied, but if we wish to understand the formation of a theory, they are unquestionably relevant.

Two sources provided the stimulus for formulating the theory that has come to be known as "the spiral of silence" (Noelle-Neumann 1984).[1] Between December 1964 and August 1965 the two major German parties were neck and neck, with the lead alternatively taken by one and then the other as reflected in expressed voter intentions. Voters were also asked: "Who do you think will win the election?"—a

---

[1] My first description of the spiral of silence theory in English was published in 1974 in the *Journal of Communications*. Several articles on the subject appeared in *Public Opinion Quarterly* between 1977 and 1980. A book on the theory was published in German in 1980, with the English translation appearing in 1984. A critical discussion of the theory in several contributions and with a response by me appeared in the *Political Communication Yearbook* in 1984. A dissertation in German (Deisenberg 1985) lists the American sources where the subject of the spiral of silence is discussed.

question that had already interested Lazarsfeld, Berelson, and Gaudet as an indicator of change in voting intentions (Lazarsfeld, Berelson, and Gaudet 1968, pp. 105–7).

The trends for the two questions left the impression that measurements had been taken in two different worlds. Until just a few weeks before the election, there was no change in voting intentions. The expectations as to who would win the election were about fifty-fifty when the first measurements were taken in December 1964, as were the voting intentions for the two major parties. In September 1965, the expectations that the Christian Democrats would win had risen to over 50 percent, with only 16 percent expecting the Social Democrats (SPD) to win. It was not until about three weeks before the election in September that voting intentions were swept along in the wake of the expectations as to who would win. The Christian Democrats won the election with a lead of 8.6 percent over the Social Democrats.

It took me more than six years to find an explanation for the absence of a change in voting intentions to match the steady increase in expectations as to who would win the election. The explanation probably only occurred to me because during the intervening years I had had to deal with student unrest in my capacity as professor of communications research at the University of Mainz. During the winter term of 1970/71 I was able to finish only one out of every two lectures. Yet the group of students who wanted to listen to the lectures in peace was larger than the opposing group which disrupted them in an attempt to influence the curriculum. It was quite evident that the majority wanted to hear the lectures, and this is also what I was told in private by students who came to my office during office hours. But though the group of protesting students was active in public—attaching fliers and slogans and stickers critical of me to the walls, the doors, the windows, and cars, and constantly interrupting my lectures—the group of students who wanted to hear the lectures grew more and more silent. They seemed increasingly to fear that supporting me would isolate them from their fellow students and make them unpopular. Thus, a false public image developed of a uniformly protesting student body which eventually occupied the Institute for Communications Research and remained there for a week.

That same month—January 1971—the first questions testing the hypothesis of the spiral of silence were used in the Allensbach public opinion questionnaire. It had occurred to me that there might be a similarity between the phenomenon I had observed at the University of Mainz and the puzzle of 1965—the fact that one camp increasingly appeared stronger in public while the other camp appeared weaker, though both groups were actually almost the same in numerical strength. I suspected that a dynamic process was at work: Those who get the impression as they observe their environment that their opinions and values are becoming more prevalent and acquiring increasing support feel strengthened by this. Because they do not fear isolation, they confidently express their opinions even where they do not know all those present by name, that is, *in public*. Those who have the impression that their views are losing ground become more cautious and keep silent, especially in situations where they are not familiar with what the others think, that is, in public. Because the one group confidently expresses its views and the other keeps silent, this in turn influences the public appearance of things. The first group seems stronger in public than it actually is, and the other group seems weaker than it actually is. This in turn convinces more people to express an opinion that appears strong, while those from the opposite camp become more and more discouraged, eventually deciding to change their opinion, until, in a spiraling process, the one side completely dominates in public while only a shunned minority is heard speaking out for the other side. Or nothing is heard at all.

A German federal election in 1972 offered the opportunity to study the hypothesis of the spiral of silence using the methods of public opinion research. The same pattern as in 1965 did in fact appear. There was almost no evidence of a change in voting intentions when the trend was observed over a period of several months. Although both the major parties were about equally strong, there again was a growing expectation of victory for one of them. This time, however, the roles were reversed—it was the Christian Democrats who took their buttons off and did without bumper stickers and took no action when their posters were defaced. Thus, fear of isolation as a result of publicly stating a political position proved to be a general human trait that had nothing to do with the particular position taken. Again, as in 1965, the party that always seemed stronger in public—in this case the Social Democrats—gained 3 percent of the votes in the final stage of the election campaign in a last-minute swing and thus became the clear victor. This brings to mind Hyman's observation that "The uniformities observed in opinions suggest that there are uniformities in the underlying intervening variables" (Hyman 1957, p. 58).

The development of the spiral of silence theory owes much to the recently developed instruments of public opinion research. The theory was tested beginning in 1971 using numerous newly developed questions: questions designed to gauge perceptions of the climate of opinion in the community, expectations of an increase or decrease in certain positions, the confidence of one camp and the insecurity of the other, the fear of being the only one to have a certain opinion, the degree of inclination to speak out or keep silent in public situations depending upon the likelihood of one's own opinion meeting with approval from others, and the fear of isolating oneself with an opinion. Our experience confirmed Hyman's assumption that, rather than being at cross-purposes, theory and practice make progress together.

But was this a theory of public opinion? Did our observations refer to public opinion? How should the concept of public opinion be understood? At this point I must introduce an irrational element. In 1965, shortly before I became a professor at the University of Mainz, I was teaching at the Free University of Berlin. One Sunday morning, just as I was beginning to work on my lecture for the next day, I suddenly saw a title in my mind and immediately noted it down: "Public Opinion and Social Control." I was very surprised because I had not done much work on social control, nor had the concept been of major importance in my academic field of German communications research. I began to investigate and soon found myself involved in a considerable amount of historical research.[2] I still cannot explain what it was that made me focus on the title, which a year later was to be the title of my inaugural lecture in Mainz (Noelle-Neumann 1966) and which got me started on the historical research. There was nothing self-evident about this, as Hyman's essay shows. The emergence of the theory of the spiral of silence was clearly based upon two sources, but neither Hyman nor Floyd Allport nor M. Brewster Smith (1971) would have expected historical studies to constitute an important source.

My historical studies showed that the concept of public opinion changed in meaning beginning in the latter part of the eighteenth century, increasingly in the nineteenth century and, finally, almost completely in the twentieth century. Encyclopedia articles on "public opinion" trace the historical roots back to the latter half of the eighteenth century in France, the period preceding the French Revolution. Necker, Louis XVI's minister of finance, is often cited as having popularized the concept (Bucher 1887, pp. 77–78). In fact, however, the Latin concept *opinionis publicae* is mentioned in the fourth century by the Spanish bishop and heretic Priscillian (1889); it is referred to several times by Montaigne in the 1588 edition of his *Essais* (Raffel 1983), and *l'opinion publique* is frequently mentioned by Rousseau beginning in 1744 (Rousseau 1964, p. 1184). There are also many similar concepts, which are used very much as Montaigne or Rousseau used *l'opinion publique*: *maioris partis sentencie* (Marsilius von Padua

[2] I am grateful to my assistant at that time in Allensbach and later in Mainz, Kurt Reumann, now an editor with the *Frankfurter Allgemeine Zeitung*, who helped me with the research.

1958, p. 723); *commune opinione, opinione universale, pubblica voce* (Machiavelli 1950) or simply *opinion* (Shakespeare, David Hume, Madison) or *vox populi vox dei* (Boas 1969); *law of opinion, law of reputation, law of fashion* (Locke 1894); *climate of opinion* (Glanvill 1661).

A phenomenon for which so many terms have been coined in so many languages must refer to something very important, to a concept, as Hyman put it, "both fundamental or deep and also *common* to a group or a society" (Hyman 1957, p. 58). And what we find in the historical texts is completely different from what Hyman criticizes as an unduly narrow definition of public opinion: "the views of the electorate on controversial issues of the day" (p. 58). In the historical texts we read about the "common presse" (Montaigne). There is not one in ten thousand who is insensible enough not to fear offending against the law of opinion (Locke 1894, p. 479). Rousseau speaks of the "yoke of opinion," which we must stoop under (1957, p. 346) and of "civil religion" (1953, p. 142). It was from Rousseau that Tocqueville derived the image of the yoke of public opinion, under which a democratic society must stoop under (Tocqueville 1948, p. 261). Bryce speaks of the tyranny of the majority (1888–89, pp. 337–44). As described by Machiavelli (1950), public opinion is a mighty power which puts the individual under its yoke and causes governments to tremble.

As the meaning of public opinion slowly changes in the course of the nineteenth century, the element of public opinion that tyrannizes the individual acquires a new name: social control. By the time Edward Ross published his book *Social Control* in 1901 (Ross 1969), the process had essentially been completed. The meaning of "public opinion" was reduced to the view well-informed and critical citizens take of the government. In the twentieth century, Hans Speier offers the following definition of public opinion: "Let us understand by public opinion, for the purposes of this historical review, opinions on matters of concern to the nation freely and publicly expressed by men outside the government who claim a right that their opinions should influence or determine the actions, personnel, or structure of their government" (1950, p. 376). Nothing of the "common presse," the "yoke of opinion," the "law of opinion" remains in the twentieth-century definition of public opinion.

What the historical sources reveal about public opinion is consistent with the empirical observations of 1965 and 1972 about the spiral of silence. It appears that we can include an entire complex of scholarly ideas on social control in a theory of public opinion based on empirical public opinion research. It is apparent that public opinion has two faces: One is the aspect of social control—the pressure to conform on issues that relate to a society's value system. The individual may not agree with conviction, but an inbred fear of isolation forces him to hide his divergent attitude. This has been well described by Tocqueville:

> Those who retained their belief in the doctrines of the Church became afraid of being alone in their allegiance and, dreading isolation more than error, professed to share the sentiments of the majority. So what was in reality the opinion of only a part . . . of the nation came to be regarded as the will of all and for this reason seemed irresistible, even to those who had given it this false appearance. [1952, p. 207 (1955, p. 155)]

The second face of public opinion is turned toward the government. As described by Machiavelli and David Hume, it demands that the government sooner or later secure the approval of the majority or that it be overthrown. Madison took Hume's account of this phenomenon and compressed it into the phrase "All governments rest on opinion" (Madison 1961, p. 340). Hume added: "this maxim extends to the most despotic and most military government, as well as to the most free and most popular" (Hume 1963, p. 29). According to this conception, public opinion is a dynamic process, assuring a society's cohesion and affecting both the government and the individual members who make up the society.

In his 1971 essay "A Psychologist's Perspective on Public Opinion Theory," M. Brewster Smith wrote with obvious impatience, "I hope that public opinion research in progress may capture enough of what is happening to advance our understanding of how the manipulation of political perception can alter the political facts" (1971, p. 39), and a little further on, "how individual opinions aggregate or articulate to produce political effects" (p. 40).

In fact, a concept of public opinion and a theory of public opinion that do *not* explain how public opinion puts pressure on the individual and how it leads to political effectiveness will have little explanatory power. In the absence of the needed explanatory power, we cannot get a better grasp of reality or provide guidance for a systematic investigation by public opinion research of how, as Hyman puts it, public opinion is created, how it takes shape, and how it disappears.

"No matter what form the analysis may ultimately take," wrote Hyman, "the unit under scrutiny is always the individual and his psychic structure" (1957, p. 55). The theory of the spiral of silence confirms this belief. The process of public opinion, which serves to maintain the common values of a society or to establish those values, functions because of the *individual's* fear of isolation. This fear of isolation causes him to keep informed at all times of prevailing views, not just the views of the general public, to be aware of what is valid and what is no longer valid—what is "in" and what is "out." This assessment of the climate of opinion influences his behavior. His behavior in turn influences the general appearance of the climate of opinion. There is thus a dynamic interaction between individual perceptions and reactions on one hand and the collective climate of opinion on the other—an interaction created by frequency distribution of publicly visible signs. Long before the existence of public opinion polls, individual members of society—and governments—regularly made "quasi-statistical" observations about the frequency distribution of opinions.

The definition of public opinion that is derived from this theory is formulated operationally, that is, in such a way that public opinion research can work with the concept. Public opinions are opinions and modes of behavior in value-laden areas which can be publicly expressed or demonstrated with the expectation that they will meet with approval or that there is no danger of thereby isolating oneself. It is obvious that this approach can serve to counteract the focus of public opinion research on issues of the day, which rightfully so bothered Hyman. Concepts such as the silent majority, pluralistic ignorance, polarization, or value change or research questions that, for example, address the relationship between public opinion and the mass media can be developed. Concepts that were formulated decades ago by Lazarsfeld, Berelson, and the research group in the Bureau of Applied Social Research at Columbia University (to which Hyman also belonged at one time)—concepts such as "opinion leader" or the "two-step flow of communication"—are more open to investigation with the theory of the spiral of silence.

In his article, Hyman states that when the demands made of a theory of public opinion are too exacting this works against establishing such a theory. He complains about the tendency to adopt "a very special view of theory, a view which equates theory with a general, even an all-embracing set of ideas and speculations about a field" (Hyman 1957, p. 54).

Such notions of grandness and generality should not frighten us. For it has been shown that other well-developed theories will follow once some parts of a theory of public opinion have been developed and tested. For example, the theory of collective action can be related to the theory of public opinion (Hardin 1982; Olson 1965). Thus, several theories can be combined to form a whole as if many islands came together to form a continent. Among the islands that could contribute to enlarging a theory of public opinion are the theoretical-empirical body of group dynamics, small group research on conformity produced during the fifties and sixties (Cartwright and Zander 1953), and the work of Erving Goffman on behavior in public places starting with his inquiry into embarrassment in the fifties (Goffman 1955, 1956, 1959, 1963, 1969, 1971, 1974).[3]

There is one respect, however, in which Hyman will probably have to wait some time yet for his demands to be fulfilled. He states that the theory is to help explain opinion formation (Hyman 1957, p. 57). The theory of the spiral of silence as it has been formulated up to now only explains how opinions and modes of behavior are established and maintained and how they decline again. But how does a new opinion begin to take shape? Socrates once said: When the music changes, the politics change. It will probably be quite some time before we have a theory to explain this.

## Bibliography

Allport, F. H. 1937. Toward a science of public opinion. *Public Opinion Quarterly* 1:7–23.

Boas, G. 1969. *Vox populi: Essays in the history of an idea.* Baltimore: Johns Hopkins University Press.

Bryce, J. 1888–89. *The American commonwealth.* 2 vols. London: Macmillan.

Bucher, L. 1887. Uber politische Kunstausdrücke. *Deutsche Revue* 12:67–80, 333–40.

Bunge, M. A. 1967. *Scientific research.* 2 vols. New York: Springer-Verlag.

Cartwright, D., and A. Zander. 1953. *Group dynamics: Research and theory.* New York: Row, Peterson.

Deisenberg, A. M. 1985. Die Schweigespirale: Die Rezeption des Models im In- und Ausland. Dissertation, University of Munich.

Glanvill, J. 1661. The vanity of dogmatizing; or, confidence in opinions: manifested in a discourse of the shortness and uncertainty of our knowledge, and its causes; with some reflexions on peripateticism; and an apology for philosophy. E. C. for H. Eversden at the Grey-Hound in St. Pauls-Church-Yard, London.

Goffman, E. 1955. On face-work: An analysis of ritual elements in social interaction. *Psychiatry* 18:213–32.

———. 1956. Embarrassment and social organization. *American Journal of Sociology* 62:264–74.

———. 1959. *The presentation of self in everyday life.* Garden City, N.Y.: Doubleday.

———. 1963. *Stigma: Notes on the management of spoiled identity.* Englewood Cliffs, N.J.: Prentice-Hall.

———. 1969. *Behavior in public places.* 4th ed. New York: Free Press.

———. 1971. *Relations in public: Microstudies of the public order.* New York: Basic Books.

[3] Sometimes formal criteria are used to determine if a concept can be considered to be a theory or not (Bunge 1967). This does not concern us here, because formalization of the theory is not intended at this point, though it could certainly be undertaken.

————. 1974. *Frame analysis: An essay on the organization of experience.* New York: Harper and Row.

Hardin, R. 1982. *Collective action.* Baltimore and London: John Hopkins University Press.

Hume, D. 1963. *Essays moral, political, and literary (1741/1742).* London: Oxford University Press.

Lazarsfeld, P. F., B. Berelson, and H. Gaudet. 1968. *The people's choice: How the voter makes up his mind in a presidential campaign.* New York: Columbia University Press. 1st. ed., New York: Duell, Sloan and Pearce, 1944.

Locke, J. 1894. *An essay concerning human understanding.* Drafted in 1671. Historical-critical ed. Edited by A. C. Fraser. 2 vols. Oxford: Oxford University Press (Clarendon Press).

Machiavelli, N. 1950. Il Principe [1514]. In M. Martelli, ed., *Tutte le opere,* Florence: Sansoni, 1971. English: *The Prince and the Discourses.* Translated by L. Ricci, E. R. P. Vincent, and C. Detmold. New York: Random House.

Madison, J. 1961. The Federalist, no. 49 [1788]. In J. F. Cooke, ed., *The Federalist,* pp. 338–47. Middletown, Conn.: Wesleyan University Press.

Noelle-Neumann, E. 1966. Öffentliche Meinung und soziale Kontrolle. *Recht und Staat* 329. Tübingen: J. C. B. Mohr (Paul Siebeck).

————. 1973. Return to the concept of powerful mass media. *Studies of Broadcasting* 9:67–112.

————. 1974. The spiral of silence: A theory of public opinion. *Journal of Communication* 24:43–51.

————. 1977. Turbulences in the climate of opinion: Methodological applications of the spiral of silence theory. *Public Opinion Quarterly* 41:143–58.

————. 1978. The dual climate of opinion: The influences of television in the 1976 West German federal election. In M. Kaase and K. von Beyme, eds., *Elections and parties,* pp. 137–69. German Political Studies, no. 3. Beverly Hills, Calif.: Sage.

————. 1979. Public opinion and the classical tradition: A re-evaluation. *Public Opinion Quarterly* 43:143–56.

————. 1980. The public opinion research correspondent. *Public Opinion Quarterly* 44:585–97.

————. 1984. *The spiral of silence: Public opinion—our social skin.* Chicago: University of Chicago Press.

————. 1985. The spiral of silence: a response. In D. Nimmo, L. L. Kaid, and K. Sanders, eds., *Political communications yearbook.* Carbondale: Southern Illinois University Press.

Olson, M. 1965. *The logic of collective action.* Cambridge, Mass.: Harvard University Press.

Padua, M. von. 1958. *Defensor pacis—der Verteidiger des Friedens* [1324]. 2 vols. Edited by Engelberg and Kusch. Leipziger Übersetzungen und Abhandlungen zum Mittelalter. East Berlin.

Priscillian. 1889. *Opera. Priscilliani quae super sunt. Maximem partem nuper detexit adiectisque commentariis criticis et indicibus primus edidit Georgius Schepss.* Pragae, Vindobonae: F. Tempsky/Lipsiae: F. Freytag.

Raffel, M. 1983. Öffentliche Meinung bei Michel de Montaigne. Master's thesis, University of Mainz.

———. 1984. Der Schöpfer des Begriffs "öffentliche Meinung": Michel de Montaigne. *Publizistik* 29:49–62.

Ross, E. A. 1969. *Social control: A survey of the foundations of order* [1901, 1929]. With an introduction by J. Weinberg, G. Hinkle, and R. Hinkle. Cleveland and London: Press of Case Western Reserve University.

Rousseau, J. J. 1953. The social contract [1762]. In *Political writings*. Edited and translated by F. Watkins. London: Nelson.

———. 1957. Emile ou de l'éducation. In *Oeuvres complètes*. Vol. 4, *La Pléiade*. Paris: Gallimard, 1964. English: *Emile*. Translated by B. Foxley. London: Dent.

———. 1964. Dépêches de Venise, XCI [1744]. *La Pléiade* 3. Paris: Gallimard.

Smith, M. B. 1971. A psychologist's perspective on public opinion theory. *Public Opinion Quarterly* 35:36–43.

Speier, H. 1950. Historical development of public opinion. *American Journal of Sociology* 55:376–88.

Tocqueville, A. de. 1948. *Democracy in America* [1835–40]. Edited by P. Bradley, translated by H. Reeve. 2 vols. New York: Knopf.

———. 1952. L'ancien régime et la révolution. In *Oeuvres complètes*. Vol. 2. Paris: Gallimard. English: *The Old Régime and the French Revolution*. Translated by S. Gilbert. New York: Doubleday (Anchor Books), 1955.

## Stephen Cole and Robert Fiorentine

# 14 The Formation of Public Opinion on Complex Issues: The Case of Nuclear Power

In a pluralistic democratic society such as the United States public opinion exerts a strong influence on public policy and on the future development of the society (Lang and Lang 1983). A good example of the significance of public opinion is the recent history of the electric utility industry. When nuclear power was first developed in the 1950s, the publicly owned utilities were uninterested in experimenting with the new technology. It was only after the government put pressure on the utility industry, threatening to build the plants itself and compete with the privately owned utilities, that the first nuclear plants were ordered (Clarke 1985). In the 1960s the government, the utility industry, and the general public all thought of nuclear power as providing the optimum solution for the future energy needs of the United States. As the environmental movement developed in the 1970s, opposition to nuclear power plants among the public grew. Public opposition substantially increased the cost of building nuclear plants by lengthening the time it took to complete the licensing.[1] Public opposition is now so great that no new nuclear plants have been ordered in the 1980s, and some completed plants such as the Shoreham plant on Long Island have not been put into service. Currently, less than one-quarter of Long Island residents favor opening the completed plant.[2]

An earlier version of this paper was presented at the annual meeting of the American Association of Public Opinion Researchers, Buck Hill Falls, Pennsylvania, May 21, 1983. We thank Hubert O'Gorman and John Gagnon for helpful comments on an earlier draft.
  [1]There were, of course, other reasons for the dramatic increase in the cost of building nuclear power plants. These include high interest rates, inflation, and changes in government regulations.
  [2]This figure is based on a survey conducted in the fall of 1985 for *Newsday* by Social Data Analysts, Inc.

Given its significance as an influence on public policy, it is important to understand how public opinion is formed. Since most public opinion research is purely descriptive, we know very little about how individuals develop their attitudes on public issues. When correlations are presented they tend to be between attitudes and basic demographic characteristics. Knowing these correlations does not enable us to understand why people with different demographic characteristics developed different attitudes.

The essential problem in studying the formation of public opinion is the difficulty of obtaining adequate longitudinal data. Studying public opinion at one point in time makes it difficult to establish causal order between variables and virtually impossible to explicate the *process* through which attitudes develop. In this paper we report the results of several surveys which were aimed at understanding the causes of attitudes toward nuclear power. The data are not longitudinal and therefore have severe limitations. Given these limitations, this paper tries to gain insight into the causes of attitudes toward nuclear power and enables us to point out the problems in trying to answer such a question with the data typically used in survey research.

Our research was in particular focused on the interplay between two broad factors influencing attitudes toward nuclear power. The first might be called "values," or an individual's personal moral beliefs about what is desirable—ethically, socially, aesthetically. The second general factor influencing the formation of public opinion might be called "information," or "facts." On the surface, nuclear power would seem to be an issue that should be heavily influenced by information. Are nuclear power plants safe? To what extent do nuclear power plants increase risks to life and health? Can the waste from nuclear plants be safely disposed of? Will nuclear power plants save us money? These questions are *presumably* capable of being factually answered by the analysis of scientific data. *If* people believed that nuclear power plants were safe and cost-effective, then the great majority would be in favor of them.[3]

The use of the term "facts" has an overly positivistic tone. There is now a large body of literature in the sociology of science that leads to the conclusion that scientific "facts" are socially constructed and an attribute of consensus formation processes rather than self-evident attributes of nature (Knorr-Cetina 1981; Latour and Woolgar 1979). It is evident that there are at least some prominent scientists who doubt

---

[3] As will be clear from the analysis below, the distinction between values and "facts" is an analytic one. We are here oversimplifying the problem. Individuals might agree upon the level of risks involved in nuclear power plants but, because of differing values, disagree upon whether these risks are acceptable.

the safety of nuclear power, as they have made their views known through organizations like the Union of Concerned Scientists.

One problem that the public has in forming opinions on complex issues like nuclear power is the difficulty in assessing what "expert" opinion is on the issue and what the "facts" are. The public learns of the opinions of experts through the media, which are journalistically committed to presenting both sides of the issue, even if one side is representative of only a small minority of opinion. This question was addressed in an important piece of research by Rothman and Lichter (1982), who conducted a series of surveys among "experts" on nuclear energy to find out whether knowledgeable scientists thought that we should continue to build nuclear power plants. The obvious problem in conducting such a study is the definition of "expert." Rothman and Lichter used three different samples, each one more narrowly defining who an "expert" was.

The first sample was drawn from all scientists listed in *American Men and Women of Science*. Since this directory includes scientists in all fields including the social sciences, it is really the most broadly defined group of "experts." The second sample consisted of those scientists who were in areas designated as energy-related (including specialties such as solar energy, conservation, and ecology), and the third sample consisted of those scientists in fields directly related to nuclear energy (including radiological health and radiation genetics as well as nuclear engineering and reactor physics). Rothman and Lichter found that 89 percent of the broad sample, 95 percent of the scientists in energy-related disciplines, and 100 percent of the scientists in disciplines directly related to nuclear energy said that we should proceed with the development of nuclear power plants. When asked whether they would be willing to have a nuclear power plant in their own "back yards," almost 70 percent of the broad sample, 80 percent of the energy experts, and 97 percent of the nuclear experts said that they would. Rothman and Lichter also analyzed their data to show that there were not significant differences in opinion among scientists who had varying levels of involvement with the nuclear industry. Thus, for example, university scientists who had not received any financial support from industry or government had essentially the same opinions as those who had received support, and they were only slightly less pronuclear than scientists employed by private industry.

What makes this study convincing to us is the fact that even the very broadly defined sample of experts, a group that has very little direct self-interest in preserving the nuclear industry, supports the continued development of nuclear power. Although some technical questions could be raised about the methods used in this study, the general conclusion seems eminently clear and well supported. A substantial majority of experts at the time the research was conducted supported the further development of nuclear power plants and believed that they were relatively safe.

Other research has shown that knowledgeable scientists, whether they think that nuclear power plants are a desirable source of energy or an undesirable source of energy, define nuclear power as a "low-level risk." Hohenemser, Kasperson, and Kates (1977) compare the risks of nuclear power with other activities. Three hundred out of a million people die each year from auto accidents; ninety out of a million from falls; thirty out of a million from drowning. The estimates of the probability of dying from a nuclear accident vary from .02 people out of a million to twenty out of a million.[4] The last estimate is that of the most skeptical critics of nuclear power. Most estimates are less than two-tenths of one person per million. Even this estimate assumes the operation of 1,000 nuclear plants—more than ten times the number currently in operation in the United States. In evidence introduced before the Nuclear Regulatory Commission by *opponents* to the Shoreham nuclear plant it was estimated that the probability of a serious accident occurring in which as many as several thousand people might be killed is only one in 500 million years.[5] To say that nuclear power represents a low-level risk does not mean that it is necessarily a risk worth taking but simply that the potential negative consequences have a low probability of occurring.

If nuclear power is a "low-level" risk, then it is possible that an individual's attitude toward it might be in part influenced by how much knowledge the individual has about nuclear energy, radiation, and the dangers involved in its use. Other researchers have shown that the public in general greatly overestimates the dangers of nuclear power. Slovic, Fischoff, and Lichtenstein (1979) found that, among a sample of the general public, nuclear power was perceived as the most dangerous hazard in a set of twenty potential hazards, when in fact probability estimates suggest that nuclear power is the least dangerous of the twenty hazards. Business leaders when given the same survey had a more realistic appraisal of the hazards of nuclear power.

The main aim of the surveys we conducted was to discover the role that information played in the development of public opinion about nuclear power plants. Do people who know more about energy and

[4] Here we are comparing risks based upon actual experience (e.g., from auto accidents, falls, or drowning) with risks based upon probability estimates made by risk assessors for nuclear power. This is necessary, because, in fact, there have never been any deaths caused by commercially operating nuclear power plants. Nonetheless, many are skeptical of the way in which these probability estimates are made (see Perrow 1985).

[5] This testimony was quoted in *Newsday*, March 27, 1983, p. 24.

nuclear power in particular have attitudes similar to the experts surveyed by Rothman and Lichter? As sociologists, we know that values will influence the way in which new information is perceived and integrated. Values play a role in our willingness to believe different interpretations of the facts. People whose values lead them to be skeptical about the motives of the "Establishment" might be less likely to believe information presented by scientists and engineers whom they might see as self-interested members of the Establishment. Despite the fact that values and perception of "facts" interact, it is possible that for some people information may influence their opinions of nuclear power.

In this paper we present data drawn from two different surveys that show how level of knowledge and values interact to influence attitudes of the public toward nuclear power plants.[6] Both surveys were conducted on the telephone using a random-digit-dialing sampling technique. The first survey was conducted for Columbia University's School of Engineering and was aimed at finding the attitudes of New York City and Westchester residents toward Con Edison's energy plans. We will refer to this study as the Con Edison survey. The second survey was conducted for an East Coast electric utility company and was aimed at measuring the attitudes of the public toward the company and toward nuclear power. We will refer to this study as the utility survey. We were able to test hypotheses developed on the basis of the Con Edison study in the utility study.

Several other surveys have attempted to measure the influence of knowledge on attitudes toward nuclear power. Although there has been some discrepancy in reported results (Melber et al. 1977), most of the studies, especially those using relatively large random samples, show the more knowledgeable people to have more favorable attitudes toward nuclear power. The best support for this hypothesis to date may be found in the data of Deborah and Carl Hensler, who studied the 1976 reactions of California residents to the antinuclear initiative, Proposition 15 (Hensler and Hensler 1979). In an analysis of these data by Kuklinski, Metlay, and Kay (1982), it was found that

---

[6]The Con Edison survey was conducted by Social Data Analysts, Inc., under a subcontract with Columbia University. Funding came from a contract between Consolidated Edison, Inc., and Columbia University. For a complete report, see Cole 1981. More than 1,500 interviews were conducted with residents of all five New York City boroughs and Westchester County. Since Westchester was overrepresented, these interviews were weighted down, making the number of cases for the whole survey equivalent to 1,181. The utility survey was conducted for the utility by Social Data Analysts, Inc., in the fall of 1981. The utility gave permission for the data to be used but preferred not to be identified. Seven hundred and six interviews were completed with a random sample of residential telephone subscribers living in the area served by the utility.

among the 111 respondents classified as more knowledgeable 24 percent voted for the antinuclear initiative, and among the 390 classified as less knowledgeable 40 percent voted for the antinuclear initiative (p. 624).[7] The level-of-knowledge questions asked, among other things, how likely it is that a nuclear power plant will explode like a bomb and whether there are any operating nuclear plants in California.

The Con Edison survey contained six questions aimed at measuring the level of the respondent's knowledge about energy in general and nuclear energy in particular. The questions and the responses given are presented in the Appendix.[8] In order to classify the respondents by their level of information on energy and nuclear power, we added up the number of correct responses given to these six questions. Only about one-quarter of the respondents knew the correct answer to four or more of the questions.[9]

The Con Edison survey contained five questions measuring atti-

[7] There is some discrepancy in the interpretation of the data between Hensler and Hensler (1979) and Kuklinski et al. (1982). This discrepancy results from differences in which questions are included in the knowledge index.

[8] It is difficult to make up unambiguous level-of-information questions on a topic like energy. The first question, as to whether oil or nuclear power is more expensive in generating electricity, is ambiguous because it did not specify whether the cost of plant construction was to be considered. The question about what proportion of Con Edison's electricity was being produced by nuclear energy has a clear and unambiguous answer, as does the question on whether a utility company can charge whatever it wants for electricity. The question on how much electricity could be generated from solar energy in the next twenty years might be considered to be an informed opinion. There are no energy experts to our knowledge who argue that more than 20 percent of the electricity in the New York area could be generated from solar energy within the next twenty years. Although no one can predict exactly, it is the near unanimous consensus of scientific experts that the generation of substantial amounts of electricity from solar energy, although feasible, is a long way from being practical. The report *Solar Photovoltaic Energy Conversion* prepared by the American Physical Society indicates that 20 percent would be an unrealistically optimistic prediction for electricity generation from solar energy in the next twenty years, even for a growing community in the Sun Belt. We therefore classified as incorrect all those answering that more than 20 percent of electricity could be generated in the New York metropolitan area from solar energy. Even anti–nuclear power scientists agree that a nuclear plant cannot blow up like an atomic bomb, and virtually all experts on nuclear energy recognize that during normal operation nuclear plants do not emit any measurable levels of radiation. Because of the ambiguity in several of the questions included in the index, caution must be used in generalizing from the results of Table 14.1.

[9] All the indexes used in this paper are simple additive ones in which each indicator is dichotomized into a one or a zero and then the number of ones are added. Since we were attempting to measure *relative* feelings on these variables as opposed to any absolute positions, this procedure is justified. Thus, for example, if a respondent is classified as being "anti–nuclear power," this simply means that compared with all the respondents in the survey this respondent had more negative feelings than others. The primary purpose of this analysis has been to explore some theoretical interpretations of how relative attitudes on issues like nuclear power develop. We have not been interested in measuring precisely either the extent of opposition or support or the various dimensions of opposition or support.

TABLE 14.1. *Attitudes toward Nuclear Power by Level of Knowledge (Con Edison Survey)*

| Knowledge index | Attitudes toward nuclear power | | | | |
|---|---|---|---|---|---|
| | Pro | Mixed | Anti | Total | N |
| 6 (high) | 65% | 30% | 5% | 100% | 32 |
| 5 | 49 | 37 | 14 | 100 | 97 |
| 4 | 41 | 40 | 19 | 100 | 172 |
| 3 | 35 | 39 | 26 | 100 | 255 |
| 2 | 29 | 52 | 19 | 100 | 294 |
| 1 | 30 | 42 | 28 | 100 | 213 |
| 0 (low) | 16 | 53 | 30 | 99 | 56 |

tudes toward nuclear power plants (see Appendix). Using these five questions, we constructed a "nuclear power" index. In Table 14.1 we show the association between the respondents' scores on the level-of-knowledge index and their scores on the nuclear power index. The data show a strong association. The more a person knows about energy, the more likely he or she is to support nuclear power; correspondingly, the less an individual knows about energy, the more likely he or she is to oppose nuclear power. Sixty-five percent of those who gave the correct answer to all six of the information questions were pro–nuclear power whereas only 16 percent of those who did not give the correct answer to any of the information questions were pro–nuclear power.

Assuming that there were no ambiguities in the questions measuring both information and attitudes toward nuclear power, would we be able to conclude on the basis of the data in Table 14.1 that there is a causal connection between these two variables? Before assuming such a connection we must consider the possibility that rather than information influencing attitudes, an individual's attitudes toward nuclear power might influence the way in which he or she perceives the facts. We are measuring both variables at one point in time and have no way of establishing causal order. Some of those whom we have labeled here as "well-informed" about energy may have scored high because their pronuclear ideological bias led them, when in doubt, to answer our informational questions in a pronuclear direction. Similarly, those who are antinuclear would tend to give answers hostile to nuclear energy and so score lower. Since these questions measured misperceptions about the *negative* aspects of nuclear power, if we assume that *every* respondent was completely ignorant, we still could have found the observed correlation between "information" and attitudes based upon ideologically determined guessing.

If we assume that level of knowledge causes attitudes, we have a rationalistic explanation that sees opposition to nuclear power as a result of ignorance of the "real" risks. If we see attitudes toward nuclear power as influencing level of information, we have what might be called a social constructionist view of how ideology comes to influence the "knowledge" that people have of the world. This alternative view needs more explication. The social constructionist view assumes correctly that there is conflicting information in the environment. Which information an individual pays attention to will be influenced by that person's ideological predisposition. Suppose that an individual is "liberal" and believes that nuclear power plants are bad things. This person sees Barry Commoner on television, Barry Commoner says that nuclear power plants are bad, and this person believes him. The same person may also see Edward Teller on television, who will say that nuclear power plants are good things. This person knows that Teller is the conservative "father of the H-bomb" and does not believe a word he says. Then suppose that this same individual is called up by a public opinion pollster and asked whether it is true or false that a nuclear power plant can blow up like an atomic bomb. Our hypothetical respondent has never thought about this and does not know the answer; but he does know that nuclear power is bad (Barry Commoner said so) and therefore it must be possible that these plants can blow up like atomic bombs. He, therefore, answers the question incorrectly. But here it can be clearly seen how the causal direction is from ideological position to "knowledge."

In fact, the relationship between attitudes and information is bidirectional. Perception of "facts" will influence opinion of nuclear power; but values on nuclear power or other related issues will probably influence the way in which an individual comes to perceive what are facts. Cross-sectional survey data cannot adequately disentangle the complex connections between these two variables. To adequately understand this process we would have to begin a longitudinal study of children in the junior high school years when they are first beginning to develop political attitudes. How do they acquire knowledge of issues like nuclear power; is the acquisition process influenced by preexisting values; does acquisition of knowledge actually cause individuals to adopt certain attitude positions?

Without access to the necessary longitudinal data we must be satisfied with inherently inadequate attempts to disentangle the complex causal web. This paper accepts as a given that values will influence information acquisition, but it attempts to present evidence that will suggest that information also has an independent influence on opinion. In the utility survey conducted among a random sample of 706 residents of an East Coast community, we attempted to replicate the findings for level of information and attitudes toward nuclear power and specify the direction of causality. We asked the respondents three questions measuring level of knowledge about nuclear power (see Appendix).[10] In classifying the respondents by how much information they had about nuclear energy, we simply added up the number of correct answers they gave. For this survey we measured attitudes toward nuclear power by two questions. Respondents were given one point for saying that they were supporters of nuclear power plants as a means of generating electricity and one point for saying they were in favor of the completion and operation of a nuclear power plant under construction in the area. Respondents who gave either one of these responses were considered to be supporters of nuclear power; others were considered to be opponents.[11]

In Table 14.2 we show the relationship between level of nuclear information and attitudes toward nuclear power in the utility survey. Once again we found a strong association: Those people who had the most knowledge were the least likely to oppose nuclear energy. It is, of course, still impossible on the basis of the data presented in Table 14.2 to say that level of information about nuclear energy "causes" attitudes toward nuclear power. In the utility survey, however, we were able to make two analyses that increase the plausibility of this interpretation. We asked three information questions on energy that had nothing to do with nuclear power (see Appendix). In order to measure the extent of the respondent's knowledge about nonnuclear energy matters, we added up the number of correct responses given to the three questions. In Table 14.3 we show the relationship between level of nonnuclear energy information and attitudes toward nuclear power.

Since this information index contained no questions dealing with nuclear energy, there is less reason to believe that attitudes toward nuclear power could have influenced the answers given to these questions. For example, there is no reason to believe that our hypothetical antinuclear respondent would be less likely to know that the utility currently generated all its electricity from oil *because* of his antinuclear attitudes. Thus, there is less ambiguity about the direction of causality between this index and attitudes toward nuclear energy. Although it is unlikely that attitudes toward nuclear power caused the respondent to know or not know the correct answers to the energy information

[10] This questionnaire underwent extensive pretesting, which included a pilot survey with 100 respondents. One goal was to develop level-of-information questions for which there were correct answers and which were not ambiguous.

[11] Again, we point out that this index is an additive one based upon dichotomies. It is aimed only at measuring relative attitudes toward nuclear power.

TABLE 14.2. *Attitudes toward Nuclear Power by Level of Nuclear Information (Utility Survey)*

| Nuclear information | Percent opposing nuclear power |
|---|---|
| 3 (high) | 26% (101) |
| 2 | 41 (211) |
| 1 | 58 (193) |
| 0 (low) | 75 (201) |

TABLE 14.3. *Attitudes toward Nuclear Power by Level of Energy Information (Utility Survey)*

| Energy information | Percent opposing nuclear power |
|---|---|
| 3, 2 (high) | 34% (131) |
| 1 | 56 (362) |
| 0 (low) | 61 (213) |

questions, we still have no way of demonstrating that energy information precedes in time attitudes toward nuclear power. If one is willing to accept this assumption, then the association observed in Table 14.3, although not as strong as that observed in Table 14.2, lends support to a tentative conclusion that level of knowledge about nuclear power may be one cause of attitudes toward nuclear power.

There is one additional piece of evidence which adds some credibility to the interpretation that, despite the bidirectionality of the relationship between knowledge and attitudes, knowledge is at least to some extent not an artifact of values. In both surveys we found attitudes toward nuclear power to be correlated with general political attitudes (this will be discussed below). In both surveys, however, we did *not* find an association between political self-identification (as a liberal, middle-of-the-roader, or conservative) and level of information. Liberals and conservatives had the *same* level of knowledge. If answers given to the level-of-information questions were merely artifacts of an individual's ideology, then we would expect to find an association between ideology and the knowledge index. The absence of an association between these two variables gives additional support to the interpretation that level of knowledge is one cause rather than simply an effect of attitudes toward nuclear power.

Why is level of information correlated with attitudes toward nuclear power? All the research that we have done on nuclear power suggests that the main reason people oppose nuclear power is that they are afraid of it. We have shown that a majority of people have relatively low levels of knowledge about the risks associated with nuclear power.[12] The less individuals know about nuclear power, the more likely they are to harbor diffuse fears about its consequences. People in general tend to be more afraid of things they do not understand and do not have a clear picture of. The utility survey contained one question that we used as an indicator of fear of nuclear power. We asked the respondents: "How much do you think living near a nuclear electricity plant would increase your chances of dying at an early age?" Nineteen percent of the sample said that it would greatly increase their chances, 20 percent said it would somewhat increase their chances, 20 percent said that it would slightly increase their chances, 34 percent said that it would hardly increase their chances at all, and 7 percent said that they did not know. Responses given to this question were very strongly related to attitudes toward nuclear power; 86 percent of those who say that living near a nuclear power plant would greatly increase their chances of dying at an early age, as compared with 26 percent of those who say that it would hardly increase their chances at all, oppose nuclear power.

Of primary importance for this paper was the association we found between fear of nuclear power and level of nuclear information. People who said that living near a nuclear power plant would greatly or somewhat increase their chances of dying at an early age were considered to have a strong fear of nuclear power. Data showing the association between these two variables are presented in Table 14.4.[13]

In the last part of this paper, we want to examine more closely the reasons why information is correlated with attitudes toward nuclear power, focusing on interaction effects between information and several values.

[12] Even if the respondents had been more familiar with this information, they still might fear nuclear power. In a classic set of papers the psychologists Tversky and Kahneman have shown that even people who use statistical reasoning in their occupations, such as social scientists, frequently do not base their everyday behavior on probabilistic reasoning. These papers, along with other relevant research, are reprinted in Kahneman, Slovik, and Tversky (1982).

[13] Given the strong correlation between level of information and both attitudes toward nuclear power and fear of nuclear power, it is relevant to ask what we know about the variables that influence the amount of knowledge an individual has on this issue. Not surprisingly, education and income were significantly correlated with level of knowledge in both surveys, as was sex. College graduates were more than twice as likely as high school dropouts to have a high level of information. Men were almost twice as likely as women to have a high level of information.

TABLE 14.4. *Fear of Nuclear Power by Level of Nuclear Information (Utility Survey)*

| Nuclear information | Percent expressing strong fear |
|---|---|
| 3 (high) | 19% (101) |
| 2 | 32 (211) |
| 1 | 47 (193) |
| 0 (low) | 64 (201) |

## Information, Values, and Attitudes toward Nuclear Power

In this section of the paper we shall present data on how three different types of values interact with information to influence attitudes toward nuclear power. The values are: liberalism/conservatism, trust in institutions, and what we shall call the value placed on human life.

### Liberalism/Conservatism

In both surveys we found a relatively strong association between attitudes toward nuclear power and various measures of the respondent's general political values [14] (see Appendix). In the Con Edison survey 25 percent of self-designated liberals, 36 percent of middle-of-the-roaders, and 44 percent of conservatives were pro−nuclear power. In the utility survey 66 percent of those who scored as most liberal on a three-item index were classified as being anti−nuclear power, whereas 48 percent who scored as most conservative were anti−nuclear power [15] (see Appendix). In this paper we are interested in any possible differential impact of information on people with differing political values. Essentially, we believe that, for those people who are ideologically sensitive and opposed to nuclear power on ideological grounds, level of information should have a weak influence.

In order to examine this hypothesis, we want to look at the relationship between attitudes toward nuclear power and level of knowledge, controlling for ideological position. Since the Con Edison survey con-

[14] "Liberalism/conservatism" is being measured by two variables. In both surveys we had a self-identification question and a series of attitude questions. See the Appendix for the exact questions used.

[15] In another paper (Fiorentine 1982), we analyze some of the reasons behind this association. Although we found ideology to be one influence on opinion formation, our data lead us to disagree with the conclusions of Kuklinski et al. (1982) that "core values . . . are the key to understanding how citizens decide" (p. 633).

TABLE 14.5. *Attitudes toward Nuclear Power by Level of Knowledge and Political Beliefs (Con Edison Survey)*

| Level of knowledge | Percent favoring nuclear power | | | Percentage difference |
|---|---|---|---|---|
| | Conservative | Moderate | Liberal | |
| 0, 1 (low) | 29% (99) | 31% (80) | 20% (123) | 9% |
| 2 | 36 (108) | 39 (67) | 24 (140) | 12 |
| 3 | 54 (62) | 39 (78) | 26 (124) | 28 |
| 4 | 64 (51) | 39 (44) | 30 (81) | 34 |
| 5, 6 (high) | 71 (48) | 57 (23) | 38 (61) | 33 |
| Percentage difference | 42% | 26% | 18% | |

tained more data on political values, we shall use this survey to analyze this point. We found essentially the same results in the utility survey. Respondents to the Con Edison survey were classified by their responses to a political self-identification question and their answers to five general attitude questions such as position on socialized medicine, opposition to the death penalty, and so on. In Table 14.5 we show attitudes toward nuclear power broken down by both level of information and political attitudes. We find an interesting specification effect. Level of knowledge has a stronger effect on conservatives and moderates and a relatively weak effect on liberals.

It is also interesting to note that in Table 14.5 ideology (or political beliefs) has a much stronger effect on those with high levels of knowledge than on those with low levels of knowledge. The people with high levels of knowledge have significantly higher levels of education and are probably more ideologically sensitive. Such people are less likely to be influenced by information.

Leaders and their ideologically sophisticated followers (a group in which many academics would probably be included) are not likely to be influenced by information. In an analysis of the ideological underpinning of both sides in the nuclear debate, Steven Del Sesto (1980) conducted a content analysis of testimony given before the Joint Committee on Atomic Energy in 1973–74. He argues that the debate is primarily over conflicting ideological positions rather than technical issues. He shows how the proponents of nuclear power have a deepseated belief that this form of energy will improve the world's standard of living and that all of the technical problems involved in the use of nuclear power can ultimately be solved by the application of science and engineering. The opposition bases its position on the belief that the use and proliferation of radioactive materials are inherently dangerous to the future health and safety of the human race and that the only safe way to use such technology would involve the imposition of a totalitarian form of government. The use of nuclear power violates the value commitment of the opposition to a decentralized democratic society that is more responsive to the input of the public (Lovins 1976).

It is unlikely that the presentation of any new information to the experts who testified before Congress or to any committed leaders of the antinuclear or pronuclear factions would have any effect on their opinions. Evidence that suggests that plants are not safe or that proposed systems for dealing with waste disposal are dangerous would not cause the pronuclear leaders to change their position because they believe that these are "only" technical problems capable of being solved if the politicians would let the scientists and engineers get on with the job. Positive evidence showing the safety of nuclear plants or the lack of harmful effects of fuel disposal will either be written off as biased by the antinuclear leaders or reinterpreted to raise questions about the data. For the opponents *any* nuclear risk is too great a risk. After a firm position on the issue has been taken, that position will determine reaction to new "facts."

As the work of Mazur (1975) and Kasperson et al. (1979) has shown, most of the leaders of the antinuclear movement had had prior experience in either other environmental causes or generally liberal consumer-oriented movements. The leading proponents of nuclear power have been either nuclear scientists or engineers, members of the nuclear industry, or government officials who have had a long history of interest in the use of nuclear energy for peaceful purposes. Thus, the opinions of the leaders of the debate can be explained by their personal backgrounds and general ideological position.

The conclusion that information will not influence the position of the leaders of the debate or their ideologically informed and sensitive followers does not mean that information will not be important in the formation of public opinion among the public at large. For most members of the public, nuclear power is not a very salient issue.[16] Also, most members of the public do not have the developed ideological positions of the leaders of the debate. For people who have to make up their minds about a complex issue with which they have minimal personal concern it is our hypothesis that level of information might be as important an influence on opinion formation as ideological positions.

[16] "Saliency" has been measured on several different surveys. In June 1982 we conducted a nationwide survey among a random sample of 1,554 for *Newsday*. Respondents were asked how often they spoke to family members or friends about a series of

## Trust in Social Institutions

Individuals differ in the extent to which they have faith in the major institutions of their society. As Lipset and Schneider (1983) have shown, there has been a general decline in recent years in the level of confidence that Americans have in major institutions. In this paper we do not attempt to explicate either the reasons for the overall decline or the causes of variation in trust among individuals; but we shall show that the extent to which individuals trust social institutions is correlated with their level of information about energy and thus their degree of fear of nuclear energy and their attitudes toward nuclear power.

In the utility survey we measured trust in social institutions by asking the respondents to tell us whether they trusted governmental leaders, business leaders, and scientific leaders to tell the truth to the public (see Appendix for question wording). Those who trusted the leaders of two or three of these institutions were treated as having a high level of trust in social institutions, those who trusted leaders of only one of the institutions were classified as having a moderate level of trust, and those who did not trust the leaders of any of the institutions were classified as having a low level of trust. Among those in the highest trust category 52 percent knew the correct answer to two or more of the nuclear information questions, as compared with 40 percent of those who scored in the lowest trust category. Although this is not a very strong association, it is significant theoretically as it points to a variable that should be more closely studied as an influence on information acquisition and thus formation of opinion.

As we had expected, trust in social institutions was also correlated with both fear of nuclear power and attitudes toward it. Among those in the highest trust category, only 30 percent expressed a strong fear of nuclear energy; among those in the middle trust category, 42 percent expressed a strong fear of nuclear energy; and among those in the lowest trust category, fully 52 percent expressed a strong fear of nuclear energy. And among those people in the lowest trust category, 59 percent oppose nuclear power, whereas among those in the highest category, 44 percent oppose nuclear power. This finding parallels that of Duncan (1978), whose secondary analysis of a 1975 Harris survey found level of confidence in the Atomic Energy Commission and

---

topics. "Nuclear power plants" was a relatively low-saliency item. Only 19 percent said that they frequently spoke about this, as compared with 62 percent about "the state of the economy," 50 percent about "crime," 34 percent about "foreign policy," and 28 percent about "nuclear war." The only topic with lower saliency was abortion; 10 percent spoke frequently about this topic.

in environmentalist groups to be significant influences on how people made up their minds on controversial aspects of the nuclear power debate.[17]

## Value Placed on Human Life

It is quite clear that information interacts significantly with values in influencing the development of attitudes toward nuclear power. The data of Table 14.5 suggest that general political ideology is one variable interacting with information. Another variable concerns willingness to accept risk to human life. Two very well-informed individuals might agree that nuclear power plants cannot blow up like atomic bombs and that the chances of a major nuclear accident are low but above zero. Even if they were to agree precisely upon what the level of risk was, they might reach different conclusions as to the acceptability of that risk. Whether or not a given risk is worth accepting depends upon another value—the value placed on human life.

Individuals differ in the value they place on human life. Almost everyone values human life; but some people are willing to consider risking human life in order to attain a particular political, social, or economic collective goal. For example, some people are more willing than others to risk lives, their own and others', in war. We hypothesized that the higher the value an individual placed on human life, the less willing that person would be to favor nuclear power.

Nuclear power plants have some advantages: They pollute the air less than any other type of existing plant; nuclear fuel will be available after oil becomes scarce; nuclear power reduces our reliance on foreign oil, thereby improving our balance of payments and lowering inflation. On the other hand, nuclear power plants cost a lot to build and as far as we currently know represent a low but nonzero risk to human life and health.[18] In a very severe accident, some people might be killed. In more minor accidents, some radiation might be released which might have negative health effects on people living in the vicinity of the plant. Do the positives outweigh the negatives? If the value placed on human life is very high, an individual will be less likely to accept *any* risk to life or health in order to achieve other goals.

[17] In the data Duncan analyzed it is questionable whether the questions on level of confidence in the AEC and environmental groups, two of the leading protagonists, were really independent of an underlying dependent variable: attitudes toward nuclear power, which might have influenced the answers given to both the specific questions on nuclear energy and the two confidence questions.

[18] The research we have done on opposition to nuclear power on the part of the public has shown that this opposition is influenced not by the cost of the power plants but almost exclusively by beliefs that they are unsafe and represent a hazard to the environment.

TABLE 14.6. *Attitudes toward Nuclear Power by Value Placed on Human Life (Utility Survey)*

| Score on human life index | Percent opposing nuclear power |
|---|---|
| 4 (high) | 68% (74) |
| 3 | 61 (200) |
| 2 | 52 (217) |
| 1 | 44 (173) |
| 0 (low) | 33 (42) |

In the utility survey we included four questions aimed at measuring the extent to which the respondents would be willing to sacrifice human lives in order to obtain some other goal (see Appendix). Using these four questions, we computed an index measuring the value placed on human life. In Table 14.6 we show the relationship between the score on this index and the respondent's attitudes toward nuclear power. The higher the value placed on human life, the more likely the respondent was to oppose nuclear power.[19]

## A Causal Analysis of the Correlation between Sex and Attitudes toward Nuclear Power

In this section of the paper we shall demonstrate how we can use both level of knowledge and value placed on human life to understand the causal connection between sex status and attitudes toward nuclear power. Virtually every survey ever conducted on attitudes toward nuclear power has found that women are more likely than men to oppose nuclear power. There has been some speculation but little empirical analysis to explain this difference. In his doctoral dissertation, Brody (1981) shows that the greater opposition of women can be explained by their greater fear of nuclear energy. Since "fear of nuclear energy" is so closely related to the dependent variable, it does not tell us a great deal more than the original association. We have to know why women fear nuclear energy more than do men.

In Table 14.7 we show the association between sex and the major variables used in our analysis. As expected, women were substantially more likely than men to oppose nuclear power. And, as Brody suggests, women are more likely to show a high fear of nuclear power.

[19] The analysis of the variable "value placed on human life" is exploratory. Further work is necessary on developing indicators for the concept. Some of our indicators could also be considered to measure "patriotism."

TABLE 14.7. *Attitudes of Men and Women (Utility Survey)*

|                                | Men    | Women  |
|--------------------------------|--------|--------|
| Attitude toward nuclear power  |        |        |
| Pronuclear (2)                 | 35%    | 15%    |
| In between (1)                 | 24     | 20     |
| Antinuclear (0)                | 41     | 65     |
|                                | (366)  | (340)  |
| Fear of nuclear power          |        |        |
| High                           | 32%    | 48%    |
| Low                            | 62     | 45     |
| Don't know                     | 6      | 7      |
|                                | (340)  | (366)  |
| Nuclear information            |        |        |
| High (3)                       | 21%    | 8%     |
| Medium-high (2)                | 37     | 24     |
| Medium-low (1)                 | 25     | 30     |
| Low (0)                        | 17     | 39     |
|                                | (340)  | (366)  |
| Value placed on human life     |        |        |
| Low (0, 1)                     | 38%    | 24%    |
| Moderate (2)                   | 33     | 29     |
| High (3, 4)                    | 29     | 48     |
|                                | (340)  | (366)  |

*Note:* Numbers in parentheses are N's. Some percentages add to 101 because of rounding.

One of the reasons for this fear can be found in the correlation between sex and nuclear information. Sixty-nine percent of the women we interviewed as compared with 42 percent of the men we interviewed knew the correct answer to one or none of the three nuclear information questions. We have shown that a low level of knowledge increases fear of nuclear power (Table 14.4) and now suggest that this is one explanation for the greater fear displayed by women.

Because this final part of our analysis entailed the simultaneous examination of four variables, we used simple correlation techniques. The zero-order correlation between sex treated as a dummy variable and attitudes to nuclear energy was $r = .18$. Computing a partial correlation coefficient holding the level of nuclear information constant reduces the correlation between sex and attitudes toward nuclear power to .08. Although substantially reduced in size, this correlation coefficient was still significant at the .05 level.

We had also hypothesized that in addition to knowing less about nuclear energy women might be more likely to oppose it because they would place a higher value on human life and therefore be less willing to engage in the rational cost–benefit analysis entailed in the acceptance of nuclear power. As we can see in Table 14.7, women do indeed place a higher value on human life ($r$ = .22). Computing a second-order partial correlation coefficient holding constant nuclear information and the value placed on human life reduces the correlation between sex and attitudes toward nuclear power to .05, a correlation that is not statistically significant at the .05 level. This analysis leads to the conclusion that the reasons why women are more likely than men to oppose nuclear power are their generally lower level of information about nuclear power, which increases their fear, and their higher value placed on human life.

Although it is possible that women's values may influence their perception of the "facts," other work in progress (Cole 1985) suggests that this is not the case and that women have lower levels of knowledge on all political issues and virtually all topics external to family life.

## Conclusion

This paper argues that level of information is an important influence on the formation of public opinion on complex issues such as nuclear power. Although there is no clear empirical as opposed to analytic distinction between values and facts, we have shown that those people who have even a rudimentary knowledge about energy and nuclear power are more likely to support nuclear power. There are two types of opponents of nuclear power: those who are ideologically opposed, and those who are not ideologically opposed but are afraid of nuclear power.

It is possible that for some the fear of nuclear power like the fear of crime is an emotional reaction in which the level of anxiety has very little relation to the probability of being a victim. The more information an individual has, the less likely he or she will be to develop a strong fear of nuclear power.[20] Other variables such as trust in institutions, general political ideology, and personal values such as the value placed on human life specify the conditions under which information will have a stronger or weaker effect. Individuals who place a very high value on human life, for example, may be informed about nuclear power but believe that any risk is too great a risk.

This paper points to the need for further studies explicating the

[20] A recent study conducted for *Newsday* has shown that more knowledgeable people take a more rational view of crime, that is, that their fear is related to the probability of being victimized. A study recently conducted for Suffolk County has found similarities in the responses of citizens to nuclear power and crime.

process through which values and information interact to influence the formation of opinion. We need to know how people get their information and what factors lead some to believe some sources and discredit others. Ultimately, longitudinal data will be necessary to better understand this process. If the analysis of level of knowledge presented in this paper is correct, then raising the level of knowledge about nuclear power should reduce the overall level of opposition. The complexity of the problem is emphasized by considering the problems one might encounter if one were interested in doing this. First, one would have to get "educators" who were credible and who could gain access to potential "learners." This would be impossible to do, for example, in television commercials sponsored by a nuclear utility. Paid spokesmen for these utilities would not be perceived as credible. Second, even if such educators could be found, opponents to nuclear power, who would emphasize the danger of the risks regardless of their size, would enter the educational arena, giving the learners the impression that nobody *really* knows what the effects of nuclear power plants are. It would probably be impossible for almost any planned educational campaign to be effective. This means that although information is an important variable in the formation of public opinion it is probably not one that can be manipulated in an open, pluralistic society. Both the acquisition of information and the attitudes such information influences are probably a result of processes over which we have little control.

## Bibliography

Brody, Charles. 1981. An analysis of sex differences in public opinion on nuclear energy. Doctoral dissertation, University of Arizona.

Clarke, Lee. 1985. The origins of nuclear power: A case of institutional conflict. *Social Problems* 32: 474–87.

Cole, Ann Harriet. 1985. The knowledge gap: Gender differences in everyday knowledge. Paper, Department of Sociology, SUNY at Stony Brook.

Cole, Stephen. 1981. Energy in the eighties: Attitudes of New York City and Westchester residents. Columbia Energy Research Center, November.

Del Sesto, Steven L. 1980. Conflicting ideologies of nuclear power: Congressional testimony on nuclear reactor safety. *Public Policy* 28: 39–70.

Duncan, Otis Dudley. 1978. Sociologists should reconsider nuclear energy. *Social Forces* 57: 1–22.

Fiorentine, Robert. 1982. Illuminating the opposition to nuclear energy: What, who and why? Master's essay, SUNY at Stony Brook.

Hensler, Deborah R., and Carl P. Hensler. 1979. *Evaluating nuclear power: Voter choice on the California Nuclear Energy Initiative.* Santa Monica, Calif.: Rand.

Hohenemser, Christoph, Roger Kasperson, and Robert Kates. 1977. The distrust of nuclear power. *Science* 196: 25–34.

Kahneman, Daniel, Paul Slovik, and Amos Tversky, eds. 1982. *Judgment under uncertainty.* Cambridge: Cambridge University Press.

Kasperson, Roger, Gerald Berk, David Pijawka, Alan B. Sharaf, and James Wood. 1979. Public opposition to nuclear energy: Retrospect and prospect. In C. T. Unseld, ed., *Sociopolitical effects of energy use and policy,* pp. 259–89, Washington, D.C.: National Academy of Sciences.

Knorr-Cetina, Karen. 1981. *The manufacture of knowledge: An essay on the constructivist and contextual nature of science.* Oxford: Pergamon Press.

Kuklinski, James H., Daniel S. Metlay, and W. D. Kay. 1982. Citizen knowledge and choices on the complex issue of nuclear energy. *American Journal of Political Science* 26:615–42.

Lang, Gladys Engel, and Kurt Lang. 1983. *The battle for public opinion: The president, the press, and the polls during Watergate.* New York: Columbia University Press.

Latour, Bruno, and Steve Woolgar. 1979. *Laboratory life: The social construction of scientific facts.* Beverly Hills, Calif.: Sage.

Lipset, Seymour Martin, and William Schneider. 1983. *The confidence gap: Business, labor, and government in the public mind.* New York: Free Press.

Lovins, Amory B. 1976. Energy strategy: The road not taken. *Foreign Affairs* 55:65–96.

Mazur, Alan. 1975. Opposition to technical innovation. *Minerva* 13:58–81.

Melber, Barbara, Stanley M. Nealey, Joy Hammersla, and William L. Rankin. 1977. *Nuclear power and the public: Analysis of collected survey research.* Seattle: Battelle Human Affairs Research Center.

Perrow, Charles. 1985. *The normal accident.* New York: Basic Books.

Rothman, Stanley, and S. Robert Lichter. 1982. The nuclear energy debate: Scientists, the media, and the public. *Public Opinion,* August/September, pp. 47–52.

Slovic, Paul, Baruch Fischoff, and Sara Lichtenstein. 1979. Rating the risks. *Environment* 21:14–39.

## Appendix: *Questions Used to Construct Indexes*

### Level of Information on Energy (Con Edison Survey)

Do you think oil or nuclear is more expensive in generating electricity?

|  |  |
|---|---|
| *Oil | 50% |
| Nuclear | 23 |
| Both the same | 6 |
| Don't know | 21 |
| Total | 100 |
|  | N = 1,181 |

What proportion of the electricity sold by Con Edison is currently produced from nuclear energy?

|  |  |
|---|---|
| None | 5% |
| Less than 10% | 12 |
| *Between 10 and 20% | 21 |
| *Between 21 and 40% | 12 |
| More than 40% | 6 |
| Don't know | 32 |
| Total | 99 |
|  | N = 1,181 |

In the next 20 years, how much electricity do you think could be generated in our area from solar energy?

|  |  |
|---|---|
| 5% or less | 9% |
| Between 5 and 10% | 16 |
| *Between 11 and 20% | 16 |
| *Between 21 and 30% | 15 |
| Between 31 and 50% | 13 |
| More than 50% | 19 |
| Don't know | 12 |
| Total | 100 |
|  | N = 1,181 |

Can utility companies charge whatever they want for electricity?

|  |  |
|---|---|
| Yes | 26% |
| *No | 71 |
| Don't know | 3 |
| Total | 100 |
|  | N = 1,181 |

Can a nuclear plant blow up like an atomic bomb?

|  |  |
|---|---|
| Yes | 58% |
| *No | 28 |
| Don't know | 14 |
| Total | 100 |
|  | N = 1,181 |

During normal operation will a person living near a nuclear power plant be exposed to as much radiation as he or she would be by taking an X-ray?

| | |
|---|---|
| Yes | 48% |
| *No | 35 |
| Don't know | 17 |
| Total | 100 |
| | N = 1,181 |

*These answers were considered to be correct.

## Attitudes toward Nuclear Power (Con Edison Survey)

In general, do you favor or oppose the building of more nuclear power plants in the United States?

| | |
|---|---|
| Favor | 32% |
| *Oppose | 55 |
| Don't know | 13 |
| Total | 100 |
| | N = 1,181 |

Which of the following comes closest to your attitude about the use of nuclear power by Con Edison?

| | |
|---|---|
| *Con Edison should immediately and permanently stop using nuclear power plants | 26% |
| Con Edison should continue to use nuclear power plants but build no more | 46 |
| Con Edison should build additional nuclear power plants | 23 |
| Don't know | 5 |
| Total | 100 |
| | N = 1,181 |

Do you think that electric companies in other parts of the country which have operating nuclear power plants should:

| | |
|---|---|
| Be allowed to continue to operate those plants | 58% |
| *Be forced to permanently close down the plants | 31 |
| Don't know | 11 |
| Total | 100 |
| | N = 1,181 |

If the United States had a choice of either continuing our current dependence on foreign oil or building more nuclear power plants, which would you favor?

| | |
|---|---|
| *Continue our dependence on foreign oil | 34% |
| Build more nuclear power plants | 51 |
| Don't know | 15 |
| Total | 100 |
| | N = 1,181 |

Would you describe yourself as:

|  |  |
|---|---|
| A supporter of nuclear power plants as a means of providing electricity | 27% |
| *An opponent of nuclear power plants as a means of providing electricity | 33 |
| You haven't made up your mind | 40 |
| Total | 100 |
|  | N = 1,181 |

*Responses coded as anti-nuclear power.

## Level of Information on Nuclear Power (Utility Survey)

Once an electricity plant is completed, do you think it costs more to operate:

|  |  |
|---|---|
| A nuclear electricity plant | 23% |
| *An oil-fired electricity plant | 29 |
| Don't know | 46 |
| Both the same | 1 |
| Total | 99 |
| N = | 706 |

During normal operation, which type of electricity plant pollutes the air the *least*?

|  |  |
|---|---|
| An oil-fired plant | 11% |
| A coal-fired plant | 6 |
| *A nuclear-fired plant | 55 |
| Don't know | 28 |
| All about the same | 1 |
| Total | 101 |
| N = | 706 |

During *normal operation*, does a nuclear power plant give off a dangerous level of radiation?

|  |  |
|---|---|
| Yes | 23% |
| *No | 47 |
| Don't know | 29 |
| Total | 99 |
| N = | 706 |

*Responses coded as correct.

## Nonnuclear Information (Utility Survey)

The most important reason for the increase in electricity rates is the increase in the price of oil.

|  |  |
|---|---|
| *Agree | 53% |
| Disagree | 41 |
| Don't know | 6 |
| Total | 100 |
| N = | 706 |

For every dollar you pay "utility," how much does "utility" pay for fuel for the plants?

| | |
|---|---|
| Less than 10 cents | 2% |
| 10 to 25 cents | 6 |
| 26 to 50 cents | 9 |
| *More than 50 cents | 8 |
| Don't know | 74 |
| Total | 99 |
| N = | 706 |

How does "utility" generate electricity?

| | |
|---|---|
| From coal | 2% |
| *From oil | 31 |
| From nuclear power | 2 |
| A combination of sources | 43 |
| Don't know | 22 |
| Total | 100 |
| N = | 706 |

*Responses coded as correct.

## Political Attitudes (Con Edison Survey)

The government should introduce a system of socialized medicine even if this means the income tax would have to be raised.

| | |
|---|---|
| *Agree | 56% |
| Disagree | 38 |
| Don't know | 6 |
| Total | 100 |
| N = | 1,181 |

Convicted murderers should be punished by the death penalty.

| | |
|---|---|
| Agree | 70% |
| *Disagree | 23 |
| Don't know | 7 |
| Total | 100 |
| N = | 1,181 |

Because of inflation, the federal government should increase welfare benefits.

| | |
|---|---|
| *Agree | 42% |
| Disagree | 52 |
| Don't know | 6 |
| Total | 100 |
| N = | 1,181 |

The United States should have used military force to obtain the release of the hostages in Iran.

| | |
|---|---|
| Agree | 52% |
| *Disagree | 41 |
| Don't know | 7 |
| Total | 100 |
| N = | 1,181 |

The United States should reinstitute the draft.

|  |  |
|---|---|
| Agree | 59% |
| *Disagree | 36 |
| Don't know | 5 |
| Total | 100 |
| N = | 1,181 |

Would you consider yourself to be politically:

|  |  |
|---|---|
| *Liberal | 32% |
| Middle-of-the-road | 43 |
| Conservative | 25 |
| Total | 100 |
| N = | 1,181 |

*Responses coded as "liberal."

## Political Attitudes (Utility Survey)

Convicted murderers should be punished by the death penalty.

|  |  |
|---|---|
| Agree | 73% |
| *Disagree | 21 |
| Don't know | 6 |
| Total | 100 |
| N = | 706 |

The government should introduce a system of socialized medicine even if this means the income tax would have to be raised.

|  |  |
|---|---|
| *Agree | 47% |
| Disagree | 42 |
| Don't know | 10 |
| Total | 99 |
| N = | 706 |

Would you consider yourself to be politically:

|  |  |
|---|---|
| *Liberal | 22% |
| Middle-of-the-road | 44 |
| Conservative | 34 |
| Total | 100 |
| N = | 706 |

*Responses coded as "liberal."

## Trust in Institutions (Utility Survey)

Do you think that most government officials can be trusted to tell the truth to the public?

|  |  |
|---|---|
| *Yes | 19% |
| No | 76 |
| Don't know | 5 |
| Total | 100 |
| N = | 706 |

Do you think that most business leaders can be trusted to tell the truth to the public?

| | |
|---|---|
| *Yes | 18% |
| No | 73 |
| Don't know | 8 |
| Total | 99 |
| N = | 706 |

Do you think that most scientific experts can be trusted to tell the truth to the public?

| | |
|---|---|
| *Yes | 60% |
| No | 28 |
| Don't know | 11 |
| Total | 99 |
| N = | 706 |

*Responses coded as indicating trust in institutions.

## Value Placed on Human Life (Utility Survey)

If Americans are held as hostages again, the government should use military force to obtain their release even if some of the hostages would be killed.

| | |
|---|---|
| Agree | 50% |
| *Disagree | 41 |
| Don't know | 9 |
| Total | 100 |
| N = | 706 |

If Cuba invaded El Salvador, the United States should send troops even if some Americans might lose their lives.

| | |
|---|---|
| Agree | 27% |
| *Disagree | 60 |
| Don't know | 13 |
| Total | 100 |
| N = | 706 |

If the United States got involved in a war which you supported, would you want your son or relative to volunteer?

| | |
|---|---|
| Yes | 51% |
| *No | 38 |
| Don't know | 12 |
| Total | 101 |
| N = | 706 |

Would you be willing to pay $500 more for a new car if this would make cars safer and thereby cut deaths from auto accidents in half?

| | |
|---|---|
| *Yes | 78% |
| No | 22 |
| Total | 100 |
| N = | 706 |

*Responses coded as placing a high value on human life.

*Part V*  Inequality

# Robin M. Williams, Jr.

## 15 Racial Attitudes and Behavior

It is difficult to take a fresh look at old questions: The weight of numerous prior discussions is heavy, and conventional wisdom warns against attempts to reinvent the wheel. Particularly intimidating is the sense that proffered answers have not been cumulative but have reiterated a limited set of possibilities. All these considerations beset this effort to appraise the state of knowledge concerning "racial attitudes and behavior."

Nevertheless, the effort may be useful, for two encouraging conditions now exist. First, the research inventory has grown rapidly, and the findings have been critically assessed in several major synoptic works. Second, the field of study can now be organized in terms of increasingly comprehensive and sophisticated conceptual frameworks—a much needed safeguard against ad hoc empiricism, fragmentation, and intellectual parochialism.

Furthermore, renewed stocktaking may be valuable in the 1980s precisely because this period combines evidence of marked reductions in racial discrimination along with equally compelling evidence of persisting and painful discrimination, prejudice, and racial disadvantage. Is the glass half full or half empty? Much current controversy represents differing evaluations of the same set of "facts." A critical review of available research will not remove such different interests and values but may help to clarify the central problems of interpretation.

This chapter reflects several successive efforts by the author to understand changes in attitudes and behavior of white and black Americans toward one another and toward their positions in American society. Even as early as 1947, a review of intergroup research showed a shift away from atomistic approaches that earlier had focused almost exclusively on individual attitudes and personality characteristics and toward analysis of social microcontexts ("situations") and of the encompassing organizational and institutional conditions (Williams 1947, chap. 2). By 1954, the task of editing a book on early school desegregation had reinforced this view, for we found in a series of community studies that social mobilization and administrative decisiveness often overweighed diffuse popular opinions; for example, "public school desegregation or integration is only loosely correlated with the attitudes or prejudices of the population" (Williams and Ryan 1954, pp. 240–41). A decade of further research showed in detail the heterogeneity of both "situations" and "attitudes" (stereotypes, evaluative beliefs, normative principles, preferences, justifications, and accounts) and the crucial importance of the *interactions* among personality characteristics, cultural codings, institutional forms, and concrete social interactions (Williams 1964; Hyman and Sheatsley 1956).

By the 1980s the long struggle to establish the reality and scientific usefulness of contextual variables—group-level effects, organizational factors, or social-system processes—seemed to have been reasonably successful. Social scientists generally were unlikely to ignore the need to pay attention to patterns of interaction and to structural opportunities and constraints in attempting to explain individual attitudes and behavior. For example, as Seeman (1981, p. 386) summarizes recent social psychological research, social learning, reinforcement through social acceptance, and differential association do seem reliable bases for explaining the origins and maintenance of "prejudice." Attitudes toward persons identified by racial labels evidently are powerfully affected by specific processes of social conformity: This is a frequently attested and robust finding. A long series of comparative and historical studies suggest further that, in general, the accuracy of intergroup attributions will be the greater the more frequent and varied the social contacts, the larger the proportion of direct personal communication as against indirect and mass media communication, and the more clearly institutionalized the statuses and collectivities within which interaction occurs. Equal-status interaction generally will produce less distortion than superordinate-subordinate relationships. The more varied the social statuses and activities of members of an identifiable ethnic category, the less homogeneous and rigid will be the stereotypes imposed on it. Accordingly, maximum inaccuracy is to be expected when ethnic groupings are spatially segregated, rarely interact directly, interact exclusively in dominant-subordinate relationships, and impinge upon one another in only one status or a few statuses or other social contexts.

Sheer spatial proximity is a crude indicator of actual ease of communication and often is negated by physical or social barriers. Functional proximity is what counts, that is, the "cost" or ease of interaction. The greater the ease of communication with, or the functional proximity of, an outgroup, the more salient it will be and the less likely it is to be regarded with indifference or neutrality. The effect of increased functional proximity, therefore, may be to increase either liking or disliking, harmonious or conflictual interaction. "Positive" outcomes will be heightened by similarity of values and beliefs, except when the similarity leads directly to increased competition for scarce goods. Dissimilarity will favor withdrawal or opposition, except when the differences are complementary, resulting in mutually rewarding interdependence.

Attitudes and behavior between members of different racial/ethnic groupings always will be affected by the character of major occupations carried out by members of each category and by the consequent relationships of trade and exchange, employer and employee, ruler and ruled, creditor and debtor, landlord and tenant, and so on. Consistent actual association of occupation and ethnic identity results in high stereotyping. Conversely, the more diverse the occupations (and other major statuses) of the members of an ethnic category, the less distinctive will it be and the less will occupational stereotypes and evaluations be generalized as attributes of the ethnic category. Furthermore, the greater the inequalities among ethnic groupings in wealth, income, power, or authority, the greater the cultural distinctiveness. In sum, ethnic/racial distinctiveness is maximized by highly visible cultural differences, by territorial separation or residential segregation, by close association with certain occupations, by separate participation in community organizations (schools, churches, voluntary associations), and by marked interethnic differences in wealth, income, power, and authority (Williams 1978, pp. 163–64).

Indeed, across the entire field of the study of ethnic or intergroup relations, the accumulation of well-supported hypotheses over the decades since World War II has been impressive. A large array of ordered data is at hand—from census reports, primary historical sources, sample surveys, field experiments, participant and nonparticipant observations, analysis of cultural products, and controlled experiments. Comparative studies have illuminated both the scope of variations and the presence of substantial cross-national and cross-cultural uniformities. Furthermore, the available knowledge has been subjected at fairly frequent intervals to systematic stocktaking and critical assessment. For example, since Myrdal's *American Dilemma* in 1944, we have seen, among others, the following inventories of the field: Berelson and Steiner 1964; Blalock 1967; Brewer and Kramer 1985; Francis 1976; Harding et. al. 1954; Hirschman 1983; Olzak

1983; Patchen 1982; Porter and Washington 1979; Rose 1947; Schermerhorn 1970; Seeman 1981; Simpson and Yinger 1985; van den Berghe 1970; Williams 1947, 1964, 1975, 1977, 1978.

What are some of the salient conclusions that can be drawn from this complex body of research and reflection?

## Aspects of Attitudes

Perhaps the first lesson—which appears easy but apparently is not—is not only that the notion of attitude is broad and multidimensional but that measured attitudes, whatever the indicators used, vary enormously with reference to different situations and objects (Hyman 1949). Although there typically are consistent positive intercorrelations—for example, among attitudes toward blacks—there is strong specificity of response. Thus, in one study of whites, 86 percent would "not mind at all" working with a black supervisor, whereas only 49 percent gave this response toward a black family (of equivalent income and education) moving in next door (Seeman 1981, p. 383). As data and analyses have developed, it has been repeatedly shown that attitudes as elicited in national interview surveys often are highly specific to particular wordings of questions and to the particular issues thereby raised. For example, white respondents differentiate sharply among different areas of life (employment, schools, intermarriage), among different means of effecting nondiscrimination or equality, and among other characteristics of the setting of action (e.g., proportions of whites and blacks in schools or in residential areas).

A second finding, seldom highlighted in its full societal importance, is that intergroup attitudes and behaviors are enormously diverse within both the black and white populations. This fact is, to be sure, unsurprising in view of the well-known heterogeneity of both categories in occupations, employment, income, residence, education, region, religious affiliation, demographic patterns (e.g., family composition), and many other social and cultural characteristics. But the diversity is a crucial social fact, cautioning strongly against the sin of overaggregation of data referring to blacks and whites.

A third substantial conclusion is that the original global conceptions of "attitudes," as against "situations," could not be sustained for long. Research rapidly revealed the many dimensions or facets of elicited attitudes. Thus, "prejudice" turned out to be a highly aggregated concept, containing a distinct component of stereotyping, another of moralistic evaluation, a third aspect of personal-social liking or aversion, a fourth component of assessment of public policy, and so on (Williams 1964, chaps. 4–5). More generally, the structure of attitudes includes the dimensions of centrality, salience, polarity, intensity, and connectedness. Ideologies, for example, are for those persons who hold them central, salient, connected, intense—but they may or may not be polarized (Kerlinger 1984, p. 9). The multidimensionality of both prejudice and discrimination has been clearly described in Seeman's comprehensive review (1981, pp. 379–81).

Just because of the intrinsic complexity of concrete opinions, the responses to direct questions as typically used in large-scale surveys rarely can be given a single clear-cut meaning. Not only are the meanings of terms often numerous and ambiguous, but the taken-for-granted contexts within which respondents frame their replies are not always obvious or easily inferred. Hence, a fourth salient feature of measured attitudes is that analytic interpretation is heavily dependent upon knowledge of a context of assumptions, beliefs, and explanatory or justificatory reasons.

In ordinary social interaction, when individuals express opinions they often give *reasons* for their statements. Analysis of such "reasons" (e.g., accounts, "explanations," justifications, elaborations, qualifications) can aid interpretation of the meaning of responses, suggest new hypotheses, and help to specify the contexts and limits of particular attitudes. Major sociological examples go back at least to Thomas and Znaniecki's *Polish Peasant in Europe and America* (1918–20) and include Samuel A. Stouffer et al., *The American Soldier* (1949; cf. vol. 1, chap. 10) and many other well-known works. Curiously, however, with the coming of repeated large-scale opinion surveys, the analysis of reasons was neglected, perhaps because of the expense and difficulty of collecting the data. More recently, the potential value of returning to explication of reasons has been illustrated by Apostle et al. (1983), *The Anatomy of Racial Attitudes*. From a sample of some 500 white persons in the San Francisco Bay area, this study elicited "explanations" of the racial attitudes expressed; these accounts could then be related to respondents' beliefs and prescriptions. For example, black/white differences in socioeconomic status or IQ were "explained" by respondents in terms of six major types of reasons: individualist, genetic, supernatural, environmental, "radical," and cultural. Reasons clustered in distinctive modes and were related in understandable ways to respondents' views on social policies and individual action concerning racial equality—for example, the "individualists" were the most likely to oppose institutional intervention against racial discrimination (Apostle et al. 1983, p. 110).

Several of the important questions used in national surveys concerning implementation of principles of equality or of integration explicitly invoke action by the federal government. Hence, if white re-

spondents endorse the principle but reject the hypothetical governmental intervention, the responses might indicate not a "superficial"
or merely symbolic orientation but rather a principled objection to or
fear of the use of federal powers. In fact, however, negative attitudes
toward federal coercion are not closely associated either with educational level or with attitudes toward implementation.

Fifth, as Kerlinger (1984) suggests, much research has assumed that
attitudes are *for* or *against* something—that they are bipolar, so that
positive and negative views are implied. But "conservative" and "liberal" attitudes toward particular referents are not necessarily opposed; lack of a positive view of something need not entail a negative
attitude. In short, although polarity does exist, the structure of many
attitudes is dualistic; two facets exist independently rather than in direct opposition or contrast (Kerlinger 1984, p. 34). This is one among
many reminders that commonsense assumptions often hide the genuine complexity of "real-life" attitudes.

A sixth set of findings centers upon categorization. The cognitive
aspects of intergroup attitudes are now much better understood than
formerly. Stereotypes enhance salience and recall: Stereotyped features are more often correctly remembered (when the categorical
information was present at the time of encoding); category identification influences inferences about individuals; stereotypes guide interpretations and judgments (e.g., tending to block new information if
inconsistent with stereotype). Categorical judgments tend to emphasize differences between categories while attenuating intracategory
differences. Further, "individuals demonstrate greater differentiation
among members of groups to which they themselves belong . . . than
they do among the members of outgroups" (Brewer and Kramer
1985, p. 223). Given initial widely shared ingroup categorization of
"others," there are strong tendencies to make category membership a
part of individuals' social identity. Given this self-identification, ingroup preferences and outgroup discrimination are facilitated, especially when intergroup rivalry is perceived (Brewer and Kramer 1985,
pp. 223–26).

The crucial role of *boundary* definition and maintenance is apparent
and has been documented in detail by other experimental and observational studies. The primordial intergroup acts are to identify, name,
and classify. Once there is a cultural (shared) definition of social categories, deep-seated social and psychological processes lead to differences
in preferences, resource allocations, sense of relative gratification or
deprivation, imputations of causes and motives, social evaluations,
and a variety of other boundary-marking phenomena. A striking example is the finding that "desirable" behavior by ingroup members

tends to be attributed by them to internal dispositions or motives, whereas such behavior on the part of outgroup persons is attributed to situational factors or unusual efforts; the converse pattern holds for undesirable behaviors (Brewer and Kramer 1985, p. 229).

Boundaries are accentuated by perceived oppositions and by threats, including expressions of hostility or negative evaluations by members of the outgroup. Boundaries are accentuated also by actual intra-category homogeneity, by dramatic public affirmations and symbols, by actual differentiation between categories (e.g., occupations), and by physical and social separateness (cf. Williams 1964, chap. 10). There is an incessant interplay between the *cultural* level of group categorization and the *social* level of interactions that either reinforce or change the definitions of boundaries, group membership, and social identity. Indeed, an important component of what is usually called racism is just the *assumption* that blacks and whites constitute two monolithic blocs with markedly different characteristics.

Still another (seventh) facet of attitudes emerges from the repeated research finding that support for general principles—norms or generalized statements of desirability—usually receives greater endorsement than specific proposals for implementing the principles ("equal rights," "open housing"), especially by means of governmental intervention. How is this finding to be interpreted? One approach assumes that the specific opinions are more trustworthy indicators of "deep" attitudes than are the endorsements of generalized values. A conspicuous case in point is provided by the massive public controversies concerning the use of busing as a means to bring about racial integration in the schools. For example, data on negative attitudes of white persons toward such busing can be interpreted as evidence of hidden or "symbolic" racism: It is noted that many whites who oppose busing do not have children who are subject to busing and that the negative attitudes are positively correlated with overt expressions of racial prejudice (Sears, Hensler, and Speer 1979). Yet the inferred racism clearly is not merely symbolic, for many of those who oppose busing also endorse expressions of overt racial prejudice—and thus are not disguising their views —and it is to be expected that avowed "racists" would oppose any antisegregation policy. The crucial question really concerns those persons who endorse integration in general but reject some specific measures ostensibly intended to promote or require integration.

The next obvious observation here is that generalized norms or values are, by definition, context-free. Concrete "implications," then, are likely to be numerous and diverse, as the principle is constrained by competing values and situational realities (resources, costs, threats, etc.). One line of interpretation, accordingly, is to examine how implementation may entail contradictory or competing values. As a case in point, it has been proposed that there is a genuine consensus among present-day American whites that racial discrimination should not be practiced or approved but that this agreement breaks down when implementation of prointegration or proequality policies involves compulsion. This situation is thought to express a contradiction between values of equality and values of individual freedom (Lipset and Schneider 1978). This interpretation gains plausibility from the historical prominence of a clash between "equality" and "freedom" in American political attitudes and behavior (Rokeach 1973; Williams 1970, chap. 11). And Jackman and Muha (1984) have focused the issue by the argument that claims based on group interests, as in preferential goals or quotas, are opposed by dominant groups (racial, gender, or class) on grounds of a principle of individual achievement. For the moment it is enough to note that contradictions or other incompatibilities of principles can diminish support for specific measures that are premised on *any* single principle. Diminished support also can arise by reason of incompatibility of proposed implementation with specific individual preferences, interests, and goals (seniority in job, residential area, property values) (Schuman, Steeh, and Bobo 1985, p. 205).

## Relations of Expressed Attitudes to Other Behaviors

There are signs of change in the long-standing and often unfruitful controversy in psychological and sociological research concerning the extent and kind of relationships between "attitudes" and "behavior." Both of the terms are problematic. If attitudes are defined in terms of expressed opinions, they *are* behavior—for such communication is a hallmark of social behavior. So the controversy needs to be rephrased. The central methodological problem has been correctly posed by Schuman and Johnson (1976, p. 161): "to what extent and in what ways attitudinal measures are related to other behaviors." The question is not whether attitudes predict behaviors but how the elicited responses we call attitudes (or opinions) are related to other responses of the same individuals or collectivities. The relationships between different kinds of responses are remarkably complex; both opinions and other behaviors are affected by measurement errors, possible falsification, distinctions among degrees of "commitment" and "realism," and questions of conceptual congruence versus correlational consistency (Schuman and Johnson 1976, pp. 163–85).

The familiar finding that generalized attitudes often do not correlate closely with actual interracial contacts and friendships is repeated in Patchen's intensive study of desegregated schools; the sheer opportunity for interracial contact strongly affected the extent of friendly interactions (1982, p. 333). Positive effects were favored by positive peer-group attitudes and by cooperative activities. A striking companion finding is that, although unfriendly contacts were correlated with negative interracial attitudes, the amount of fighting and arguing was essentially independent of the amount of friendly contact (Patchen 1982, pp. 335–36). Thus, individuals have different experiences with different members of the other racial category and adjust their behavior to these differences.

These brief examples serve to illustrate the possible interactive effects of attitudes, ideologies, institutional structures, and social interactions in localized situations. The relationships between public policies and "popular" attitudes and values (i.e., those diffusely present in the general population) are nonobvious because they are complex and variable.

Although only a beginning has been made in the needed empirical analysis, the generic problem can now be more clearly seen than hitherto. Many of the data we review here refer to attitudes as indicated by specific opinions, usually expressed in interview situations. We suggest that such opinions often are short-run, volatile phenomena; they can shift drastically in response to *both* microcontexts ("situations") and macroevents (war, depression, national elections, international crises). If we study opinions for other than topical purposes, then, we must hope to infer from them something about more basic values and beliefs or about important social relationships and networks. "Racial attitudes" are not synonymous with "racial relations." The latter are *constituted by* actual social interactions: Repetitive *interactions* constitute *relationships*, which in turn become patterned as *networks*. The boundaries of networks are defined by frequencies of interactions of given types. What those types are will be partially defined by *social categories* (black, white; immigrant, native)—which over time may be altered by changes in interactions and by changes in beliefs and values. To conceptualize ethnic/racial relations adequately requires close attention simultaneously to beliefs (including categories), values, interactions, relationships, networks, and environing macrostructures.

## Attitudes toward Segregation and Integration: Characteristics and Changes

Attempts to develop analyses of trends in ethnic/racial attitudes have to deal with several possible artifacts in the data. Outstanding is the need to separate cohort effects from aging and from change due to alterations in context ("historical" change). Evidently, for example, some changes over time in survey results can represent changing response rates in different sectors of the population, for example, decreasing responses from persons of lower socioeconomic status (SES), interview refusals from the more (or the less) militant blacks. Responses can be affected by changes in the interviewing staffs, for example, changing proportions of blacks, of women, of young and older. Other conceivable artifacts can be easily imagined.

The most systematic available analysis of the national survey data has been able to disentangle cohort effects from the gross changes (Schuman, Steeh, and Bobo 1985). The study shows that changes in the attitudes of whites on racial questions during the last decade have been largely the result of the maturing of cohorts with more "liberal" attitudes rather than of changes in attitudes of individuals. For example, the largest changes in individual attitudes occurred during the years of the civil rights movements (mainly the 1960s). Thus, the younger generations have been more liberal than the older and have raised the level of liberalism as the younger have replaced the older. Most recently, however, there are signs of declines in such items as favoring governmental action to insure school integration or being unfavorable to the Ku Klux Klan. An increasingly conservative political period may be having negative effects upon attitudes toward racial equality. One indication is found in the fact that since the early 1970s national surveys show that it is not just among whites that support has decreased for federal intervention to aid minorities and to enforce school desegregation. Although such support remains much higher among blacks than among whites, substantial declines occurred in both populations between 1970 and 1982 (Schuman, Steeh, and Bobo 1985, chap. 4). White support for employment rights, however, did not show a negative trend.

Schuman, Steeh, and Bobo (1985) have identified three broad types of interpretation of recent change in racial attitudes and behavior in the United States. The first, Progressive Trend, holds that the data reflect real and consistent changes. The second line of interpretation— Underlying Racism—proposes that many of the apparent changes are endorsements of general principles, representing a more sophisticated rhetoric, that leave intact a deeper commitment to group position and correlative resistance to realistic change (rather than "merely symbolic" concessions). The third approach, which may be called Meaningful Patterns of Progress and Resistance, attempts to specify both the complex profile of change and resistance to change and the probable causes of that pattern.

The Progressive Trend accepts at face value the reported decreases in negative attitudes among whites. The Underlying Racism argument attempts to discount the apparent changes. Such discounting may refer to various lines of evidence: (1) Lower proportions of whites approve "implementation" than approve "principle" items; (2) lower proportions of whites accept integration when large rather than small proportions of blacks are specified; (3) approval of integration is less for close, personalized relations than for impersonal, public contexts; (4) whites are more likely to give prointegration responses to black than to white interviewers; (5) responses vary greatly with changes in the specific wordings of questions.

Nevertheless, there is no plausible reason to doubt that whites' acceptance of blacks' rights to "equality of opportunity" has greatly increased during the last four decades. The same is true of racial integration in public accommodations, in public education, and, to a lesser extent, in residential areas. The great variations in apparent levels of acceptance do not belie the pervasive shifts in norms of legitimacy and appropriateness since the end of World War II. The changes are evident in overt behavior as well as in "testimony" (e.g., survey responses) and simply cannot be dismissed as hypocrisy, as sophisticated tactics to maintain social peace, or as mere ritualistic lip service.

By the 1970s, very few whites still overtly favored racial discrimination in employment, and only small and declining proportions were willing to support segregation in public accommodations and transportation, or even in public schools. Residential choice has remained an area of considerable resistance, although the principle of nondiscrimination has gained ground. "Boundary maintenance" is strongest with regard to intermarriage, but support for laws against intermarriage has declined from the levels of the 1950s.

To appreciate the significance of those massive changes, we have only to remember that the *majority* of American whites in the early 1940s overtly supported racial segregation and discrimination in principle and as a matter of public policy. Over the last three decades the central fact of change is the acceptance of a whole normative framework that rejects racial discrimination either as a mode of interpersonal behavior or as public policy.

Although the evidence on changes in stereotypes comes largely from scattered studies, it also rather consistently indicates that black/white stereotyping has become less uniform and that the content has changed. Whites' stereotypes of blacks have dropped some "negative" traits and have added other characterizations, both "positive" (progressive, ambitious) and of uncertain valence (religious, quick-tempered). Both blacks and whites have increased the favorability of their images of blacks, but both have decreased the favorability of the image of whites. The content of stereotypes of whites has remained more stable than the image of blacks (cf. Clark and Pearson 1982).

This is not to say that the changes have been total or undifferentiated. Not only are there differences among life areas, but the extent of change varies greatly among segments of the population. Thus, among white adults, *trends* in attitudes concerning racial integration have been similar among all educational levels, from low to high, but the better-educated generally show greatest change, both positive and negative (Schuman, Steeh, and Bobo 1985, chap. 6); higher education usually correlates with prointegration position, but in recent years the better-educated have decreased their support for governmental intervention to bring about school integration, converging in attitude toward the less-educated.

Also, attitudes vary greatly from one specific social situation to another. In general, acceptance of integration is most likely when sense of threat is low and perceived similarity is high. In the case of schools, for instance, Patchen (1982, pp. 330–31) concluded that in desegregated schools negative attitudes of black toward white students centered upon perceptions of whites as acting superior, being stuck-up, not wishing to be friendly. Thus, fear of rejection was a central issue with black students. On the other hand, for whites—especially for males—the central basis students cited for negative attitudes was the perception of blacks as dangerous and disruptive. Anticipation of attack or molestation thus paralleled blacks' anticipation of unfriendliness and social contempt. At the level of generalized intergroup stereotypes, these images lay the basis for a continuing cycle of hostile interactions and avoidances.

Blacks in high schools had the most positive attitudes when they had experienced early positive interracial relations, when their white peers were accepting or friendly, when they were not a small minority in the school or class, when they received fair treatment by teachers and school administrators. Patchen (1982, p. 331) says that blacks were most likely to have positive attitudes when they were in situations in which they were likely "to feel accepted and treated on an equal basis by both white students and the school staff." Among white students, positive attitudes were most likely when there was least sensed threat of physical attack or of blacks "taking over" the school. Among both blacks and whites, attitudes were related to early interracial experiences and to perceived attitudes of family and peers.

Blacks and whites do differ in a number of sociopolitical attitudes, even when controls are introduced for class, self-identification, and income. In both populations, however, there are similar structures of interrelations among the sociopolitical attitudes: political-economic conservatism, "social issues" (women's rights, abortion, marijuana, rights of the accused), military affairs, racial attitudes, "law and order." Whites are more "conservative" on most items, but blacks are more conservative with regard to "social issues" and military affairs, once the correlations of these two clusters with other attitudes are taken into account (in a multiple regression analysis). Factor analysis suggests that attitudes of whites are organized around a single factor of liberalism/conservatism, whereas for blacks there are two main clusters—one indicating positive attitudes toward the military, and the other dominated by racial, "law and order," and "social" issues (Sidanius 1984). What is most striking, however, even given the distinctiveness of many elements of black experience and black culture, is the similarity of many goals and values shared by blacks and whites.

Research on black identity and self-concepts in the 1930–60 decades emphasized putative effects of the negative racial images held by whites upon blacks' self-esteem. It was often assumed—and considerable evidence in those years supported the presumption—that blacks developed unfavorable and ambivalent conceptions of racial identity as well as low self-esteem in response to pervasive discrimination, subordination, and segregation. Some scholars did recognize that these effects were complex and by no means universal (Porter and Washington 1979, p. 54). From the mid-1960s onward, research increasingly emphasized positive coping, black militancy, and the existence of strong ingroup identification and protective sociopsychological processes (Williams 1964). An important distinction was developed between *racial* self-esteem and *personal* self-esteem, and both were shown to be strongly influenced by the specific local settings and social circles in which individuals grow up and establish their social identities. Studies in this complicated field have encountered many methodological problems: Many seemingly "inconsistent" findings probably derive from problems in sampling, research techniques, and methods of analysis—as well as from real changes in self-concepts over time. Among the reliable findings two of the most important are these: (1) Personal and racial self-esteem are positively related but vary independently to an important extent; (2) both black militancy and a supportive black community are positively correlated with favorable self-concepts and evaluations (Porter and Washington 1979, pp. 63–69). *Personal* self-esteem among children seems to be influenced by comparisons much narrower than supposed in early research (Seeman 1981, p. 393) and hence may be only loosely connected with categorical racial or ethnic evaluations. Self-esteem of black children can be quite high in situations of strong negative attitudes on the part of whites. These conclusions are consistent with the evidence that shows especially high levels of both racial and personal self-esteem among the younger black people, especially those from middle-class families. The possibility that defensive psychological mechanisms may be involved in this situation does not alter the fact of substantial increases in black self-esteem since the end of World War II.

In spite of the widely accepted assumption among both black and white Americans that the two massive racial categories are distinct, clear, and enduring, there is abundant evidence of vagueness of boundaries and of commonalities of orientation. The facts of great differences of experience and social location are not in question. But beside the histories of discrimination, segregation, and prejudice are the common histories of interdependence and shared destiny. As a consequence, blacks and whites have many similar conceptions of desirable family and community life, share basic religious beliefs and organizational forms, participate to a substantial and increasing extent in a common public life (Taylor 1979). Across a wide range of generalized value commitments, blacks and whites manifest essentially the same positions (Prager 1982, p. 116; Rokeach 1973, pp. 66–72). Where the two populations diverge most sharply is precisely on the value of *equality*. When blacks and whites are matched for income and education, most value differences diminish; those that remain are what we would expect between people who have or have not experienced discrimination and unwelcome segregation.

## Modes of Explanation

Ethnic and racial relations illustrate every conceivable type of social process and may affect and be affected by every kind of social and cultural structure. Such relations, accordingly, vary enormously in detail in differing social contexts. Concrete empirical generalizations, therefore, tend to be situation-specific and historically conditioned. Given these characteristics, ethnic/racial relations resist simple explanations: Adequate accounts require careful *analytic* formulations that explicitly allow for contextual variations.

Three examples may help to specify what we mean. First, the many efforts to specify the antecedents of indexed prejudice in socioeconomic status (as indicated by occupation, income, education) have had only modest success. In Seeman's assessment, the patterns of correlations "are not very dependable and quite complex"; for example, the reported associations differ for various ethnic groups, dimensions of attitudes, and specific SES indicators (1981, p. 383). The second illustration is provided by recent work that reinforces earlier findings that urban experience increases generalized tolerance of outgroups. Even when socioeconomic status, life-cycle stage, and race are statistically controlled, urbanism (size of respondent's community of residence) is associated with willingness to grant civil liberties to holders of unpopular (or "deviant") ideas and interests (Wilson 1985). A third example moves into detailed examination of the outcomes of desegregation of public schools in the analysis by Patchen (1982) of the 1970–72 experience in the Indianapolis public schools. The study is consistent with earlier summaries of research evidence (e.g., St. John 1975; Williams 1975, 1977) in showing the extreme diversity and complexity of situations and outcomes. In general, the apparent effects (correlates) of interracial exposure to potential contacts and of actual interactions upon academic performance were small. Although a very high proportion of black students in a school predicted to lesser academic achievements, the exceptions in predominantly black classes suggest that factors other than the sheer amount of interracial contact were the more important influences. Where unfavorable effects were inferred, the circumstances suggested that lowered standards and discipline may have been mediating factors (Patchen 1982, pp. 292–94, 325–26).

Efforts to explain intergroup attitudes, especially prejudice, on psychological grounds have a complicated history, but many approaches have shared two basic assumptions: (1) "The individual" is a unit separable from "society"; (2) prejudices involve distortions of an external reality or departures from rationality. Both assumptions were congenial to an individualistic and experimental psychology that wished to exclude complex and "vague" sociocultural factors from laboratory studies and detached individual subjects. Both assumptions also were congruent with a cultural framework in which power relationships and "macro" social structures were obscured by a focus on individuals—their needs, desires, errors, perceptions, personality structures, socialization, and so on. In terms of political implications, an emphasis on prejudice could avoid confronting structures of domination and vested interests by focusing instead on education, information, therapy, and personal contacts as means of altering attitudes and behavior (cf. Henriques et al. 1984, pp. 60–89; Williams 1947, chaps. 1–3).

## Correlates and Effects of Education

The long-standing popularity in the United States of "education" as a means of dealing with social problems helps to explain the persistent hope that higher levels of formal education will reduce racial discrimination and prejudice. And, indeed, much evidence points to the greater tolerance, cosmopolitan outlook, and complexity of judgments among the better-educated (cf. Hyman, Wright, and Reed 1975). But critics have been quick to note that correlation does not demonstrate causation and have pointed to inconsistent or contradictory findings.

It is a sociological commonplace that formal education cannot be fully value-neutral but rather necessarily transmits a more or less organized set of beliefs, values, and assumptions concerning human beings and society—in short, an ideology. The claimed absence of ideology usually means either a doctrine of avoiding extremism and permitting all views to be heard or a somewhat more systematic commitment to norms of rationalism and tolerance. There is considerable evidence that higher levels of formal education are accompanied by lesser endorsement of negative stereotypes and evaluations of ethnic and racial minorities. It is plausible that an educational system exposing students to a diversity of views and to complex cognitive tasks would result in greater complexity and lessened dogmatism in attitudes concerning race and ethnicity.

But it was clear all along that no simple formula relating higher levels of education to diminished prejudice would do. Most obviously, "education" is not a clean unitary variable with an unequivocal meaning but rather a label for many enormously varied processes and cultural contents. Furthermore, as we noted above, attitudes toward ethnic/racial categories or objects have long been known to be multidimensional, including, for example, stereotyping, positive and negative affects, evaluations of public policies, personal preferences for close or distant social interaction, and many other aspects. Thus, both the independent and the dependent terms in the education/attitude equations are congeries of analytically separable variables. In the third place, the effects of education—it can confidently be predicted—will be confounded with and modified by other independent or mediating variables, such as SES, sex, age, place of residence, extent of interaction with persons of different ethnic or racial groups. Finally, the racial and ethnic objects of attention and concern exhibit numerous characteristics, any one of which may be salient in some contexts and not in others.

Accordingly, one expects the research results to be complex, and that expectation is fulfilled. A multiple classification analysis of national samples of adults in the United States and in Canada (1968) found two main patterns of association between education and "liberal" attitudes. In Canada higher levels of schooling were associated with greatly reduced prevalence of negative attitudes toward ethnic (nationality, language) minorities, Jews, and blacks; the relationships held among French-Canadians and among English-speaking Catholics and Protestants (Curtis, Kuhn, and Lambert 1976, p. 129). On the other hand, the higher the level of education, the more frequent are negative attitudes toward labor unions and "right-wingers," whereas views of big business and left-wingers showed a more complex pattern. In a parallel analysis of a 1968 national U.S. survey, more education predicted to greater favorability toward blacks and, among Protestants, toward Catholics, but there was no trend in attitudes toward Jews, and white Protestants with higher education showed especially high levels of hostility toward labor unions. In the Canadian study, even with controls for seven other factors, higher education consistently goes along with lesser preference for cultural uniformity and sociopolitical authoritarianism (Curtis, Kuhn, and Lambert 1976, p. 133). The authors conclude: "In any event, it appears that for two modern nations said to be characterized by cultural and political pluralism, the 'education leads to less negative out-group affect' proposition requires some qualifications both in terms of (1) differences in the institutional locations and types of the attitude object (groups) referred to and (2) the subcultural backgrounds of the respondent groups" (Curtis, Kuhn, and Lambert 1976, p. 138).

This conclusion is compatible with the findings of Schuman, Steeh, and Bobo (1985) that in national U.S. surveys the more highly educated whites led the movement to accept racial nondiscrimination and integration but that they also led the 1970s decline in support for implementation of school integration, converging toward the less-educated. Although the data do not tell us why, a plausible expectation is that some of the better-educated whites feared a loss of competitive advantage of their children under desegregation. Withdrawal from central-city schools containing large proportions of black pupils from low-income households is an expectable response from some status-oriented white parents who want their children to gain advantages in the struggle for economic and social position. At the minimum, most parents want the kind of education for their children that will give some substantial insurance against downward social mobility. For this reason alone they would tend to want schools of "good reputation," that are orderly and not dangerous, that encourage learning, and that prepare pupils for successful entry into the job market or into higher education.

The most vigorous attack on the proposition that higher education reduces negative attitudes toward "outgroups" involves the argument that formal education inculcates the ideologies of "dominant groups" and hence cannot be "liberating" (Jackman and Muha 1984, p. 752). It is granted that education leads to greater knowledge and to awareness of "social desirability," but the changes in ethnic attitudes are seen as superficial. Jackman and Muha use a 1975 national survey to provide data for investigating the correlates of education. Although higher levels of education are associated with greater acceptance of the general principle of racial integration, of black residential rights, and of women's job rights, only ten of some forty other items show substantial positive correlations. Jackman and Muha (1984, p. 758) interpret the positive associations to indicate attachment to the principle of individual rights rather than consistent commitment to a principle of equal rights. With these findings established, the authors explicitly leave the data behind to speculate broadly on the possible interpretations. In their view, the higher acceptance of racial integration and black rights by the well-educated whites is a sophisticated way of avoiding offense and confrontation by emphasizing individualized rights while evading commitment to group equality. Indeed, "By upholding individualism as a guiding principle in the empirical and normative interpretation of social life, the rights of *groups* are thus rendered illegitimate and unreasonable" (Jackman and Muha 1984, p. 760). The "broader and more sophisticated knowledge" and greater cognitive complexity of the well-educated are seen not as liberating but rather as means to enable them to better protect their privileged interests in the status quo. The primary outcome, then, is "ideological sophistication rather than moral liberation."

The argument just sketched rests upon a single (1975) survey, in which—as usual—there is little information on the contextual meaning of responses and no direct link between those responses and group-level or macroinstitutional factors. A major theme of this chapter has been the importance of providing specification of both the institutional setting and the contextual meanings to interpret survey responses adequately. Thus, an important issue must remain unresolved until we have more *specific* and *systematic* evidence on the putative linkages among the educational system, social class position, sociopolitical ideology, the persisting inequalities in American society, and the reality of large-scale changes in the status of blacks since World War II.

To say that racial and ethnic relations are inherently parts of more inclusive social systems may appear to be one of the simplest of platitudes. Yet a failure to take that statement seriously and specifically can lead and often does lead to massive distortions and lapses in understanding of interethnic relationships. Persisting controversies about the changing status of black Americans have centered upon the concepts of "race" versus "class." It is difficult to doubt that racial categorization is important, that stratification position in the Marxian sense is important, and that the two structural locations are strongly interactive. Unproductive arguments would be minimized if this view could be accepted, if both class and race were specified within the encompassing social system, and if empirical tests were more systematically applied to factual claims.

Consider how the position of a given ethnic/racial population (a "minority") in the United States is linked to the dynamic interrelations of major institutions. Political hegemony of a dominant grouping excludes the minority from voting and officeholding. As a consequence of lack of authority and influence, the minority is excluded from access to public services and facilities, including education. Inadequate education restricts economic opportunities. Poverty and unemployment and subjection to domination in menial work tend to produce unstable families and arbitrary parental authoritarianism. Residential segregation accentuates competitive deficits and concentrates a "culture of poverty." To the degree that these interrelated processes operate, stereotypes are encouraged and discrimination and segregation are facilitated. Resultant group-sanctioned prejudice reinforces political exclusion and economic discrimination. Consequent disruptive social conditions in the ethnic enclave generate political apathy, frequent intragroup violence, and endemic insecurity.

In the simplified model just sketched, the feedback loops continually recycle and thus reproduce the system. Were the model fully representative of the actual society, a suppressed minority could never break out of its position of political and economic disadvantage. In contrast, the history of real societies shows both impressive continuity and stability of ethnic stratification and numerous contrary processes that produce change. To better understand both is the challenge.

This chapter has had a modest aim: to present a limited and highly selective critical sketch of several apparently quite disparate lines of sociological and social psychological study. Our aim has been to locate descriptions and hypotheses within two encompassing contexts: (1) a complex, dynamic societal system having its own distinctive exigencies and constraints; (2) a cultural framework of beliefs and values—partially organized as ideologies—that stands in complex and changing relationships to the social system.

## Bibliography

Apostle, Richard A., Charles Y. Glock, Thomas Piazza, and Marijean Suelzle. 1983. *The anatomy of racial attitudes.* Berkeley: University of California Press.
Backman, Jerold G., and Patrick M. O'Malley. 1984. Black-white differences

in self-esteem: Are they affected by response styles? *American Journal of Sociology* 90:624–39.

Berelson, Bernard, and Gary A. Steiner. 1964. *Human behavior: An inventory of scientific findings*. New York: Harcourt Brace and World.

Blalock, Hubert M., Jr. 1967. *Toward a theory of minority-group relations*. New York: Wiley.

Brewer, Marilynn B., and Roderick M. Kramer. 1985. The psychology of intergroup attitudes and behavior. In Mark R. Rosenzweig and Lyman W. Porter, eds., *Annual review of psychology*, pp. 219–43. Palo Alto, Calif.: Annual Reviews, Inc.

Clark, M. L., and Willie Pearson, Jr. 1982. Racial stereotypes revisited. *International Journal of Intercultural Relations* 6:381–93.

Curtis, James, Martin Kuhn, and Ronald Lambert. 1976. Education and the pluralist perspective. R. A. Carlton et al., eds., *Education, change, and society: A sociology of Canadian education*, pp. 124–39. Toronto: Gage.

Ehrlich, Howard J. 1973. *The social psychology of prejudice*. New York: Wiley.

Francis, E. K. 1976. *Interethnic relations: An essay in sociological theory*. New York: Elsevier.

Harding, John, Bernard Kutner, Harold Proshansky, and Isidor Chein. 1954. Prejudice and ethnic relations. In Gardner Lindzey, ed., *Handbook of social psychology*, 2:1021–61. Reading, Mass.: Addison-Wesley.

Henriques, Julian, Wendy Hollway, Cathy Urwin, Couze Venn, and Valerie Walkerdine. 1984. *Changing the subject: Psychology, social regulation, and subjectivity*. London and New York: Methuen.

Hirschman, Charles. 1983. America's melting pot reconsidered. In Ralph H. Turner and James F. Short, Jr., eds., *Annual review of sociology*, 9:397–423. Palo Alto, Calif.: Annual Reviews.

Jackman, Mary R. 1978. General and applied tolerance: Does education increase commitment to racial integration? *American Journal of Political Science* 22:302–24.

Jackman, Mary R., and Michael J. Muha. 1984. Education and intergroup attitudes: Moral enlightenment, superficial democratic commitment, or ideological refinement? *American Sociological Review* 49:751–69.

Kerlinger, Fred N. 1984. *Liberalism and conservatism: The nature and structure of attitudes*. Hillsdale, N.J.: Erlbaum.

Le Vine, Robert A., and Donald T. Campbell. 1972. *Ethnocentrism: Theories of conflict, ethnic attitudes, and group behavior*. New York: Wiley.

Lipset, Seymour Martin, and W. Schneider. 1978. Racial equality in America. *New Society* 44:28–31.

Myrdal, Gunnar, with the assistance of Richard Sterner and Arnold Rose. 1944. *An American dilemma: The Negro problem and modern democracy*. Vols. 1 and 2. New York: Harper.

Olzak, Susan. 1983. Contemporary ethnic mobilization. In Ralph H. Turner and James F. Short, Jr., eds., *Annual review of sociology*, 9:355–74. Palo Alto, Calif.: Annual Reviews.

Patchen, Martin. 1982. *Black-white contact in schools: Its social and academic effects*. West Lafayette, Ind.: Purdue University Press.

Porter, Judith R., and Robert E. Washington. 1979. Black identity and self-esteem: A review of studies of black self-concept, 1968–1978. In Alex Inkeles, James Coleman, and Ralph H. Turner, eds., *Annual review of sociology*, 5:53–74. Palo Alto, Calif.: Annual Reviews.

Prager, Jeffrey. 1982. American racial ideology as collective representation. *Ethnic and Racial Studies* 5:99–119.

Rokeach, Milton. 1973. *The nature of human values.* New York: Free Press.

Rose, Arnold. 1947. *Studies in reduction of prejudice.* Chicago: American Council on Race Relations.

St. John, Nancy H. 1975. *School desegregation.* New York: Wiley.

Schermerhorn, R. A. 1970. *Comparative ethnic relations: A framework for theory and research.* New York: Random House.

Schuman, Howard, and Michael P. Johnson. 1976. Attitudes and behavior. In Alex Inkeles, James Coleman, and Neil Smelser, eds., *Annual review of sociology*, 2:161–207. Palo Alto, Calif.: Annual Reviews.

Schuman, Howard, Charlotte Steeh, and Lawrence Bobo. 1985. *Racial attitudes in America: Trends and interpretations.* Cambridge, Mass.: Harvard University Press.

Sears, D. O., C. P. Hensler, and L. Speer. 1979. Whites' opposition to busing: Self-interest or symbolic politics? *American Political Science Review* 73: 369–84.

Seeman, Melvin. 1981. Intergroup relations. In Morris Rosenberg and Ralph H. Turner, eds., *Social psychology*, pp. 378–410. New York: Basic Books.

Sidanius, Jim. 1984. Race and ideology in America: An exploratory study. Report no. 625, Department of Psychology, University of Stockholm.

Simpson, George Eaton, and J. Milton Yinger. 1985. *Racial and cultural minorities.* 5th ed. New York: Plenum.

Stouffer, Samuel A., et al. 1949. *The American soldier.* Vols. 1 and 2. Princeton, N.J.: Princeton University Press.

Taylor, Ronald L. 1979. Black ethnicity and the persistence of ethnogenesis. *American Journal of Sociology* 84:1401–23.

Thomas, William I., and Florian Znaniecki. 1918–20. *The Polish peasant in Europe and America.* 5 vols. Chicago: University of Chicago Press.

van den Berghe, Pierre. 1970. *Race and ethnicity: Essays in comparative sociology.* New York: Basic Books.

Williams, Robin M., Jr. 1947. *The reduction of intergroup tensions.* Bulletin 57. New York: Social Science Research Council.

———. 1964. *Strangers next door.* Englewood Cliffs, N.J.: Prentice-Hall.

———. 1970. *American society.* 3rd ed. New York: Knopf. (1st ed., 1951; 2nd ed., 1960.)

———. 1975. Race and ethnic relations. In Alex Inkeles, Neil Smelser, and James S. Coleman, eds., *Annual review of sociology*, 1:125–64. Palo Alto, Calif.: Annual Reviews.

———. 1977. *Mutual accommodation: Ethnic conflict and cooperation.* Minneapolis: University of Minnesota Press.

———. 1978. Intergroup relations: Problems of conflict and accommodation.

In T. Lynn Smith and Man Singh Das, eds., *Sociocultural change since 1950,* pp. 153–92. New Delhi: Vikas.

Williams, Robin M., Jr., and Margaret Ryan, eds. 1954. *Schools in transition.* Chapel Hill: University of North Carolina Press.

Wilson, Thomas C. 1985. Urbanism and tolerance: A test of some hypotheses drawn from Wirth and Stouffer. *American Sociological Review* 50:117–23.

# Robert B. Hill

## 16 Structural Discrimination: The Unintended Consequences of Institutional Processes

### Introduction

This nation is currently experiencing a "paradox" regarding the circumstances of blacks and other racial minorities. In spite of record-level government expenditures to combat unemployment and poverty, the racial gap in economic conditions was wider during the 1980s than it had been over a decade ago (Farley 1984; Hill 1981; Jones 1981). Between 1970 and 1982, for example, the unemployment rate for blacks increased from 1.7 to 2.4 times the white jobless rate, while the ratio of black to white family income dropped from 61 to 55 percent.

What are the reasons for this widening racial cleavage? Some observers attribute it to increased racism in America (Blauner 1972; National Advisory Commission on Civil Disorders 1968; Pinkney 1984). But national polls and surveys have shown sharp declines in negative racial attitudes among whites over the past four decades (Allport 1954; Hyman and Sheatsley 1956, 1964; Smith and Sheatsley 1984). Proponents of "symbolic racism" argue that these declines reflect not genuine reductions but greater sophistication on the part of whites in disguising their true feelings by attributing their hostility to "proxy" symbols, such as welfare, busing, open housing, and quotas (Jackman 1973; Kinder and Sears 1981; McConahay and Hough 1976; McConahay et al. 1981).

However, even if there has been a significant drop in prejudicial attitudes, it need not follow that there has been a similar decline in discriminatory behavior. Numerous studies of race relations have revealed wide discrepancies between attitudes and actions (Gross and

353

Niman 1975; LaPiere 1934; Linn 1965; O'Gorman 1975; Wicker 1969). On the other hand, reviews of the literature by Hyman and other analysts identify several innovative studies that obtained high correlations between prejudiced attitudes and discriminatory actions (DeFleur and Westie 1958; Hyman 1969).

I offer the hypothesis that the persistence of racial inequities today is due primarily to institutional structures and processes and only secondarily to individual prejudice and discrimination. This thesis was stated by Friedman (1975, p. 385) as follows:

Even more frequently, we observe patterns of black-white inequality which no one seems to have planned, or designed. The reduction of prejudice and legal discrimination over the past decades has not produced the across-the-board increases in equality folk wisdom would have us expect. In short, racial inequality seems to be becoming less dependent on individual choice. Rather than looking to the individual for the source of racial inequality, we must look to those forces which coordinate and direct individual attitudes and behavior in modern societies. Racial inequality, like economic depressions, must be explained in terms of the processes of human organization, their invisible laws and unique characteristics.

This perspective was also set forth by Williams (1977, p. 15) in his discussion of the impact of broad societal changes in the economy, technology, and population shifts on race and ethnic relations:

Many changes in intergroup relations, then, are due not to direct effects of actions intended to influence those relations but to indirect, unintended (and usually unanticipated) effects of actions undertaken for quite different reasons and under the influence of considerations far removed from race and ethnicity.

Consequently, I contend that the persisting racial cleavage in this nation is due, increasingly, to "structural discrimination," that is, the unintended adverse consequences of societal changes, events (such as recessions, inflation, urbanization, industrialization), and institutional policies (i.e., laws, edicts, and regulations in such areas as taxes, housing, employment, health, government, trade, immigration, etc.) on racial minorities. Two examples of structural discrimination due to societal changes in the area of employment are "cyclical" and "structural" unemployment:

Cyclical unemployment refers to a situation in which workers are laid off or can't find jobs because of a general economic recession and an overall shortage of jobs. Structural unemployment refers to a situation in which certain groups of workers cannot compete successfully in the labor market because of a deficiency of skills or education, a depressed regional economy, or discriminatory hiring practices. Such workers have difficulty finding satisfactory jobs even during periods of high overall employment. [U.S. Congress, Joint Economic Committee 1976]

Blacks are disproportionately laid off during recessionary or cyclical unemployment because of the seniority principle of "the last hired is the first fired." But they are also differentially affected by structural unemployment due to technological changes, because of their disadvantaged educational attainment, jobs skills, and racial characteristics.

An example of structural discrimination due to social policies is the law enacted by Congress in 1983 to raise the eligible age for retirement at full social security benefits to ages sixty-six and sixty-seven between 2000 and 2022. Since the overriding purpose of this policy change was to increase the solvency of the trust fund for all future retirees, it was racially neutral in intent. Nevertheless, it will have disparate adverse impact on minorities with lower life expectancies than whites—most especially, black males, whose current life expectancy of sixty-four years prevents most of them from receiving full retirement benefits today.

Because unintentional discrimination appears to be an important key to understanding the persistent patterns of racial inequality, it needs to be carefully examined. An in-depth assessment of the nature, causes, and consequences of structural discrimination may enhance interracial understanding and cooperation. It may help blacks to understand that not all discriminatory actions or policies are racially motivated. Traditionally, the civil rights movement has employed strategies to combat *intentional* discrimination—at both individual and group levels. Though this must continue to be an overriding goal, different tactics will be needed to combat the unintended but disparate adverse effects of societal trends and policies. Such an analysis may also help the American public and decision makers to realize that it is possible for racially neutral trends and policies to have racially discriminatory consequences. With this in mind, I attempt to answer the following questions:

1. Which societal changes and social policies have major unintended discriminatory consequences for racial minorities?

2. Which institutional structures and processes exacerbate and sustain structural discrimination?

3. What is the legal status of structural discrimination involving civil rights issues such as school segregation, employment bias, and voting disenfranchisement?

Before examining these questions, a brief review of pertinent theoretical formulations related to unintended adverse consequences will be undertaken. This essay will conclude with a brief consideration of strategies that policy makers and civil rights groups might adopt to prevent or minimize the disparate negative effects of social changes and policies on racial minorities.

## Unintended Adverse Consequences

The concept of "structural discrimination" is based mainly on Merton's analyses of latent functions and dysfunctions. His article, "The Unanticipated Consequences of Purposive Social Action," identifies several constraints and processes that lead social policies to have unintended and unanticipated effects (Merton 1936). In *Social Theory and Social Structure*, Merton (1957) went on to introduce the related concepts of "latent functions and dysfunctions"; the latter in order to take explicit account of unintended consequences that have adverse effects on subsystems or groups. This concept was later elaborated in his discussion of "latent social problems":

A major function of the sociologist, then, is to make latent social problems manifest. By discovering unwanted consequences of institutionalized arrangements, the sociologist inevitably becomes a social critic. . . . It allows us to examine social conditions in terms of their consequences for people diversely located in this society.

. . . by uncovering latent social problems and clarifying manifest ones, sociological inquiry helps make people accountable for the outcomes of their individual, collective and institutionalized actions. [Merton 1976, p. 14]

The concept of structural discrimination attempts to link Merton's analyses of latent functions and dysfunctions with his paradigm of prejudice and discrimination. In his essay, "Discrimination and the American Creed," Merton (1948) set forth a typology that yields four possible relationships between prejudiced attitudes and discriminatory behavior on the part of individuals: (I) the absence of both, (II) discrimination without prejudice, (III) prejudice without discrimination, and (IV) the presence of both. He refers to "Type II: the unprejudiced discriminator" as "fair-weather liberals." These unprejudiced individuals manifest discriminatory behavior when it is expedient to do so. Such individuals are said to be subjected to feelings of guilt and shame because of their conformity to pressure from prejudiced individuals and groups.

Yet Merton failed to identify instances of discrimination without prejudice that might not involve any feelings of guilt, that is, when unprejudiced persons engage in behavior that has unintended discriminatory consequences of which they are *unaware*. In short, some unprejudiced individuals might engage in *latent* discriminatory actions. Moreover, by transposing Merton's typology from the individual to the institutional level, Type II now encompasses our concept of structural discrimination—disparate adverse consequences of social structures that were unintended.

Although Merton's formulations provide the theoretical foundation for unintentional discrimination, this phenomenon has been identified most often in social science assessments of "institutional racism" (Carmichael and Hamilton 1967; Feagin 1978; Jones 1974; Shaw 1976). For example, Friedman (1975, pp. 386–87) characterizes institutional bias as follows:

When we speak of institutional racism, then, we mean *any action, policy, ideology or structure of an institution which works to the relative disadvantage of blacks as compared to whites, or to the relative advantage of whites as compared to blacks.* When the options allowed by the structure and function of institutions are exercised by one race so as to limit the choice of another, such operations constitute racism. Thus racism may be overt or covert, conscious or unconscious, intentional or unintentional, attitudinal or behavioral. It may be the result of malice or the best intentions; it may be based on the direct apprehension of the race of a person or group, or it may be based on criteria only peripherally related to race; it may be the result of no more than apathy, ignorance and inertia.

Similarly, Pettigrew (1973, p. 275), notes:

Institutional racism avidly supports individual racism. . . . racist institutions need not be headed by racists or designed with racist intentions to limit black choices. Indeed, it makes little difference to Black Americans what the formal intentions are, for the restrictive consequences are the same.

And Baron (1969, pp. 142–43) observes:

*Maintenance of the basic racial controls is now less dependent upon specific discriminatory decisions. Such behavior has become so well institutionalized that the individual generally does not have to exercise a choice to operate in a racist manner. The rules and procedures of the large organization have already prestructured the choice.* The individual only has to conform to the operating norms of the organization and the institution will do the discriminating for him.

But it is Feagin who has gone farthest in applying the distinction between intentional ("direct") and unintentional ("indirect") discrimination at the institutional level in his studies (Feagin 1978; Feagin and Feagin 1978) of racial, ethnic, and sex discrimination:

*direct institutionalized discrimination,* refers to organizationally-prescribed or community-prescribed actions that by intention have a differential and negative impact on members of subordinate race and ethnic groups. Typically, these actions are not episodic or sporadic, but are continually and routinely carried out by a large number of individuals guided by the norms of a large-scale organization or community. . . .

*indirect institutionalized discrimination,* refers to practices having a negative and differential impact on members of subordinate race and ethnic groups even though the organizationally-prescribed or community-prescribed norms or regulations guiding these actions were established, and are carried out, with no intent to harm the members of those groups. [Feagin 1978, pp. 15–16]

The pre-Reagan U.S. Commission on Civil Rights also distinguished between intentional and unintentional discrimination in several of its works (U.S. Commission on Civil Rights 1981). More specifically, it identified three types of discrimination: individual, organizational, and structural:

*Individual Discrimination* . . . Although open and intentional prejudice per-sists, individual discriminatory conduct is often hidden and sometimes un-intentional. . . . unintentionally discriminatory actions [are] taken by persons who may not believe themselves to be prejudiced but whose decisions con-tinue to be guided by deeply ingrained discriminatory customs. . . .

*Organizational Discrimination* . . . Discrimination, though prescribed by indi-viduals, is often reinforced by the well established rules, policies and practices of organizations. These actions are often regarded simply as part of the orga-nization's way of doing business and are carried out by individuals as just part of their day's work. . . .

*Structural Discrimination* . . . Such self-sustaining ("organizational") discrimi-natory processes occur not only within the fields of employment, education, housing, and government but also between these structural areas. There is a classic cycle of structural discrimination that reproduces itself. [U.S. Commis-sion on Civil Rights 1981, pp. 35–36]

The commission's use of the term "structural discrimination" is anal-ogous to Feagin's "side-effect" or indirect institutional discrimination; that is, it refers to the impact that discrimination (often intentional) in one sector (such as education) has on the denial of equal opportunity in another sector (such as employment) (Feagin 1978). But "side-effect" bias is only a subset of our concept of structural discrimination, since we also encompass unintentional "organizational" discrimina-tion—occurring within the same sector—in our operational defini-tion of structural discrimination. Thus, our terminology is consistent with Mayhew's (1968) distinction between intentional and uninten-tional ("structural") institutionalized discrimination in his study of the work of the Massachusetts Commission Against Discrimination.

It is essential, however, to underscore the fact that many unin-tended consequences of structural discrimination are anticipatable and acceptable. For example, the differential impact of raising the eligible age for social security benefits on minorities may be undesirable but tolerable in order to insure the solvency of the trust fund for future generations. Similarly, many legislators may consider the disproportionate effects on minorities of recent budget cuts in social programs to be a necessary and acceptable short-term evil for the long-term good of the American economy.

And, to the extent that specific public policies have positive consequences for the majority, any negative side effects for minorities are likely to be ignored or tolerated. Furthermore, since most decision makers define only *intended* harmful effects on minorities as racism or discrimination, they do not feel a moral or legal obligation to mitigate unintended side effects of public policies. It is for these and related reasons that civil rights and other advocates for minorities and the poor will have to adopt different strategies to combat the unintended consequences of institutional processes and policies in the coming decades.

I shall identify key societal changes and social policies that have unintended adverse consequences for racial minorities. Then I shall describe the institutional structures and processes that make for structural discrimination.

## Forms of Structural Discrimination

To facilitate our discussion of the forms and processes of structural discrimination, I introduce the paradigm depicted in Figure 16.1. This typology relates the negative ("discrimination") and positive ("benevolence") effects of institutional patterns on racial minorities to the state of underlying intentions. Four types of institutional bias are revealed; intentional discrimination, unintentional discrimination, intentional benevolence, and unintentional benevolence.

### Intentional Discrimination

Intentional institutional discrimination is overt or covert. The overt form refers to discrimination involving the mistreatment of minorities on *explicitly* racial and ethnic grounds. Examples include: slavery, the subjugation of blacks after emancipation through the Black Codes, and the imposition of de jure segregation in all aspects of southern life after Reconstruction (Woodward 1966).

Covert intentional discrimination refers to differential adverse treatment of minorities based on criteria which, though nonracial, strongly correlate with race. Thus, such discrimination is a kind of "patterned evasion," that is, the deliberate use of racial "proxies" to deny equal opportunities to minorities. The "grandfather clauses," lit-

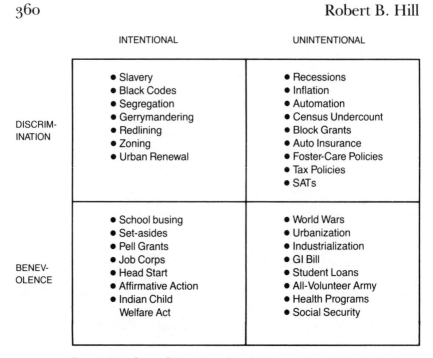

|  | INTENTIONAL | UNINTENTIONAL |
|---|---|---|
| DISCRIM-INATION | • Slavery<br>• Black Codes<br>• Segregation<br>• Gerrymandering<br>• Redlining<br>• Zoning<br>• Urban Renewal | • Recessions<br>• Inflation<br>• Automation<br>• Census Undercount<br>• Block Grants<br>• Auto Insurance<br>• Foster-Care Policies<br>• Tax Policies<br>• SATs |
| BENEV-OLENCE | • School busing<br>• Set-asides<br>• Pell Grants<br>• Job Corps<br>• Head Start<br>• Affirmative Action<br>• Indian Child<br>  Welfare Act | • World Wars<br>• Urbanization<br>• Industrialization<br>• GI Bill<br>• Student Loans<br>• All-Volunteer Army<br>• Health Programs<br>• Social Security |

FIGURE 16.1. *A Typology of Intentional and Unintentional Discrimination and Benevolence.*

eracy tests, and poll taxes are early examples of such patterned evasions in the area of voting rights (Myrdal 1944; Woodward 1966). More recently, many jurisdictions—in the North and South—interested in diluting the voting impact of minorities have found it expedient to use such devices as at-large elections, run-off primaries, and gerrymandering. Many of these electoral procedures have been declared invalid by local and federal courts as *intentionally* racially discriminatory (Simpson and Yinger 1985). It should be made clear, however, that many run-off primaries and at-large election districts were not established with the intent of undermining the voting power of racial minorities, although they may have such consequences.

Examples of covert intentional discrimination abound in other areas as well. Numerous court cases have uncovered intentional discriminatory actions by local authorities concerning: (*a*) urban renewal that resulted in the differential dislocation of racial minorities from their homes and communities; (*b*) redlining, that is, the differential refusal by banks, insurance companies, and so on, to grant home mortgage loans, commercial credit, and insurance for fire, property, and automobile coverage to racial minorities living in designated ("redlined") neighborhoods and communities; and (*c*) zoning, that is, the differential denial of housing options to racial minorities due to zoning ordinances prohibiting low-income and multifamily dwellings in predominantly white communities (Heimer 1982; Newman et al. 1978; Pettigrew 1975). Once again, however, it should be emphasized that not *all* instances of urban renewal or zoning are intentionally discriminatory.

Covert intentional discrimination is also manifested through (*a*) dilatory tactics (such as tokenism, the formation of study commissions, and laxity in complying with or enforcing civil rights laws or affirmative action guidelines), and (*b*) differential withholding of important information about program eligibility from racial minorities. An example of the latter bias is reflected in the widespread lack of knowledge among low-income blacks and other minorities about the existence of an important welfare program for poor two-parent families—Aid to Families with Dependent Children of Unemployed Parents (Levitan 1980). Although the AFDC-UP program has been in existence since 1961 (when it was set up for poor families with jobless fathers), most poor black and Hispanic families (as well as the general American public) are aware only of the regular AFDC program (for which unemployed fathers are not eligible). The sharp underrepresentation of unemployed black fathers on the AFDC-UP rolls suggests some intentional racial discrimination by local welfare agencies (Hill 1981).

## Unintentional Discrimination

Unintentional or structural discrimination comprises two institutional patterns: societal changes and social policies. Examples of societal trends having differential adverse effects on minorities are provided by recessions, automation, and inflation. Because of their relatively low and fixed incomes, minorities are affected by inflation more adversely than whites (Cross 1984). And, since automation results in a larger reduction in lower-skilled jobs compared to higher-skilled ones, minorities are affected disproportionately (Johnson 1932; Randolph 1931). It should be emphasized, however, that during certain periods of this nation's history, some technological changes (especially the shift from agriculture to manufacturing) have had disproportionately *favorable* effects by way of upgrading the occupations of blacks. I shall elaborate on such positive latent consequences in the discussion of "unintentional benevolence," below.

Social policies that have unintentional adverse effects on minorities include (*a*) the allocation of legislative seats and federal aid to localities based on census figures with a differential black undercount; (*b*) the distribution of funds to states and local areas through block rather than categorical grants; (c) social work practices that result in minority children remaining in foster care for longer periods of time than white children; (d) tax policies favoring middle- and upper-income individuals over low-income persons; and (e) the use of scores on the Scholastic Aptitude Test (SAT) as a primary criterion for college admissions (Boyd 1977).

## Intentional Benevolence

The typology in Figure 16.1 reminds us that societal institutions can have disparate *positive* as well as adverse effects on minorities. Thus, as Merton (1957, p. 51) noted, it is important to examine the "net balance" of positive *and* negative consequences. Consider, then, some circumstances in which societal changes and policies have various favorable consequences for minorities both intended and unintended.

Intentional benevolence refers to policies, practices, and actions of institutions and organizations that are designed to have disproportionate beneficial effects on minorities. Examples of deliberate benevolence include: (a) the busing of minority children to predominantly white schools in order to enhance school integration; (b) "set-aside" programs to increase the number of awards of government contracts to minority businesses; (c) federal scholarships, such as Pell grants, designed to help youth from low-income families attend college; (d) Job Corps, one of the original "War on Poverty" programs designed to provide remedial education and marketable job skills to minority youth from inner-city areas; (e) Head Start, another "Great Society" program designed to provide quality preschool learning and development experiences for low-income and minority children; (f) the Indian Child Welfare Act, passed in 1980 to insure that American Indian children in need of foster care would be placed within their extended families or tribes; and (g) affirmative action, which includes goals, timetables, guidelines, quotas, et cetera, that are designed to insure good-faith compliance with provision of equal opportunities for minorities (Levitan 1980; Newman et al. 1978).

## Unintentional Benevolence

Unintentional benevolence refers to societal trends and institutional policies that have differential positive effects on minorities, though not explicitly designed to do so. For example, World Wars I and II accelerated the occupational mobility of blacks. The shortages of labor during both wars forced American industries to hire blacks (as well as women) in positions closed to them during peacetime—and in large part, after those wars (Johnson 1932; Newman et al. 1978). The shift from agriculture to manufacturing between 1890 and 1940 induced large-scale migration of blacks (from rural to urban areas and from the South to the North and West) that greatly raised the occupational and earnings levels of blacks as they moved from farm to factory jobs (Randolph 1931).

Government policies that have had unintended, disparate favorable effects on racial minorities include the GI bill, guaranteed student loans, the all-volunteer army, Medicare and social security cost-of-living adjustments (COLAs) (Newman et al. 1978). The GI bill and special financial aid programs for college students, for example, facilitated access to higher education for thousands of minority and low-income youth (Levitan 1980). Moreover, the sharp decline in poverty among the black elderly during the 1970s was due, in large part, to the institution of COLAs that kept social security pensions abreast with spiraling inflation. As a result, some black aged had higher and more stable incomes during retirement than throughout their years of work (Hill 1983). Clearly, the structural sources and processes of unintentional benevolence merit further study. However, in the rest of this essay, I will restrict my discussion to an assessment of structural mechanisms that exacerbate and sustain unintentional discrimination.

## Processes of Structural Discrimination

The institutional mechanisms that exacerbate and sustain unintentional discrimination are normative and structural (Mayhew 1968). The key normative factor is the dominant-group ideology, and the main structural factor is social stratification. Each of these variously facilitates the operation of structural discrimination.

### Dominant Ideology

Dominant ideology refers to sets of values, beliefs, and norms of dominant groups that are used to legitimate and justify current dominant-subordinate group relations. As Jackman and Muha (1984, p. 759) note, such an ideology need not be malicious in intent:

Dominant groups develop such an ideology without contrivance; it flows naturally from their side of experience as they seek to impose a sense of order on the pattern of social relations and to persuade both themselves and their subordinates that the current organization of relationships is appropriate and equitable.

Dominant-group ideology facilitates structural discrimination when it assigns high priority to values or norms that impede the advancement of minority groups. As Jackman and Muha (1984, p. 760) observe, for example, undue emphasis on individualism may hinder the progress of minorities:

The problem is that when the members of one group operate from a disadvantaged position, the principle of individualism does little to promote their advancement and it often stands as an obstacle . . . because it does not correct for systematic inequalities that exist in resources, access to information and general political knowledge, all of which predetermine the ability of different groups to participate effectively. . . .
Yet individualism provides a general, privileged, seemingly neutral basis for the rejection of aggregate group demands. The rights of the individual are endorsed vehemently, as there is a systematic aversion to any representation of social problems in group terms. . . . By upholding individualism as a guiding principle in the empirical and normative interpretation of social life, the rights of *groups* are thus rendered illegitimate and unreasonable.

The conflict between individual and group rights is at the core of such controversial issues as affirmative action, welfare, busing, and standardized testing. Proponents of "symbolic racism" contend that dominant-group ideology diverts attention from group grievances by upholding such values as self-sufficiency and individual merit. In fact, the notion of "reverse discrimination" is based on the assumed violation of the rights of white individuals in favor of the rights of minority groups.

Strong emphasis on "color blindness" by dominant-group ideology can also contribute to the perpetuation of racial inequities. Mayhew (1968, p. 67) observes how color-blind policies in the area of employment facilitate structural discrimination:

The demand for equal treatment led to considerable business acceptance of the obligation to be color blind. One factor that supported acceptance of this obligation was the discovery on the part of business that a change in attitude and policy in the upper echelons does not usually upset the status quo. A color-blind management can let the established social structure do the work of discrimination, leaving clear consciences. Color blindness does lead to some change. . . . But change will be gradual because mere color blindness permits many of the forces of the status quo to continue operation. *Structural* or *passive* discrimination remains.

Color blindness is invariably accompanied by norms prescribing universalistic criteria for all individuals and groups, regardless of race or ethnicity. Yet as Mayhew notes, "An unprejudiced person can apply standards in a completely universalistic and equitable manner and still exclude Negroes" (1968, p. 57). Racial inequalities are reinforced when one uses universalistic qualifications to which nonwhites have less access than whites. Examples of such standards include seniority, neighborhood school attendance zones, standardized test scores for college admission, and other unequally distributed qualifying criteria.

Another example of the role of dominant-group ideology in sustaining structural discrimination is the "deficit model"—an intellectual perspective that attributes the social problems of minority and low-income groups to internal rather than to external factors. It is popularly known as the "blaming-the-victim" syndrome. As Valentine (1968, p. 18) observes, this ideology has a long tradition:

> [These are] doctrines that point to presumed defects in the mentality of behavior of disadvantaged classes, then go on to explain their social position and deprivation as resulting from their internal deficiencies. There is of course a long philosophical evolution behind the modern emergence of those doctrines.

The deficit perspective is reflected in studies that attribute high unemployment rates among racial minorities to psychological deficiencies (such as low self-esteem or lack of work ethic) without examining such external factors as a shortage of jobs or employment discrimination (Auletta 1982). The blaming-the-victim syndrome is also exemplified by analyses that identify the female-headed family structure as the "principle source" of the "tangle of pathology" in the black community without assessing the impact of such factors as periodic recessions, inflation, or the suburbanization of jobs (Rainwater and Yancey 1967, p. 76). The deficit model exempts the dominant society of any responsibility for sustaining the disadvantages of minorities by identifying the need for change in minority individuals and groups and not in dominant-group institutions, structures, or policies (Coe 1982).

## Social Stratification

Social stratification refers to the differential ranking of individuals and groups in a hierarchy on the basis of power, property, and prestige (Duberman 1976). Since it distributes these scarce resources unequally, social stratification is a form of institutionalized inequality found in all societies (Miller and Roby 1970). Individuals and groups occupying different positions in the hierarchy have unequal life chances and opportunities to achieve societal goals and rewards.

Three forms of stratification have special relevance for aiding structural discrimination: class, racial-ethnic, and sectoral. Class stratification involves differential ranking of individuals and groups, regardless of race or ethnicity, on the basis of power, property, and prestige. The most frequently used groupings of class strata probably are upperclass, middle-class, working-class, and lower-class. Racial-ethnic stratification refers to the differential ranking of groups on the basis of their racial or ethnic affiliation. Key racial-ethnic strata are commonly classified (in order of increasing disadvantaged) as (*a*) white Protestants ("WASPs"); (*b*) white Catholics and Jews ("white ethnics"); (*c*) Asians and Hispanic whites; and (*d*) Hispanic blacks, non-Hispanic blacks, and native Americans (Barron 1957; Hill 1975). The convergence of class and ethnic stratification accounts, in part, for the greater disadvantages of certain middle-class minorities compared with middle-class and often with working-class whites on various social and economic indicators (Cross 1984).

Sectoral stratification refers to the differential ranking of subsectors within major institutional areas, such as employment, housing, education, health, and so on. The most widely studied form of sectoral stratification has been "dual labor markets," which Baron (1969, p. 146) describes as follows:

> In practice, the metropolitan labor market consists of two sectors: a primary job market in which firms recruit white workers and white workers look for jobs and a smaller secondary market in which firms recruit black workers and black workers look for jobs. There are distinct sets of demand and supply forces determining earnings and occupational distribution in each for the white and black sectors of the job markets; the two sectors also differ as to practices and procedures for the recruitment, hiring, training and promotion of workers.

Primary and secondary subsectors can be identified in other institutional areas as well. The primary subsectors are characterized by (*a*) high representation of whites and (*b*) goods and services for which middle- and upper-income groups are the primary recipients. Secondary subsectors, on the other hand, are characterized by (*a*) high representation of minorities and (*b*) goods and services for which low-income groups are the primary recipients (Cross 1984).

### *"Past-in-present" Discrimination*

As Feagin and Feagin (1978) observe, unintentional (or "indirect") discrimination can operate through one of two means: "past-in-present" or "side effects." Past-in-present discrimination refers to racially "neutral" practices in an institutional area that indirectly have differential negative impact on minorities because of past intentional discrimination in the same institutional area. For example, the long history of de jure segregation that restricted blacks to separate and *unequal* subsectors in education for hundreds of years contributes to their lower performance relative to whites on most standardized tests today (Boyd 1977; Cross 1984). Similarly, the inadequate health care received by blacks in secondary subsectors of health care in the past is partly responsible for their lower life expectancies—and fewer years of *full* retirement social security benefits—relative to whites today (Hill 1983; Newman et al. 1978).

## "Side-Effect" Discrimination

Side-effect discrimination refers to practices in an institutional area that have an unintentional adverse impact on minorities because they are linked to intentional or unintentional discriminatory practices in another institutional area. For example, intentional discrimination in the field of higher education may impede minority access to higher-paying jobs because minorities lack the proper educational credentials (Cole and Cole 1973; Morris 1979). Similarly, residential (de jure or de facto) segregation of minorities in central cities may prevent them from attaining quality education or good jobs in suburban areas (Friedman 1975).

Myrdal (1944) refers to the side-effect phenomenon as the "vicious circle" or "the principle of cumulation." According to this thesis, since institutional areas are interlocked with one another, the disadvantages (or advantages) of groups in one area are likely to contribute to their disadvantages (or advantages) in another area. For example, low education is likely to be linked with low-paying jobs which, in turn, are likely to be linked with substandard housing which, in turn, is likely to be linked with inferior education, which repeats the cycle once again.

The vicious circle is one manifestation of Merton's (1948, 1957) "self-fulfilling prophecy." In the past, whites justified racial discrimination on the basis of inferior achievements of blacks. Denying blacks opportunities to improve their status in turn makes for lower average achievements, which are then used as grounds for further denial of equality. Thus, side-effect discrimination is one of the most frequent mediums for structural discrimination, since groups who are largely confined to secondary subsectors in one institutional area are likely to be concentrated in inferior subsectors in other areas as well.

## The Matthew Effect

A related process that may facilitate structural discrimination is the "Matthew effect," a phenomenon that Merton (1968) identified from the following passage in the Gospel according to Saint Matthew: "For unto every one that hath shall be given, and he shall have abundance; but from him that hath not shall be taken away even that which he hath." In short, Merton sought to apply the notion of "the rich get richer while the poor get poorer" to stratification in the field of science. According to the principle of "accumulative advantage," scientists of high status and prestige are more likely to obtain additional resources and rewards for their research than scientists of low status. Many scholars—notably Allison (1976), Cole and Cole (1973), and Zuckerman (1972)—have attempted to examine the degree of empirical support for the notion of "accumulative disadvantage" as well. For example, Cole and Cole observe (1973, pp. 146–47):

Critics of the reward system of science hypothesize that women scientists suffer from the processes of accumulating disadvantage. Once denied access to resources and facilities, they are forever more involved in a struggle simply to reach parity with their male colleagues. Harriet Zuckerman has recently referred to this process as the "principle of the double penalty," a principle which holds that groups like blacks and women not only suffer from direct discrimination but also from the second penalty of being placed initially into second-rate structural positions which make it almost impossible for them to produce the outstanding work that is necessary for moving out of such positions.

A major distinction between the Matthew effect and the vicious-circle hypothesis is that the former focuses on cumulative advantages and disadvantages in one institutional sphere whereas the latter emphasizes reinforcing advantages and disadvantages between institutional areas. More research is needed to determine the extent to which the Matthew effect sustains structural discrimination against racial minorities (Blau and Schwartz 1984).

## Legal Status

What is the legal status of structural discrimination? To what extent are policies and actions that have unintentional discriminatory consequences considered unconstitutional? The issue of "intent" versus "effects" continues to generate much controversy in all branches of government.

In the area of school segregation, the U.S. Supreme Court has refused to declare de facto school segregation (i.e., racial isolation resulting from racially segregated neighborhoods) unconstitutional, unless direct evidence of racially discriminatory intent by school authorities is available (Graglia 1980). In the first "northern" case, *Keyes* v. *School District No. 1*, Denver, Colorado (1973), to reach the court, the Supreme Court ordered citywide busing to achieve racial balance. Nevertheless, it retained the de jure/de facto distinction by requiring the elimination of only that segregation resulting from school-related actions. In his concurring opinion in *Keyes*, however, Justice Douglas attacked the de facto/de jure distinction by quoting Judge Wisdom in an earlier case: "when school authorities by their actions contribute to segregation in education, whether by any additional segregation or maintaining existing segregation, they deny to the students equal protection of the law" (Sullivan 1983, p. 273). Thus, Douglas argued that the act of imposing attendance zones on racially segregated neighborhoods automatically implicated the school authorities in racial discrimination. Although this view has been adopted by many lower courts, it has not prevailed in any of the Supreme Court's subsequent cases involving de facto segregation without proof of discriminatory intent.

The initial breakthrough for advocates of the "effects" standard—regardless of intent—was in the area of employment discrimination in the *Griggs* v. *Duke Power Co.* (1971) case. In *Griggs*, the U.S. Supreme Court declared that the company's employment tests, which had a disparate adverse impact on the hiring and promotion of minority workers, was a constitutional violation. However, the unconstitutionality was found not in the tests' disproportionate impact but in the lack of relevance in their content to actual job performance. Nevertheless, in a later case, *Washington* v. *Davis,* the Court of Appeals declared employment tests for police officers in the District of Columbia to be discriminatory—solely because of their disproportionate impact on black policemen. That decree was reversed by the Supreme Court (1973), which mainly found that the lower court erred in not providing evidence of discriminatory intent and/or lack of relevance to job performance.

The greatest consensus in support of the "effects" standard exists among the courts—and Congress—in the area of voting rights. The courts at all levels have declared various forms of electoral procedures (e.g., at-large elections, run-off primaries, and multimember districts) unconstitutional because of their disparate adverse impact on minority political participation.

In 1980, a setback occurred in *Mobile* v. *Bolden,* when the Supreme Court refused to declare an at-large election unconstitutional because discriminatory intent had not been proven. In order to prevent similar decisions in the future, the U.S. Congress inserted an "effects" amendment in its renewal of the Voting Rights Act on June 18, 1982. Consequently, in 1985, a federal judge declared run-off primaries in New York City unconstitutional—even though the original 1972 law had not been designed to have such consequences.

## Conclusions and Implications

The persisting social and economic cleavages between whites and nonwhites in America cannot be explained solely in terms of intentional discrimination by individuals, groups, or institutions. Unintentional racially discriminatory consequences of societal changes (such as recessions, inflation, technological changes, etc.) and social policies (in such areas as employment, housing, taxes, social welfare, health, etc.) are additional major contributing factors in need of further study.

Consequently, civil rights groups will have to employ strategies tailored to counteract the effects of unintentional discrimination, while they continue to use traditional methods to eliminate intentional discrimination. For example, they should give serious consideration to employing tactics involving the use of "nonracial" proxies (in such areas as taxes, health, business development, etc.) that may convert unintentional discrimination into unintentional benevolence. For example, the newly formed Council for a Black Economic Agenda places top priority on enacting tax and other policies that reinforce innovative community-based efforts to create jobs for inner-city youths and adults, stimulate black business formation, allow residents to manage their public housing projects, permit welfare recipients to develop day-care cooperatives, and reduce the number of minority children in foster care by increasing incentives to use informal extended family networks.

Since most decision makers feel little obligation to redress the unintentional consequences of their actions for minorities, different approaches may be needed for different types of policy makers. For example, information and moral suasion may be effective for the "fair-weather liberals"—unprejudiced persons who enact discriminatory policies when it is expedient or when they are unaware of the negative effects on minorities. Administrators and legislators who are genuinely interested in reducing racial inequities may modify such policies after being informed of their adverse side effects.

However, more coercion may be needed for the "all-weather illiberals"—decision makers who are passionately antiminority and antipoor. Further litigation may be needed to persuade the courts and Congress to expand the scope of the "effects" standard beyond voting rights to include de facto (school and residential) segregation and employment discrimination.

Finally, civil rights advocates might insist that federal, state, and local governments conduct "impact analyses" for minorities and low-income groups somewhat similar to risk assessments of the effects of technology on the environment. Clearly, a concerted effort is needed by all segments of American society in order to reduce structural discrimination against racially and economically disadvantaged groups.

# Bibliography

Allison, Paul D. 1976. *Processes of stratification in science*. New York: Arno Press, 1980.

Allport, Gordon W. 1954. *The nature of prejudice*. Reading, Mass.: Addison-Wesley.

Auletta, Ken. 1982. *The underclass*. New York: Random House.

Baron, Harold M. 1969. The web of urban racism. In Louis L. Knowles and Kenneth Prewitt, eds., *Institutional racism in America*, pp. 134–76. Englewood Cliffs, N.J.: Prentice-Hall.

Barron, Milton L. 1957. *American minorities*. New York: Knopf.

Blau, Peter M., and Joseph E. Schwartz. 1984. *Crosscutting social circles: Testing a macrostructural theory of intergroup relations*. New York: Academic Press.

Blauner, Robert. 1972. *Racial oppression in America*. New York: Harper and Row.

Bogardus, Emory S. 1959. Racial distance changes in the U.S. during the past thirty years. *Sociology and Social Research* 43:286–90.

Boyd, William. 1977. SAT's and minorities: The danger of underprediction. *Change*, November, 9:48–49, 64.

Carmichael, Stokeley, and Charles Hamilton. 1967. *Black power*. New York: Random House (Vintage Books).

Coe, Richard D. 1982. Welfare dependency: Fact or myth? *Challenge* 25: 43–49.

Cole, Jonathan, and Stephen Cole. 1973. *Social stratification in science*. Chicago: University of Chicago Press.

Cross, Theodore. 1984. *The black power imperative*. New York: Faulkner.

Davidson, Mary. 1983. Achieving simple justice: Identifying discrimination in the delivery of social services. *Journal of Intergroup Relations* 11:3–22.

DeFleur, M. L., and F. R. Westie. 1958. Verbal attitudes and overt acts: An experiment on the salience of attitudes. *American Sociological Review* 23: 667–73.

Duberman, Lucile. 1976. *Social inequality: Class and caste in America*. Philadelphia: Lippincott.

Farley, Reynolds. 1984. *Blacks and whites: Narrowing the gap?* Cambridge, Mass: Harvard University Press.

Fasman, Zachary, and R. Theodore Clark. 1974. Non-discriminatory discrimination: An overview of the discrimination problem. *Journal of Intergroup Relations* 3:25–44.

Feagin, Joe R. 1978. *Racial and ethnic relations*. Englewood Cliffs, N.J.: Prentice-Hall.

Feagin, Joe R., and Clairece B. Feagin. 1978. *Discrimination American style: Institutional racism and sexism*. Englewood Cliffs, N.J.: Prentice-Hall.

Frazier, E. Franklin. 1926. Three scourges of the Negro family. *Opportunity* 4:210–13, 234.

———. 1931. Family disorganization among Negroes. *Opportunity* 9:204–7.

Friedman, Robert. 1975. Institutional racism: How to discriminate without really trying. In Thomas F. Pettigrew, ed., *Racial discrimination in the U.S.*, pp. 384–407. New York: Harper and Row.

Graglia, Lino A. 1980. From prohibiting segregation to requiring integration. In Walter G. Stephen and Joe R. Feagin, eds., *School desegregation*, pp. 69–96. New York: Plenum.

Gross, Steven J., and C. Michael Niman. 1975. Attitude-behavior consistency: A review. *Public Opinion Quarterly* 39:358–68.

Harris, Louis, and Associates. 1978. *A study of attitudes towards racial and religious minorities and toward women.* New York: National Conference of Christians and Jews.

Heimer, Carol A. 1982. The racial and organizational origins of insurance redlining. *Journal of Intergroup Relations* 10:42–60.

Hiestand, Dale L. 1964. *Economic growth and employment opportunities.* New York: Columbia University Press.

Hill, Robert B. 1975. Who are more prejudiced: WASP's or white ethnics? *Urban League Review* 1:26–29.

———. 1981. *Economic policies and black progress.* Washington, D.C.: National Urban League Research Department.

———. 1983. Income maintenance programs and the minority elderly. In R. L. McNeely and John L. Colen, eds., *Aging in minority groups*, pp. 195–211. Beverly Hills, Calif.: Sage.

———. 1984. The polls and ethnic minorities. *Annals* 472:155–66.

Jackman, Mary R. 1973. Education and prejudice or education and response set? *American Sociological Review* 38:327–39.

Jackman, Mary R., and Michael J. Muha. 1984. Education and intergroup attitudes. *American Sociological Review* 49:751–69.

Johnson, Charles S. 1932. The new frontier of Negro labor. *Opportunity* 10:168–73.

Jones, Faustine A. 1981. External crosscurrents and internal diversity: An assessment of black progress, 1960–1980. *Daedalus* 110:71–101.

Jones, James M. 1972. *Prejudice and racism.* Reading, Mass.: Addison-Wesley.

Jones, Terry. 1974. Institutional racism in the United States. *Social Work* 19:218–25.

Kendall, Diane, and Joe R. Feagin. 1983. Blatant and subtle patterns of discrimination: Minority women in medical schools. *Journal of Intergroup Relations* 11:8–33.

Killingsworth, Charles C. 1966. Structural unemployment in the U.S. In Jack Steiber, ed., *Employment problems of automation and advanced technology*, pp. 128–55. New York: St. Martin's Press.

Kinder, D. R., and David O. Sears. 1981. Prejudice and politics: Symbolic racism versus racial threats to the good life. *Journal of Personality and Social Psychology* 40:414–31.

LaPiere, Robert T. 1934. Attitudes vs. actions. *Social Forces* 13:230–37.

Lehner, J. Christopher, Jr. 1980. *A losing battle: The decline in black participation in graduate and professional education.* Washington, D.C.: National Advisory Committee on Black Higher Education and Black Colleges and Universities.

Levitan, Sar A. 1980. *Programs in aid of the poor for the 1980's.* Baltimore: Johns Hopkins University Press.

Linn, L. S. 1965. Verbal attitudes and overt behavior: A study of racial discrimination. *Social Forces* 43:353–64.

Lohman, Joseph D., and Dietrich C. Reitzes. 1952. Note on race relations in mass society. *American Journal of Sociology* 58:240–46.

Marrett, Cora B., and Cheryl Leggon, eds. 1979. *Research in race and ethnic relations*. Greenwich, Conn.: JAI Press.

Mayer, Robert R. 1979. *Social science and institutional change*. Washington, D.C.: U.S. Public Health Service, National Institute of Mental Health.

Mayhew, Leon H. 1968. *Law and equal opportunity: A study of the Massachusetts Commission Against Discrimination*. Cambridge, Mass.: Harvard University Press.

McConahay, John B., and J. S. Hough, Jr. 1976. Symbolic racism. *Journal of Social Issues* 32:23–45.

McConahay, John B., et al. 1981. Has racism declined in America? *Journal of Conflict Resolution* 25:563–79.

Merton, Robert K. 1936. The unanticipated consequences of purposive social action. *American Sociological Review* 1:894–904.

———. 1942. The normative structure of science. Reprinted in Robert K. Merton, *The sociology of science*. Chicago: University of Chicago Press, 1973.

———. 1948. Discrimination and the American creed. In R. M. MacIver, ed., *Discrimination and the national welfare*, pp. 99–126. New York: Harper.

———. 1957. Social theory and social structure. Rev. ed. Glencoe, Ill.: Free Press.

———. 1968. The Matthew effect in science. *Science* 159:56–63.

———. 1972. Insiders and outsiders: A chapter in the sociology of knowledge. *American Journal of Sociology* 78:9–47.

———. 1976. The sociology of social problems. In Robert K. Merton and Robert Nisbet, eds., *Contemporary social problems*, pp. 5–43. New York: Harcourt Brace Jovanovich.

———. 1984. Texts, contexts, and subtexts: An epistolary foreword. In Louis Schneider, *The grammar of social relations*, ed. Jay Weinstein, pp. ix–xiv. New Brunswick, N.J.: Transaction Books.

Miller, S. M., and Pamela Roby. 1970. *The future of inequality*. New York: Basic Books.

Morris, Lorenzo. 1979. *Elusive equality: The status of black Americans in higher education*. Washington, D.C.: Howard University Press.

Murray, Charles. 1984. *Losing ground*. New York: Basic Books.

Myrdal, Gunnar. 1944. *An American dilemma: The Negro problem and modern democracy*. Vols. 1 and 2. New York: Harper and Brothers.

National Advisory Commission on Civil Disorders. 1968. *Report of the National Advisory Commission on Civil Disorders*. Washington, D.C.: Government Printing Office.

National Urban League Research Department. 1980. Initial black pulse findings. *Black Pulse* Bulletin no. 1.

Newman, Dorothy K., et al. 1978. *Protest, politics, and prosperity: Black Americans and white institutions, 1940–75*. New York: Pantheon Books.

O'Gorman, Hubert J. 1975. Pluralistic ignorance and white estimates of white support for racial segregation. *Public Opinion Quarterly* 39:313–30.

Parsons, Talcott. 1965. Full citizenship for the Negro American? *Daedalus* 94:1009–54.

Pettigrew, Thomas F. 1973. Racism and the mental health of white Americans. In Charles Willie, et al., eds., *Racism and mental health*, pp. 274–75. Pittsburgh: University of Pittsburgh Press.

———. 1975. *Racial discrimination in the United States.* New York: Harper and Row.

Pettigrew, Thomas F., ed. 1980. *The sociology of race relations.* New York: Free Press.

Pinkney, Alphonso. 1984. *The myth of black progress.* Cambridge: Cambridge University Press.

Piven, Frances, and Richard Cloward. 1971. *Regulating the poor.* New York: Pantheon Books.

Rainwater, Lee, and William L. Yancey. 1967. *The Moynihan Report and the politics of controversy.* Cambridge, Mass.: MIT Press.

Randolph, A. Philip. 1931. The economic crisis of the Negro. *Opportunity* 9:145–49.

Reitzes, Dietrich C. 1959. Institutional structure and race relations. *Phylon* 20:48–66.

Shaw, Van B. 1976. The concept of institutional racism. *Journal of Intergroup Relations* 5:3–12.

Sieber, Sam D. 1980. *Fatal remedies: The ironies of social intervention.* New York: Plenum.

Simpson, George E., and J. Milton Yinger. 1985. *Racial and cultural minorities.* 5th ed. New York: Harper and Row.

Smith, Tom, and Paul B. Sheatsley. 1984. American attitudes toward race relations. *Public Opinion Quarterly* 7:15–53.

Stephen, Charles. 1961. *Education and attitude change.* New York: Institute of Human Relations Press.

Sullivan, Harold J. 1983. Formula for failure: A critique of the intent requirement in school segregation litigation. *Journal of Negro Education* 52:270–89.

U.S. Commission on Civil Rights. 1981. *Affirmative action in the 1980's: Dismantling the process of discrimination.* Washington, D.C.: Government Printing Office.

U.S. Congress, Joint Economic Committee. 1976. *The 1976 Joint Economic Report.* Washington, D.C.: Government Printing Office.

U.S. Office of Personnel Management. 1979. *Equal employment opportunity court cases.* Washington, D.C.: Government Printing Office.

———. 1980. *Equal employment opportunity court cases: 1980 supplement.* Washington, D.C.: Government Printing Office.

Valentine, Charles. 1968. *Culture and poverty.* Chicago: University of Chicago Press.

Wicker, Allan W. 1969. Attitudes versus actions. *Journal of Social Issues* 25:41–78.

Williams, Robin M., Jr. 1947. *The reduction of intergroup tensions.* Bulletin 57. New York: Social Science Research Council.

———. 1977. *Mutual accommodation: Ethnic conflict and cooperation.* Minneapolis: University of Minnesota Press.

Wilson, William J. 1973. *Power, racism, and privilege.* New York: Free Press.

———. 1978. *The declining significance of race.* Chicago: University of Chicago Press.

Woodward, C. Vann. 1966. *The strange career of Jim Crow.* New York: Oxford University Press.

Zuckerman, Harriet. 1977. *Scientific elite: Nobel laureates in the United States.* New York: Free Press.

# James S. Coleman

## 17 Equality and Excellence in Education

Herbert Hyman's empirical research with survey data has been characterized by a kind of skill rarely found in social science: the skill of bringing together evidence of different kinds, each providing partial confirmation of an inference and each adding weight to the inference. Most researchers depend on statistical tests from a single type of evidence to confirm or deny an inference. The ingenuity and painstaking effort involved in taking the alternate path of testing an inference through a range of different implications is a hallmark of Hyman's work.

I hope that the analysis carried out in this paper reflects these qualities, for these are important elements of what Herb Hyman taught me about data analysis. The paper is related to Hyman's work in another way as well, for it deals with education, a long-standing concern of his, exhibited in his research. Thus, I hope that the analysis presented here pays tribute to Hyman's work both in method and in substance. The issue I want to examine concerns the compatibility of excellence in education with quality of educational opportunity.

Two fundamental questions have been posed in recent years for education in the United States and, I think, for education in other developed countries as well. The questions have been posed by events; yet we can thank the events for focusing our attention on matters central to the purposes of education. It remains to be seen whether we will use this focused attention in a productive way.

The two questions are simple and straightforward: Can there be equality of educational opportunity? And can the public school system foster high levels of achievement? Stated in such a way, it becomes evident that these two questions are directed to the twin goals of education in a democratic society. But they have arisen with intensity in recent years, not as abstract and academic questions but as very practical ones. The first of these arose principally in the United States in relation to blacks, and in Europe in relation to lower classes: Given the prima facie historical and continuing inequality of educational opportunity confronted by the disadvantaged, is it possible for the educational system to overcome such inequality? The second question has arisen prominently with some force in the United States, first in connection with the achievement test score decline. This decline was first evident with Scholastic Aptitude Test scores but has also become evident in the standardized testing programs carried out by states and school systems and in the National Assessment testing programs. A recent study of my own, on public and private schools, has reinforced this by showing that Catholic schools, long considered inferior to public schools, now produce higher achievement test scores than public schools (Coleman, Hoffer, and Kilgore 1982; Coleman and Hoffer 1987). It is clear that performance in the United States with respect to each of these two goals is less than perfect. But I want to raise the further question: Are these goals fundamentally in conflict? Is inequality necessarily produced in pursuing a goal of excellence? Is mediocrity necessarily the result of the pursuit of equality? I shall examine some evidence as to whether there is such conflict and, if there is, just how serious it is.

A useful way to begin is to look comparatively at American and European education. There has been, from the very beginning, a major difference between educational systems in Europe and those in the United States. In every European country, the educational system has had two tiers and, within those two, sometimes other subdivisions. There was established an elite tier, the *Gymnasium* in Germany, the *lycée* in France, and the grammar school and public school in England. And there was established a tier for the masses, which was of shorter duration, involved manual, commercial, and technical skills, and reduced academic requirements. The United States, from the beginning, has had a system of *common* schools. This was in part a matter of the absence of a history of feudalism in America but also in part derivative from the use of the school in creating a single cohesive nation from a polyglot of immigrants. The school's role as a "melting pot" has been long noted, and I will not belabor it here, but it should be apparent that this role is incompatible with a two-level school system of the sort that existed in Europe.

From the beginning, a higher value was placed on equality in American schools than was true in European schools. It does not directly follow, of course, that a lower value was placed on achievement. But anyone who is familiar with the academic demands of the Gymnasium or the lycée or the grammar school knows that in the upper tier, at least, European educational systems required more of students and maintained far more rigid requirements than have American schools, either in the present or in the past. For example, in France, a very large proportion of students have traditionally received outside tutoring in order to pass, and a very large proportion fail a year or more before they finish. Although "failing a grade in school" was once well known in schools in the United States, it was never as frequent an occurrence, by an enormous margin, as in France. (In England, the pattern was different: If a child did not do well, he or she was merely relegated to the lower tier of schooling or sent to a private school.)

It takes only a little knowledge of these systems to know that the standards of performance required in the European upper tier exceeded those in the American "common" or "comprehensive" high school. But this does not in itself mean that the *average* levels of achievement were higher in those systems, when all students are taken into account.

Some evidence on that does exist, however. The International Educational Achievement (IEA) studies, which have done comparative testing across countries first in the 1960s in mathematics and then in the 1970s in science, reading comprehension, and other subjects, allow international comparisons (Comber and Keeves 1973; Husen 1967; Thorndike 1973).

Students in twelve developed countries were tested at ages ten and fourteen. Growth in average achievement in science between ages ten and fourteen differed sharply in these countries. The highest growth, in Hungary, was eight times the lowest growth, in French-speaking Belgium.[1] Similarly, growth in inequality differed sharply. In the country with the highest growth in inequality, Japan, the fourteen-year-olds were almost *twice* as dispersed in science achievement as were the ten-year-olds. That is, the standard deviation of achievement in science at age fourteen was nearly twice that at age ten. In the country with the lowest growth in inequality, Italy, the fourteen-year-olds were almost as homogeneous as the ten-year-olds, only 20 percent more dispersed. Figure 17.1 shows the relation between growth in average achievement and growth in inequality of achievement, over all countries. There are two clusters of countries, one cluster showing high growth in average achievement and high growth in inequality, and the other cluster showing low growth in average achievement and

[1] Hungary is perhaps not appropriately involved in the comparison, as it was the only country not to have nearly all of the cohort still in school and tested at age fourteen. Next in science growth was Japan, where growth was over six times that in French Belgium.

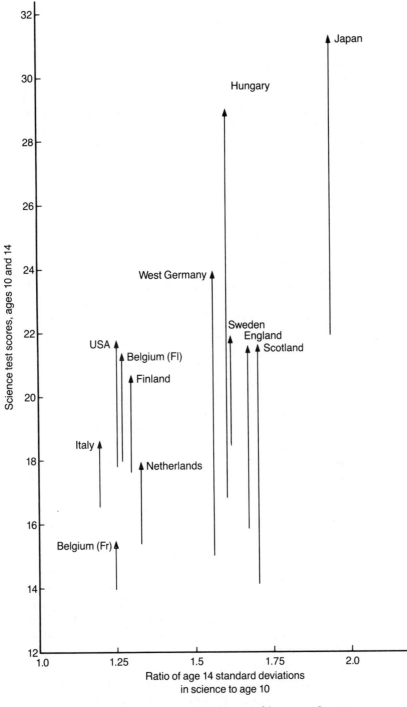

FIGURE 17.1. *Increase in Science Achievement Scores.*

Source: Coleman 1985, Figure 2 and Table 1.

low growth in inequality. The first cluster consists of Japan, West Germany, England, Scotland, Hungary, and Sweden. The second consists of the Netherlands, Finland, the United States, Italy, French Belgium, and Flemish Belgium. It appears clear that the first group of countries pursue an educational policy—explicitly and openly or not— that differentiates students before the age of fourteen and sacrifices equality of achievement for higher achievement among the best-performing students. The policies of the second group sacrifice high achievement at the top for equality. A by-product of these choices is that the first group gets a higher growth in *average* performance, not merely in the top students' performance.

Note that the United States lies in the group of countries with low growth in inequality and low growth in achievement. Its growth in inequality is third-lowest, lying right in the middle of the low-growth-in-inequality group. Its growth in achievement is lower than in all but one of the other cluster of countries, Sweden. Nevertheless, there is not complete correspondence between growth in inequality and growth in average performance: Although the United States is third from lowest in growth in inequality, it has the highest growth in average achievement of any country in that group.

A further question can be asked about these systems, because in eleven of the countries science achievement was tested in the last year of secondary school as well. At this level, different countries had widely different proportions of the age cohort in school, so that we can only look at portions of the cohort. One question we can ask concerns the very highest-performing students, taking the top 1 percent of the total cohort in each country. What are the consequences of these two different educational strategies for achievement of the top 1 percent?

Figure 17.2 shows this relation. Those countries that have high growth in inequality at early ages—between ages ten and fourteen— also have higher achievement of their science elites at the end of secondary school—ordinarily at age eighteen.

Finally, we can ask how much this educational strategy of differentiation is related to selectivity at the secondary level. A first reaction might be that these are one and the same, but a little reflection will show that this is not the case. For example, both England and France have relatively selective academic secondary school systems. But English A-level examinations (the examinations at the end of upper secondary school) and the curriculum to prepare for these examinations in upper secondary school are very differentiated, with students choosing which examinations they take. Some students will take none

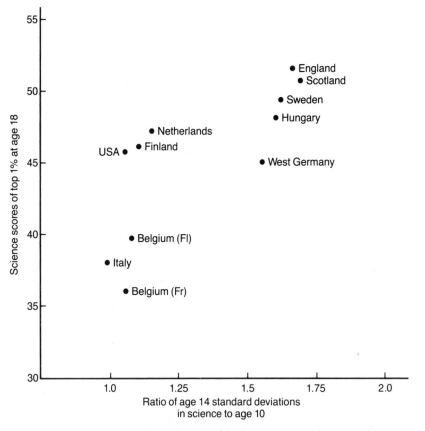

FIGURE 17.2. *Increase in Science Achievement Scores of Science Elites.*
Source: Data from Coleman 1985, Table 1.

at all in science. In France, however, the equivalent examination has traditionally been the same examination for all.

Figure 17.3 shows the relation between the proportion remaining in school through the last year of secondary school and the growth in science achievement between ages ten and fourteen. There is a negative relation, but it is not strong. Those countries that have a high growth rate in science between ages ten and fourteen keep, on average, a smaller fraction of the cohort in academic secondary school until the end, but the difference is not large. As indicated in the examples of England and France, there are two modes of differentiation, one between an elite (academic) stratum and a lower stratum, and the other between scientific and humanistic streams. The proportion of the co-

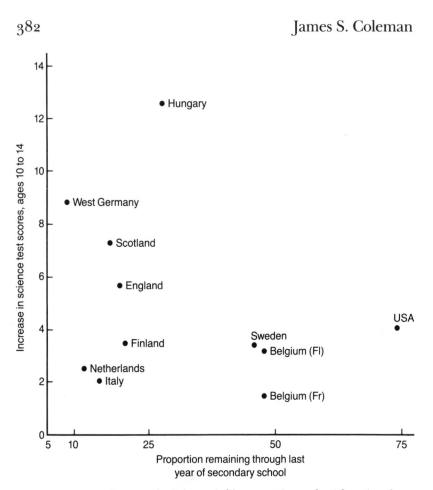

FIGURE 17.3. *Increase in Science Achievement Scores by Educational Selectivity.*

Source: Data from Comber and Keeves 1973.

hort in secondary school until the end captures only the first of these, whereas the growth in science scores may result from either.

The relation between a slower and less demanding educational system, on the one hand, and a system that is nonselective, keeping the whole cohort in a common school, can also be seen by looking at changes in education in the United States. In 1900, only a small proportion of the U.S. high-school-age population was in high school; but a very large proportion of high school graduates went on to college. The high schools were, in effect, preparatory schools for college, with demands imposed accordingly. Thus, despite the ideology of the common school, the fact that high school was attended primarily by the small segment of youth preparing for college meant that the standards and demands imposed in those schools were the more rigid ones of the "selective" school systems. After 1900, as increasing proportions of the age cohort moved into high school instead of the labor force, the practice of education changed, bringing "life adjustment" components into the curriculum and reducing its wholly academic flavor. The shift in practice was necessitated by the influx of a mass of elementary school graduates who were not preparing for college but for whom high school was an educational preliminary to nonprofessional white-collar and blue-collar occupations. The common-school ideology characteristic of U.S. education dictated that this new audience at secondary level would not be relegated to a second tier of education; rather, the curriculum and requirements of the common school, the comprehensive high school, would be modified to accommodate them.

This egalitarian modification of secondary education found its philosophical justification in John Dewey's works. The end result was a transformation of the high school by the necessities imposed by its new mass audience—who came to high school more poorly equipped than their predecessors (not that their own counterparts in previous years would have been better equipped but rather that they would have not entered high school, so that the predecessors in high school were a more select group) and whose futures required fewer academic skills than had been true for their predecessors.

This transformation of the high school consisted in part of changes in the curriculum in the direction of "life adjustment" and in part of reduced demands in the traditional subjects of the curriculum. The high school, if it was to be truly comprehensive, must have both a curriculum and a set of standards that would hold its new audience.

To be sure, this transformation was never complete, and there was not a full homogenization of secondary school. Heterogeneity still obtained in one of two ways: Some schools had, because of their clientele, largely a college-bound and academically intense student body, which allowed the demands and standards in these schools to rise accordingly. And in many "comprehensive" schools there were explicit tracks, which allowed differentiated standards and curricula within the school. For example, when I went, in 1957, to a high school in an affluent North Shore Chicago suburb, I noticed that in the homeroom there was a small subset of students, self-segregated from the others by at least a row and column of seats, in a rear corner. When I inquired about this apparently distinct group that was found in most homerooms, I learned that they were from the neighboring town, working-class, a service community for the affluent suburb, and that most of them had a curricular program that was completely distinct from the other students (see Coleman 1961).

Thus, there were various kinds of accommodation of the high school to its mass audience, some of which did not impose a homogeneous set of reduced standards. Nevertheless, the central tendency was toward a maintenance of the common school, with accommodations generally in the direction of a softened and less demanding curriculum.

There is, however, another potential impact, which is more difficult to document but is suggested both by the nature of the situation and by the IEA results I referred to earlier in science. Low growth in achievement among countries that did not engage in differentiation in science occurred *before* high school—between ages ten and fourteen. The suggestion is that the reduced demands and greater flexibility in high school have a strong impact in reducing the achievement demanded in elementary school. Or, more generally, when one educational level modifies the demands it makes either for admission or in its own curriculum, these modifications reverberate downward to the next level, causing it in turn to modify its demands. In particular cases, we can see clearly how that is true: When selective universities in the United States began in the 1960s no longer to require foreign language for admission, then, as if by magic, foreign languages drifted into obscurity in the high school curriculum. And when high school teachers began no longer to demand good handwriting of their students, the teaching of penmanship in the early grades lost its force. But the IEA results comparing achievement in different educational systems suggest that this may be operative on a very broad scale. That is, greater demands on the part of teachers at the higher levels appear to have produced greater demands at the lower levels and sufficient response to those demands by students that the overall average achievement is raised.

Such a conclusion as applied broadly to a whole educational system and to a whole curriculum is certainly not a firm one and deserves further examination, through comparative studies like those of the IEA. It does, however, have sufficient initial confirmation to allow examining its applicability to the current situation in academic achievement in the United States. It is to that situation that I now turn.

I turn to that situation not in an attempt to account wholly for recent declines in academic achievement but rather to suggest that a process similar to what I have described for the elementary level in an earlier period of U.S. history has now been occurring at a secondary level. That is, my premise will be that the enormous growth of a college population in the 1960s produced a reduction in the demands imposed by colleges on their entrants and on their students and that those reduced demands reverberated downward into the high schools, allowing a relaxation of teacher demands, an increased flexibility of curriculum, and a reduced intensity of effort, leading to lower achievement on the part of the high school population as a whole.

But, first, it is useful to say something about the nature of the declines in achievement in U.S. schools. As Willard Wirtz's (1977) commission on the Scholastic Aptitude Test found, about half the recent decline can be accounted for as "compositional effect," that is, by the changing composition of the student populations taking the SATs and going on to college. That is, lower-performing students who would not have taken the tests or attended college in the past were now doing so, thus dragging down the average. However, half is not due to changing composition but is due to lower scores on the part of students whose counterparts in the earlier periods *would* have taken the tests and attended college. This half can be thought of as a "real" decline, in which the same students are performing less well than they would have a decade and a half ago.

The reality of the decline has been confirmed by looking at other data as well. For example, standardized test scores given the total student bodies in given grades, as part of districtwide or statewide testing programs, show the same declines in high school (Coleman and Kelly 1976). Even here, one might be tempted to conjecture that if there has been a decline in New York City or in Dade County, Florida (as there has, when scores on the same tests are compared over the period in question), it might be due to the exodus of a middle-class white population or the influx of a black or Hispanic population. But such conjectures are stifled by the fact that the same tests given in New York City were also given, in those same years, throughout New York State. And, in all cases of cities, towns, villages, and rural areas (some of which might have been expected to profit in achievement levels by the middle-class exodus from the central cities), there was a similar decline in achievement. This, along with other evidence like it (such as the comparison of first and later waves of National Assessment testing in the United States, which showed declines among nearly all groups of students), reaffirms the reality of the achievement decline.

Other changes in high schools in the United States in recent years parallel the reduction in achievement, and some authors have suggested that they are proximate causes of the declines. These are changes in the courses taken by students. Most pronounced is the reduction in the taking of foreign languages. Another change is the substitution for the standard English course of a variety of diverse courses that as a whole can be characterized as easier and less demanding. Although it is difficult to make a direct causal connection between these curricular softenings and the achievement declines, the parallel between them strongly suggests such a connection.

Now I would like to hold these matters aside for a moment and say something about the source of changes in the college population in the United States. In 1946 a baby boom began. This meant, beginning in 1963, a vastly increased number of seventeen-year-olds leaving high school and ready to enter college or the labor market. One might have predicted in 1960 that, based on the rate of new job formation in the economy in the preceding decade and on the number of young persons who would enter the labor force in the next decade due to the baby boom that began in 1946, there would be a vast surplus of youth without jobs. The predictions turned out not to be accurate, but for only one reason: There *was* a surplus of youth for the labor force, but that surplus was soaked up by community colleges, state colleges, and municipal colleges. Not only did the number of college students greatly increase in the decade of the 1960s; the proportion of the age cohort attending college did as well.

In the 1960s, then, there was a parallel at the college level to what had occurred earlier in the century at the high school level. There was a vast influx of students who in earlier years would not have continued in school but would have entered the labor force.

There was a second force in the United States, which in addition to the demographically induced change had its own special effects. This is the force resulting from the long-deferred attempt to accord blacks equality of educational opportunity and to bring them into full parity with whites in the educational system. Because this movement aims to end the nation's history of discriminatory treatment of blacks, it exerted a strong force in the direction of eliminating all barriers to the upward movement of blacks. Given the historical educational treatment of blacks, this inevitably meant that certain of these barriers were those of educational standards and demands themselves. As a result, there came to be an especially potent augmentation of the pressure already on educational institutions, for the reasons I have given earlier, to reduce demands to the point where they did not constitute a barrier to disadvantaged blacks. Sometimes this led to a double standard, which would not have the effect of generally reducing standards; but elimination of that double standard takes the form that it seems always to take: not adoption by the lower group of the more rigid and demanding standards once imposed upon the higher group, but relaxation of these demanding standards in favor of the reduced ones.

It is worth pointing out in passing that the movement of blacks into equality of educational opportunity has come remarkably rapidly in the United States. In 1966, 48 percent of the eighteen- and nineteen-year-old white youth were in school or college, and only 38 percent of blacks. By 1981, the proportion of white youth remained unchanged at 48 percent, but the proportion of black youth aged eighteen and nineteen in school or college had *increased* by 10 percent to 48 percent, the same as the attendance rate for white youth. Thus, there has been a dramatic increase in the educational attainment of blacks during this period. Consistent with this, the only groups that showed increased achievement in the results of the second National Assessment testing were nine- and thirteen-year-old blacks, groups that had in the first testing been the lowest groups in performance. Achievement continued to decline among the higher-performing segments of the youth population.

From the set of observations, I think it is possible to state three generalizations. None of the three generalizations can be regarded as "proved" by these observations, but for each the evidence is rather strongly suggestive.

The first generalization: A change in demands or requirements at one institutional level has powerful effects in changing both the institutional demands and the student response at the next-lower level, from which the students will come. In particular, a change in demands and requirements in high school transmits itself downward to elementary school; and a change in demands or requirements at the college level transmits itself downward to high school. The process works both in increasing demands and in decreasing demands. For example, for many decades, the "Carnegie unit" of instruction imposed by the colleges (determining the number of credit hours toward graduation) had dictated the demands made by the high schools on their students; and the "college boards," designed by an association founded by elite colleges (College Entrance Board), have had a strong impact on the approach to subject matter by high schools. A contrast in point is the much greater concentration of English secondary schools on matters involving *knowledge* (rather than basic verbal and quantitative *skills*), certainly in part as a result of the concentration of the English universities' common entrance examination, as well as the A-level exams, on knowledge instead of basic skills.

The second generalization: A change in the student body composition, which creates a so-called compositional effect, will produce a noncompositional effect, probably through reduction of demands. A reduction in skills of the student body, such as that due to the broader coverage of schooling, will lead to a lowering of the average achievement of students at all levels of skill. That is, if in a given school there is an influx of lower-achieving students, not only will their own lower performance reduce the school average but the achievement of others will decline as a consequence of their presence. The principal mechanism—assuming that the generalization is true—is very likely the changed demands imposed by the teachers as a consequence of the changed composition of their student body.

The third generalization is that educational differentiation—which may be used as a way of coping with a more diverse student population, covering a larger fraction of the cohort—increases both average achievement levels and inequality in achievement. The IEA studies, showing that growth in average achievement and growth in inequality of achievement go hand in hand and that these seem to result from policies of differentiation, strongly suggest this generalization.

These three generalizations lead to a single very blunt question: What are the conflicts between equality and achievement? How severe are the incompatibilities, and how inherent are they?

The answer to this simple question is not simple. Another result from the IEA studies provides some evidence of the complexity. Just as ten-year-olds and fourteen-year-olds were given tests in science, they were given reading comprehension tests in their native languages. Ten countries gave reading comprehension tests at both age ten and age fourteen, most of them the same countries that gave science tests. Unlike the science tests, these tests differed because the languages differed. Thus, the absolute levels of achievement cannot be compared. However, the average growth in reading comprehension can be compared, as can the growth in dispersion of achievement.

Thus, we can ask the same question for reading comprehension as for science achievement: Is the growth in inequality related to the growth in achievement?

The results can be seen in Table 17.1: First the left hand column shows that there is considerable variation in average growth in reading comprehension. Hungary is first, followed by the United States. Both countries, together with French-speaking Belgium and Scotland, show over twice the growth of Sweden, the country with lowest growth in reading comprehension.

But when we look at the right-hand column of Table 17.1, showing growth in dispersion of achievement, to see its relation to growth in average achievement, the results are striking. There is not only no relation of growth in dispersion to growth in average achievement but almost no growth in dispersion in any country. In one, there is even slightly *less* dispersion at age fourteen than at age ten. In the others, there is virtually no increase in dispersion.

This result indicates that the relation found in science between

TABLE 17.1. *Growth in Average Achievement and in Inequality of Achievement in Reading Comprehension between Ages 10 and 14*

|  | Achievement growth | Ratio of dispersion age 10/age 14 |
|---|---|---|
| Hungary | 11.3 | 1.01 |
| U.S.A. | 10.5 | 1.00 |
| Belgium (French) | 9.5 | 0.94 |
| Scotland | 9.5 | 1.04 |
| Italy | 7.9 | 1.06 |
| Finland | 7.5 | 1.01 |
| Netherlands | 7.4 | 1.07 |
| Belgium (Flemish) | 7.0 | 1.05 |
| England | 6.6 | 1.03 |
| Sweden | 4.0 | 1.03 |

*Source:* Data from Coleman 1985, Figure 2 and Table 1.

growth in average achievement and growth in inequality of achievement is not at all true for reading comprehension. The apparent incompatibility between excellence and equality found in science does not hold for reading comprehension. The reason for the difference is not clear. It is true that the variation in growth in average achievement among countries is considerably less in reading achievement than in science. It appears that there was much less specialization, much less differentiation of curriculum, in reading achievement in these countries than in some of the countries in science. This may be responsible in part for the strikingly different results for science and reading comprehension.

There may, however, be another important factor. This is what might be called the "technology of teaching." An example will illustrate what I mean. There is a usual finding with a new teaching program that presents material in a somewhat different way or involves other minor modifications: If it is better, in the sense that students learn more, the students that are benefited most are those who are already doing well. The correlation between prior performance and achievement is increased. This correlation at the level of individuals is precisely consistent with the results for science I have described at the level of countries: the positive relation between growth in inequality and growth in average achievement.

However, some major modifications in the method of instruction have the reverse effect. For example, Robert Slavin and his colleagues at Johns Hopkins have carried out well-controlled experiments on the effects of *games* and *teams* in learning mathematics (Slavin 1983). They found that both use of the game and the additional introduction of a team structure dramatically increased achievement compared to the usual methods of instruction. But there was not a positive correlation between achievement and prior performance. High- and low-performing students performed better than before, but those students gained most who had been performing most poorly before.

I use this example to illustrate what I think is more generally true: When there is a radical change in the structure by which learning takes place, as is true in the shift from a usual classroom to a game structure, there can be both an increase in achievement and an increase in equality. This of course imposes more difficult requirements on an educational system—to find changes sufficiently fundamental that they can move toward both of these goals. But nevertheless the opportunity does exist.

Another example exists from a study of public, Catholic, and other private high schools in the United States which I have been carrying out recently. The Catholic schools taken as a group produced both higher levels of achievement *and* smaller differences in achievement between whites and blacks, Anglos and Hispanics, or students from high and low parental educational backgrounds. They seem to have done so by a combination of stronger academic demands *in general* and less tracking or differentiation of students. Thus, in comparing types of schools as well as types of classroom structure, it is again apparent that the general incompatibility between quality and equality can be partially overcome. Some educational settings are better on both counts than are others.

## Conclusion

It is clear from the material I have presented that there can be incompatibility between high levels of performance—on the average as well as at the upper end of the distribution—and equality of educational performance. But it is equally clear from the evidence that this incompatibility is not inherent, that high average levels of performance can occur without leaving a segment of students far behind.

The queston of how to bring about high achievement without leaving some students far behind is not satisfactorily answered, but some points appear to be clear. One has to do with demands. If demands for achievement in an area are largely relaxed for a set of students, through tracking, through a shift into vocational education unaccompanied by continued demands in academic subjects, or through mere failure to require academically demanding courses, then these students will not achieve, and the distance between them and others may grow if there is a demanding program at the upper end of the curriculum. On the other hand, if demands for academic achievement remain as strong for students at lower ends of the performance distribution as for those at the upper end, the evidence at hand does not indicate that dispersion in achievement will grow.

A second point is that a change in the technology of teaching, as exemplified in the use of games and teams in learning but not confined to these particular tools, can have powerful effects, not merely in preventing a growth in inequality as achievement grows but in reducing the existing degree of inequality. Different children are motivated and stimulated by different kinds of social and intellectual environments. Children who respond poorly in the teacher–student relation may be highly motivated by the competitive structure of a game. Others may thrive on the structure of mutual help that occurs in a team. If the learning environment is sufficiently varied to provide stimulation for a variety of personalities, then this may aid in reducing the disparities in performance.

More generally, what is necessary is to carry out a sufficiently deep analysis of the educational process that the sources of incompatibilities between quality and equality become clearer, thus pointing the way to educational strategies that can make use of this understanding. We are only starting along this road but are far enough, I believe, to see both that excellence in education is not inherently incompatible with equality of opportunity, and that as schools curently function, there is a high degree of incompatibility.

## Bibliography

Coleman, James. 1961. *The adolescent society.* New York: Free Press.

———. 1985. International comparisons of cognitive achievement. *Phi Delta Kappan*, February, pp. 403–6.

Coleman, James, Thomas Hoffer, and Sally Kilgore. 1982. *High school achievement: Public, Catholic, and other private schools compared.* New York: Basic Books.

Coleman, James, and Thomas Hoffer. 1987. *Public and private schools.* New York: Basic.

Coleman, James, and S. Keliy. 1976. Education. In W. Gorham and N. Glazer, eds., *The urban predicament*, pp. 231–80. Washington, D.C.: Urban Institute.

Comber, L. C., and John P. Keeves. 1973. *Science education in nineteen countries.* Stockholm: Almqvist and Wiksell; New York: Wiley.

Husen, Torsten, ed. 1967. *International study of achievement in mathematics.* 2 vols. Stockholm: Almqvist and Wiksell; New York: Wiley.

Slavin, Robert. 1983. *Cooperative learning.* New York: Longman.

Thorndike, R. L. 1973. *Reading comprehension in fifteen countries.* Stockholm: Almqvist and Wiksell.

Wirtz, Willard, chairman. 1977. *On further examination: Report of the Advisory Panel on the Scholastic Aptitude Test Score Decline.* New York: College Entrance Examination Board.

# Stanley Lebergott

## 18  Income Equality: Some Missing Dimensions

Shortly before the War on Poverty exploded in American politics, America's best-known economist declared, with regrettable clarity: "Inequality has ceased to preoccupy men's minds."[1] But few economists agreed with Galbraith. Most believed (with Henry Simons) that "there is something unlovely to modern, as against mediaeval minds, about marked inequality of either" power or income (Simons 1948, p. 51).

Income inequality has long evoked fierce, and direct, comment ("Woe unto ye, rich men"). Relative deprivation theory, and class analysis, were then invoked. And in recent decades discussions of the subject menace listeners with statistical "proofs" as well. (These involve ingenious, and difficult to explain, measures such as the share of income going to those with "income less by 44 percent of the median," Gini coefficients, and so on.)[2]

I should like to discuss three truisms about inequality in America. Two usually are proved by relying on income statistics, while the third is usually embedded in anecdotes and adjectives. (1) The usual distributions of money income reveal how inequality has increased in an era of corporate merger and monopoly. (2) Survey data demonstrate how unequally U.S. income is distributed. (3) Poverty in the United States has been "passed down from generation to generation along family lines."

---

[1] Galbraith 1958, p. 82: "While it continues to have a large ritualistic role in the conventional wisdom of conservatives and liberals, inequality has ceased to preoccupy free men's minds."

[2] Poverty "is a comparative status. . . . If being poor means that family income is less by 44 percent of the median (middle) income of the nation there has been virtually no reduction of poverty for the last 10 years" (Heilbroner and Thurow 1977).

393

Closer consideration suggests that the empirical basis for these truisms is uncertain, in part because of a failure to consider basic demographic forces. Proposals to redistribute income, of course, are not endangered by the fragility of these three conclusions. But our understanding of what redistributive policies can achieve may be affected.

For a few centuries capitalism interrupted an ancient tradition. Precapitalist modes of production typically emphasized nonmonetary incomes. Feudal lords and slave owners exacted services in kind. Monks lived on gifts in kind. So did artists, peripatetic philosophers, and generations of peasants.

But under capitalism incomes were increasingly monetized. That may have provided unexampled freedoms to the average worker and advanced his income by advancing productive efficiency. But there was a distinct flaw. Monetization labeled every participant by a single, simple number—his money income (or wealth). As Simmel wrote, there is an "uncompromising objectivity" about a definite sum of money (1978, p. 373). It became singularly easy to compare one's "well-being" with persons in other income groups, particularly as income tax and survey reports began to proliferate. Americans most often seem to use these data to compare their own status with that of "the rich"—but not as frequently with the poor. Unfortunately, scholars of reference groups have not yet gotten around to deciphering this choice. Does envy have more evolutionary value than gratitude?[3]

Dislike for "the rich" has long been widespread. That feeling does not arise because the rich consume too much of the nation's output. If anything, the prudent but generous rich—for example, J. D. Rockefeller—were disliked more than the "Coal Oil Johnnies" who lit cigars with $100 bills. Dislike links to the simple fact that they are rich. And money income figures demonstrate and dimension their riches.

Historic changes flowed from such dislike. The role of nonmonetary income increased. And the meaning of money income distributions was steadily eroded. The pattern differed in capitalist and noncapitalist nations.

In capitalist nations, that dislike helped bring on the income tax. The initial U.S. rates were low—so low that Robert La Follette, the Senate radical, shocked his colleagues when he proposed that marginal incomes over $100,000 should be taxed at the (then) unbelievably high rate of 10 percent. That proposal collected a mere handful

[3] As far as economic evolution is concerned, it is of interest that the Central Committee of the Communist party of China announced (October 1984) that "egalitarian thinking is a serious obstacle to . . . the forces of production."

of votes (U.S. Congress 1913, pp. 3807, 3819). Time marched on. Under the New Deal the top marginal rate was moved to 90 percent. When the Republicans swept into office in 1953, after two decades out of power, they did triumphantly cut the 90 percent rate—but only to 89 percent. They could not reverse the tide of history.

Not surprisingly, the rich reacted to decades of rising tax rates. They substituted away from the receipt of money income—to capital gains, stock options, and deferred compensation; to the company automobile, dining room, and fishing camp. But matters did not end there.

By a process of mimicry natural in a democracy lower-income people also began to convert money income to nonmonetary form as their tax rates rose. As James R. Hoffa remarked in 1963: "Our guys are going home with $200 a week in their pockets, and it might be better to put most of an increase we negotiate into fringes instead of wages."[4] (Such fringes were not taxed.)

Fringe benefits averaged less than 2 percent of wages in 1931 when tax rates began to rise. By 1984 benefits had reached 20 percent (U.S. President 1985, p. 256). An important share of national output was obviously being diverted to middle- and lower-income families, in the form, for example, of medical insurance payments. They collected other subsidies in the form of life insurance, in-plant cafeterias, professional trips to Europe, company bowling teams, cars for personal use, and so on. The salaried employee became a part-time insurance salesman—charging off the family car as a business expense. Impecunious college teachers, imitating pecunious lawyers, discovered they too had to pursue their professional endeavors in fascinating places to which the less intellectual could resort only without offsetting tax advantages.

Direct consumption expanded at the expense of money income receipt. The income tax created a lively industry devoted to tax avoidance. That is well known. What is less well known is that the tax code increasingly distorted the pattern of real income receipt. That outcome has been ignored by those who invoke Gini coefficients, using the standard estimates of money income distribution to discuss "inequality."

But it is in noncapitalist nations that the dislike of large, and measurable, money incomes has had the most spectacular results. The political, military, or intellectual leaders have learned the basic lesson for

---

[4]Quoted in Lester 1964, p. 340. As Lester notes (p. 332–33), "The sharp upward trend in nonwage benefits commenced in World War II. . . . In mid-1942 the National War Labor Board imposed definite limits on wage increases . . . but no such restraints were placed on reasonable contributions to employee benefit programs. . . . as a result employer contributions to private pensions and other benefit programs rose."

survival today. They therefore take little or no money income. Workers are still plucked to benefit the elite; but leaders collect the fruits of their power and position in nonmonetized form.

That elegant simplification of the usual sequence (effort-income-consumption) surely anticipates the world's future. It recognizes that consumption is the simple goal of production, as Adam Smith and Irving Fisher declared. But elites in noncapitalist nations consume far more efficiently than capitalists. For they cut out the intermediary stage of making money income. Have the socialist ruling classes, then, returned to barter? Not at all. They have created something much more like an Aladdin's lamp economy—for themselves. They have protected themselves against the dangerous malaise produced by high incomes—by removing high incomes. That single, brilliant change ended the ever-increasing protest that high money incomes in the capitalist world appear to create.

Michael Voslensky (1984) describes the effective ingenuity of the system by which Soviet officials buy rare and otherwise unavailable products at moderate prices in stores where they alone can trade; use official cars; enjoy vacation dachas and servants provided by the state; receive protection from specially assigned police and physicians. In China the construction cost per square meter of houses for "high-level intelligentsia" is about double that for ordinary houses and dormitories. But "rentals do not differ greatly for houses of differing quality."[5] In Laos "Government and party officials and soldiers enjoy numerous privileges not available to others, including access to stores where government controlled low-priced goods can be bought" (*New York Times*, May 3, 1977). Such privileges are so varied that the most myopic cost accountant could not easily sum their shadow prices into a single figure for (imputed) income. Thus, there need be no barbarously rich people, no high-income recipients, in any command economy—communist, "Marxist," or barefoot military directorate—even though its leaders consume as lavishly as capitalists.

How does the same consumption take place under capitalism? Few members of the Establishment reach the age of discretion without knowing that their status and income are apparent to sellers, who chalk up their prices. In Rolls Royce showrooms, Elizabeth Arden salons, couturier establishments, law and real estate offices, capitalists pay full market rates, or better. The rich, the American Medical Association assures us, even pay for medical care at above market rates. (Insofar as Park Avenue physicians devote some free time to the poor,

---

[5] Chao 1968, pp. 106, 101. Chao notes that, in turn, department heads of the Ministry of Railways were assigned housing space more than double that of professors at Tsinghua University.

they are indeed not likely to do so at their own expense but by charging the rich higher rates.)

The incomes the rich acquire to buy these goods are first whittled down by taxes, local, state, and federal, plus a socially obligatory level of charitable contributions. Finally, the Establishment saves. Such savings are income that capitalism awards its leaders on condition (as Keynes noted) that they never consume it.[6] These items sum to a single, simple number. The gap separating that figure and the income of the least well-paid member is easy to measure in capitalist society, and blatant. Systems that do not enmesh their leaders in so bold a confrontation may prove far more palatable than capitalism.

## Income Size Distributions

"The nation is heading for a taxpayer's revolt." That heartrending cliché was not uttered by Jack Kemp, nor by the National Association of Manufacturers. It was expressed by the Retail Clerks International Union. And they were responding to a Treasury Department proposal to tax workers' total income (i.e., not merely their money income). Were the retail clerks fighting for the working class? Or only for their own perquisites? They held as a clear moral principle that they should be able to buy goods at a discount where they worked—and not be taxed on such saving. Concurrently, "many of the nation's 300,000 airline employees [also] fired off telegrams of protest . . . 'I just sent off four,'" said one employee. For Treasury had also proposed to tax airline employees on the value of the free airline tickets given them.[7]

One-third of U.S. workers receive free or discounted merchandise.[8] Yet such perquisites are never included in studies of inequality. For income distributions almost inevitably deal only with money income—first, because income in the West is typically received in money, and second, because analysts are trained on studies made in monetary units. But who ever maintained that "only money matters"? Not the most obdurate monetarist. And what competent economist contends that money maximization is *the* goal of human behavior? (Even without reading Adam Smith, most people know that workers substitute between money income and other sources of utility when choosing jobs.)

---

[6] A contemporary estimated that the robber baron millionaires saved 84 percent of their incomes. Cf. Shearman 1895, pp. 185, 150.

[7] *New York Times*, December 16, 1976. Community groups in New York City upbraided their school custodians—not for their salaries (which ran up to $32,500) but because they kept for themselves the vacuum cleaners, floor sanders, and other capital equipment they bought with taxpayers' money (*New York Times*, February 6, 1977).

[8] In 1977 free or discounted merchandise was a fringe benefit for 34 percent of U.S. workers, and meals for 16 percent. Cf. Quinn and Staines 1979, p. 8.

Much of the interest in the U.S. income distribution involves how it changes over time. But steady changes in the substitution between legal money income and other sources of utility distort such comparisons. Six can be readily noted.

1. The growing preference for leisure: American workers now work about 2,200 hours a year. Their grandfathers worked almost 50 percent more hours in 1900 (Lebergott 1975, p. 92). Hours declined most for low-income workers—common labor, unskilled factory workers. (Entrepreneurs and corporate executives probably still work as many hours as in 1900.) If unskilled workers still worked sixty hours a week and took all their work income in money, the ranks of those with (money) incomes below, say, $10,000 would be far smaller.

2. A growing preference for life rather than money: Thaler and Rosen have estimated that workers give up $1,760 a year for each reduction in the risk of death on the job by 1 percent (1975, p. 292). Now, workmen's compensation has expanded in recent decades; and workers have drifted away from the riskiest jobs. All this has cut the risk of death on the job, and also wages. For when employers spend to reduce suck risk they reduce worker incomes that would otherwise maintain. Since official income distributions relate to a single year, they ignore the fact that workers live longer.[9]

3. A growing preference for being a hired hand: From 1900 to 1975 the number of employees rose more than sixfold. Meanwhile, the self-employed declined significantly (Lebergott 1964, p. 511; U.S. Department of Labor 1986; table 20). (Between 1950 and 1970 alone the farm group fell 70 percent; U.S. Census 1975, p. 139.) Now the self-employed—who ran farms, groceries, shoe repair shops—had lower money incomes than workers. Their lower money incomes reflected the greater freedom of decision they had over their own workday than did wage earners, and their chance of striking it rich. Moreover, farmers—the largest self-employed group—typically collected one-quarter of their income in nonmonetary form (as imputed rent and food). If we added the distribution margin needed to make it equivalent to the income of urban workers, we would find that farmers really collected one-third of their income in such form. The twentieth-century shift to employee status, therefore, has created a shift toward higher money income even if real incomes had not changed.

4. In the United States, and even more clearly in Africa and Asia, development enabled minority groups to move out of their traditional occupations. Younger workers no longer accepted jobs as domestic

---

[9] Other safety costs are required by law or custom, but they do not improve health enough to yield dollar-for-dollar compensating increases in worker incomes.

servants, newspaper boys, crossing sweepers, water carriers, rickshaw pullers. Their alternative turned out to be urban unemployment plus the receipt of illegal income, none of which, in principle, appears in the income distribution figures. The *Manpower Report of the President* quotes a "study of Harlem [which] estimates that roughly 2 out of every 5 adult inhabitants had some illegal income in 1966 and that 1 out of every 5 appeared to exist entirely on money derived from illegal sources" (U.S. President 1971, pp. 2, 98).

5. A fifth element is home ownership. The aged now constitute one-fifth of the entire class officially estimated as in poverty. But more than half the aged own their own homes (U.S. Census 1970a, table 36). The Department of Health, Education, and Welfare estimates "income requirements" in order to make up its poverty count. In doing so, it necessarily includes a substantial budget item to cover rent. Since half the aged do not pay rent the poverty count is biased upward, and significantly so.

6. A sixth force has become increasingly vital in recent years: the categorical public programs. To a striking degree U.S. economists agree it is better to give money than specific assistance. (They did not when Stigler first suggested it. But ever since Friedman and Tobin agreed that giving money is the thing, U.S. economists have typically followed their lead. Most congressmen and interest groups normally disagree.) The job opportunities for social workers, and the wages paid to workers in food service and construction would certainly be less inspiriting under a negative income tax than the network of categorical programs now permits (which may help explain why these programs constitute the heart of the public redistribution effort today.) Yet the billions of dollars in real income such programs provide, particularly those expanded in the 1960s, are omitted from income distributions.[10]

We suggested above some of the issues in which "income" involves us. But the concept of "distribution" is no clearer. Distribution among whom? Inequality among whom? The fundamental units in human existence are not groups or classes but individuals. It is the person who has a psyche and who may revel in utility. It is a human being who consumes goods and leisure. Measures of individual economic welfare, however, are drastically limited by a social factor: Individuals usually exist in families. And that is probably the primary process by which individuals maximize their utility.

[10] If one included the value of food stamps, subsidized housing, and similar programs at what families could buy in the market, the official poverty rate of 11.6 percent for 1984 would fall to 7.7 percent, according to U.S. Census 1984a.

Now, the family is an odd combination of commune, dictatorship, and summer camp. It endlessly redistributes income among its members. How can an outsider decide which individuals benefit from which items? Is the encyclopedia for the children—or for their loving but unrealistic parents? The piano lessons? Visits to the dentist? Is the new stove for the wife, or for the gourmet desires of her husband? How can the cost of the family home be partitioned? Of the television set? Allocating joint family consumption raises as many problems as allocating joint production costs. Pareto set an unfortunate precedent by creating a neat mathematical coefficient to compare income distributions while ignoring what he said elsewhere about interpersonal utility comparisons.

Such problems cannot be vanquished by assuming that every individual gets an aliquot share of every family expenditure. Families are not uniform. Individuals are not fungible. One does not have to be a member of the National Organization for Women to question whether women share equally in family expenditure. We could not even get far studying the subset of nuclear families. Even assuming that "Happy families are all alike," one would have to confront Tolstoy's addition: "Every family is unhappy in its own way."

Even ignoring individual incomes to focus on family incomes does not solve such conceptual problems. It only creates new ones. For the family itself produces welfare. And it does so whether it consists of a couple with children or a ménage à trois. This, of course, is why individuals spend much of their lives changing the family unit itself. They manipulate its size, shape, and existence to increase their well-being.

Sometimes they do so for tax or subsidy purposes. The son may live apart to get lower university tuition—and the father to qualify his family for Aid to Families with Dependent Children. But by far the commonest reason is the direct emotional return that ensues when single persons marry. Married persons have children. Men desert their families. Grandparents are moved into (or out of) families. The nation has a generally free market in economic transactions. Decisions with respect to who lives with whom are no less freely made. Hence, one may conclude that decisions that change family composition normally improve the welfare of most of the persons involved.

Yet the usual comparisons of family income distributions at different dates—numbers, quintile shares, and so on—ignore all this. Can comparisons that boldly ignore family creation, change, and dissolution really yield meaningful insights into welfare changes over time?

In 1970 less than one American husband in a thousand lived with his mother-in-law. Presumably 999 passed up the opportunity to do so. Suppose, however, that government restrictions on new construction expanded that group fourteenfold—to the figure that prevails in the Soviet Union (Raitsin 1969, p. 25). Would that improve the level of welfare in the United States? The usual Gini coefficients and comparison of family income distributions would insist that it had: for fewer low-income, one-person families would exist. Yet how many spouses would find their well-being the same if their income increased ten dollars a year but their mother-in-law came to live with them?

A growing American preference for living alone is evident in the expanding count of single-person families as income rose. In 1930 they constituted 5 percent of American families and unrelated individuals; they now total 46 percent.[11] Single-person families typically earn less income than other families. Their income needs and goals are less (they are typically younger or aged); and their desires for income, as their abilities to earn it, also seem to be less.[12] In 1945, as in 1976, about half of single-person families were in the bottom fifth of the family income distribution.[13]

Suppose every individual in a nation got the same basket of goods in each of two periods, but families split off members between periods. The usual family income distribution data would report that poverty and inequality had increased. Thus, even identical incomes per person are seen as increased income inequality when screened through income distribution data.

Suppose two other regimes. In one, incomes of the poor rise markedly—but young people set up families of their own at a still faster rate. In the second regime, the income of the poor falls markedly—but family composition remains unchanged. The widely used family income distributions would not declare that poverty fell in one case and rose in the other. They could even report the same change in inequality under both regimes, measured by the usual indicators—quintile shares, proportions under 44 percent of the median, and so on.

Most income distribution data are collected for public policy purposes. But are these the ways in which the public understands these data? Or the economist concerned with policy analysis? And if the social process simply does not stand still, what are we to make of the usual intertemporal comparisons between family income distributions?

[11] 1930: U.S. Census 1940, table 11. 1984: U.S. Census 1984*b*, P-60, no. 149, tables 1, 4. For convenience, we use the 1930 category of single-person families as equivalent to the "unrelated individuals" category used in more recent years.

[12] Taking merely the 14–24 group: Of those who were in families, 93 percent in 1970 had income below $4,000, and 83 percent of those not in families also had such low incomes. U.S. Census 1970*b*, table 10; 1970*c*, table 4.

[13] The figures were 55 percent and 47 percent, respectively (U.S. Census 1945, P-60, no. 2, tables 1, 7, and P-60, no. 103, table A, combining family and unrelated individual data into a single distribution).

## Inheritance of Poverty

"Poverty in modern nations . . . is a way of life, remarkably stable and persistent, passed down from generation to generation along family lines." So said Oscar Lewis (1961, p. xxiv). Society, Lester Thurow stated, "would probably tolerate a much more unequal income distribution if the same individuals, families and social groups were not consistently at the top or bottom." But unfortunately, he added, "most families are consistently at the bottom of the distribution" (1969, pp. 13, 16).

Dozens of anecdotes reinforce such comments. Since Booth described London, and the eugenics movement warned about the Jukeses and Kallikaks, we have been told that families inherit immorality, fecklessness—and poverty. More than that, we have been presented with data. For example, an extended survey of New York City families on welfare reported data for those reared in the city (Podell 1966). These demonstrate that parents of 20 percent of the whites on welfare had themselves been on welfare; 40 percent of the Puerto Ricans; and 48 percent of the blacks (Podell 1966, p. 95).[14]

The surveys are retrospective. But the question of acute public interest is prospective. It concerns a probability: What chance do children have of moving up and out if their parents lived in poverty? Was Thoreau right when he described an immigrant as "a poor man, born to be poor, with his inherited Irish poverty . . . his Adam's grandfather and boggy ways; not to rise in this world, he nor his posterity."[15]

The sharpest test would seem to be the experience of major groups that historians, memoirists, and pressure groups tell us were disadvantaged. They were presumably menaced by the native white American majority. Now, surely, those most likely to have been kept down economically would be their descendants. Our test can be a direct one. We ascertain the income figure that marks off the lowest decile in a given year. In 1900, 10 percent of native white husband–wife families had incomes under $285. The major immigrant groups in that year inevitably had a far higher percentage. For northern Italians the figure was 28 percent. So too for Jews, Slovenes, and Croats. It was 33 percent for Poles, Slovaks, Hungarians; about 40 percent for southern Italians, Japanese, Chinese—and 40 percent for American blacks (Lebergott 1976, p. 47).

Now, if poverty were inherited by social groups, then grandchildren

[14] Those few responding "don't know" were distributed in proportion to the numbers responding "ever" or "never" on welfare.

[15] "Till their wading, webbed, bog-trotting feet get *talaria* to their heels" (Thoreau 1971, chap. 10).

of these ethnic groups would report percentages well above the 10 percent for native whites in the bottom decile in 1970. But what do the data actually show? For every nativity group mentioned, the proportion below the 1970 lowest decile income figure ($4,000) for native whites turns out to be just about 10 percent. Indeed, the proportions for the Japanese, the Chinese, and many others are actually less than 10 percent (Lebergott 1976).[16] For blacks the proportion is 14 percent. An enormous literature has described these groups as victims of a heritage of discrimination. Yet their percentage in the lower depths dwindled, and markedly so, from the grandparents' generation to that of the grandchildren. Data for these important groups provide little warrant for general assertions that poverty in the United States has been inherited from generation to generation.

Some shorter-term comparisons can likewise be made. One set appeared in the *Economic Report of the President*. Many of the forty-odd such *Reports* have discussed low incomes, but only one presented a comparison following a given cohort of poverty families. The data were taken from the annual income survey of the Census Bureau. And they indicate that of all poverty families in 1962 some 19 percent had left poverty by 1963 (U.S. President 1965, p. 195). The President's Commission on Income Maintenance made a similar calculation for 1965–66 and discovered that not 19 percent but "35.6 percent of those classified as poor in 1965 became nonpoor in 1966."[17] Had the annual rate of departure from poverty nearly doubled as the War on Poverty escalated? The commission did not even comment on the change. "Surprisingly," or "inevitably"—depending on one's prejudices—it did not express interest in this apparently large, and increasing, rate of exit from poverty. After prolonged study it concluded that poverty was a major issue, whatever the numbers showed (a conclusion obvious to some before its report).[18]

[16] We have not discussed the major immigrant groups—Irish and German. The proportion for each in 1910 did not exceed that for native whites. Nor did that for the Irish in 1970. For Germans, however, the 1970 percentage is greater. Yet its excess cannot be taken as an indication of low income before one allows for the fact that an unusually large proportion of German descendants were rural residents. An important share of their income in kind—including their housing and food—is omitted from the U.S. Census money income figures we are using.

[17] President's Commission on Income Maintenance 1970, p. 24. The commission hastens to add: "from this it should not be inferred that the poverty problem is less serious than has previously been supposed, however. On the contrary, the data suggest that the risk of an experience of poverty for any family is much greater than is generally imagined. Indeed, if monthly . . . flow data were available, the problem would doubtless be seen even to be worse" (p. 24).

[18] The commission's report, *Poverty amid plenty: The American paradox* (1969, p. 32), found "More striking than the recorded successes are the failures," emphasizing that "much of the movement into and out of poverty is really movement close to the line." And its conclusion to chapter 2 began: "The persistence of poverty and the extensive

TABLE 18.1. *Percentage of Children in Poverty,*
*1983, by Type of Family*

|  | White | Black |
|---|---|---|
| Male head |  |  |
| 1–2 children | 7 | 15 |
| 3+ children | 19 | 32 |
| Female head |  |  |
| 1–2 children | 38 | 54 |
| 3+ children | 67 | 88 |

*Source:* Computed from U.S. Census 1983, P-60, no. 147, table 18
("Children under 18").

A solid and sufficiently broad survey of the changing fortunes of individual Americans from 1968 to 1978 provides our most reliable and relevant information on "permanent poverty" in the United States today. It reports less than 5 percent of all Americans in poverty for as long as ten years,[19] and less than that in "permanent poverty" if by permanent we mean a period longer than ten years.[20]

We get further light on generational changes by comparing the incomes of fathers in 1948 (aged twenty-five to thirty-four) with sons in 1979 (then aged twenty-five to thirty-four).[21] Less than half the fathers (42 percent) had incomes that could support a family of four above the poverty line. But over 80 percent of the sons could do so. Surely that generational change was marked, and socially significant.

Do these few inquiries confirm the general judgment that "most" U.S. families remain "consistently at the bottom of the distribution"? Surely not. Does the rate at which poverty is "perpetuated" in the United States today exceed that for any other nation, at any period? We have no reason to think so. And suppose we ask what rate of out-mobility would distinguish between a society in which families (*a*) did or (*b*) did not remain "consistently at the bottom"? An answer requires

---

movements into and out of poverty testify to the fact that problems of income inadequacy and income insecurity are common to large segments of the population."

[19] Morgan et al. (1981) report that 3 percent of the U.S. population were in poverty throughout 1968–78. A study of nonelderly poor, using the same data, finds that of these poor during any given year 25 percent would have been poor for more than eight years, whereas twice that proportion would be poor in the completed distribution (Bane and Ellwood 1983, table 2).

[20] About the same percentage of Americans received Aid to Families with Dependent Children.

[21] In 1948, 42 percent of the fathers had incomes above the poverty line of $2,952 for a family of four. Price increases had raised the poverty line to $7,412 by 1979 (U.S. Census 1980, P-60, no. 6, table 12; no. 103, tables 11, 16; no. 125, table 12).

translating adjectives into numbers, and to it the poverty specialists have given little attention.

The twentieth-century record, then, provides little evidence of any broad "inheritance of poverty from generation to generation" in the United States, and much evidence to the contrary. However, the intellectual and emotional deficits generated by a childhood in poverty warrant some comments on the links between parental actions and child poverty. Some striking differences appear if we make a simple cross-classification (see Table 18.1).

We take as our reference base the poverty rate for families with male heads and one to two children. The margins by which poverty rates for other categories exceed those bases are as follows:

|  | *White Heads* | *Black Heads* |
|---|---|---|
| More children | + 12% | + 17% |
| Female head, 1–2 children | + 31 | + 39 |
| Female head, 3+ children | + 60 | + 73 |

1. *Additional children* add 12 percent for white couples—and 17 percent for blacks. It is worth remembering that the *Children of Sanchez* (Lewis 1961), who lived in such bitter poverty, numbered fifteen.

2. *Race*—a proxy for discrimination (plus lack of human capital plus distant social inheritance)—adds 8 percent (i.e., 15 percent − 7 percent) for families with male heads.

3. *Desertion:* The surest way men guarantee that their children will be raised in poverty is failure to marry or desertion. (It adds 31 percent for those in the white families with one to two children and 60 percent for the larger ones—and adds 39 percent and 73 percent for black families.) The phenomenon has been tellingly caricatured by V. S. Naipaul: "On this island I was telling you about . . . they had this woman, pretty but malevolent. She make two–three children for me, and bam, you know what, she want to rush me into marriage" (1965, p. 175). Our national code of accepted behavior includes the right of men to propagate children—and desert them.[22] So doing, of course, they help increase poverty. Women find it difficult to earn any income when they have young children. If they get a job they must drop their work whenever the children fall ill. They therefore end up with less responsible jobs, at lower wage rates—and are paid for fewer hours. And the children who became poor when their mother was deserted or divorced will remain in poverty five years, some more, some less (Bane and Ellwood 1983, table 4). In King Canute's day housewife and

---

[22] This is hardly to imply that the United States is an exception among nations. One need only remember Rousseau, or the enormous death rate among foundlings in Paris.

"house-bound" lived together, the man being "bound" to the ties of marriage—and children (Hale 1853, p. cv). But the tide eventually rolled in.

The earlier discussion of long-term changes for ethnic groups dealt with husband–wife families. Data for persons—as distinct from families with both husband and wife—lead to the same conclusions for every group but one: blacks. What accounts for that difference? The percentage of black husband–wife families in the lowest income decile did fall significantly from 1900 to 1983. Between 1962 and 1975 alone the number of black families with male heads in poverty was cut almost two-thirds, by the vigorous endeavors of the families themselves, by advancing wage rates, and by some lessening of discrimination. But the percentage of all black families with female heads rose from 18 percent in 1900 to 43 percent by 1983 (U. S. Census 1980, P-60, no. 81, table 1, no. 103, table 19). Hence, the number of black persons in poverty rose, even though the percentage of black families (with male heads) declined sharply.

The inheritance of poverty seems to elicit three basic attitudes. One was suggested, with desperate humor, by Edward Fitzgerald in 1844:

If we could but feed our poor! It is now the 8th of December; it has blown a most desperate East wind, all razors. . . . What are all the poor folks to do during the winter? And they persist in having the same enormous families they used to do; a woman came to me two days ago who had seventeen children. What farmers are to employ all these? What landlord can find room for them? The law of generation must be repealed [Rees 1919, p. 308].

More than a century later, and thousands of miles away, Indira Gandhi heard—and began compulsory sterilization. Of course, if "the national interest," or the five-year plan, demands rising per capita incomes her route offers one alternative. For per capita income does decline in a nation whenever children are born. And the more children born, the greater the decline. To block that result, China has imposed powerful economic and social penalties against families with more than two children. Other nations have taken the somewhat milder policy of deterring births by limiting housing construction.

A second viewpoint is that of parents. They act as though expenditures to raise children produce satisfactions at least as surely as spending to raise dogs or goldfish. Ever since the Flood, parents have produced and raised children—to satisfy their own desires. As one of Congreve's characters tells his disobedient son:

Why, Sirrah, mayn't I do what I please? . . . Did I not beget you? And might not I have chosen whether I would have begot you or no? . . . How came you here, Sir? . . . Did you come a volunteer into the World? Or did I, with the lawful Authority of a Parent, press you to the Service? [Congreve 1966, act 2]

The desertion of children simply italicizes the role of parental self-interest in deciding how many children will be born, and into what economic circumstances. The annual campaigns in the United States to raise money for the starving children in the Third World have one rock-hard component. They can confidently assume that millions of children will be starving five years hence—none of whom is yet born. Future food campaigns will have suitable objects of distress.

There exists a third viewpoint—that of the child. Presumably, no child would choose to be born into poverty. It is parents who conscript their children into poverty. For one group of fathers the persistent odds that their children will grow up in poverty are 7 in 100. But fathers in another group, who generate and desert many children, can guarantee odds of 88 in 100.

Economists have no professional basis for choosing among these three views. But they can observe that priority to the child's future welfare is not primary in most contemporary societies.

## Bibliography

Bane, Mary Jo, and David Ellwood. 1983. *Slipping into and out of poverty: The dynamics of spells*. Cambridge, Mass.: National Bureau of Economic Research.

Chao, Kang. 1968. *The construction industry in Communist China*. Hawthorne, N.Y.: Aldine.

Congreve, William. 1966. *Love for love*. Edited by Emmett L. Avery. Lincoln: University of Nebraska Press.

Galbraith, John K. 1958. *The affluent society*. Boston: Houghton Mifflin.

Hale, William. 1853. *The Domesday of St. Pauls*. London: Camden Society Publications.

Heilbroner, Robert, and Lester Thurow. 1977. *The Economic Problem Newsletter* (Winter). New York: Prentice-Hall.

Lebergott, Stanley. 1964. *Manpower in economic growth*. New York: McGraw-Hill.

———. 1975. *Wealth and want*. Princeton, N.J.: Princeton University Press.

———. 1976. *The American economy: Income wealth and want*. Princeton, N.J.: Princeton University Press.

Lester, Richard. 1964. *The economics of labor*. New York: Macmillan.

Lewis, Oscar. 1961. *Children of Sanchez*. New York: Random House.

Morgan, James, et al. 1981, *Five thousand American families: Patterns of economic progress*. Ann Arbor, Mich.: Institute of Survey Research.

Naipaul, V. S. 1965. *A flag on the island*. London: Deutsch.

*New York Times*, December 16, 1976; February 6, May 3, 1977.

Podell, Lawrence. 1966. *Families on welfare in New York City*. New York: City

University of New York, Center for the Study of Urban Problems, n.d. (1966 or 1967).

President's Commission on Income Maintenance. 1969. *Poverty amid plenty: The American paradox.*

————. 1970. *Technical Studies.* Washington, D.C.

Quinn, Robert, and Graham Staines. 1979. American workers evaluate the quality of their jobs. *Monthly Labor Review,* January, p. 8.

Raitsin, V. I. 1969. *Planning and the standard of living according to consumption norms.* White Plains, N.Y.: International Arts and Sciences Press.

Rees, Byron. 1919. *Nineteenth century letters.* New York: Scribner.

Shearman, Thomas S. 1895. *Natural taxation.* New York: Doubleday and McClure.

Simmel, Georg. 1978. *The philosophy of money.* London: Routledge and Kegan Paul.

Simons, Henry. 1948. *Economic policy for a free society.* Chicago: University of Chicago Press.

Thaler, Richard, and Sherwin Rosen. 1975. The value of saving a life: Evidence from the labor market. In Nestor Terlecky, ed., *Household production and consumption,* p. 292. New York: Columbia University Press.

Thoreau, Henry David. 1971. *Walden.* Edited by Lyndon Shanley. Princeton, N.J.: Princeton University Press.

Thurow, Lester. 1969. *Poverty and discrimination.* Washington, D.C.: Brookings Institution.

U.S. Census Bureau. 1940. *Size of family and age of head.* Washington, D.C.: Government Printing Office.

————. 1945. *Family and individual money income in the United States, 1945.* P-60, nos. 2, 103. Washington, D.C.: Government Printing Office.

————. 1970*a*. *Low-income population.* Washington, D.C.: Government Printing Office.

————. 1970*b*. *Persons by family characteristics.* Washington, D.C.: Government Printing Office.

————. 1970*c*. *Sources and structure of family income.* Washington, D.C.: Government Printing Office.

————. 1975. *Historical Statistics of the United States . . . to 1970.* Washington, D.C.: Government Printing Office.

————. 1980. *Current Population Reports.* P-60, nos. 6, 81, 103, 125. Washington, D.C.: Government Printing Office.

————. 1983. *Characteristics of the population below the poverty level, 1983,* P-60, no. 147. Washington, D.C.: Government Printing Office.

————. 1984*a*. *Estimates of poverty including the value of noncash benefits, 1984.* Tech. Paper 55. Washington, D.C.: Government Printing Office.

————. 1984*b*. *Money income and poverty status . . . 1984.* P-60, no. 149. Washington, D.C.: Government Printing Office.

U.S. Congress, Senate. 1913. *Congressional Record,* August 27. Washington, D.C.: Government Printing Office.

U.S. Department of Labor, Bureau of Labor Statistics. *Special Labor Force Report,* no. 185. 1986.

U.S. President. 1965. *Economic Report of the President, 1965.* Washington, D.C.: Government Printing Office.

————. 1971. *Manpower Report of the President.* April. Washington, D.C.: Government Printing Office.

————. 1985. *Economic Report of the President, 1985.* Washington, D.C.: Government Printing Office.

Voslensky, Michael. 1984. *Nomenklatura.* Garden City, N.Y.: Doubleday.

*Part VI*  **Mass Media**

## Eleanor Singer

# 19 Surveys in the Mass Media

Opinion polls and surveys have succeeded in capturing the attention of the media beyond the wildest dreams of their early practitioners, representing the most visible application of social science methods today. In 1944, when Hadley Cantril, then director of Princeton's Office of Public Opinion Research, carried out the first poll on the polls, about 9 percent of the people surveyed said that they regularly followed poll results in any newspaper or magazine; 44 percent had never heard or read about polls (Goldman 1944). Forty years later, in the spring of 1985, Gallup found that the percentage of the population that follows polls regularly had almost tripled, to 25 percent; and everyone, apparently, had heard about them. Small wonder: Turner and Martin (1984*b*) estimated that over 200 million copies of newspapers containing poll results reached the American public in a one-month period from July 1 to July 30, 1980. About half of all social science studies reported during a five-month period in 1982 in ten national news media consisted of attitude or opinion surveys; surveys made up 81 percent of all social science studies in which the method used was explicitly identified (Weiss and Singer with Endreny, forthcoming).[1]

This paper is based on a larger study of the reporting of social science in the media, carried out in collaboration with Carol Weiss and Phyllis Endreny. The support of the Russell Sage Foundation is gratefully acknowledged. I would like to express my appreciation to our research assistants Kathleen Allen, Kathy Cole, Anna Di Lellio, Diane Elebe, Doris Newman, Anastasios Kalomiris, and Thuy Tranthi, and to Marc Glassman, for statistical consultation and data processing. I would also like to thank Hubert J. O'Gorman for his generous spirit and astute editing.

[1] For some estimates of the size of contemporary survey research activities, see Rossi, Wright, and Anderson 1983; Turner and Martin 1984*b*.

413

Despite persistent concerns about the reliability and validity of the survey method in general (for a tiny recent sampling, see, e.g., Lang 1981; Schuman and Presser 1981; Sudman and Bradburn 1974; Turner and Martin 1984*b*)—and political polling in particular (see, e.g., Wheeler 1976)—it has established itself as preeminently suited for the investigation of public opinion. And public opinion, whether measured by traditional "man-in-the-street" interviews or by "scientific" polls, or, most recently, by electronic pseudo polls, is what the press is in the business of reporting as well as attempting to mold.

Indeed, some say that public opinion polls are performing this function all too well; that the incessant din of feeding their own opinions back to the public serves to control and shape as well as inform opinion, and perhaps even to discourage its expression (e.g., Beniger 1983; Bogart 1972; Boorstin 1978; Field 1971; Noelle-Neumann 1984). But this criticism is leveled at the polls only in part; in larger part, it is addressed to the media, without whose amplification the pollster's would be only a voice crying in the wilderness.

It is easy to imagine that this concern is new, the result of the polls' increasing visibility. But, in commenting on Cantril's first survey of opinion on the polls, Goldman (1944, p. 461) wrote:

For the first time, public opinion polls are the subject of serious and widespread criticism. Polling men themselves are intensely concerned with inadequacies in their techniques, but surprisingly little of the attack is directed against these inadequacies. The spectacular success of the polls in predicting elections seems to have stamped deeply the impression that the polls can, if they want to, get accurate results. The criticism is moving chiefly along two other lines. Do all of the polls want to get accurate results and interpret them fairly all of the time? Are the polls, even if accurate and fair, contributing to the successful functioning of democracy? . . . [N]ever have the questions been asked so widely, so persistently, and with so much rancor as in the months surrounding the bitter election of 1944.

But it is not only surveys of public opinion that flourish in the media. Health, relationship, and life-style pages also occasionally feature social science research, and though surveys make up a less prominent part of the studies mentioned there, they are by no means absent. Because of the social invention of surveys and their deployment in the mass media of communication, the pictures of others' lives that we carry in our heads have been immeasurably enriched and the cognitive framework of millions of human beings has been greatly enlarged. Furthermore, the results of polls and surveys are used by policy makers at all levels of government as well as by politicians seeking access to government positions. Survey findings enter into economic predictions prepared by private and public forecasting firms.

Polls and surveys are, thus, inextricably linked to the social sciences, on the one hand, and to the polity, on the other.[2] And because they are becoming a standard feature of an increasing number of news organizations, they are heard or seen every day by millions of ordinary people who otherwise would have little or no contact with any other aspect of the social sciences. But what is it that they see?

For several years, Carol Weiss, Phyllis Endreny, and I have been engaged in a study of the reporting of social science. The study, which looks at social science reporting in ten news media—the *New York Times,* the *Washington Post,* the *Wall Street Journal,* the *Boston Globe, Newsweek, Time, U.S. News and World Report,* and the three network evening newscasts—consisted of two major components: a content analysis of the media in 1982 and a corresponding period in 1970, and interviews with reporters, social scientists, and editors on selected social science stories. For the content analysis, we selected every story that met our definition of social science during a five-month period in 1982 and a three-month period in 1970 in which we monitored every third week of media coverage—a total of 3,107 stories. We defined social science as the intersection of two dimensions: Every story that mentioned a social science element (research, a social scientist, data, a social science organization, theory, method, or institutional concerns) pertaining to one of seventeen specified fields (e.g., economics, psychology, sociology) was included in our sample. For each item, we coded a set of media variables—the media name and date, the amount of space or time devoted to the item, the prominence with which it was featured, and so on. For each item, we also coded a set of content variables, including such information as the topic of the story and the nature of the item (book review, obituary, news story, etc.). The remaining information coded varied depending on the particular social science element involved. For research reports, for example, we coded such information as the kind of study involved (opinion and attitude survey, laboratory experiment, economic forecast, etc.), the institutional origins of the study, the discipline of the investigator, whether or not the investigator was named or identified as a social scientist, whether or not information was given about the methods used in the study, and so on.[3] (For further details about the research design as well as the findings, see Weiss and Singer with Endreny, forthcoming.)

[2] As Boyd with Hyman (1975, pp. 306–7) points out, "The history of survey methodology illustrates the close connection between the research and the policy interests of those who pioneered the development of surveys."

[3] For the content items, our measure of reliability (kappa) averaged .66 at the beginning of coding and .77 at the end; for the study-specific items, .32 and .52. Because kappa, which measures the agreement among *n* coders after adjusting for chance agreement, is a much more stringent test of intercoder reliability than is ordinarily em-

As will become apparent, we allowed the media to define both a "study" in general and a "survey" in particular. That is, we did not set any methodological criteria that the research had to meet in order to be classified as a piece of social science research.[4] This was done for two reasons: because a paucity of information about methods ordinarily made it impossible to apply such criteria; and because, if the media defined something as a "survey," that is how it was probably perceived by the public. Nor did we distinguish between censuses and sample surveys but included both data collection methods in our count.

In this paper, I do three things. First, I examine some characteristics of the opinion and attitude surveys reported in the national media, contrasting them with other kinds of social science studies reported there.[5] What subjects are covered in the surveys reported? Who sponsors them, and who carries them out? Are they reported more or less often than other kinds of social science studies, and is the quality of reporting better or worse? Where appropriate, I compare 1982 findings with those for 1970.

Second, I compare in some detail the presentation of opinion and attitude surveys in the mass media with the norms for their presentation in scholarly journals, again contrasting this with the reporting of other types of social science studies. By these criteria, is the reporting of surveys in the mass media better or worse, more or less complete, than the reporting of other kinds of social science research? I also draw on a study of surveys in the scholarly literature by Presser (1984), which makes it possible to compare the reporting of surveys in the media with their treatment by social scientists themselves. Finally, I look at some instances of the reporting of surveys in the media that appear to me to be problematic and ask what some of the consequences of such reporting are likely to be for public attitudes toward public opinion research.[6]

In 1980, Paletz and his colleagues examined the reporting of poll stories in three media (Paletz et al. 1980). But, aside from providing a more recent reading (Paletz's study is based on polls reported in 1973,

---

ployed, values of .21–.40 are considered fair, .41–.60 moderate, .61–.80 substantial, and anything over .81 almost perfect (Landis and Koch 1977).

[4]Hyman (1973) defines a survey as "an inquiry of a large number of people, selected by rigorous sampling, conducted in normal life settings by explicit, standardized procedures yielding quantitative measurements." The definition is also adopted by Boyd with Hyman (1975, p. 266).

[5]The presence of a social science study was the most frequent reason for selecting stories focused on social science in 1982 and the second most frequent, after mention of a social scientist, for selecting stories that mentioned social science in an ancillary context.

[6]Some sections of this final part of the paper are based on Singer and Endreny, forthcoming.

1975, and 1977), the present study differs from the earlier one in a number of respects.

In the first place, it draws on a wider sampling of media. Second, it draws on an actual monitoring of the media, instead of a search of the *New York Times* and the Vanderbilt Television Indexes. As a result, it is based on a larger *number* of stories (concentrated in a shorter period of time), as well as on different *kinds* of stories from those analyzed by Paletz.[7]

Finally, the two studies have somewhat different perspectives. Paletz supplies an implicit frame of reference for his analysis, according to which polls—or the way they are reported in the media—are found wanting. In the present study, the frame of reference is provided by several explicit comparisons: norms for the reporting of social science research in the scholarly literature; the actual reporting of survey methods in scholarly journals; and the reporting of social science research other than surveys in the media. By these criteria, too, the reporting of surveys is found wanting. But whereas Paletz, a political scientist, is concerned primarily with the potential of poll reporting for the trivialization of politics, I am concerned primarily with its potential for the trivialization of social research.

## Some Characteristics of Surveys in the Media

During the five-month period in 1982 in which we monitored the media every third week, we coded 853 stories containing a reference to social science studies; 421 of these studies were coded as surveys or polls of opinions or attitudes.[8] In 193, or a little less than half of the 421, the survey was the focus of the news story; the rest were what we called "ancillary" stories, in which the reference to a survey was subsidiary to the story's main theme. One-half of all the focus social science studies reported by newspapers in 1982 were coded as opinion

[7] For example, we picked up many more stories in which the survey was a subsidiary element in a larger news story, and we probably picked up a larger proportion of stories which, though focused on a survey, were of relatively minor importance. Furthermore, although a precise comparison is difficult because of differences in the coding scheme, it appears that Paletz's sample of stories includes a much larger percentage devoted to polls about the presidency and about political parties than does our own.

[8] By opinion and attitude surveys, we meant to include what is generally regarded as public opinion research; more specialized studies—for example, evaluation studies and studies of audience shares—were excluded from this category even if they used survey methods, provided we recognized them as such. Although some studies may have been incorrectly classified as a result, the error was probably not large; evaluation studies, for example, were estimated to have made up 7.9 percent of all studies in 1982. The most likely errors we made were to classify as opinion or attitude surveys some studies that dealt primarily or exclusively with reports of behavior rather than attitudes, but we cannot estimate the magnitude of this confusion.

or attitude surveys; this was true of 36 percent of those reported on television and of 17 percent of those reported by newsmagazines. The proportions of surveys were even higher for studies mentioned in an ancillary role: 49 percent of such studies in newspapers, 59 percent of those in newsmagazines, and 71 percent of those on television were coded as attitude or opinion surveys. None of these proportions represents a substantial change from 1970. In short, in 1982 as in 1970, opinion surveys were the dominant type of study referred to by the national news media in their coverage of social science research.

Although these were surveys of opinion, and ordinarily of opinion about public rather than private life, they were not, with rare exceptions, election polls. We deliberately selected 1982 and 1970 as our comparison years in order to avoid inflating the count of social science studies with the flood of polls that characterize reporting in an election year.

Some flavor of the range of opinion research reported in the media in 1982 can be gleaned from the following partial list of specific survey topics: presidential preferences, presidential approval, political parties; drugs and drug usage; confidence in and evaluations of the economy; social security; welfare and poverty; drinking age; punishment for drunk drivers; unemployment; satisfaction with life and work; threat of nuclear war; nuclear weapons, arms control, and the proposed nuclear freeze; the Middle East; the Soviet Union; civil liberties; terrorism; the environmental movement, environmental protection and regulation; residential segregation and bias. If a topic is newsworthy, the news media are likely, at some time, to report survey results pertaining to it. Much more rarely do they report surveys that have no clear link with currently salient events—for example, surveys of satisfaction with life and work.

Compared to other social science research, the surveys reported in the media in 1982 (1) *were much less likely to originate at a university, and much more likely to originate with the media themselves* (cf. Table 19.1).[9] The proportion of media surveys has increased substantially since 1970, at the expense of those originating with government and other research organizations. About 20 percent of surveys reported in newspapers in 1982, and an even higher percentage of those reported in newsmagazines or on television, were surveys initiated and, in most cases, carried out by the media themselves.[10] Thus, increasingly, the surveys

[9] Throughout, data are shown for 1982 surveys; tables permitting comparisons with studies other than surveys in 1982, and between surveys and other studies in 1970, are available from the author on request.

[10] In contrast, Paletz et al. (1980) found that 40 percent of the television polls were done by Gallup or Harris; and Gallup, Harris, and other established polling organizations conducted 65 percent of those reported in the *New York Times!*

TABLE 19.1. *Institutional Origin of Survey, by Type of Media and Whether Study Is Focus or Ancillary (1982)*

| Institutional origin | Focus | | | Ancillary | | |
|---|---|---|---|---|---|---|
| | News-papers | News-maga-zines | TV | News-papers | News-maga-zines | TV |
| University | 11.6% | — | — | 7.0% | 6.3% | — |
| Government | 17.7 | — | 37.5% | 8.6 | 6.3 | — |
| Other research organization | 21.5 | 50.0% | — | 28.5 | 25.0 | 30.0% |
| Media-initiated poll, self-executed | 20.4 | 25.0 | 62.5 | 15.6 | 21.9 | 40.0 |
| Media-initiated poll, other-executed | 1.1 | 25.0 | — | 2.7 | 6.3 | — |
| Other | 19.3 | — | — | 16.1 | 12.5 | — |
| D.K. | 8.3 | — | — | 21.5 | 21.9 | 30.0 |
| (N) | (181) | (4) | (8) | (186) | (32) | (10) |

the public is exposed to in the media are carried out to serve the imperatives of news organizations. Other social science studies reported in the media are much more likely to reflect the interests of academic social scientists; only about 2 percent of such studies were reported as originating with the media themselves.

(2) The surveys *were more likely to identify the sponsor of the research.* This statement is to some extent misleading: Television and newsmagazines were much more likely to identify sponsors of surveys than of other studies, but this was because they were often talking about their *own* surveys. Newspapers were no more likely to identify survey sponsors than those of other studies—in both cases, only about one-quarter of the time (cf. Table 19.2).[11]

(3) The surveys *were more likely to be about some aspect of government and politics.* The modal public opinion story in 1982 was about government or politics. By way of contrast, about half of all studies other than opinion surveys that were reported in the media in 1982 were rather evenly divided between economics and health, with another 20 percent or so falling into the area we labeled integration and social control, which consists, on the one hand, of stories devoted to religion, education, and other activities relevant to socialization and, on the other, to stories about law enforcement and crime. Compared

[11] Paletz et al. (1980) report that sponsors were identified in 25 percent of the *New York Times* poll stories, and in even fewer of those on television.

TABLE 19.2. *Details of Reporting, by Type of Media and Whether Survey Story Is Focus or Ancillary (1982)*

| Detail | Focus | | | Ancillary | | |
|---|---|---|---|---|---|---|
| | News-papers | News-magazines | TV | News-papers | News-magazines | TV |
| Reference to a published source | | | | | | |
| Yes | 29.8% | 25.0% | 0.0% | 12.4% | 12.5% | 10.0% |
| No | 64.6 | 25.0 | 37.5 | 83.3 | 84.4 | 80.0 |
| DNA; media poll | 5.5 | 50.0 | 62.5 | 4.3 | 3.1 | 10.0 |
| Information about method | | | | | | |
| Yes, detail | 46.4 | 50.0 | 50.0 | 11.8 | 9.4 | — |
| Yes, name only | 48.1 | 50.0 | 37.5 | 82.3 | 84.4 | 100.0 |
| No | 5.5 | — | 12.5 | 5.9 | 6.3 | 0.0 |
| Mention of discrepant information | | | | | | |
| Yes | 3.9 | 25.0 | 12.5 | 2.2 | 3.1 | 0.0 |
| Mention of supporting findings | | | | | | |
| Yes | 11.6 | 0.0 | 0.0 | 6.5 | 18.8 | 0.0 |
| Number of investigators | | | | | | |
| Unknown | 83.4 | 75.0 | 100.0 | 91.4 | 93.8 | 100.0 |
| Sponsor named | | | | | | |
| Yes | 32.6 | 75.0 | 75.0 | 21.0 | 25.0 | 40.0 |
| Mention of data | | | | | | |
| Yes | 93.4 | 100.0 | 100.0 | 88.2 | 96.9 | 90.0 |
| Information about subgroups | | | | | | |
| Yes | 39.8 | 100.0 | 62.5 | 16.7 | 12.5 | 10.0 |
| Information about change over time | | | | | | |
| Yes | 40.9 | 50.0 | 50.0 | 19.9 | 25.0 | 10.0 |
| Interpretation or analysis | | | | | | |
| Yes | 30.9 | 25.0 | 0.0 | 18.3 | 15.6 | 10.0 |
| (N) | (181) | (4) | (8) | (186) | (32) | (10) |

with 1970, proportionately more focus opinion surveys reported in newspapers in 1982 were devoted to economic issues, with a corresponding decline in surveys related to demographic trends. There was little change with respect to other topics.

(4) The surveys *were much more likely to include some mention of data.* More than 90 percent of all opinion surveys reported in the media included some mention of data in 1982—a proportion substantially higher than that for other types of studies and up slightly from 1970 (cf. Table 19.2).

(5). *They were much less likely to include any interpretation or analysis of the findings.* Only 31 percent of focus newspaper stories about surveys, 25 percent of those in newsmagazines, and none of those reported on television included such interpretation or analysis in 1982, compared with 46 percent of focus stories about studies other than surveys, regardless of where they appeared (cf. Table 19.2). (There was much less difference between ancillary reports of surveys and ancillary reports of other studies: 18 percent of the former and 20 percent of the latter included some interpretation or analysis of the findings in 1982.)

Most opinion surveys reported in the media, like most other kinds of studies reported there, originated in the United States. The single exception is the category of ancillary surveys reported on television; 71 percent of these, consisting for the most part of foreign public opinion polls, originated *outside* the United States in 1982.

What conclusions can we draw from the portrait presented so far? Most obvious but perhaps most important is the fact that the agenda for surveys reported in the media is set by the *public* agenda, not by that of social science. Although to some extent this is true for all social science research reported there (cf. Weiss and Singer with Endreny, forthcoming), it is especially evident in the case of survey research. As a result, the findings reported tend to be relatively ephemeral. Furthermore, although social scientists have learned to pay less attention to simple marginals in favor of much more complex analyses (Schuman and Kalton 1985), so far marginals remain the staple of media reporting. And although in 1982 between 36 and 45 percent of all focus social science studies, including surveys, provided information about subgroups or about changes over time, this information was generally presented without analysis or interpretation.

Furthermore, as we have seen, the media themselves have become more frequent originators of surveys, which they then have an economic incentive to report (Roper 1983). And, to the extent that the media report on their own research, media needs—for speedy as well as topically relevant results—increasingly shape the methodology as well as the content of the surveys reported there.

## Some Characteristics of Survey Reporting

Elsewhere, I have noted that by far the most significant difference between social science research as written for the general public and as written for other social scientists has to do with the way research findings are presented (Singer and Endreny 1986). In newspapers, newsmagazines, and on television, findings resulting from one piece of research, done in a particular time and place with a distinct sample and a specified research instrument, are often presented as if they were universal truths, holding for all people everywhere.

In the original analysis of these data, we identified several media practices that contribute to the image of a disembodied social science: failure to identify a published source, failure to name the researcher, failure to discuss the methods used, and failure to place the research findings in context by providing supporting or discrepant evidence from other research. Here, I look separately at the category of attitude and opinion surveys, comparing their reporting to that of all other social science studies with respect to the media practices identified above. Implicit in that analysis is a comparison between certain media *practices* and the *norms* governing the reporting of social science research in scholarly journals. By this criterion, the reporting of surveys is in some respects better, in most respects worse, than the reporting of other kinds of social science studies. Subsequently, I use Presser's analysis (1985) to compare certain aspects of the reporting of surveys in the mass media with their reporting by social scientists themselves. In this comparison, the mass media fare better—and the scholarly journals worse—than might have been supposed.

### Identification of a Published Source

When an article in a scholarly journal presents findings from prior research, the source of those findings is expected to be clearly indicated, either in a footnote or in a list of references. (That the findings may not always be accurately reported, even in a scholarly journal, is another matter; cf. Garfield, 1977–78.)

In media reports of surveys, however, a published source was indicated only 30 percent of the time in focus newspaper stories and only about 12 percent of the time in ancillary stories in all media (see Table 19.2). Media reports of studies other than surveys were somewhat more punctilious in citing a published source. Between 50 and 60 percent of all stories about focus studies other than surveys referred to a published source in 1982, and about a quarter of all ancillary stories did so, as well.

It can be argued that reference to a published source is less feasible for an opinion survey than for other kinds of social science studies, since many survey and poll findings are presented as press releases or client reports and are not available in published form. Nevertheless, it remains true that the information ordinarily presented in a news account of a survey is insufficient to enable readers easily to track down the original release or full report.[12] And, as we shall see, the details ordinarily provided in the media account of a survey are no substitute for such source materials.

## Identification of the Researcher

When writing for a scholarly journal, it is customary to cite those responsible for prior relevant research (e.g., Garfield 1977–78; Kaplan 1965). But identification of the scientists who carried out the research being reported is far from accepted practice in the media (cf. Borman 1978). The author is likely to be unknown to a mass audience; the institution under whose auspices the study was done is much more likely to be familiar. Hence, media references to institutional auspices are used both to locate and to legitimate the research being reported.

As it turns out, however, failure to identify the researcher is much more common in the reporting of opinion and attitude surveys than in the reporting of other kinds of social science research. For each media story, we coded how many scientists were identified as carrying out the study in question. In 1982, this number was *unknown* for 88 percent of newspaper reports of surveys, for 92 percent of newsmagazine reports, and for 100 percent of reports of surveys on television. By way of contrast, the figures for other kinds of social science research were considerably lower, though still not trivial: 67 percent for newspaper stories; 59.5 percent for newsmagazine stories; and 78 percent for television stories.

In part, of course, the tendency not to identify an individual as the researcher responsible for an opinion or attitude survey reflects the reality of how many surveys are conceived and carried out. Such surveys are large, collective enterprises; they are done by "Gallup," "Harris," or "Yankelovich," rather than by individual researchers employed by these organizations (Paletz et al. [1980] refer to these organizations as "conductors"). Although one individual may ultimately be responsible for a particular survey, the collective attribution fairly reflects the complexity of its creation.

Other surveys, however, are done by survey organizations for indi-

---

[12] Reference to a "Gallup poll released yesterday," or to "figures from the latest Survey of Consumer Confidence, released yesterday by the Conference Board," were coded as *not* referring to a published source.

vidual investigators; they reflect an individual, not a bureaucratic, sensibility. After all, the *Midtown Manhattan Study* (Srole et al. 1962), *The Academic Mind* (Lazarsfeld and Thielens 1958), and *The Civic Culture* (Almond and Verba 1963) were all studies done by means of survey research. In such cases, an individual researcher can be identified in the media account. Unfortunately, we were unable to distinguish those surveys that are appropriately identified only by an organization's name from those in which an individual could have been identified as well. But it does seem to be true that, especially in the case of surveys, the news media substitute organizational for individual identification. Whereas most stories left the identity of the researcher in doubt, fewer than 10 percent of focus stories failed to identify the type of institution in which a survey originated.

## Placing Research Findings in Context

In a scholarly article, it is considered customary to put one's findings in context: to provide an indication of whether they accord with, or depart from, the findings of related research (Kaplan 1965; Wilson 1952). We have, unfortunately, no information about how regularly this norm is obeyed in practice. We do know, however, that the proportion of media stories that provide such a context is very small. In 1982, between 0 and 15 percent of focus stories about social science research (depending on the medium) provided supporting information, as did between 0 and 24 percent of ancillary stories; the figures were about the same for discrepant information.

When we examined these practices separately for opinion surveys and other social science studies, we found that they were somewhat more common in the reporting of other studies than in the reporting of surveys. In newspaper reports, for example, 13 percent of stories about focus studies other than surveys included some discussion of discrepant findings, compared with 4 percent of survey stories; and 19 percent of stories about "other" studies included supporting findings, compared with 12 percent of stories about surveys. The same trends, though on a reduced scale, were apparent for surveys and other studies reported in an ancillary context. I return to the implications of this later.

## Discussion of the Methods Used

Very few reports of social science research in the media discuss the methods used in any detail—only 18 percent of the studies we analyzed in 1982—and only thirty (of 853) stories about research contained any evaluation of those methods.

Surveys of public opinion were considerably *more* likely than other types of social science studies to provide some information about the method used. Just about half the focus surveys in our sample provided some detail about methods; all but a handful of the rest at least named the method used, though an unknown number of these "surveys" were in fact instances of what I have called pseudo research (see below). Among surveys reported in an ancillary context, only about 10 percent provided any methodological detail, but, again, virtually all the rest named the method used.[13]

By contrast, only 14 percent of stories about studies other than surveys provided any details about the methods used, even when the study was the focus of the news story. An additional 20 percent named the method (e.g., experiment, secondary analysis), whereas the rest provided no information whatever. Among studies other than surveys that were reported in an ancillary context, almost 80 percent provided no methodological information at all.

Media reports of surveys thus provide more information than other studies about the method used. But how adequate is the information provided?

Paletz et al. (1980, p. 505) found that 67 percent of their *New York Times* articles reported sample size and 43 percent gave the dates of the survey; the figures for the NBC and CBS evening news programs were lower. But aside from sample size and survey dates, information was minimal. In 95 percent of the television stories and 70 percent of those in the *Times,* for example, none of the polling questions was quoted in its entirety, though words or phrases from some of the questions were often quoted. Sampling error was given in only 7 percent of the stories in the *Times.*

We did not record the precise details provided by media stories about surveys. But we did stipulate that mention of *any two* of the following would qualify a survey as providing "details" about methods: sample size, interviewing dates, wording of any question, and response rate. Thus, we know that at least half the focus surveys and 90 percent of the ancillary surveys failed to provide even two bits of information about how the survey was done. Interestingly enough, surveys reported on television were no less likely to provide details, according to this crude classification system, than those reported in newspapers.

[13] To some extent, this finding may be an artifact. Studies labeled as surveys were easily classified as opinion or attitude surveys; some surveys not so labeled may have been misclassified into another category, where they would have contributed to the "no information about methods" category. However, we believe that such instances of misclassification, if they occurred, were rare.

Our standards for "detailed" reporting were, of course, very lax. A somewhat more stringent set of standards for minimal disclosure is that of the American Association for Public Opinion Research (AAPOR), which stipulates that information about the following should be incorporated in the text of any release about surveys:

1. Identity of *who sponsored* the survey.
2. The *exact wording* of question asked.
3. A *definition of the population* actually sampled.
4. *Size of sample.* For mail surveys, this should include the number of questionnaires mailed out *and* the number returned.
5. An indication of what allowance should be made for *sampling error.*
6. *Which results are based on parts of the sample,* rather than the total sample. (For example: likely voters only, those aware of an event, those who answered other questions in a certain way.)
7. Whether *interviewing* was done personally, by telephone, or by mail; at home or on street corners.
8. *Timing* of the interviewing in relation to relevant events.

Although news media are "strongly urged" to ask for and to include all the information above when preparing final copy for publication or broadcast, most of the stories falling into our sample did not meet these standards.

But, as it turns out, the media differ less in this respect from scholarly journals than might have been supposed. Noting that concern about the reporting of survey procedures has focused mainly on the mass media, Presser (1985) asks whether such details are ordinarily included in scholarly articles drawing on survey data. He points out that there is evidence that this has not always been the case in the past, quoting a 1967 National Research Council committee's report and an analysis of sociology articles by Alwin and Stephens (1979). His own analysis of articles based on survey data that have appeared in the leading journals of four social science disciplines indicates that the problem persists and that there has been little improvement with the passage of time. Even restricting the analysis to those articles reporting data the authors themselves had collected or that had been collected by other individuals (i.e., excluding data collected by large survey organizations, for which extensive documentation is ordinarily available but is not necessarily presented in detail in any given article) reveals that *fewer than half* of them reported on each of the following: sampling method, response rate, the wording of any question, year of the survey, or interviewer characteristics. "These reporting levels," writes Presser, "are not markedly better than those of the much criticized mass media, despite the considerably greater space available in journals."

This section has tried to answer the question "How is survey research reported in the media?" by comparing it with several reference points. In the first place, there is the set of norms that applies to the reporting of research in the scholarly literature and that prescribes such practices as the citing of a published source for prior work, identification of the researcher responsible for such work, detailed description of the methods used, and placing the research in context by citing discrepant or supporting findings from the work of others. Compared to this set of standards, the reporting of all social research in the media falls short. But reports of surveys are even less likely to include such details than news stories about other kinds of social research, with one exception: They provide more information about the methods used. With respect to methods, the reporting of surveys in the media is superior to the reporting of other social research, and it is not markedly inferior to the reporting of surveys in scholarly journals. But, as Presser (1985) and Paletz et al. (1980) have pointed out, the information provided in both places is ordinarily far from adequate for permitting an informed evaluation of the results.

## Surveys, Pseudo Surveys, and Discrepant Poll Results

In a 1983 book entitled *Superstition and the Press*, Curtis MacDougall documents the coverage of paranormal events that appeared in the newspapers of Chicago, Washington, and Los Angeles and sporadically in other newspapers and periodicals over the last thirty years and asks whether the press, by its coverage of such phenomena, helps perpetuate superstition and ignorance.

Here, I pose an analogous question, asking whether the press, by its uncritical reporting of "surveys," helps foster ignorance and skepticism about public opinion research. The answer is that I believe it does, although there is some evidence to indicate that certain practices may be changing. In this section, I focus on some problematic aspects of the reporting of public opinion surveys, discussing these under two headings: the reporting of phone-ins, write-ins, and "electronic polls"; and the reporting of discrepancies among poll results. Both of these are linked to a lack of concern about methods, which has already been noted.

### Phone-ins, Write-ins, and Electronic Polls

Some "surveys" reported in the popular press result from activities that most social scientists would agree do not constitute legitimate research at all: "surveys" of a magazine's readers, based on responses by self-selected subscribers; phone-ins to 900 (or 800) numbers, sponsored by television networks; or interviews or questionnaires administered to convenience samples. Even though the number of "respondents" to such "surveys" can sometimes reach several hundred thousand, the method of phone-ins or write-ins violates all the rules of sampling on which legitimate surveys are based.

Although phone-ins are a relatively recent innovation, magazines such as *Ladies' Home Journal* and *Psychology Today* (and, most recently, *Science 1985!*) have for a long time conducted "surveys" of their readers, using the results as the basis for substantive reports subsequently published in the magazine. Such "surveys" obtain information about readers' opinions and, sometimes, demographic characteristics at a fraction of the cost of a real survey. The trouble is that there is no way of knowing how closely characteristics and attitudes of readers who voluntarily fill out the questionnaire printed in the magazine match those of all the magazine's readers. Still less confidence can be placed in projections from write-in responses to the general population, which includes nonreaders as well as readers.

Phone-ins are a more recent version of this procedure, especially adapted to the broadcast media. The television or radio station that sponsors such a call-in announces today's question over the air and provides two different call-in numbers. If a viewer is willing to have fifty cents charged to his phone bill, he can call one 900 number to register a "yes" answer or another 900 number to register a "no" answer. A variant of this procedure uses two 800 numbers, in which the sponsor of the call-in bears the cost. The phone companies, which have strenuously marketed phone-ins to the networks, make money either way, and so do the networks, who stand to increase their share of audience and, potentially, advertising revenue by the novelty and drama of these "instant polls."

But there are many defects to this procedure. In the first place, a person must be a viewer of the channel in question to be aware of the phone-in and to know what the two 900 numbers are. Then, in order to register an opinion, respondents must be willing to take the initiative and call the number, and to pay fifty cents. But if it is important enough and they are willing to pay the price, they can make as many calls as they like and have their opinion counted not once but many times. On a controversial issue, organized interest groups can create a "phone yes" or "phone no" campaign, urging their members to call early and often.

A variation on this procedure uses the capabilities of two-way cable. Writing in the *New York Times* of August 29, 1982, Larry Sabato commented on NBC News' use of Qube, a two-way cable hookup earlier installed in 29,000 homes in Columbus, Ohio. After President Carter's "crisis of confidence" speech in July 1979, the reactions of these 29,000 Ohioans were given national attention on NBC's "Prime Time Sunday" program. Viewers were asked a series of questions about their evaluation of Mr. Carter's speech and his presidency, and within seconds the percentage results of the responses were tabulated and flashed on the screen.

"While NBC advised the home audience that this nonrandom, unscientific sample was the equivalent of a 'man on the street' interview," Sabato wrote, "the definition was probably lost on most viewers, especially because the host of the program . . . referred to Qube as an 'electronic poll.'" Along with Roper (1983) and others, I believe that such devices cheapen the process of public opinion measurement and undermine the credibility of social science research in general.

## Discrepancies among Survey Results

Survey researchers know only too well the many factors, besides true differences in opinion, that can lead to discrepant poll results. The most easily quantified of these is sampling error, the difference attributable to the fact that opinion is measured on a sample of a certain size rather than the population as a whole. But sampling error is hardly the only factor involved. Preeminent among sources of nonsampling error are question wording, variations in the response alternatives offered, inclusion of an explicit "don't know" category, variations in the definition of eligible respondents, and a myriad of other factors that can bring about differences in response in the absence of any real difference in the underlying opinion or attitude (e.g., Andrews 1984; Bishop, Oldendick, and Tuchfarber 1983; Boyd with Hyman 1975; Schuman and Presser 1981; Sudman and Bradburn 1974).[14]

In 1978, Turner and Krauss set off a wave of unease among survey researchers and others involved in the social indicators movement by demonstrating apparent "house effects" in a number of questions asked in identical form by several different survey organizations ("Fallible Indicators of the Subjective State of the Nation"). This report triggered a flurry of self-examination (e.g., Smith 1982), culminating

[14] Whether this is to be regarded as a methodological defect remains to some extent an open question. Davis (1982), for example, points to it (only partly in jest) as an indication of the sensitivity of the survey method as a measurement tool: To change the wording or order of a question or the response alternatives offered is, in his view, to ask a different question, which *should* elicit a different answer. Furthermore, "measurement error" is hardly peculiar to survey research (e.g., Turner and Martin 1984*a*, pp. 14–17).

in a mammoth two-volume report finally published for the National Academy of Science by the Russell Sage Foundation (Turner and Martin 1984*b*). That report concluded that surveys are uniquely capable of shedding light on what people think and believe about themselves and their world and are generally capable of reasonably reliable and reproducible measurements. But it also urged more research into non-sampling survey errors and cautioned users against attaching undue significance to simple marginals—the stuff that most survey reports in the media are made of.

Thus, in the nature of the case, discrepant poll results are often obtained and widely disseminated. But the media, as political scientist Anthony Broh pointed out in a letter to the *New York Times* on October 30, 1980, present such results with little sensitivity to the different methods used by different survey organizations. And, as we saw earlier, there is a virtual absence of news stories in which discrepant survey results are juxtaposed in the same account, or, more significantly, in which any analysis or interpretation of the discrepant findings is offered.

In 1967, Philip Meyer in an article entitled "Social Science: A New Beat?" pointed to the transformation of social science from an armchair to an empirical science and urged journalists to develop the critical sophistication needed to separate the wheat from the chaff. "Social science," he said, "has not yet shaken down to the point where it is easy to identify the fringe operators. There is no equivalent of a local medical society to put the finger on a quack pollster. Many newspapers," he went on to point out,

blandly report the outcomes of polls as if all polls were alike. . . . Earlier this year, [Harris and Gallup] produced opposite results on the relative popularity of Richard Nixon and George Romney among Republican voters. Papers which subscribed to both polls shrugged their editorial shoulders and ran the conflicting reports side by side without comment, in the time-honored tradition of "letting the reader decide." If the highly educated staff of a metropolitan newspaper cannot interpret such a discrepancy, how can the poor reader be expected to do it? [Meyer 1967: pp. 5–6]

Thirteen years later, Noelle-Neumann (1980: p. 586), the well-known German survey researcher, wrote:

Whenever results stemming from different sources clash, this should serve as a signal to journalists that something important is going on, perhaps some progress or variation in methodology that deserves attention. . . . [E]xactly what it means can only be decided in the context of long-term, systematic observation of the institutes publishing the results. But this is rarely done in Germany.

Nevertheless, there are some signs that this situation is slowly beginning to change. On August 15, 1984, the *New York Times* ran a front-page story, by Robert Reinhold, which examined at length the methodological variations that might have accounted for the discrepant presidential poll results then being reported. On the following day, the *Wall Street Journal,* on page 2, featured a similar analysis by political scientist Carl Everett Ladd, executive director of the Roper Center for Public Opinion Research. And, in reporting the results of the *Times*–CBS polls, the *Times* now regularly includes a boxed statement indicating that sampling error is only one part of total survey error.

Noelle-Neumann, in the same article quoted earlier, reports on a contract between her public opinion research institute and a leading German daily newspaper, the *Frankfurter Allgemeine,* and comments on its impact:

The number of articles dealing with public opinion research results has increased markedly, not only on the editorial pages of the *Frankfurter Allgemeine* but also in the competing daily newspaper. . . . "Ambivalent" results are fully represented, while a subtle comparison of different methods of reaching an investigative goal is not only accepted but expressly solicited. The publication of essays about indicators or spurious correlations, about multilevel analyses or Guttman scales may also soon be possible. [1980, p. 596]

## Some Implications of the Findings

I began this examination of how opinion and attitude surveys are reported by asking: If the public had access only, or primarily, to the mass media for information about current survey research, what image would they confront? How do surveys reported in the media differ from those reported in scholarly journals? And what are some of the problematic aspects of the reporting of surveys and polls in the public press?

In view of the rich variety and number of surveys reported in the national media, it may seem ungracious to cavil about shortcomings in the quality of the reporting. The diffusion of sample survey findings has made more human beings aware of other people than at any time in history. Societies that now rely routinely on survey research are probably, in Shils's words, "more integrated in the sense that there is more mutual awareness, more perception of others, more imaginative empathy about the stages of mind and motivations of others" than in the past (Shils 1961). But, just because of their pervasive presence, concern about the way surveys are reported—about the quality of information that inevitably touches all of us—is an appropriate preoccupation of social scientists. This concern might well focus on three interrelated shortcomings in the reporting of survey research:

1. First, as we have seen, reporters pay very little attention to the details of how surveys were designed, carried out, or analyzed. This lack of attention is not peculiar to survey research; on the contrary, reporters tend to include more details in their accounts of surveys than in their description of other social research. Nor is the inclusion of methodological detail markedly better in many scholarly journals than it is in the popular press. Nevertheless, the amount of information provided about a survey in the media is generally inadequate to permit readers to evaluate the results.

2. Second, the media do not attempt to distinguish "good" surveys from "bad"; they are concerned less with the scientific value of the information communicated than with its entertainment value (cf. also Broh 1980; Noelle-Neumann 1980; Rokeach 1968; Wheeler 1976). The most blatant example is the recent attention given by the media to phone-ins, write-ins, and electronic "polls," but other examples could readily be cited. When journalists describe as "surveys" anything from a casual questioning of a handful of airplane passengers to standardized interviews with a probability sample of the adult population of the United States, the reader cannot be blamed for failing to discriminate between them.

In the last few years, surveys have been used in major investigations of mental health (e.g., National Institutes of Mental Health 1984; Kessler and McLeod 1984); group consciousness and identification (e.g., Jackman and Senter 1980); and judgments of equity with respect to income (e.g., Dubnoff 1985; Jasso and Rossi 1977), to mention only a tiny sampling of significant research. Secondary analyses of surveys have been used to investigate the long-term effects of education (Hyman and Wright 1979; Hyman, Wright, and Reed 1975); and the effects of widowhood (Hyman 1983). Yet, to the best of my knowledge, only the NIMH report has been reported in any of the media we monitored.

3. Related to the shortcomings just described are the media's failure to provide a context of relevant findings for those from a particular survey and the general absence of analysis and interpretation of survey results. Others (e.g., Broh 1980; Crespi 1980; Noelle-Neumann 1980; Paletz et al. 1980) have commented on this shortcoming as well. Crespi (1980), for example, sees it as the flip side of such generally positive effects of the collaboration of journalists and survey researchers as an emphasis on factual documentation of results and a sensitivity to changes in public opinion over time.

What, if anything, can be done to correct these shortcomings? Here, I briefly mention three things.[15]

1. One corrective is better training for reporters in the methods of social research—training designed to help them sort the wheat from the chaff (cf. also MacDonald 1978; Wheeler 1980; Wilhoit and Weaver 1980; all cited in Gollin 1980). Although some social scientists have expressed skepticism about the value of this approach (e.g., Noelle-Neumann 1980), others have attempted to put it into practice. Social scientists from the University of Michigan Survey Research Center, for example, conduct regular seminars in survey methods for editors and reporters of the *Detroit Free Press* (Michael Traugott, personal communication). And the Russell Sage Foundation, mindful of the extraordinarily complex skills needed in the reporting of risks, is supporting the work of Victor Cohn, a veteran science reporter for the *Washington Post*, in developing a primer for reporters on the statistical methods used by scientists (including social scientists) (Russell Sage Foundation *Newsletter*, no. 5 [1984], p. 4). If reporters are trained to ask the hard questions, researchers will increasingly have to answer them. As a result, the reporting of surveys may become more critical and more selective.

2. But reporters can hardly be expected to carry the whole burden. Therefore, survey researchers themselves must be prepared to play a more active role in improving the reporting of research results. One obvious way is to adhere strictly to AAPOR's "Standards of Disclosure," making available to journalists on a routine basis information crucial to evaluating a survey's quality. If journalists come to expect such information, its absence can be treated by them as a tip-off to poor quality and as an aid in screening out inadequate and misleading research, however dramatic its results may seem.

We also need more attention by social scientists to accurate reporting—to the inclusion of qualifications and caveats in material prepared for the press. Though some social scientists are dubious about the ability to woo journalists to a problematic view of the world ("Social research . . . can only make observations with a higher or lower probability of accuracy. This is something journalists abhor"; Noelle-Neumann 1980), and some journalists appear to support this view ("We don't especially like caveats; we wouldn't take caveats very seriously"; Rick Flaste, science editor of the *New York Times*, personal communication), I believe that the delimiting and qualification of research findings in

[15] Not surprisingly, there is a resemblance between these independently arrived at recommendations and those offered by Turner and Martin (1984*a*; see esp. pp. 44–48).

the media are absolutely essential for the proper regard and future esteem of the social sciences. Social scientists will have to learn how to qualify their findings when talking to reporters, and reporters will have to learn how to probe and report the reasons for discrepant results.

3. We need more cooperation by social scientists, social science organizations, and media organizations to eliminate the reporting of "pseudo" research. When ABC both conducts a phone-in and subsequently reports the results on television, it is not the ABC reporters who are to blame. It is the network that must be persuaded to abandon a practice it considers lucrative. There are, of course, plenty of "surveys" reported in the media that are not surveys at all and that better methodological training for reporters might eliminate from public view. But the issues often go beyond methodological sophistication to competition among individual and organizational interests, a competition in which social science values may well lose out. The solution may have to come as a result of deliberate public relations efforts by survey and other social science organizations to educate the public about the difference between social science and entertainment. In the long run, this may be more effective than attempts to get media and other organizations to abandon practices they consider economically attractive.

## Bibliography

Almond, Gabriel, and Sidney Verba. 1963. *The civic culture.* Princeton, N.J.: Princeton University Press.

Alwin, Duane, and S. Stephens. 1979. The use of sample surveys in the social sciences. Paper presented at the 145th Meeting of the American Association for the Advancement of Science.

Andrews, Frank M. 1984. Construct validity and error components of survey measures: A structural modeling approach. *Public Opinion Quarterly* 48: 409–42.

Ball-Rokeach, Sandra, and Muriel Cantor, eds. 1986. *The media and the social fabric.* Los Angeles: Sage.

Beniger, James. 1983. Comment on James Tilly: The popular symbolic repertoire and mass communication. *Public Opinion Quarterly* 47:479–84.

Bishop, George F., Robert W. Oldendick, and Alfred J. Tuchfarber. 1983. Effects of filter questions on public opinion surveys. *Public Opinion Quarterly* 47:528–46.

Bogart, Leo. 1972. *Silent politics: Polls and the awareness of public opinion.* New York: Wiley Interscience.

Boorstin, Daniel J. 1978 [1961]. *The image: A guide to pseudo-events in America.* New York: Atheneum.

Borman, Susan Gray. 1978. Communication accuracy in magazine science reporting. *Journalism Quarterly* 55:345–46.

Boyd, Richard A., with Herbert H. Hyman. 1975. Survey research. In Fred E. Greenstein and Nelson W. Polsby, eds., *Handbook of political science*, vol. 7. Reading, Mass.: Addison-Wesley.

Broh, C. Anthony. 1980. Horse-race journalism: Reporting the polls in the 1976 election. *Public Opinion Quarterly* 44:514–29.

Crespi, Irving. 1980. Polls as journalism. *Public Opinion Quarterly* 44:462–76.

Davis, James A. 1982. Is item order the quota sampling of the 80's? Paper presented at the 37th Annual Meeting of the American Association for Public Opinion Research.

Dubnoff, Steven. 1985. How much income is enough? *Public Opinion Quarterly* 49:285–99.

Field, Mervin D. 1971. The researcher's view. *Public Opinion Quarterly* 35:342–46.

Garfield, Eugene. 1977–78. *Essays of an information scientist.* Vol. 3. Philadelphia: ISI Press.

Goldman, Eric F. 1944. Poll on the polls. *Public Opinion Quarterly* 8:461–67.

Gollin, Albert E. 1980. Exploring the liaison between polling and the press. *Public Opinion Quarterly* 44:445–61.

Jackman, Mary R., and Mary S. Senter. 1980. Images of social groups: Categorical or qualified? *Public Opinion Quarterly* 44:341–61.

Jasso, G., and P. H. Rossi. 1977. Distributive justice and earned income. *American Sociological Review* 49:639–51.

Kaplan, Norman. 1965. The norms of citation behavior: Prolegomena to the footnote. *American Documentation* 16(3): 179–84.

Kessler, Ronald C., and Jane D. McLeod. 1984. Sex differences in vulnerability to undesirable life events. *American Sociological Review* 49:620–29.

Landis, J. P., and G. G. Koch. 1977. The measurement of observer agreement for categorical data. *Biometrics* 33:159–74.

Lang, Serge. 1981. *The file.* New York: Springer-Verlag.

Lazarsfeld, Paul F., and Wagner Thielens, Jr. 1958. *The academic mind.* New York: Free Press.

MacDonald, Dick. 1978. Reporting on polls: Some helpful hints. Toronto: Canadian Daily Newspaper Publishers Association.

MacDougall, Curtis. 1983. *Superstition and the press.* New York: Prometheus Books.

Meadows, Robert G. 1980. The public opinion of public opinion. Paper.

Meyer, Philip. 1967. Social science: A new beat? *Neiman Reports,* June 3–8.

NIMH. 1984. Epidemiologic catchment area study. *Archives of General Psychiatry* 41:pp. 934–89.

Noelle-Neumann, Elisabeth. 1980. The public opinion research correspondent. *Public Opinion Quarterly* 44:585–97.

———. 1984. *The spiral of silence: Public opinion—our social skin.* Chicago: University of Chicago Press.

Paletz, David L., et al. 1980. Polls in the media: Content, credibility, and consequences. *Public Opinion Quarterly* 44:495–513.

Presser, Stanley. 1984. The use of survey data in basic research in the social sciences. In Charles F. Turner and Elizabeth Martin, eds., *Surveying subjective phenomena.* New York: Russell Sage Foundation. 2:93–114.

Rokeach, Milton. 1968. The role of values in public opinion research. *Public Opinion Quarterly* 32:547–59.

Roper, Burns W. 1983. Polls and the media: For good or ill. Talk to the National Council on Public Polls, November 11. New York City.

Rossi, Peter H., James D. Wright, and Andy B. Anderson. 1983. *Handbook of survey research*. New York: Academic Press.

Schuman, Howard, and Graham Kalton. 1985. Survey methods. In Gardner Lindzey and Elliot Aronson, eds., *Handbook of social psychology*, 1:635–97. 3d ed. New York: Random House.

Schuman, Howard, and Stanley Presser. 1981. *Questions and answers in attitude surveys*. New York: Academic Press.

Shils, Edward. 1961. The calling of sociology. In *Theories of society*, ed. Talcott Parsons, pp. 1405–47. New York: Free Press.

Singer, Eleanor, and Phyllis M. Endreny. 1986. The reporting of social science research in the mass media. In Ball-Rokeach and Cantor.

Smith, Tom W. 1982. House effects and the reproducibility of survey measurements: A comparison of the 1980 GSS and the 1980 NES. *Public Opinion Quarterly* 46:54–68.

Srole, Leo, et al. 1962. *Mental health in the metropolis*. New York: Harper Torchbooks.

Sudman, Seymour, and Norman M. Bradburn. 1974. *Response effects in surveys*. Chicago: Aldine.

Turner, Charles F., and Elissa Krauss. 1978. Fallible indicators of the subjective state of the nation. *American Psychologist* 33:456–70.

Turner, Charles F., and Elizabeth Martin, eds. 1984a. *Surveys of subjective phenomena: Summary report*. Washington, D.C.: National Academy Press.

———. 1984b. *Surveying subjective phenomena*. New York: Russell Sage Foundation.

Weiss, Carol, and Eleanor Singer, with Phyllis Endreny. Forthcoming. *The reporting of social science in the media*. New York: Russell Sage Foundation.

Wheeler, Michael. 1976. *Lies, damned lies, and statistics: The manipulation of public opinion*. New York: Liveright.

———. 1980. Reining in horserace journalism. *Public Opinion Quarterly* 3: 41–45.

Wilhoit, G. Cleveland, and David H. Weaver. 1980. Newsroom guide to polls and surveys. Washington, D.C.: ANCA.

Wilson, E. Bright, Jr. 1952. *An introduction to scientific research*. New York: McGraw-Hill.

*Jonathan R. Cole*

## 20 Dietary Cholesterol and Heart Disease: The Construction of a Medical "Fact"

The mass media play a critical role in transmitting health-risk information from knowledge producers to consumers. But do those reporting on health risks present an accurate picture of the state of scientific knowledge on these risks? More specifically, if there are biases and distortions of scientific information, what is the character of these problems in reporting? And what properties of the institutions of science and the mass media help us understand the types and sources of bias and distortion? To answer such questions we would need an extensive data base of health-risk studies reported in the various media.[1] Such a set of data does not exist. Here I will present material on one case—the reporting of health risks purported to be associated with dietary cholesterol. The basic analytic problem of this paper can be stated quite simply: How is a questionable claim to truth, or medical "fact," transformed into an unquestionable one? What role do health scientists and the mass media play in this process?[2]

A brief version of this paper appeared in *Columbia Magazine;* a second was presented at the 1985 AAPOR Conference, McAfee, N.J., May 17, 1985. The work has been supported by a grant from the Josiah Macy, Jr., Foundation. I thank Dr. John Bruer for his support throughout the project. For extensive comments on an earlier draft of this paper, I thank E. H. Ahrens, Jr., Bernard Barber, Stephen Cole, Robert K. Merton, Hubert J. O'Gorman, Eleanor Singer, Stanley Schachter, and Harriet Zuckerman. A substantially elaborated and more detailed version of this paper, entitled, "Health Risks in the Media: Some Food for Thought," can be obtained from the author at the Center for the Social Sciences, 420 West 118th Street, New York, NY 10027. This work was supported also by a grant from the National Science Foundation, NSF (SES–80–08609).

[1] For a discussion of the distinction between the frontiers of research and the "core" of knowledge, see Cole and Cole 1973; Cole 1983.

[2] The paper represents one effort in a larger program of research focusing on the sociology of risk assessment. I have examined material for other cases, and although all of the cases examined to date lead to similar conclusions, we must be cautious about

The focus is on reporting by scientists and reporters of recent studies on the relationship between cholesterol and coronary heart disease. The first section describes the recent results from a major, long-term study of cholesterol and notes what types of information were not transferred from the medical research community to the public via the media. The second section examines the recent history of the controversy over the health risks associated with dietary cholesterol and describes the development of a "scientific fact" that cholesterol intake is a major cause of heart disease and of the normative conclusion that it should be uniformly minimized in American diets. A final section discusses some possible sources of explanation for the distortion of health risks in the media.

## The Cholesterol Case

In January 1984 the *Journal of the American Medical Association* (*JAMA* 251, no. 3) published the results of a recently completed ten-year, $150 million study of the link between lowering cholesterol levels and a reduction in heart attack deaths. Prior to this publication, several scientists from the Lipid Research Clinics (LRC) team who conducted the study on 3,806 subjects gave the media an extensive briefing on their research methods and the study's results (Brensike et al. 1982, 1984; Levy et al. 1984; Lipid Research Clinics Program, 1984*a*, 1984*b*).

Almost all the major newspapers and magazines in the United States carried reports on the scientists' findings, and the principal investigators were interviewed extensively on radio and television. The *Los Angeles Times* ran a typical headline: "Cholesterol Decisively Linked to Heart Attacks." The *Times* reported: "The average participant who received the [cholesterol-reducing] drug for between seven and 10 years had 19% lower risk of having a heart attack and was 24% less apt to die of a heart attack than those who received only the placebo."

Plainly a breakthrough for medical science. Now doctors could recommend reducing cholesterol intake and feel confident that this would reduce risks to their patients. And those of us who rarely see a physician could make our own decisions about cutting down on eggs and beef. But we should consider first what major newspapers and network television news programs failed to discuss about this major medical study.

To this end, I took the 1984 *JAMA* publications of the lipid research group's major findings as a point of departure. I examined all news

---

generalizations from a few cases before more extensive work on larger samples is completed.

stories, columns, editorials, and opinion pieces appearing in the *New York Times,* the *Wall Street Journal,* the *Washington Post, Newsweek, Time,* and a less systematically collected set of additional reports by the wire services and television news programs.[3] I also traced back to 1980 the news treatment of the relationship between cholesterol and coronary heart disease and death, and traced it forward since January 1984. Portions of the scientific and scholarly literature (particularly the clinical trial and epidemiological research) and assessments of the risks of dietary cholesterol by the National Research Council, the research arm of the National Academy of Sciences, were examined.[4]

Here, then, are seven features of the research that were given little or no space in the press reports following the 1984 Lipid Research Clinics' publications:

1. Because the media reported the data as "% reduction in risk," the reader was not made aware of the difference in the number of coronary heart deaths (CHD) in the two groups studied. The control group's 1,900 members were matched with the 1,906 in the experimental group for a variety of factors but were not given cholestyramine, a cholesterol-reducing drug given to the experimental group. Over the ten-year period of the study, there were thirty-eight CHDs in the control group and thirty in the experimental group. In short, there was a difference of eight deaths in an experiment involving 3,806 people, or a death rate of 2 percent in the first group and 1.6 percent in the second. Of course, if we take the difference between the two—that is, 0.4 of 1 percent—and state it as a ratio of .4 to 1.6, we obtain, as was reported in the scientists' abstract, a 24 percent reduction in risk. Thus, a major conclusion of the study on the harmful nature of cholesterol rests on this 0.4 of 1 percent.[5]

2. Although the scientists reported this difference to be significant at the .05 level for a one-sided test of their hypothesis, they neglected to report in the *JAMA* article that chi-square and other tests of significance do not show any significant difference between the experimental and control groups.

[3] In all, over 100 cholesterol news stories were reviewed between 1980 and 1984. Twenty-two were located in the *Washington Post,* forty-six in the *New York Times,* ten in the *Wall Street Journal;* nineteen were from CBS Morning and Evening News, five from ABC News, and more than twenty-five from various news magazines and news services. These stories varied, of course, in length, depth, and type—from straight news reports to opinion columns. References to "the media" and "the press" throughout this paper are restricted to these data sources.

[4] David Gerwin, an undergraduate student at Columbia College, helped collect these materials.

[5] Epidemiologists are quick to point out that very small fractions can represent large numbers of cases when extrapolated to the entire population. But this is so, of course, only if the small differences are to be treated as a real "signal" rather than "noise."

3. Most reportage of the study failed to state that the overall mortality rate in the two groups was not significantly different.[6] In short, the control group members were no less likely than those in the experimental group to live through the ten-year period (3.7 versus 3.6 percent), a fact reported in the *JAMA* article but rarely picked up by the press.

4. Virtually no news stories examined the gastrointestinal side effects of the treatment, which, though ostensibly not severe, did occur more often in the experimental group. Indeed, the data on gallbladder disease (one potential consequence from using lipid-reducing drugs) show insignificant effects, but if we apply the method of ratio of increased risk adopted by the scientists in presenting the data on coronary disease, it appears that the cholestyramine group had an increased risk of 46.1 percent over the placebo group of having "operations involving the gallbladder" (36 versus 25) (Lipid Research Clinics Program 1984*a*, p. 357).

5. Although the *JAMA* article gave plenty of information about the criteria used to select subjects for the study, the press gave little or none. For instance, few reports cited the fact that the study concentrated on those in the top 5 percent of the population in terms of their cholesterol level—hardly a representative sample of the United States population or of those apt to read about the results.

6. There was no discussion in more than 100 news stories and analysis columns or in the *JAMA* papers of varying results among the score of lipid research clinics. In fact, there was substantial variability, making the pooling of the data for all of the clinics a somewhat questionable method of analysis.

7. The news and health column stories did not deal with a set of other questions that, although not considered in the *JAMA* article, are relevant to readers attempting to make decisions about their cholesterol intake. For example, what is the relationship between dietary intake of cholesterol, on the one hand, and cholesterol plasma levels on the other? What scientific problems are there in extrapolating from dietary intake of cholesterol and cholesterol plasma levels? How do the rates of death within specific age groups from all causes in this study differ from those in the population of American men during the same period of time? How do women, children, blacks, and whites react to the treatment?

Not having any training in medicine, I am not suggesting, of course,

[6]This conclusion, as well as others drawn throughout this paper, is limited to the journals and media that I examined, which were noted above (n. 3). Thus, when I speak of the media with regard to the cholesterol case, I am limiting myself to these sources in the media.

that any given level of cholesterol consumption is appropriate for all or any of us. I am saying that the conclusions about the risks of cholesterol intake were raised by some to a level of scientific certainty ("definitive," according to the principal investigators and quoted in the press) prematurely. And I am suggesting that this type of distortion might lead in turn to significant changes in the public's dietary habits—especially after it has been bombarded with "news" of the risks and newly spawned advertising campaigns about the dangers of cholesterol.

From my limited evidence, it appears that reporters of health risks working for leading newspapers, newsmagazines, and television network news programs have difficulty in incorporating scientific disagreement and uncertainty into their stories. In fact, among leading experts in the field of cholesterol research, there is substantial scientific disagreement about the value of changing dietary habits and about cholesterol-reducing drugs as means of influencing rates of coronary heart disease. None of the alternative views from the one calling for dramatic dietary change was given prominent airing in the news articles following the 1984 LRC publications.

Take the views of Edward H. Ahrens, Jr., Frederick Henry Leonhardt Professor of Rockefeller University, who has been working in the "murky business of lipids" since the 1940s, as an example. He has studied how cholesterol metabolism is regulated in different types of people. Cholesterol is necessary of course in normal body functioning: It is a good thing. The question is, Do we have "too much of a good thing"? As Ahrens puts it:

Blood levels of cholesterol are useful indicators of people at risk . . . but the important question to ask about such a person, once identified, is *why* the level is elevated; is the body making or absorbing too much cholesterol or not excreting enough? Most treatment is aimed simply at lowering blood lipid levels, which is not necessarily beneficial. [Rockefeller University Research Profiles 1984, p. 4]

Considering the ten-year cholesterol study from this angle of vision, Ahrens makes the point that it is "not scientifically sound to extrapolate drug results to advice on diet for people in whom synthesis-absorption feedback regulation works efficiently" (p. 6). In a recent paper in the *Lancet*, Ahrens questions some overly broad extrapolations from the results of clinical trial and epidemiological studies of cholesterol. The past evidence appears, in fact, weak:

Over the past 25 years this hypothesis [that CHD rates will drop if plasma cholesterol levels are reduced] has been put to the test in more than 20 trials which attempted to lower plasma cholesterol levels by dietary manipulations or by the administration of plasma-cholesterol-lowering drugs. Only the Lipid Research Clinic's coronary prevention trial (LRC–CPPT) . . . produced evidence for benefit that was any more than suggestive. [Ahrens 1985, p. 1085]

Extrapolations by scientists from limitedly supported hypotheses to proof is disquieting to Ahrens, not only because these extrapolations can mislead reporters who include them in their stories but also because major agencies in the scientific community, for example, the National Institutes for Health (NIH), are reinforcing these leaps. Ahrens makes several additional points.

He questions whether the results from research on cholesterol can be applied to all subgroups in the population.

I cannot accept the recommendation that the prudent diet be adopted by everyone over the age of 2 years. That viewpoint was rationalized on two grounds: (1) the generalization by the CPPT authors that any 1% reduction in plasma cholesterol level will lead to a 2% reduction in CHD incidence in all segments of the population; and (2) the public health view that dietary interventions are more feasible if adopted by a whole family than singly by a high-risk member of a family. . . . I know of no evidence that the prudent diet will prevent the development of arterial atheroma at any age: the hypothesis is reasonable but not proven. [Ahrens 1985, p. 1086]

Perhaps most tellingly, Ahrens is also worried

that drastic changes in fat consumption, both in quality and quantity, which have been observed to change cell-membrane structure, may have undesirable effects on an individual's immunologic responsiveness and susceptibility to other diseases. [Rockefeller University Research Profiles 1984, p. 6]

He would prefer the health community to focus its attention on

the twenty percent or so of the population at the top end of the blood cholesterol level scale who need vigorous, *individualized* testing and treatment. It is not a popular theme song these days . . . but more and more experts are learning the tune. [P. 6]

This cautionary position, which would limit extensive treatment to the people at "real" risk, is shared by Michael S. Brown and Joseph L. Goldstein, who recently received the Nobel prize for their work on LDL (low-density lipoprotein) receptors. These receptors bind particles that carry cholesterol and remove them from the body's circulatory system. Brown and Goldstein take a far more cautious stance toward sharp dietary changes than do the Lipid Research Clinics researchers:

If the LDL-receptor hypothesis is correct, the human receptor system is designed to function in the presence of an exceedingly low LDL level. The kind of diet necessary to maintain such a level would be markedly different from the customary diet in Western industrial countries (and much more stringent than moderate low-cholesterol diets of the kind recommended by the American Heart Association). It would call for the total elimination of dairy products as well as eggs, and for a severely limited intake of meat and other sources of saturated fats. [Brown and Goldstein 1984, p. 65]

Then, the authors make the critical point about the consequences of drastic changes in our eating habits:

We believe such an extreme dietary change is not warranted for the entire population. There are several reasons. First, such a radical change in diet would have severe economic and social consequences. Second, it might well expose the population to other diseases now prevented by a moderate intake of fats. Third, experience shows most Americans will not adhere voluntarily to an extreme low-fat diet. Fourth, and most compelling, people vary genetically. Among those who consume the current high-fat diet of Western industrial societies, only 50 percent will die of atherosclerosis; the other 50 percent are resistant to the disease. Some individuals resist atherosclerosis because their LDL level does not rise dangerously even though they consume a high-fat diet. [Pp. 65–66]

Elsewhere, Goldstein and Brown specifically note that the positive benefits of lowering blood cholesterol remain unproven.

In some subjects with high serum cholesterol levels . . . , atherosclerosis to some degree always develops with time. In other people, cholesterol accumulates even when their blood cholesterol level is within the normal range; their arteries seem to be sensitized by unknown factors. It can be argued that such individuals would benefit from a lowering of their blood cholesterol levels, *but that has not yet been demonstrated scientifically.* [Goldstein and Brown 1985, p. 46; emphasis added]

Putting aside the questions of economic and social cost–benefit analysis associated with dietary change, the fact is there exists substantial scientific disagreement about its consequences among highly reputable scientists. Ahrens, as well as Brown and Goldstein, views the scientific problems and related policy recommendation for cholesterol intake in different terms from the authors of the ten-year cholesterol study. The former group allows that dietary recommendations may be in order, but they emphasize that these should be highly individualized, dependent upon detailed knowledge of individual histories and other risk factors. The lipids research group was far more willing to generalize its results to the entire U.S. population, suggesting in several interviews that significant dietary changes should begin for all children beyond the age of two. The central point here is not who is right or wrong but that the reportage neglected these alternative perspectives and failed to give the reader any idea that there might be disagreement within the scientific community over the meaning and implications of the results of the ten-year study.

Today we find almost no discussion in the news media of the scientific disagreement over the hypothesized relationships between cholesterol intake, plasma lowering of cholesterol, and atherosclerosis. The harmful effects of cholesterol in the diet are not only taken as a given but, based largely on the Lipid Research Clinics findings, are given the following felicitous functional form: For every 1 percent reduction in cholesterol there is a 2 percent reduction in the risk of coronary heart deaths. This has become a scientific "fact"—at least in news stories and probably in the minds of many concerned Americans who attend to this news. Yet, as I have suggested, such consensus simply does not yet exist in the scientific community. In the following section, I take up the question of how scientific disagreement about the effects of dietary intake of cholesterol was transformed in the press into apparent consensus, how it became a "fact."

## From Possibility to Probability to Fact: The Cholesterol Case in Detail

Elevating important but inconclusive scientific results to the level of "definitive fact" is often facilitated by certification through institutional authority. For example, the National Institutes of Health recently have formed "consensus committees," on which a panel of "experts" sit and "weigh" evidence, attempt to reach a "consensus," and publish a set of conclusions and recommendations. Such a committee was formed to review cholesterol data.

Thorny problems can arise in selecting members of consensus committees, and these choices can affect what the media receive as "best evidence." The cholesterol consensus conference is a good example of this problem. Among the members of the planning committee who set up the NIH consensus panel were Dr. Basil M. Rifkind, the associate deputy director for atherogenesis lipid metabolism, Atherogenesis Branch of the NIH's National Heart, Lung, and Blood Institute. And it included Dr. Kenneth Lippel from the same NIH unit, as well as Dr. Charles Gluck of the Lipid Research Clinic in Cincinnati. Each of these three is undoubtedly an expert in this field. But they also happen to have been deeply involved in the ten-year cholesterol study. In the end, the essential question is, Were we really obtaining "peer review" from the most knowledgeable experts on cholesterol research?

If this consensus conference was composed of unbiased experts, it surely did not appear so to M. F. Oliver of the Cardiovascular Research Unit of the University of Edinburgh, who concluded:

Clearly, the aims of both the consensus development conferences were to develop a consensus view and, not surprisingly, the final statements prepared at the end of each 2½ day meeting were biased. How could they have been otherwise? Those who initiated the idea were either naive or determined to use the forum for special pleading, or both. The panel of jurists . . . was selected to include experts who would, predictably, say that . . . all levels of blood cholesterol in the United States are too high and should be lowered. [Oliver 1985, p. 1088]

Regardless of their makeup, when NIH consensus panels talk, the media listen. And the *New York Times* on December 13, 1984, ran a front-page story on the conclusions reached. The National Institutes of Health, as a leading scientific authority, are now supporting the "fact" that there is a direct causal link between cholesterol and CHD. And few caveats enter into the news story. A paragraph in the *Times* story states: "The most recent study showed that reducing cholesterol levels in the blood could prevent deaths from heart disease, with every 1 percent reduction in cholesterol lowering the coronary risk by 2 percent." No mention any longer of the subpopulation on which this questionable result is based; no discussion any longer of the statistical or other problems we have already noted. This ratio of 1 : 2 is gaining "cognitive independence" from the original study.

The progression of scientific evidence from the status of possibility to probability to fact occurs, I suggest, with some frequency in the media. This would hardly be significant if the progression were coupled with notable improvement in the quality of scientific evidence, but, in the case we are dealing with, it is not. By tracing briefly the historical journey of the standing of cholesterol vis-à-vis coronary heart disease, we can develop a picture of how the values and cultural ideology of scientists, scientific organizations, and members of the media influence the public's perception of scientific "facts."

An abbreviated sketch of the 1980 to 1985 media presentation of the link between cholesterol and coronary heart deaths, triggered by new epidemiological and clinical trial studies, will demonstrate how the construction of this fact is accomplished.

## Phase One: Possibility

*Toward Healthful Diets*—In 1980 the National Research Council (NRC) published a report of the Food and Nutrition Board, *Toward Healthful Diets* (National Academy of Sciences 1980). The board evaluated existing scientific evidence on aspects of diet and obesity, cardiovascular disease, hypertension, cancer, and diabetes mellitus. The board took a cautious position on the link between cholesterol and atherosclerosis.

The causes of atherosclerosis are unknown. . . . A number of risk factors for cardiovascular disease have been identified from epidemiological studies. . . . Risk factors are those factors found to be statistically associated with an increased incidence of disease. They cannot, without independent evidence, be considered to be causative agents of the disease. . . . Diet modification as recommended for the prevention of atherosclerosis is based upon the assumption, not yet adequately tested, that reduction of high serum cholesterol levels . . . will reduce the probability of cardiovascular disease. [Pp. 8–9]

Now consider a truncated presentation of the critical reception of this work by the media.

1. May 28, 1980: Jane E. Brody of the *New York Times* writes a front-page story with the following lead: "In a sharp departure from recent dietary recommendations, the Food and Nutrition Board of the National Research Council said yesterday that it found no reason for the average healthy American to restrict consumption of cholesterol. . . . For human beings . . . the link between cholesterol and fat in the diet and heart disease is largely circumstantial."

2. On the same day, however, Lawrence K. Altman of the *Times* writes an article on an inside page entitled: "Report about Cholesterol Draws Agreement and Dissent." He presents a scenario of disagreement within the scientific community. There is the spokesman for the American Heart Association: "We stand firmly behind our dietary evidence to the American public—eating a maximum of 300 milligrams of cholesterol and 30 to 35 percent of calories from fat . . . These recommendations represent the work of hundreds of experts who have sifted carefully through the available scientific evidence." With a contrasting view is Dr. Norman Spitz, professor at the NYU Medical School and "a recognized expert on nutrition": "it turns out that our bodies manufacture much of our cholesterol and that the effect of diet is 'relatively small.' . . . Clinical studies that tried to lower cholesterol directly by dietary and drug means were not successful in lowering the death rates."

3. On May 29, we have Susan Okie, writing in the *Washington Post:* "A scientific panel's finding that healthy Americans need not lower the amount of fat and cholesterol in their diet was welcomed by milk, meat and egg producers yesterday but caused some chagrin at the American Heart Association." Later she quotes the rising chorus of dissenters: "Dr. William Kannel . . . head of the Framingham study that first produced evidence on the relation of life-style to heart disease, said the latest report was inconsistent in its recommendations. . . . 'It makes me wonder . . . at their objectivity.'" Michael Jacobson, director of the Center for Science in the Public Interest is quoted: "It stinks. It reads as if it was written by the meat, dairy, and egg industries."

4. May 29, 1980: Jane Brody of the *New York Times* writes a story headlined "Dispute on Americans' Diets." The story details the scientific disagreement on the effects of cholesterol.

5. June 1, 1980: the *New York Times* has this front-page headline, "Experts Assail Report Declaring Curb on Cholesterol Isn't Needed." The counterattack on the National Academy of Sciences (NAS) begins in earnest. The following points are made. (*a*) *The NAS is attacked for its lack of representatives on the board of different perspectives.* Robert Levy, director of the National Heart, Lung, and Blood Institute of the NIH is quoted: "It's true that not all the facts are in. . . . But to recommend doing nothing in the meantime is inappropriate . . . Americans should hedge their bets and seek a diet lower in saturated fats and cholesterol, at least until more evidence is available." (*b*) *The Nutrition Board members had ties to the food industry.* (*c*) *The board's recommendations were inconsistent.*

6. June 1, 1980: the *New York Times'* "Week in Review" runs a story, "Sunny Side Up for Cholesterol," in which it briefly summarizes the NAS report.

7. On the same day, Jane Brody, under the headline, "When Scientists Disagree, Cholesterol Is in Fat City," notes:

Lacking ironclad proof that changing one's diet can prevent heart disease in otherwise healthy persons, the board recommended no restrictions in cholesterol intake. . . . the board's advice is contrary to that offered by at least 18 organizations concerned with nutrition and health.

Thus far, the presentation of information on cholesterol reflects the existing disagreement within the scientific and medical community. There is a possibility that large cholesterol intake is harmful, but it is neither proven nor beyond scientific dispute. But it is also plain that there is a growing interest in the press, at least in some quarters, in debunking the NAS findings altogether. For example, on Monday, June 2, 1980, a *Washington Post* editorial entitled "Cholesterol Does Count" states: "'Toward Healthful Diets' . . . not only has increased public confusion over proper diet. It has also soiled the reputation both of the board and of the academy for rendering careful scientific advice" (p. A-18). The *Post* seems to be asking that a subject that, *in fact,* generates real scientific disagreement and some confusion be simplified and made easily digestible for the American public, even if the reports are not true to the controversy.

The *New York Times* follows with an editorial on June 3, entitled "A Confusing Diet of Fact." It admonishes the academy:

The National Academy of Sciences is supposed to be an authoritative, impartial source of scientific advice to both the public and government—a Supreme

Court of Science. But its latest report on health diets is so one-sided that it makes a dubious guide to nutritional policies. . . . The Academy should be espousing more than a single view.

And in fact subsequent articles do reflect existing disagreement. Consider just a few additional headlines: "A Few Kind Words for Cholesterol" (*Time*, June 9, 1980, p. 51); "How Bad Is Cholesterol?" (*Newsweek*, June 9, 1980, p. 111), which presents the conflicting opinions of various authorities; "Lower Fat Diet Affirmed Despite Recent Findings" (*Washington Post*, June 10), which is based upon testimony at the National Academy by Dr. William Castelli, "medical director of the famed Framingham, Mass. study of life-style and disease." On June 11, 1980, Mimi Sheraton, a food and dining specialist for the *Times*, writes under the headline, "Conflicting Nutrition Advice Bewilders U.S. Consumers." A variety of points of view are expressed, including Dr. Michael De Bakey's: "A good 60 percent of the people who have arteriosclerosis do not have elevated serum cholesterol levels . . . why then are we basing our assumptions on the 40 percent minority?"

The *Washington Post*, June 12, 1980, headline for a story by Victor Cohn: "Panel Quits to Protest Advice on Cholesterol." The *New York Times*, June 18, 1980, headline for a column by Jane E. Brody: "Hidden Fat: The Hazards." The *New York Times*, June 20, 1980, "Scientists Clash on Academy's Cholesterol Advice," reports that "scientists . . . agreed that there was no scientific correlation between lowering of cholesterol and a reduction in coronary disease, they disagreed on whether Americans should have dietary advice on cholesterol." Suffice it to say that in June of 1980 the public was presented with a spate of news stories emphasizing the scientific disagreement over the effects of cholesterol.

Several points emerge from the plethora of stories. The NRC–NAS report's findings questioned the "received wisdom" about cholesterol and heart disease. Consequently, the media present a sense of a lively, and often confusing, debate over what constitutes scientific fact on this issue. They explicitly call for the presentation of diverse points of view and take the academy to task for its supposedly unbalanced presentation of this scientific conflict. But, as we shall see, when subsequent scientific studies present findings that appear to support the prevailing received wisdom, the press fails to present any similar discussion of conflicting points of view. And the fundamental point is that no critical experiments or results of scientific work were done in the intervening years to warrant a shift in position from a possible to a probable linkage between cholesterol and coronary heart deaths.

*The Framingham Study*—The controversial academy report was not the only cholesterol and atherosclerosis news in 1980. In that year, the results of the Framingham study, a massive twenty-four-year epidemiological effort "to determine the risk factors for coronary heart disease and other atherosclerotic disorders" (the results of which had been published in more than 150 scientific papers between 1950 and 1978), were pulled together and summarized in a book by Thomas Royle Dawber (1980), one of the study's principal investigators. The Framingham study followed 5,127 men and women between ages thirty and fifty-nine. Initial examinations of subjects began in the spring of 1950. Individuals who were free of coronary heart disease at the initial physical examination constituted the population to be followed (pp. 20–21).[7]

On the effects of blood cholesterol levels, Dawber states: "Observations from the Framingham study over 24 years clearly indicate that serum cholesterol plays a role in the incidence of coronary heart disease. . . . The average annual rate during the entire 24 years for men with cholesterol levels 260 mg % or more was twice that of those with levels below 200" (1980, pp. 129–30).

Now consider these results in greater detail. For women, the findings are wholly inconclusive. "Analysis of the 24-year risk in women . . . shows [that], in both the youngest and oldest decades examined, no significant differences in incidence of coronary heart disease on the basis of cholesterol levels were observed" (Dawber 1980, p. 130).[8] Even in the middle-aged group there is no difference in incidence of coronary heart disease for every cholesterol category except for the highest cholesterol group, representing a relatively small proportion of the population (see Dawber 1980, fig. 8.4, p. 133). For most of the population of women there is no relation between cholesterol and heart disease.

Even for men the relationship is tenuous. Of course, men in all age groups are far more apt than women to develop heart disease. But for men with cholesterol levels in the lowest group, the average annual rate of coronary heart disease was 7.4 per 1,000; 8.4 in the next group; 12.7 in the midgroup; 10.1 in the next-to-highest; and 14.6 in the highest. The incidence of heart disease is about double between the extremes, but the relationship is less marked when comparing the other groups—for example 1.7 persons per thousand between the second-lowest and next-to-highest cholesterol groups. These rates are simple bivariate distributions. Multivariate analysis describing the independent effect of cholesterol on coronary heart disease and mortality by cholesterol levels is not presented. Dawber never indicates the

[7] The various methodological problems of the study, such as dropout rates and representativeness of the sample, require more elaborate discussion that can be found in Cole 1986.

[8] The book omits discussion of mortality rates and discusses morbidity only.

percentage of variance explained by dietary cholesterol. He does suggest that diet had little to do with coronary heart disease in the Framingham population:

> The expectation that the intrapopulation differences in cholesterol level could be attributed to individual dietary habits has not been fulfilled. The variability of blood cholesterol values within the Framingham population appears to reflect inherent or constitutional traits rather than differences in life habits. . . . Differences in dietary intake that could affect the blood cholesterol level did not account for the intrapopulation differences nor for the effect of cholesterol level on the *relative* risk within this population. [Dawber 1980, pp. 138–39; emphasis in original]

The relatively small differences in risk associated with varying cholesterol levels in men; the virtual absence of any relationship among women; and that differences in cholesterol were unrelated to diet have been almost totally ignored in the media's presentation of the Framingham study. The message of Framingham has been that the intake of cholesterol in diet produces significantly increased risk of heart disease and death.

## Phase II: From Possibility to Probability, 1981–1984

Between 1981 and the Lipid Research Clinics trial results in 1984, the media transform the possible linkage into a highly probable one. This progression is again associated with the publication of results of scientific research.

*The Western Electric Study*—In January 1981, *The New England Journal of Medicine* publishes a paper, "Diet, Serum Cholesterol, and Death from Coronary Heart Disease: The Western Electric Study." Based on a twenty-year follow-up physical examination of 1,900 middle-aged men, this study investigated "the associations of dietary saturated fatty acids, polyunsaturated fatty acids, and cholesterol with serum cholesterol level and risk of death from coronary heart disease (CHD)" (Shekelle et al. 1981, pp. 65–70). There are design problems with this study. For example, there was only one follow-up over a twenty-year period and no monitoring of changing patterns of health, diet, and life-style variables in the intervening years. Women, children, members of varying occupations and social classes are not studied at all, or are underrepresented. But more importantly, the percentage difference in coronary heart deaths between the lowest and highest third of the 1,900 men in terms of saturated fats was 10.9 versus 11.8 percent and in terms of dietary cholesterol, 10.9 versus 13.6 percent. In short, these small substantive differences mean that cholesterol explained little variance in death rates, although the authors choose to interpret the effects very generously indeed. "The correlations between dietary variables and serum cholesterol concentration in our study were small" (p. 69). But the media that I examined treat the results otherwise.

*Time*, January 19, 1981: "Cholesterol: The Stigma Is Back—New Report Reaffirms the Link to Heart Disease." The story states: "The main finding: those who had consumed large amounts of cholesterol and saturated fat suffered upwards of a third more deaths from heart disease than those who consumed relatively small amounts." Although this is a misleading summary, *Time* acknowledges that the debate over cholesterol will probably continue. A *Newsweek* article contends that the Western Electric study "demonstrated a specific link between individual eating habits and fatal heart attacks" (*Newsweek*, January 19, 1981, p. 74).

*The "MRFIT" Study*— In September 1982, the *Journal of the American Medical Association* (*JAMA*) published the results of a randomized primary prevention trial to examine the effects of changes in hypertension, cigarette smoking, and dietary advice for lowering blood cholesterol on mortality from coronary heart disease. Almost 13,000 high-risk men aged thirty-five to fifty-seven were chosen from 361,000 initially screened and randomly assigned to "special intervention" groups, who received counseling to alter existing habits, and a "usual care" group, which represented a control. To become a participant, a person had to be at "increased risk," that is, in the upper 15 percent of a risk distribution based upon cigarette smoking, serum cholesterol, and blood pressure (based upon data from the Framingham study). This Multiple Risk Factor Intervention Trial (MRFIT) encountered methodological problems, as had the previous major epidemiological and clinical trial studies. For one, the experimental and control groups differed little on a set of risk factors, even after attempted interventions. Members of both groups had lowered their smoking levels and their intake of cholesterol during the ten years of study.

The results were dramatic—but at variance with the wisdom being placed in print and on the air by the media. For example, the mortality rate from coronaries in the special intervention (SI) and usual care (UC) groups were almost identical, and the difference in overall mortality obtained went in the opposite direction from what had been predicted. The death rate was actually 2.1 percent higher in the special intervention group. The effects of serum cholesterol on CHD deaths were nonexistent or minimal. In short, cholesterol levels had no significant effect on the death rates, even considering statistical interactions among the three risk factors.

This was a major, $115 million, ten-year study reporting a "negative finding" on cholesterol. MRFIT did not go unnoticed by major news organizations. As far back as 1980, there was keen interest in the potential of the MRFIT study.

Several months before the MRFIT results are published, Jane Brody discusses a Norwegian study of about 1,200 healthy men between forty and forty-nine years old with high cholesterol levels. Under the headline, "Life-Saving Benefits of Low-Cholesterol Diet Affirmed in Rigorous Study," Brody begins her story:

A major, well-designed study has shown more persuasively than any previous experiment that eating less fats and cholesterol can reduce the chances of suffering a heart attack or of dying suddenly from heart disease. . . . Though their blood pressure was normal, their cholesterol levels were considered high—from 290 to 380 milligrams of cholesterol per 100 milliliters of blood—and 80 percent of them smoked cigarettes. . . . The team [of scientists conducting the research] . . . calculated that dietary changes accounted for 60 percent of the difference in the number of heart attacks and heart deaths suffered by the two groups of men. [*New York Times*, January 5, 1982, p. C-1]

No mention whatsoever is made that men of this age with levels of cholesterol averaging well over 300 mg/100 ml would have been in the upper 1 to 5 percent of the Framingham distribution—hardly typical people. And, in the penultimate paragraph, nestled away in an inside page, Brody adds: "The researchers conceded that 'if this had been a diet trial only, the difference in MI [myocardial infarction, or heart attack] incidence in the two groups would probably not have reached statistical significance.'"

As it turns out, cholesterol intake (even in this extreme group) is not a strong predictor of subsequent coronary heart disease and deaths. That certainly is not the tone or direction of the article. Not one scientific expert, apart from the study director, is asked to evaluate the quality of the work or its limitations. The results support the probable relationship and the prevailing presuppositions.

In reporting the MRFIT study (*New York Times*, September 17, 1982, p. A-10), Jane Brody's story details the methods used and several of the negative findings. Brody does a good job of this. But the article focuses on the various limitations of the study—a focus totally absent from the treatment of the Western Electric and other studies showing "positive" results. Brody notes the study director's own skepticism.

Americans should not interpret the inconclusive results to mean it was all right to smoke, to be on a high fat diet and to have high blood pressure. "It is our judgment that the public should continue to reduce these risk factors associated with heart disease," said Dr. Oglesby Paul, professor emeritus of medicine at Harvard Medical School, chairman of the study's steering committee. . . . The researchers were also surprised to find that one treatment subgroup suffered a higher death rate than those getting regular treatment.

The criticism of MRFIT continues on October 10, 1982. The *New York Times* reports methodological problems enumerated by study officials.

Although caution and skepticism are no less in order for MRFIT than for the other studies, why is a "negative" or "inconclusive" result presented as a failing? Indeed, it is puzzling why the reporters covering the cholesterol question seemed committed to the point of view that cholesterol intake was a substantial health risk. To be sure, they were following the lead of health scientists, but why was the opposing point of view given less space and weight in their stories—especially since reporters find reports of controversy appealing?

In 1983 the probable link is stressed once again. The *New York Times,* January 11, 1983: In a brief article, "Reversing Heart Disease," this probability is suggested. "A newly published study indicates that significant improvement in cardiovascular health can occur after just 24 days of a radically changed diet and life style." This conclusion was reported on the basis of "a pilot study" of forty-six patients. Jane E. Brody in her "Personal Health" column of March 16, 1983:

> For a while it seemed as if the advice to lower cholesterol levels had fallen on hard times. . . . But before anyone could even digest a cholesterol rich meal, more meaningful data poured in. . . . The main recommendation is to eat less fat, in total, and especially less saturated fat, since this kind of fat raises cholesterol levels in the blood and increases the risk of heart disease. . . . So the heart-saving advice to reduce consumption of fats and cholesterol still holds. As a bonus, it may help protect you against cancer as well.

Brody fails to mention a single one of these new studies that "poured in"; no longer mentions skepticism about the results; omits all qualifiers about people at risk or the types of people who were enlisted in the research studies. The recommendation is apparently now applicable to all readers of the *Times.* Similar stories appear in other newspapers and on television news programs.

A week before *JAMA* publishes the Lipid Research Clinics' result, Peter Jennings on "ABC World News Tonight" anticipates the cholesterol publications when he and reporter George Strait interviewed Dr. R. Basil Rifkind of the NIH. Probability is now being transformed into fact:

> *Jennings:* Scientists now have conclusive proof that lowering the amount of cholesterol or fat that we eat can significantly reduce the chance of heart attacks. . . .
>
> *George Strait:* For more than a decade Americans have been warned to cut back on red meat, eggs and other foods high in cholesterol because scientists suspected that cholesterol was a prime cause of heart disease. Well, now they are sure. The new federal study confirms the definitive link between cholesterol and heart disease.

*R. Basil Rifkind/NIH:* The greater the reduction in cholesterol, the greater the reduction in coronary heart disease. And that a 25 percent reduction in blood cholesterol cuts risk by half. ["ABC World News Tonight," January 12, 1984]

The Lipid Research Clinics papers are published at this point. The media assumption that these studies provide a conclusive causal link between cholesterol and mortality from coronaries has been documented. What has happened since the scientific papers were published? As far as the media are concerned, we now are dealing with fact. So what has happened to the "fact" once "established"?

## Phase III: From Probability to "Fact"

Since the publication of the LRC results, the media have moved still farther away from discussion of the study's limitations, have generalized from the limited findings, and have rarely seen fit to present opposing views. The same sources that condemned the National Academy for not reporting the full spectrum of opinion in *Toward Healthful Diets* have now totally abandoned the presentation of scientific disagreement. Thus:

*Time*, January 23, 1984: "Sorry, It's True, Cholesterol Really Is a Killer." And on March 26, 1984, *Time*'s cover story reads, "Cholesterol, and Now the Bad News." The *Reader's Digest* story is entitled "Cholesterol Is the Culprit." The statement that "every 1% cholesterol drop in the bloodstream means a 2% decrease in the likelihood of a heart attack in people with high cholesterol levels" is becoming a medical aphorism.

Victor Cohn in the January 29, 1984, *Washington Post:* "So now cholesterol is real. Government scientists have said so." The *Wall Street Journal*, March 15, 1984: "Cholesterol Levels in American Children Should Be Lowered, Heart Specialists Say." Jane Brody in the *New York Times*, May 16, 1984: "Diet to Prevent Heart Attacks Aims to Cut Blood Fat Levels." On March 27, 1984, Ted Koppel devotes ABC News' "Nightline" to cholesterol and heart disease. Dr. Robert Levy, a principal investigator in the Lipid Research Clinics study, states:

We've always known that cholesterol was a risk factor. We've always known that we've had diets and drugs that could lower cholesterol, but now for the first time in man, we have that conclusive evidence that if you lower your cholesterol your risk of heart attack and death . . . will decrease. . . . As you know, as with the tobacco story, there will be some who will never believe. But I think that the evidence that my family should act on, and I think all Americans should act on, is now in hand.

The views of other scientists who perceive the data differently are not presented or alluded to. The rule is now a general one. Finally, Jane Brody in a 1985 story discussing "new" findings from the Framingham heart study presents the health aphorism ("For every 1 percent change in cholesterol, the risk of heart disease changes by 2 to 3 percent") without any mention of the original source. It has now diffused into the culture.[9]

## A Research Agenda for Understanding Distortions of Health Risks in the Media

The cholesterol case and others like it raise fundamental issues that need to be addressed before we can understand better what determines the distortion of health risks in the media. In this section questions are raised that might enter a research agenda on the presentation of health risks in the media. Specifically, processes at work in the development of scientific facts are examined, and a discussion follows on how the social organization of science and the media can influence the presentation of health-risk information.

### Cholesterol and Coronary Heart Deaths: the Development of a Scientific Fact

The cholesterol case history is an exemplar for how values, intellectual conflicts, and socially structured interests influence the development of a scientific fact. The hypothesis we are considering for its fact status is: Dietary intake of cholesterol causes coronary heart disease and death. In its most graphic reportage form, the "fact" is that for every 1 percent reduction in cholesterol intake there is a 2 percent reduction in the risk of coronary heart deaths. Let us examine several elements in the struggle for fact status.[10]

The principal characters in this drama include a set of medical research scientists (the LRC group) who are proposing, in effect, that the results of their ten-year, $150 million study be accepted as a medical fact. Other actors include scientists who dispute this claim to fact, regarding the assertion as too strong an extrapolation from the available evidence and too sweeping in its claims to generality. Still others

[9] Even the National Research Council's Committee on Nutrition in Medical Education had changed its tune by 1985. See the National Academy of Sciences report, *Nutrition Education in U.S. Medical Schools* (1985).

[10] Space limits this section to the briefest elaboration of the relevance of ideas of Ludwik Fleck, Thomas Kuhn, Imre Lakatos, Bruno Latour and Steve Woolgar, Karen Knorr-Cetina, Robert K. Merton, and earlier work by Stephen Cole and myself as they bear on the development of "medical facts." See Cole 1986 for a broader discussion.

include powerful organizations and interest groups, among others, the American Heart Association, the National Institutes of Health, the National Academy of Sciences, and lobbies for the food industry, which had definite interests in the outcome of the fact dispute. The cast of characters is fleshed out by members of the press, science writers, editors, and reporters working the science beat, who transfer the content of this debate to the general public, and others with varying degrees of knowledge of the scholarly literature on which the fact claims are based. The contest is over the extent to which the fact claim is (a) accepted among influential members of the medical research community; (b) accepted for some duration of time by the research community to a degree that effectively eliminates disagreement from the scientific discourse; (c) accepted by science reporters as "definitive"; and (d) accepted by the public as a medical "fact."

The outcome of the contest can have significant effects on careers of scientists involved in the dispute, on the allocation of scientific resources for future research (and on processes of accumulating advantages and disadvantages), on the public's perception of health risks and what can be done about them, and on the economy of businesses whose products are affected by the public's perception of the effects of cholesterol.

How is the drama surrounding cholesterol related to current views about the social processes at work in the development of scientific facts? At least since Ludwik Fleck's work in 1935 on the development of the Wasserman reaction,[11] there is a recognition and growing acceptance that, at least in some measure, the choice of scientific problems, modes of presenting experimental evidence, acceptance or rejection of theories, selective evaluation of experimental results as a function of selective perception are socially conditioned.

More recently, Bruno Latour and Steve Woolgar (1979), as well as Karen Knorr-Cetina (1981), have suggested that the processes of "persuasion" and "negotiation" are central elements in the construction of scientific facts. Each of these elements plays a role in the fact dispute over the effects of cholesterol in the diet. In analyzing sixteen drafts of a single scientific paper on potato protein concentrates, Knorr-Cetina suggests that the actual difference in content had little to do with changes in evidence but was largely a consequence of extended negotiations between author and critics, including, among others, collaborators, laboratory directors, reference individuals, and authori-

---

[11] Fleck's (1935) work has become well known to American sociologists of science since its recent translation by Fred Bradley and Thaddeus J. Trenn, edited by Trenn and Robert K. Merton (1979).

ties in the scientific speciality (Knorr-Cetina 1981, pp. 94–135, esp. p. 104).

Knorr-Cetina suggests that the typical outcome from negotiation in science is the changing of modalities of certain assertions, toning down of claims, movement from over- to understatement, from more to less dramatic styles of presentation, from assertions to caveats. In short, the early or original draft is stripped typically of some of its dramatic content—without any changes in evidence. The normative structure of science enjoins scientists toward such outcomes of negotiations.[12]

The published news story or broadcast is the analog to scientific publication. The final content of this story is, surely to some extent, also a process of negotiation. The critics with whom the reporter must negotiate include possible collaborators, science editors, and general editors. However, the norms governing negotiations in the news business tend to run counter to those operating in science (Goodell 1975; Nelkin 1985; Winsten 1985). Unlike most scientists, competent science reporters face pressures in negotiation to tone their stories up rather than down. Consequently, health-risk stories hitting the newsstand or reaching the air tend toward fewer modalities, qualifications, caveats, and statements of limitations. To get stories in print or on the air, science reporters are apt to have to expunge rather than add qualifying statements.

The differences in normative structures between science and news become particularly problematic for the final story when the earlier negotiation over the scientific paper has resulted in a highly "dramatic" and possibly exaggerated claim about experimental results. This dramatic and possibly distorted presentation can be exacerbated still further by the negotiation process in the newsroom.

Akin to negotiation is what Latour and Woolgar (1979) describe as the process of persuasion, that is, an ongoing contest between scientists, one set trying to change the modalities of statements so that the statement holds an increasing "factlike status" and another trying to be more restrained about claims to fact status. Some scientists, generally the authors of papers, are pushing statements that have a greater factlike quality; critics are frequently pushing for greater caution and qualification. Latour and Woolgar discuss five types of statements

---

[12] It is not self-evident that toned-down outcomes of negotiation facilitate the development of knowledge. We know little about the incidence of truly important papers that go largely unnoticed because negotiations led to overly restrained claims and, correlatively, the incidence of exorbitant claims that led to significant false starts and unproductive research programs.

found in scientific papers, ranging from statements of "facts" that everyone takes for granted (Type 5) to far less definite, limited, and more qualified statements, such as "*A* has a certain relationship to *B*," and finally to the fully qualified modality of conjectures and speculations (Type 1 statements). Latour and Woolgar characterize laboratory activity in terms of pushes and pulls toward fact status that result from interaction between fact claimants and their critics.

They are fully aware, of course, that sociological factors (such as power, authority, theoretical and methodological orientations, and personal values) play a critical role in the persuasion or negotiation process. But they do not consider the influence of structural features of science beyond the laboratory, or more macrolevel factors that may influence the outcomes of contests and struggles about fact status.[13]

This work bears directly on the recent cholesterol papers and publicity, because we see in the cholesterol controversy an ongoing contest about what should be granted fact status. We witness an effort by one set of researchers, most recently those associated with the Lipid Research Clinics' long-term clinical trial, who are attempting to persuade others—scientists, journalists, and the wider public—of the unadorned *fact* that dietary intake of cholesterol causes heart deaths. They are asserting with increasing frequency Type 5 statements that label cholesterol as a major cause of heart deaths for all members of the U.S. population. If they are the protagonists in this drama, the antagonists are those scientists, such as Ahrens as well as Brown and Goldstein, who are advocating scientific statements that continue to include strong qualifying modalities. It is important to emphasize that contests over fact status often take place with new empirical or experimental evidence continually influencing the dialogue, but in the recent cholesterol case the contest seems to be proceeding quite independently of additional evidence.

Throughout this paper examples have been presented of efforts by investigators associated with the LRC trial to reduce the number and types of qualifying statements, which have the effect of enhancing the fact claims by the authors. These actions suggest efforts by the prin-

---

[13] Knorr-Cetina (1981) and Latour and Woolgar (1979) concentrate on changes in texts that are attributed to different interests of authors and critics. They underplay changes that result from an awareness gained by authors through criticism that they have overgeneralized or have made statements which, upon reflection, are viewed by the authors as errors. Furthermore, they fail to see the act of writing as a creative process that represents an action quite distinct from the activities in the laboratory. This process of creating a text can itself lead to new ideas, some of which appear upon critical reflection to be too strong, too weak, imprecise, or in error. Thus, changing modalities of statements in scientific papers are not purely a result of a clash of interests, values, and so on.

cipal investigators to persuade potential critics and the public of the fact status of their findings.

Here is where science reporters and the media in general enter the negotiation and persuasion process. They are recipients of the statements that emerge from scientific papers published in prestigious journals, such as *JAMA* or the *New England Journal of Medicine,* from personal interviews with scientists, and from formal news conferences and briefings. They are an important audience in the contest over fact status, because indirectly they influence opinion formation, not only in the larger public but in the attentive publics of physicians who offer advice to patients (but who do not necessarily read the scholarly literature on cholesterol), other scientists, health administrators, staff members of congressmen and administrative agencies, and decision makers at federal funding agencies who oversee the funding of large-scale laboratory and clinical trial programs.

When dealing with the press, scientists interested in changing the modality of statements about research results are often not subject to the same mechanisms of social control that operate within their discipline.[14] A simplification may involve only the omission of a strategically placed "could" or "maybe" or "applies only to . . ." from earlier, more cautionary statements. Reporters can hardly be expected to be familiar with much, or all, of the detailed work that comes out of a laboratory, or with the details of the published data.[15] When acceptance of less tentative statements is coupled with the normative tendency within journalism to strengthen rather than weaken stories through further reduction of qualifying modalities, there is an increased probability of "premature facts" being elevated to "fact" status and being widely accepted as such.[16]

## Institutional Properties Influencing the Distortion of Health Risks in the Media

At least three institutional properties of both science and the media are apt to increase the probability of distorted representations of sci-

[14] We do not have any extensive data that can demonstrate this; there is plainly a need to develop systematic data to go beyond the impressions based upon more limited inquiries by Winsten and others.

[15] There are probably a few specific research areas that each science reporter is familiar with. Based upon the reporters' own science background and subsequent interests, this may allow them to be highly informed critics in these specialty areas. To cite only one notable example, Walter Sullivan of the *New York Times* has extensive knowledge and has written important books on the geology of plate tectonics.

[16] Ludwik Fleck has an extraordinary discussion of the simplification process and its consequences for fact development as we move from scientific papers to textbooks to popular accounts. See Fleck (1979), pp. 111–24.

entific "discoveries." The first of these is the structure of the reward and opportunity systems in *both* institutions; the second, inadequate training of reporters as critical observers of scientific information; and the third, ineffective mechanisms in the media and science to forestall the distribution of premature results or distorted news.

*The Reward Systems*—There are, of course, many forms of scientific recognition: prestigious positions; honorific awards, such as Nobel prizes or election to leading academies of science; and visibility and peer esteem (see Cole and Cole 1973; Merton 1942, 1973; Zuckerman 1977). There is a substantial overlap among the recipients of these various forms: The few receive the lion's share. But with increasing frequency, scientific and public visibility, if not notoriety, can be attained through extensive media exposure—and sometimes even by conducting scientific controversies through the media (see Cole 1979; Goodell 1975).

Scientists, like others, seek recognition from important reference groups. Although precise figures do not exist, we may ask what proportion of scientists completely eschew media attention of their work; what proportion accept it without seeking it; and what proportion actively seek representation in the media. For the group, however small, who seek visibility through the press, what determines their interest? Some scientists may have a personal and professional interest in being "represented" in the press.

The consequences of representation in the press can extend, of course, beyond personal psychic gratification. Press exposure may aid scientists in obtaining continued resources for their research—especially if the research program is extremely expensive and is directly reviewed by congressional committees and directors of funding agencies.

The problem goes deeper than passivity among scientists because some (again, the exact proportion is surely unknown) contribute directly to media distortions by tailoring their own results through incomplete and misleading paper abstracts, news releases, and press conferences that give the media what the scientist has defined as "strong" news stories—even at the expense of complete summaries and inclusion of essential limitations. In the cholesterol case, we see the principal investigators in television interviews and newspaper stories making extreme claims for the results without acknowledging the limits to the data. But for the medical research and larger scientific community, we know little about the sources of distortion in reporting.

Jay A. Winsten (1985) recently completed focused interviews with twenty-seven science reporters, editors, and television producers at leading news organizations. Many of the reporters interviewed were authors of stories addressing health risks associated with cholesterol. The reporters repeatedly told Winsten that the competitive pressures of journalism and interest in recognition often led to altered stories, creating the appearance of either greater conflict and tension or greater consensus than in fact existed, and to other significant alterations in stories to meet the requirements of editors who were gate-keepers in opening or shutting off opportunities for advancement and recognition. For example, one reporter told Winsten of tension between building a "strong" story while maintaining credibility:

I'm in competition with literally hundreds of stories each day, political and economic stories of compelling interest. In science, especially, we sometimes have to argue [with editors], pound the table, and say, "This is an important story. It turns a key of understanding, it affects a lot of people," or "it's just interesting, it's part of the unfolding romance of science." But we have to make that clear in our copy. We have to almost overstate, we have to come as close as we can within the boundaries of truth to a dramatic, compelling statement. A weak statement will go no place. [Winsten 1985, p. 9]

Science editors, Winsten reports, are aware of the tension and the competing values associated with tension and accuracy.

The pressures for recognition among reporters and science editors are summarized in Winsten, but we surely cannot tell from the twenty-seven interviews, however instructive, how generalizable the results are, that is, with what frequency reporters and editors push beyond the boundaries of truth as they come to know it.

## Structural Problems that Can Lead to Distortion

*Problems of the Training Necessary to Report on Scientific and Medical Research*— A potential source for the publication of biased or distorted health-risk information lies in the quality and quantity of training of those on the "science beat." In fact, for most newspapers and broadcast journalism, general assignment reporters far outnumber science reporters in covering science topics. This was not true for the sources we used in tracing the cholesterol controversy, but it is the general case. Even if we focus exclusively on science reporters, what proportion of them and their editors can be sufficiently knowledgeable about the sciences covered in their stories to assume a critical posture toward the scientists who are making claims of fact? Given that science has become so highly specialized and technical, we can hardly expect that the majority of reporters would have specific knowledge of most of the sciences about which they write. Of course, it remains unclear how much detailed knowledge a reporter needs about the basic canons of scientific inquiry, of proof and evidence, of scientific

Jonathan R. Cole

skepticism, and of how facts and theories develop in the scientific community to write stories that correctly depict the fact claims and the extent to which these claims are matters of contention within the research community. Short of extraordinary knowledge, reporters must, of course, rely heavily on scientific authority, on the "word" and reputations of the principal investigators and scientific institutions, and on the peer review system. This can be problematic for several reasons, especially in dealing with health risks and medical research.

First, many flawed papers pass through the peer review system and are published without adequate attention to methodological or substantive inaccuracy—and this is so for the journals of the highest rank as well as those of lesser stature. Recently, DerSimonian et al. (1982) studied the reporting of clinical trials in the *New England Journal of Medicine, British Medical Journal, Journal of the American Medical Association,* and *Lancet.* They chose eleven basic topics and examined whether each one had been discussed in the paper reporting the clinical trial experiment.[17] Of the sixty-seven papers reviewed, only 1 percent gave information on all eleven items; more than 50 percent provided information on six or fewer. In short, many papers that have passed through the peer review process fail to provide basic information that allows readers to assess the quality of the study.

Second, the peer review system is marked by honest, intellectual disagreement among scientists about what constitutes "high-quality work" and what is a valuable paper. Published papers often had one or more referees who identified substantial problems with the papers (among many others, see Ingelfinger 1974; Stinchcombe and Ofshe 1969; Zuckerman and Merton 1971). Such disagreements in appraisals may actually be healthy for a science and, in any event, are common when people evaluate new scientific work at the frontier of knowledge, but as a consequence, acceptance or rejection will depend significantly on the "luck of the reviewer draw" (see Cole and Cole 1985; Cole, Cole, and NAS Committee on Science and Public Policy 1981; Cole 1983; Cole, Cole, and Simon 1981). Thus, peer review may represent the best of all possible but highly imperfect worlds. In sum, the fact that a paper appears in a prestigious medical journal offers no strong guarantee against the appearance of poorly analyzed or distorted results of medical and scientific research.

What is the media to do about such problems? They surely cannot develop an independent refereeing system, but it may be possible

[17] The eleven items were: eligibility criteria, admission before allocation, random allocation, method of randomization, patient's blindness to treatment, blind assessment of outcome, treatment complications, loss to follow-up, statistical analysis, statistical methods, and power (quoted in Mosteller 1985).

to extend the training of experienced reporters in the methods used in research and experiments as well as new analytic and statistical techniques.

*Problems of Timing*— Television and newspaper reporters are often under considerable pressure to get stories out in a timely way. Constraints of time and space in storytelling can work against adequate presentation of the limitations of scientific findings, which often require a longer period of time to investigate the adequacy of the evidence. However, data do not exist that address the relationship among the length of news stories, the speed with which they must be developed, and the level of distortion in the final presentation of health risks.

## Value Commitments of Scientists and Reporters in the Reporting of Science News

Personal values can also affect the handling of scientific data and preparation of science news stories. Work in the history and sociology of science over the past two decades supplies us with evidence that ideological presuppositions and values influence the perceptions of scientists; their choice of problems; their choices in examining one source of possible errors as opposed to another; their reading and interpretation of the data and results (Barber 1961; Gould 1981; Holton 1978; Merton 1972; Polanyi 1963). These cognitive tendencies, which do not necessarily involve motivated deception, may be exacerbated when personal rewards and resources are more apt to accrue to those who conform to the received wisdom in the scientific community.

Pressure for the presentation of eye-catching and somewhat overblown results may also come today from the sources for funding science. With increased interest in fiscal "accountability," with populist pressures for more egalitarian distribution of scarce federal dollars for researchers, it is probably difficult for science programs that spend upward of $100 million on research to conclude: "The results are inconclusive." This is a hard position to argue and sustain, especially when entire laboratories and scores of scientists depend upon the government's support for their continuing research. Such pressures may produce a strain toward early or premature publication and an attempt to characterize results for the press and scientist colleagues more dramatically than they warrant.

Finally, if scientists and medical researchers have their set of presuppositions that influence the conduct of their research and its outcome, surely reporters and health columnists have their own presuppositions and ideological beliefs. Logically, this should influence their choice of stories and their selective perception and use of evidence, although little empirical work exists to specify this claim. Thus, the values, biases, and attitudes of both reporters and scientists can interact to create conditions under which the probability for significant distortion of health risks and other science news is increased.

### The Absence of Effective Social Control

The absence of effective mechanisms of social control can also influence distortions about health risks. High-quality monitoring and feedback systems do not yet exist. Public "taste" for stories is plainly not a sufficient barometer of how well the media are doing.

One mechanism of social control is through complaints. However, the system of reporting health risks tends to reduce the effectiveness of this mechanism because scientists whose stories are covered tend to be a highly self-selected lot who are apt to be pleased by the coverage. Furthermore, those scientists who are skeptical about the likelihood of distorted reporting probably shy away from coverage.

Except for self-criticism within the media, there are few mechanisms to my knowledge that operate to minimize distortion. Jay A. Winsten's interviews suggest that editors' insistence on producing "strong" stories has the frequent consequence of distorting them:

The desk editors are the ones who always want you to push it a little harder. . . . I go to the desk, and they say, "Well, can't you make it a little stronger?" And then they give you an alternative. And I say, "No, you've just eliminated a qualifier, or you've added that word there that's just not true." And you go back and forth like that. So there is movement in the direction of a stronger statement—running out to the boundaries at which you've overgeneralized, at which you've just overdone it. [Winsten 1985]

Thus, the forces operating to produce an engaging and readable newspaper story or television news program appear to work against accurate and balanced reporting of health risks. More effective feedback mechanisms about balance and accuracy need to be constructed, if we are to reduce distortions.

### Bibliography

Ahrens, E. H., Jr. 1985. The diet–heart question in 1985: Has it really been settled? *Lancet,* May 11, pp. 1085–87.

Barber, B. 1961. Resistance by scientists to scientific discovery. *Science* 134: 596–602.

———. 1971. Function, variability, and change in ideological systems. In Bernard Barber and Alex Inkeles, eds., *Stability and social change,* pp. 244–62. Boston: Little, Brown.

Brensike, J. F., et al. 1982. National Heart, Lung, and Blood Institute Type II Coronary Intervention Study: Design, methods, and baseline characteristics. *Controlled Clinical Trials* 3:91–111.

————. 1984. Effects of therapy with cholestyramine on progression of coronary arteriosclerosis: Results of the NHLBI Type II Coronary Intervention Study. *Circulation* 69 (2):313–24.

Brown, M.S., and J. L. Goldstein. 1984. How LDL receptors influence cholesterol and atherosclerosis. *Scientific American* 251 (5):58–66.

Cole, J. R. 1979. *Fair science: Women in the scientific community.* New York: Free Press.

————. 1986. Health risks in the media: Some food for thought. Center for the Social Sciences, Columbia University, Preprint no. 108.

Cole, J. R., and S. Cole. 1973. *Social stratification in science.* Chicago: University of Chicago Press.

————. 1985. Experts' "consensus" and decision-making at the National Science Foundation. In Kenneth S. Warren, ed., *Selectivity in information systems: Survival of the fittest,* pp. 27–63. New York: Praeger.

Cole, J. R., S. Cole, and the Committee on Science and Public Policy, National Academy of Sciences. 1981. *Peer review in the National Science Foundation: Phase two of a study.* Washington, D.C.: National Academy of Sciences.

Cole, S. 1983. The hierarchy of the sciences. *American Journal of Sociology* 89:111–39.

Cole, S., J. R. Cole, and G. A. Simon. 1981. Chance and consensus in peer review. *Science* 214:881–86.

Dawber, T. R. 1980. *The Framingham Study: The epidemiology of atherosclerotic disease.* Cambridge, Mass.: Harvard University Press.

DerSimonian, R., L. J. Charette, B. McPeek, and F. Mosteller. 1982. Reporting on methods in clinical trials. *New England Journal of Medicine* 306:1332–37.

Fleck, L. 1979 [1935]. *Genesis and development of a scientific fact.* Translated by F. Bradley and T. J. Trenn; edited by T. J. Trenn and R. K. Merton. Chicago: University of Chicago Press.

Goldstein, J. L., and M. S. Brown. 1985. Familia hypercholesterolemia: A genetic receptor disease. *Hospital Practice,* November 15, pp. 35–46.

Goodell, R. 1975. *The visible scientists.* Boston: Little, Brown.

Gould, S. J. 1981. *The mismeasure of man.* New York: Norton.

Holton, G. 1978. *The scientific imagination.* Cambridge: Cambridge University Press.

Ingelfinger, F. J. 1974. Peer review in biomedical publication. *American Journal of Medicine* 56:686 ff.

Knorr-Cetina, K. D. 1981. *The manufacture of knowledge. An essay on the constructivist and contextual nature of science.* Oxford: Pergamon Press.

Latour, B., and S. Woolgar. 1979. *Laboratory life: The social construction of scientific facts.* Beverly Hills, Calif.: Sage.

Levy, R. I., et al. 1984. The influence of changes in lipid values induced by cholestyramine and diet on progression of coronary artery disease: Results of the NHLBI Type II Coronary Intervention Study. *Circulation* 69 (2):325–37.

Lipid Research Clinics Program. 1984a. The Lipid Research Clinics Coronary Primary Prevention Trial results. I. Reduction in incidence of coronary heart disease. *JAMA* 251 (3):351–64.

———. 1984b. The Lipid Research Clinics Coronary Primary Prevention Trial results. II. The relationship of incidence of coronary heart disease to cholesterol lowering. *JAMA* 251 (3):365–74.

Merton, R. K. 1942. Science and technology in a democratic order. *Journal of Legal and Political Sociology* 1:115–26. Reprinted in R. K. Merton, *The sociology of science: Theoretical and empirical investigations*, pp. 266–78. Chicago: University of Chicago Press, 1973.

———. 1968. Social structure and anomie. In R. K. Merton, *Social theory and social structure*, pp. 185–214. Enlarged ed. New York: Free Press.

———. 1972. The perspectives of insiders and outsiders. *American Journal of Sociology* 77:9–47.

———. 1973 [1957]. Priorities in scientific discovery. In R. K. Merton, *The sociology of science*, pp. 286–324. Chicago: University of Chicago Press.

Mosteller, F. 1985. Selection of papers by quality of design, analysis, and reporting. In K. E. Warren, ed., *Selectivity in information systems*, pp. 98–116. New York: Praeger.

Multiple Risk Factor Intervention Trial Research Group. 1982. Multiple Risk Factor Intervention Trial: Risk factor changes and mortality rates. *JAMA* 248 (12):1465–77.

National Academy of Sciences. 1980. *Toward healthful diets*. Washington, D.C.: National Academy Press.

———. 1985. *Nutrition education in U.S. medical schools*. Washington, D.C.: National Academy Press.

National Center for Health Statistics. 1984. Monthly vital statistics report. 33 (9), December 20.

Nelkin, D. 1985. Managing biomedical news. *Social Research* 52 (3):625–46.

Oliver, M. F. 1985. Consensus or nonsensus conferences on coronary heart disease. *Lancet,* May 11, pp. 1087–89.

Polanyi, M. 1963. The potential theory of adsorption. *Science* 141:1010–13.

Rockefeller University Research Profiles. 1984. Edward H. Ahrens, Jr. (Fall.)

Shekelle, R. B., et al. 1981. Diet, serum cholesterol, and death from coronary heart disease: The Western Electric Study. *New England Journal of Medicine* 304 (2):65–70.

Stinchcombe, A. L., and R. Ofshe. 1969. On journal editing as a probabilistic process. *American Sociologist* 4 (2):116–17.

Winsten, J. A. 1985. Science and the media: The boundaries of truth. *Health Affairs* 3:5–23.

Zuckerman, H. 1977. *Scientific elite: Nobel laureates in the United States*. New York: Free Press.

Zuckerman, H., and R. K. Merton. 1971. Patterns of evaluation in science: Institutionalization, structure, and function of the refereeing system. *Minerva* 9:66 ff.

## Charles R. Wright

## 21 Social Surveys and the Use of the Mass Media: The Case of the Aged

On the occasion of the twentieth-anniversary issue of the *Public Opinion Quarterly* in 1957, an issue devoted to twenty years of public opinion research, Herbert Hyman reflected on the existing state of theory about public opinion (Hyman, 1957; pp. 54–60). The state of theory was bleak, he commented, if one looked for a grand theory that integrated the vast empirical findings of past and contemporary studies of public opinion. Things looked brighter, however, if one looked for theoretical orientations of more modest scope, for example, theories of the middle range, a phrase suggested by Robert K. Merton (Merton 1949; pp. 4–5).

### Hyman's Ideas about Opinion Polls and Theories of Public Opinion

Hyman offered several suggestions as to how future survey research could contribute theoretically relevant data that, over time, would strengthen sociological theories about public opinion formation and its social consequences. We review them here because they provide useful guides to ways in which survey research also can contribute to our theoretical understanding of mass communication audiences.

One reason for the difficulty in developing theories of public opinion formation and change, Hyman argued, is that public opinion surveys, especially public opinion polls, tend to focus on current social

I wish to acknowledge, with thanks, the helpful editorial and sociological comments of Hubert J. O'Gorman and the research assistance of Chien Joanna Lei and Michael Lightfoot.

issues and thus do not provide a running account of public opinion about topics not yet socially or politically salient or about former issues no longer "hot." Because of this, analyses tend to focus on immediate, short-term factors relating to current public opinion. There is limited opportunity to relate public opinion to such macroscopic social determinants as the law, social change, and so on. We miss the social determinants of opinion formation and change.

Second, he states, public opinion polls by and large concentrate on adults—as if their opinions appeared with no history. Public opinion theory would be enriched by data on the various precursors to adult opinions, by research on socialization and the stabilization (or change) of views, and the mechanisms through which such socialization and stabilization occur.

Theories of public opinion need to go beyond their usual focus on the individual person and his or her views. One needs to search for what is fundamental and also common to a group or society, such as social values. Hyman saw promise in the secondary analysis of surveys that contain clues to determinants of public opinion rooted in social structural factors, group membership, and reference group phenomena.

Survey analyses could benefit, too, from attempts to conceptualize and measure units of public opinion going beyond the individual. It would be constructive, for example, to develop indexes of public opinion (in addition to scales of individual opinions) reflecting the social distribution of opinions among groups, regions, or other units of society.

Finally, what is the point of all these efforts? Not, Hyman implies, merely to describe the general state of the population's opinions on a particular issue but rather to link public opinion to the political process—to understand, so to speak, the larger social consequences of public opinion formation, maintenance, and change.

To summarize, Hyman argued that our theories of public opinion would be enriched by social surveys that provided for continuity over time, a broader range of population, examination of data at the level of social groups rather than individuals only, the development of measures to reflect the social distribution of opinions within and between units of society, and attempts to link the data to larger social issues of social order and change.

## Relevance for the Study of Mass Communication Behavior

Hyman's insights into these opportunities for the inductive development of public opinion theory from public opinion polls also illuminate the strengths and weaknesses of trying to develop middle-range theories about mass communication behavior from survey research. The similarities between public opinion polls and surveys of communication behavior are readily apparent.

Both fields have been active in recent years. Yet both share the tendency to focus on matters of the moment. Just as we tend to begin collecting public opinion data about new topics such as toxic waste, abortion, and other matters only after they become social issues, so too we tend to gather data on various features of mass media audiences only when they become timely. As a result, we often lack valuable baseline data that would contribute to our understanding of consistencies and variability in audience behavior over time. National surveys of television behavior in the 1950s and 1960s, for example, rarely focused on the aged, a group now of considerable social and sociological interest.

Audience measures also tend to report on the individual's mass communication behavior rather than on patterns of behavior of social segments or groups. Just as public opinion polls have transformed the empirical study of public opinion—once conceived as a social phenomenon—into the precise science of measuring and enumerating the individual's opinions, so too mass communication surveys tell us more about the individual's mass media habits than about mass communication as a social phenomenon.

There are exceptions. Some surveys have examined communication patterns at the household level, but these are rare. Studies of the role of mass communication in even larger social units, such as friendship and peer groups, should enrich our theoretical understanding of the processes and consequences of media behavior.

Indexes of communication behavior that characterize and summarize group differences also should strengthen theoretical analyses. Just as it has proven useful, for example, to classify individuals according to their patterns of media behavior (heavy or light users of print, television, both, or neither), so it might be of interest to develop indexes of media behavior that allow trend studies and contrasts among age groupings, social classes, ethnic groups, even entire societies.

Surveys shedding light on institutionalized patterns of mass communication also have theoretical interest. Surveys can contribute, for example, to our sociological knowledge of the social norms and folkways surrounding media use by persons differentially located in the social structure—as by social class or age, for example.

Hyman's suggestion to broaden the range of respondents also applies to communication surveys. Communication theory could benefit from more studies that relate earlier behavior to the patterns of media usage, gratifications, and functions found among persons later in life. Surveys also could give greater attention, for example, to the very elderly population than has been done in the past. Furthermore, certain segments of the population—institutionalized adults, for example—tend to be systematically excluded from most regularly conducted national audience surveys.

Finally, it seems clear that the study of mass communication relates to our sociological interest in the larger topics of social control, stability, and social change. Surveys can contribute to this effort. For example, attention is being given to how mass media are used during the process of adult socialization. (For one discussion, see Wright 1985, pp. 185–201.) These studies, usually local and often exploratory in nature, have begun to link media behavior to larger sociological interests in social class differences and in the assimilation of adult immigrants, as examples. As another example, previous and recent surveys of the media's role in affecting individuals' opinions on social issues have been reexamined in terms of larger issues of public opinion and public agenda building.

On balance, then, the prospect for building and strengthening our theoretical understanding of mass communication behavior through survey research seems good. We have yet, as Hyman observed for the field of public opinion, to build a comprehensive theory. That day is yet to come. Its arrival, we suggest, may depend greatly on firmly established foundations of data collection, sociologically oriented descriptive accounts of mass communication behavior, and middle-range theory—accomplishments now within the reach of survey design and analysis.

One of the more promising strategies of survey research that can assist in this enterprise is secondary analysis of sample surveys originally conducted for other purposes. This strategy, as readers of this volume are sure to recognize, is one widely promoted and codified by Herbert Hyman in his own research (Hyman 1972). We will employ it here, together with a mode of descriptive survey analysis that I have introduced elsewhere, called *constructional analysis* (Wright 1975, pp. 379–413), in search of patterns in the mass media behavior of the aged, a topic that is of interest to both sociologists and mass communication researchers today.[1]

## Constructional Analysis

Constructional analysis, unlike traditional multivariate analysis, does not seek to determine how much variance is statistically explained, di-

[1] See, for example, Davis and Davis 1985; Atkin 1976.

rectly or indirectly, by the independent variables under study. Rather, the approach is descriptive and comparative. It resembles, to some extent, the use of surveys for what Hyman (1955, p. 119) has termed "differentiated descriptions." The strategy of constructional analysis is to search for, describe, and contrast patterns of communication behavior between types of people classified according to constructed combinations of social characteristics. These social characteristics are selected because they promise to be theoretically important or sociologically interesting. By and large, they are indicators of people's positions in the social structure.

The relevance of these social categories for the study of mass communication behavior comes from the theoretical expectation that such social locations provide differential access to the mass media and differential norms concerning their use. Category selection is guided by sociological theory or experience. In previous analyses using one sample survey, for example, I found it useful to contrast the media behavior of persons classified according to intergenerational occupational mobility, cumulative intergenerational levels of education, educational achievements of husbands and wives, and status sets of aging, retirement, and widowhood.

The strategy of contrasting carefully constructed types of respondents is one that Hyman has used advantageously in his own survey analyses, sometimes colorfully referring to the process as a horse race. Respondents' views and opinions were contrasted according to constructed types that reflected differences in social position and social experiences. (As examples, see Hyman 1983; Hyman, Levine, and Wright 1967, pp. 165–70; Hyman, Wright, and Hopkins 1962, pp. 288–89; Hyman, Wright, and Reed 1975, pp. 73–74.) In these instances, contrasts were made in order to demonstrate the influence of a specific key variable under comparatively favorable or adverse conditions. For example, the impact of an educational program in citizenship was shown to endure even among its graduates who later lived in communities where public sentiments might not support some of the values encouraged by the program, in addition to enduring for respondents living in more supportive social contexts.

The strategy of constructional analysis used here seeks more to discover patterns of behavior associated with certain combinations of variables, such as status sets, than to determine the impact of one key variable. In the section that follows I shall further demonstrate constructional analysis by exploring, through secondary analysis of national surveys, data on the mass media behavior of the elderly population in America.

## Mass Media Behavior of the Aged: Some Prior Research

Relatively few national studies in the past provide specific data about the mass media behavior of our nation's very elderly or moderately elderly people.[2] There are some major exceptions to be noted.

An important national survey of noninstitutionalized older Americans, in 1974, gives data on mass media behavior measured in broad terms, such as whether or not respondents *ever* spend any time watching television, reading newspapers, or listening to the radio. By these measures, the proportion of people using various mass media dropped somewhat among the very elderly in comparison to others. Nevertheless, a majority—and often a sizable majority—of relatively old people reported spending time with the mass media (National Council on the Aging 1975).[3]

Robert Bower's studies of television and the public provide an unusual example of planned continuity in sociological audience surveys, being based on national surveys conducted in 1960, 1970, and 1980. He reports that, by and large, the amount of time spent watching television in the evenings and on weekends increases for people in their twenties, falls off for those in their thirties and forties, increases for people in their fifties, and then drops a bit for people of age sixty and over (Bower 1973, 1985).

Leo Bogart cites data from marketing surveys showing that about three-fourths of respondents of age sixty-five or older said that they read a newspaper "yesterday." About the same percentage of younger old people (aged 55–64) also said they had read a paper. Somewhat fewer people in their twenties and thirties said so (Bogart 1981, p. 116).

These exceptions (there may be others; a complete review of the literature is beyond our purposes here) provide glimpses into the mass media behavior of our nation's elderly population. They spur our interest to learn more. It is not easy to do so, however, from any available single national survey. Therefore, the strategy of secondary analysis of several comparable surveys seems worth exploring.

---

[2] Data through the late 1960s are reviewed by Riley and Foner (1968) and by Schramm (1969). Riley and Foner concluded that television viewing and radio listening received increased time in older age. More recent data, mostly from local surveys, are given by Atkin (1976) and Davis (1980). Data from commercial surveys also can provide sociologically useful information on the media habits of the aged.

[3] The 1974 survey was replicated in 1981, but some of the earlier mass media questions were not repeated. The 1981 data show a decline in the proportion of respondents who believe that the media accurately report the condition of the elderly. See National Council on the Aging 1981.

## Data for Secondary Analysis

One reason that detailed data on the mass media behavior of the more elderly are rarely presented is that relatively few very old people are captured in general cross-sectional probability samples.[4] This limitation also applies to the surveys that we use here for our secondary analysis. But by pooling data from several national samples we can obtain sufficient numbers of elderly respondents for some comparisons.[5]

The *General Social Surveys* of the National Opinion Research Center provide the necessary data. We draw upon these national sample surveys for the past decade, using data from 1975, 1977, 1978, 1980, 1982, and 1983—years when questions were asked about mass media use (National Opinion Research Center 1983).

Our first problem is to determine what age categories to use. Transitions in age status in our society are only crudely and arbitrarily indexed by chronological age. Because age sixty-five has certain legal and social consequences, many surveys classify respondents aged sixty-five or more as elderly. But that convention may not provide an appropriate sociological criterion for other research purposes. It is difficult to determine who should be classified as old independent of the survey research problem at hand. We will classify persons aged seventy to seventy-nine as moderately elderly, octogenarians and nonagenarians as more elderly.[6]

Each of the National Opinion Research Center (NORC) national samples of about 1,500 respondents contains only about forty-five respondents who are eighty or more years of age. Therefore, we have pooled data from our six surveys for a combined yield of slightly more than 260 cases from this rare population. We also have a total of approximately 750 septuagenarians.

Each of the NORC surveys selected also contains questions on the mass media behavior of American adults. The questions have the advantage of calling for direct and simple reports of overall media ex-

[4]Those who are, of course, are usually persons living in private households and therefore do not represent the institutionalized or hospitalized elderly. This limitation applies also to the data used here for our secondary analysis of the use of mass media by the aged.

[5]We assume, for our purposes here, that pooling the data does not distort the patterns of media behavior that accompany various age categories. On this point, see Reed (1975), who presents an example of studying "rare" populations by pooling survey data for secondary analysis and a discussion of some of the methodological considerations.

[6]As a check on possible distortions caused by defining old age as beginning at seventy rather than at the conventional age of sixty-five, the following analyses also were run for the moderately elderly, defined as aged sixty-five to seventy-nine and then as seventy to seventy-nine. Raising the threshold to seventy made no appreciable difference in the findings.

posure from the respondents.[7] They record what respondents tell survey researchers about their media behavior. These data can be compared across age groups and other categories of people to discover similarities and differences in reported media behavior. The surveys provide more data on the amount of reading, viewing, and listening that elderly people say they do than are available in any single prior survey cited above. They make it possible, therefore, to examine whether regular, even heavy use of these mass media is more or less common among the elderly than among other age groups.

The surveys (which cover a variety of topics, some repeated each year) inquired as to how often the respondents read a newspaper, watched television, and listened to the radio. These are the communication behaviors that will concern us here. The specific questions were as follows:

How often do you read the newspaper—every day, a few times a week, once a week, less than once a week, or never?

On the average day, about how many hours do you personally watch television?

Do you ever listen to the radio? [if *Yes*]: On the average, about how many hours a day do you usually listen to the radio?

The surveys also contain data on various social characteristics of interest to us, such as marital status, thus making them suitable resources for our secondary analysis and construction of contrast types.

## Patterns of Mass Media Use among the Aged

Popular stereotypes of the aged may lead to contradictory expectations about their mass media behavior.[8] On the one hand, it may be expected that elderly persons—especially the most elderly—disengage from many social roles and lose some of their interest in social events. Freed from certain social responsibilities, the elderly may reduce their mass media use too, no longer having to keep up with current events through daily newspaper reading, for example. On the other hand, social disengagement and increased leisure time might combine to lead elderly persons to increase their use of the mass media

---

[7] All self-reports on behavior have certain limitations, of course. But the data presented here, taken in the aggregate and used in conjunction with broad response categories of use, seem adequate for our purposes. The simplicity of the questions makes it unlikely that responses would be systematically biased between age groups or between the other social categories that we have constructed for comparisons.

[8] For data on the public's image of the aged, see *The Myth and Reality of Aging* (National Council on the Aging 1975). For an analysis of some factors leading to misconceptions about the elderly, by the general public and by the elderly themselves, see O'Gorman 1980, 1985.

TABLE 21.1. *Daily Mass Communication Behavior of Elderly and Younger Adults*

| Age of respondent | Read a newspaper | | Watch TV 3 hrs. & up | | Listen to radio 2 hrs. & up | |
|---|---|---|---|---|---|---|
| | Pct. | (N) | Pct. | (N) | Pct. | (N) |
| 80 or older | 62% | (215) | 56% | (258) | 51% | (122) |
| 70–79 | 72 | (637) | 61 | (747) | 58 | (319) |
| 60–69 | 73 | (980) | 57 | (1181) | 57 | (504) |
| 50–59 | 72 | (1201) | 46 | (1409) | 62 | (631) |
| 40–49 | 65 | (1202) | 42 | (1409) | 56 | (639) |
| 30–39 | 53 | (1634) | 45 | (1949) | 63 | (1015) |
| 18–29 | 39 | (2088) | 55 | (2439) | 71 | (1250) |
| All respondents | 58% | (7959) | 50% | (9392) | 63% | (4480) |

*Source:* Data from the *General Social Surveys,* National Opinion Research Center, for various years from 1975 through 1983.

for mass entertainment, to "escape" into the world of television, for example. Early social researchers, as Davis and Davis (1985, pp. 79–80) point out, characterized the aged as "embracers" of television, like very young children.

Our first task is to examine the communication behavior of the older respondents to discover whether in fact they are heavy or light users of the mass media. We also want to see whether the most elderly differ greatly from less elderly and younger respondents.[9] Data on daily mass media use by persons in different age categories are presented in Table 21.1

First let us consider newspaper reading. Does increasing age, with its presumed disengagement from many of society's role obligations, seem to be accompanied by a sharp drop in the proportion of people who keep up with the daily newspaper? Apparently not.

The majority (62 percent) of the respondents who were eighty or older said they read a newspaper every day (68 percent read a paper at least a few times a week). This compares favorably with the proportion of people in their forties who read a newspaper every day (65 percent) and is higher than the figures for people in their twenties and thirties. Likewise, 72 percent of the septuagenarians are daily readers (and 82 percent read a newspaper at least a few times a week), a figure similar

[9] Our purpose here and in subsequent analyses is descriptive and comparative. We wish to examine the patterns of media use by persons in various age categories without statistically "controlling" for other differences among them, such as varieties of education, state of health, or income. In other words, we are not concerned with determining the amount of variance in media behavior that is statistically "explained" by age as an independent variable.

to that for persons in their fifties and sixties. (It is the case, however, that 19 percent of the respondents aged eighty or more said that they never read a newspaper, as compared to only 4 to 7 percent among younger respondents.)

These findings show that daily newspaper readership is about as common among the aged as among the rest of the population. A substantial majority of our older respondents usually read a newspaper every day; an overwhelming majority read a paper at least once a week. Although our data cannot tell us what people read in their newspapers, the strong pattern of frequent newspaper readership suggests that most elderly people do remain in touch with current news and world events, at least through daily exposure to newspapers.

Television provides another look at the world, for both news and entertainment. One plausible expectation is that television provides a convenient at-home medium for escape from boredom, and therefore very old people may be especially dependent upon it for mass entertainment.

Our survey data suggest that life does become less exciting (although no less precious) with changes in age status. Though a little more than half of both the young and the middle-aged respondents found life to be routine or even dull, 64 percent of the septuagenarians (N = 377) and 66 percent of the oldest respondents (N = 134) found it so. But more to the point concerning escape from boredom, 33 percent of the most elderly respondents (N = 58) said that they often have time on their hands, as do 26 percent of the moderately elderly (N = 136). It needs to be noted, however, that the most elderly respondents are not generally less happy than others, 35 percent saying that they are very happy (N = 258), as compared with 40 percent among the moderately elderly (N = 742). Nor are very old people more likely to condone suicide for someone who is tired of living. So the aged, as a group, are not necessarily more depressed than others. More of them are simply likely to have time on their hands and to find daily life falling into a routine.

Whatever very old people may be doing to fill their hours, they are not television addicts, at least no more so than others. Nearly everyone in the surveys reported watching some television each day. The average (median) respondent reported watching television for about three hours a day. Table 21.1 presents data on the percentage of respondents from each age category whose viewing was average or more. Of the oldest respondents, 56 percent watched television for three or more hours every day, but so did 55 percent of young adults in their twenties. It is true that slightly lower percentages of respondents aged thirty to sixty spent this much time watching television (probably because of other time-consuming duties of work and family). But the increase in proportion of regular viewers among the aged is modest. Very heavy viewing (six or more hours a day, reported by 10 percent of the total population) is engaged in by 17 percent of the oldest respondents and by 13 or 14 percent of the people in their twenties, sixties, and seventies. As might be anticipated, such heavy viewing was less common (about 7 percent) among persons in their middle years. With these minor exceptions, then, the aged resemble other adults rather than differing markedly from them in amounts of television exposure.

It is worth remembering, however, that nearly all of the elderly watch television for several hours a day and therefore have this second channel of news and entertainment to keep in touch with the world.

Finally, we consider radio listening. Radio, at least during the period of these surveys, was a young person's medium, probably because of its music format. Still, some of its fare—news, sports, talk shows, telephone call-ins, classical and nostalgic music—might be expected to appeal to the elderly and very old people, especially during the potentially sleepless late-night hours. And radio use depends less on good eyesight than does newspaper reading or television viewing.

Nearly everyone said they listened to the radio for some time every day. The average (median) respondent in our surveys reported listening to the radio between two and three hours a day. Table 21.1 presents data on the percentage of persons in each age category who listened this much or more per day.

Clearly, young adults favor radio, 71 percent listening for two or more hours a day. Beyond that, however, there are only minor and unsystematic differences in the percentage of "moderately heavy" radio listeners (ranging from 56 to 63 percent) up to the oldest age category. A bare majority of respondents of age eighty or more listened that long. Still, all of them did listen to the radio every day, if only for a few minutes or an hour or so, and therefore they too made use of this mass medium, adding a third possible avenue for news and entertainment.

These findings, unrefined though they may be, are quite informative about the mass media behavior of the very old population. The proportion of people who are regular, even heavy, users of television, newspapers, and radio drops only slightly among the most elderly population. This suggests, on the one hand, that, perhaps contrary to popular beliefs, the very old, as a group, are no more (but no less) media-dependent than others. On the other hand, it is important to note that a sizable majority of older people make regular use of the mass media and, to that extent, remain in contact with the world around them.

Thus, secondary analysis adds to what was known before about the media habits of the aged. Nevertheless, we would hope for more continuity in research on media behavior, as Hyman urged in his case for continuity in public opinion polling. Future primary surveys that focus more regularly on the mass media habits of the heterogeneous elderly population would provide the continuity essential to trend studies and would produce adequate numbers of cases for more refined analyses. A similar call for regular general surveys of the aged is made by Pearlin (1982).[10]

In the meantime, in order to obtain sufficient cases for further secondary analysis here, it is necessary to broaden our category of elderly to include both moderately elderly and older persons. We will set it at age seventy and above. Combining people moderately elderly and older into one category necessarily obscures any differences in mass media behavior between these two age groupings. Nevertheless, given the findings reported above, these differences are relatively small and not qualitatively radical. We proceed, then, to construct our next comparison groups by adding a social contextual condition—size of household.

## To Be Old and Alone

One of life's changes that may accompany aging is a reduction in household size, perhaps to the point where one is living alone. To be living by oneself while young may be exciting—one's first fling at freedom—but to be old and alone may add up to just plain lonely. (Being old and living alone do not necessarily lead to loneliness, however. On this point, see Peplau and Perlman 1982, pp. 327–47.)[11]

Peter Townsend and Sylvia Tunstall (1968) have observed that people who are old and living alone seem likely to use the mass media. In an analysis of a national survey of the elderly in 1962 these authors report that 53 percent of elderly persons living alone in America had watched television during the previous day, and 56 percent had lis-

---

[10] Pearlin (1982) argues for the need for comparative analysis of age cohorts, preferably longitudinal studies but also independent cross-national surveys, as a basis for the development of theory and as a protection against falsely generalizing from experience with a particular age cohort.

[11] Also see other chapters in Peplau and Perlman (1982) for reviews of the literature on loneliness and discussions of theoretical and methodological issues. On conceptualization and measurement of loneliness, also see Wenger 1983.

tened to the radio. Jeremy Tunstall also reports that old people living alone in Great Britain make frequent use of the home-centered mass media, namely newspapers, radio, and television. "The mass media," he suggests, "appear to affect isolated old people in two separate ways. Some of these old people are very well informed about recent political events and trends in popular entertainment. . . . On the other hand, another strong impression . . . is that the mass media serve to emphasize to these old people their own isolated state" (1966, p. 197).

Various combinations of age status and social circumstances provide their own special context for the likely use of mass media. We will examine mass media use for nine constructed combinations of age status and living conditions: people living alone who are young (18–29), middle-aged (30–69), or elderly (70–89); people living with one other person, who are young, middle-aged, or elderly; and young, middle-aged, or elderly people living with two or more other persons. In this analysis our attention will be focused on the three elderly types, but data on the six other types are considered occasionally for contrast.

The number of cases in each of these constructed types varies because some of the dependent questions were not asked each year and therefore did not involve the total pool of 9,429 respondents. The smallest group from the combined samples was ninety-nine cases of elderly persons living in households with two or more other people.

Before examining media use, it is helpful to get some ideas about what living alone may signify for the quality of the respondent's life. Whatever the age group, people who live alone are less likely to say that they are *very* happy than are people who live with others. (Surprisingly, perhaps, the group who is least likely to report happiness is not the young or the old but middle-aged people who live alone.) Older people who live with someone (or with several people) are the most likely to report general happiness.[12]

To be old and alone is not necessarily more likely to mean time on one's hands than is being old and living with others. Elderly respondents, as noted earlier, were more likely than others to find themselves with extra time on their hands, and this holds regardless of the presence or absence of others in the household. (The only others equally likely to have "idle" hours were young people living alone.)

To be old and living alone is not associated with fear or with approval of suicide if one is tired of living. Old respondents living alone

[12]One study, in Cleveland, Ohio, reports that morale among elderly persons living alone was somewhat lower than among those living with a spouse but higher than among those living with their grown children (Mindel and Wright 1983).

were about as likely as others to say that they felt safe and secure at home. And old people in general were the least likely group to approve of suicide.

These data suggest, then, that to be old and living alone is to have time on one's hands, but no more so than other elderly people, and to be about as happy and secure at home as other people. In general, our nine constructed groups do not differ greatly along the few psychological characteristics examined. Nevertheless, different combinations of age and living arrangements may be associated with differences in mass media behavior, thus reflecting the social aspects of these arrangements. That is, the presence or absence of others in the household might contribute to different patterns of mass media use.

Newspaper reading is one possibility. The presence of others in the household might increase the likelihood of a newspaper being available, either through subscription by a household member or through someone carrying a paper home. Television viewing also might reflect the presence or absence of others. At the very least, one is likely to be exposed to the television set turned on by others, unless one is able to escape to another part of the house. Radio listening seems the least likely to be affected by surrounding social relationships. It has become a personalized medium when one wishes—with earphones—and even if one lives among others, radio can be privately turned to for music, talk shows, news, and sports, late into the sleepless nights. On the other hand, radio listening can be a socially shared experience, voluntary or not—boombox and all.

The media behavior for our nine types is contrasted in Table 21.2. Certain patterns can be discerned, two of which seem relevant to our concern about media use and the aged.

First, it is clear that the previously demonstrated finding that the aged are regular daily users of the mass media is sustained even for those who are living alone and therefore possibly more disengaged. The findings suggest that to be old and living alone means keeping in touch with life aided by regular use of the mass media. A majority of our elderly alones read newspapers everyday, watch television for three hours or more each day, and listen to the radio for two hours or more a day. No other type matches this consistency of media use across the board. Only elderly respondents living with two or more other people come close to it.

Second, by contrast, to be young and living alone is to be mainly radio-oriented, among the mass media studied. (We regret the absence of data on movie attendance.) In no other type is there so high a percentage (77 percent) who listen so much to the radio each day and so low a percentage of television and/or newspaper "fans." Also, rela-

TABLE 21.2. *Daily Mass Communication Behavior of Nine Constructed Types of Age and Living Arrangements*

| Type[a] | Read a newspaper | | Watch TV 3 hrs. & up | | Listen to radio 2 hrs. & up | |
|---|---|---|---|---|---|---|
| | Pct. | (N) | Pct. | (N) | Pct. | (N) |
| Young, alone | 39% | (254) | 37% | (297) | 77% | (167) |
| Middle-aged, alone | 58 | (802) | 47 | (958) | 68 | (500) |
| Old, alone | 68 | (406) | 61 | (487) | 67 | (216) |
| Young, twosome | 39 | (577) | 50 | (679) | 73 | (362) |
| Middle-aged, twosome | 70 | (1494) | 51 | (1810) | 60 | (834) |
| Old, twosome | 73 | (360) | 59 | (419) | 42 | (181) |
| Young, group | 39 | (1257) | 61 | (1463) | 70 | (721) |
| Middle-aged, group | 63 | (2721) | 45 | (3180) | 57 | (1455) |
| Old, group | 69 | (86) | 58 | (99) | 64 | (44) |

*Source:* Data from the *General Social Surveys,* National Opinion Research Center, for various years from 1975 through 1983.

[a] For details on construction of types, see text.

tively fewer young people are daily newspaper readers, whatever the size of the household where they live.

It is not contended that either age or residential status causes or explains these observed differences in media behavior. Rather, constructional analysis has led us to *compare* media behavior of carefully constructed types of respondents. These types combine one indicator of the respondent's position in the life course—age—with an indicator of social context—size of one's household. This research strategy has disclosed some interesting differences in mass media behavior that may serve to correct popular misconceptions about the elderly and that, in themselves, warrant further examination.

## Young and Old Men and Women Alone: The Single and the Widowed

In the space remaining in this chapter, we shall explore only a few additionally constructed types with no attempt at a fuller description or analysis. We first consider gender.

For the total sample, much as expected on the basis of prior research, men and women differ in their mass media behavior. A higher percentage of men than women are likely to say that they read a newspaper every day, whereas a smaller percentage of men than women report relatively heavy television viewing. Gender makes little or no difference in the percentage of people who listen to the radio for several hours a day.

Our focus here, however, is on people living alone. And for them, further contrast by gender does not disclose different patterns of mass media use. The general patterns described above prevail. There are no important statistical differences between men and women living alone in the percentage of each who read a newspaper every day or watch television more than average, or listen to the radio regularly. (See Table 21.3.)

We extend the construction by adding another social status to our typology of age and household size: marital status. Complications arise in constructing these additional combinations, however, because of practical limitations. One finds few cases in certain potential types, even when starting with large total samples pooled from several national surveys. For example, nearly all of the young people living alone are single; there are (fortunately, from our human point of view) hardly any cases of young people living alone who are widows or widowers. Nevertheless, there are sufficient cases of certain interesting types to permit description and contrast here. We continue to focus on respondents who are living alone, first the young and then the elderly and middle-aged.

Most young people living alone are single and have never been married. Their mass media behavior shows a pattern similar to youth in the aggregate. That is, radio is their medium. A relatively small portion of them read newspapers (41 percent) or watch a lot of television each day (36 percent), but many more (75 percent) listen to the radio for several hours a day. This pattern holds for both young men and young women.

Most elderly respondents living alone are widowed. These respondents, it might be argued, face day-to-day life with triple social "handicaps." They are elderly, live by themselves, and are without the daily support and interaction of their chosen mates. They seem likely candidates, on the one hand, to withdraw from interest in newspaper events and, on the other hand, to escape into heavy viewing of television entertainment. The data, however, suggest they do neither—at least no more so than others. (See Table 21.4.) Their mass media behavior follows a pattern similar to elderly respondents in general. That is, a majority of them (67 percent) read a newspaper every day; thus, they have not withdrawn from this contact with the world. A majority of them, but not an extraordinarily high proportion (61 percent) watch television for three or more hours a day; there is no sign of massive addiction to television. And a comparable majority (64 percent) listen to the radio for several hours each day. This pattern is similar for both widows and widowers.

Middle-aged widows and widowers living alone also show a pattern of moderately heavy daily exposure to the mass media—64 percent

TABLE 21.3. *Daily Mass Communication Behavior of Men and Women Living Alone*

| Type[a] | Read a newspaper | | Watch TV 3 hrs. & up | | Listen to radio 2 hrs. & up | |
|---|---|---|---|---|---|---|
| | Pct. | (N) | Pct. | (N) | Pct. | (N) |
| Young men, alone | 41% | (152) | 39% | (179) | 73% | (97) |
| Young women, alone | 35 | (102) | 34 | (118) | 71 | (70) |
| Middle-aged men, alone | 56 | (346) | 39 | (421) | 67 | (219) |
| Middle-aged women, alone | 60 | (456) | 53 | (537)[b] | 68 | (281) |
| Older men, alone | 70 | (92) | 54 | (110) | 67 | (48) |
| Older women, alone | 67 | (314) | 63 | (377) | 67 | (168) |

*Source:* Data from the *General Social Surveys,* National Opinion Research Center, for various years from 1975 through 1983.
[a]For details on construction of types, see text.
[b]$p < .0001$ (chi-square test). No other differences between men's and women's media behavior were significant at the .01 level.

TABLE 21.4. *Daily Mass Communication Behavior of Widowed Persons, Middle-aged and Older, Living Alone or with Others*

| Type[a] | Read a newspaper | | Watch TV 3 hrs. & up | | Listen to radio 2 hrs. & up | |
|---|---|---|---|---|---|---|
| | Pct. | (N) | Pct. | (N) | Pct. | (N) |
| Middle-aged, widowed, & alone | 64% | (250) | 57% | (296) | 69% | (130) |
| Old, widowed, & alone | 67 | (335) | 61 | (400) | 64 | (176) |
| Middle-aged, widowed, and with others | 65 | (151) | 51 | (183) | 68 | (74) |
| Old, widowed, and with others | 62 | (85) | 57 | (97) | 55 | (40) |

*Source:* Data from the *General Social Surveys,* National Opinion Research Center, for various years from 1975 through 1983.
[a]For details on construction of types, see text.

reading a daily newspaper, 57 percent watching television, and 69 percent listening to the radio for several hours each day.

It seems fitting that our demonstration end with this look at the media behavior of elderly widows and widowers, for this is a group of special concern in one of Herbert Hyman's recent research projects (Hyman 1983, pp. 34–38). As part of his larger study on the enduring effects of widowhood, Hyman reports (on the basis of secondary analysis of several national sample surveys) no appreciable difference in the percentage of elderly widowed (aged 60–79) and younger widowed (aged 40–59) who read the newspaper daily or who watch television for four or more hours a day. He comments that "surely such activity connects the individual to the larger social world; brings the person into contact, albeit at a distance, with great events and small happenings involving others."

Thus, mass communication behavior is linked to larger social matters. In this way too our survey data on the mass communication behavior of the aged and others—contrasting data on men and women who are elderly and alone, single or widowed—sheds light on their potential links to the larger society and current events through their daily use of the mass media.

## Conclusion

Our essay began by drawing upon Hyman's earlier remarks on public opinion polling and extending them to suggest ways in which future social surveys can contribute sociologically useful data about people's mass media behavior. It is my optimistic hope—as it was Hyman's hope concerning the future of public opinion polling and theory—that in time we will have a wealth of systematic, theoretically relevant survey data about our mass communication behavior from which to work.

These developments will be most welcome. But while awaiting their arrival we can do much through exploiting currently available resources. In particular, we can begin to explore the relations between mass communication use and social structure by following a strategy of secondary analysis of previous national surveys.

I have suggested one research tactic for the discovery, description, and comparative analysis of patterns of mass communication behavior through secondary analysis—constructional analysis—and have illustrated its usefulness in the study of such special and often "rare" survey populations as the aged, people living alone, the widowed, and persons combining these statuses. Such comparative descriptive accounts help to dispel, refine, or support popular preconceptions and stereotypes about mass media use by persons of various social types. In this way they provide the empirical base necessary for future theoretically directed survey analyses aimed at explaining genuine differences and similarities in the use of the mass media by people differentially located in the social structure.

## Bibliography

Atkin, Charles K. 1976. Mass media and the aging. In Herbert J. Oyer, and E. Jane Oyer, eds., *Aging and communication*, pp. 99–118. Baltimore: University Park Press.

Bogart, Leo. 1981. *Press and public: Who reads what, when, where, and why in American newspapers*. Hillsdale, N.J.: Erlbaum.

Bower, Robert T. 1973. *Television and the public*. New York: Holt, Rinehart and Winston.

————. 1985. *The changing television audience in America*. New York: Columbia University Press.

Davis, Richard H. 1980. *Television and the aging audience*. Los Angeles: University of Southern California Press.

Davis, Richard H., and James A. Davis. 1985. *TV's image of the elderly: A practical guide for change*. Lexington, Mass.: Heath.

Merton, Robert K. 1949. *Social theory and social structure*. Glencoe, Ill.: Free Press.

Mindel, Charles H., and Roosevelt Wright, Jr. 1983. Differential living arrangements among the elderly and their subjective well-being. In Phyllis M. Foster, ed., *Activities and the "well elderly,"* pp. 25–34. New York: Hawthorn Books.

National Council on the Aging. 1975. *The myth and reality of aging in America*. Washington, D.C.

————. 1981. *Aging in the eighties*. Washington, D.C.

National Opinion Research Center. 1983. *General Social Surveys, 1972–1983: Cumulative Codebook*. University of Chicago.

O'Gorman, Hubert J. 1980. False consciousness of kind: Pluralistic ignorance among the aged. *Research on Aging* 2 (1): 105–28.

————. 1985. Pluralistic ignorance and false consciousness of kind: The impact of perceived personal problems on the perception of others' problems. Paper presented to the 55th Annual Meeting of the Eastern Sociological Society, Philadelphia, March 17.

Pearlin, Leonard I. 1982. Discontinuities in the study of aging. In T. K. Hareven and K. J. Adams, eds., *Aging and life course transitions: An interdisciplinary perspective*, pp. 55–74. London: Tavistock.

Peplau, Letitia Anne, and Daniel Perlman, eds. 1982. *Loneliness: A sourcebook of current theory, research, and therapy*. New York: Wiley.

Reed, John Shelton. 1975. Needles in haystacks: Studying "rare" populations by secondary analysis of national sample surveys. *Public Opinion Quarterly* 39:514–22.

Riley, Matilda White, and Anne Foner, eds. 1968. *Aging and society*. Vol. 1: *An inventory of research findings*. New York: Russell Sage Foundation.

Schramm, Wilbur, 1969. Aging and mass communication. In Matilda White Riley, John W. Riley, Jr., and Marilyn E. Johnson, eds. *Aging and society*. Vol. 2: *Aging and the professions*, pp. 352–75. New York: Russell Sage Foundation.

Townsend, Peter, and Sylvia Tunstall. 1968. Isolation, desolation, and loneliness. In Ethel Shanas, P. Townsend, D. Wedderburn, H. Friis, P. Milhoj, and J. Stehouwer, eds., *Old people in three industrial societies*, pp. 258–87. New York: Atherton.

Tunstall, Jeremy. 1966. *Old and alone: A sociological study of old people*. London: Routledge and Kegan Paul.

Wenger, Clare. 1983. Loneliness: A problem of measurement. In Dorothy Jerrome, ed., *Aging in modern society: Contemporary approaches*, pp. 145–67. New York: St. Martin's Press.

Wright, Charles R. 1975. Social structure and mass communications behavior: Exploring patterns through constructional analysis. In Lewis A. Coser, ed., *The idea of social structure: Papers in honor of Robert K. Merton*, pp. 379–413. New York: Harcourt Brace Jovanovich.

———. 1985. *Mass communication: A sociological perspective*. 3rd ed. New York: Random House.

## Leo Bogart

## 22 The Return of Hollywood's Mass Audience: How a Social Institution Adapts to Technological Change

Mass communication provides common symbols for a complex and impersonal society. Sociologists approach the study of mass communication from a number of different angles. They examine the structures and functions of media as institutions. They analyze media content both as an expression of social values and as a force that shapes values. They differentiate media audience characteristics, describe and explain audience motivations and tastes, and attempt to trace media effects on the socialization of children and on the personal, social, and economic behavior of both children and adults.[1]

Mass communication may also be considered from the perspective of another line of sociological inquiry: the study of social change and especially of the social impact of technology. From this perspective, the conventional study of media institutions, content, and audiences deals in ephemeral phenomena, since all are constantly being transformed by the emergence of new and different means of communication. Technical inventions that change the forms through which information is disseminated also change the character of the information itself and thus change the society. This paper reports on a national survey made at one moment in an evolving process through which a powerful medium, the motion picture, is being profoundly altered as a result of new inventions in the field of communication. The findings reveal how the public persists in established patterns of communications behavior at the same time that it embraces the new forms of experience made possible by advancing technology. This

[1] Most sociological research on film audiences had focused on motivations rather than on characteristics. For a compilation of source material, cf. Austin 1983. For an exceptionally interesting discussion of the sociology of the film, cf. Jarvie 1978, p. 24.

process affects the producers as well as the consumers of communication. The film studios have reoriented their output to the new markets opened up by cable television and the video recorder, illustrating how powerful institutions adapt to their changing environment.

## The Film Industry in the Age of Television

The movies have exerted intense fascination for twentieth-century America. They have shaped its fantasy life, provided some of its most notable heroes, enriched the content of innumerable conversations, and induced an illusion of familiarity with people and places remote in time or geography. America's movie experience changed with the coming of television. Forty years later, with the advent of new technology in the form of cable television and the videocassette recorder, the movie experience was changing again.

In 1946 the average American (including children) went to the movies twenty-nine times a year. Television provided a cheaper, more readily accessible source of entertainment. By 1985, per capita movie attendance had declined to a rate of five times a year.

While the frequency of moviegoing plummeted, the pattern of American life was undergoing great change. American cities were losing population during the years of television's growth (from its commercial introduction in 1948 to the time it reached virtual saturation in the early 1960s). Their ethnic composition was changing, and their downtown retail structure was crumbling as the middle class moved to the suburbs. For several generations, moviegoing had been a family activity that brought people to city centers on expeditions that included eating out and shopping. The presence of crowds attracted crowds. Theaters closed when downtown pedestrian traffic dwindled after business hours, but the very fact that fewer theaters were open reduced pedestrian traffic and discouraged attendance. The process fed on itself.

Theater owners followed their customers and moved into suburban shopping centers. They sought to cut costs and increase their revenues by transforming their large houses into multiscreen film complexes, operated by a single small staff of employees. Their expanded food and drink concessions became ever more important to their profits.

The motion picture studios fought back the competition from television by emphasizing the differences between films in the theater and the black and white images on the tiny tube. Color became almost universal in film making, where it had been the exception. The theater screen became wider and larger. Multichannel sound was introduced, and three-dimensional projection techniques were tried and abandoned. Casts became larger, locales more exotic, and budgets ever more extravagant; in 1986 a typical movie cost nearly $15 million to produce.

Most important, Hollywood dramatically changed the content of films themselves to differentiate them as much as possible from the blander programming material permitted by television network censors. Violence became both more prevalent and more gory, sex progressively more explicit (especially after court rulings that restricted censorship), vulgar and obscene language more commonplace. Violence, sex, and obscenity often seemed to be introduced gratuitously, not as an essential component of the plot or character depiction but to titillate the audience in ways that had long been forbidden by the old Hays Code and that the self-imposed codes of television still discouraged. Perhaps of even greater moral significance was the abandonment of a fundamental theatrical convention that long antedated the movies themselves: the requirement that wrongdoing be punished at the end. For the first time in the history of fiction, antisocial actions were glorified in those films whose heroes were criminals and whose villains were the forces of justice, depicted as incompetent, petty, and vindictive.

By the time the film rating system was introduced by the Motion Picture Association of America in 1968, these changes were already well underway, but they have accelerated since, as Table 22.1 shows. Of the films rated in 1968–69, 32 percent received a G rating (approved for a general audience). A dozen years earlier, every film released by Hollywood might have qualified for such a rating by its propriety. Of the films in 1968–69, 6 percent were rated X for their sexual content. In 1985, only one film was rated X, not because erotic films were not being made but because they simply bypassed the ratings systems altogether and found their way into their own channels of distribution. Only 4 percent of the films in 1985 were rated G, since it was widely believed in the industry that this rating discouraged attendance.

The changes in film content facilitated and legitimated the changes that took place during the same period in standards of language use and sexual mores. These changes were induced by a variety of complex forces: the new technology of contraception; the massive entry of women into the work force, with the consequent alteration of sex roles, household composition, and living patterns; the coming of age of the postwar "baby boom" generation, whose sheer size put pressure on existing institutions and whose rebelliousness was spurred by the strains of the Vietnam War. Film content reflected the transformation

TABLE 22.1. *Film Ratings*

| Rating | 1968–69 | 1985 |
|--------|---------|------|
| G | 32% | 4% |
| PG[a] | 39 | 21 |
| PG-13 | — | 18 |
| R | 23 | 56 |
| X | 6 | 0 |
| (N) | (441) | (356) |

[a]Parental Guidance suggested. The PG-13 designation was added in 1984 to indicate the age at which the guidance was apparently no longer required. R-rated films are restricted to adults. Film ratings are assigned by the Motion Picture Association of America.

in values, but, as always, films also provided role models and guidance for behavior. Film reflected the changes in society, but through a distorting lens. As always, the media are a force for change as well as an indicator of change.

Television network programming practices also changed in direct response to the examples set by Hollywood. In spite of recurrent government protests and investigations, violence remained an important element of prime-time TV drama (Signorielli, Gross, and Morgan 1982). Extramarital sex became a principal preoccupation of daytime serials. Sexual innuendos and "jiggly" breasts were casually introduced into comedy programs, obscenities came easily to the lips of guests on late-night talk shows. In short, behavior and speech that had been adopted by the film industry as a defense against the prudery of television became staple fare on television itself.

The production of television drama has been concentrated in Hollywood, forging close links between the film makers and the networks. The same actors, writers, and directors work interchangeably for the two media in the same studio facilities. Made-for-TV movies have been released after broadcast for theatrical runs, further obscuring the distinction between the two media.

From the beginning of television, movies have been a major element of its programming, though for many years most of the films shown were of ancient vintage. Thus, movies continued to be very much a part of the average American's mainstream entertainment, even though they were typically enjoyed at home on the television set rather than in the theater. Films have been so popular that television networks and stations have been willing to pay substantial sums for permission to air them a few years after they have finished their theatrical runs. As independent stations and cable channels have captured more of the television audience, the demand for films to fill time on the air has grown steadily, increasing the value of the studios' film libraries and prompting a wave of corporate takeovers by media tycoons. In 1985, under complicated financing arrangements, Rupert Murdoch purchased 20th Century-Fox, and Ted Turner bought MGM.

Going out to the movies remains a very different form of entertainment from watching movies on TV. The sheer size of the screen in relation to the viewer, reinforced by the magnified sound level, gives the images an extraordinary power that diminishes when they are reduced to the dimensions of a cathode ray tube. Seeing a film in the theater is an intense experience, with attention focused in the darkness and without domestic distractions and commercial interruptions.

The darkness of the theater provides the privacy needed for courting, a principal motivation for moviegoing, which remains a highly popular form of dating. Not surprisingly, therefore, the theatrical movie audience has become progressively more youthful. Teenagers spend 27 percent less time watching television than does the average American (Nielsen 1985). They spend more time out of the house, and their moviegoing reflects this. In 1985, a survey found that individuals aged twelve to seventeen went to the movies twice as often as adults. The data indicate that they accounted for over a fifth of all movie admissions among people aged twelve and over (Opinion Research Corporation 1985).

Like the teenagers, young adults account for a substantial part of the movie industry's theatrical revenues. Individuals between eighteen and twenty-four represent 18 percent of all adults but account for more than double that proportion of the frequent moviegoers— whom we define as those who have been to the movies within the past month. This finding comes from a May 1985 telephone survey (conducted under my direction by Henry Senft Associates) among a national cross-section of 1,000 people aged eighteen and over.[2] The survey covered both the current state of theatrical moviegoing and the impact of the new media.

## Going Out to the Movies

The study confirms the observation that motion picture attendance has become rare among substantial parts of the population. Forty-four percent of the respondents have not been to the movies within

[2] This study, done for the Newspaper Advertising Bureau, used a probability sampling design based on random digit dialing within a cross-section of residential telephone exchanges. One respondent per household was chosen by a random procedure, and up to six call-backs were made, with a final completion rate of 34 percent. The sample was statistically balanced for age and sex to compensate for varying probabilities of access. B. Stuart Tolley supervised the execution of the research.

TABLE 22.2. *Moviegoing Frequency, by Age*

| Age of moviegoer | Frequent moviegoers[a] | Infrequent moviegoers | All other adults | All U.S. adults |
|---|---|---|---|---|
| 18–24 | 39% | 18% | 6% | 18% |
| 25–34 | 31 | 36 | 18 | 26 |
| 35–44 | 16 | 20 | 16 | 17 |
| 45–54 | 6 | 13 | 16 | 13 |
| 55–64 | 4 | 9 | 18 | 12 |
| 65+ | 4 | 4 | 26 | 14 |
| (N) | (259) | (332) | (406) | (1000) |

[a]Frequent moviegoers have gone within the past month, infrequent moviegoers less often but within the past year.

the past year, and this proportion rises to 72 percent among the one out of three adults who is over fifty. Frequent moviegoers (who have been to the movies at least once in the last month) account for 24 percent of the public, but it can be estimated that they represent 83 percent of all adult movie admissions. Seventy percent of them are under thirty-five (see Table 22.2)

Being younger, 47 percent of the frequent moviegoers are single (compared with 22 percent of all adults). They are also above average in education, with 43 percent (compared to 34 percent of all adults) having had at least some college. This group of movie buffs has for years been the prime target for Hollywood's marketing effort and the audience for whom films are designed.

As the film makers well understand, the tastes of young people differ from those of older ones. A 1981 study by the Newspaper Advertising Bureau found that they particularly like comedies and are far more likely than average to be drawn to horror films. Twice as many moviegoers aged eighteen to thirty-four as of those thirty-five to forty-nine said they like "vivid horror scenes" and "vivid sex scenes," and they are also much more attracted to "wounding and killing scenes" and to scenes of fires, explosions, and crashes. The film industry has not neglected these interests.

Movies are not an obsession, even among movie buffs. As a favorite way of spending free time, filmgoing ranks higher among the frequent moviegoers than among other members of the public, but it ranks well below reading and television. For the public at large, it is also far less important than outdoor activities. (See the tables in the Appendix to this chapter for data on this and subsequent findings.)

As a matter of fact, frequent filmgoers differ very little from those who go less frequently in the way they make up their minds to see a film or in what they want to know about it. Our survey asked all those who had been to the movies within the past year a series of questions about the last film they had seen. Four out of five left for the theater from home rather than from work or a shopping expedition, and a majority went with another member of the household. Even among the frequent moviegoers, only about half went with a date or other companion outside the family. Three out of five filmgoers went out for a meal or refreshments either before or after the show, and two out of three bought something to eat or drink at the theater itself.

Thus, in most cases, people go to the movies not merely to be entertained, informed, inspired, amused, aroused, or titillated by the actual content of the film they are about to see but as a social event that provides an occasion for conversation, shared emotions, and diversion from normal daily routine.

The desire to go someplace may be a strong incentive for moviegoers, but 59 percent say they last decided to go to the movies because they wanted to see a particular film rather than because they just felt like going out (41 percent). Even among those who gave the latter answer, 59 percent knew what film was playing. This kind of expedition does not take a lot of advance planning. In two out of three cases it is made the same day or the night before.

Typically (in 56 percent of the cases), people go to a theater in their own neighborhood and have a choice of about five different films to see at that location. But 44 percent travel outside the immediate vicinity to catch a film they don't want to miss. The films they see are usually the heavily promoted new ones that generate publicity, reviews, and discussion. Seven out of ten saw their last movie within a month after it first opened, more than four out of ten within the first week. Only 10 percent saw a film that was over three months old. To keep up with the latest films is to be *au courant,* which is one reason why the frequent moviegoers want to see current films in the theater instead of waiting for them to show up on TV.

The new movies remain, in fact, a reliable topic of conversation, though few people admit that they have "above-average interest" in the private lives of the stars. Thirty-nine percent of all filmgoers recall discussing the last film they saw before they went to see it, and 71 percent have talked about it since.

In spite of all the conversation about movies, the public gets most of its information on the subject from mass media. People first find out about new films from the newspapers and from television, more often before the film is launched (31 percent) or at the time of release (28 percent) than after it has been in circulation.

A majority (53 percent) say they usually pay attention to movie reviews, and 36 percent had read or heard reviews or commentary on the last film they saw. Also, 61 percent remember coming across advertising for that film before they saw it, with equal numbers (55 percent) mentioning newspapers and TV and surprisingly few (4 percent) referring to the preview or "coming attractions" trailers in the theater itself. The information filmgoers say they look for in movie ads (when given a checklist that did not include the names of the stars) is primarily utilitarian: Starting times, the address of the theater, the rating, and the admission price rank high.

What are the kinds of things people want to know about a film before they decide to go to see it? The answers to an open-ended question reveal that the plot and the actors (32 percent) are of most importance. Only a small number spontaneously refer to what the reviews have said, presumably because the reviews are regarded as a source of information rather than as information itself.

People think of their moviegoing as a positive form of social enjoyment rather than as a negative means of escaping the pressures of everyday life. An earlier survey we did in 1978 found that "to laugh and be happy" was the principal reason picked for moviegoing. Not too many people (and especially few frequent moviegoers) acknowledged that they went "to get away from everyday problems," and hardly anyone said the main motive was "self-improvement and to think."

People feel good about the movies that they see, with the frequent moviegoers only slightly more positive than the rest of the public (not much more positive, as we hypothesized). In the 1985 study, three out of five rate the last film they saw as outstanding or as above average; only 7 percent rate it below average or poor.

In summary, the young people who go to the movies most often follow a pattern very similar to that of the rest of the filmgoing public on any particular trip to the theater, even though they have very distinctive tastes and interests in specific kinds of film content.

## Films on the Tube

For over half a century, theatergoing was the channel through which Hollywood made its impact on American culture. The personalities of the "silver screen" were perceived as larger than life, their passions of supranormal intensity, the settings more opulent or exotic than everyday reality. The magnificent downtown film palaces of the Golden Era enshrined these heroic images and made going out to the movies a special experience—even a compelling one. But although the theatrical filmgoing experience changed and the film audience changed and dwindled too, movies on television have continued to be a universal medium of entertainment for every age group.

Watching films on television is a widespread activity, but film buffs do it somewhat more often. Thirty-four percent of the public have watched a movie on TV within the last seven days (and 5 percent have seen more than one). The proportion goes up to 39 percent among frequent moviegoers, even though they would rather be out at the theater. Seventy-seven percent of the frequent moviegoers, compared with only 43 percent of the general public, prefer to go out to see a new movie rather than to watch it on TV.

Films viewed on television in the intimate setting of the home represent a different form of communication than those seen in the theater. But apart from the differences that I noted earlier in the perceptual and social environment, our survey reminds us that films seen in the theater are generally approached as experiences that are fresh and new, whereas those seen on television have, until quite recently, been relics of another era, culled from those ancient film libraries that the studios have been willing to release.

Access to movies on television was profoundly affected by the spread of cable television, which started as a service to isolated communities with signal reception problems and has grown into a facility that brings clear images on a great number of channels.[3] By 1986 more than seven out of ten American homes were in areas that had been wired for cable television, and half (48 percent) were cable subscribers. Over half of these elected to pay extra for one or more pay tiers, notably from Home Box Office and Showtime, which offered feature films that had been released to theaters about a year earlier. About 5 million households also had access to pay-per-view systems with no fixed subscription fee.

The presence of relatively recent films on pay cable (some of them coproduced for that purpose by the cable companies) spurred the television networks to offer higher prices to the studios for broadcast rights and eventually to commission their own "made-for-TV" movies. Partly as cause and partly as effect, prime-time network television program schedules increasingly departed from the predictable regular half-hour weekly format. Feature films accounted for 15 percent of network prime-time hours in 1985.

How does the television audience for movies compare in character with the theater audience? To answer this question requires a preliminary look at who the cable subscribers are. Noncable households con-

[3] In 1984, 78 percent of all cable households could receive twenty-two or more channels, and 28 percent could receive thirty-six or more.

TABLE 22.3. *Geographic Location of Cable and Noncable Households*

|  | Passed by cable | | | Not passed |
|  | Pay | Basic | None | |
|---|---|---|---|---|
| Central city | 27% | 28% | 35% | 29% |
| Suburban | 54 | 42 | 51 | 35 |
| Nonmetropolitan | 19 | 30 | 14 | 36 |
| (N) (100%, in 000s)= | (38,179) | (37,837) | (50,378) | (44,811) |

*Note:* These data are drawn from the 1986 SMRB Survey of Media and Markets, based on a national probability sample of 19,000 adults. Base *N*s represent sample respondents projected to total U.S. adults. Extensive statistical adjustments were made, as is commonly done in commercial research. Households passed by cable are those in areas that have been wired.

TABLE 22.4. *Characteristics of Cable and Noncable Households*

|  | Passed by cable | | | Not passed |
|  | Pay | Basic | None | |
|---|---|---|---|---|
| $30,000+ households income | 58% | 39% | 36% | 33% |
| 3+ persons in household | 71 | 55 | 49 | 56 |
| Household head under 35 | 30 | 23 | 41 | 27 |

stitute the whole population in regions that are geographically remote (and therefore costly to wire) and in cities like Philadelphia and Chicago where cable wiring has been delayed by economic difficulties or political wrangles. But in the bulk of the country, the households that are willing to pay for cable, and especially the surcharge for pay cable, tend to be those that both can afford it and are the most heavily oriented to entertainment.

The differences between cable and noncable households have been generally obscured by the fact that published sources lump together those noncable households that are located in wired neighborhoods and those that are not passed at all. As might be expected, those not passed by cable in 1986 included a highly disproportionate number of households in nonmetropolitan areas (Table 22.3). Within regions accessible by cable, a relatively high percentage of pay-cable subscribers were located in the suburbs, compared with those who subscribed only to a basic cable service. To some extent, this reflected the different social composition of central cities and suburbs. Pay cable in 1986 was present in a much larger proportion of high-income households and of larger families with children (Table 22.4).

In areas passed by cable, households that chose not to subscribe

TABLE 22.5. *Percentage Who Have Gone to the Movies in Past Month*

|              | Percent | (N)   |
|--------------|---------|-------|
| Noncable     | 21%     | (512) |
| Basic cable  | 24      | (211) |
| Pay cable    | 27      | (279) |
| VCR owners   | 29      | (278) |

even to a basic service were markedly smaller than nonsubscribing households in noncable areas. The adults in pay-cable households were also considerably more youthful than the average (a condition that is, of course, associated with the presence of children at home).

Since motion pictures represent the lion's share of pay-cable programming, it is not surprising that among people with pay cable in our own survey, 64 percent had watched a movie on it within the past week, and 33 percent had watched three or more.

Cable subscribers (especially those to pay cable) are also above average in their theatrical moviegoing (Table 22.5). This finding is worth emphasis because the availability of more programming choices on cable television—especially the films on pay cable—might be expected to produce a difference in the opposite direction, diverting these subscribers from the theater. The explanation is that they can better afford it, and they are more interested in audiovisual entertainment, which they watch any way they can. However, subscribers to both regular cable and pay cable are not narrowly concentrated in any particular age group to the degree that frequent moviegoers are. As a result, pay cable has made reasonably current motion pictures available to mass audiences again, in contrast to the narrow age range of the theatrical film audience. The coming of the videocassette recorder makes this reorientation even more significant.

By 1987, 40 percent of the homes in the country owned a VCR, according to an estimate by the A. C. Nielsen Company. Our 1985 survey found that 40 percent of the owners had acquired them within the past year. Although that kind of annual growth rate was likely to taper off, it appears to be only a question of time before VCRs are almost as common as TV sets. In 1986, VCR owners were still concentrated in high-income households, especially larger ones. They were also slightly more youthful (Table 22.6).

VCRs were most often found in the homes of entertainment-minded people—those who are frequent moviegoers (34 percent) and those who subscribe to pay cable (33 percent). (These proportions compare with a level of 27 percent for the entire sample at the time of our sur-

TABLE 22.6. *How VCR Owners Compare with Others*

|  | VCR owners | Total U.S. |
|---|---|---|
| $30,000+ household income | 61% | 41% |
| 3+ persons in household | 70 | 57 |
| Household head under 35 | 6 | 40 |

TABLE 22.7. *Daily Hours Spent Viewing Television*

|  | VCR owners | Nonowners |
|---|---|---|
| Noncable | 2:38 hrs. | 3:00 hrs. |
| Basic cable | 2:19 | 3:09 |
| Pay cable | 2:35 | 3:11 |

vey.) The time spent with the VCR was eating into the audience for television. Although the broadcasters took comfort in ratings reports that showed VCR ownership had no adverse effect on television viewing time, our survey showed that this was not the case, when due allowance was made for the relationship between VCR ownership and cable subscription—both associated with above-average viewing. When people without cable are compared with subscribers to basic or pay cable, VCR owners in each group viewed television approximately 10 percent less (Table 22.7).

Of course, VCRs were being used to record and play back sportscasts and regular TV programs at more convenient times (17 percent had done this within the past week), as well as for an occasional home video. But it is clear that a principal use of the VCR is to watch movies.[4] Although VCR owners indicate that their outside moviegoing has been affected more than their TV viewing (Table 22.8), the presence of the VCR has made movies an ever more significant feature of their lives.

Just within the past week, two out of five watched a movie they had previously recorded off the air. Nearly two out of five owned videocassettes of movies—an average of ten. Three out of five had rented a videocassette within the past month—an average of nine. One in four had borrowed or exchanged videocassettes with friends. Not surprisingly, these proportions were higher among the VCR owners who are frequent moviegoers (Table 22.9).

[4]A 1985 survey of 1,350 individuals in VCR households, conducted by Statistical Research, Inc., found that half of all VCR viewing was of home-recorded television programming, and half was of rented and owned tapes (Metzger 1986).

TABLE 22.8. *Effects of VCR Ownership on Moviegoing and TV Use*

|           | Moviegoing | TV viewing |
|-----------|-----------|------------|
| More      | 2%        | 6%         |
| Unchanged | 56        | 66         |
| Less      | 41        | 28         |
| (N)       | (278)     | (278)      |

TABLE 22.9. *Uses of VCR*

|                                                      | Frequent movie-goers w/VCRs | All VCR owners |
|------------------------------------------------------|------------------------------|----------------|
| Watched film previously recorded off TV              | 39%                          | 40%            |
| Own film videocassettes (average of 10)              | 44                           | 36             |
| Rented videocassette in past month (average of 9)    | 65                           | 58             |
| Borrowed or exchanged videocassette                  | 30                           | 25             |
| Recorded and played back TV programs/sportscasts     | 15                           | 17             |
| (N)                                                  | (85)                         | (278)          |

Videocassettes were being bought and rented much as books are bought or borrowed from a library, on impulse more often than by specific intent. When VCR owners were asked how they made their decision on what cassettes to get, only 6 percent said they had seen the particular film before and another 37 percent said they knew their choice ahead of time. Fifty-nine percent said they decided after browsing in the store. (Some gave more than one answer.)

In 1986, videocassettes of a film were generally available about six months after its theatrical release, six months before it was shown on pay TV, and a year and a half before its availability on broadcast television. The number of videocassette sales and rental shops had climbed to 24,000—greater than the number of movie theaters (20,000). Each stocked an average of 1,900 titles. Even with rentals as low as ninety-nine cents, they accounted for an estimated 79 percent of sales and for 98 percent of the transactions. (Typically, the shop broke even with eighteen rentals.) In 1985, 670 million rentals took place. A family of four could rent nine cassettes for little more than the cost of a single night out at the movies.

TABLE 22.10. *Sources of Studio Revenues, 1985*

| Source | Percentage |
|---|---|
| Theatrical showings | |
|     Domestic | 36% |
|     Foreign | 12 |
| Television rights | |
|     Pay cable | 23 |
|     Networks | 7 |
|     Syndication | 5 |
| Videocassettes | 18 |

*Source:* 1986 Video Software Directory Annual.

The availability of pornographic videocassettes sharply reduced attendance at movie theaters specializing in X-rated movies, forcing substantial numbers of them to close down. Pornographic films initially accounted for a high proportion of videocassette rentals, but they receded into a secondary position as VCR ownership broadened.

A 1986 survey by Market Facts reported that 40 percent of all films seen by the American public were being seen on VCRs. The public's expenditures on videocassettes (the range of estimates for 1985 was between $2.3 and $4.5 billion) were fast approaching (or perhaps surpassing) the $3.7 billion spent at the theater box office. Theatrical showings still represented Hollywood's major single source of income, but they now accounted for less than half of the studio's total revenues (Table 22.10).

Obviously, the appeal of "going out," as well as the attraction of brand-new releases, will continue to bring people, especially young people, to the movie houses. "Blockbusters"—the most successful 10 percent of all films produced—account for 45 percent of box office receipts, and most of the theatrical revenues are generated in the first few weeks after a film is launched. These facts guarantee that competition from VCRs and pay cable will not destroy the audience for theatrical movies. But the indications were clear that motion pictures, as a form of communication, were in a radically new and much more complex phase of their history.

As revenues from cassettes and cable come to surpass its income from theatrical showings, Hollywood inevitably will have to start thinking again in terms of the broad mass audience that it had before the advent of TV. The expansion of the market may reverse the trend for fewer films to be produced each year and broaden the range of choice for the public. More important, it may strengthen the appeal of film as a shared family experience for children and adults. This should not necessarily mean a return to the innocuous formulas of Hollywood's Golden Era, but it does suggest a shift away from the images and techniques that the film makers adopted to defend their turf during the years of television's ascendancy. In a society whose values have been portrayed and influenced by Hollywood, the alteration of imagery was bound to have significant consequences. This illustrates how technology and culture interact and how a major social institution, the American film industry, has adapted its production and marketing methods to meet the challenge of new communications forms.

## Bibliography

Austin, Bruce A. 1983. *The film audience: An international bibliography of research.* Metuchen, N.J.: Scarecrow Press.

Jarvie, Ian C. 1978. *Movies as social criticism: Aspects of their social psychology.* Metuchen, N.J.: Scarecrow Press.

Metzger, Gale. 1986. Contam's VCR research. *Journal of Advertising Research* 26(2):RC 8–12.

Nielsen, A. C. 1985. *Television 1985.*

Opinion Research Corporation. 1985. Incidence of motion picture attendance. July.

Signorielli, Nancy, Larry Gross, and Michael Morgan. 1982. Violence in television programs: Ten years later. In David Pearl, Lorraine Bouthilet, and Joyce Lazar, eds., *Television and behavior: Ten years of scientific progress and implications for the eighties,* 2:158–74. Rockville, Md.: NIMN.

## Appendix: *Tables 22.11–13*

TABLE 22.11. *Favorite Ways to Spend Free Time*

|  | Frequent moviegoers | All other adults |
|---|---|---|
| Watching TV | 18% | 21% |
| Going to movies | 11 | 5 |
| Reading | 19 | 21 |
| Working outdoors | 8 | 13 |
| Fishing/hunting | 6 | 13 |
| (N) | (259) | (741) |

TABLE 22.12. *Preference for Films in Theater and on TV*

|  | Frequent moviegoers | All other adults |
|---|---|---|
| Going out to see a new movie | 77% | 31% |
| Waiting to see it on TV | 22 | 68 |

TABLE 22.13. *Frequent and Infrequent Moviegoers Compared*

|  | Frequent moviegoers | Infrequent moviegoers |
|---|---|---|
| A. The last trip to the movies |  |  |
| Went with someone else | 94% | 95% |
| (Of these) |  |  |
| Went with other household member | 47 | 64 |
| Went with a date or friend | 53 | 36 |
| Left from home | 79 | 90 |
| Went for a meal or drink before or after the show | 66 | 64 |
| Bought food or drink at theater | 64 | 64 |
| (N) | (259) | (332) |
| B. When they decided to go |  |  |
| One day or less ahead of time | 65% | 66% |
| Several days before | 19 | 21 |
| About a week before | 13 | 10 |
| Longer | 3 | 3 |
| C. Where they first learned about last film seen[a] |  |  |
| Newspapers | 37% | 33% |
| Television | 32 | 35 |
| Friends | 20 | 20 |
| Coming attractions | 3 | 3 |
| Posters | 3 | 5 |
| No answer | 11 | 10 |

TABLE 22.13. *(continued)*

|  | Frequent moviegoers | Infrequent moviegoers |
|---|---|---|
| D. Sources of review or commentary on last film seen (of those who remember one) | | |
| Newspaper | 51% | 56% |
| Television | 41 | 39 |
| Magazine | 11 | 12 |
| Radio | 6 | 2 |
| (N) | (99) | (126) |
| E. Information wanted in movie ads | | |
| Starting times | 84% | 85% |
| Address of theater | 69 | 75 |
| Rating | 67 | 71 |
| Description of plot | 53 | 54 |
| Admission price | 51 | 55 |
| Names of supporting cast | 44 | 53 |
| Pictures of stars | 29 | 32 |
| Director's name | 19 | 17 |
| F. What they want to know about a new film | | |
| Plot | 36% | 29% |
| Actors | 32 | 29 |
| Rating | 22 | 23 |
| What kind? | 14 | 16 |
| Worth seeing? | 13 | 14 |
| "Clean?" | 9 | 13 |
| Is it a comedy? | 5 | 12 |
| What did reviews say? | 7 | 6 |
| Nothing, don't care | 3 | 7 |
| G. Quality of last film seen | | |
| Outstanding | 28% | 24% |
| Above average | 37 | 34 |
| Average | 25 | 35 |
| Below average | 5 | 5 |
| Very poor | 4 | 2 |

[a]More than one response was permitted.

*Compiled by Irene Spinnler*

# The Writings of Herbert H. Hyman: A Bibliography

## Books and Monographs

1983. *Of time and widowhood: Nationwide studies of enduring effects.* Durham, N.C.: Duke University Press.

1979. *Education's lasting influence on values.* With Charles Wright. Chicago: University of Chicago Press.

1975. *The enduring effects of education.* With Charles Wright and John S. Reed. Chicago: University of Chicago Press. Phoenix Books, 1978.

1972. *Secondary analysis of sample surveys: Principles, procedures, and potentialities.* New York: Wiley.

1968. *Readings in reference group theory and research.* With Eleanor Singer. New York: Macmillan, Free Press. Introductory Essay reprinted in E. P. Hollander, *Current perspectives in social psychology,* pp. 87–97. 3rd and 4th eds. Oxford: Oxford University Press, 1976.

1967. *Inducing social change in developing communities.* With Gene Levine and Charles Wright. Geneva: United Nations Research Institute for Social Development. Spanish and French eds., 1967. Portion reprinted in *Development Digest* 8 (2) (1970): 107–19.

1962. *Applications of methods of evaluations.* With Charles R. Wright and Terence K. Hopkins. Berkeley: University of California Press.

1961. *Evaluation of statistical methods used in obtaining broadcast ratings.* With William Madow and Raymond Jessen. Washington, D.C.: Government Printing Office.

1959. *Political socialization.* New York: Macmillan, Free Press. Paperback ed., 1969. Indian ed., Delhi: Amerind, 1971. Portion reprinted in George Balch and Leroy Rieselbach, eds., *Psychology and politics: An introductory reader,* pp. 107–20. New York: Holt, Rinehart and Winston, 1969.

1955. *Survey design and analysis.* New York: Macmillan, Free Press, first printing; ninth printing, 1974. Portuguese ed., Editora Lidador Rio de Janeiro, 1967. Italian ed., Marsilio-Editori of Padova, 1968. Spanish ed., Amorrortu Editores, Buenos Aires, 1972. Portions reprinted in: Bernard Berelson and

Morris Janowitz, eds., *Reader in public opinion and communication*, pp. 623–48. 2nd ed. New York: Free Press, 1966. P. M. Worsley, ed., *Modern sociology: Introductory readings*, pp. 82–91. New York: Penguin Books, 1970.

1954. *Interviewing in social research*. With William J. Cobb, Jacob J. Feldman, Clyde W. Hart, and Charles Herbert Stember. Chicago: University of Chicago Press, first printing; sixth printing, 1970. Phoenix Books, 1975. Portion reprinted in P. M. Worsley, *Reader in sociology*, pp. 92–102. New York: Penguin Books, 1971.

1949. *The pre-election polls of 1948*. With Frederick Mosteller et al. New York: Social Science Research Council, Bulletin no. 60.

1942. *The psychology of status*. New York: Archives of Psychology, no. 269. New York: New York Times–Arno Press Reprint ed., 1980.

## Articles

1985. Strategies in comparative survey research. In Robert B. Smith, ed. *Quantitative methods, focused survey research, and causal modeling*, pp. 97–151. New York: Praeger.

1979. The effects of unemployment: A neglected problem in modern social research. In Robert K. Merton, James S. Coleman, and Peter Rossi, eds., *Qualitative and quantitative social research: Papers in honor of Paul F. Lazarsfeld*, pp. 282–98. New York: Free Press, Macmillan.

1975. Survey research. With Richard Boyd. In Fred Greenstein and Nelson Polsby, *Handbook of political science*, 7:265–350. Reading, Mass.: Addison-Wesley.

1975. Reference individuals and reference idols. In L. Coser, ed., *The idea of social structure: Papers in honor of Robert K. Merton*, pp. 265–82. New York: Harcourt Brace Jovanovich.

1974. Mass communication and socialization. In W. P. Davison and F. T. C. Yu, eds., *Mass communication research: Major issues and future directions*, pp. 36–65. New York: Praeger.

1973–74. Mass communication and socialization. *Public Opinion Quarterly* 37:524–40.

1973. Surveys in the study of political psychology. In J. Knutson, ed., *Handbook of political psychology*, pp. 322–55. San Francisco: Jossey-Bass.

1973. Occupational aspirations of the totally blind. With Janet Stokes and Helen Strauss. *Social Forces* 51:403–16.

1972. Dimensions of social psychological change in the Negro population. In Angus Campbell and P. E. Converse, eds., *The human meaning of social change*, pp. 339–90. New York: Russell Sage Foundation.

1971. Voluntary association memberships of American adults: A replication and trend study based on secondary analysis of national sample surveys. With Charles Wright. *American Sociological Review* 36:191–206. Reprinted in Richard Taub and Doris Taub, *American society in Tocqueville's time and today*, pp. 92–116. Chicago: Rand McNally, 1974.

1969. Black matriarchy reconsidered: Evidence from secondary analysis of sample surveys. With John Reed. *Public Opinion Quarterly* 33:346–54. Reprinted in: John Bracey, August Meier, and Elliott Rudwick, eds., *Black matriarchy: Myth or reality?* pp. 186–93. Belmont, Calif.: Wadsworth, 1971. Richard Evans and Richard Rozelle, eds., *Social psychology in life*, pp. 163–73. Boston: Allyn and Bacon, 1973. Lawrence Rosen and Robert West, *A reader for research methods*, pp. 59–67. New York: Random House.

1969. Social psychology and race relations. In Irwin Katz and Patricia Gurin, eds., *Race relations and the social sciences*, pp. 3–48. New York: Basic Books.

1968. Reference groups. In *International encyclopedia of the social sciences*, 13: 353–66.

1967. Evaluating social action programs. With Charles Wright. In P. F. Lazarsfeld, ed., *The uses of sociology*, pp. 741–82. New York: Basic Books. Reprinted in F. Caro, ed., *Readings in evaluation research*, pp. 185–220. New York: Russell Sage Foundation, 1971.

1967. Studying expert informants by survey methods: A cross-national inquiry. *Public Opinion Quarterly* 31: 9–26.

1966. Metodi di valutazione dei programmi di azione sociale. *La Rivista Di Servicio Sociale* 6 (1): 89–104.

1964. The evaluators. With Charles Wright. In Phillip Hammond, ed., *Sociologists at work*, pp. 121–41. New York: Basic Books. Paperback ed., New York: Doubleday (Anchor Books), 1967.

1964. Attitudes on desegregation. With Paul Sheatsley. *Scientific American* 211: 16–23. Reprinted in: R. A. Dentler, *Major American social problems*, pp. 205–17. Chicago: Rand McNally, 1967. John Kessel, Robert Seddig, and George Cole, eds., *Micropolitics*, pp. 405–18. New York: Holt, Rinehart and Winston, 1970. Melvin Tumin, ed., *Comparative perspectives on race relations*, pp. 277–92. Boston: Little, Brown, 1969.

1964. Research design. In Robert Ward, ed., *Studying politics abroad*, pp. 153–88. Boston: Little, Brown.

1963. Reflections on the relation between theory and research. *Centennial Review* 7: 431–53. Reprinted in Billy Franklin and Harold Osborne, eds., *Research methods: Issues and insights*, pp. 39–47. Belmont, Calif.: Wadsworth, 1970.

1963. England and America: Climates of tolerance and intolerance. In Daniel Bell, ed., *The radical right*, pp. 227–57. Garden City, N.Y.: Doubleday.

1963. Problems of research on the corporate image. In John W. Riley, ed., *The modern corporation and its publics*, pp. 64–76. New York: Wiley.

1963. Mass media and political socialization: The role of patterns of communication. In Lucian Pye, ed., *Communications and political development*, pp. 128–48. Princeton, N.J.: Princeton University Press.

1962. Samuel A. Stouffer and social research. *Public Opinion Quarterly* 26: 323–28.

1961. The role of the mass media in the formation of public opinion. In De Witt C. Reddick, ed., *The role of the mass media in a democratic society*, pp. 11–24. Austin: University of Texas Press.

1960. Reflections on reference groups. *Public Opinion Quarterly* 24: 383–96.

1959. Turk yuksek Tahsil Gencliginin Degerler Sistemi. With A. Payaslioglu and F. W. Frey. *Siyasal Benilgiler Fakultesi Dergisi* 14: 95–121.

1958. Voluntary association memberships of American adults: Evidence from national sample surveys. With Charles Wright. *American Sociological Review* 23:284–94. Reprinted in: Robert O'Brien, Clarence Schrag, and Walter T. Martin, *Readings in general sociology*, pp. 139–48. Boston: Houghton Mifflin, 3rd ed., 1964, 4th ed., 1969. Eric Larrabee and Rolf Meyersohn, eds., *Mass leisure*, pp. 315–27. New York: Free Press, 1958. Kimball Young and Raymond Mack, *Principles of sociology*, pp. 20–30. New York: American Book Co., 1960. Murray Strauss and Joel Nelson, *Sociological analysis: An empirical approach through readings and replication*, 1966. David Sills and William Glaser, eds., *The government of associations*, pp. 31–37. Totowa, N.J.: Bedminster Press, 1966. Roland L. Warren, ed., *Perspectives on the American community*, pp. 448–61. Chicago: Rand McNally, 1966. Peter I. Rose, ed., *The study of society: An integrated anthology*, pp. 207–19. 2nd ed. New York: Random House, 1970. Betty Zisk, ed., *American political interest groups: Readings in theory and research*, pp. 300–15. Belmont, Calif.: Wadsworth, 1969.

1958. The values of Turkish college youth. With F. Frey and Arif Payaslioglu. *Public Opinion Quarterly* 22:275–91.

1957. An exploration into opinions and personality. *World Politics* 10:144–53.

1957. Toward a theory of public opinion. *Public Opinion Quarterly* 21:54–60. Reprinted in Robert Carlson, ed., *Communications and public opinion*, pp. 96–102. New York: Praeger, 1975.

1957. Utilization of questionnaire, interview, and biographical data. In *Admissions information*, pp. 15–24. New York: College Entrance Examination Board.

1956. Attitudes toward desegregation. With Paul Sheatsley. *Scientific American* 195:35–39.

1955. The Cochran-Mosteller-Tukey Report on the Kinsey Study. *Journal of the American Statistical Association* 50:314–15.

1954. The methodology of sexual behavior in the human female. With Paul Sheatsley. In Donald P. Geddes, ed., *An analysis of the Kinsey reports on sexual behavior in the human male and female*, pp. 91–117. New York: Dutton.

1953. Trends in public opinion on civil liberties. With Paul Sheatsley. *Journal on Social Issues*. 9:6–16.

1953. The use of surveys to predict behavior. With Paul Sheatsley. *International Social Science Bulletin* 5:474–81.

1953. The authoritarian personality: A methodological critique. With Paul Sheatsley. In Richard Christie and Marie Jahoda, eds., *Studies in the scope and method of the authoritarian personality*, pp. 50–122. New York: Free Press.

1953. The political appeal of President Eisenhower. With Paul Sheatsley. *Public Opinion Quarterly* 17:443–60. Reprinted in N. Polsby, R. Dentler, and P. Smith, eds., *Politics and social life*, pp. 453–65. Boston: Houghton Mifflin, 1963.

1953. The value systems of different classes. In Reinhard Bendix and S. M. Lipset, eds., *Class, status, and power*, pp. 426–42 (1st ed.), pp. 488–99 (2nd ed.). New York: Free Press, 1966. Reprinted in: Raymond Boudon and Paul Lazarsfeld, *Le vocabulaire des sciences sociales*, pp. 260–82. Paris: Mouton, 1965. Eduardo Hamuy, *Antologia sobre estratificación social*, pp. 173–217.

Santiago, Chile: Editorial Universitaria, S.A., 1958. Herman D. Stein and Richard Cloward, eds., *Social perspectives on behavior*, pp. 315–30. Glencoe, Ill.: Free Press, 1958. Peter Rose, ed., *The study of society: A collection of readings*, pp. 371–93. New York: Random House, 1967. Melvin Tumin, ed., *Readings on social stratification*, pp. 186–203. Englewood Cliffs, N.J.: Prentice-Hall, 1970.

1952. Trends in public opinion polling since 1948 and their probable effect on 1952 election predictions. In *Proceedings of the Invitational Conference on Testing Problems*, pp. 64–69. Princeton, N.J.: Educational Testing Service.

1951. A field study of interviewer effects on the quality of survey data. With Jacob Feldman and Clyde Hart. *Public Opinion Quarterly* 15:734–61.

1951. Interviewing as a scientific procedure. In Daniel Lerner and Harold Lasswell, eds., *The policy sciences*, pp. 203–16. Stanford, Calif.: Stanford University Press.

1950. The biasing effect of interviewer expectations on survey results. With Harry Smith. *Public Opinion Quarterly* 14:491–506.

1950. The current status of American public opinion. With Paul Sheatsley. *21st Yearbook of the National Council for the Social Studies*, pp. 11–34. Reprinted in Daniel Katz, ed., *Public opinion and propaganda*, pp. 33–48. New York: Holt, 1954.

1950. Problems in the collection of opinion research data. *American Journal of Sociology* 4:362–71. Reprinted in: Milton Barron, ed., *Contemporary sociology*, pp. 513–24. New York: Dodd, Mead, 1964. Carl Backman and Paul Secord, eds., *Problems in social psychology*, pp. 21–28. New York: McGraw-Hill, 1965.

1949–50. Interviewer effects in the classification of responses. With Herbert Stember. *Public Opinion Quarterly* 13:669–83.

1949. Inconsistencies as a problem in attitude measurement. *Journal on Social Issues* 5:38–42.

1949. How interviewer effects operate through question form. With Herbert Stember. *International Journal of Opinion and Attitude Research* 3:493–513.

1949. Isolation, measurement, and control of interviewer effect. *Items* 3:15–17.

1949. Interviewer performance in area sampling. With Dean Manheimer. *Public Opinion Quarterly* 13:83–92.

1948. The Kinsey Report and survey methodology. With Paul Sheatsley. *International Journal of Opinion and Attitude Research* 2:183–95.

1947. Some reasons why information campaigns fail. With Paul Sheatsley. *Public Opinion Quarterly* 11:412–23. Reprinted in: Guy Swanson, Theodore Newcomb, and E. L. Hartley, eds., *Readings in social psychology*, pp. 86–95. New York: Holt, 1952. Daniel Katz, ed., *Public opinion and propaganda*, pp. 522–31. New York: Holt, 1954. Eleanor Maccoby, Theodore Newcomb, and E. L. Hartley, eds., *Readings in social psychology*, pp. 164–73. New York: Holt, 1958. W. Schramm and Donald Roberts, eds., *Process and effects of mass communication*, pp. 448–66. Rev. ed. Urbana: University of Illinois Press, 1972. Dunod, *Psychologie sociales: Textes fondamenteaux anglais et americains*.

Barcelona: Editorial Laia, 1972. Susan Welch and John Comer, eds., *Public opinion*, pp. 290–302. Palo Alto, Calif.: Mayfield, 1975.

1947. World surveys: The Japanese angle. *International Journal of Opinion and Attitude Research* 1 (2):3–14.

1947. Industrial morale and public opinion methods. With Daniel Katz. *International Journal of Opinion and Attitude Research* 1 (3):13–40.

1947. Morale in war industry. With Daniel Katz. In Theodore Newcomb and Eugene Hartley, eds., *Readings in social psychology*, pp. 437–41. New York: Holt.

1945. Community background in public opinion research. *Journal of Abnormal Social Psychology* 40:411–13.

1944–45. Do they tell the truth? *Public Opinion Quarterly* 8:557–59.

## Book Reviews

1978. "A banquet for secondary analysts." A feature review of the NORC General Social Survey. *Contemporary Sociology*, September, pp. 545–49.

1977. Review of Elisabeth Noelle-Neumann, *Allensbacher Jahrbuch der Demoskopie, 1976–1977*. *Public Opinion Quarterly* 41:572–73.

1975. Review of Elisabeth Noelle and Erich Peter Neumann, *Jahrbuch der öffentlichen Meinung, 1968–1973*. *Public Opinion Quarterly* 39:584–86.

1975. Review of Jean M. Converse and Howard Schuman, *Conversations at random: Survey research as interviewers see it*. *Public Opinion Quarterly* 39:277–78.

1974. Review of Alexander Szalai et al., "The use of time." *Science* 185 (4151):605–7.

1970. Review of Matilda Riley et al., *Aging and society*, vol. 1: *An inventory of research findings*. *Public Opinion Quarterly* 34:506–8.

1968. Review of *Survey research in the social sciences*, ed. Charles Glock. *Public Opinion Quarterly* 32:532–33.

1966. Review of *Comparing nations: The use of quantitative data in cross-national research*, ed. Richard L. Merritt and Stein Rokkan. *Political Science Quarterly* 81:633–35.

1961–62. Review of Angus Campbell, Philip E. Converse, Warren E. Miller, and Donald C. Stokes, *The American voter*. *American Psychologist* 2:202–4.

1957. Review of Elisabeth Noelle and Erich Peter Neumann, *Jahrbuch der öffentlichen Meinung, 1947–1955*. *Public Opinion Quarterly* 21:401–3.

1954. Sexual behavior in the human female: A special review. With Joseph Barmack. *Psychology Bulletin* 51:418–27. Reprinted in Bernhardt Lieberman, ed., *Human sexual behavior*, pp. 421–33. New York: Wiley, 1971.

## Miscellaneous Writings

1980. Samuel A. Stouffer. *Dictionary of American biography, Supplement Six, 1956–60*, pp. 604–6. New York: Scribner.

1979. Otto Klineberg. *Biographical supplement, International encyclopedia of the social sciences* 18:381–88. New York: Macmillan.

1965. Discussion. In O. Klineberg and R. Christie, eds., *Perspectives in social psychology,* pp. 49–52. New York: Holt.

1963. How whites view Negroes, 1942–1963. With Paul Sheatsley. *Herald Tribune,* November 10, p. 8.

1963. Preface to Mary Jean Cornish, Florence A. Ruderman, and Sydney S. Spivack, *Doctors and family planning.* Publication no. 19. New York: National Committee on Maternal Health.

1954. Introduction to "Cross-national research: A case study." With Daniel Katz. Special number of *Journal of Social Issues* 10 (4).

1940. An experimental approach to the problem of functional autonomy. Unpublished master's thesis. New York: Columbia University.

# Index

## About the Book

*Surveying Social Life* was composed on the Mergenthaler 202 in Baskerville, with Baskerville and Schneidler display type. The Mergenthaler 202 Baskerville is a contemporary rendering of a fine transitional typeface named for the eighteenth-century English printer John Baskerville. It was adapted for the 202 from the Linotype version by the Mergenthaler Corporation. The book was composed by G & S Typesetters, Inc. of Austin, Texas, and designed and produced by Kachergis Book Design, Pittsboro, North Carolina.

Wesleyan University Press, 1988